Tangled Titans

The United States and China

Edited by
David Shambaugh

ROWMAN & LITTLEFIELD PUBLISHERS, INC.
Lanham • Boulder • New York • Toronto • Plymouth, UK

Published by Rowman & Littlefield Publishers, Inc.
A wholly owned subsidiary of The Rowman & Littlefield Publishing Group, Inc.
4501 Forbes Boulevard, Suite 200, Lanham, Maryland 20706
www.rowman.com

10 Thornbury Road, Plymouth PL6 7PP, United Kingdom

British Library Cataloguing in Publication Information Available

Library of Congress Cataloging-in-Publication Data
Tangled titans : the United States and China / edited by David Shambaugh.
        p. cm.
    Includes bibliographical references and index.
    ISBN 978-1-4422-1969-4 (cloth : alk. paper) — ISBN 978-1-4422-1970-0
(pbk. : alk. paper) — ISBN 978-1-4422-1971-7 (electronic)
    1. United States—Foreign relations—China.   2. China—Foreign relations—
United States.   I. Shambaugh, David L.
    E183.8.C5T289 2013
    327.73051—dc23

                                                                 2012021175

∞^{TM} The paper used in this publication meets the minimum requirements of
American National Standard for Information Sciences—Permanence of Paper
for Printed Library Materials, ANSI/NISO Z39.48-1992.

Printed in the United States of America

Tangled Titans

To America's China watchers
and China's America watchers,
in their continual and challenging effort
to interpret the "Other"

Contents

List of Abbreviations and Acronyms   ix

Preface and Acknowledgments   xv

Part I Introduction

1. Tangled Titans: Conceptualizing the U.S.-China Relationship   3
   David Shambaugh

Part II The Historical Context

2. The Evolution of U.S.-China Relations   29
   Nancy Bernkopf Tucker

Part III The Theoretical Context

3. The Rise of China, the United States, and the Future of the Liberal International Order   53
   G. John Ikenberry

4. U.S.-China Relations in a Realist World   75
   Ashley J. Tellis

Part IV The Domestic Context

5. Domestic American Influences on U.S.-China Relations   103
   Robert Sutter

6. Domestic Chinese Influences on U.S.-China Relations   125
   Yufan Hao

Part V The Bilateral Context

7. The Diplomatic Relationship: Substance and Process   151
   Bonnie S. Glaser

8. The Commercial and Economic Relationship   181
   Charles W. Freeman III

9. The Cultural Relationship   211
   Terry Lautz

10. The Military-Security Relationship   235
    Christopher P. Twomey

Part VI The Regional Context

11. U.S.-China Interactions in Asia 263
Avery Goldstein

12. Taiwan in U.S.-China Relations 293
Shelley Rigger

Part VII The Global Context

13. U.S.-China Interactions in the Middle East, Africa, Europe,
and Latin America 315
David Shambaugh and Dawn Murphy

14. U.S.-China Interactions in Global Governance and
International Organizations 347
Rosemary Foot

Part VIII Visions for the Future

15. Chinese Visions of the Future of U.S.-China Relations 371
Wu Xinbo

16. American Visions of the Future of U.S.-China Relations:
Competition, Cooperation, and Conflict 389
Harry Harding

Index 411
About the Editor and Contributors 429

Abbreviations and Acronyms

A2/AD (AA/AD)	anti-access/area-denial
AEI	American Enterprise Institute
AFP	Agence France-Presse
AFRICOM	U.S. Africa Command
APEC	Asia-Pacific Economic Cooperation
AQSIQ	Administration of Quality Supervision, Inspection, and Quarantine
ARATS	Association for Relations Across the Taiwan Strait
ARF	ASEAN Regional Forum
ASBM	anti-ship ballistic missile
ASEAN	Association of Southeast Asian Nations
ASEAN+3	ASEAN plus China, Japan, and South Korea
ASW	anti-submarine warfare
BBS	bulletin boards
BRICs	Brazil, Russia, India, and China
CASCF	China-Arab States Cooperation Forum
CASS	Chinese Academy of Social Sciences
CCP	Chinese Communist Party
CFIUS	Committee on Foreign Investment in the United States
CIA	Central Intelligence Agency
CIC	China Investment Corporation
CICIR	China Institutes of Contemporary International Relations
CIIS	China Institute of International Studies
CIRSPRC	Committee on International Relations Studies with the People's Republic of China
CPE	Consultation on People-to-People Exchange
CPP	China Policy Program
CRS	Congressional Research Service
CSBA	Center for Strategic and Budgetary Assessments
CSC	China Scholarship Council

CSIS	Center for Strategic and International Studies
CTBT	Comprehensive Nuclear Test Ban Treaty
CUSP	China-U.S. Strategic Philanthropy Partnership
DC	Deputies Committee
DCT	Defense Consultative Talks
DMZ	Demilitarized Zone
DOC	Declaration on the Conduct of Parties in the South China Sea
DoD	Department of Defense
DPCT	Defense Policy Coordination Talks
DPP	Democratic Progressive Party
DPRK	Democratic People's Republic of Korea
EAS	East Asia Summit
ECA	Bureau of Educational and Cultural Affairs
ECFA	Economic Cooperation Framework Agreement
ECLAC	Economic Commission for Latin America and the Caribbean
EEZ	Exclusive Economic Zone
ETIM	East Turkestan Islamic Movement
EU	European Union
FALSG	Foreign Affairs Leading Small Group
FAO	Foreign Affairs Office
FAPA	Formosan Association for Public Affairs
FDI	foreign direct investment
FAS	Federation of American Scientists
FOCAC	Forum on China-Africa Cooperation
FTA	Free Trade Agreement
G-2	Group of 2
G-20	Group of 20
G4	Brazil, Germany, India, and Japan
GCC	Gulf Cooperation Council
GDP	gross domestic product
GFC	global financial crisis
GNP	gross national product
GPCR	Great Proletarian Cultural Revolution
HA/DR	humanitarian aid/disaster relief
HRD	Human Rights Dialogue
IADB	Inter-American Development Bank
ICBM	intercontinental ballistic missile
IGO	intergovernmental organization
IIE	Institute of International Education

IMF	International Monetary Fund
INTERPOL	International Criminal Police Organization
IPC	Interagency Policy Committee
IPR	intellectual property rights
IR	international relations
ISAF	International Security Assistance Force
ISR	intelligence, surveillance, and reconnaissance
JCCT	Joint Commission on Commerce and Trade
KEI	Korea Economic Institute
KMT	Kuomintang
LSG	Leading Small Group
M&A	mergers and acquisitions
MEF	Major Economies Forum
MERCOSUR	Mercado Comun del Cono Sur (Southern Cone Common Market)
MES	market economy status
MFA	Ministry of Foreign Affairs
MFN	most favored nation
MIT	Massachusetts Institute of Technology
MMCA	Military Maritime Cooperation Agreement
MOFCOM	Ministry of Commerce
MOU	Memorandum of Understanding
NATO	North Atlantic Treaty Organization
NBA	National Basketball Association
NBR	National Bureau of Asian Research
NBS	National Bureau of Statistics
NDRC	National Development and Reform Commission
NGO	nongovernmental organization
NPC	National People's Congress
NPR	National Public Radio
NPT	Non-Proliferation Treaty
NDRC	National Development and Reform Commission
NSC	National Security Council
NSLSG	National Security Leading Small Group
NTR	normal trade relations
NYU	New York University
OAS	Organization of American States
ODA	official development assistance
ODI	outbound direct investment
OECD	Organization for Economic Cooperation and Development
OFDI	outward foreign direct investment

ONI	Office of Naval Intelligence
P-5	Permanent 5 Members of the United Nations Security Council
PBOC	People's Bank of China
PBSC	Standing Committee of the Politburo
PC	Principals Committee
PKO	peacekeeping operation
PLA	People's Liberation Army
PLAAF	People's Liberation Army Air Force
PLAN	People's Liberation Army Navy
PNTR	permanent normal trade relations
PRC	People's Republic of China
R&D	research and development
R2P	responsibility to protect
RAT	remote access tool
RBF	Rockefeller Brothers Fund
RFA	Radio Free Asia
RIMPAC	Rim of the Pacific
RMB	*renminbi*
ROC	Republic of China
RSIS	Rajaratnam School of International Studies
S&ED	Strategic and Economic Dialogue
SAFE	State Administration of Foreign Exchange
SAIS	School of Advanced International Studies
SAM	surface-to-air missile
SARS	severe acute respiratory syndrome
SCS	South China Sea
SD	Senior Dialogue
SED	Strategic Economic Dialogue
SEF	Straits Exchange Foundation
SEZ	special economic zone
SIPRI	Stockholm International Peace Research Institute
SLOC	sea lines of communication
SOAS	School of Oriental and African Studies
SOEs	state-owned enterprises
SRBM	short-range ballistic missile
SRO	surveillance, reconnaissance, and observation
SSBN	nuclear-powered, ballistic missile carrying submarine
SSD	Strategic Security Dialogue
SSN	nuclear powered attack submarine
TAC	Treaty of Amity and Cooperation

TAF	The Asia Foundation
TFC	Teach for China
TPP	Trans-Pacific Partnership
TRA	Taiwan Relations Act
TYF	Ten Year Framework
UAV	unmanned aerial vehicle
UMSL	University of Missouri–St. Louis
UN	United Nations
UNCLOS	United Nations Convention on the Law of the Sea
UNFCCC	United Nations Framework Convention on Climate Change
UNPKO	United Nations Peacekeeping Operation
UNSC	United Nations Security Council
UNSCR	United Nations Security Council Resolution
USCBC	U.S.-China Business Council
USCET	U.S.-China Education Trust
USD	U.S. dollar
USITC	U.S. International Trade Commission
VOA	Voice of America
WAPI	WLAN Authentication and Privacy Infrastructure
WIPO	World Intellectual Property Organization
WMD	weapons of mass destruction
WTO	World Trade Organization
WWF	World Wildlife Fund

Preface and Acknowledgments

The origins of this volume lay in my own uneasy, but growing, sense that many of the fundamental elements of United States–China relations had shifted since the 1990s and there was a real need for a reassessment of the relationship. I had this sense before spending 2009–2010 on sabbatical as a senior Fulbright scholar in China, but it crystallized during this time.

During that year I experienced and witnessed many things that led me to understand things were changing and all was not well in the U.S.-China relationship. I witnessed the frosty reception offered President Barack Obama when he paid a state visit to Beijing and Shanghai in November 2009, and the excessive controls put on every aspect of his schedule by the Chinese government. Having witnessed other presidential visits to China, in which citizens and officials alike welcomed his predecessors effusively, the cool reception offered Obama and his entourage was a distinct rebuff—but also symptomatic of subterranean strains in the relationship. A month before, as I sat in Tiananmen Square on the sixtieth anniversary of the People's Republic and witnessed hours of advanced military hardware roll down Chang'an Avenue (much of the weaponry had been developed to deter the United States), a new robust Chinese nationalism was very much on display. Throughout the year I wrestled with stubborn apparatchik-bureaucrats in the Chinese Academy of Social Sciences who did little to help facilitate my research—with a senior CASS official telling me at the end of the year, "Unlike the 1980s we do not feel we need to do this for Americans any longer." In conversations with professional Chinese colleagues as well as average citizens across the country—from taxi drivers to shopkeepers to students—it became clear that the appealing allure of the United States, so present previously, had worn off and been replaced by a combination of disinterest and disgust. Other Americans I knew recounted similar stories, and American Embassy personnel complained of being "frozen out" of contacts with Chinese society and government. I was treated to regular doses in the Chinese media and academic meetings about the "China Model"—which was being touted as the alternative to the failed "American

Preface and Acknowledgments

Model" in the wake of the 2008 U.S.-triggered global financial crisis. The anti-Americanism and hubris over China's own rise was palpable in many different venues. Throughout the year a series of seemingly random events buffeted the Sino-American relationship—including the Google case, the Copenhagen Climate Change Conference, U.S. arms sales to Taiwan, President Obama's meeting with the Dalai Lama, increased imprisonment of dissidents, a deteriorating business climate for U.S. and foreign businesses, retaliatory trade tariffs, tense encounters between Secretary of State Hillary Clinton and Chinese Foreign Minister Yang Jiechi, and assertive Chinese diplomacy in Asia. Whatever aspirations for a "global partnership" the U.S. and Chinese governments professed only a few months earlier at the conclusion of President Obama's visit to Beijing[1] had been quickly bashed and dashed by intervening events.

All of this left me with a very unsettled feeling about the state and future of U.S.-China relations. Having visited China for thirty-two consecutive years and having witnessed repetitive cycles of ups-and-downs in Sino-American relations, part of my lengthy experience told me that this was just another "bad patch" that would pass in time. But another part of my experience in 2009–2010 told me that something more basic—and something very negative—was transpiring in U.S.-China relations. Fundamental changes in China were causing qualitative changes in the U.S.-China relationship, and not necessarily for the better. Before leaving China I gave a speech at the American Chamber of Commerce in Beijing and wrote an article outlining these changes and calling for a new American strategy toward China to reflect the new realities.[2] To be sure, wrenching changes in the United States were also contributing to a changed relationship with China—the searing impact of the financial crisis on America and its standing in the world, the lingering effects of two wars in Iraq and Afghanistan, but also rising concerns about China: its military modernization, assertive and uncooperative diplomacy, cyber attacks, espionage, unfair trading practices, abuse of ethnic minorities and dissidents, currency valuation, and other troubling issues.

When I returned to Washington from the sabbatical year in China, I also found that a shift in perceptions had occurred. China's "year of assertiveness" had produced a "paradigm shift" among Washington China watchers. A new edge was also apparent in conversations with Obama administration officials—who had come into office in 2008 hoping to forge a global partnership with China. Beijing had not "stepped up to the plate" in their view and, taken together with a range of contentious issues that had surfaced during 2009–2010, the relationship seemed to be on tenuous footing from the U.S. perspective.

The return to the United States thus only served to strengthen my unsettled sense of the trajectory of U.S.-China relations—but it also left me with the conviction to organize an effort to better understand the deeper dynamics at work and to take stock of the state of the relationship. But how to conceptualize and organize this effort? What was required was a fresh investigation that really dug into the extraordinary complexities of the relationship, probed its deeper dynamics and the forces driving the relationship, looked at it from different perspectives, examined the different contexts and arenas in which the U.S. and China interact, and to avoid a "temperature taking" exercise.[3] I thus spent several months during the fall of 2010 thinking through how to organize such a research effort, who to involve, and where to find funding to support it.

This volume is the result. This book came about through the efforts and support of many individuals and institutions, who I wish to gratefully acknowledge.

First, I wish to deeply thank all of the fifteen contributors for their time and efforts. These are all extremely busy scholars and leading experts in the field of Sino-American relations who took a year and a half of their time to prepare their chapters. This not only involved researching and thinking about their chapters but writing multiple drafts. In this process, they not only were politely responsive to my various editorial suggestions and prodding about deadlines but also to the critical comments of external reviewers and each other on earlier chapter drafts. This was truly a team effort in the best sense of academic collegiality. We all entered the project unsure where we would come out—but we all sensed that the foundations of Sino-American relations had shifted in the 2000s and that, as scholars specializing in the subject, we needed to understand the nature of those changes and to produce a study that was both up-to-date on the various aspects of the relationship and captured its changing dynamics. There was no attempt to come to any joint conclusions, although readers will see that consensus emerged on several important themes.

In December 2010 we convened an intensive two-day conference at the Elliott School of International Affairs at George Washington University to present and critique the initial draft chapters. This was done in a collegial "peer review" fashion. In this process we were joined by many of Washington, D.C.'s leading China experts who gave generously of their time and expertise to serve as designated discussants and join the general discussion of different topics. This group of experts included: David M. Lampton (Johns Hopkins SAIS), Charles Glaser (George Washington University), Douglas H. Paal (Carnegie Endowment for International Peace), John Frisbie (U.S.-China Business Council), Cheng Li (The Brookings Institution), Jonathan Pollack (The Brookings Institution), Richard Bush (The Brookings Institution), J. Stapleton Roy (Woodrow Wilson International Center for Scholars), Michael Yahuda (George Washington University), and Kenneth Lieberthal (The Brookings Institution). I am most grateful to each for their important contributions.

I am also most grateful to the Sigur Center for Asian Studies, particularly its Director Edward McCord and staff members Matt Grieger and Christopher Wong, for their efforts in organizing the many complicated logistics of this international conference. The smooth and collegial flow of the proceedings reflected their hard work behind the scenes. Thanks also go to Christopher Wong for compiling the list of abbreviations and acronyms.

Finally, no project of this nature could materialize without significant financial support. In this case I am most grateful to two sources. First, I wish to thank the Ford Foundation for a generous grant (No. 115-0202), and particularly Ford's Beijing Representative John Fitzgerald for his personal support and understanding of the importance of the project. Second, the book benefited from support from the China Policy Program (CPP) of the Elliott School at George Washington—and I would particularly like to acknowledge the ongoing support for the CPP from Elliott School International Council member and alumnus Christopher J. Fussner. Without Chris's continuing support over many years, the CPP would not have achieved all that it has since its establishment in 1998.

All of those who have contributed to the publication of this volume hope that it advances understanding of Sino-American relations, so that these two major powers and great nations can forge a peaceful and productive future together (even if our analysis leads us to different conclusions). I therefore wish to dedicate this book to the broader group of America's China specialists and China's America specialists, who have labored daily for decades to improve the relationship through interpreting the "other" for their respective societies and governments. Our respective work will never be done, and it has never been more challenging, but it has also never been more important.

David Shambaugh
Washington, D.C.
May 2012

NOTES

1. See "U.S.-China Joint Statement," available at: http://www.whitehouse.gov/the-press-office/us-china-joint-statement.
2. David Shambaugh, "The State of U.S.-China Relations on the Eve of S&ED Talks," available at: http://www.amchamchina.org/article/index/6271; David Shambaugh, "A New China Requires a New U.S. Strategy," *Current History* (September 2010), pp. 219–226.
3. All too often, journalists wish to get a simplistic snapshot of the relationship—is it warm or cold, up or down, getting better or getting worse, and so forth—and thus fail to understand the deeper dynamics at work.

Part I

Introduction

1

Tangled Titans

Conceptualizing the U.S.-China Relationship

David Shambaugh

The relationship between the United States and People's Republic of China has rightly been described by officials and experts in both countries as the most important relationship in world affairs.

It is also the most complex one. These two titans are tangled together in innumerable ways—strategically, diplomatically, economically, socially, culturally, environmentally, regionally, internationally, educationally, and in many other domains. The two nations are the principal powers in the Asia-Pacific region and globally. The two possess the world's two largest economies in aggregate, two largest military budgets and navies, are the two largest consumers of energy and importers of oil in the world, are the two largest national emitters of greenhouse gasses and contributors to climate change, contribute the two largest numbers of Ph.D.s and patent applications in the world, and are the only two true global actors on the world stage today. They are each other's second largest trading partner, the U.S. is the largest source of foreign direct investment in China, while China is the largest foreign creditor of the United States; China is the world's largest exporting nation, and the United States the largest importer. Every day about 9,000 people travel between the two countries, nearly 150,000 Chinese students study in American universities with about 20,000 Americans studying in China. There are 38 sister province/state and 169 sister city relationships binding localities together and offering opportunities for exchanges. There are 300 million Chinese learning English and approximately 200,000 Americans learning Chinese.[1]

By these and many other measures, the United States and China are inextricably tied together and exert the greatest impact of any two nations on international relations today. It is therefore of vital importance to understand the complexities and dynamics that underlie and drive this relationship. Yet, the elements of the relationship are in flux and have changed significantly over the past decade, making many previous studies outdated.[2] This book attempts to update, unpack, and explain these complexities. Following this introductory chapter, this is done through the prism of seven distinct contexts: the historical context, the theoretical context, the domestic context, the bilateral context, the regional context, the global context, and alternative Sino-American visions for the future evolution of the relationship.

"COOPETITION" AND "COMPETITIVE COEXISTENCE"

The main argument in the volume, and what we see as the principal theme in the relationship at present and into the medium term future, is that the United States and China are inextricably tied together, that they cooperate extensively, but that there is also rising competition in the relationship. This leads to a mixed picture of cooperation and competition—a condition I call "coopetition." Just as Zalmay Khalilzad and his Rand Corporation colleagues coined the term "congagement" several years ago to denote the mixture of engagement and containment in U.S. policy towards China,[3] I believe that "coopetition" captures the contradictory dual nature—and the "new normal"—of the relationship today. This is empirically demonstrated in all of the following chapters. To be sure, mixed cooperation and competition is not an unusual condition for two countries—but it *is* an unusual condition for the two major powers in the world to find themselves in. Historically, it is more normal that the two leading powers display minimal cooperation—while being locked into an asymmetrical, competitive, and often adversarial relationship. Sometimes leading powers can coexist in a kind of "concert" of multiple states (as in Europe during the nineteenth century) where the competitive dynamics of the two leading states are somewhat buffered and offset by the other members of the concert, while security and commerce is shared among them. Yet, concerts are inherently fragile as mutual security dilemmas and strategic suspicions germinate like weeds in a spring rain. As they do, the competition and tensions between the two leading powers becomes increasingly acute. As the comprehensive capabilities of the two leading powers begin to "separate" from the other members of the concert, and the capabilities of the secondary power begin to approach that of the primary power, a "power transition" looms on the horizon and an increasingly unstable strategic environment emerges. Even in more classic bipolar orders, such as the Cold War between the United States and former Soviet Union, cooperation between the two primary powers is minimal and rather pro forma—whereas the competitive and adversarial dynamics predominate.

One senses that this situation is occurring today between the United States and China and in international affairs. And there is ample evidence to support this sense. The competitive elements in the relationship are growing and now becoming primary, while the cooperative ones are secondary and declining. The areas of cooperation are narrowing and inter-governmental meetings meant to forge cooperation are becoming more pro forma and acrimonious. Mutual distrust is pervasive in both governments, and one now finds few bureaucratic actors in either government with a strong mission to cooperate. (The educational sphere is one exception.)

This increasingly uneasy situation has been brought about by a number of factors intrinsic to both nations, but also as the result of systemic changes in world affairs. U.S.-China relations are simultaneously conditioned by the structures (and institutions) of the international system, the shifting power balance between them, as well as substantial bilateral linkages—a condition I describe as *structural interdependence*. This condition recognizes that interdependencies bind both together, but *simultaneously* they exacerbate existing frictions and produce new competition. This leads to the odd mixture of a cooperative-competitive dynamic—but a relationship where the *balance* between cooperation and competition is shifting from the former to the latter. I describe this new phase of Sino-American relations as *competitive coexistence*. While increasingly competitive, though, the two powers still coexist in a deeply interdependent fashion. Thus, the overriding policy task for Washington and Beijing is to *manage the competition and maximize the cooperation*, so that the relationship does not lurch decidedly in an adversarial direction.

The implications of this situation are further elaborated at the end of this chapter and throughout subsequent chapters in the volume. First, however, the remainder of this introductory chapter offers a range of alternative paradigms for conceptualizing this complex relationship. Theories can help to illuminate and categorize empirical realities. That many different alternative frameworks compete to explain the macro dynamics of the relationship today is in itself further evidence of its complexity—as *each* offers important insights and holds some validity. No single theory explains all. But, for the sake of simplicity, this chapter first adopts a historical/cultural approach and then utilizes the three principal international relations theories—realism, liberalism, and constructivism—for understanding the U.S.-China relationship today.

THE HISTORICAL AND CULTURAL APPROACH

The first prism through which to view contemporary Sino-American relations involves the two nations' respective modern historical experiences and cultures. These are, of course, not easily generalized, but they are important to understanding the psychological and experiential "baggage" that each brings to the relationship. Nancy Bernkopf Tucker's subsequent chapter elucidates a number of the historical events and factors in an impressive overview of the past century of Sino-American relations. But I would like to add several further considerations. At least five historical and cultural features can be identified that, I suggest, continue to affect Beijing's approaches to the United States and vice versa.

The first is the longstanding Chinese sensitivity to encroachments on its continental and maritime borders by foreign intruders and invaders.[4] This is, after all, the reason the Great Wall was built and rebuilt between the fifth century B.C. and sixteenth century A.D.[5] Territorial fragmentation resulting from external incursions was a longstanding reality for much of China's pre-modern history. More recently in its modern history, particularly during the eighteenth through twentieth centuries, China suffered territorial partition and occupation at the hands of several European colonial powers, Japan, and Russia. Concomitantly, one must consider the longstanding fragmentation of national political authority and the perpetual tug and pull of centrifugal versus centripetal forces throughout Chinese history. This was always exacerbated by foreign incursions on the periphery, leading to a condition the Chinese describe as "internal disorder, external pressure" (内乱, 外环).

These two traditional concerns have particular pertinence for Sino-American relations today. Many Chinese perceive attempts by Washington to strategically pressure their periphery, keep Taiwan separate, while seeking to subvert the Chinese Communist Party's political power by sowing instability among elements of the populace (notably intellectuals and ethnic minorities).

A second element has been China's 150-year search for "wealth and power" (福强) and restoration of its great power status. In this eternal quest, foreign countries are measured by a simple metric: Are they contributing to, or trying to impede, China's grand national mission? By the calculus of many Chinese, the United States' record is mixed at best. While knowledgeable Americans believe that the U.S. has contributed significantly in the pre-1949 and post-1978 periods to China's modernization, there seems to be little awareness of this or sense of gratitude among Chinese society. If anything, there seems to be ingratitude for not doing more, while believing that the United States has strategically, politically, culturally, and technologically attempted to impede China's rightful rise.

This raises the third historical element: American exceptionalism and paternalism. These twin attitudes were explicitly on display during the Republic of China (1911–1949) and implicitly during the "reform and opening" period of the People's Republic of China (1978–). The former holds that the American national identity and experience is unique and is premised on individualism, populism, and laissez-faire capitalism. These all fueled the American liberal ethos, particularly during the interwar period, and led to a distinct paternalism towards China during the Republican (Nationalist) era. This "missionary impulse" to assist but *shape* China's evolution was notably manifest in medicine and the sciences, agriculture, education, religion, government and military organization, and the economy.[6]

As the chapter by Terry Lautz in this volume makes clear, this American paternalistic "mission" to transform China in its image did not die in 1949 with the Communist revolutionary victory—it lived on: first, in continuing support for the rump Nationalist regime on Taiwan and, second (after a period of "hibernation") in an enormous wave of governmental and private philanthropic largesse to mainland China after 1978.[7] During both periods the United States poured incalculable amounts of human and financial resources into China to help it modernize and democratize. At times—notably during the 1920s–1930s and 1980s—the American liberal mission resonated among Chinese elites and intellectuals, with the result that the eager Chinese "student" patronized the paternalist impulse of the American "teacher." These liberal interludes both came to unfortunate ends with the erosion of Nationalist power and victory of the Communists in 1949 (resulting in the recriminations and purges over who "lost China"), and the military suppression of popular uprisings in June 1989. Despite these two searing events, the sense of American exceptionalism and paternalism towards China remained deeply ingrained in the American psyche. America sought to "shape" China's evolution in directions that are politically, economically, culturally, intellectually, and strategically commensurate with liberal American traditions and interests.[8] But China's stubborn resistance to "conform" to American expectations has caused repeated disillusionment in the United States. I sense, though, that this long-standing paternalism in American society towards China and aiding China's development has waned significantly during the past twenty years. The aftereffects of 1989 linger, but more important has been China's own rise and increasing challenges to the United States. Many Americans wonder "why should we assist China to become strong, when it will only challenge us?" If one believes that the two countries are locked in a zero-sum competition—economically, ideologically, politically, militarily, strategically—then this perspective holds considerable validity.

Chinese exceptionalism also endures. Many observers argue that Sino-American relations are now free of ideology since the end of the Cold War, but I would not agree. China may have discredited Maoist ideology, but the Chinese Communist Party (CCP) has definitely not abandoned Marxist socialism or Leninist authoritarianism—and it certainly has not abandoned the ideology of being a great power. Beijing also certainly still sees direct ideological threats coming from the United States. As President Hu Jintao made clear in his speech to the Sixth Plenary Session of the 17th Central Committee in October 2011: "We must be sober enough to see that international hostile forces are stepping up their strategic plots to westernize and divide China, and that the ideological and cultural sectors are the main areas through which they commit long-term infiltration."[9] For their part, Americans remain anti-communist. The innate beliefs in democracy, freedom, individualism, and human rights all still undergird America's approach to China. Thus there remains an underlying ideological struggle between American exceptionalism and liberal paternalism, on the one hand, and Chinese exceptionalism and its socialist political system on the other. The ideological/political divide between the two nations has always been there but was often sublimated in the cause of greater strategic interests. But in the absence of greater strategic commonality today, the ideological and political differences have returned from the background to the foreground of the relationship.

 The fourth historical factor affecting Sino-American relations is the Chinese sense of "face" (面子) that is deeply rooted in Chinese culture. Providing "face" means to give others status and respect. Chinese go to extraordinary lengths to give others "face," maintain their own, and avoid losing face. It is a form of social theater domestically but becomes diplomatic theater internationally. It fundamentally affects Chinese foreign policy, including (especially) towards stronger powers like the United States.[10] Chinese officials crave the protocol and trappings of being treated as a great power, largely to reinforce their image and political legitimacy at home, and they go to extraordinary lengths to avoid international embarrassment. Thus, issues such as how many cannons are fired on the south lawn of the White House, whether visiting Chinese leaders are offered a working luncheon or a state dinner, who gets invited to the meals, what level official meets them at the airport, whether they are provided a Secret Service motorcade, whether they are subjected to public demonstrations, and if they are made to take unscripted questions at a press conference—all become major diplomatic issues for the Chinese side when their president or vice president visits Washington, D.C. They are often far more concerned with the *symbols* of diplomacy than the substance of it. American officials are the opposite and are eager to get down to business and hammer out agreements in tough negotiations. This derives from the American litigious culture. In negotiations, American impatience and desire to get to a substantive outcome frequently bumps up against famous Chinese patience, bureaucratic impediments, and the desire to maintain "face." For Chinese, to negotiate across a (rectangular) table is in itself a confrontational encounter and loss of face—it is far preferable for Chinese to cut a deal informally over a (round) dinner table.

What this means practically for China's relations with other countries (including the United States) is that, in Chinese culture, confrontation is a severe form of losing face and stigmatization. Thus, the American penchant to publicly confront China on various issues—whether human rights, currency appreciation, trade deficit, military modernization, whatever—is tantamount to public shaming (a tactic Chinese reserve only to scold and deter deviant behavior).[11] Chinese much prefer to deal with sensitive subjects behind closed doors, so as to maintain public "face." Disputes and dirty linen should be hidden, not aired, in Chinese culture—whereas American custom is just the opposite.

The final historical factor concerns geography. More specifically, it concerns the Chinese sense of its role in Asia, and the American belief that it is an "Asia-Pacific power." Just as the United States once claimed a "Manifest Destiny" over the western hemisphere, China similarly presided over a several-centuries-long sphere of influence in Asia that became euphemistically known as the imperial "tribute system" and "Sinocentric" world order.[12] Some scholars believe that this is the "natural" Asian regional order and that, having endured a three-century hiatus, it is now returning as China grows stronger and attracts other regional nations back into a de facto sphere of influence.[13] Some even go so far as to provocatively argue that China will soon "rule the world."[14]

Yet, since the nineteenth century, and particularly after World War II (precisely the period when China was in decline), the United States established its presence in the Asia-Pacific and has very much considered itself to be a legitimate regional actor and major power. More recently, the Obama administration has made much of its strategic "pivot" to the region. It is not clear, but unlikely, that China accepts this American position. If it does accept some U.S. presence, it surely does not accept American "primacy" or "hegemony" over the Asia-Pacific. Many in China certainly resent the American presence—although its officials occasionally (usually when prompted by the U.S.) offer verbal reassurances that China "recognizes" American interests in the region. Such lukewarm recognitions reflect tolerance more than genuine acceptance. Some senior Chinese officials are more reassuring. "We have no intention to drive the U.S. out of Asia. There is no need for this. You are already in our house (in China)—why would we like to drive you out of the neighborhood," observed Vice Foreign Minister Cui Tiankai in an interview with the author.[15] Moreover, the majority of China's Asia-Pacific neighbors publicly and privately welcome the American presence—increasingly as a means to "balance" a growing and sometimes "assertive" China.

So there exists a strategic "contradiction," as Marxists would say. From the Chinese perspective, the United States is a Johnny-Come-Lately interloper—while China's geographic and cultural centrality has anchored Asia for six millennia. While the tribute system of old is just as impractical to reassert today as the Monroe Doctrine is for the United States, it nonetheless lurks in the strategic background of the Sino-American relationship.

There are many other important aspects of, and differences between, Chinese and American histories and cultures which are enduring features that still underlie and affect Sino-American relations today.[16] These subliminal macro factors usually go unnoticed by those who track Sino-American relations, but I am convinced they continue to have an operative impact. Having considered these, the remainder of the discussion below pertains to the three principal theories in the field of international relations (IR)—realism, liberalism, constructivism—and briefly discusses how each is a vector through which to view different aspects of the Sino-American relationship.[17]

REALISM

Realism is the longest extant paradigm of international relations. Ancient realism had its origins simultaneously in Greece with Thucydides' classic study of the Peloponnesian War (431–404 B.C.), and in China during the Warring States period (475–221 B.C.) in the thinking of Han Feizi (280–233 B.C.). While there are indeed important variations among different realists and in each phase of the theory's development, all realists share certain core assumptions: a generally pessimistic view of human nature; the centrality of states as actors in international relations; an emphasis on the material capabilities of states; the essential insecurity of states; the uncertainty of states' intentions; a prevailing condition of anarchy in the international order; an emphasis on the structure and polarity of the international system; the pursuit of power; and the struggle to ensure security in this environment. Regardless of variations, all realists tend to view power politics as a zero-sum game and anticipate conflicts of interests between established major power and rising challengers. Some believe that a conflict can be postponed, and a rising peer competitor deterred in the short to medium term, but in the longer term the intrinsic imperative of survival drives states into prolonged—and dangerous—competition. As Ashley Tellis succinctly puts it in chapter 4: "Heightened competition is inevitable—the only argument [among realists] is over the degree of its intensity."

Because realists see the structure of the international system as a key variable, they focus closely on polarity in the international system.[18] They identify major powers that constitute the system's poles, as well as middle powers and smaller states that seek to either align (bandwagon) with or against (balancing) the major powers. Realists disagree about whether unipolarity, bipolarity, tripolarity, or multipolarity is the most stable or unstable system. But many realists argue that *transitions* from one system to another are likely to be unstable periods in which miscalculations frequently occur, tensions are aggravated, and conflicts often erupt. This is known in neo-realist thinking as *power transition theory*. Power transition theory holds that the period when a rising power *approaches parity* with the established power is *the most* unstable and prone to conflict—what Organski and Kugler described as the "crossover" point.[19] In this transitional period, either the predominant power is likely to launch a preemptive war to stave off the challenge of the rising power *or*, more commonly, the challenger may strike first. This is what Robert Gilpin labels "hegemonic wars."[20]

John Mearsheimer's *The Tragedy of Great Power Politics* is Exhibit A of "offensive realism" or hegemony theory. In this book and his other writings, Professor Mearsheimer expounds his "iron law" that all powers seek hegemony, are discontent with balances of power, and the U.S. and China are no exceptions. This presents, in his view, a grave and future danger to the United States and its own hegemonic position in Asia and the world. He goes so far as to claim, "What makes a future Chinese threat so worrisome is that it might be far more powerful and dangerous than any of the previous hegemons that the United States confronted in the twentieth century."[21] Mearsheimer is therefore unabashed and explicit in his policy prescription that Washington should move forthwith to impede and counter China's rise—what can be described as "preemptive containment." Mearsheimer's analysis is anchored on assessing material capabilities of states and the assumption that all states seek absolute hegemony—where culture, traditions, ideologies, or domestic political systems play little role. As such, China's protestations of its "peaceful rise" or "peaceful development," its ancient traditions and statecraft, its historical experience of subjugation by foreign powers, and its current political system are seen as unimportant or irrelevant.

Aaron Friedberg essentially shares Mearsheimer's view that the U.S. and China are locked in a "contest for supremacy," as he puts it, but his analysis is born less out of asymmetrical power transitions than geopolitical competition in Asia.[22] He sees Asia's future through a realist's historical prism of geopolitical rivalry in Europe—arguing in previous writings that "Asia's future is Europe's past."[23] Yet, unlike Mearsheimer, Friedberg's analysis places great weight on the nature of the Chinese communist regime as a key variable and underlying source of friction with the United States. Says Professor Friedberg:

> Deep-seated patterns of power politics are driving the United States and China toward mistrust and competition, if not toward open conflict. The fact that one is a liberal democracy and the other remains under authoritarian rule is a significant additional impetus to rivalry. The yawning ideological chasm that separates the two nations is both an obstacle to measures that might reduce uncertainty and dampen competition, and a source of mutual hostility and mistrust. . . . Ideology inclines the United States to be more suspicious and hostile toward China than it would be for strategic reasons alone.[24]

In this regard, Friedberg borrows from "democratic peace theory" in the Liberal tradition, which argues that democracies do not fight each other while autocracies and democracies do.

While Mearsheimer and Friedberg are illustrative of the most alarmist realist assessments of China's rise, there is no shortage of such studies that predict an inevitable conflict between the United States and China.[25] Realists tend to focus almost exclusively on the security and military variable in the relationship, while neglecting the economic and cultural variables that enmesh the two countries in webs of interdependence. Most such assessments tend to view the United States as a benign hegemon, but treat China as an assertive destabilizing power. As such, they see China as the "expanding" and "revisionist" power, while the United States is assumed to be the "status quo" power that must "respond" to China's rise and occasional provocations. Analogies are frequently drawn between previous rising powers' challenge to the reigning hegemon, for example, Wilhemine Germany's challenge to imperial Britain at the end of the nineteenth century. The counseled response by realists is to sustain American primacy through "balancing" and "strategic hedging" tactics by the United States together with its Asian allies and partners.[26]

These assessments are all good examples of a realist view that emphasizes the asymmetrical nature of the Sino-American power balance, as well as the power transition taking place as America's power relatively declines while China's rises. Ashley Tellis' insightful chapter in this volume falls squarely in this genre. However, not all power transition theorists foresee an inevitable Sino-American clash.[27]

In addition to the relative shifts in the balance of power, central to realist analysis is the logic of the "security dilemma." Popularized by Robert Jervis in 1978,[28] this concept posits that even if states seek to augment their security by internal and external means for purely defensive reasons, other states must worry that these efforts could mask motives that are actually offensive and threatening. At present, this is particularly argued to be the case with China's naval, cyber, anti-satellite, and ballistic missile modernization programs. In each case, China's actions are perceived as destabilizing and even aggressive by many American strategists.[29] Christopher Twomey's chapter in this volume is a perfect illustration of the security dilemma at work in Sino-American relations. It makes the reader realize just how hair-trigger and prone to accidental conflict the U.S.-China military relationship has become.

Other observers are more optimistic. They believe that, when faced with a security dilemma, a state's best option is restraint and/or cooperation. International security scholar Charles Glaser argues that the U.S.-China security dilemma—both at the conventional and nuclear level—is *not* acute and may not even exist, as both states have many reasons to feel essential *security*, both can coexist in a bipolar environment, and there is ample room for both sides to take steps to enhance confidence and reduce strategic mistrust.[30] Some China scholars who specialize in security relations, such as Michael Swaine, are also confident that the strategic competition can be managed.[31] While arguing that competition is the most likely feature of future U.S.-China relations, Harry Harding's concluding chapter in this volume is also more sanguine about keeping strategic tensions from escalating to conflict. Bonnie Glaser's chapter and part of Christopher Twomey's chapter detail the wide range of existing inter-governmental diplomatic mechanisms that are designed to reduce mis-perception and mistrust while forging strategic cooperation. Avery Goldstein's chapter also describes well the complex web of issues the two must manage in Asia. A joint study by leading American and Chinese scholars also argues that managing competition is possible, but only if both sides exercise restraint by inadvertently or intentionally provoking the other and infringing on each side's core interest.[32] Finally, none other than Henry Kissinger also recognizes the rising dangers of Sino-American strategic competition and counsels a "co-operative approach of mutual restraint" by both nations:

> They need to recognize that some competition is inherent and inevitable, but also that it can be conducted within defined limits. They should seek together to circumscribe the sphere in which their peaceful competition is taking place. If that is managed wisely, both military confrontation and abdication can be avoided; if not, escalating tension is inevitable. It is the task of diplomacy to discover this space, to expand it if possible, and to prevent the relationship from being overwhelmed by tactical and domestic imperatives.[33]

Finally, a group of scholars led by Robert Ross and Zhu Feng examined the applicability of power transition theory to the rise of China. Unlike the prevailing consensus among power transition theorists that war between the rising and established power is highly likely precisely in the period in which the former approaches parity with the latter, this set of scholars came to the conclusion that war between the United States and China is not inevitable dur-ing the transition period: "Structural variables, including global unipolarity, regional bipolarity, geography, and weapons systems combine to mitigate both security dilemma dynamics and the prospect for war."[34]

The discussion above is illustrative of the predominant position that real-ism holds in the U.S. discourse on China. As is seen below, no other paradigm has generated anywhere near as much literature on the Sino-American rela-tionship. Needless to say, with such diversity "within the family" of realism it is not unsurprising that there is also diversity in the analyses, prescriptions, and predictions from realist scholars who study Sino-American relations. But there is one common dominator across the neorealist spectrum—that contemporary and future Sino-American relations have been, and will continue to be, characterized predominantly by strategic competition, geopolitical rivalry, and the possibility of military conflict.

Despite the dominance of realism in the discourse, readers of this volume and observers of the U.S.-China relationship should be aware that this has much to do with the American analytical fixation on grand strategy, meta trends, and military power. A focus on other dimensions of the relationship, which this volume intentionally does, leads one to different conclusions. If one draws on other theories and focuses on other levels of analysis, variables, and actors, one comes to other—less threatening and pessimistic—conclusions.

LIBERALISM

The other prevalent school of international relations theory is liberalism. Classical liberal theory has its origins in the Enlightenment and the thought of Montesquieu, Locke, Kant, and Adam Smith. Anchored in the belief of societal progress, human reason, moral values and ethics, liberals believe that the pursuit of power can be constrained and promethean energies can be channeled for the collective good of society. For liberals, ideas and values matter, domestic politics matter, civil society matters, and institutions matter.

For liberals, the world of international relations is not in a state of Hobbesian anarchy, relations between states are not zero-sum and all about power maximization—rather they are about building a just world, deepening transnational linkages, and conditioning behavior through institutionalized norms and laws. Unlike Realist theorists who focus on external systemic factors in shaping states' behavior in international relations, Liberals tend to look *inside* the state and society for the sources of external behavior. Individual liberty and freedoms are seen as the fundamental source of progress (the belief in progress is a core liberal assumption) and modernity. Representative and constrained democracies are the embodiment of liberal beliefs and norms. Liberalism is closely connected with the emergence of the modern constitutional state. Liberals further believe in "democratic peace theory," the idea that democracies do not go to war with each other, even if they do compete in various realms. Conversely, they tend to believe that autocracies are inherently aggressive—if, for no other reason, because they are not accountable to their people. Liberals also have a strong belief in free trade.

At the same time that liberals focus on variables internal to states, a key dimension of neoliberalism involves international institutions, external constraints on states, and the concept of "global governance." Unlike Realists who believe that international relations exist in a state of anarchy in which there is no global authority, Liberals believe that states' Darwinian impulses can be constrained through structures and laws, and that global governance is possible.

A distinct sub-theory of interdependence grew out of the Liberal tradition, but also as a reaction to the Realist School of IR theory and its exclusive focus on states and interstate relations. Pioneered by Robert Keohane and Joseph Nye in the 1970s,[35] interdependence theory focuses on transnational relations and primarily non-state actors, particularly in the economic domain. It was the forerunner to globalization theory.[36] Over time the concept of interdependence has come to embrace both state-to-state and sub-state actors.

These variations of Liberal theory find a number of applications in Sino-American relations. Three areas stand out.

The first is the nature of the Chinese political system. Given their predisposition in favor of democracy and predilection against authoritarianism, it is little surprise that American liberals have been discontent with the Chinese Communist Party's rule. This can be described as "republican liberalism." It is important to remember, though, that the American desire to liberalize and democratize China dates back to the pre-communist period. As discussed above, American paternalism towards China is deeply rooted in liberalism. This is why there was such deep national angst over the "loss of China" when the Nationalists were defeated by the Chinese Communists. This was followed, as described in Nancy Tucker's chapter, by several decades of U.S. support for "Free China" (Taiwan) against "Red China." It also helps to explain the continuing American support for Taiwan, which has genuinely democratized since the lifting of martial law in 1987. American liberalism was also reflected in the strong revulsion and reaction Americans felt over the military suppression of the pro-democratic uprising in China in June 1989. With Chinese students quoting Benjamin Franklin, Thomas Jefferson, Nathan Hale, and other American democrats, their erection of a replica of the Statue of Liberty in the center of Tiananmen Square, and their unprecedented demonstrations across China in favor of free speech, free press, and democratic reforms, all resonated deeply with the American liberal impulse—only to be suppressed by the tanks of an intolerant communist regime. The liberal "end of history" thesis was applied to China in the wake of the Tiananmen debacle.[37] Some Sinologists predicted that it was only a matter of time before the Chinese communist regime joined its East European and Soviet comrades in the Marxist-Leninist "dustbin of history,"[38] while others argued that the CCP was "adaptive," "resilient," and had staying power.[39]

The liberal emphasis on the authoritarian Chinese political system is linked directly to the issue of human rights in China. This has been a highly contentious dimension of Sino-American relations over time, although it has become somewhat "routinized" through intergovernmental dialogues—while the Chinese security state continues to routinely detain, arrest, harass, and imprison political dissidents. The 2010 Nobel Peace Prize recipient, Liu Xiaobo (serving an 11-year prison sentence for "inciting subversion of state power"), is the symbol of an increasingly large number of those who speak out in favor of human rights in China, only to have those rights completely deprived.[40]

The American discontent with the Chinese political system and human rights situation is not limited to liberals. As we noted above, the ideological/political dimension of the relationship is rising in importance and realists like Aaron Friedberg place Chinese politics at the center of their critiques. Realists and neoconservatives are some of the staunchest anti-communists.

The second key realm in which liberalism has an impact on Sino-American relations is in the realm of trade. This is "commercial liberalism." It has been a key element of American strategy for more than three decades to integrate China into the international trading and financial systems (epitomized by the World Trade Organization and Bretton Woods institutions). The premise has been that it would force China to "play by the rules" of international commerce—particularly breaking down protectionist barriers and domestic subsidies while maximizing economies of scale and comparative advantages. But both liberals and realists, Democrats and Republicans, have also believed that trade would have a transformative effect *inside* China—economically, socially, and politically. It has been an assumption—articulated by several American presidents (most forcefully by George W. Bush)—that the sheer strength of the international trading systems would empower Chinese society and ultimately liberalize Chinese politics.

The third element has to do with China's participation in international institutions and "global governance." This can be described as "liberal institutionalism." G. John Ikenberry's and Rosemary Foot's chapters in this volume (chapters 3 and 14 respectively) deal directly with this issue, albeit in different ways. Professor Ikenberry makes the very strong case that China's evolution over the past three decades of reform, at present, and well into the future is profoundly conditioned by the international liberal order. In making this case he puts forth a "double bind" argument that China is deeply and irreversibly institutionalized in the order itself, and if China wished to mount an alternative challenge of an illiberal order it would fail. Says Ikenberry:

> The existing international order is deeply entrenched. It is a layered system of Westphalian and liberal rules and institutions. It is an order that is wide and deep. It is not simply a political formation tied to American power. The constraints and obstacles on China's ability to overturn and reorganize international order are multiple: the Chinese "model" is unsustainable as a global system, Chinese revisionism will generate self-encirclement, and, in the background, the grand mechanism for overturning old international orders—great power war—has disappeared.

Ikenberry makes a strong case that, even *if* China did wish to replace the existing global liberal order with an illiberal order of its own making, it would confront insurmountable difficulties in doing so.

Rosemary Foot's chapter, as elaborated more fully in her book *China, the United States, and Global Order*,[41] extends the analysis in several important ways. Sharing the general conclusions of several other scholars,[42] Professor Foot finds that China has willingly and thoroughly integrated into the international institutional order and, thereby, in most ways has been a "status quo" power.[43] Yet, despite China's integration, Professor Foot concludes, "Beijing generally remains ambivalent about the liberal international order and uncomfortable in bodies that act too independently of the states that make up their membership." Her conclusion echoes the assessments of Ann Kent, Gregory Chin, this author, and other scholars, that China continues to exhibit significant ambivalence, shallow normative conformity, and tactical cooperation in certain international regimes (particularly in the areas of security and human rights). Thus, while China may have been co-opted into the international institutional order (a key element in U.S. and European strategy over four decades), it still has not been fully "socialized" into the underlying liberal norms of that order. Given the nature of China's authoritarian political system, lack of transparency in both the economic and military realms, and historical experiences with the West, it is highly unlikely that it will ever fully accommodate itself to the liberal order—and therefore to American and Western desires and demands.

Thus, like Realist theory, an examination of the application of liberal theory to U.S.-China relations reveals a number of discomforting conclusions. Unlike realists, liberals are not particularly worried about the potential outbreak for conflict between the United States and China, as they place a far higher value on the ability of the liberal international order to constrain and shape China's choices and behavior. But they are nonetheless troubled by the nature of China's authoritarian political system, its partial compliance with global trade rules, and Beijing's less than full commitment to international norms and regimes based on liberal principles.

On the other hand, many liberals argue that China and the United States share a large number of global issues and responsibilities in common, including: regional and global security, the environment, transnational crime, access to energy supplies, open trade and investment, nuclear proliferation, and so on. These transnational issues form the core cooperative agenda for U.S.-China relations. Presidential summits and the annual Strategic and Economic Dialogue offer evidence of this bilateral cooperative agenda in the form of lengthy joint statements and communiqués. The cooperative agenda between the two countries is tangible and important. Bonnie Glaser's chapter is proof positive of the wide range of issues and mechanisms that sustain it. Periodically, in more heady days of the relationship, this gives rise to speculations about a U.S.-China partnership or "G-2" condominium.[44]

This all argues for a continued mixture of cooperation and competition in Sino-American relations. The key question, as Harry Harding's concluding chapter discusses and I further elaborate below, is the *balance* between the cooperative and competitive elements and the *management* of them.

CONSTRUCTIVISM

Unlike liberalism and realism, which emphasize material factors among states, constructivist theory emphasizes the realm of ideas—and, particularly, how ideas are "socially constructed" in societies and become socialized as behavioral "norms" within and between societies.[45] The formation, socialization, and transmission of individual and national identities are important processes for constructivists. While constructivism is rooted in domestic cultures and societies, it thus "travels" across national boundaries and shapes behavior within "international society." Constructivism has its origins in the Frankfurt School of critical social theory and the sociology of knowledge,[46] developed in "national character" studies of the early Cold War period, but popularized in international relations theory by Alexander Wendt, Ian Hurd, Martha Finnemore, and others during the 1990s. In the post–Cold War period, constructivist theory has wrestled with the interplay of national interests and transnational imperatives.[47] Much constructivist literature also explores norm socialization and diffusion via informal and formal institutions.

One manifestation of constructivism occurred during the late Cold War period when U.S. and Soviet experts sought to forge "epistemic communities" between the two adversarial societies (mainly in the fields of science and arms control) to advance détente. The premise was that if the two could establish professional linkages it would be easier to identify and agree on mutually acceptable norms of behavior—thus stabilizing relations. The American-Soviet experience of building epistemic communities was applied to U.S.-China exchanges, but in a much wider set of professional fields. As in the Soviet case, groups of American and Chinese scientists and arms control experts began a set of exchanges in the early 1980s (although China and the United States were not engaged in arms control negotiations). These were quickly supplemented by a broad range of so-called "Track II" (nongovernmental) exchanges between international relations and security specialists, as well as economists.

What distinguished China from the Soviet case was, of course, the open opportunities for educational exchange between the two nations following the normalization of diplomatic relations in 1979 (the author was, in fact, the first

American and foreign student permitted to study international politics in a Chinese university). Immediately, with core funding from the Ford Foundation, three committees of American experts were established to oversee and fund exchanges in the fields of international relations, law, and economics.[48] The operational premise of these committees was precisely that to train Chinese students and scholars in these fields would, first, infuse them with American (and prevailing international) concepts and, second, build epistemic communities between the two societies. The National Academy of Sciences and other professional organizations also became involved in the process. This was part and parcel of the revitalized mission to "shape" China's evolution, discussed above.

Today, more than 30 years later, countless numbers of students and scholars have been exchanged in these and other professional fields. Strong bonds of personal familiarity and professional collaboration have been forged. While American and Chinese scholars and professionals do not always agree, they are conversant on the same concepts—thus providing evidence of constructivist connections between the two societies. While scholars such as Alastair Iain Johnston and Ann Kent have studied the socialization of China and its officials in international organizations, there has not yet been any systematic study of Sino-American epistemic communities.[49] The important work of Rosemary Foot and Andrew Walter do explore Sino-American interactions in various global regimes and on various global governance issues (also see Professor Foot's chapter in this volume).[50]

MANAGING "COOPETITION" AND "COMPETITIVE COEXISTENCE" IN SINO-AMERICAN RELATIONS

Through these illustrations I have sought to show how historical factors and these three main bodies of theory in international relations studies—realism and neo-realism, liberalism and neoliberalism, and constructivism—can be applied to understand contemporary Sino-American relations. While each offers insights into some aspects of this exceedingly complex relationship, no single theory explains all. Analysts must draw on *all* four approaches discussed above. Indeed, other theories (which have not been discussed) also offer additional prisms and insights—such as the English School, rationalism, critical theory, post-modernism, feminism, Marxism, psychological theories, decision-making theories, and others. Taken together, by drawing in these paradigms, observers will gain a clearer composite view of the Sino-American relationship. The relationship is far more than an assemblage of data points, facts, events, actors, and interactions—there exist distinct and definite patterns to these isolated phenomena that are illuminated through these theoretical approaches.

Despite the utility of diverse theories, the subsequent chapters in this volume collectively demonstrate that two variables above all characterize the present and future of the relationship: *structuralism* and *interdependence*. Whether from a realist, a liberal, or constructivist perspective, it is clear that *international structures* (security structures, diplomatic structures, normative structures, commercial structures) do much to condition and shape Sino-American relations. U.S.-China relations do not operate in a vacuum, immune from broader forces in the world—quite to the contrary, it is evident that both nations are considerably constrained and influenced in their approaches to the other because of these structures. In general, international security structures tend to contribute to the competitive/adversarial dynamics in the relationship, while international economic structures and normative regimes tend to ameliorate security tensions and constrain competition. In terms of the balance of power, there is a clear structural contradiction between China's rise and America's primacy. As China increasingly becomes a global actor,[51] it is likely to exacerbate structural conflicts of interest as it increasingly bumps up against American equities and interests in various parts of the globe.

At the same time, the subsequent chapters in this book also make abundantly clear that the Sino-American relationship is extraordinarily *interdependent* and tied together through numerous bilateral and multilateral interactions, intergovernmental mechanisms, and inter-societal linkages. The chapters by Charles Freeman and Terry Lautz detail the dense webs of economic and cultural linkages between the two economies and societies respectively, while Bonnie Glaser's chapter is an exemplary illustration of the dense network of inter-governmental interactions. Moreover, G. John Ikenberry's and Rosemary Foot's chapters illustrate how the U.S. and Chinese governments are enmeshed in a thick web of international institutions and regimes. This bureaucratic institutionalization at the bilateral and multilateral levels provides an important foundation and buffer against "strategic shocks" and episodic disruptions to the relationship. Conversely, deep interdependencies can also spawn frictions (particularly in the economic realm). Shelley Rigger's chapter shows that, while the Taiwan issue has seemingly stabilized in recent years and thus been removed as a central thorn in U.S.-China relations, it remains a dynamic and volatile issue.

Because Sino-American relations predominantly reflect these dual characteristics, it leads to the observation that the relationship is increasingly one of "coopetition" and *competitive coexistence*. While the two powers coexist, they do so in an increasingly competitive manner. Despite the many linkages, many of the contributors to this volume (and other observers of the relationship) share the view that the U.S.-China relationship has increasingly tended towards competition in recent years. This is plainly evident in the economic, ideological, normative, security, and geopolitical realms. *Divergence* rather than *convergence* of interests, approaches, and policies increasingly characterize the relationship. As many have noted, there exists a significant deficit of "strategic trust."[52] In the diplomatic domain one sees few attempts by both governments to cooperate and coordinate policies bilaterally and multilaterally, although various institutional mechanisms exist to pursue cooperation and coordination. This is true of the economic and security spheres as well.

It must be said that these institutionalized efforts are increasingly ephemeral and episodic, while the deeper competitive forces threaten to overwhelm the efforts for cooperation. Indeed, the mechanisms themselves seem to have changed from their original purpose to forge cooperation to forums for discussing differences and managing competition. In virtually *every* subject area of the two governments' 60-plus dialogues, substantive differences and frictions are now evident. What these dialogues really amount to is *consultation*, where each side informs the other of its (differing) preferences and policies, rather than forging real cooperation or coordination. In these intergovernmental dialogues, as well as high-level diplomacy, it seems that both sides attempt to present a façade of cooperation and harmonious exchanges, but under the surface of these dialogues—indeed the entire relationship—there exists deepening distrust. Sometimes the differences bubble to the surface and transcend the protocol of diplomacy.[53] The two governments simply do not agree on how to approach many international problems, and powerful domestic interests in both countries limit the ability of both to manage bilateral problems. The two governments sometimes seem subliminally locked in a titanic struggle over competing visions of world order: the United States seeks to expand the liberal order (which very much includes liberal states), whereas China is highly ambivalent about and often opposed to the liberal order (particularly when liberal states seek to use coercion and intervention against illiberal regimes). In short, the two are *tangled titans*.

This is not good news for the future of U.S.-China relations or the world. But it is the reality at present and likely into the near to medium term future. The sphere of cooperation seems to be shrinking while the zone of competition is expanding. As Henry Kissinger notes (above), serious efforts need to be made to expand the zone of cooperation and to more clearly demarcate the zone of competition. It is important to grasp that these are not mutually exclusive or zero-sum zones—they are *coexistent*. Both cooperation and competition coexist *simultaneously*. What changes is the *balance* between these two features. At some points in time the cooperative dimension is more apparent, at others the competitive dimension is ascendant. If one simply conceptualizes the relationship along a spectrum with the extremes of conflict and accord at the two ends, then the middle is composed of the band between competition and cooperation. The U.S.-China relationship today operates in the center of the spectrum between the competition-cooperation bands, never achieving real accord and (hopefully) avoiding conflict.

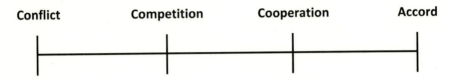

Figure 1.1. A Simple Spectrum of U.S.-China Relations.

Some of the following chapters argue that the structural and competitive dimensions of Sino-American relations have become more apparent and that this trend is likely to continue into the future—absent a newly emergent global threat that challenges both nations to forge greater cooperation. U.S.-China relations have really not faced such a common threat since the 1970s–1980s (despite common opposition to al-Qaeda and terrorism). Absent such a galvanizing mutual threat, the cooperative dimension of relations is diminished and the competitive realm enlarged. As Henry Kissinger also observes: "Absent common goals coupled with agreed rules of restraint, institutionalized rivalry is likely to escalate beyond the calculations and intentions of its advocates."[54]

As such, the *key future challenge* in U.S.-China relations is to *manage competition*, keep it from edging towards the conflictual end of the spectrum, while trying to expand the zone of genuine cooperation (recognizing that complete accord is illusive and impossible). Kissinger hopes for and envisions what he calls "co-evolution" between the two powers, but even he concludes that this will require "wisdom and patience."[55] It will also require mutual pragmatism, acceptance, and tolerance. It is not at all clear to me that the respective political cultures and existing political systems, national identities, social values, and worldviews will afford such a strategic Grand Bargain today as existed during the years of Nixon-Kissinger led *rapprochement*.

Thus, these two "tangled titans" are likely to find it increasingly difficult to coexist—yet they must. However complicated and fraught, this is a marriage in which divorce is not an option. As in marriages, there is one truism in U.S.-China relations: the relationship is never as good or as bad as it seems or is said to be. Reality lies somewhere in the middle. As long as there is no fundamental conflict of national interest, the United States and China should (hopefully) be able to continue to manage their complex relationship. The titans will remain tangled.

NOTES

I am very grateful to Martha Finnemore, Charles Glaser, Avery Goldstein, Katherine Morton, Gilbert Rozman, Robert Sutter, and an anonymous reviewer for their most helpful comments on previous drafts of this chapter.

1. Some statistics in this paragraph are from Chinese Ambassador to the United States Zhang Yesui in a speech at Texas A & M University. See "China-U.S. Relationship Complex," *China Daily*, October 24, 2011.

2. See Patrick Tyler, *A Great Wall: Six Presidents and China* (New York: Public Affairs, 2000); David M. Lampton, *Same Bed, Different Dreams: Managing U.S.-China Relations, 1989–2000* (Berkeley: University of California Press, 2002); James Mann, *About Face: A History of America's Curious Relationship with China, from Nixon to Clinton* (New York: Vintage, 2000); Ramon Myers, Michel C. Oksenberg, and David Shambaugh (eds.), *Making China Policy: Lessons from the Bush and Clinton Administrations* (Lanham, MD: Rowman & Littlefield, 2001); Robert Suettinger, *Beyond Tiananmen: The Politics of U.S.-China Relations, 1989–2000* (Washington, D.C.: Brookings Institution Press, 2004); Rosemary Foot, *The Practice of Power: U.S. Relations with China Since 1949* (Oxford: Oxford University Press, 1997). For more recent studies see, Yufan Hao (ed.), *Sino-American Relations: Challenges Ahead* (London: Ashgate, 2010); Robert G. Sutter, *U.S.-Chinese Relations: Perilous Past, Pragmatic Present* (Lanham, MD: Rowman & Littlefield, 2010); Michael D. Swaine, *America's Challenge: Engaging a Rising China in the 21st Century* (Washington, D.C.: Carnegie Endowment for International Peace, 2011); Jeffrey A. Bader, *Obama and China's Rise: An Insider's Account of America's Asia Strategy* (Washington, D.C.: Brookings Institution Press, 2012).

3. See Roger Cliff, Abram N. Shulsky, Zalmay M. Khalilzad, and Daniel L. Byman (eds.), *The United States and a Rising China: Strategic and Military Implications* (Santa Monica: The Rand Corporation, 1999).

4. See Thomas J. Barfield, *The Perilous Frontier: Nomadic Empires and China, 221 B.C. to A.D. 1757* (London: Wiley-Blackwell, 1992). For a study of contemporary China's management of its borders, see M. Taylor Fravel, *Strong Borders, Secure Nation: Cooperation and Conflict in China's Territorial Disputes* (Princeton: Princeton University Press, 2008).

5. See Julia Lovell, *The Great Wall: China Against the World, 1000 B.C. to A.D. 2000* (New York: Grove Press, 2007).

6. See James C. Thompson, *When China Faced West: American Reformers in Nationalist China* (Cambridge, MA: Harvard University Press, 1969); Peter Buck, *American Science and Modern China* (Cambridge: Cambridge University Press, 2010).

7. See Richard Madsen, *China and the American Dream: A Moral Inquiry* (Berkeley: University of California Press, 1995).

8. For further discussion of this strategy, see David Shambaugh, "A New China Requires a New U.S. Strategy," *Current History* (September 2010).

9. Hu Jintao, "Unswervingly Take the Path of Socialist Cultural Development with Chinese Characteristics, Strive to Build a Socialist Cultural Power," *Qiushi Online*, No. 1, January 1, 2012; translation by the Open Source Center CPP20120103704003.

10. For studies of this phenomenon, see Yong Deng, *China's Struggle for Status: The Realignment of International Relations* (Cambridge: Cambridge University Press, 2008); and Peter Gries, *China's New Nationalism: Pride, Politics, and Diplomacy* (Berkeley: University of California Press, 2004).

11. This occurred, for example, in Vice President Joe Biden's welcoming luncheon toast for Vice President Xi Jinping on February 14, 2012.

12. The classic studies are John King Fairbank (ed.), *The Chinese World Order: Traditional Chinese Foreign Relations* (Cambridge, MA: Harvard University Press, 1968), and Mark Mancall, *China at the Center: 300 Years of Foreign Relations* (New York: Free Press, 1984). For a more recent study see David Kang, *East Asia Before the West: Five Centuries of Trade and Tribute* (New York: Columbia University Press, 2010).

13. See, in particular, David C. Kang, *China Rising: Peace, Power, and Order in East Asia* (New York: Columbia University Press, 2007). Also see David Shambaugh, "China Engages Asia: Reshaping the Regional Order," *International Security*, Vol. 29, No. 3 (Winter 2004/05); David Shambaugh (ed.), *Power Shift: China and the New Dynamics of East Asia* (Berkeley: University of California Press, 2005).

14. Martin Jacques, *When China Rules the World: The Rise of the Middle Kingdom and End of the Western World* (London: The Penguin Group, 2009).

15. Interview with Vice Foreign Minister Cui Tiankai, Ministry of Foreign Affairs, May 18, 2010, Beijing.

16. The best assessments of Chinese political culture are by Lucian W. Pye, *The Mandarin and the Cadre* (Ann Arbor: Michigan Monographs in Chinese Studies, 1988); *Chinese Negotiating Style: Commercial Approaches and Cultural Principles* (Boston: Quorum Books, 1992); *The Dynamics of Chinese Politics* (Boston: Oelgesschlager, Guun & Hain, 1982). Also see Alastair I. Johnston, *Cultural Realism: Strategic Culture and Grand Strategy in Chinese History* (Princeton: Princeton University Press, 1995).

17. While there are many other applications of IR theory to the rise of China, a recommended survey can be found in Avery Goldstein, *Rising to the Challenge: China's Grand Strategy and International Security* (Stanford: Stanford University Press, 2005).

18. The relevant literature is enormous, but a good survey can be found in Nuno P. Monteiro, "Unrest Assured: Why Unipolarity Is Not Peaceful," *International Security*, Vol. 36, No. 3 (Winter 2011/2012), pp. 9–40.

19. A. F. K. Organski and Jacek Kugler, *The War Ledger* (Chicago: University of Chicago Press, 1980).

20. Robert Gilpin, *War and Change in World Politics* (New York: Cambridge University Press, 1981).

21. John J. Mearsheimer, *The Tragedy of Great Power Politics*, op. cit., p. 401.

22. Aaron L. Friedberg, *A Contest for Supremacy: China, America, and the Struggle for Mastery in Asia* (New York: W.W. Norton, 2011).

23. Friedberg makes this case in several previous articles. See Aaron Friedberg, "Ripe for Rivalry: Prospects for Peace in a Multipolar Asia," *International Security*, Vol. 18, No. 3 (Winter 1993/1994), pp. 5–33; "Will Europe's Past Be Asia's Future?" *Survival*, Vol. 42, No. 3 (2000), pp. 147–160; "The Future of U.S.-China Relations: Is Conflict Inevitable?" *International Security*, Vol. 30, No. 2 (Fall 2005), pp. 7–45.

24. Friedberg, "The Future of U.S.-China Relations," pp. 42–43.

25. See, for example, Richard Bernstein and Ross Munro, *The Coming Conflict with China* (New York: Alfred Knopf, 1997); Ted Galen Carpenter, *America's Coming War with China* (New York: Palgrave Macmillan, 2006); Peter Navarro and Greg Autry, *Death by China: Confronting the Dragon—A Global Call to Action* (Upper Saddle River, NJ: Pearson Education, 2011).

26. See, for example, Evan Medeiros, "Strategic Hedging and the Future of the Asia-Pacific Region," *The Washington Quarterly*, Vol. 29, No. 1 (2005), pp. 145–167.

27. See, for example, Steve Chan, *China, The U.S., and the Power Transition Theory: A Critique* (London: Routledge, 2008); David Lai, *The United States and China in Power Transition* (Carlisle Barracks, PA: U.S. Army War College Strategic Studies Institute, 2011).

28. See John H. Herz, "Idealist Internationalism and the Security Dilemma," *World Politics*, Vol. 2, No. 2 (January 1950), pp. 157–180; Robert Jervis, "Cooperation Under the Security Dilemma," *World Politics*, Vol. 30 (1978), pp. 167–214.

29. See, for example, Robert D. Kaplan, "The Geography of Chinese Power," *Foreign Affairs*, Vol. 89, No. 3 (May/June 2010), pp. 22–41.

30. Charles Glaser, *Rational Theory of International Politics* (Princeton: Princeton University Press, 2010), pp. 272–281; Charles Glaser, "Will China's Rise Lead to War?" *Foreign Affairs*, Vol. 90, No. 2 (March/April 2011), pp. 80–91.

31. See Michael D. Swaine, *America's Challenge: Engaging a Rising China in the 21st Century* (Washington, D.C.: Carnegie Endowment for International Peace, 2011).

32. Richard Rosecrance and Gu Guoliang (eds.), *Power and Restraint: A Shared Vision for the U.S.-China Relationship* (New York: Public Affairs, 2009).

33. Henry A. Kissinger, *On China* (New York: Penguin, 2012, revised edition), p. 542. The same quotation, with slightly different wording, can be found in Henry A. Kissinger, "The Future of U.S.-China Relations: Conflict Is a Choice, Not a Necessity," *Foreign Affairs* (March/April 2012), p. 52.

34. Robert S. Ross and Zhu Feng (eds.), *China's Ascent: Power, Security, and the Future of International Politics* (Ithaca: Cornell University Press, 2008), p. 314. In particular, see the chapter by Jack Levy, "Power Transition Theory and the Rise of China."

35. Robert O. Keohane and Joseph S. Nye (eds.), *Transnational Relations and World Politics* (Cambridge, MA: Harvard University Press, 1971); *Power and Interdependence* (Boston: Little, Brown, 1977).

36. See James N. Rosenau and Ernst Otto Czempiel (eds.), *Governance Without Governments: Order and Change in World Politics* (Cambridge: Cambridge University Press, 1992); Thomas Friedman, *The Lexus and the Olive Tree: Understanding Globalization* (New York: Anchor Books, 2000).

37. The original thesis is put forward in Francis Fukuyama, *The End of History and the Last Man* (New York: Free Press, 2002).

38. See, in particular, Roderick MacFarquhar, "The Anatomy of Collapse," *New York Review of Books*, September 26, 1991, pp. 5–9; Gordon Chang, *The Coming Collapse of China* (New York: Random House, 2001); Arthur Waldron, "After Deng, the Deluge," *Foreign Affairs* (September/October 1995), pp. 148–153; Bruce Gilley, *China's Democratic Future: How It Will Happen and Where It Will Lead* (New York: Columbia University Press, 2004); Minxin Pei, *China's Trapped Transition: The Limits of Developmental Autocracy* (Cambridge, MA: Harvard University Press, 2006); Will Hutton, *The Writing on the Wall* (New York: Free Press, 2006).

39. See David Shambaugh, *China's Communist Party: Atrophy and Adaptation* (Washington, D.C., and Berkeley: Woodrow Wilson Center Press and University of California Press, 2008); and Andrew Nathan, "China's Resilient Authoritarianism," *Journal of Democracy*, Vol. 14, No. 1 (January 2003), pp. 6–17.

40. See Perry Link, Tienchi Martin-Liao, and Liu Xia (eds.), *Liu Xiaobo: No Enemies, No Hatred* (Cambridge, MA: Belknap Press of Harvard University Press, 2012).

41. Rosemary Foot and Andrew Walter, *China, the United States, and Global Order* (Oxford: Oxford University Press, 2011).

42. See, in particular, Ann Kent, *Beyond Compliance: China, International Organizations, and Global Security* (Stanford: Stanford University Press, 2007); Alastair I. Johnston, *Social States: China in International Institutions, 1980–2000* (Princeton: Princeton University Press, 2007).

43. See Alastair I. Johnston, "Is China a Status Quo Power?" *International Security*, Vol. 27, No. 4 (2003), pp. 5–56.

44. For criticism of this concept, see Elizabeth Economy and Adam Segal, "The G-2 Mirage," *Foreign Affairs*, Vol. 88, No. 3 (May/June 1989).

45. The classic works are Alexander Wendt, *Social Theory of International Politics* (Cambridge: Cambridge University Press, 1999); and Martha Finnemore, *National Interests in International Society* (Ithaca: Cornell University Press, 1996).

46. See Anthony Giddens, *The Constitution of Society: Outline of the Theory of Structuration* (Cambridge: Polity Press, 1984); Jurgen Habermas, *The Theory of Communicative Action* (Boston: Beacon Press, 1984).

47. See Martha Finnemore, *National Interests in International Society* (Ithaca: Cornell University Press, 1996).

48. The history of the Committee on International Relations Studies with the People's Republic of China (CIRSPRC) is recounted in David Shambaugh, "International Relations Studies in China: History, Trends, and Prospects," *International Relations of the Asia-Pacific* (September 2011).

49. Alastair I. Johnston, *Social States*, op. cit.; Ann Kent, *Beyond Compliance*, op. cit.

50. Rosemary Foot and Andrew Walter, *China, the United States, and Global Order* (Oxford: Oxford University Press, 2011).

51. See David Shambaugh, *China Goes Global: The Partial Power* (Oxford and New York: Oxford University Press, 2012).

52. For an excellent discussion of the issue of "strategic trust" see Kenneth Lieberthal and Wang Jisi, *Addressing U.S.-China Strategic Distrust* (Washington, D.C., and Beijing: John L. Thornton China Center and Peking University Center for International and Strategic Studies, 2012). Also see David M. Lampton, *Power Constrained: Sources of Mutual Strategic Suspicion in U.S.-China Relations* (Seattle: National Bureau of Asian Research, 2010).

53. Such was the case, for example, with Vice President Biden's remarks in welcoming Vice President Xi Jinping in February 2012. See: http://www.whitehouse .gov/the-press-office/2012/02/14/remarks-vice-president-biden-and-chinese-vice-president-xi-state-departm.

54. Henry Kissinger, *On China*, op. cit., p. 543.

55. Ibid, p. 548.

Part II

The Historical Context

2

The Evolution of U.S.-China Relations

Nancy Bernkopf Tucker

For more than a century the emergence of a strong China has dominated the ambitions of China's leaders and people alike. In establishing the People's Republic of China (PRC) on October 1, 1949, Mao Zedong memorably proclaimed that "the Chinese people, comprising one quarter of humanity, have now stood up!" Chairman Mao argued China would again be "a great, courageous and industrious nation" as it recovered from the havoc of "oppression and exploitation by foreign imperialism and domestic reactionary governments."[1]

Less obviously, a strong China—unified, prosperous, and secure—has also been the goal of the United States throughout most, though not all, of its relationship with the PRC. In 1979, on a visit to Beijing, Vice President Walter Mondale evoked Teddy Roosevelt to assure his Chinese hosts of Washington's good intentions.

> It is to the advantage, and not to the disadvantage of other nations when any nation becomes stable and prosperous, able to keep the peace within its own borders, and strong enough not to invite aggression from without. We heartily hope for the progress of China, and so far as by peaceable and legitimate means we will do our part toward furthering that progress.[2]

The key difference between the Chinese and American visions has been the American assumption that a strong China should and would be friendly to, even aligned with, the United States.

To see this clearly, it is vital to understand the history of Sino-American interaction. Until 1949, Americans saw their support for a stronger China as a beneficent gesture, and one that conveniently protected U.S. interests from the depredations of foreign powers. As historian Michael Hunt has pointed out, they fashioned a myth of a "special relationship" between the U.S. and China comprised of "American benevolence, Chinese gratitude, and mutual good will."[3] Americans congratulated themselves for trying to change China, believing they could make it better by making it more like the U.S. They hoped to prevent China's collapse, worrying that a chaotic China would invite international competition, colonization and disorder. But for Washington, until the late twentieth century, China was at best a useful pawn in a broader, more serious game that focused largely on Europe.[4] Accordingly, President Franklin Delano Roosevelt named China one of "Four Policemen" to keep peace after World War II—but in Winston Churchill's view this was just a "faggot vote" he could control in future international organizations.[5] Although Americans lamented its weakness, China was not important enough to elicit serious remedial action.

From the Chinese perspective, although Americans might not have been as rapacious as the British or Japanese, they were still imperialists who did little to curtail exploitation of China (except when necessary to protect U.S. trade and investments). With the advent of the communist era, moreover, the U.S. sided with Mao Zedong's opponents and called them "Free Chinese"—despite Chiang Kai-shek's authoritarian, corrupt and inept rule on Taiwan. Historian Tu Wei-ming observed that the early "image of America as a model of science and democracy" was "displaced by an image of a greedy and violent nation, struggling to remain the wealthiest and the strongest on earth."[6] Beijing never shed its conviction that Washington was determined to contain and transform China, keeping it weak and divided.[7]

All of this has special resonance today because the U.S.-China relationship has emerged as the most "complex and consequential relationship" of the twenty-first century—economically, strategically, environmentally and politically.[8] As Rosemary Foot demonstrates later in this volume, the U.S. and China are interdependent societies with quite different cultures contending over the norms in, and organization of, the international system. Whether China's rise—its evolution into a strong power, perhaps a superpower—will be a good thing for Americans remains uncertain. China's rise not only means a necessary and unavoidable readjustment in U.S. influence and behavior, but also requires the Chinese to assume some of America's responsibilities for world affairs. Washington's willingness to concede gracefully, and Beijing's ability and capacity to undertake these tasks without trying to use its strength to dominate East Asia or the world, will define the decades ahead.

1949–1969: TURMOIL AND SUSPICION

As the Chinese Communist Party (CCP) came to power in China in 1949, its determination to make China a strong and prosperous state aroused widespread anxiety in the United States. As much as Americans had encouraged China to reform and modernize, the strength displayed by a "new China" whose ideological bent allied it with the Soviet Union comprised a threat. Washington feared that China's growing power would be used to carry out destabilizing interventions, sparking revolutions—and eventually—military confrontations. Rather than encourage a strong China, the United States hoped, and sought to ensure that, China would remain weak.

Hostility may not have been inevitable—but history, ideology, culture and expediency made it difficult to avoid. Antagonism served the purposes of leaders in China and the United States better than conciliation. For the Chinese, particularly Mao, anti-Americanism was essential to eradicate imperialism, to rally a vast population in support of the revolution, to defeat and eliminate the Kuomintang and to realize international communist solidarity and national pride. On the American side, the takeover of China by communists looked like a betrayal. Decades of assistance from the U.S. government, missionaries, businessmen and soldiers had been discarded to follow a false faith and retreat behind the "iron curtain." In the early days of the Cold War, with World War II only recently won, a China lobby vociferously argued that China's decision to "go communist" could not have been voluntary, but rather had resulted from a grand conspiracy led by fanatics whose loyalties were to the Soviet Union not China.

Yet, the so-called "loss of China" did have two advantages. First, it rendered Washington's charges of a rapacious monolithic communism menacing the free world credible. Second, as diplomat George Kennan reasoned, China would "more closely resemble a strategic morass than a strategic springboard." Moscow would regret China's dependence regardless of ideological affinity. The U.S., Kennan averred, "need neither covet the favor, nor fear the enmity, of any Chinese regime."[9]

Washington's dismay at the success of the "Red Chinese" did not reflect naiveté about the corruption and ineptitude of Chiang Kai-shek's Kuomintang forces. Americans had found Chiang's troops inadequate in fighting Japan and his government callous about the poverty, hunger and disease that beset the Chinese people. Some acknowledged the greater popularity of Mao's CCP, crediting it with fiercer opposition to Tokyo and stronger interest in the welfare of China's millions. Washington's disillusionment brought it close to jettisoning the Kuomintang and establishing relations with Beijing. In fact, President Harry Truman and Secretary of State Dean Acheson expected that Chiang's government would fail, that the Chinese civil war would end, that Beijing and Moscow might split and that the period after the November 1950 midterm elections would be a good time to launch trade and diplomatic intercourse with China.[10]

The Korean War saved Chiang and derailed any idea of a U.S.-China relationship. Washington immediately threw its support behind South Korea under attack by the North and ordered the U.S. Seventh Fleet into the Taiwan Strait. Although the Truman administration intended this to be temporary, it proved easier to get in than get out. The Chinese Communists, who crossed the Yalu River and struck massively against U.S. forces in October 1950, appeared nothing less than Moscow's minions, and bloodshed on the battlefield made reconciliation difficult for two decades thereafter. Beijing feared for China's security and Washington concluded that all its friends and allies in Asia were vulnerable to a mobilized communist bloc.

The difficulty of fighting the war in Korea came as a surprise to the U.S. Americans had fought alongside incompetent Kuomintang armies during the anti-Japanese war and watched their rapid defeat in the civil war. Rather than a CCP victory, they concluded Mao's 1949 triumph had been a Kuomintang loss. Thus the powerful drive of Chinese Communist armies across the Korean peninsula came as a shock. Chinese Communist soldiers proved capable, dedicated and determined, elevating estimates of China's strength and menace. Washington imposed a strict economic embargo on China and Beijing expelled or imprisoned the last of the American intruders living on the mainland, reaching diplomatic accords primarily with communist states.[11] Beyond the political and military implications of the clash on the Korean peninsula, moreover, the brutality of the war rekindled and reflected strident racism in the U.S. (racism that had been pervasive during the struggle against Japan).[12] As Chinese troops stormed across the Yalu River Americans decried the merger of a long dreaded Asian "yellow peril" with a Nazi-style "red fascism."[13]

War in Korea also had powerful repercussions in the domestic affairs of both the United States and China. In the U.S., it invigorated the scurrilous campaign of Senator Joseph McCarthy who attacked Harry Truman and his administration for cultivating communism in China and in the government at home. McCarthy hounded diplomats, soldiers and scholars for accurately predicting the communist victory and allegedly exposing Americans to unimaginable danger. Anxiety about the Chinese Communists produced lurid images captured in the novel and movie *The Manchurian Candidate* that made the dangers of exposure to communism clear: you would be mistreated, exploited, even brain-washed, emerging as a dupe, a spy or an assassin.[14]

Mao Zedong similarly used the war as a vehicle for manipulating domestic politics, eliminating pro-American sentiment and eradicating anti-communist opposition. His "Resist America, Aid Korea" (*Kang-Mei, Yuan Chao*) campaign ruthlessly attacked so-called reactionaries who, he believed, stood in the way of land reform and reconstruction.[15] It would be followed periodically by other anti-American campaigns such as his "Hate America" week in the summer of 1960.[16]

In the years following the 1953 Korean Armistice, the U.S. seemed devoted to isolating and destabilizing China. President Dwight D. Eisenhower authorized Chiang Kai-shek to attack the mainland, signed a Mutual Defense Treaty with Taipei and stationed troops on Taiwan. But contemporary politics, popular culture and historical writing portray a rigid Sino-American relationship that did not exist. For instance, although Eisenhower proclaimed the U.S. Seventh Fleet would no longer "shield Communist China" by preventing a Kuomintang attack, a policy mislabeled "unleashing Chiang Kai-shek," the administration immediately imposed restraints to prevent him from trying to "retake the mainland" (*guangfu dalu*).[17]

Contact also persisted. The Chinese communist regime might have been viewed as repugnant, but U.S. leaders recognized that they could not topple it—that it was thriving, unified and would endure. Hesitant feelers for a *modus vivendi* occurred periodically. Such proposals, however, never captured the imagination of the opposing leaders at the same time. Ambassadorial talks in Geneva and Warsaw began in 1954, for instance, and facilitated the release of prisoners, insured regular communication and occasionally defused explosive tensions, but otherwise made few substantive changes in relations. Officials flirted with possible initiatives, particularly as the Sino-Soviet bloc began to disintegrate, but those who did—such as Eisenhower, who favored recognition, UN seating and trade with China—did not do enough to surmount political opposition at home.[18]

Contact more often came through confrontation. Between 1954 and 1962 three Taiwan Strait crises raised the specter of war. Sovereignty claims in the aftermath of a still incomplete Chinese civil war triggered the clashes. The offshore islands held by the Republic of China (ROC) were within sight of the Chinese mainland, and Chiang Kai-shek garrisoned a large contingent of his best forces there to harass and sabotage the PRC. His government succeeded in enlisting U.S. military help to sustain his troops under fire, but he could not entrap or persuade Washington into support for recovering the mainland.

More critical to the American experience than crises in the Taiwan Strait was the Vietnam War, which elevated anxiety about Chinese capabilities and intentions. Washington recognized that China was rendering valuable support to Ho Chi Minh. Beijing encouraged the fighting to deplete U.S. resources and manpower. But the U.S. dreaded a reprise of the bloody clashes in Korea and minimized assaults on Chinese soldiers and across the border. Beijing meanwhile sent supplies and manpower to protect its vulnerable frontier, fortify an ideological compatriot, disrupt U.S. containment and establish its international credentials as the leader of the "third world" against both the U.S. and the Soviet Union. The Vietnam conflict contributed to the radicalization of China as Mao used it internally to revive class struggle, reinvigorate the revolution and incite mass mobilization against revisionism and American imperialism.[19] Even as U.S. national unity and international influence suffered because of the war, the PRC moved toward the far more devastating disarray of the Great Proletarian Cultural Revolution (GPCR).The Sino-Soviet Split slowed Beijing's efforts to strengthen China, forcing it to become even more self-reliant. But American fear of the Sino-Soviet alliance did not diminish. When evidence began to accumulate that a rift had developed, Washington accepted its authenticity only slowly. National Intelligence Estimates as late as 1960 asserted that there would be no open break between Moscow and Beijing for the next five years and the army, navy, air force and Joint Chiefs of Staff concurred.[20] Analysts in the government and the scholarly world believed the dispute was not fundamental but rather over how best to confront the U.S. Once persuaded that its roots ran far deeper, Washington lamented that the more rational Soviets could no longer apply any check on Mao Zedong's fanaticism.

The assumption that Chinese leaders were fanatics and ruled recklessly shaped American perceptions of China's behavior. The 1962 Cuban Missile Crisis and the Sino-Indian war following the disastrous Great Leap Forward and the collapse of the Hundred Flowers campaign all seemed to confirm that Mao was an irresponsible extremist. Americans believed Chinese pressure contributed to Soviet Premier Nikita Khrushchev's foolhardy placement of missiles in Cuba. They also blamed China for launching an army across its border with India (although New Delhi had provoked the attack and many judged China's limited response prudent).

The idea that China might become a strong power seemed more credible and more alarming as Beijing developed a nuclear weapon. Moscow refused to give China a prototype bomb and withdrew technicians as a result of fraying ties. Nevertheless, Americans, who did not know the details of Sino-Soviet nuclear cooperation, nervously concluded a Chinese bomb would render Beijing more influential and intimidating. As feared, detonation of a device in 1964 won Beijing respect across the "third world" and especially among overseas Chinese. Washington's efforts to minimize the achievement proved largely irrelevant. Still there were no indications that Beijing or Washington intended to use nuclear weapons against each other.

Throughout it all, even as Washington maintained diplomatic relations with Chiang Kai-shek's rump regime on Taiwan, the U.S. pragmatically dealt with two Chinas much to the chagrin of Taipei and Beijing. This policy suited Eisenhower and Secretary of State John Foster Dulles, who saw it as logical and realistic. Their successors adhered to the "two China policy" even though neither Beijing nor Taipei sanctioned it and the PRC protested the interference in its internal affairs.

Simultaneously, the U.S. moved slowly toward better relations with China in the 1960s. Amid moderating popular opinion—pursuit of better relations was favored by a 53 to 32 percent margin early in the decade—congressional hearings warned that isolating China was unproductive and dangerous. President John F. Kennedy had hinted that he planned to reach out to Beijing, but secretly pledged to veto China's admission to the United Nations and worried about development of a Chinese nuclear bomb.[21] By 1966 President Lyndon Johnson publicly called for "cooperation, not hostility" and congressional hearings explored the idea of a "new policy"—which China specialist A. Doak Barnett dubbed "containment without isolation."[22] Washington worried less about direct Chinese involvement in Vietnam, having successfully exchanged signals with Beijing regarding the limits of the war.

What the U.S. and China might have achieved with a breakthrough will never be known. Mao's Cultural Revolution intervened. It significantly weakened China economically, politically and militarily, and rendered it a pariah internationally. Mao empowered a seemingly maniacal people to assault China's culture and history as well as its educated, and allegedly pro-Western, elite.[23] The Cultural Revolution turned Chinese foreign policy into a xenophobic tirade against everything foreign, capitalist or revisionist. The British embassy in Beijing was ransacked and burned; the U.S. being spared only because it had yet to establish a representative office inside China.[24]

1969–1979: WIDER HORIZONS

The U.S.-China relationship had shifted enough during the 1960s so that by the end of the decade both Washington and Beijing sought to use their common opposition against Moscow rather than continue countering each other. Both the U.S. and China had much to gain geopolitically and strategically through normalization. China anticipated an end to U.S. support for Chiang Kai-shek and unification of Taiwan with the PRC. Normalization would facilitate China's entrance into the United Nations. The U.S.-Japan alliance would be less a threat to Beijing and more an insurance policy against future Japanese aggression. And Mao wanted the U.S. on China's side of the Sino-Soviet rift so that Moscow would not dare attack China. Domestically, normalization freed Mao to redouble efforts to eradicate capitalist resurgence.[25]

After years of fearing China's growing power, U.S. leaders once again believed that a strong China—one that felt confident, prosperous and secure—would serve U.S. interests. Washington sought to use China to make Moscow responsive to Washington's priorities, nervous about its security and less adventuresome in the "third world." Washington hoped normalization would help to end the Vietnam War and strengthen the U.S. position in Asia. Richard Nixon also believed the opening to China would win plaudits even from his erstwhile, liberal enemies and help ensure his reelection.

Ping-pong diplomacy, Henry Kissinger's 1971 trip to Beijing and the signing of the Shanghai Communiqué in 1972 accomplished much of what Nixon sought (with the not insignificant exception of ending the Vietnam War). Nixon and Kissinger secretly promised to remove U.S. troops from Taiwan, not to pursue a "two Chinas" or "one China, one Taiwan" policy, and not support independence—all without pressing Beijing to renounce the use of force against Taiwan. But with these concessions hidden, Nixon's China visit created euphoria that swept the U.S., encompassing enthusiasm for its food, clothing, furniture and medicine (acupuncture). China gained admission to the United Nations and in 1973 the U.S. and China established Liaison Offices in lieu of embassies in each other's capitals.

But despite the China craze, diplomatic relations did not come quickly. The Watergate scandal made it impossible for Richard Nixon, and then Gerald Ford, to contend with anti-communist/conservative Republicans still trying to protect Taiwan. In China, after initial impatience, leaders felt less urgency as the Soviet threat diminished. U.S. opposition to Soviet policies weakened, the Nixon Doctrine signaled U.S. troop reductions in Asia and a succession struggle (including the brief rise of the Gang of Four) materialized.

Not until the election of Jimmy Carter in 1976, and passage of the Panama Canal Treaties, did Washington secretly resume the push for diplomatic relations and feel confident about helping to strengthen China. National Security Adviser Zbigniew Brzezinski, like Kissinger, intended to play the "China card" against the Soviet Union, although he approached the game with greater zeal and lifelong malice against Moscow. Brzezinski did not want simple diplomatic accommodation, he wanted military ties. Accordingly, the Carter administration sold Beijing weapons and technology and wherever the U.S. could not make a sale, Brzezinski proved willing to find a European supplier. The administration also provided the Chinese with intelligence regarding Soviet troop deployments and military facilities and sought China's agreement to host a monitoring station in Xinjiang to replace facilities lost to the Iranian revolution. A strong, cooperative, anti-Soviet China would promote U.S. interests and security.[26]

Beijing also had complex motives. Above all, Deng Xiaoping pursued a new era of self-strengthening, seeking a supportive international environment within which to implement multifaceted and radical economic reforms. Beijing needed the U.S. as a market and a source of technology. Further, Deng wanted a U.S. counterweight to Moscow in order to mount a punitive invasion of Vietnam to punish Hanoi for aligning itself with the Soviet Union and toppling the Chinese-supported Pol Pot regime in Cambodia. So much did Deng require U.S. economic and security cooperation, that he grudgingly acquiesced in the resumption of arms sales to Taiwan (after a one year hiatus) and did not disrupt relations when Congress passed the Taiwan Relations Act in 1979. That legislation, much to Deng's irritation and embarrassment, provided the mechanisms for continued, if informal, U.S.-Taiwan interaction, sustained defensive weapons sales and potential U.S. aid in the event of an attack. Finally, although China got Washington to reiterate the Shanghai Communiqué acknowledgment that both sides of the Taiwan Strait took a "one China" position, Deng could not get the U.S. explicitly to accept it.[27]

China, however, was not alone in agreeing to awkward compromises to cultivate the Sino-American relationship. Jimmy Carter's reputation as the "human rights president" was tarnished when, just weeks after diplomatic recognition, Deng Xiaoping cracked down on the Democracy Wall movement, sending its best known activist Wei Jingsheng to prison for 15 years. Thereafter Congress would seek to hold trade benefits hostage to China's human rights record, but repeatedly failed.

1980–1989: OPTIMISM

Establishing relations on January 1, 1979 did not resolve all Sino-American differences, but Washington could congratulate itself on having a friendly China strong enough to pose problems for the Soviet Union. This seemed especially fortunate when in December the Soviets invaded Afghanistan and rekindled the Cold War. First Jimmy Carter, and then more readily Ronald Reagan, substantially increased defense spending. China, by contrast, found the Afghanistan episode less disturbing and more advantageous. The U.S. military buildup and its active opposition to Moscow reassured Beijing.

China saw an opportunity to resolve troubling Taiwan issues, demanding concessions without fear that Washington would disrupt Sino-American ties.[28] The result became the August 17, 1982 Communiqué through which Beijing sought to reduce and ultimately eliminate U.S. arms sales. Negotiation of the agreement proved arduous, particularly since various members of the Reagan administration were sympathetic to Taiwan. The president himself had talked about restoring diplomatic relations during his election campaign. China ultimately got a Joint Communiqué in 1982, but arms sales to Taiwan did not decline significantly as U.S. officials used financial and other mechanisms to bypass it. Moreover, Reagan gave Taiwan "Six Assurances"—including that Washington had not set a date for ending arms sales and would not consult Beijing prior to sales or pressure Taipei into negotiating with Beijing. Further,

Reagan signed a secret memo asserting that the "willingness to reduce ... arms sales to Taiwan is conditioned absolutely upon the continued commitment of China to the peaceful solution of Taiwan-PRC differences."[29]

Of course, a strong China appealed to Washington only so long as the U.S. and China worked together to thwart the Soviet Union. The flurry of American programs to reform China's socialist economy, upgrade its educational institutions, restore its legal system and facilitate cultural exchange marked a honeymoon period in Sino-American relations in the 1980s that dissipated as Sino-American interests diverged over issues like the Persian Gulf. Beijing became a major weapons merchant in the mid-1980s supplying both sides in the Iran-Iraq War. Of greatest concern to the U.S., China sold Iran "Silkworm" anti-ship missiles capable of striking Kuwaiti oil tankers under U.S. protection in the Gulf. In response to fervent Chinese denials, some Pentagon officials were not simply angered—they stopped advocating more fulsome military relations with the Chinese. "This lack of candor ... eroded the earlier goodwill toward China felt by many in the U.S. defense establishment," according to U.S. Air Force envoy Eden Woon. Misgivings ran so deep that "some even questioned the basic worth of a military relationship."[30]

Magnifying differences between Washington and Beijing, China began to repair relations with the Soviet Union. Although the U.S. publicly hailed the prospect of reconciliation, China's growing strength would be far less desirable if tied to Moscow. Mikhail Gorbachev's decision to end the sometimes violent and often vicious internecine struggle and travel to Beijing for a summit with Deng in May 1989 promised to be a dramatic watershed. The world press descended on Beijing to report the momentous event.

Instead, student demonstrations greeted the journalists in Beijing and some 80 cities across China. Complaints ranged widely but focused on corruption, social instability, inadequate employment, absence of the rule of law and lack of media freedom.[31] By the time Gorbachev arrived there were as many as 500,000 protestors in Tiananmen Square and the crowds continued to swell.

1989–2001: DISARRAY

The Tiananmen Massacre on the night of June 3–4, 1989 shattered the U.S. national consensus on the merits and importance of ties with China. How could the U.S. look favorably upon, or trust, a China that brutalized its own citizens? Economic and military assistance that had promoted China's strengthening for the common struggle against Moscow suddenly looked foolhardy. The profound impact of Tiananmen can be attributed to circumstance and coincidence. First of all, the accidental television coverage broadcast vivid pictures worldwide of heroic but terrified citizens fired upon by ferocious soldiers. Images of a lone man blocking tanks on Beijing's central avenue and the military's tearing down of a Statue of Liberty lookalike (the "Goddess of Democracy") symbolized for Americans the failures of the Chinese communist state. Secondly, American belief in a liberalizing and democratizing China vanished amid repression.

Disillusionment, however, was not the only cause of changed relations. With Sino-Soviet reconciliation, the strategic rationale for U.S.-China rapprochement crumbled, leaving the relationship without a clear purpose—a "strategic glue"—that could counter rancor over cultural, political and security differences. The ultimate collapse of the Soviet Union in 1991 and, with it, the end of the Cold War, rendered China's communism and authoritarianism more noticeable and troubling. Enthusiasm for a strong China evaporated.

After Tiananmen, President George H. W. Bush dreaded the possible rupture of U.S.-China relations in the newly toxic environment. He secretly dispatched representatives to Beijing. National Security Adviser Brent Scowcroft and Deputy Secretary of State Lawrence Eagleburger encountered a surprisingly calm, confident but resistant Deng Xiaoping who assumed that businessmen would pressure foreign governments to reenter the China market.[32] Deng bluntly told Scowcroft not only that irresponsible U.S. media had encouraged Chinese counterrevolutionaries but that wrongful congressional actions created the problem in U.S.-China relations—so Washington would have to "untie the knot."[33] But Americans were outraged by Bush's perceived "kowtowing," preferring stiff sanctions. As a result, Bill Clinton won the presidency in 1992 in part by decrying the president's coddling of the "butchers of Beijing."

In the wake of Tiananmen, accordingly, the human rights agenda—which had often been overlooked by Washington—drew more attention and support. There had, of course, been eruptions of dismay in previous years. Deng Xiaoping's attacks on spiritual pollution (1983) and bourgeois liberalization (1987), for instance, primed Americans, especially in Congress, to deplore China's behavior. Between 1990 and 1994, Congress unsuccessfully sought to link economic policies to progress on human rights, and the U.S. tried fruitlessly to condemn Beijing through the United Nations Commission on Human Rights.[34] China saw all this as hypocritical and self-serving. In fact, China's commercial relations resumed quickly with Japan and Taiwan.[35] By 1993 American and European investors returned to China attracted by breakneck growth stimulated by Deng Xiaoping's 1992 "southern journey."[36] The human rights issue would again threaten commercial relations when Congress wrestled over granting China permanent normal trade relations (PNTR) in 2000 in conjunction with China's accession to the World Trade Organization (WTO), but Deng was right to believe that private interests would prevent effective action. He had predicted already in 1989 that China was a "big piece of meat" and foreign business could not resist.

Other conflicts, large and small, roiled Sino-American relations during the 1990s. In 1993 a Chinese ship, the *Yin He*, sailed from China bound for Iran carrying, according to U.S. intelligence, a large cargo of precursor components for chemical weapons. Beijing rejected U.S. charges, and although U.S. ships shadowed the *Yin He*, it carried no chemicals when it arrived in the Middle East. The incident not only damaged the credibility of American intelligence, it strained Sino-American relations.[37] In 1996 charges of illegal contributions to the Clinton re-election campaign focused on China, Taiwan and Asian Americans. Turmoil from "Donorgate" persisted after the election fueled by claims that access to President Clinton had been purchased with illicit funds. Then came allegations of espionage involving theft of highly classified designs for U.S. nuclear weapons allowing China effectively to duplicate the W-88, a sophisticated miniature warhead. Further, China angered U.S. nonproliferation and defense officials by selling weapons of mass destruction to Pakistan and Iran while steadfastly denying it.

Overshadowing all these disputes, Taiwan became, as it had been in the past, a source of disagreement, dismay and danger. In the 1990s Beijing still lacked the military capabilities for overwhelming the island, but accelerated military modernization to make that goal possible. The display of sophisticated U.S. technology in the Persian Gulf War 1990–1991 and changes in U.S.-Taiwan relations stimulated its sense of urgency.

Washington and Taipei had sustained active informal ties in the 1980s, but Americans felt little enthusiasm for the relationship. The Tiananmen Massacre did what the U.S. government would not—it rekindled interest in, and sympathy for, Taiwan (whose newly democratizing political system contrasted profoundly with China's brutal repressiveness). Then in 1992, trapped in a rancorous and losing presidential race, incumbent President Bush decided to sell 150 F-16 advanced fighter aircraft to Taiwan. Bush had been a friend to China since serving as head of the Liaison Office in Beijing and explained the sale was vital to his re-election (the planes would be manufactured in vote-rich Texas). Later the Chinese leadership would regret having accepted Bush's excuses lamenting that their passiveness opened the way for other unwanted initiatives.

And other initiatives followed quickly. In 1995, Taiwan President Lee Teng-hui secured an invitation to his alma mater Cornell University and the Clinton administration granted a visa. The decision followed manipulation by a weak client state (Taiwan) capable of a tough lobbying effort that used the American Congress against the executive branch, but also reflected U.S. respect for freedom of speech and democratically elected leaders. In retaliation, the Chinese fired missiles into the waters around Taiwan hoping to punish Lee and intimidate the Taiwan electorate by reducing his margin of victory in the 1996 presidential contest.[38] Failing at this, they sought reaffirmation of U.S. policy during Clinton's 1998 visit to China—where, in Shanghai, Clinton delivered the so-called "Three No's": "we don't support independence for Taiwan, or two Chinas, or one-China-one Taiwan. And we don't believe that Taiwan should be a member in any organization for which statehood is a requirement."[39] Not to be outdone, Lee proclaimed the "two-state theory" in July 1999 which asserted that relations between China and Taiwan ought to be conducted on a state-to-state basis and not as relations within one country.

By then, however, the U.S.-China relationship had significantly worsened. In the course of air campaigns over Serbia in the Balkan War, the U.S. bombed the Chinese Embassy in May 1999. Washington insisted this had been a dreadful accident. China's government decried the U.S. assault, rejecting American explanations, and crowds of ordinary Chinese poured into the streets, attacking the U.S. embassy in protest. To many commentators this appeared to be just a new chapter in the U.S. effort to keep China weak and distracted.

2001 AND AFTER: NEW GLOBAL REALITIES

Among the most stunning developments of the twenty-first century has been the shifting balance of power between the U.S. and China. Although the U.S. remains far stronger militarily, its multi-year economic crisis and divided politics have undermined U.S. international leadership, causing commentators around the world to predict America's decline. Simultaneously, the strengthening of China's economic, military and soft power commands considerable admiration and respect. China bears little resemblance to the struggling communist experiment of 1949 facing poverty, disarray and American dominance. Less often do Chinese officials complain about the "century of humiliation," demanding compensation for imperialist exploitation. On the contrary, China is proud of its "capacity to influence the world," which China analyst Michael Swaine observes has "expanded exponentially" in the new globalized environment linked for good and ill by an information revolution.[40]

The rise of China poses new challenges and makes any effort to ensure Sino-American friendship or, at least, prevent an adversarial relationship more important. The inherent difficulties became apparent at the beginning of the George W. Bush administration. Bush had campaigned against coddling China, which he labeled America's strategic competitor to distance himself from Clinton's touting it as a strategic partner. As was true of many new presidents, Bush felt his predecessors had conceded too much to what was then perceived as a middling power with questionable values and institutions. Evidence of Chinese enmity came in April 2001 when a Chinese fighter plane collided with a U.S. reconnaissance aircraft (EP-3), forcing the Americans to land on Hainan Island and killing the Chinese pilot. Relations spiraled downward faster after Bush granted a huge arms sales package to Taiwan and declared publicly he would "do whatever it takes" to assist Taipei in the face of Chinese aggression.

Although the U.S. and China sought to reverse the damage to their relationship even before the 9/11 terrorist strikes in New York and Washington, these grim developments facilitated reconciliation. China provided support for the "war on terrorism" particularly by fighting money laundering, sharing intelligence, enhancing port security and helping to rebuild Afghanistan after defeat of the Taliban. The U.S. welcomed China's actions even though Beijing used anti-terror activities as cover for suppression of domestic separatist movements. But China, at the same time, recognized the advantages of Washington's preoccupation with homeland security and Bush's pursuit of war in Iraq. While Washington focused on Islam and the Middle East and many in Asia concluded that the U.S. had forsaken them, China mounted a successful regional soft power strategy fueled by economic largesse to boost its influence and win friends.

China's growing power also led to expectations about how that power would be used. The U.S. put those expectations into words in 2005 when Deputy Secretary of State Robert Zoellick challenged China to become a "responsible stakeholder" in the international community, abandoning narrow national preoccupations to uphold international norms and institutions. Some of these broader concerns, like peacekeeping and economic stability, fit easily with Beijing's international priorities. Others discomforted the Chinese and led them to question the meaning of, and the motives behind, the stakeholder concept. Once again fundamental distrust led some Chinese to interpret Washington's injunction as a mechanism to overburden China and undermine its rise.

In reality, neither the U.S. nor China have had the ability or the will to subvert the other. For better and worse, their economies have become too deeply intertwined. Historian Niall Ferguson dubbed their intimate embrace "Chimerica."[41] Clearly the interconnected dynamic of Chinese exports, foreign exchange earnings, U.S. consumerism and U.S. debt have magnified ordinary economic friction. Massive exports to the U.S. facilitated by an artificially undervalued currency and non-tariff trade barriers that depressed U.S. sales to China generated a huge Chinese surplus. As of 2008, Beijing had some 70 percent of its foreign exchange in dollar denominated holdings and became the United States' most important creditor. Accordingly it acquired enormous potential leverage over Washington. To some Americans there is no doubt that China will "weaponize its dollar hoard."[42] But this power has been largely unusable since selling any meaningful part of its dollar assets would lower the value of what China retains.[43] Instead, Beijing urges Americans to spend less and save more, rightly insisting that internal U.S. policies and practices have been largely to blame for the economic recession. On the other side, Americans blame China for job losses and threaten punitive tariffs.

But despite these problems vigorous trade and investment continues. American industry still rushes to take advantage of cheap and plentiful Chinese labor,[44] skilled technicians, inexpensive land and weak environmental regulations, hollowing out U.S. factory towns and transferring technology as a condition of doing business in China. Chinese enterprises eagerly seek to invest more heavily in the U.S., chafing at restrictions on sensitive sectors such as energy and purchases of certain high-tech goods.

Beijing's success in fighting the global recession, as the U.S. and Europe succumbed, shaped more nationalistic, confident, assertive, some say truculent, behavior beginning in 2008. China engaged in confrontational actions in the East and South China Seas with Japan, Vietnam and the Philippines over underwater resources, scattered islands and maritime rights including fishing, surveillance and navigation. It harassed the U.S. over conflicting interpretations of maritime rights. It refused to condemn North Korea for sinking a South Korean warship (the *Cheonan*) and shelling an island (Yeonpyeong) or put in place effective economic sanctions to stop nuclear and missile tests. And Beijing angered the Western business community as theft of intellectual property rights, indigenous innovation and censorship of the internet made operations in China more difficult.[45]

Surprisingly, the cross-Strait Taiwan situation became the major exception to this string of damaging developments. With the election of Ma Ying-jeou as president of Taiwan and his assurance that he accepted the idea of "one China," reserving only the definition of that one China, dialogue began and led to more than a dozen agreements. Washington welcomed the change since it appeared to be mutually desired and economically beneficial. Internationally observers anticipated the probability of war in the Taiwan Strait would be reduced, although China never stopped deploying missiles on its coast (now more than 1,200), maintaining a military threat to thwart independence activities and acquiring capabilities to prevent U.S. intervention.

China's overall lack of transparency, however, has made it difficult to judge its intentions regarding Taiwan, the South and East China Seas or other points of friction. Beijing has continued to assert that Deng Xiaoping's injunction to "keep a low profile and bide its time" (*tao guang yang hui*) guides decision making.[46] Analysts outside China disagree on Beijing's ambitions. Will China continue to adhere to an international system put in place by Washington without Chinese participation or will it seek to rewrite the rules? Will China remain preoccupied with domestic instability or expand its global reach and ambitions? Observers like Alastair Iain Johnston, of Harvard University, argue that China might "wish to be richer and more powerful [but] has not translated [that wish] into a concerted military effort to replace the United States as the predominant state regionally or globally."[47] By contrast, others, including Aaron Friedberg of Princeton University see a belligerent and ambitious China, one that wants to "establish itself as Asia's dominant power by eroding the credibility of America's security guarantees, hollowing out its alliances and eventually easing it out of the region.[48] David Shambaugh and Dawn Murphy's chapter in this volume examines this issue.

Challenged by China's rising strength and influence, in 2012 Washington began rebalancing military, economic and diplomatic priorities to emphasize America's presence and interests in Asia. The so-called pivot away from the Atlantic world, the Middle East and terrorism sparked political and security initiatives to reassure friends and deter potential adversaries. Among other things, it meant giving more visibility to troop deployments, including stationing forces in Australia and sending the navy on exercises in the seas around China despite shrinking U.S. defense budgets. President Barack Obama also berated Beijing for its economic policies telling reporters "China [must] operate by the same rules as everyone else. We don't want them taking advantage of the United States."[49] China's official Xinhua News Agency unsurprisingly rejected this American pivot, insisting, "The U.S. sees a growing threat to its hegemony from China. Therefore, America's strategic move east is aimed in practical terms at pinning down and containing China and counterbalancing China's development."[50]

Meanwhile, China's neighbors want the U.S. deeply involved in the region to counterbalance China. They do not seek a new Cold War, having for decades disparaged frenetic U.S. anti-communism. Indeed they would not support an effort to contain China today even if that were possible. They do not believe that Washington ought to treat China as an adversary lest it become one. But they do not want to be swept up in China's orbit or mount a new arms race, perhaps including nuclear capabilities, to preserve their autonomy. They want to be able to profit commercially while remaining free politically and strategically. To facilitate this outcome they look to the United States. But what they want from Washington is neither antagonism nor a U.S.-China condominium. Washington-Beijing dialogue in venues such as the annual Strategic and Economic Dialogue have not caused distress; closer collaboration would. Beginning in 2006 proposals for a "G-2" as a more efficient way to solve problems multiplied in the U.S., especially when former National Security Adviser Zbigniew Brzezinski began to advocate it. The idea, however, dismayed other countries and overestimated China's capabilities even in the eyes of the Chinese.

CONCLUSION

In the many decades of relations between the U.S. and China there has not been an occasion until the eve of the twenty-first century when both countries could simultaneously claim to be strong, prosperous and influential. There has also never been a moment when the two have been so interdependent and rarely a time when China has posed even an incipient challenge to U.S. power and primacy. The United States still leads an international system to which China generally adheres, but one from which it may increasingly deviate. China—so long an afterthought—has become a central preoccupation of a new era.

Amid these altered realities there are nevertheless critical continuities that will inform the future. Washington remains a source of inspiration and knowledge. Chinese still flock to the U.S. for education and training, and even as they go home in greater numbers, they do so with skills critical to China's modernization. Americans continue their quest to reform China, seeking to make it more democratic, liberal, transparent and market oriented. On both sides domestic politics intrude so that shared goals are difficult to agree on. Ill-informed or ill-willed interests romanticize and demonize each other, exaggerating expectations and amplifying threats. But perhaps most disturbingly, mutual distrust lingers—impeding cooperation and progress. Americans complain about China's opacity and Chinese insist that the U.S. still seeks to contain China.[51]

Whether Beijing and Washington can and will find common ground remains unclear. Popular views of China among Americans and of the U.S. among Chinese are contradictory. In a CBS News poll in the autumn of 2011, though 48 percent of Americans thought of China as friendly, 61 percent considered its economic expansion bad for the U.S. and 67 percent saw China as a moderate or serious military threat.[52] Their Chinese counterparts share this wariness. Polling can be especially unreliable in China, but it appears that between 2010 and 2011 favorability ratings of the U.S. declined 14 percent from 58 to 44.[53] It would seem that constant interaction and mutual dependency have not effectively ameliorated tension and suspicion.

Americans face an enormous adjustment in accepting a strong China, but the Chinese themselves are struggling with the implications of the nation's growing strength. China has not yet adjusted to its changing status, unwilling to embrace many of the responsibilities that come with international leadership. Ordinary Chinese, who perceive their national policies and intentions as benign, do not appreciate that others fear them. Charges that China has been provocative or confrontational are interpreted as part of a conspiracy to damage China's reputation and constrain it.

Furthermore, in the years ahead, a strong China and a weaker United States will be viewed quite differently. Internationally, many countries already believe that "China either will replace or already has replaced the United States as the world's leading superpower." And, the Pew Global Attitudes Project attests that this "view is especially widespread in Western Europe."[54] Accordingly in 2011, Europe turned to China for help in solving its economic crisis, not to the U.S. In the twentieth century Washington helped rebuild Europe after the devastation of World War II with the Marshall Plan. Today, however, Europeans no longer believe the U.S. has the means or the will to assist them.

China could, of course, be undone by economic upheaval and civil strife brought on by a financial collapse, a real estate bubble, soaring inflation, pollution, a political crisis and/or corruption.[55] For the U.S., a chaotic China would likely be more perilous than a strong China. As in the past, a break in China's unity would invite foreign meddling or could even empower a new version of Chinese warlords.

Sino-American relations are rarely as bad or good as they seem. There always appear to be optimists extolling a new closeness, greater cooperation and shared interests or pessimists warning of fragility, xenophobia and isolationism. Underlying cultural, strategic and economic differences persist even as China and the United States understand each other better and need each other more. The U.S. will remain a critical player in Asia rejecting the advice of those who insist "that Washington should read the writing on the Great Wall and begin to draw down its presence."[56] Whether China outstrips the U.S. or Washington sustains its influence, these two will dominate for decades to come. The course of U.S.-China relations has repeatedly been shaped by China's weakness and strength; that is the reality of the future as well as the past.

NOTES

1. Opening address by Mao Zedong, Chairman of the Chinese Communist Party, at the First Plenary Session of the Chinese People's Political Consultative Conference, September 21, 1949, available at: http://www.international.ucla.edu/eas/documents/mao490921.htm.

2. Warren I. Cohen, *America's Response to China* (New York: Columbia University Press, fourth edition, 2000), p. 242.

3. Michael Hunt, *The Making of a Special Relationship* (New York: Columbia University Press, 1983), p. x.

4. Nancy Bernkopf Tucker, "China and America 1941–1991," *Foreign Affairs* (Winter 1991/92).

5. Robert Dallek, *Franklin D. Roosevelt and American Foreign Policy, 1932–1945* (New York: Oxford University Press, 1979), p. 389.

6. Tu Wei-ming, "Chinese Perceptions of America," in Michel Oksenberg and Robert B. Oxnam (eds.), *Dragon and Eagle* (New York: Basic Books, 1973), p. 104.

7. Jonathan D. Spence wrote of the long tradition of American outreach in *To Change China: Western Advisers in China* (New York: Penguin, 1980).

8. Kurt Campbell, Remarks by the Assistant Secretary for East Asian and Pacific Affairs, speech at the National Chinese Language Conference, Asia Society, San Francisco, April 2011, available at: http://sites.asiasociety.org/nclc2011/conference/presentations/remarks-by-assistant-secretary-of-state-for-east-asian-and-pacific-affairs-kurt-campbell.

9. David Allan Mayers, *George Kennan and the Dilemmas of U.S. Foreign Policy* (New York: Oxford, 1988), p. 173, n. 40 and 41.

10. Nancy Bernkopf Tucker, *Patterns in the Dust* (New York: Columbia University Press, 1983).

11. "The Story of a U.S. Prisoner in a Chinese Jail," *Leninist Vanguard*, June 6, 2007, available at: http://s7.invisionfree.com/Revolutionary_Pravda/ar/t124.htm.

12. John W. Dower, *War Without Mercy* (New York: Pantheon, 1986).

13. Thomas G. Paterson and Les K. Adler, "Red Fascism: The Merger of Nazi Germany and Soviet Russia in the American Image of Totalitarianism, 1930's–1950's," *American Historical Review* 75 (1970).

14. The book by Richard Condon was published in 1960. The original film, starring Frank Sinatra, Laurence Harvey, Janet Leigh and Angela Landsbury was released in 1962 and then remade in 2004.

15. Chen Jian, *China's Road to the Korean War* (New York: Columbia University Press, 1994), pp. 140–41.

16. Leonard A. Kusnitz, *Public Opinion and Foreign Policy* (Westport, CT: Greenwood Press, 1984), p. 96.

17. Robert Accinelli, *Crisis and Commitment* (Chapel Hill: University of North Carolina Press, 1996), pp. 111–18.

18. Nancy Bernkopf Tucker, *The China Threat: Memory, Myth and Reality in the 1950s* (New York: Columbia University Press, 2012).

19. Qiang Zhai, *China and the Vietnam Wars, 1950–1975* (Chapel Hill: University of North Carolina Press, 2000), pp. 1–5, 115–16, 152.

20. Robert L. Hutchings, ed., *Tracking the Dragon: National Intelligence Estimates on China During the Era of Mao, 1948–1976* (Washington, D.C.: National Intelligence Council, 2006), xxii, 218, 220–21, 231; Tucker, *The China Threat*, pp. 103–10, 175.

21. Warren I. Cohen, *Dean Rusk* (Totowa, NJ: Cooper Square, 1980), pp. 166–67, and see Noam Kochavi, *A Conflict Perpetuated: China Policy during the Kennedy Years* (Westport, CT: Praeger, 2002).

22. Kusnitz, *Public Opinion and Foreign Policy*, 116, and see Michael Lumbers, *Piercing the Bamboo Curtain: Tentative Bridge-building to China during the Johnson Years* (Manchester: Manchester University Press, 2008).

23. Warren I. Cohen, "American Perceptions of China," Oksenberg and Oxnam, eds., *Dragon and Eagle*, p. 81.

24. CIA, "Mao's Red Guard Diplomacy: 1967," June 21, 1968, RSS 0029/68, available at: http://www.foia.cia.gov/CPE/POLO/polo-21.pdf.

25. Chen Jian, *Mao's China and the Cold War* (Chapel Hill: University of North Carolina Press, 2001), 238–44.

26. James Mann, *About Face* (New York: Alfred A. Knopf, 1998), pp. 109–14.

27. For a careful history of the origin and evolution on the "one China" policy, see Shirley Kan, *China/Taiwan: Evolution of the "One China" Policy —Key Statements from Washington, Beijing and Taipei* (Washington, D.C., CRS RL30341, June 24, 2010).

28. Robert Ross, *Negotiating Cooperation* (Stanford: Stanford University Press, 1995), pp. 170–75.

29. Nancy Bernkopf Tucker, *Strait Talk* (Cambridge: Harvard University Press, 2009), pp. 148–50, 152, 155–58.

30. Eden Y. Woon, "Chinese Arms Sales and U.S.-China Military Relations," *Asian Survey* 29 (June 1989), pp. 603–05, 611–12 (quote p. 612).

31. Richard Madsen, *China and the American Dream: A Moral Inquiry* (Berkeley: University of California Press, 1995), pp. 18–26.

32. Ezra F. Vogel, *Deng Xiaoping and the Transformation of China* (Cambridge: Belknap Press, 2011), p. 643.

33. Robert L. Suettinger, *Beyond Tiananmen: The Politics of U.S.-China Relations, 1989–2000* (Washington, D.C.: Brookings Institution, 2003), p. 81.

34. Rosemary Foot, *Rights Beyond Borders: The Global Community and the Struggle Over Human Rights in China* (New York: Oxford University Press, 2001), pp. 22–23.

35. Nancy Bernkopf Tucker, *China Confidential* (New York: Columbia University Press, 2001), p. 449.

36. Mann, *About Face*, pp. 284–85.

37. Suettinger, *Beyond Tiananmen*, op. cit., pp. 174–77.

38. China knew Lee would win but hoped to deprive him of a mandate. Tucker, *Strait Talk,* pp. 213–30; Alan Romberg, *Rein In at the Brink of the Precipice* (Washington, DC: Henry L. Stimson Center, 2003), pp. 175–76.

39. Romberg, *Rein In at the Brink,* p. 184.

40. Michael Swaine, *America's Challenge: Engaging a Rising China in the Twenty-first Century* (Washington, D.C.: Carnegie Endowment for International Peace, 2011), p. 3.

41. Nathan Gardels, "Niall Ferguson: Is U.S.-China Economic Marriage on the Rocks?" *The Huffington Post,* July 27, 2009, available at: http://www.huffingtonpost.com/nathan-gardels/niall-ferguson-is-us-chin_b_245470.html.

42. Walter Russell Mead, "Softly, Softly: Beijing Turns Other Cheek—For Now," *The American Interest,* November 19, 2011, available at: http://blogs.the-american-interest.com/wrm/2011/11/19/softly-softly-beijing-turns-other-cheek-for-now.

43. Patrick Chovanec, Tsinghua University, "NPR: Will China Dump U.S. Debt?" July 31, 2011, available at: http://chovanec.wordpress.com/2011/07/31/npr-will-china-dump-u-s-debt.

44. Demographic trends in China mean the workforce has begun to shrink and labor is becoming more expensive.

45. Michael Swaine, "Perceptions of an Assertive China," *China Leadership Monitor,* 32 (Spring 2010), pp. 1–4, 9–10, available at: http://www.hoover.org/publications/china-leadership-monitor/article/5297; Michael D. Swaine and M. Taylor Fravel, "China's Assertive Behavior: Part Two: The Maritime Periphery," *China Leadership Monitor,* 35 (Summer 2011), available at: http://www.hoover.org/publications/china-leadership-monitor/article/93591.

46. See Swaine, "Perceptions of an Assertive China," op. cit., pp. 4–8. See also analysis of the debate over peaceful rise/peaceful development in Bonnie Glaser and Evan Medeiros, "The Ecology of Foreign Policy Decision-making in China: The Ascension and Demise of the Theory of Peaceful Rise," *China Quarterly* 190 (June 2007), pp. 291–310.

47. Alastair Iain Johnston, "Is China a Status Quo Power?" *International Security* 27 (spring 2003), pp. 6, 47, 56, *available at:* http://0-www.jstor.org.library.lausys.georgetown.edu/stable/pdfplus/4137603.pdf?acceptTC=true.

48. Aaron Friedberg, "China's Challenge at Sea," *New York Times* (September 5, 2011), A17.

49. News Conference by President Obama, Kapolei, Hawaii, November 14, 2011, *available at:* http://www.whitehouse.gov/the-press-office/2011/11/14/news-confer ence-president-obama.

50. Christopher Bodeen, "Beijing Is Wary of Obama's Assertive China Policy," Associated Press online, November 17, 2011.

51. The impact of China's concerns about containment on foreign policy is analyzed in Evan S. Medeiros, *China's International Behavior* (Santa Monica: RAND Corporation, 2009), pp. 53–56. See also Kenneth Lieberthal and Wang Jisi, "Addressing U.S.-China Strategic Distrust," Brookings Institution John L. Thornton China Center Monograph Series, Number 4, March 2012.

52. CBS News Poll, November 6–10, 2011, *available at:* http://www.pollingreport. com/china.htm.

53. "China Seen Overtaking U.S. as Global Superpower," Pew Global Attitudes Project, July 13, 2011.

54. Ibid.

55. The China collapse school has repeatedly warned of impending disaster. See Gordon Chang, *The Coming Collapse of China* (New York: Random House, 2001); and Huang Yasheng, "Why China Will Not Collapse," *Foreign Policy* 99 (June 1995), pp. 54–69.

56. David Pilling, "How America Should Adjust to the Pacific Century," *Financial Times*, November 16, 2011, *available at:* http://www.ft.com/intl/cms/s/0/72bec88e-103e-11e1-8211-00144feabdc0.html#axzz1eArcQcWe.

Part III

The Theoretical Context

3

The Rise of China, the United States, and the Future of the Liberal International Order

G. John Ikenberry

The United States and China increasingly loom as the two great powers that will dominate the international system in the coming decades. For over a century, American power has been a central reality in world politics—but China is catching up. If current growth trends continue, China's economy could overtake the United States by as early as 2020. China is now the leading trade partner with most of the countries in Asia and it is rapidly building a commercial and investment presence around the world. China's military is dwarfed by the United States but it is the fastest growing among the major states. The United States is still the only global superpower. Yet if there is a rising state that will someday challenge it as a global rival and peer competitor, it is China. Indeed, it is not an exaggeration to say that U.S.-China relations, more than any other bilateral relationship, will shape the overall character of twenty-first-century world politics. If U.S.-China relations become beset with geopolitical conflict, arms competition, and zero-sum rivalry, the peace and stability of the wider global system will be at risk. But if the United States and China succeed in finding ways to manage their differences and to develop an expansive agenda of economic, political, and security cooperation, the prospects for peace and stability within Asia and across the globe will be strengthened as well.

So how will the strategic relationship between China and the United States unfold? This is a question about the evolving relationship between two great powers. But it is also a question about China's relationship to the wider liberal-oriented system that the United States has led since the end of World War II. China is rising up as a non-Western developing country that until the 1980s existed for the most part outside this American-led order. Will the rise of

China necessarily lead to a grand clash between the two states? Will China seek to integrate into the existing American-led international order or seek to transform it? Does the rise of China—and Asia more generally—signal the emergence of a rival non-Western way of organizing the international system or simply the arrival of new stakeholders seeking greater authority and leadership within the existing international order? As Paul Kennedy observed, the "weights and balances" of the global system are shifting. What is less clear is how the global political order will look in the aftermath of these redistributed capabilities. Will China and other rising states embrace the core features of the liberal international order or seek new rules and institutions?

Obviously, there are many observers who see trouble ahead. As realist theory suggests, power transitions, such as the one underway today between China and the United States, are fraught with danger. As power shifts and Western and Asian great powers rise and decline, stable order is put at risk. Insecurity, competition, and conflict—which are staples of world politics even when the global distribution of power is not rapidly transforming—threaten the old order. The United States will feel threatened by the rise of China, and China will be emboldened to see its growing economic and military capabilities transformed into influence and leadership. Out of this classic predicament, the U.S.-China relationship will increasingly become antagonistic. And the wider world will also become more fragmented and divided. But how inevitable is this realist vision of geopolitical discord and global fracture?

This chapter acknowledges this realist predicament, but goes on to look at U.S-China relations from a liberal internationalist point of view. It focuses on the ways in which democracy, capitalism, institutions, and diplomatic engagement matter in shaping U.S.-Chinese relations and reinforcing stability and cooperation. It does not dismiss the very real—that is, realist—sources of antagonism and competition. But it attempts to place these forces and pressures within a wider perspective that identifies an array of international-level structural incentives and constraints that might mitigate full-scale hostility and security competition. This liberal point of view looks at the bilateral U.S.-China relations and the ways in which economic interdependence, mutual vulnerabilities, norms and institutions, and diplomacy can shape and constrain conflict. But just as importantly, the liberal perspective also looks at the more general ways in which the prevailing global liberal world order creates the setting for the rise of China and the terrain upon which the rise and decline of states and the struggles over rules and institutions of order proceeds.

In thinking about U.S-China relations and the impact of the rise of China on the international order, observers tend to focus on China itself. What does it want? Is it a status quo or revisionist state? How will China seek to turn power into purpose? These are "inside out" questions. But it is also useful to reverse the perspective and ask: What will be the impact of the existing Western liberal-oriented international order on China? How will the "weight and character" of the American-led postwar international order shape and constrain Chinese choices? What are the existing order's attractions and obstacles? These are "outside in" questions. States rise up and seek to shape the international order—but states also rise up and find themselves being shaped and constrained by the prevailing international order.

I explore the ways in which the rise of China will impact the liberal international order—and, just as importantly, the ways in which the liberal international order will influence and orient China's rise. I argue that there is reason to think that the liberal international order will survive the growth of Chinese power, providing far-reaching constraints and shaping influences on China's ascent. China faces a very different sort of "existing international order" than past rising states. It is more institutionally embedded, functionally articulated, and globalized in scope than past international orders. It is a complex and multifaceted order that will have a "double effect" on China. On the one hand, it will provide attractions, incentives, and opportunities for China—thereby encouraging Beijing to integrate further into the existing order. On the other hand, it is a deeply rooted and expansive order that is difficult to undermine or circumvent—thereby making it difficult for Beijing to oppose it or offer a viable alternative vision of international order.

In my view, the liberal international order is more durable than many observers think. China and the other rising non-Western development states are not inevitable enemies of Western-style liberal order. Indeed, the ideas embedded in this order are as much universal as they are Western. Great alternatives to liberal international order do not exist. To put it simply, the pathway to the future still runs through the rules, institutions, and relationships created over the last half century during the era of American dominance. American dominance may be ending, and power and authority may be shifting to other states within the global system. But China does not have the ideas, capacities, or incentives to tear down the existing international order and build a new one.

In this chapter I make five arguments. First, I offer a way of thinking about the rise of China and liberal international order. It is useful to see these grand shifts in power and order as "power transitions." In the most simple view states rises up, wins wars, and build international order—only to subsequently decline and be challenged by a new rising state that seeks dominance and remakes international order. But the characteristics of international order can vary greatly, and therefore so too will the logic of power transitions. In depicting international order, it is important to distinguish between different layers and levels. At the deepest level, there is the bedrock of the modern international order—the Westphalian state system. It is upon this foundation that liberal international order has been built—that is, order that is *open and at least loosely rule-based.* Liberal international order itself can—and has—varied in character. The American-led hegemonic organization of liberal international order may be giving way but the more general organizing rules and principles of liberal international order will still endure.

Second, the existing international order is indeed a massive and formidable system, significantly different than previous international orders that rising states in those earlier eras encountered. It is wider and deeper. It is more integrated and institutionalized. It is an order that is rooted in the deep structures of modern industrial society. A rising China does not just face the United States or the West. It faces a massive and far-flung global system of capitalism and democracy that continues to expand and integrate. It is an order that is not simply tied to American power but is more deeply entrenched in the structures of the modern state system and the expanding realms of liberal democracy and global capitalism. The far-reaching scale and scope of this global order complicate simple ideas about "power transitions" and the rise and decline of international order.

Third, the current international order is not just the American-led order created after World War II. It is best seen as the result of two longer-term and evolving world order building "projects." One is the Westphalian project—the 500-year growth and evolution of the rules and institutions of the modern state system. This order building project has enshrined rules and norms about sovereignty, non-intervention, self-determination, and great power authority. The other is order building associated with the "liberal ascendency." This is the 200-year growth of liberal democracies from a position of weakness and peripheral status to global dominance—and the repeated and evolving efforts of these states to build open and rule-based international order. These two order building "projects" have worked together and unfolded over the decades and centuries to generate a complex and deeply rooted system of rules and institutions—a liberal Westphalian order.

Fourth, to a remarkable extent, China is already in this order—and it will become more so. China embraces the rules and norms of sovereignty, and it is a permanent member of the United Nations Security Council. China's participation in this order—most notably in the world's trading system—has allowed it to achieve its remarkable growth and progress. In this sense, China is already a stakeholder in the liberal international order. For China and other rising non-Western developing countries, an open and rule-based international order has attractions. Openness allows access to other societies for trade, investment, and mutually beneficial cooperation. Rules and multilateral frameworks—such as the World Trade Organization—provide rights and protections for these countries as they get more involved in the world economy and confront discrimination. The rules and institutions of liberal internationalism offer platforms for these states to project their influence and acquire legitimacy at home and abroad.

Fifth, a Chinese alternative to this liberal logic of order is simply not available or sustainable. There is a serious question what such an alternative would actually be or who would join it. The Chinese themselves have not offered one. But an alternative order—a "Beijing model"—would seemingly be one organized around more or less exclusive blocs, spheres of influence, and mercantilist networks. It would be an illiberal order. It would be less open, less rule-based, and dominated by arrays of state-to-state ties. But organized on a global scale, such a system would not advance the interests of any of the major states, including China. The Beijing model does not offer a set of ideas and principles around which the world economy can function. It is a model for working within—and working around—a liberal world system.

Taken together, these arguments suggest that China will find itself increasingly rising up *within* the existing international order—rather than rising up and challenging this order from the outside. The United States and China will compete for power and influence, but they will do so within a structural setting shaped by liberal and Westphalian systems. Great powers—the United States, China, and others—will continue to rise and decline, but the international order itself has become too complex and deeply entrenched to be captured or overturned by one country—even a powerful country. It is this structural setting that will shape and constrain the growth of Chinese power and the terms of U.S-Chinese relations.

POWER TRANSITIONS AND LIBERAL INTERNATIONAL ORDER

There is general agreement that the global distribution of power is shifting. China—together with other rising non-Western states, such as India and Brazil—are gaining in wealth and power. The distribution of material capabilities among major states is being rearranged. In the decades after the end of the Cold War, the United States had unrivaled and unprecedented power capabilities. What is happening today is that this unipolar distribution of power is eroding. The distribution of power is becoming less centralized and concentrated. This gradual shift in the distribution of power is frequently described as a "return to multipolarity." Some see multipolarity as simply a move to a less concentrated system of global power. Others see the process leading to the rise of rival "poles" manifest most clearly with the rise of China.[1]

Within Asia, a regional power transition is also taking place. For decades, East Asia has been dominated by the United States. America's military power, forward-deployed forces, alliance pacts, and trade and investment ties served to bind the United States to the countries in the region. The United States was at the center of a partial hegemonic order. The United States exported security and imported goods. China existed for the most part outside of this regional economic-security order. But today that partial hegemonic order is giving way to a more complex system that has the markings of a partial balance of power system. This is a dual shift. The geopolitical "space" of the region is expanding to include countries such India, Australia, as well as the United States. And, under the shadow of the rise of Chinese economic and military capacities, the region is taking on more multipolar and less hegemonic identity. Power is shifting and the political relations within the region are evolving.

Many of these grand narratives about the global power transition suggest that the "American era" of global leadership is passing away. The shift in power is paving the way for a shift in the rules and institutions of international order. The "political formation" that was built around American power is breaking down as power capabilities diffuse outward to other states. In this view, we are witnessing the rise of rival global powers with their own order building agendas. The United States was the most powerful state through most of the twentieth century, and with this power it built international order. It was an order that reflected American ideas and interests. Today, as other countries gain power, they will look for opportunities to recast and reorganize the rules and institutions of the system to reflect their ideas and interests.[2]

In this grand narrative, the struggle that is unfolding today is between a rising China and a declining America. As American power declines, China will increasingly be in a position to advance new ideas about the rules and institutions of global order. American-inspired liberal rules and institutions may increasingly be contested by China. In effect, world politics is a struggle over the "political formation" within which states operate. That political formation reflects the values and interests of the leading state. As power shifts from an old leading state to a new one, the political formation of world politics will also shift. As China grows in power, its willingness and ability to reshape global rules and institutions will increase. The United States will resist these shifts—and struggle and conflict between the U.S. and China will ensue.

Behind these arguments about the decline of unipolarity, the rise of China, and struggles over international order are theories of hegemony and power transition. Robert Gilpin has provided a classic realist account of the rise and fall of international order.[3] In Gilpin's vision, the global system can be seen as a sequence of historical cycles or eras punctuated by great power wars. War destroys the old order—indeed, war itself reflects the failure of the old order. Winners and losers emerge. The power distribution shifts. A new leading state or group of states make peace and, in one way or another, establishes a new international order. As Gilpin argues, these periodic wars "resolve the question of which state will govern the system, as well as what ideas and values will predominate."[4] At these rare moments, such as 1945, basic questions are placed on the world diplomatic table about who commands and who benefits. The rules and institutions of order are hammered out.

In this sense, to talk about international order—its rise, fall, and evolution in character—is to focus on the organizational logic of international relations. The character of states and the nature of their relations are defined, embedded in the rules and norms of the system. International order provides settled answers to the big questions. How is sovereignty arrayed across the system? What is the distribution of rights and authority among states? What are the rules and institutions for "doing business," that is, facilitating cooperation, fostering collective action, resolving conflicts, avoiding war? More generally, international order is a functioning political order—however primitive and power-based—which establishes the terms by which states interact.

Several considerations follow from this discussion of order creation and change that are relevant to the question of how the rise of China will impact the global system. First, the arguments on hegemony and power transition highlight the way in which international order—its stability and character—can be tied to a specific powerful state. This is a two-fold claim. One is that the rise and decline of international orders are linked to the rise and decline of a dominant state. A powerful state rises up and creates international order and the fate of that order is tied to the fate of that state. When that powerful state declines so too will the international order. The other claim is that the resulting international order reflects the interests and values of the leading state that led in the creation of the order. This is why the subsequent leading state, which emerges after war or upheaval in the system, will seek to create a new international order. It will want to create an order that reflects its interests and values.

Second, international orders can be more or less *liberal* in character. A liberal international order is one that is relatively open and rule-based. Openness is manifest when states trade and exchange on the basis of mutual gain. Rules and institutions operate as mechanisms of governance—and they are at least partially autonomous from the exercise of state power. In its ideal form, liberal international order creates a foundation in which states can engage in diffuse reciprocity and institutionalized multilateral cooperation. As such, liberal international order can be contrasted with closed and non-rule-based relations—whether geopolitical blocs, exclusive regional spheres, closed imperial systems.[5] But liberal international order itself can be organized in different ways. Liberal international order can be more or less tied to norms and institutions of national sovereignty and self-determination. Liberal international order can be more or less open, it can be more or less rule-based, it can be more or less institutionalized, it can be more or less global, and it can be more or less hierarchical.[6]

Finally, we can make a distinction between the distribution of authority and status within an international order and more basic rules and organizational principles of order. Within the postwar liberal international order, the United States positioned itself as a hegemonic leader. It had the rights and responsibility to organize and run the order. It provided public goods—such as open markets and security—and other states cooperated with the United States. In this way, the United States turned liberal international order into an American-led liberal hegemonic order. It was hierarchically organized and directed from Washington. This hegemonic organization of liberal international order is now in transition—and some would argue it is rapidly passing away. The rights and authority within liberal international order are being redistributed. Other states are seeking to acquire rights and authority. But a struggle over leadership and authority within liberal international order needs to be distinguished from a struggle over the deeper logic and character of liberal internationalism as an open and rule-based order.

The big question that cuts through the debate about the rise of China and the fate of liberal international order is whether the current struggle over the governance of the global system is a struggle over rights and authority or over the deeper principles and norms of world order. To clarify this question, it is necessary to look more closely at the layers and levels of the existing international order.

WESTPHALIA AND THE LIBERAL ASCENDENCY

China and the United States do not just face each other as great powers that are rising and declining. There is a structural setting that is shaping and constraining the rise of China and the resulting relationship between the United States and China. China and other non-Western developing states do not simply face an "American-led order" and a "Western system." They face a wider and deeper international order that is the product of centuries of struggle and innovation. It is an international order that is highly developed, expansive, integrated, institutionalized, and deeply rooted in the societies and economies of advanced capitalist states and parts of the developing world. It is an order that has characteristics that make it particularly robust and durable. It is an evolving order that has been unusually capable of assimilating rising powers and reconciling political and cultural diversity. Embedded in this modern international order are principles, rules, and institutions that have the potential to be universal in scope and global in appeal.

Today's international order is the product not just of United States leadership in the wake of World War II, but of two multi-century order building "projects." One is the Westphalian project associated with the creation and expansion of the modern state system. This is the unfolding movement in which states have developed rules and principles defining the terms of state sovereignty and norms of great power conduct. The other is the liberal order building project led by Great Britain and the United States, in turn, over the last two centuries. This project has been pushed forward by the rise of liberal democratic states to global dominance in the twentieth century. Both these order building projects have unfolded in waves, phases, and historical turning points, marked most importantly at postwar moments of peacemaking and reconstruction. The two order building projects also have worked together. The Westphalian project has been focused on solving "realist" problems of creating stable and cooperative inter-state relations under conditions of anarchy. The liberal order building project has only been possible when the great power relations have been stabilized.

The Westphalian project has involved the development of rules and institutions that give coherence to the system of sovereign states. At the heart of this order is the notion of state sovereignty and great power relations. The founding moment of this project was, of course, the Westphalian peace of 1648, but the rules and norms of state relations have continued to evolve. The founding location of this project was, of course, Western Europe. Great powers, empires, and universal religious authority competed for dominance on the continent. Through wars and peace settlements, rules and norms of the Westphalian order took shape and evolved. The result has been the rise and evolution of the so-called Westphalian system of states. The great powers compete, cooperate, and balance each other within a wider framework of rules and norms. In the background, Westphalian norms of sovereignty enshrine states as formally equal and independent, possessing the ultimate authority over their own people and territory.

Over the centuries, the Westphalian system has evolved as a set of principles and practices and expanded outward from its European origins to encompass the entire globe. Despite this unfolding, however, states have retained their claims of political and legal authority. The founding principles of the Westphalian system—sovereignty, territorial integrity, and non-intervention—reflected an emerging consensus that states were the rightful political units for the establishment of legitimate rule. Norms and principles that subsequently evolved within the Westphalian system—such as self-determination and non-discrimination—served to further reinforce the primacy of states and state authority. These norms and principles have served as the organizing logic for Westphalian order and provided the ideational source of political authority within it. Under the banner of sovereignty and self-determination, political movements for decolonization and independence were set in motion in the non-Western developing world. Westphalian norms have been violated and ignored but they have, nonetheless, been the most salient and agreed upon rules and principles of international order in the modern era.[7]

The succession of postwar settlements—1815, 1919, 1945, 1989—also provided moments for the great powers to develop principles and practices that have shaped and updated the functioning of great power relations. Along this historical pathway—through war and settlement, learning and adaptation—it is possible to see an evolution in how the great powers have operated within a multipolar balance of power system. The source of order remained rooted in a decentralized states system in which major states compete and balance each other. But the practices and principles of competition and balance have evolved to incorporate strategic notions of restraint and accommodation, providing the great powers—Western and non-Western, rising and falling—with an accumulation of mutual understandings and experiences with which to manage their relations.[8]

The liberal order building project followed from and built upon this evolving system of Westphalian relations. In the nineteenth century, liberal internationalism was manifest in Britain's championing of free trade and freedom of the seas, but it was limited and coexisted with imperialism and colonialism. In the twentieth century, liberal order building was pushed forward by the United States in several phases. After World War I, Woodrow Wilson and other liberals pushed for an international order organized around a global collective security body in which sovereign states would act together to uphold a system of territorial peace. Open trade, national self-determination, and a belief in progressive global change also informed the Wilsonian worldview. It was a "one world" vision of nation-states that trade and interact in a multilateral system of laws creating an orderly international community. But this experiment in liberal order collapsed into an inter-war period of closed economic systems and imperial blocs.

After World War II, the Roosevelt administration again engaged in liberal order building, embracing a vision of an open trading system and a world organization in which the great powers would cooperate to keep the peace. American architects of postwar order—drawing lessons from the Wilsonian failure and incorporating ideas from the New Deal period—also advanced more ambitious ideas about economic and political cooperation embodied in the Bretton Woods institutions. This vision was originally global in scope and spirit, but it evolved into a more American-led and Western-centered system as a result of the weakness of postwar Europe and rising tensions with the Soviet Union. As the Cold War unfolded, the United States took command of organizing and running the system, taking on new commitments and functional roles in both security and economics. Its own economic and political system became, in effect, the central component of the larger liberal hegemonic order.

The liberal project also elaborated progressive ideals and notions of universal human rights, enshrined in the United Nations and the Universal Declaration of Human Rights. This human rights revolution is deeply embedded in the postwar liberal international project. A steady stream of conventions and treaties followed that together constitute an extraordinary vision of rights, individuals, sovereignty, and global order. In the decades since the end of the Cold War, notions of "responsibility to protect" have given the international community legal rights and obligations to intervene into the affairs of sovereign states—one more ingredient in the layer cake of ideas, norms, rules, and institutions that has resulted from two centuries of the Westphalian and liberal international projects.[9]

Liberal and Westphalian ideas and institutions did emerge, geographically speaking, in the West but they are not in any intrinsic sense Western ideas and institutions. Free trade, democracy, sovereignty, multilateral cooperation—these are now global ideas with wide appeal. The idea, for example, that world politics should be organized—at least loosely—around the rule of law has champions in all parts of the world. There is a struggle worldwide between actors that want to support and expand the existing rule-based global order and others who want some sort of less cooperative order built around spheres of influence and power balances. The fault lines between these opposing views, however, do not map onto geography nor do they split Asia and the West. There are voices that favor a loosely rule-based order in China, and there are opponents of it in the United States.

In the post-WWII decades, the United States did step forward as the hegemonic leader, taking on the privileges and responsibilities of organizing and running the system. It presided over a far-flung international order organized around multilateral institutions, alliances, special relationships, and client states—a hierarchical order with liberal characteristics. But as this American hegemonic organization of liberal international order starts to change, the hierarchical aspects are fading while the liberal aspects persist. So even as China and other rising states may seek to contest American leadership—and today there is indeed a struggle taking place over the rights, privileges, and responsibilities of leading states within the system— the deeper international order remains intact. And even if China and other states were seized with illiberal ambitions, they would find it very difficult— indeed impossible—to contemplate overturning this order or offer a serious alternative to it.

Incentives and Opportunities

The existing multilayered liberal Westphalian order offers China and the other non-Western rising states with a variety of attractions and opportunities, creating incentives for these states to integrate and operate within it. These incentives and attractions are of various sorts: club benefits, growth opportunities, institutional protections, and credibility tools.

One general incentive that rising non-Western states have for being "inside" the liberal order—rather than on the "outside"—relates to the general advantages that accrue from membership. We can call these "club benefits." Liberal international order is not just a collection of liberal democratic states. It is a highly developed political system with evolved rules and institutions that facilitate cooperation and mutual advancement. It is an order that might be seen as an international "mutual aid society," that is, it is a sort of global political community or club that provides members with tools and resources to add in their economic and political advancement. Participants in the order gain trading opportunities, dispute resolution mechanisms, frameworks for collective action, regulatory agreements, alliance security protection, and resources and mutual assistance in times of crisis. To be in the liberal internationalist club is to gain access to these tools, resources, and safeguards. To be outside of the club is to operate at a disadvantage.

To be sure, there are some problems that China has in fully integrating into this club. It is not a liberal democracy—and, as a result, it is not able to join some groupings, such as the Organization for Economic Cooperation and Development (OECD). But the WTO and the Bretton Woods institutions are all part of this club system that provide tools and resources for China. For example, China has taken steps to get more involved in the IMF. In July 2011 it was announced that the first Chinese official—Zhu Min—has been named as a new IMF deputy managing director.[10] The IMF also has plans to elevate the official role of other emerging countries—including Brazil, India, and South Africa—on the IMF board. China is also seeking membership in the OECD, which will allow it access to technical knowledge and policy experience in areas such as agriculture subsidies, innovation policy, and science and education programs. China's interest in the OECD is a microcosm of the more general ways in which involvement in the liberal order's multilateral organizations and networks advances China's ability to manage and govern its economy.

Second, there are more direct growth opportunities that come from pursuing economic development within an open world system. These are gains that come from operating within an open and loosely rule-based order. Openness allows these states access to other societies—for trade, investment, knowledge, and political support. China is already deeply enmeshed in the global trading system. Although Chinese leaders are seeking to stimulate domestic consumption and reduce dependence on trade as a source of growth, the world trade system remains vital to China's economic fortunes. China entered the world economy in the 1980s after decades of efforts by the leading capitalist states to open and stabilize the world economy. The successes of the United States, Western Europe, Japan, and other states to build on open trading provided the bases for China's subsequent and ongoing economic ascent. It is not surprising, therefore, that there are growing constituencies within China and the other emerging economies for participation in the liberal order.[11]

Third, rules and multilateral frameworks of cooperation are essential for developing states as well. As countries like China, India, and Brazil grow they will encounter protectionist and discriminatory reactions from abroad. As a result, rules and institutions that uphold non-discrimination and equal access become critical. The WTO—the most formal and developed rule-based institution of the liberal international order—enshrines these rules and norms, and rising developing states have been eager to join the WTO and operate with the rights and protections that it affords. WTO principles, such as non-discrimination, reciprocity, and transparency, and the dispute settlement mechanism provide tools for states to protect their economic interests and keep the global trading system open. China, which gained membership in the WTO in 2001, has both won and lost trade dispute decisions. But it is the framework of rules that is of value to China and other rising developing states. On the one hand, the United States and other Western liberal states hope that the WTO will act as a sort of pressure on China to open up, promote transparency, and strengthen the domestic rule of law. China, on the other hand, hopes that the WTO will provide a set of institutional rules that allow it to blunt unfair discrimination against its export sectors and reinforce trade openness.

The sovereignty norms of the Westphalian system are also an important tool for China and other non-Western states as they navigate their rise. China has consistently appealed to the norms of sovereignty—non-intervention, self-determination, and non-discrimination—in both regional territorial disputes and in resisting Western liberal interventionist ambitions. In pushing back against the "responsibility to protect" norm, China is making use of other norms and ideas in the system. In doing so, it is being driven further into the existing international order—not away from it. There are tensions that exist in this order—tensions between Westphalian and liberal interventionist aspirations. But this creates a sort of invitation to struggle. It is a situation not unlike that which exists within Western democracies. These domestic orders also have tensions in their norms and ideas—between, for example, norms of social equality and market freedom, on the other. Both of these are legitimate norms, and day-to-day politics involves the struggle over them.

Fourth, the rules and institutions of the liberal order are also useful to China and other rising states as tools to signal commitment and leadership credibility. Some observers argue that China's authoritarian state gives its leaders advantages in pursuing expansive social and economic goals. But a political order that lacks transparency and the rule of law is also at a disadvantage when that state seeks to establish itself as a global leader. Other states worry about the credibility of its commitments—and it is more difficult for these states to establish close institutional ties. To the extent China wants to establish itself as a global leader, it will have incentives to acquire more liberal-style features, opening itself up and strengthening rule of law institutions. By operating within the complex of liberal and Westphalian institutions, China is signaling its peaceful intentions. It is signaling that it is not a revisionist state. These institutions are valuable to China as a strategic tool for reassuring the outside world that it can be trusted and is capable of leadership.

The general dynamic is clear. As China seeks to establish itself as a responsible and influential great power, it will need to move more fully into the existing liberal Westphalian order—not away from it. In some instances, China's use of these institutions is simply defensive. It seeks to protect its sovereignty and autonomy. For example, China has used its veto in the United Nations Security Council to undercut efforts by the United States and other Western states to gain UN support for various humanitarian interventions. This allows China a way of helping to shape the global debate on principles such as the "responsibility to protect" and the evolving norms of sovereignty and non-intervention. More generally, China has incentives to get involved in global institutions, becoming a "player" so that it can achieve their goals. The complexity and density of global institutions makes it difficult for China to simply pull back from the existing order and seek partners who might help build an alternative order.

Overall, China and the other non-Western rising states were not party to the "grand bargains" that lay behind the founding of the liberal order in the early postwar decades. But they do have incentives to embrace the rules and institutions of the old order so as to protect and advance their various interests. They want the protections and rights that come from the international order's Westphalian defense of sovereignty. They care about sovereignty and great power authority and these are norms that exist within the prevailing system. They want the protections and rights relating to trade and investment—and these are fundamental rules and norms of liberal internationalism. They also want to use the rules and institutions of liberal internationalism as platforms to project their influence and acquire legitimacy at home and abroad.

Constraints and Obstacles

If China were in fact to seek to use its growing geopolitical power to overturn the existing international order and push for fundamentally different rules and institutions, it will find enormous constraints and obstacles. Indeed, such an endeavor is essentially impossible. As I have argued, the existing international order is deeply entrenched. It is a layered system of Westphalian and liberal rules and institutions. It is an order that is wide and deep. It is not simply a political formation tied to American power. The constraints and obstacles on China's ability to overturn and reorganize international order are multiple: the Chinese "model" is unsustainable as a global system, Chinese revisionism will generate self-encirclement, and, in the background, the grand mechanism for overturning old international orders—great power war—has disappeared.

First, some observers do talk about a Chinese model. The recent financial crisis and economic downturn has hit the Western economies while China and other Asian countries have appeared to weather the crisis. The crisis of the "neo-liberal" model has led some people to talk about the rise of a Chinese-led authoritarian capitalist alternative. As the Chinese scholar Wang Jisi notes, "It is a popular notion among Chinese political elites, including some national leaders, that China's development model provides an alternative to Western democracy and experiences for other developing countries to learn from, while many developing countries that have introduced Western values and political systems are experiencing disorder and chaos. The China Model, or Beijing Consensus, features an all-powerful political leadership that effectively manages social and economic affairs, in sharp contrast to some countries where 'color revolutions' typically have led to national disunity and Western infringement on their sovereign rights."[12] But this Chinese model is simply not sustainable as a global system. There is a serious question what such an alternative world would actually be or who would join it. An alternative order—a "Beijing model"—would presumably be organized around more or less exclusive blocs, spheres of influence, and mercantilist networks. It would be an illiberal order. It would be less open, less rule-based, and dominated by an array of state-to-state ties. But organized on a global scale, such a system would not advance the interests of any of the major states, including China. The Beijing model only works when one or a few states opportunistically exploit an open system of markets. Raised to the level of a world organizational type, it breaks down. One or a few states can exploit an open system but if everyone does, it is no longer an open system—and everyone suffers.

It is possible that China could nonetheless move in this direction. This is a future in which China is not an illiberal hegemon that reorganizes the global rules and institutions. It is simply a spoiler. It attempts to operate both inside and outside of the liberal international order. It is opportunistic in seeking special deals with resource-exporting developing countries. In this instance, China would be successful enough with its authoritarian model of development to resist the pressures to liberalize and democratize. But if this is not a model that the rest of the world gravitates to, China will find itself subjected to pressures from both advanced democratic and rising states to open up and play by agreed upon rules. A hint of this was seen in February 2011 when the Brazilian President Rousseff joined U.S. Treasury Secretary Geithner to express concern over Chinese currency policy. China can exploit and free ride on liberal international order but it will pay a cost—and it will not be able to impose its illiberal vision on the world.

Beyond this, there is little evidence that authoritarian states can become truly advanced societies without moving in a liberal democratic direction. The legitimacy of one-party rule within China is widely seen as resting more on the state's ability to deliver economic growth and full employment than on authoritarian—let alone communist—political principles. Kishore Mahbubani, a Singaporean intellectual who has championed China's rise, admits that "China cannot succeed in its goal of becoming a modern developed society until it can take the leap and allow the Chinese people to choose their own rulers."[13] No one knows how far or fast democratic reforms will unfold in China, but pressures for doing so will persist from a growing middle class, business elites, and human rights groups. In the background, as Amartya Sen notes, despite the recent troubles encountered by established and emerging democracies, democracy has become a near universal ideal. "While democracy is not yet universally practiced, nor indeed universally accepted, in the general climate of world opinion democratic governance has achieved the status of being taken to be generally right."[14] All the leading institutions of the global system enshrine democracy as the proper and just form of governance—and no competing or alternative political ideals even lurk on the edges.

Second, China will also face another sort of constraint if it seeks to mount a full-fledged geopolitical challenge to the prevailing order. This is the problem of self-encirclement. To overcome this problem, China will find incentives to reaffirm its adherence of global rules and norms. To some extent, China has already acted on this incentive. In various political and military realms, China has taken steps to operate within existing regional forums and institutions so as to reassure neighbors of its peaceful intentions.

As China itself realizes, its rise makes neighboring states potentially less secure. A more powerful China that asserts itself, acts aggressively, and exhibits revisionist ambitions will generate even more insecurity—triggering a balancing backlash and Chinese self-encirclement. In these circumstances, China has incentives to signal restraint and moderation. It will find ways to do so by showing its participation in various existing regional and global institutions. In some areas, China already has acted on this incentive. As Rosemary Foot and Andrew Walter argue, "China's leadership has an evident desire to be perceived by others as a peaceful, non-threatening country and a responsible great power. Its involvement in UN PKOs, its signature of the NPT and CTBT, and its acceptance of the UN Charter and the 2005 World Summit Outcome document as authoritative texts are examples of this signaling and suggest that concerns about international image have been strong prompts behind China's commitment to many global order norms."[15] The principles and practices of great power restraint and accommodation enshrined in the Westphalian system will also be useful to Beijing as it grows in power. If China is serious about convincing its neighbors that it is embarked on a "peaceful rise," it will inevitably need to become more—not less—integrated into the existing international order.

The danger to China of a balancing backlash was exposed in 2010 with Beijing's pronouncements regarding in the South China Sea and in the fishing boat clash with Japan, episodes which seemed to signal a more bellicose and aggressive foreign policy. This has triggered a reaction in the region. ASEAN, Japan, and South Korea have all moved closer to the United States. In effect, there has been a balancing reaction to China when it has tried to act too aggressively. But China should have incentives to avoid these reactions. It has incentives to try to reassure other states in the region as it rises. It may want to redouble its participation in existing institutions, such as the ASEAN Regional Forum (ARF) and the East Asia Summit (EAS) or work with the other great powers in the region to build new ones. This is, of course, precisely what the United States did in the decades after World War II, building and operating within layers of regional and global economic, political, and security institutions—thereby making itself more predictable and approachable, and reducing the incentives that other states would otherwise have to resist or undermine the United States by building countervailing coalitions.

Finally, in the background, China will find it difficult to build a radically new international order because the old and classic mechanism for overturning old international orders—great power war—has disappeared. The United States was able to have such a far-reaching impact on post-1945 international order because world war had destroyed the old order. The war itself had discredited the old order. In the meantime, the United States has grown powerful during the war while other states have been diminished. Postwar "moments" create unusual and fleeting opportunities for a leading state to organize global rules and institutions. But China may not have a postwar "moment" available to it—and so its ability to use its growing power to restructure global relations will be constrained.

The absence of great power war is certainly due to several factors not present in earlier eras, including the existence of nuclear deterrence and the dominance of liberal democracies. Nuclear weapons—and the deterrence they generate—give great powers some confidence that they will not be dominated or invaded by other major states. They make war among major states less rational and therefore less likely. Nuclear weapons have a double-edged effect. They put limits on the power of even the most preeminent state in the system. The United States may be a unipolar power, but it is not capable of engaging in conquest against other major powers. In this sense, great military powers of the past may have been less dominant than the United States defined in terms of share of material capabilities and military expenditures. But they were nonetheless more threatening to other major states because the threat of war was real. Nuclear deterrence removes the threat of war and makes American unipolar power less existentially threatening to other great powers. At the same time, the removal of great power war as a tool of overturning international order tends to reinforce the status quo. The United States was lucky to have emerged as a global power in the nuclear age because it puts rival great powers at a disadvantage if they seek to overturn the American-led system. The cost-benefit calculation of rival would-be hegemonic powers is altered in favor of working for change within the system. But, again, the fact that great power deterrence sets limits of the projection of American power also, presumably, makes the existing international order more tolerable. It removes a type of behavior in the system—war, invasion, and conquest between great powers—that historically provided the motive for seeking to overturn order.

CONCLUSION

How will U.S.-China relations unfold over the next several decades? This chapter argues that the key dynamic to watch is China's relationship with the U.S.-led postwar liberal order. It is this encounter between China and the prevailing liberal and Westphalian rules and institutions of global order that matter most in shaping the pathway of U.S-China relations. The U.S. and China will struggle and compete in various economic, political, and security domains. But the larger drama of their relationship—poised as they are to be the two most powerful states in the world—is how China makes decisions about joining and opposing the rules and institutions of the modern world order. Will China integrate into and become a leader within this complex set of rules and institutions? Or will it seek to build alternative rules and relationships, offering a revisionist vision of global order?

I argue that China and other non-Western rising states are finding incentives and opportunities to engage and integrate into this order, doing so to advance and protect their own interests. Westphalian norms of sovereignty and non-discrimination are available to China and other rising states as tools to defend their national interests. An open and rule-based international order is an indispensable environment in which to trade and develop. It provides rising non-Western states with an institutional platform for them to acquire and project influence and authority. The road of a modern future for rising states runs through—not away from—the rules and institutions of international order laid over the previous decades and centuries.

In the debate about what the rise of China means for U.S.-China relations and the existing liberal world order, there is a lot of attention paid to China's growing economy and capabilities. But there is less attention paid to the complex logic and expansive character of liberal international order itself. This order is more than simply "America's world order." It is an order built around and by American power—and it continues to be led by the United States and other leading liberal democratic states. But the order itself has a semi-independent standing and logic. It is more expansive, institutionalized, and functional than past international orders. China does not just face America or the West, it faces the globalized embodiment of modernity itself.

The realist vision of a coming U.S.-China clash is quite compelling. The United States does not just seek to protect the liberal international order—it seeks to protect its own position within it. As China grows in power, it will seek to challenge the American geopolitical position in East Asia. It will seek to extend its own dominance throughout the region and in other regions of the world, such as Latin America, Africa, and the Middle East. If China surpasses the United States in economic size and if its military capacities become world class, a grand U.S.-China struggle will unfold. In the realist view, this clash is generated by two dynamics. First, as China grows more powerful, it will want to play a more dominant role in world politics and it will want to organize rules and institutions in a way that accord with its values and interests. This is, after all, what the United States did after 1945. Second, the United States and other liberal democratic states will grow increasingly insecure in the face of Chinese advancements and encroachments. In response, the United States will redouble its efforts to project power into Asia and reinforce its alliance partnerships. Out of these dynamics, geopolitical conflict will follow.

No doubt, as realist theory predicts, the U.S.-China power transition will generate tensions and conflict. But the realist account misses other features of modern world politics. China and the United States are not only potential rivals. They are also states that are deeply interdependent with each other and mutually dependent on an open and stable world order. As rivals who seek to be the singular and dominant world leader, they are playing a zero-sum game. For one to win, the other needs to lose. Both cannot be the top state. But as great powers that need a congenial international environment—rules, institutions, partnerships, legitimate authority—in which to advance and protect their interests, they are in a non-zero-sum situation. For one to win, the other state will also need to win. The liberal perspective asks the observer to look at both sets of dynamics. There are deep sources of conflict and mistrust generated by the anarchic and competitive structures of world politics. But there are also deep sources of stability and cooperation generated by the interdependence and mutual vulnerability that come with living in the modern era. U.S.-China relations will be shaped by how these leading states navigate between these dual dynamics.

NOTES

This chapter draws on some of my earlier writings, including G. John Ikenberry, "The Future of Liberal World Order, *Foreign Affairs* (May/June 2011); and *Liberal Leviathan: The Origins, Crisis, and Transformation of the American World Order* (Princeton: Princeton University Press, 2011).

1. On anticipations of a return to multipolarity and the end of American dominance, see Charles Kupchan, *The End of the American Era: U.S. Foreign Policy and the Geopolitics of the Twenty-First Century* (New York: Knopf, 2003); Parag Khanna, *The Second World: Empires and Influence in the New Global Age* (New York: Random House, 2008); Paul Starobin, *After America: Narratives for the New Global Age* (New York: Penguin Group, 2009); Kishore Mahbubani, *The New Asian Hemisphere: The Irresistible Shift in Global Power to the East* (New York: Public Affairs, 2009); and Fareed Zakaria, *The Post-American World* (New York: Norton, 2009).

2. See Charles Kupchan, *No One's World: The West, the Rising Rest, and the Coming Global Turn* (New York: Oxford University Press, 2012).

3. Robert Gilpin, *War and Change in World Politics* (New York: Cambridge University Press, 1981).

4. Gilpin, *War and Change*, p. 203.

5. For a survey of types of international orders, including non-liberal varieties, see essays in Greg Fry and Jocinta O'Hagan, eds., *Contending Images of World Politics* (New York: St. Martin's/Macmillan, 2000).

6. See G. John Ikenberry, "Liberal Internationalism 3.0: America and the Dilemmas of Liberal World Order," *Perspectives on Politics*, Vol. 7, No. 1 (March 2009), pp. 71–87.

7. For depictions of the Westphalian state system, see F. H. Hinsley, *Power and the Pursuit of Peace* (Cambridge: Cambridge University Press, 1963); and Hedley Bull, *The Anarchical Society: A Study of Order in World Politics* (London: Macmillan Press, 1977).

8. Moderate realist accounts of great power balancing and the evolution of its practices and principles include: Henry Kissinger, *A World Restored: Metternich, Castlereagh and the Problem of Peace, 1812–22* (Boston: Houghton Mifflin Co., 1957); Gordon A. Craig and Alexander L. George, *Force and Statecraft: Diplomatic Problems of Our Time* (New York: Oxford University Press, 1981); and Paul Schroeder, *The Trans-*

formation of European Politics, 1763–1848 (Oxford: Oxford University Press, 1994). For "society of states" perspectives on the evolution of the state system see: Bull, *The Anarchical Society*; Barry Buzan and Richard Little, *International Systems in World History: Remaking the Study of International Relations* (Oxford: Oxford University Press, 2000); Barry Buzan, *From International to World Society: English School Theory and the Social Structure of Globalization* (Cambridge: Cambridge University Press, 2004); Ian Clark, *The Hierarchy of States: Reform and Resistance in the International Order* (Cambridge: Cambridge University Press, 1989); and Andrew Hurrell, *On Global Order: Power Values, and the Constitution of International Society* (Oxford: Oxford University Press, 2007).

9. See Ikenberry, "Liberal Internationalism 3.0," pp. 71–81.

10. "U.S. and Chinese Officials Named in I.M.F. Posts," *The New York Times*, 12 July 2011.

11. See Edward S. Steinfeld, *Playing Our Game: Why China's Rise Doesn't Threaten the West* (Oxford: Oxford University Press, 2010).

12. Kennth Lieberthal and Wang Jisi, *Addressing U.S.-China Strategic Distrust* (Washington, D.C.: The Brookings Institution, 2012), p. 10.

13. Quoted in Gideon Rachman, *Zero-Sum Future: American Power in an Age of Anxiety* (New York: Simon and Schuster, 2011), p. 283.

14. Amartya Sen, "Democracy as a Universal Value," *Journal of Democracy*, Vol. 10, No. 3 (July 1999), pp. 3–17.

15. Rosemary Foot and Andrew Walter, *China, the United States, and Global Order* (New York: Cambridge University Press, 2011), p. 291.

4

U.S.-China Relations in a Realist World

Ashley J. Tellis

M anaging the rise of China remains the central geopolitical challenge facing the United States. The economic growth and technological modernization unleashed by Deng Xiaoping's reforms in 1978 have resulted in a
dramatic expansion of Chinese power which, if sustained, could enable China
to overtake the United States, not least by measures such as the gross national
product (GNP). This eclipse, by itself, would be symbolically significant because relative GNP still remains the simplest and most easily recognized measure of power in international politics. The displacement of the United States
as the world's largest productive system would, therefore, signal the dawning
of a new era—and a return to an earlier age when China possessed the world's
largest economy.[1]

That China might already be on the way to recreating this achievement
raises the prospect of a possible "power transition" within the international
system, a situation where the currently dominant power, the United States, is
gradually displaced by a new rising entity, China, whose ascent to primacy
would challenge the existing international order because that dispensation
is built around the interests and the values of the existing hegemon. It does
not require a slavish adherence to the canon of power transition theory—that
major interstate war is likely because the reigning primate will be confronted
by a dissatisfied challenger as it increases in relative strength—to accept the
key realist insight that significant power shifts in international politics are
periods of stress and intensified security competition, as both the existing
system leader and the new rising power struggle to adjust to changing political realities.[2]

This chapter explores the structural character of U.S.-China relations in
the decades ahead from the viewpoint of political realism. Political realism,
in this context, refers to the venerable tradition of understanding politics as

a permanent struggle for power arising from the perennial quest for security. Although encompassing many diverse approaches, methods, and formulations, it is unified by its focus on explaining:

> how [political] entities seek to preserve themselves in an environment characterized by pervasive egoism and the ever-present possibility of harm. The presence of egoism implies that all entities value only themselves; the interaction of many such entities creates a situation in which each becomes a limitation on the security, freedom, and ambitions of the others; and the competition which results is characterized by each entity constantly jostling with other entities in an attempt to preserve its own power and enhance its own safety. Realist approaches thus perceive politics primarily as a conflictual interaction.[3]

In a strict sense, political realism constitutes, in the terminology of Imre Lakatos, a "research program"[4] rather than a singular theory. Its metaphysical core is centered on the notion of a disordered human nature, and its "positive heuristic" consists of various formulations or theories that hypothesize how the ataxia characterizing the created order is manifested in social, political, and interstate relations. Accordingly, the earliest variants of political realism—which might be labeled "traditional realism"—were eclectic in their units of analysis: they focused on individuals as well as social wholes, such as kingdoms, republics, or the larger system of states, depending on their immediate object of interest. Over the centuries, traditional realism appeared in two variants: the secular, exemplified by the works of Thucydides, Kautilya, Machiavelli, Nietzsche (with many qualifications), and Morgenthau, and the religious, embodied in the enquiries of first Augustine and later Reinhold Niebuhr.[5] Although these individuals constitute a diverse group, they are united broadly by their conviction that the disorder of the human condition creates social strife which is overcome only by a political domination that produces a semblance of order at all levels of political activity.

The marriage of political realism to modern social science fragmented the realist tradition. After the demise of systems theory, one broad stream incorporated structuralism in an attempt to mimic the method of modern economics, while the second emphasized macro-historical analysis to uncover recurrent trends in modern history. Both schools, however, jettisoned the core that animated the traditional realists—the production of order in human society—in order to concentrate primarily on relations between states. The neorealist synthesis, associated with the work of Kenneth Waltz, thus emphasized the interaction of anarchy and polarity in the production of recurring balances of power,[6] while the macro-historical schools, exemplified by the "long cycle" and "power transition" theories of George Modelski and A.F.K. Organski respectively, viewed hegemony as the natural equilibrium in competitive international politics.[7]

Whatever their differences, then, all realists hold in common the understanding that, in the competitive environment of political action, power is the means by which conflicts of interest between egoistic entities are decided. Divergences within realism stem in the first instance from the question of motivations—traditional realists see the self-interested behavior of states as grounded in humanity's natural drive for security, power, or glory, while structural realists see the self-serving behavior of states as a product of the structure of the international system.[8] Traditional realists would not necessarily disagree with structural realists on this score, but the latter's commitment to a parsimonious social science leads them ineluctably to adopt the most limited assumption, namely, that states are motivated merely by self-preservation.

In this pursuit of security, a second order consideration—the means by which states can best secure their survival—leads to a further division within the realist family. If the state-of-nature competition at any level of political aggregation and on the sparsest assumptions is modeled through situational logic, it is possible to demonstrate that the drive to domination becomes the equilibrium outcome of anarchic rivalry.[9] This outcome, which unifies the traditional realist insight with the macro-historical schools of realism, implies that the structural diktats of the system make the quest for security necessarily a zero-sum game that compels all rational states to maximize their power.[10]

The opposing argument, on the other hand, contends that power maximization is *not* necessarily synonymous with security maximization, and thus that states' intentions matter. Whether a state is a status quo power or one that seeks to revise the international system then becomes a critical issue, along with a state's ability to credibly signal its intentions to other states in order to mitigate the security dilemma. The logical durability of this claim hinges considerably on the introduction of additional variables that mitigate conflict in the state of nature, such as the offense-defense balance and regional geography, producing thereby both a less-parsimonious theory and one that reaches more optimistic—but heterodox—conclusions in comparison to the larger realist tradition.[11]

Whatever the theoretical disagreements between orthodox realists, however, all would agree on the natural—and competitive—course that the U.S.-China relationship will follow if Chinese power continues to increase, and disagree only over the extent to which this course can be slowed or diverted. Heightened competition is inevitable—the only argument is over the degree of its intensity.

The vision of security competition that informs the analysis in this chapter is derived from traditional realism, primarily the works of Thucydides and

Machiavelli, but in a rationalist form that explains rivalry as the unintended consequence of particular agents seeking to maximize their physical security and political autonomy. The "single-exit" outcome produced by such contention is a struggle for domination in diverse realms because security, like power, is always relative in the state of nature, an insight conveyed most acutely in the penetrating work of Thomas Hobbes.[12] The assessment of U.S.-China relations that follows is thus anchored in the expectation that as China's power continues to grow, this distention will intensify security competition and pose complex challenges to the United States because the actions undertaken by *both* Washington and Beijing interactively will produce a rivalry that strains the international system and tests each protagonist (as well as their allies and neutral bystanders) in different ways.

THE UNIQUE RISE OF CHINA— AND ITS IMPLICATIONS FOR COMPETITION

China's ascent has been distinctive when compared with the rise of other great powers in the modern period. Most of the states that dominated Western history after the fifteenth century acquired their great power capabilities through a combination of military expansion beyond their national borders coupled with autarkic economic and political transformations at home. These transmutations usually involved significant increases in population, the harnessing of domestic technological innovations that drove the creation of new leading sectors in the global economy, and momentous changes in state capacity and state-society relations, usually characterized by the increasing penetration of the state in society and an expanded capacity to extract resources from the population at large for national purposes. In general, these revolutionary developments were embedded in a grand dialectic of "war making" and "state making," where violent international politics either drove domestic innovation and deepened state power, or where indigenous transformations enhanced national capabilities that in turn were pressed into the service of conflict and territorial expansion.[13]

In contrast, the rise of China, which is but part and parcel of the larger rise of Asia, is different because it has been engendered in great measure by the permissive benefits of American hegemony in the postwar period. China, accordingly, did not require any war-making abroad to fuel its economic expansion. And while its meteoric growth has undoubtedly required a measure of effective state-making for success, the benefits of being embedded in a larger liberal economic order sustained by the United States implied that China could actually grow not by the autarkic processes that dominated the rise of previous great powers, but rather by exploiting the interdependence arising from deliberate American investments in producing an open international trading system.[14]

This American effort to create a free market system internationally after the Second World War was driven by a combination of liberal and realist impulses that had nothing to do with China. The liberal belief, arising from its own domestic experience, held that an open trading system provided the best device for increasing global prosperity and ensuring peace through deepened interdependence.[15] The realist calculation, driven by the growing threat from the Soviet Union, also converged on promoting free trade—even if it was initially asymmetric—because it offered the best device, in tandem with economic aid, for bolstering the economies of America's friends and allies in the coming struggle with communism. This investment resuscitated Western Europe while creating the first wave of Asian success, as exemplified by the early regeneration of Japan, South Korea, Taiwan, and the smaller Southeast Asian states.

Although the rise of these allies implied the relative decline of the United States, it contributed to advancing the most important U.S. grand strategic objective of the time—containing the Soviet Union and its Communist bloc. In the last decade before Soviet disintegration, the United States took the first tentative steps towards integrating China into this containment system. This effort was driven by the need—felt equally by both countries—to bolster containment at a time when Moscow exhibited increased aggressiveness in Europe, Africa, and Asia, and when it was not at all clear that the Cold War was destined to end peacefully and with a decisive victory for the West.

After China had begun its own economic reforms (which increased its foreign trade explosively) and the Cold War had been brought to a successful close, the United States was confronted by the question of whether the rapprochement with Beijing ought to be reinforced by supporting its quest for permanent membership in the World Trade Organization (WTO). Distaste about China's authoritarian political system and fears that WTO membership might sharply accelerate its material capabilities weighed heavily on the minds of U.S. policymakers. The first issue would come as no surprise to traditional realists, given their conviction that domestic politics affects foreign policy, while the second was something realists of all stripes would readily appreciate. At the end of the day, however, the Clinton administration, seeking to avoid the painful ritual of extending "most favored nation" status to China after heated national debates year after year, granted China permanent normal trade relations (PNTR), thus paving the way for China's accession to the WTO in December 2001.[16]

There is, thus, little doubt that the United States has aided China's growth in power through considered and deliberate policy choices. This wager has been unquestionably successful in economic terms, as evidenced by the fact that over thirty years of phenomenal growth has lifted millions of Chinese out of poverty, contributed indispensably to wider Asian economic development, created a steady source of finance for America's vast trade and budget deficits, and congealed a dense set of new manufacturing, trading, and financial linkages throughout the Asian continent, with China as its central hub.

The Asian economic miracle has, accordingly, enjoyed a second iteration, but with an important difference this time around. In the first wave of success, the political necessity of containing Soviet expansion comported perfectly with the economic desirability of strengthening allies and neutrals—if necessary at the relative expense of American power. But the prospective rise of China promises to be more problematic because, while Beijing's continued prosperity depends on its participation in the trading order managed by Washington, China also remains enmeshed in a variety of disputes with major American allies in Asia (as well as many other neighbors) and increasingly poses a serious and growing military threat to the principal guardian of that order, America itself.[17] In other words, the structural contradiction between the United States and China is defined by the awkward reality that Washington sustains an international economic system that, although producing great benefits for itself and others, simultaneously fuels the growth of what could be its most significant geopolitical rival over time. This phenomenon is unique in contemporary history: although something similar was witnessed prior to the First World War, when both Britain and Germany found themselves bound by economic linkages despite geopolitical competition, the extent and the density of interdependence witnessed today between the United States and China has no parallel in the modern era.

This reality, which Catherine Mann has aptly described in another context as "global co-dependency,"[18] shapes the U.S.-China relationship in distinctive ways. Most critically, it will not eliminate the possibility of deep geopolitical rivalry or intense military competition. Both the experience of the First World War and contemporary politics suggest that states can—and will—resolutely pursue their strategic interests, despite the enmeshing bonds of trade and commerce, because security competition directly implicates *immediate* national or regime survival in a way that has no counterpart in economic interactions.

There is now also impressive empirical evidence to suggest that a country like the United States has not been restrained from pursuing important political objectives by its financial dependence on China, and it must be similarly expected that when critical Chinese strategic interests, such as preventing Taiwanese independence, are at stake, Beijing too will not be restrained from the use of force, no matter how that might affect its trade with the United States.[19] Both the United States and China can, therefore, be expected to pursue their core strategic interests—even to gunpoint—under the shadow of economic interdependence. If current economic trends persist, both sides will undoubtedly be careful to avoid any commercial rupture on a whim, but neither one will be deterred from putting at risk these ties should any serious challenges emerge to their national security from the other.

U.S.-CHINA SECURITY COMPETITION "BETWEEN THE TIMES"

The Indeterminacy of China's Rise

Although U.S.-China relations will continue to embody the inherent contradiction where Beijing's rise is sustained by an international order subsidized by Washington, it must be remembered that China's definitive success as an emerging power is not yet certain. In fact, it is likely that China will be unable to sustain its historically high growth rates for several reasons.

As neoclassical economic theory suggests, growth ultimately derives from the interaction of three variables: capital accumulation, labor force increases, and technical change. The miracle of Chinese growth during the last three decades, which has been driven in part by impressive rates of national savings—generally exceeding 50 percent of GNP—is likely to be constrained in the decades to come because societal aging, the poor national social safety net, a precarious financial system, and increased consumption associated with economic development, all combine to potentially diminish the impressive rates of capital accumulation witnessed in the past.[20]

China's historical "one child policy" also threatens to undermine its capacity for labor force growth because the proportion of working-age individuals is contracting at precisely the same time when the dependency ratio—the number of people of non-working age, both young and old, as a proportion of those of working age—is certain to almost double. This development makes it certain that China will grow old before it grows rich, at least in per capita terms.[21]

And while China has made impressive strides in some—narrow—areas through technical innovation, this is by no means pervasive in the economy writ large; in fact, there is no evidence that China is on the cusp of creating new leading sectors in the global economy, the single most important driver propelling the rise of any great power in the international system.[22] These considerations taken together, then, suggest that while China will continue to grow in absolute terms, it may not be able to sustain its abnormally high rates of growth long enough to actually produce a genuine power transition that involves overtaking the United States.

The prospects for future U.S.-China relations are thus clouded by substantial indeterminacy about the durability of rising Chinese power. This implies that even if the open economic order underwritten by the United States were to survive unhampered, China may not develop the "comprehensive national power" it seeks—and which any great power of consequence must of necessity possess. Even if China succeeds in sustaining a steadily expanding GNP, as is likely for a long time to come, its per capita income will lag behind the United States for many decades and so, from a strict power transition perspective, Beijing will not even be deemed a nominal challenger, given that per capita income is the standard measure favored by many power transition theorists and for good reason.[23]

This narrow conceptual issue aside, there are nonetheless many reasons to believe that although its GNP growth will be prolonged, China will still not be able to mimic the United States any time soon where national power in span and depth are concerned.[24] In other words, even if China's aggregate GNP were to exceed that of the United States at some future point, it will almost certainly still lack the encompassing capacities that mark American power: economic strength as measured by pervasive national well-being; military capabilities permitting the application of force in a sustained way at great distances from one's national borders; geopolitical advantages arising from a network of powerful allies who share both interests and values; ideational influence deriving from an international admiration for the cultural and symbolic artifacts of its society; and, finally, institutional strength as manifested through the global regimes that preserve and promote its political influence.

However, the fact that China is still some way from threatening a genuine power transition within the international system does not imply that U.S.-China relations are destined to remain harmonious until the moment a geopolitical displacement appears inevitable. Rather, they are ordained to veer in the direction of rivalry not because a transition is certain, but because it is *possible*. As Thomas Hobbes understood clearly—and demonstrated persuasively—in the *Leviathan*, competition in the state of nature arises not necessarily because of malicious intentions on the part of rational egoists, but because uncertainty about their intentions creates rivalries that can be mitigated only by the acquisition of superior power. Long before Hobbes clarified this micro-logic of social competition, both Thucydides and Machiavelli demonstrated that the quest for dominance in any competitive political environment is, by necessity, continuous and relentless, with all political entities, whether they be individuals or states, seeking to expand their power whenever they can do so without undue penalty because their circumstances simply permit it.[25]

In the case of U.S.-China relations, this competitive dimension becomes particularly significant because American and Chinese interests are at least sometimes orthogonal, if not directly opposed. The United States seeks to preserve its hegemony, despite the realities of increasing interdependence with

China and the countervailing pressures imposed by rising Chinese power. China, at the very least, seeks to preserve its territorial integrity and to increase its national power comprehensively. Although the ends to which these growing material capabilities may be directed are not yet clear, their potential for undermining U.S. interests in Asia and globally creates exactly the conditions—as Thucydides might have expected—for a coming "contest for supremacy."[26]

Even if a real power transition is therefore averted during the next two decades, the United States and China are likely to experience increasing competition in three broad areas: economic relations, military operations, and regional geopolitics.

Economic Relations

The plethora of economic benefits accruing to the United States from China's economic growth are undeniable. It is clearly understood by most policymakers that the growth in U.S.-China trade over the last two decades—the value of the total trade stood at $457 billion in 2010—is intimately connected to the expanding Chinese economy. China is now America's second largest trading partner after Canada, its third largest export market, and its largest supplier of imported goods. The welfare gains to American consumers deriving from the supply of inexpensive Chinese goods are undeniable, even as the lower costs of Chinese labor also contribute towards the improved competitiveness of U.S. companies manufacturing goods in China either for local consumption or for re-export. Moreover, China's huge trade surpluses have partly financed the large U.S. budget deficits witnessed in recent years.[27]

Despite all these benefits, however, there is a growing fear in the United States that the economic relationship with China is undermining American interests by contributing to deindustrialization and the loss of jobs at home, while simultaneously propelling China's emergence as a high-technology rival over time. The argument about deindustrialization and the loss of jobs is a complex one, but in its simplest version, it takes the following form: the Chinese ability to manufacture goods at lower costs and export them freely to the United States results in the destruction of traditional manufacturing, which then produces an irreversible loss of jobs. While cheaper Chinese goods may therefore benefit U.S. citizens *qua* consumers, these imports undermine their interests as employees. If American firms are to effectively compete with these low-cost Chinese products, they can either move their manufacturing operations to China in order to benefit from the availability of cheaper labor abroad—in the process further increasing job losses at home—or they can reduce the wages offered to American labor—thereby protecting jobs but at the cost of diminishing the standards of living.[28]

Either way, the simple deindustrialization thesis contends that rising U.S. imports from China, arising as a result of expanded U.S.-China trade, undermine the American labor force which, once lacking jobs, cannot enjoy the benefits of cheaper Chinese goods. This argument quickly increases in complexity because of the complications produced by the contraction in manufacturing and the wage stagnation that has affected the American middle class for some time now—problems that are only exacerbated by the strong perception that China's export effectiveness is aided by various unfair trade practices, ranging from undervalued exchange rates to domestic protectionism to widespread dumping.

There is no doubt that manufacturing employment in the United States has steadily dropped over the years and average real wages, especially from the mid-1970s to the late 1990s, grew all too slowly. It is not clear, however, that these problems can be attributed to increased U.S. dependence on trade for GNP growth. Diminishing manufacturing employment in particular seems to be driven by the productivity growth in that sector in the United States, and the long-term decline of manufacturing itself as a generator of employment is intimately linked to endogenous increases in technological intensity, as well as to shifting patterns of comparative advantage globally. While this last fact does imply that at least some U.S. manufacturing losses may be linked to China's internal transformations and its rising export effectiveness, those casualties should normally be offset by job creation in other sectors arising from increased efficiencies in the economy as a whole.[29]

There is good evidence, however, that even if growing import penetration does not cause a net loss of jobs in the country, the effects in specific sectors can be significant. The manufacturing and job losses suffered by the United States in textiles, apparel, leather and allied products, computer and electronic products, and electrical equipment and appliances thus acquire larger-than-life consequences because they affect key electoral blocs that are important in American politics.[30] Even if academic economists can demonstrate with great cogency that these sectors' depredations—which are to be expected in any dynamic trading system—are rarely attributable to unfair Chinese trade practices and that, in any event, they are invariably compensated by the larger wealth and welfare gains enjoyed by the United States writ large, these conclusions will not defuse the anxiety resident in the body politic nor will it fully restrain America's leaders from seeking to mitigate economic losses through political actions against China. Such behavior would be readily appreciated by all traditional realists who understood correctly that the domestic struggle for power was intimately connected to the external quest for security. Not surprisingly, then, issues of economic advantage remain matters of contestation in U.S.-China relations, and these will grow in intensity as China enjoys further increases in its national power.

While the problems of deindustrialization arising from trade might be dismissed simply as gnawing pains associated with changing comparative advantage, the threat that the open international economic system underwritten by U.S. power might levitate China into becoming an advanced technology competitor remains a serious problem that realists of all stripes would appreciate.[31] Such levitation would occur in many ways: increased high technology trade between sources in the United States or North America, Europe, Japan, and recipients in China; increasing American (or Western) foreign direct investment (FDI) in China, to include the location (or relocation) of advanced Western or American research and development or manufacturing facilities; Chinese purchases of, or investments in, American (or Western) advanced technology companies; American (or Western) transfers of advanced technology to China as part of commercial responses to Chinese tenders; illegal Chinese reverse engineering of technology that has been otherwise legitimately purchased, albeit in small numbers, for the express purpose of analyzing its structure, function, and operation; and, finally, Chinese pilfering or espionage of American (or Western) high technology through private or governmental instruments. Limiting China's access to high technology in an open trading system will be a difficult challenge, but it may be among the most important problems facing the United States because it could make a fundamental difference as to whether a nominal power transition actually becomes a real one.

Concerns about how the current trading system supports China's technological transformation have grown in recent years because of the disturbing trends that have gathered steam on almost every one of the mechanisms identified above. For example, U.S. exports of high technology products to China today—defined by the U.S. Census Bureau as referring to advanced materials, aerospace technologies, biotechnology, electronics, flexible manufacturing, information and communications, life science, nuclear technology, opto-electronics, and weapons—constituted close to a third of the total U.S. exports to China in 2010.[32] Outside of Hong Kong, the United States remains the fourth largest source of non-financial FDI in China, with private firms, both American and international, playing a critical role in driving China's remarkably rapid technological growth. Today, most of the world's 500 largest companies have investments in China, including those noted for leading-edge innovation in advanced technologies, such as Motorola, General Electric, Sony, Boeing, Matsushita, Siemens, Toshiba, Intel, Kodak, Hewlett-Packard, and IBM.

In accordance with Chinese state directives, many of these firms have structured at least part of their operations as joint ventures with Chinese partners or universities that are often under the direct control of—or responsible to—central or local government entities. The goal of domesticating the best Western technology to advance Chinese commercial and military aims has now been widely documented, but this mechanism has also been consciously supplemented by extensive espionage, illegal reverse engineering, and coerced transfers of technology "from U.S. companies engaged in normal business practices and joint ventures in China in exchange for access to China's market."[33] These unlawful routines appear to have intensified ever since the China National Offshore Oil Corporation's bid to buy UNOCAL, a U.S. energy company, fell through in the face of heightened American fears about the national security impact of Chinese state-owned or state-connected companies seeking to take over major U.S. firms.

In the years to come, therefore, U.S. efforts to control the transfer of specific advanced technologies to China, even as Beijing seeks to acquire these through legitimate means or otherwise, will become an important component of the U.S-Chinese rivalry, even if Washington is otherwise committed to sustaining an open trade regime. Irrespective of the merits of any specific trade disputes or the gains from expanded trade overall, the growing Chinese dominance in manufacturing will also continue to unnerve the United States because of the economic and strategic vulnerabilities it produces. The United States will, above all else, respond to the rising Chinese economic challenge— and the economic elements of the evolving competition—by concerted internal balancing. This will include efforts to better manage national expenditures and to invest in promoting new technological revolutions, such as 3-D manufacturing. If these efforts succeed, the threats of an early power transition will be defused. But if they do not, the debate about relative gains vis-à-vis China will only intensify over the long-term, raising once again the question long thought to be settled: Does an open trading system really serve America's interests as a great power?[34]

Military Operations

The economic challenge posed by China, which affects millions of Americans in their everyday lives, is increasingly complemented by new and unsettling threats in the arena of military operations, deriving fundamentally from the rapid modernization of the People's Liberation Army (PLA).[35] This modernization already threatens American friends and partners along the Indo-Pacific littoral and, when complete, will undermine a key precondition for strategic stability in Pacific Asia—the unimpeded U.S. ability to assist its allies when they are threatened by external dangers.

The postwar U.S. security system in Asia is often described as a "hub and spokes" arrangement, but its underlying strategic concept is better captured by Jonathan Pollack's metaphor of "holding the ring."[36] This metaphor describes a situation where no regional power possesses military instruments capable of inflicting "high-leverage strategic harm" on another, while the only external entity possessing such capabilities—the United States—lacks the incentives to use them abusively, because it employs its power to serve larger political and economic interests. The strategy of "holding the ring" thus capitalizes on America's geographical distance from East Asia: it puts the United States in the role of a non-threatening but engaged external protector with forward de-ployed forces that reduce the incentives for regional states to acquire any mili-tary capabilities that would make its protective task either more compelling or more difficult.[37]

The American forces operating around or committed to the Asian littorals are critical to this strategy because, on the one hand, they serve to prevent any other power from being able to dominate the Indo-Pacific while, on the other hand, they create the region-wide order that enables local states to avoid frit-tering away resources in ill-conceived attempts at producing security unilater-ally. In this context, the superior war fighting capability of the U.S. military essentially serves as a reminder to all local states that attempts at hegemonic dominance would be extremely costly and, ultimately, unfruitful. Should a prospective challenger fail to get this message, American forward deployed forces quickly become the means to bolster the defense of its regional allies, and the instruments by which a larger containment strategy can be operation-alized, if necessary. To the degree that these objectives are successfully real-ized, they contribute towards sustaining the ongoing Asian economic miracle by permitting regional states to concentrate on economic intercourse at the expense of security competition.[38]

The history of the last several decades suggests that the United States, de-spite many challenges, managed to successfully hold the ring: it prevented the rise of threatening regional hegemonies, averted dangerous local securi-ty competitions that had potential strategic consequences, and nurtured the permissive conditions for sustained economic cooperation—all because the forward deployed and forward operating U.S. military forces were fundamen-tally unchallenged in their task of protecting American allies and important neutrals along the Asian littoral.

For the first time now, however, there is a grave risk that China's new ac-quisition of dedicated anti-access and area-denial (AA/AD) capabilities will fundamentally threaten the principal U.S. surface components and their asso-ciated land bases in ways that would actually prevent Washington from being able to discharge its security obligations in Asia.[39] Such a failure would not only undermine the traditional system of extended deterrence that the United States has relied upon to dampen local security competition and sustain wider economic growth, but it would also, over time, lead to even more pernicious outcomes, such as further regional nuclear proliferation and eventually the consolidation of a Chinese regional hegemony that would undermine U.S. interests not only in Asia but also globally.

The original reason for the concerted Chinese acquisition of AA/AD capabilities was rooted in the desire to prevent U.S. naval and air forces from being able to intervene effectively on Taipei's behalf in the context of any future war in the Taiwan Strait. This objective, embedded in the intense Chinese desire to prevent Taiwanese "secession" at all costs, has evolved—given both operational and political imperatives—into a larger requirement aimed at constraining the capacity of the U.S. military along a wider territorial swath.[40] Chinese military aims now include enforcing complete area denial throughout the Yellow, East China, and South China Seas and their littorals—the "Near Seas" defined by what the PLA refers to as the "first island chain"—along with depriving access to their approaches by reaching far into the "second island chain"—which includes the Japan, Philippine, and Indonesian Seas, covering the Kuriles, Kokkaido, and Marianas and Palau Islands in the south, and reaching to Guam in the western Pacific. While these aspirations are encompassed by the Chinese doctrine of "offshore active defense," the means being developed to implement these goals exemplify what Chinese planners call "non-linear," "non-contact," and "asymmetric" operations, which, if successful, would transform the western Pacific into a hermetic enclosure where Chinese dominance is assured because of its ability to hold American military power at risk.[41]

Given this interest—not surprising in light of China's rising power and the resulting desire for an appropriate sphere of control radiating outwards from its boundaries—Beijing has invested in a formidable land-based "reconnaissance-strike complex." This capability is anchored in an extensive intelligence, surveillance, and reconnaissance (ISR) system that includes terrestrial and space-based sensors employing multiple phenomenologies to detect, fix, track, and target mobile U.S. military systems operating at great distances from Chinese territory, as well as activities at fixed bases throughout the Pacific. This information, supplemented by other intelligence collected by Chinese naval and air elements, is then disseminated to Chinese offensive forces through a national command and control grid. The command echelons at various levels, thereafter, direct China's most potent weapons—including its anti-ship ballistic missiles, and more generally its large and growing ballistic and cruise missile inventory—in mass raids on the U.S. surface fleet and its supporting bases throughout the theater. These offensives will, in all probability, be accompanied by ancillary "kinetic" and "non-kinetic" attacks on America's larger space, intelligence, and computer networks.[42]

This last category of operations, although driven in the first instance by regional contingencies, will by necessity have global impact because of the highly integrated nature of the U.S. C4ISR system. Even if the deleterious consequences of such Chinese attacks can be avoided universally, there is a growing consensus among U.S. planners that American forward deployed and operating surface forces—especially its carrier battle groups—will be at severe risk even in limited conventional conflicts over Taiwan. As the Chinese "reconnaissance-strike complex" expands to include other orientations beyond the western Pacific (for example, the Indian Ocean), the battlespaces wherein the United States traditionally enjoyed unconstrained freedom of action will steadily diminish, and with such diminutions will come further reductions in American potency and influence. Beijing's expanding military capabilities thus not only threaten to undermine the U.S. ability to service its extended deterrence guarantees in the Indo-Pacific, but they also threaten to alter the existing military balances between China and its major regional rivals such as Japan, India, and Russia.[43]

The uninterrupted continuation of these strategic trends bodes ill for future stability in Asia. Consequently, Beijing's increasing military prowess will be determinedly contested by the United States in the years to come. The American struggle to dominate the offense-defense balance is already underway, and is materializing in three different but complementary directions: first, through the search for technological solutions aimed at neutralizing various Chinese weapon systems at either the tactical or the operational levels of warfare; second, through the modification of U.S. war plans against China, which are shifting away from the earlier emphasis on mounting a pure standoff or *in situ* defense of American allies towards attacking critical nodes on the Chinese mainland; and third, through an effort at more systematically incorporating various options focused on counteracting the larger Chinese nuclear deterrent and other supporting capabilities through offensive and defensive means. These actions, in turn, will stimulate further Chinese military responses that will, once again, provoke additional U.S. initiatives in what will be an open-ended struggle for strategic dominance in Asia. Therefore, for as far as the eye can see—and even if a consequential power transition is not imminent—the United States and China will be locked into a technical and operational rivalry to secure freedom of action in the Asian battlespaces that are important, albeit for different reasons, to each country.[44]

Regional Geopolitics

Finally, the competition for military advantage is embedded in an equally significant rivalry over geopolitical positioning. This contest derives from two interacting sources: first, the unease in the United States that China's continued growth—if uninterrupted—could eventually result in a broad challenge to American hegemony in a systemic sense, initially in Asia and thereafter (or in parallel) globally; and, second, the growing fear throughout the Indo-Pacific region, especially in the capitals of China's major competitors, that expanding Chinese power presages rising threats to their physical security and their political autonomy. These dangers arise not only because of the extant disputes with China but also because of the natural Asian fears that a rising China will eventually seek to recreate a modern version of the "tributary" system that will naturally limit their freedoms and subordinate their preferences to those of Beijing. The strategic concerns of China's neighbors, thus, dovetail perfectly with those of the United States, leading both sides to search for solutions that will permit growing Chinese power to be effectively balanced even as all the concerned parties seek to continue to profit economically from China's rapid economic growth.[45]

This challenge was simply not significant for most of the postwar period. Until the last decade of the twentieth century, U.S. power and influence in Asia was uncontested, thanks to the United States' unrivalled economic strength, its strong economic ties with key Asian states, and the robust American security umbrella manifested through the holding the ring arrangement. Even at the high tide of Soviet supremacy, Moscow's coercive reach in Asia was more limited compared to its capabilities in Europe and, consequently, the fears in the littoral about the threat of Soviet political domination were much more attenuated given that Moscow had neither a history of controlling the Asian periphery nor the maritime power that could have sustained control in these spaces in the face of American opposition. The prospective rise of China is different in this regard. China has a long history of enjoying suzerainty in the East and Southeast Asian littorals, which its neighbors remember all too clearly and which they are also determined now to resist, if propitious conditions for such resistance can be created. China also has active political disputes with key regional powers such as Japan and India, and it poses a long-term threat to Russia, especially in its vulnerable Far East. And China, thanks to both geography and technology, is better positioned to resist American military power in Asia in a way that the Soviet Union was not.

While China's growing power, its emerging military capabilities, and its critical locational advantages all combine to provoke U.S. and regional disquiet, that the fate of Asia itself is at stake in this rivalry makes all the difference.[46] This is because for the first time in modern history, the Asian continent is certain to become the single largest locus of economic power in the international system—producing some 43 percent of global production of goods and services by 2025—and as such will become exactly as attractive to global politics in this century as Europe was in the last. Consequently, realists believe that the United States is faced with exactly the same task that it confronted in the previous era: preventing the domination of the continent by any indigenous power that might, over time, accumulate sufficient strength to control Asia's resources and threaten local American allies, important neutral powers, or even U.S. security itself. U.S. interests are deeply threatened by the prospect that China might integrate the Indo-Pacific periphery through a network of trading relations that could become the foundation for an impermeable sphere of influence centered on Chinese economic, geopolitical, and cultural primacy in Asia.

Because China's steady growth in power could enable it to configure just such a world in the future—assuming that it has not begun to do so already—the United States has attempted since the beginning of this century to develop a new strategy for managing China's rise. This endeavor was not driven by the view that Beijing was a malicious power as the Soviet Union had previously been. Rather, it was given impetus by the terrible curse of uncertainty—what Hobbes labeled "diffidence" or "anticipation"—which prevents any rational egoist from knowing with certainty what the future behavior of its competitors might be. Thus, it was feared that a growing China might evolve into an unyielding competitor as it accumulated more national power, and that it might develop an obduracy that would become manifest either through future efforts to resolve territorial disputes through coercive diplomacy or the use of force, or through prospective demands for a greater recognition of China's prerogatives as a function of its size and power. The American conviction that a strategy for coping with China was indispensable was only deepened by the troubling rise of nationalism in the Chinese polity, as well as the presence of an authoritarian regime in Beijing which has survived remarkably despite the social change otherwise occurring in China. Beijing's dramatic military modernization, combined with the pervasive opacity suffusing its military programs, finally proved to be the conclusive driver bolstering the necessity for a calculated response to China's rise, because the security dilemmas accentuated by Chinese rearmament implied that the United States could no longer sustain the early post–Cold War policy of watchful waiting.

Cognizant that China's reemergence could prove to be highly disruptive if it were not shaped in a way that enhanced peace and stability in Asia, the Bush administration set out to develop and implement a new strategy that would accommodate the benefits of growing economic interdependence between the United States (and others) and China, while simultaneously hedging against the downside of growing Chinese strength.[47] It was understood clearly that the old strategy of containment, which had served the United States well in its previous competition with the Soviet Union, was inutile in the emerging geopolitical environment which was instead characterized by tight and growing economic bonds between the United States and its Asian partners on the one hand, and China on the other.

Given this reality, the Bush administration settled on a strategy of continuing to deepen economic ties with China and its other global partners, even as it deliberately embarked on an effort to strengthen the democratic states on China's periphery in order that their growth in capabilities would serve as objective constraints on Beijing's misuse of power. Consistent with this policy, the United States revitalized its alliances with Japan, South Korea, and Australia, deepened ties with key Southeast Asian partners such as Singapore, the Philippines, and Vietnam, and in a dramatic breakthrough, transformed the previously estranged relationship with India, the one major Asian continental power that had both the capacity and the incentives to balance China, and by so doing, help to preserve a regional equilibrium that favored Washington.[48]

The genius of the Bush approach resided in the fact that it permitted all—the United States, its allies and partners, and China—to enjoy continued benefits from trade among themselves, while at the same time creating the foundations for constraining potential Chinese misbehavior without containing China. This strategy of broad "alliance making," however, was viewed in China—correctly—as a none-too-subtle effort at restraining Beijing. As this American effort increasingly gathers steam over time, deepened both by growing regional fears of Chinese power and American anxieties over the global balance, it is certain to trigger various Chinese efforts at "alliance breaking," many of which have already begun.

Beijing's rejoinders to the evolving American strategy will appear in diverse but predictable forms. China will, whenever possible or necessary, attempt to drive wedges among U.S. alliance partners in order to prevent a unified and coherent response in disputes of importance to China. Beijing will also seek, whenever possible, to prevent neutral powers from supporting Washington and its allies in any confrontation with China, even as it uses its deep and growing economic linkages with other nations, including the United States, to threaten a loss of access (or to promise enhanced asymmetric access) to its markets in order to shape the behavior of its competitors. Finally, *in extremis*, China will use force in an exemplary and deliberate way, when the benefits are judged to be worth the costs, to intimidate challengers who might otherwise collaborate to undermine vital Chinese interests.

Irrespective of how Beijing's responses are manifested in any given case, the fact remains that it will utilize all the time-honored stratagems of "alliance breaking"—side payments, discriminate intimidation, or, when necessary, all-out confrontation—to deny the United States the benefits it seeks through its policies of polite balancing. These initiatives will, in turn, provoke Washington to focus on strengthening the capability and commitment of its alliance partners, even as both sides attempt to navigate the treacherous push and pull exerted by the competing pressures of free-riding on one hand, and fears of either entrapment or abandonment on the other. Sustaining coalitions, even in the face of a dangerous adversary, is a dynamic and oftentimes precarious process that is not always assured of success. As a result, the United States and China will be locked into a constant and calculating competition for influence over the choices made by the major Asian states, both allies and bystanders, because their decisions will make—along with, obviously, the courses of action pursued in Beijing and Washington—an important difference to the ease with which the United States can preserve its primacy in the face of growing Chinese power. The struggle over geopolitical positioning, too, will therefore persist for some time to come, abating in intensity only when either Washington or Beijing ceases to pursue their interests at the expense of the other.[49]

CONCLUSION: WHAT NEXT?

China's emergence as a great power has undoubtedly been unique because it has risen under the aegis of American power and through integration with the liberal international economic order sustained by the United States. Whether China can sustain this ascendency indefinitely still remains an open question, because its myriad internal weaknesses could conspire to slow down its economic growth considerably.[50] Even if overtaking the United States in terms of GNP were to occur, in all probability China would not be able to match its Western rival in per capita income and it may not be able to compete with Washington where "comprehensive national power" is concerned for quite some time to come.

In spite of such relative inferiority persisting for as far as the eye can see, U.S.-China relations promise to remain troubled, competitive, and vexatious because of a variety of serious near-term problems in the arenas of economic relations, military operations, and regional geopolitics. Although the presence of nuclear weapons on both sides will likely prevent any conflict—if one were to occur—from degenerating into unlimited war, any realist would predict that the broad bilateral relationship is nonetheless likely to remain anything but harmonious. The growing American fear that China might consequentially challenge its power one day leads it to inevitably follow strategies designed to tacitly constrain the free exercise of Chinese strength and influence, even as Beijing's fears of exactly that outcome push it in the direction of protecting its regional and global interests through greater assertiveness.

This pattern of interaction will continue indefinitely so long as the current distribution of power, or some facsimile thereof, obtains. If Chinese power, however, declines in relative terms at some point, either because of internal crises, a defeat in war either with the United States or a third country, or some other "wild card," or simply because American power enjoys dramatic resuscitation as a result of new technological breakthroughs or effective economic restructuring, then the intensity of bilateral competition will inevitably moderate.

If, in contrast, American power continually declines in relative terms over the long run, then the impact on the U.S.-China relationship will depend, in the first instance, on what happens to other major powers in the international system. A significant American decline that is accompanied by the rise of a third power—say, India—in the face of continued Chinese growth will create novel patterns of tripolar politics characterized either by stable joint U.S.-Indian balancing of China, or by continually unstable and revolving balances, where different combinations of two-on-one materialize depending on the issue in contention.[51] Chinese behaviors in this situation will play a critical role in determining whether stable or unstable tripolarity remains the "equilibrium" outcome. If American relative decline occurs amid the rise of more than two other powers, then the patterns of interaction that are likely to occur will be the extraordinarily complex ones associated with multipolarity, where the nature of the issues, the intensity of the competing interests, and the differences in relative power (both individually and in different combinations) will shape how U.S-China relations play out.

If significant American decline relative to China occurs, however, in relative isolation—meaning that no other power acquires material capabilities that place in it in a similar league to either the United States or China—then U.S.-China relations will be determined by the relative *rates* of rise and decline affecting the two states. If the Chinese rise and American decline are comparatively slow, then the current systemic configuration will gradually evolve in the direction of bipolarity for at least some time to come. This iteration of bipolarity, however, will not necessarily mimic the erstwhile U.S.-Soviet competition unless the liberal international order that currently ties both Washington and Beijing together were to decay and be reconstituted into competing trading blocs, each underwritten by one of these two global powers. In such circumstances, depending on the absolute and relative economic performance of both rivals, the ensuing bipolarity could persist for a while, with increased geopolitical competition neatly superimposed on the economic realities in a broad reproduction of Cold War dynamics. This situation would create the greatest incentives for intense great power competition. However, if the open international trading order survives and continues to entwine both competing great powers—a difficult outcome to imagine unless the gains from cooperation were perfectly symmetrical—then rivalry will still ensue, but each state will be more constrained because of the constant need to balance the benefits of power-political rivalry against the potential for economic losses.

If, in contrast to the previous scenario, China's rise and the United States' decline were to be both substantive and rapid—in a world where there were no other rising powers—then the bipolarity that surfaces would be fundamentally transient and at best an evanescent waypoint on the road to a new world order called Chinese hegemony. This universe would share important similarities with the current U.S.-dominated global order in its arterial characteristics, though obviously not in its style or in its detail—and, of course, centered on the critical transposition that replaces the United States with China. Whether an open international economic system will survive in this situation will depend greatly on whether China as the new hegemon would be willing to bear the costs of maintaining such a regime, which would involve everything from making disproportionate contributions to the production of global public goods to bearing the structural deficits necessary to sustain systemic liquidity.

The United States, in this world, would probably still remain an important power, but a decidedly subordinate one that is continually anxious about the threats that Beijing and its allies could mount against Washington and its interests. Irrespective of what happened to American conventional forces, the United States would of necessity take even deeper refuge in its nuclear weapons—assuming that these still remain "ultimate" weapons that are not superseded by other devices. The United States would obviously attempt to resist China in concert with other powers sharing similar interests, but the distribution of capabilities would, by definition in this scenario, prevent any constraints from effectively limiting the exercise of Chinese power.

Irrespective of what the systemic benefits of such an outcome might be, Chinese hegemony would be decidedly disadvantageous to the United States and its friends. The possibility that this realm might actually be instantiated in a time to come only ensures that Washington will do everything in its power in the interim—meaning now, while China still subsists "between the times"—to prevent this eventuality from coming to pass. Because Beijing expects just this response from the United States, U.S.-China relations are doomed to be competitive now and well into the future. No other epitaph could be inscribed by a traditional realist reading of politics.

NOTES

The author is deeply grateful to Charles Glaser, David Shambaugh, Christopher Twomey, and especially Sean Mirski for their helpful comments on this chapter.

1. For a work that seeks to demonstrate the inevitability of this outcome, see Arvind Subramanian, *Eclipse: Living in the Shadow of China's Economic Dominance* (Washington, D.C.: Peterson Institute for International Economics, 2011).

2. The "power transition" approach in international relations theory has been articulated by several generations of scholars, and key works in this tradition include A. F. K. Organski, *World Politics* (New York: Knopf, 1958); A. F. K. Organski and Jacek Kugler, *The War Ledger* (Chicago: University of Chicago Press, 1980); Jacek Kugler

and A. F. K. Organski, "The Power Transition," in *Handbook of War Studies*, ed. Manus Midlarsky (Boston: Unwin Hyman, 1989); and Jacek Kugler and Douglas Lemke, eds., *Parity and War: Evaluations and Extensions of the War Ledger* (Ann Arbor: University of Michigan Press, 1996).

3. Ashley J. Tellis, "Reconstructing Political Realism: The Long March to Scientific Theory," *Security Studies* (Winter 1995/96), p. 3.

4. The key source is Imre Lakatos, "Falsification and the Methodology of Scientific Research Programmes," in *Criticism and the Growth of Knowledge*, eds. Imre Lakatos and Alan Musgrave (Cambridge: Cambridge University Press, 1970).

5. See Thucydides, *History of the Peloponnesian War*, trans. Rex Warner (Harmondsworth: Penguin, 1954); Kautilya, *The Arthashastra*, trans. L. N. Rangarajan (New York: Penguin Books India, 1992); Niccolo Machiavelli, *The Prince and the Discourses*, trans. Luigi Ricci (New York: Modern Library, 1950); Friedrich Nietzsche, *On the Genealogy of Morals*, trans. ed. Douglas Smith (Oxford: Oxford World's Classics, 1996); Hans J. Morgenthau, *Politics Among Nations: The Struggle for Power and Peace* (New York: A. A. Knopf, 1950); Augustine of Hippo, *The City of God*, trans. John Healey (New York: E. P. Dutton, 1945); and Reinhold Niebuhr, *Moral Man and Immoral Society: A Study in Ethics and Politics* (New York: Charles Scribner's Sons, 1932).

6. Kenneth Neal Waltz, *Theory of International Politics* (Reading: Addison-Wesley Publishing Co., 1979).

7. See Organski, *World Politics*; Organski and Kugler, *The War Ledger*; and George Modelski, *Long Cycles in World Politics* (Seattle: University of Washington Press, 1987).

8. For prominent modern writings on traditional realism, see Edward Hallett Carr, *The Twenty Years' Crisis, 1919–1939: An Introduction to the Study of International Relations* (London: MacMillan, 1939) and Morgenthau, *Politics Among Nations*. For the definitive writing on structural realism, see Kenneth Waltz, *Theory of International Politics* (New York: Cambridge University Press, 1986).

9. This claim was first formally demonstrated in Ashley J. Tellis, *The Drive to Domination: Towards a Pure Realist Theory of Politics* (Ph.D. dissertation, University of Chicago, Illinois, 1994), which established that the traditional realist insight about domination being the natural outcome of state-of-nature struggles not only undermined the Waltzian claim that recurring balances of power constituted the equilibrium under anarchy, but also elucidated how political realism in its rationalist variant could explain state formation as a product of individual competition (cf. Bradley A. Thayer, *Darwin and International Relations: On the Evolutionary Origins of War and Ethnic Conflict* [Lexington: University Press of Kentucky, 2004], p. 303).

10. This argument is advanced via multiple exit-models in Ashley J. Tellis, "The Quest for Security in International Politics: Explaining Security in a Universe of Stable States," chapter in Tellis, *The Drive to Domination*, pp. 340–386. The definitive exposition of how power maximization has occurred in history, an approach now labeled "offensive realism," can be found in John J. Mearsheimer, *The Tragedy of Great Power Politics* (New York: Norton, 2001).

11. This approach, now labeled "defensive realism," has spawned a large literature which includes Robert Jervis, "Cooperation under the Security Dilemma," *World Politics* (January 1978), pp. 167–214; Stephen M. Walt, *The Origins of Alliances* (Ithaca: Cornell University Press, 1984); Barry R. Posen, *The Sources of Military Doctrine: France, Britain, and Germany between the World Wars* (Ithaca: Cornell University Press, 1984); and, most recently, Charles L. Glaser, *Rational Theory of International*

Politics: The Logic of Competition and Cooperation (Princeton: Princeton University Press, 2010).

12. For a detailed examination of Hobbes' contribution to understanding conflict, see Jean Hampton, *Hobbes and the Social Contract Tradition* (New York: Cambridge University Press, 1986).

13. On the relations between a state, its society, and other states, as well as on the imperatives of state-building, see Joseph R. Strayer, *On the Medieval Origins of the Modern State* (Princeton: Princeton University Press, 1970); Charles Tilly (ed.), *The Formation of National States in Western Europe* (Princeton: Princeton University Press, 1975); Douglass C. North and Robert Paul Thomas, *The Rise of the Western World: A New Economic History* (Cambridge: Cambridge University Press, 1973); Richard Bean, "War and the Birth of the Nation State," *Journal of Economic History* (March, 1973), pp. 203–221; Karen A. Rasler and William R. Thompson, *War and State Making: The Shaping of the Global Powers* (Boston: Unwin Hyman, 1989); and Charles Tilly, *Coercion, Capital, and European States, AD 900–1900* (Cambridge: B. Blackwell, 1990).

14. Ashley J. Tellis et al., "Sources of Conflict in Asia," in *Sources of Conflict in the 21st Century: Regional Futures and U.S. Strategy*, ed. Zalmay Khalilzad and Ian O. Lesser (Santa Monica: RAND Corporation, 1998), pp. 46–52.

15. For a further elucidation of the liberal viewpoint, see G. John Ikenberry's chapter in this volume.

16. For an overview of the debate, see Vladimir N. Pregelj, *Most-Favored-Nation Status of the People's Republic of China* (Washington, D.C.: Congressional Research Service Report for Congress RL 30225, June 7, 2001), available at: http://digital.library .unt.edu/ark:/67531/metacrs2000/m1/1/high_res_d/RL30225_2001Jun07.pdf.

17. Ashley J. Tellis, *Power Shift: How the West Can Adapt and Thrive in an Asian Century* (Washington, D.C.: The German Marshall Fund of the United States, *Asia Paper Series*, January 2010).

18. Catherine L. Mann, "Breaking Up Is Hard to Do: Global Co-Dependency, Collective Action, and the Challenges of Global Adjustment," *CESifo Forum*, January 2005, p. 16, available at: http://www.iie.com/publications/papers/mann0105b.pdf.

19. Daniel W. Drezner, "Bad Debts: Assessing China's Financial Influence in Great Power Politics," *International Security* (Fall 2009), pp. 7–45; Thomas J. Christensen, "The Contemporary Security Dilemma: Deterring a Taiwan Conflict," *The Washington Quarterly* (Autumn 2002), pp. 7–21. The Tiananmen Square incident in June 1989 is another apt demonstration of Beijing's willingness to risk its economic ties when it perceives a danger to the security of its regime.

20. Gabe Collins and Andrew Erickson, "China's S-Curve Trajectory: Structural Factors Will Likely Slow the Growth of China's Economy and Comprehensive National Power," *China SignPost* (August 15, 2011). Also see Charles Freeman's chapter in this volume.

21. Nicholas Eberstadt, "Asia-Pacific Demographics in 2010–2040: Implications for Strategic Balance," in *Strategic Asia 2010–11: Asia's Rising Power and America's Continued Purpose*, ed. Ashley J. Tellis, Andrew Marble, and Travis Tanner (Seattle: National Bureau of Asian Research, 2010), pp. 247–250.

22. Adam Segal, "Chinese Technology Policy and American Innovation," Prepared Statement for the U.S.-China Economic and Security Review Commission, June 15, 2011, available at: http://www.uscc.gov/hearings/2011hearings/written_testimonies/11_06_15_wrt/11_06_15_segal_testimony.pdf; George Modelski and William R.

Thompson, *Leading Sectors and World Powers: The Coevolution of Global Politics and Economics* (Columbia: University of South Carolina Press, 1996).

23. See the discussion in David Rapkin and William R. Thompson, "Power Transition, Challenge, and the (Re)Emergence of China," *International Interactions* (2003), pp. 324–325.

24. See Ashley J. Tellis, "Preserving Hegemony: The Strategic Choices Facing the United States," in *Strategic Asia 2008–09: Challenges and Choices*, ed. Ashley J. Tellis, Mercy Kuo, and Andrew Marble (Seattle: National Bureau of Asian Research, 2008), pp. 3–37.

25. For Hobbes, see Ashley J. Tellis, "Resolving the Hobbesian Problem: The Limits of Liberal Theories of Order Production," chapter in Tellis, *The Drive to Domination*, pp. 161–198. For Thucydides, see Jacqueline de Romilly, *The Rise and Fall of States According to Greek Authors* (Ann Arbor: University of Michigan Press 1991), and for Machiavelli, see Markus Fischer, *Well-Ordered License: On the Unity of Machiavelli's Thought* (Lanham: Lexington Books, 2000).

26. Aaron L. Friedberg, *A Contest for Supremacy: China, America, and the Struggle for Mastery in Asia* (New York: W.W. Norton & Company, 2011).

27. For this point and more, see the extended discussion in Charles Freeman's chapter in this volume.

28. Bob Baugh and Joel Yudken, "Is Deindustrialization Inevitable?," *New Labor Forum* (Summer 2006), pp. 55–64. For a criticism of this story, also see Charles Freeman's chapter in this volume.

29. David Brauer, "What Accounts for the Decline in Manufacturing Employment?," *Economic and Budget Issue Brief*, Congressional Budget Office, February 18, 2004, available at: http://www.cbo.gov/ftpdocs/50xx/doc5078/02-18-Manufacturing Employment.pdf.

30. Douglas Holtz-Eakin, "Economic Relationships between the United States and China," Written Testimony Before the United States House of Representatives Committee on Ways and Means, April 14, 2005, see Footnote #11, available at: http://www.cbo.gov/ftpdocs/62xx/doc6274/04-14-ChinaTestimony.pdf.

31. For more on this issue, see Charles W. McMillion, "China's Very Rapid Economic, Industrial and Technological Emergence," Prepared for the U.S.-China Security Review Commission, June 5, 2002, available at: http://www.uscc.gov/researchpapers/2000_2003/pdfs/26rpt.pdf.

32. U.S. Census Bureau, "U.S. Trade with China in Advanced Technology Products – Monthly and Cumulative Data (in Thousands US $)," July 12, 2011, available at: http://www.census.gov/foreign-trade/statistics/product/atp/2010/12/ctryatp/atp5700 .html. For a more thorough investigation, see Michael J. Ferrantino, Robert B. Koopman, Zhi Wang, and Falan Yinug, "The Nature of US-China Trade in Advanced Technology Products," *Comparative Economic Studies* (2010): 207–224.

33. Bureau of Export Administration, Office of Strategic Industries and Economic Security, Defense Market Research Report, *U.S. Commercial Technology Transfers to the People's Republic of China*, January 1999, available at: http://www.fas.org/nuke/guide/china/doctrine/dmrr_chinatech.htm.

34. Robert J. Samuelson, "The Real Economic Threat from China," *Newsweek*, August 20, 2008, available at: http://www.signonsandiego.com/uniontrib/20080820/news_lz1e20samuels.html.

35. See Office of the Secretary of Defense, *Annual Report to Congress: Military and Security Developments Involving the People's Republic of China 2011* (Washington, D.C.:

U.S. Government Printing Office, 2011) and previous annual reports for a good survey of these developments. See also Richard D. Fisher, *China's Military Modernization: Building for Regional and Global Reach* (Stanford: Stanford University Press, 2010).

36. Jonathan D. Pollack, "The United States in East Asia," in *Asia's International Role in the Post-Cold War Era* (London: IISS Adelphi Paper No. 275, 1993), pp. 69–82.

37. Although this is an accurate characterization of the United States' role in the Asian security architecture, it is worth noting that Beijing—unsurprisingly—has a different perspective on the U.S. role in Asia. Indeed, this divergence in viewpoints is part and parcel of the larger polarization of perceptions that is inherent in any security dilemma—what one state views as its defensive or beneficent actions is perceived by another as a potential security threat that necessitates a firm response.

38. These paragraphs are drawn from Ashley J. Tellis, "Military Technology Acquisition and Regional Stability in East Asia," in Jonathan D. Pollack and Hyun-Dong Kim (eds.), *East Asia's Potential for Instability and Crisis: Implications for the United States and Korea* (Santa Monica: RAND Corporation, 1995), pp. 43–73.

39. See Roger Cliff, Mark Burles, Michael S. Chase, Derek Eaton, and Kevin L. Pollpeter, *Entering the Dragon's Lair: Chinese Anti-Access Strategies and Their Implications for the United States* (Santa Monica: RAND Corporation, 2007) for a useful survey.

40. Michael Glosny, "Getting Beyond Taiwan? Chinese Foreign Policy and PLA Modernization," *Strategic Forum* (January 2011); Michael D. Swaine, "China's Regional Military Posture," in *Power Shift: China and Asia's New Dynamics*, ed. David Shambaugh (Berkeley: University of California Press, 2005), pp. 266–285; and Michael D. Swaine, Andrew N. D. Yang, and Evan S. Medeiros, *Assessing the Threat: The Chinese Military and Taiwan's Security* (Washington, D.C.: Carnegie Endowment for International Peace, 2007).

41. See, for instance, Office of the Secretary of Defense, *Annual Report to Congress 2011*; Office of Naval Intelligence, *The People's Liberation Army Navy: A Modern Navy with Chinese Characteristics* (Washington, D.C.: U.S. Office of Naval Intelligence, 2009); and Nan Li, "The Evolution of China's Naval Strategy and Capabilities: From 'Near Coast' and 'Near Seas' to 'Far Seas,'" *Asian Security* (2009), pp. 144–169.

42. Mark A. Stokes, *China's Evolving Conventional Strategic Strike Capability: The Anti-Ship Ballistic Missile Challenge to U.S. Maritime Operations in the Western Pacific and Beyond*, Project 2049 Institute, September 14, 2009, available at: http://project2049.net/documents/chinese_anti_ship_ballistic_missile_asbm.pdf. Also, see Mark A. Stokes, *China's Strategic Modernization: Implications for the United States* (Carlisle Barracks, PA: U.S. Army War College Strategic Studies Institute, 1999).

43. See Roger Cliff et al., *Entering the Dragon's Lair*, as well as Andrew Scobell and Larry M. Wortzel (eds.), *China's Growing Military Power: Perspectives on Security, Ballistic Missiles, and Conventional Capabilities* (Carlisle Barracks, PA: U.S. Army War College Strategic Studies Institute, 2002); Jonathan D. Pollack (ed.), *Asia Eyes America: Regional Perspectives on U.S. Asia-Pacific Strategy in the Twenty-First Century* (Newport: Naval War College Press, 2007); and Ashley J. Tellis, Travis Tanner, and Jessica Keough (eds.), *Strategic Asia 2011–12: Asia Responds to Its Rising Powers—China and India* (Seattle: National Bureau of Asian Research, 2011).

44. Friedberg, *The Contest for Supremacy*, pp. 215–284.

45. Dan Blumenthal, Randall Schriver, Mark Stokes, L. C. Russell Hsiao, and Michael Mazza, "Asian Alliances in the 21st Century," Project 2049 Institute, 2011, available at: http://project2049.net/documents/Asian_Alliances_21st_Century.pdf.

46. Aaron L. Friedberg, "The Struggle for Mastery in Asia," *Commentary* (November 2000), pp. 17–26. This theme is explored penetratingly in David Shambaugh, ed., *Power Shift: China and Asia's New Dynamics* (Berkeley: University of California Press, 2005).

47. Ashley J. Tellis, "Ebb and Tide: Has the US-Indian Strategic Partnership Bombed?" *Force* (December 2011), pp. 36–41; Evan S. Medeiros, "Strategic Hedging and the Future of Asia-Pacific Stability," *The Washington Quarterly* (Winter 2005/6), pp. 145–167; and Tellis, "Power Shift."

48. Ashley J. Tellis, "Ebb and Tide."

49. Friedberg, *The Contest for Supremacy*, pp. 182–214.

50. Charles Wolf, Jr., K. C. Yeh, Benjamin Zycher, Nicholas Eberstadt, and Sung-Ho Lee, *Fault Lines in China's Economic Terrain* (Santa Monica: RAND Corporation, 2003).

51. Arvind Virmani, "A Tripolar World: India, China and US," Indian Council for Research on International Economic Relations, May 18, 2005, available at: http://www.icrier.org/pdf/TripolarWrld_IHC5.pdf; R. Harrison Wagner, "Bargaining, War, and Alliances," *Conflict Management and Peace Science* (2004), pp. 215–231.

Part IV

The Domestic Context

5

Domestic American Influences on U.S.-China Relations

Robert Sutter

Scholarship explaining domestic influences on American foreign policy discerns several key sources of domestic influence in recent decades. Among them are public opinion; the media; the political parties and related partisanship; interest groups involved with economic issues, national defense, values and ethnic groups, among others; and think tanks that reflect and sometimes foster the viewpoints of particular interests. The influence of these domestic American forces often is reflected in the deliberations and actions of the president and executive branch in the making of foreign policy. However, the president and his administration at times impose discipline, secrecy, or other means in order to carry out foreign policy while keeping domestic American influences at arms length. In contrast, the U.S. Congress is much more open to and dependent on domestic American constituencies. The Congress has diffused authority, poor central control, and many more access points than the executive administration for domestic American forces to influence its policy deliberations. In practice, the Congress generally more closely reflects the concerns of domestic American groups or organizations with perspectives regarding particular issues in American foreign policy.[1]

This chapter assesses key developments in the influence of domestic American forces on U.S.-China relations since the opening of U.S.-China relations in the 1970s in order to explain their contemporary and future importance. A prevailing pattern has been for the president and the administration to lead the formation and implementation of U.S. policy as they endeavor to manage and develop the U.S. relationship with China in often complicated and challenging international circumstances. Preoccupied with international statecraft, the president and the administration have tended to devote lower priority to domestic American influences in the making of U.S. policy toward China. As domestic American influences often have reflected differences between the United States and China, they have been commonly viewed as obstacles to the administration's objectives in fostering cooperative relations with China and broader international interests.

This chapter judges that even though the president and the administration have encountered domestic American influences on China policy through various channels, the main avenue for such encounters has been in relations with Congress. Thus, the record of how domestic American influences have actually had an impact on U.S. policy toward China can be seen in large measure during the course of congressional-executive relations over China policy.[2]

EPISODIC DOMESTIC INFLUENCES ON
U.S. POLICY TOWARD CHINA

While they have sometimes supported forward movement and other policy initiatives toward China carried out by the president and administration, domestic American influences have had more importance as sources of differences with China, posing obstacles to administration policies and prompting debate in the United States over the proper course in U.S. policy toward China. A review of the record of the past four decades and analysis of contemporary developments lead to these summary findings:

- The domestic influences and interests sometimes have prompted debate that proved to be a key determinant or "driver" of the direction of U.S. policy toward China. More commonly, they have constituted a "brake," a factor that slowed forward momentum in U.S. policy toward China.
- From the Richard Nixon administration through the early years of Ronald Reagan's administration, domestic American factors generally were a brake slowing efforts led by the administration to move closer to China and away from past American ties with Taiwan. The struggles between the administration and congressional opposition became intense and lasted for several years during the Jimmy Carter and early Reagan administrations, with both sides firmly committed to conflicting agendas.
- For a few years after the Tiananmen crackdown and the end of the Cold War, domestic American forces drove U.S. efforts in opposing China's policies and in improving ties with Taiwan. However, domestic support for a tough U.S. stance toward China and strong support for Taiwan proved thin and fickle by the mid-1990s in the face of serious adverse consequences posed notably by China's strong and increasingly powerful opposition. An analysis of the congressional debates over China policy

in the late 1970s–early 1980s and in the 1990s shows that the commitments of congressional opponents to administration China policy were significantly weaker in the latter period.

- American domestic influences in opposition to generally pragmatic and positive U.S. administration China policy were weaker still as a result of U.S. preoccupation over the past decade with the struggle against terrorism, wars in Iraq and Afghanistan, nuclear proliferation crises in North Korea and Iran, domestic and international economic stagnation and China's rising as a world economic and growing military power. Adding to the mix was an overall sharp decline in congressional commitment to defend the foreign policy prerogatives of Congress, including regarding policy toward China.
- Congressional specialists offer muddled predictions of Congress possibly reasserting its role in foreign affairs. Conflicting domestic American interests in favor of and opposed to tougher U.S. policy toward China add to indicators that the overall effect of American domestic influences on China policy will remain secondary, providing a source of periodic debate and an overall drag on forward movement in U.S. relations with China.[3]

The Nixon Administration through the Reagan Administration

Prior to the normalization of U.S. relations with China begun by President Richard Nixon and Chinese Communist Party Chairman Mao Zedong, domestic American forces at times showed considerable influence in the making of U.S. China policy. As the Cold War emerged in Asia and U.S. policy in support of Chiang Kai-shek's Chinese Nationalist regime failed in the face of Communist victory on the Chinese mainland, the American "loss" of China became a salient and often partisan issue in the media, the Congress, and during congressional and presidential elections. The full-scale war between U.S. and Chinese forces in Korea lasted from 1950 to 1953; it was followed by almost two decades of Cold War confrontation and conflict. The early years of this period saw often intense congressional, media, and executive branch scrutiny designed to purge from government ranks and isolate advocates seen as moderate and accommodating toward the Communist regime in China. In this context, proposed initiatives for a more moderate and constructive U.S. relationship with China were considered behind closed doors, if they were considered at all.[4]

Against this background, President Nixon, his National Security Adviser Henry Kissinger and the small group of U.S. officers involved in the early efforts to open U.S. relations with China resorted to secret diplomacy, in part out of concern that prevailing domestic forces in the United States opposed to moderation and accommodation of the People's Republic of China (PRC) would react strongly and undercut the hoped for breakthrough with China. In fact, however, Nixon's initial opening seen in his February 1972 visit to China was broadly welcomed by American popular and elite opinion. Congressional leaders, media representatives, business people, and other opinion leaders began an active series of trips to China for positive exchanges with Chinese representatives.[5]

U.S. leaders in the Nixon and later governments through the early period of the Reagan administration generally followed a perceived strategic need to move closer to China in order to benefit the United States, especially in competition with the Soviet Union. Nixon, Kissinger, and later leaders understood that the United States had to cut back ties with Taiwan if it wanted to move ahead with China against the USSR. As the process of improving relations with China at the expense of Taiwan and U.S. relations with the Soviet Union became more apparent, it met with strong domestic opposition, notably in the U.S. Congress.

The debate was protracted and intense. Officials in the U.S. administrations and their critics in Congress judged that there was a lot at stake for the United States in conducting these policies effectively. On the one hand, U.S. administration officials and their supporters tended to see the United States as weaker than before and in urgent need of support from China in order to deal with the perceived rising threat from the USSR. On the other hand, many in the Congress and supporting American constituencies were concerned that a sharp U.S. break with Taiwan, as required by Beijing, would extinguish Taiwan—a longstanding U.S. ally—as an international entity. Others, including a minority of administration senior officials, were concerned that the drive to improve relations with China would have serious counterproductive effects on American relations with the Soviet Union.[6]

The momentum was on the side of those who were pushing to sacrifice U.S. ties with Taiwan in order to build ties with the PRC against the USSR. However, there was determined opposition to this momentum from several U.S. domestic quarters that resulted in a strong and continuing domestic U.S. debate that slowed and modified the U.S. move away from Taiwan and toward the PRC. Salient elements of the resistance included:

- Conservatives in Congress, media, and other opinion leaders who supported Taiwan as a longstanding ally and were deeply suspicious of Communism and the PRC leadership.
- Strategists who judged that it was foolish for the United States to rely on China to leverage the USSR, or strategists who favored a more accommodating U.S. stance designed to build common ground and détente with Moscow.

- A spectrum of opinion in the Congress, media, and other groups judged that expediency in cutting ties with Taiwan would seriously undermine U.S. credibility in regard to support for Israel and other friends, including allies around China's rim.
- Opinion in Congress and elsewhere that objected to the intense secrecy that surrounded administration efforts to cut back ties with Taiwan and develop ties with Beijing. Congressional representatives judged that the secrecy was used to carry out policies without appropriate consideration of congressional prerogatives in the making and implementing of foreign policy.[7]

The opposition slowed the movement in U.S. policy but in fact the United States did break all official ties with Taiwan, including the U.S.-Taiwan defense treaty, and even signed a communiqué with China in 1982 that appeared to mark the beginning of the end of U.S. arms sales to Taiwan. The opposition did achieve some notable victories along the way, in particular the Taiwan Relations Act of 1979 that served as a marker that the administration policy makers could not easily cross in their efforts to accommodate China over Taiwan.

Policy Shift: 1982–1989

The U.S. dynamic toward China changed markedly in the rest of the Reagan administration, but not because of domestic U.S. pressures. Rather, the administration leaders headed by Secretary of State George Shultz (1982–1989) recalculated the strategic importance of China against the USSR and judged that China was less important for the United States and that the United States was in relatively good shape in competition with Moscow. A major U.S. military build-up, strong support from U.S. allies like Japan, and perceived Soviet decline coincided with an assessment that China was a difficult partner. There was much less urgency in the U.S. administration about the need to seek China's support against the rising Soviet threat. The U.S. domestic forces that supported Taiwan and opposed advances in relations with China that sacrificed other U.S. interests continued to do so; but they sensed the flagging of the U.S. administration interest to cater to PRC demands and accordingly saw less need to take countermeasures to brake the momentum and protect U.S. interests in Taiwan and elsewhere. Meanwhile, China's post-Mao Zedong (d. 1976) economic opening coincided with Taiwan's more gradual opening to China, prompting Beijing to pursue its Taiwan agenda more through cross-Strait contacts than through pressure on the United States.[8]

In sum, the debate in the Nixon-Reagan period involved important tangible costs and benefits for the United States. The U.S. strategic posture vis-à-vis the Soviet Union and the future of Taiwan headed the list of the serious issues at stake for the United States. Reflecting deep uncertainty about U.S. power and purpose in world affairs, U.S. policy advocates were prepared to make major sacrifices in order to pursue respective paths in the debate. In the end, U.S. policy ultimately sacrificed official relations with Taiwan and took the unprecedented step of ending a defense treaty with a loyal ally for the sake of the benefits to be derived from official relations with the PRC, notably in regard to assisting the United States in dealing with expanding Soviet power.[9]

The major protagonists in the U.S. domestic debate over policy toward the PRC and Taiwan at this time argued their case mainly because they were sincerely concerned about the serious implications and consequences of the direction of U.S. policy. Partisan interests and the influence of interest groups or constituent groups generally were not important. The fact that a Democratic-controlled Congress took the lead in writing the Taiwan Relations Act and in taking later actions in modifying the perceived oversights and excesses of the Democratic administration of President Jimmy Carter in tilting in favor of Beijing and against Taiwan in the late 1970s and 1980 showed that partisan interests played a relatively unimportant role in the U.S. domestic debate.[10]

The late 1970s and early 1980s represented a high point of Congress's assertiveness in foreign affairs against what was seen as presidential dominance of American foreign policy decision making. Congress appeared determined to protect its perceived prerogatives in U.S. foreign policy, while U.S. administration officials were equally determined to protect the prerogatives of the executive branch in foreign affairs. This competition for power added to friction between Congress and the administration over China policy.[11]

POST–COLD WAR—THE IMPACT OF TIANANMEN AND TAIWAN DEMOCRACY

The U.S. domestic debate became more prominent and important in influencing the course of U.S. policy toward China and Taiwan and related issues after the Tiananmen incident of 1989 and the end of the Cold War in the late 1980s and the early 1990s. Public opinion turned sharply against the Chinese administration, and was slow to improve as majorities tended to disapprove of the Chinese administration up to the present.[12] Similarly, American media and public opinion turned against China after a honeymoon period in the 1980s; their coverage eventually became somewhat more balanced in more recent years but sustained a tendency to emphasize the negative about developments in China and their implications for the United States. By contrast, Taiwan's emerging democracy at this time improved its standing with American media and elite and public opinion.[13]

The end of the Cold War undermined the U.S. focus on the strategic competition with the Soviet Union and eliminated what had been the main reason for American accommodation with China in the previous two decades. Interest groups and related media and think tanks emerged to new prominence stressing a variety of often narrow or particular security, economic, and values issues. Many of these issues emphasized differences between the United States and China over such questions as human rights, Tibet, proliferation of weapons of mass destruction, and trade practices. Administration departments and agencies that had played a secondary role in U.S. foreign policy making during the Cold War also rose to the fore. In this context, setting a coherent agenda with distinct priorities in American foreign policy seemed impossible.[14]

The importance of the post–Cold War debates on China policy turned out to be less than it appeared at first, and their influence diminished after a few years. Analysis shows that the resolve and commitment of many congressional and other protagonists pushing for a harder or less accommodating posture to China and a more favorable posture toward Taiwan generally were weaker in the 1990s than in the 1970s.[15] U.S. policy makers in the executive branch and the Congress were confident of U.S. power and influence in the world, especially now that the Soviet empire had collapsed—a marked contrast from the U.S. strategic uncertainty that drove the American policy debates in the late 1970s and early 1980s. In the 1970s U.S. officials faced and made major sacrifices in pursuit of American policy toward the PRC and Taiwan. The protagonists pressing a tougher line toward China after the Cold War had little inclination to sacrifice tangible American interests. Thus, congressional attacks on China stopped abruptly following the Iraqi invasion of Kuwait in 1990. Once the U.S.-led war to drive Iraqi forces from Kuwait was over and the need for Chinese acquiescence in the United Nations over the U.S. war effort against Iraq ended in 1991, the congressional attacks on China immediately resumed. There was some disappointment but no serious opposition in Congress to President Clinton terminating in 1994 his administration's efforts to place conditions on the annual approval of most-favored-nation trade status for China. The hundreds of vocal congressional advocates supporting a U.S. visa for the Taiwan president in 1995 largely fell silent when Beijing reacted with force. Even some of the most prominent leaders among congressional members opposing the annual waiver granting continued most favored nation tariff treatment to China made clear they had no intention of seeking a serious cutoff of U.S.-China trade.[16] Many active in the U.S. domestic debate in the 1990s sought partisan or other ulterior motives—a marked contrast from the 1970s when the foreign policy issues themselves seemed to be the prime drivers in the U.S. domestic debate. Presidential candidate Bill Clinton used the China issue to attack the record of the incumbent George H. W. Bush administration in order to win the 1992 presidential election. The strident rhetoric coming from Republican congressional leaders critical of the Clinton administration's engagement policy in its second term had similarly partisan motives.[17]

THE GEORGE W. BUSH ADMINISTRATION

The influence of domestic American critics of China and cooperative U.S.-Chinese relations on U.S. China policy reached new lows with the Republican-controlled Congress during much of the George W. Bush administration. The September 11, 2001 terrorist attack on America sharply curtailed U.S. domestic debate over China policy, which was then focused notably on the threat to U.S. security interests posed by a rising China. U.S. foreign policy shifted to getting along with China as the United States dealt with terrorism-related issues and U.S.-led wars in Afghanistan and Iraq.[18] President Bush showed extraordinary ability to control congressional interference with his preferred foreign policies. Congress broadly deferred to presidential leadership during this time of war.

The strong victory of the Democratic Party in the November 2006 congressional elections underlined a broad desire of the American electorate for change in the policies and priorities of the George W. Bush administration. At first, the implications of the Democratic victory seemed serious for U.S. policy toward China. In particular, the Democratic majority was forecast to pursue strong trade measures that if successful would seriously disrupt U.S. economic relations with China. Mainstream commentator Thomas Friedman predicted a civil war in American politics over the massive U.S. trade deficit and related economic issues with China.[19]

In contrast with such dire warnings, however, circumstances diluted the push for substantial change in U.S. policy toward China. In particular, in the face of a determined president like George W. Bush, the Democratic-led Congress appeared to have only a few levers to force change in relations with China. Morevoer, a prevailing focus in Congress on domestic issues and the controversial wars in Iraq and Afghanistan meant that most issues involving China received lower priority. Even if House Speaker Nancy Pelosi and Senate Majority Leader Harry Reid had wanted to pressure congressional Democrats to follow their past leanings to be tough in relations with China, the makeup of the Democratic majority and committee leadership strongly suggested less than uniform support. Conservative Democratic members increased as a result of the 2006 election and were reluctant to press too hard on differences with China when important U.S. business and security interests were at stake. Many Democratic members supported free trade and resisted what they saw as protectionist measures of Democratic colleagues against China and other trading partners. They were backed by polling data which showed that Americans were fairly comfortable with the economic rise of China.[20] Trade hawks and critics of China's human rights practices among Democrats leading key congressional committees were offset by moderates on trade headed by the Ways and Means Committee's leading Democrat Charles Rangel and Senate Finance Committee leading Democrat Max Baucus, and by the large number of Democratic members who joined various working groups designed to foster pragmatic exchanges with and more informed and effective U.S. policy toward China.

In the end, what the Democratic-led Congress could actually accomplish in changing U.S. policies and practices regarding China turned out to be limited. On the one hand, there were frequent congressional proposals, postures, and maneuvers regarding toughening U.S. policies and practices concerning China. On the other hand, the impact of these congressional actions seemed not to change the course of U.S. relations with China in major ways. Overall, the experience showed that the publicly positive equilibrium that emerged in relations between the U.S. and Chinese governments during the Bush administration was not to be substantially challenged by the continuing U.S. domestic debate over priorities in policy toward China.[21]

A key determinant at this time that served to weaken the importance of American domestic influences that were at odds with administration China policy was a notable decline in congressional assertiveness over foreign policy. Expert commentators and scholars showed the Congress to have lost interest in the efforts after the Vietnam War to curb the power of the executive in foreign affairs. In effect, the pattern of Congress asserting its rights in foreign affairs seen in the Taiwan Relations Act and other congressional practice after the end of Vietnam War was no more.

The shift to congressional acquiescence reached a point where the results included the most serious challenges to congressional constitutional rights in many decades carried out by Bush administration leaders in dealing with issues of war powers, use of coercive interrogation widely seen as torture, detaining suspects, and other sensitive issues. Congress did little in the face of these challenges.[22] By the middle of the past decade, Congress was accused by veteran bipartisan observers of irresponsibly ignoring its constitutional responsibilities, allowing strong advocates of presidential powers in foreign affairs in the George W. Bush administration to pursue their agendas without the "checks and balances" sought by the American founding fathers.[23] The Democratic leadership of the 110th Congress endeavored to reverse this marked decline in congressional passivity on foreign affairs, but as noted above, their focus was on domestic issues and more salient foreign policy issues involving Southwest Asia and the Middle East, resulting in little concrete action on China policy.

Congressional Dialogues with China

The growth of congressional dialogues with China at this time reflected a pragmatic congressional tendency to deal with issues and differences in China policy posed by domestic U.S. influences and other factors in less disruptive ways. The congressional channels mimicked and reinforced concurrent Bush administration dialogues with the Chinese administration. As explained in the chapters on U.S.-China diplomatic and economic interactions by Bonnie Glaser and Charles Freeman respectively, by 2003 the Bush administration actively sought stability and cooperation in relations with China as the United States deepened military involvement in the Middle East following the attack on Iraq in 2003 and faced a major crisis caused by North Korea's public break with past nonproliferation agreements and active push to develop nuclear weapons. For its part, China was anxious to sustain a cooperative relationship with the United States and in the process build interdependencies that would constrain future U.S. pressure against China. Soon the two governments were working closely together and dealing with differences through a rapidly growing array of official dialogues and sub-dialogues.[24]

A concurrent rise of official dialogues linking the U.S. Congress and its Chinese counterparts represented a significant change from Congress's long-standing position reflecting domestic American influences at odds with U.S. administration efforts to manage and develop closer relations with the Chinese administration. As explained earlier, for decades Congress led the domestic U.S.-China debates over Taiwan, trade, human rights, and security issues. Even as Congress (at the end of the Clinton administration) moved to approve China's entry into the World Trade Organization and grant Permanent Normal Trade Relations (PNTR) status to China, it remained the scene of often very partisan debate on China policy. The debate focused on such issues as Chinese spying, influence peddling, human rights and economic practices, and the threat posed by Chinese military advances. In this context, legislation was passed that restricted U.S. defense exchanges with China that would facilitate Chinese military advances.[25]

Against this background, the exchanges that developed between Congress and Chinese counterparts in the recent decade appeared remarkable. Scholars have identified several key reasons for the change. One involved the pragmatic recognition that China's international importance, especially as a trade partner and recipient of ever-growing investment by U.S. firms, meant that constructive U.S. interaction with China was important to protect and foster the interests of various congressional constituencies. A second involved the impact of the terrorist attack on America in September 2001 and the following wars in Afghanistan and Iraq and the overall war on terrorism. Preoccupied

with these wide-ranging endeavors of central importance to U.S. national security, Congress followed the lead of the president in pragmatically seeking
better dialogue and cooperation with China.[26]

In short, an increasingly pragmatic, preoccupied, and acquiescent Congress
saw benefit in developing channels of interchange with China in parallel with
the growth of official dialogues between the U.S. administration and the Chinese
government. Because of the diffused authority and weak institutional structure
in the Congress and the fact that congressional initiatives toward China often
depended on the initiative and interests of individual members, the various
forms of exchange and dialogue changed over time. But the overall increase in
these constructive exchanges was clearly registered in the following ways.[27]

The U.S. House of Representatives Inter-Parliamentary Exchange was notably active under the leadership of Representative Donald Manzullo (R.-Ill.).
The Manzullo-led delegation to China in 2005 marked the seventh U.S.-China
parliamentary dialogue which the U.S. and Chinese sides agreed had provided
"the most efficient way to deepen mutual understanding." The Senate U.S.-
China Inter-Parliamentary Exchange program was established in 2004 with
the aim of exchanging views on salient issues in U.S.-China relations. During
a 2006 visit, President Hu Jintao met with the Senate leaders and underlined
that the exchanges between Chinese and U.S. legislative bodies "served as a
vigorous driving force for bilateral relations." Representative Randy Forbes (R-
Va.) worked with Representative Ike Skelton (D-Mo.) to establish the Congressional China Caucus, which had a membership of 35 House members. Both
Forbes and Skelton were leaders of the House Armed Services Committee and
their interests seen during visits to China and interchange with Chinese counterparts focused on the strategic importance of China's rising influence in regional and world affairs as well as longstanding bilateral issues in U.S.-China
relations.

Also in 2005, Representative Mark Kirk (R-Ill.) and Representative Rick
Larsen (D-Wash.) established the U.S.-China Congressional Working Group
which had a membership of 30 House members. The group followed an active
agenda of seminars, trips to China, and interchange with Chinese visitors that
focused on discussion and understanding of China-related issues with the belief that "it is vital for Congress to increase its dialogue" with China.

DOMESTIC INFLUENCES DURING THE OBAMA ADMINISTRATION

Other chapters in this volume explain in detail the diplomatic, economic, and
other accomplishments and shortcomings in Sino-American relations during
the Obama administration. The record shows that as a presidential candidate
Barack Obama was unusual in recent U.S. presidential campaign politics in

not making an issue of his predecessor's China policy. Like outgoing President Bush, candidate Obama and his Democratic election team seemed to reflect less domestic American division over China policy than in the recent past. He forecast a course with China involving pursuing constructive contacts, preserving and protecting American interests, and dealing effectively with challenges posed by rising Chinese influence and power.

Over time, the president came to shift from his initial focus on seeking the cooperation of China to deal with salient international concerns such as the global economic crisis and recession, climate change, nuclear weapons proliferation, and terrorism. He and his administration adopted a publicly tougher stance on Chinese trade, economic and foreign policies, and practices notably involving North Korea, Iran, and maritime security in Asia.

The president's shift was in line with an increase in domestic pressure for tougher U.S. measures against China. The continued economic stagnation in the United States, Europe, and elsewhere made China's practices on currency, market access, and intellectual property rights more salient in the domestic American debates leading to the presidential elections in 2012. The Senate in October 2011 passed by a wide margin a bill that would impose some measures to punish Chinese currency manipulation. President Obama said China was "gaming" the international trade system to its advantage, and other senior administration leaders sharply criticized Chinese trade practices. The most vocal advocates for stronger measures against China were the aspirants for the Republican presidential nomination for 2012. One of the more moderate leaders in the race, former Massachusetts Governor Mitt Romney, offered stern rebuke of Chinese practices as he listed a systematic series of steps he would enact as president in order to curb perceived Chinese trade and economic abuses. Meanwhile, the first congressional hearings on Taiwan in many years were held by the House Foreign Affairs Committee in September and October 2011 in order to review U.S. interests in Taiwan and the continuing sale of arms to Taiwan. Many in Congress and among the Republican presidential aspirants criticized President Obama's decision not to sell F-16 jet fighters despite strong requests from Taiwan's president. The committee approved legislation supporting the sale of the jet fighters and other U.S. measures of stronger support for Taiwan.[28]

STATUS AND OUTLOOK FOR DOMESTIC AMERICAN INFLUENCES ON U.S.-CHINA RELATIONS

In order to gauge the significance of the above-noted signs representing a broader upswing in domestic pressure for a more critical American policy toward China, this chapter has assessed various determinants of contemporary domestic American influence on foreign policy toward China. What emerges is a muddled picture featuring contradictions within and among these deter-minants. The elements of domestic American influence generally appear suffi-ciently negative toward China that they are likely to sustain patterns of periodic episodes of strong American criticism and pressure on China and on the U.S. government to be tougher in relations with China. But, overall, they do not mirror the episodes of U.S. domestic resistance to closer or cooperative rela-tions with China seen during the late 1970s, early 1980s, or in the 1990s. On balance, rather than driving U.S. policy toward China in a strongly negative direction, they are more likely to serve as a drag slowing and impeding possible improvements in U.S. relations with China.

This forecast is contingent on certain circumstances and conditions. It as-sumes that China's recent pattern of assertiveness toward the United States and in foreign affairs more generally will remain subordinate to the Chinese government's stated emphasis on peaceful development in order to reassure neighbors, the United States, and other concerned powers. A persistent and publicly truculent Chinese posture toward the United States very likely would be widely seen in the Congress and among domestic American constituencies as posing a major challenge requiring strong U.S. response.

The assessment also is premised on the United States avoiding another major economic recession or a collapse of effective governance, notably on account of prolonged deadlock on how to deal with growing U.S. government indebtedness, tax policy and massive entitlement programs. Such prolonged economic decline or governance collapse could add strongly to domestic pres-sures for trade protection against China. And it assumes that the United States and China will avoid war over such regional hot spots as North Korea and Taiwan; and that the two powers will avoid a major military clash or incident, such as the 2001 crash between a Chinese jet fighter and a U.S. reconnais-sance plane and the 1999 bombing of the Chinese embassy in Belgrade by a U.S. stealth bomber. Such incidents risk escalation amid widespread calls from within both countries for strong military actions.

In assessing different elements of American domestic influences on con-temporary China policy, the analysis first looks at the impact of partisanship and the 2012 presidential election campaign. It then treats the prospects of a resurgent Congress taking a stronger role in influencing U.S. policy toward China. To determine which policy direction Congress and the broader U.S. government would likely favor, it assesses the influence on congressional and broader American leanings on policy toward China of such elements of Amer-ican domestic influence as public opinion, media opinion, the massive U.S. government and non-government national security apparatus, and those lob-bying for more critical and more cooperative relations with China, including salient interest groups and think tanks.

In early 2012, domestic political partisanship appeared to be the strongest domestic element in support of a tougher U.S. policy toward China. The Republican presidential campaign rhetoric repeatedly criticized President Obama's alleged weakness and ineffectiveness in countering Chinese trade and other economic policies deemed unfair to the United States. And the Republican candidates strongly supported the sale of F-16 jet fighters to Taiwan despite the strenuous objections of China; they sharply attacked President Obama for refusing to make the sale in a large arms sales package announced in 2011.[29]

It remains to be seen whether or not a Republican candidate, if elected, would actually follow through with such campaign promises that seriously risk strong retaliation from China. The last Republican president, George W. Bush, entered office with tough rhetoric about China and in support of Taiwan, but he soon switched to a pragmatic approach emphasizing constructive dialogue and engagement. While known for his unilateral and often controversial foreign policies, Bush came to an understanding of the importance for American interests of a balanced approach to Taiwan and China. Another strong supporter of Taiwan, President Ronald Reagan, reluctantly came to a similar understanding and backed away from a controversial promise to reestablish diplomatic relations with Taiwan made during his presidential election campaign in 1980. Thus, the record suggests that controversial China policy statements made during the heat of the election campaign will be superseded by more pragmatic pursuit of national interest.

Meanwhile, Bush's record of military support in the form of arms sales to Taiwan in his eight years in office was comparatively less than President Obama's record of sales to Taiwan in his first four years. On trade matters, despite the campaign rhetoric and partisan attacks, the Republican leadership remains divided on the wisdom of tougher trade and economic measures toward China. Reflecting the free trade preferences strongly supported by some Republican leaders, the House Republican leadership fended off pressure from domestic American constituencies to adopt the Senate-passed bill calling for trade and other countermeasures against China's currency manipulation.[30]

As in the recent past, domestic pressures for a tougher China policy tend to be reflected in congressional actions, debates, and other disagreements with the president. The congressional elections of 2010 were a landslide victory for the Republicans. They took control of the House of Representatives by a wide margin and the Democrats narrowly held the leadership of the Senate. Under Republican leadership, the House strongly asserted its prerogatives against the president on such issues as government debt, government spending, and entitlements including health care, Social Security, and Medicare.

The pressures forced consideration of major cuts in U.S. spending on foreign affairs and defense well beyond cuts planned by the Obama government.

If enacted, these larger cuts could weaken U.S. government efforts to sustain a security and diplomatic environment in the Asia-Pacific region advantageous to the United States and supportive of U.S. objectives in dealing with China. The actual impact of the budget cutting on U.S. relations with China remains to be seen, especially as the president and his administration have publicly pledged to allocate, if necessary, funds for programs in the Asian region taken from other accounts.[31] Apart from creating uncertainty about the impact of undetermined budget cuts on U.S. defense and foreign policy efforts related to China, a newly assertive Congress on budget and related issues foreshadows a possible resurgence of Congress strongly pushing its prerogatives in foreign policy and especially policy toward China.

Even in the event that Congress judged its interests were best served with a more assertive stance regarding China policy, it is hard to discern with much precision in which direction Congress would move. As noted above, tougher trade and economic measures do not enjoy uniform support on either side of the aisle and are subject to cross pressures from various quarters. Republicans supporting a free trade agenda remain influential.

As shown in Charles Freeman's chapter on U.S.-China economic relations, China has grown to become the world's second largest trader, America's second largest trading partner, the largest foreign holder of U.S. government securities, a rapidly growing market for U.S. exports, and a rising source of investment in the United States. Against this backdrop, many Members of Congress have become keenly aware of the serious negative consequences for them and their constituents of strong U.S. measures against Chinese trading and economic practices. They have participated in trips to China and discussions in various congressional working groups regarding China. They have listened to lobbying urging moderation in dealing with China by constituent business interests, Chinese embassy and other Chinese officials and lobbyists hired by China, and a broad range of American business groups.

American public opinion remains more negative than positive regarding the policies and practices of China, but it is not in a position, as it was in the aftermath of the Tiananmen crackdown, to prompt serious negative change in American China policy. The most authoritative and comprehensive study of American public opinion toward China in 2010 provided a careful assessment of various reliable polls going back many years. It found the U.S. public somewhat anxious about Chinese economic and military power and policies, and its authoritarian political system and human rights practices. While the American public favors U.S. efforts to strengthen American influence in Asia as a counterweight to China, it eschews confrontation and conflict as it is "prepared to live peacefully and cooperatively" with China. The study underlined the traditionally low level of American public support for U.S. military conflict with China over Taiwan.[32]

Similarly, mainstream American media has become more moderate in its extensive coverage of developments in China than was the case in the years following the Tiananmen crackdown. On the whole, the U.S. media has reflected trends in American public opinion in demonstrating a continuing tendency to highlight the negative implications of Chinese developments for American interests and values, but the intensity seen in U.S. media coverage for many years after Tiananmen has faded markedly. A recent scholarly study indicated that the perceived growth of freedom and development in China, economically, politically, and socially, and markedly expanded cooperative U.S. interactions with China have been reflected in more positive coverage of Chinese developments in American media.[33]

As seen in Charles Freeman's chapter on U.S.-China economic relations, American business groups have been seeking U.S. government support against various perceived unfair Chinese economic practices involving market access, intellectual property rights, widespread subsidies from state banks, and other issues. Some also have criticized Chinese currency manipulation and have supported the recent Senate bill threatening retaliation on account of Chinese currency manipulation. However, divisions within the business community over what to do about China remain profound. A prevailing sentiment is to sustain stability in the Chinese business environment which has proven advantageous for many American companies that invest, manufacture, and trade in China. The drive for stability often causes American business interests to place differences and disputes with China in second place as they lobby American officials in Washington and China.

The American military-security community involves the armed services at home and abroad, the Department of Defense, various intelligence agencies, other security agencies, and in recent years the Department of Homeland Security. Outside of government are businesses which support the national security efforts through weapons, technology, information, analysis, and other services.

The chief responsibility of these institutions is to guard against threats to American security and security interests. Rising Chinese military power combined with rampant espionage activities and widespread cyber attacks is seen warily by this important segment of America. U.S. defense secretaries and senior military commanders sometimes aver that they do not view China as an enemy and a threat. Some recently retired senior flag officers and defense officials have urged stronger U.S. efforts to accommodate China's rise as a world military power.[34] Overall, however, the armed services, government departments, and related businesses spend vast amounts of time and money developing military capabilities and other measures that can deter Chinese aggressiveness and deal with military conflict with China, if necessary. They tend to enjoy strong support from congressional committees that provide funding and oversee their activities. The American media routinely portray their statements on China's worrisome military activities as well as espionage and cyber attacks as authoritative and good reason for American concern. American public opinion shares concerns about Chinese military buildup and foreign intentions. Some commentators assert that some in the U.S. "military-industrial complex" seek to sustain a level of tension with China in order to ease the approval process and funding for expensive weapons and related systems including advanced aircraft, naval surface warships and submarines, advanced missiles and missile defense, and sophisticated cyber warfare efforts. Defense contractors also are seen by some to support efforts to sell advanced weapons to Taiwan for the sake of business profit.[35]

Studies have shown that congressional opinion has been more negative about China than that of other U.S. elites and broader public opinion.[36] One reason congressional opinion has been more negative probably relates to the fact that most domestic American influences endeavoring to use Congress to change American China policy take a negative view of the Chinese government and its policies and practices. Moreover, while congressional action on China has been episodic, Congress has continued support to two commissions that have focused for over a decade on policies and practices in China viewed negatively in the United States.

The Congressional-Executive Commission on China was created by Congress in October 2000 with the legislative mandate to monitor human rights and the development of the rule of law in China, and to submit an annual report to the president and the Congress. The commission consists of nine Senators, nine Members of the House of Representatives, and five senior administration officials appointed by the president. It has a staff of well-trained specialists to research and assess Chinese developments within the scope of the commission's concerns. As the Chinese authorities repeatedly emphasize their determination to sustain one-party Communist rule in China and to deal strongly with challenges to the one-party system, the annual report and the overall orientation of the commission emphasizes negative implications for U.S. interests.

The U.S.-China Economic and Security Review Commission was created by the Congress in October 2000 with a legislative mandate to monitor, investigate, and submit to Congress an annual report on the national security implications of the bilateral trade and economic relationship between the United States and the People's Republic of China, and to provide recommendations, where appropriate, to Congress for legislative and administrative action. This commission holds periodic in-depth hearings on Chinese developments with important and often negative implications for American interests. The commission's annual report reviews the findings of the hearings and other investigations that alert readers to what are often seen as Chinese policies and behavior having negative implications for U.S. interests, especially national security interests.

Registered lobbyists and interest group representatives seeking to influence congressional opinion on China often focus on special issues that have negative implications for U.S. interests and values and complicate U.S. relations with China. The issues emphasize differences between the United States and China over such questions as human rights, Tibet, Taiwan, Xinjiang, proliferation of weapons of mass destruction, and trade practices.[37]

Nevertheless, the negative impact of these commissions and lobbying activities is offset to some degree by efforts to influence Congress to adopt more positive approaches to China. Supporting Chinese interests and smooth U.S.-China relations are lobbyists and interest group representatives for American business and other interests with a broad stake in continuing stable and profitable U.S.-China relations. A pillar in this community is the National Committee on U.S.-China Relations which has worked with Congress, the U.S. administration and a variety of specialists with an interest in China and their Chinese counterparts in order to foster better mutual understanding and broader common ground in U.S.-China relations. Business groups that have long been involved in fostering closer American economic engagement with China include the U.S. China Business Council.

The Chinese embassy in Washington has had a congressional relations section that has grown markedly in size and scope since the normalization of diplomatic relations. Working with nongovernment groups like the U.S.-Asia Institute in Washington, this contingent in the Chinese embassy has partnered with Chinese institutes in arranging and paying for well over 100 congressional staff delegations to visit China for consultations with relevant Chinese officials and experts and sightseeing. Chinese embassy officials were particularly pleased with the breakthrough in arranging the various congressional working groups and exchanges between Members of Congress and their Chinese counterparts during the past decade.[38]

Chinese embassy lobbying—including paid trips to China for staff members and Congressional Members—took a page out of Taiwan's well-known playbook on how to influence and gain closer access to Congress. China also followed Taiwan in using so-called buying missions to the United States to make widely publicized deals purchasing various American goods. The positive publicity helped to overshadow attention to the large annual trade deficits that Taiwan used to run with the United States and that China now runs with the United States.

Taiwan used to be a formidable opponent of China in lobbying on Capitol Hill. Its ability to mobilize congressional support against aspects of U.S.

China policy reached a high point when every congressional member except for Senator Bennett Johnson (D.-La.) voted for legislation in 1995 supporting the controversial step of granting the Taiwan president a visa to visit the United States. Unfortunately for Taiwan's interests in Congress, its lobbying effort came to reflect the wide political divide that developed between the pan-blue forces of the Nationalist or Kuomintang Party currently ruling Taiwan and the pan-green forces of the Democratic Progressive Party. The latter party struggled for ascendance against the dominant Kuomintang through the 1980s and 1990s, and won the presidency in 2000, holding the office for eight years. During the strident political struggle between the two camps in Taiwan politics since 2000, the pan-blue and the pan-green camps set up separate offices to lobby Congress for their respective interests. As their objectives tended to clash, congressional members interested in helping Taiwan became frustrated and confused with the pan-blue/pan-green competition, reducing Taiwan's overall influence. The decline in the Taiwan lobbying of Congress continued under Kuomintang President Ma Ying-jeou (2008–) whose administration relied more strongly on nurturing close and reliable relations with the U.S. administration, giving less attention to Congress. President Ma also seemed to do little to resolve the differences between the pan-blue and pan-green camps in their lobbying efforts, especially when he appointed the head of the pan-blue Washington office as the head (de-facto ambassador) of the Taiwan representative office in Washington.[39]

Ethnic lobbies or ethnic interest groups traditionally have not had a big impact on congressional consideration of China policy. Though Chinese Americans have been a significant part of American society for many decades, they have not pursued lobbying or advanced in American politics to the degree of other more motivated and better organized ethnic groups such as Indian Americans. Groups like the Committee of 100 have endeavored to close this gap and raise the profile of ethnic Chinese in American politics. In general, the committee advocates cooperative and smooth American relations with China. The most active and arguably most influential ethnic group dealing with China issue represents Taiwan citizens who have settled in the United States. Members of this relatively small but highly motivated and economically successful group pooled resources and organized the Formosan Association for Public Affairs (FAPA) in 1982. FAPA stresses Taiwan's right to self-determination and cooperates with the pan-green camp in Taiwan politics in pushing initiatives supporting their agenda.[40]

Many of the major Washington-based think tanks have tended to be generally aligned with the administration's overall pragmatic efforts to sustain a business-like relationship with China and to manage differences diplomatically. The Brookings Institution, the Center for Strategic and International Studies

(CSIS), the Carnegie Endowment for International Peace, the Heritage Foundation, the Peterson Institute for International Economics, and the American Enterprise Institute (AEI) all have China experts on staff, many of whom have played important roles in the engagement policies toward China pursued by U.S. administrations in recent years, with some having experience going back to the Tiananmen incident. Former Republican administration Asian experts at CSIS and AEI joined the recent criticism of President Obama's decision not to sell F-16 fighters to Taiwan, and some of these think tank experts have taken a strongly negative view of China's military and other national security policies and practices. The Heritage Foundation, which works closely with Congress, also is strongly supportive of Taiwan and critical of Chinese security policies. Think tanks associated with organized labor in the United States have tended to call for tougher policies against perceived unfair Chinese trade and economic policies. In contrast, Heritage Foundation reports are in the lead in stressing the importance of continued U.S. free trade policies toward China. The CATO Institute is a leading advocate of large-scale withdrawal from American military commitments and other costly involvement in Asia, which remains a minority view among think tank specialists in Washington.[41]

CONCLUSION

In conclusion, the path ahead in U.S. policy toward China shows promise that recent pragmatic and business-like relations with China pursued by the Bush and Obama governments will be strong enough to avoid serious setbacks because of pressures in the United States emphasizing differences with Chinese policies and practices. Nevertheless, the road to progress and forward movement in U.S. relations with China will remain hampered. American public opinion, media opinion, interest groups, and congressional attention remain focused on salient differences with China over security, economic, and political issues. These domestic American influences will continue to make it difficult to argue in favor of substantial forward movement involving American compromise and accommodation of China's government unless the Chinese government's policies and behaviors seen at odds with U.S. interests and values were to change substantially. The likelihood of the latter over the short term seems low.

NOTES

This chapter benefited greatly from suggestions of Douglas Paal, David Shambaugh, three anonymous reviewers, and participants at a workshop sponsored by the China Policy Program at George Washington University, Washington, D.C., December 15–16, 2011. The author also thanks Nicholas Bellomy for timely research assistance.

1. James McCormick, *American Foreign Policy and Process* (Boston: Wadsworth, Cengage Learning, 2010); James Lindsay, *Congress and the Politics of U.S. Foreign Policy* (Baltimore: Johns Hopkins University Press, 1994).

2. Warren I. Cohen, *America's Response to China: A History of Sino-American Relations* (New York: Columbia University Press, 2000); Harry Harding, *A Fragile Relationship: The US and China Since 1972* (Washington, D.C.: Brookings Institution, 1992); David M. Lampton, *Same Bed, Different Dreams: Managing US-China Relations, 1989–2000* (Berkeley: University of California, 2001); James Mann, *About Face: A History of America's Curious Relationship with China, from Nixon to Clinton* (New York: Knopf, 1999); Robert Sutter, *U.S.-Chinese Relations: Perilous Past, Pragmatic Present* (Lanham, MD: Rowman & Littlefield, 2010); Nancy B. Tucker, *Strait Talk: United States–Taiwan Relations and the Crisis with China* (Cambridge, MA: Harvard University Press, 2009).

3. Sutter, *U.S.-Chinese Relations,* pp. 99–104, 111–114, 133–136.

4. Cohen, *America's Response to China,* pp. 177–194.

5. Michael Schaller, *The United States and China: Into the Twenty-First Century* (New York: Oxford University Press, 2002), pp. 178–184.

6. U.S. Congress, House Committee on Foreign Affairs, *Executive-Legislative Consultations over China Policy, 1978–1979* (Washington, D.C.: U.S. Government Printing Office, 1980).

7. Robert Sutter, *The China Quandary* (Boulder, CO: Westview Press, 1983), pp. 89–92.

8. Robert Ross, *U.S.-China Relations 1969–1989* (Stanford: Stanford University Press, 1995), pp. 201–245.

9. Tucker, *Strait Talk,* pp. 29–52.

10. Tucker, *Strait Talk,* pp. 116–128; Sutter, *China Quandary,* pp. 5, 19, 85, and 146.

11. *Executive-Legislative Consultations over China Policy, 1978–1979.*

12. Benjamin Page and Tiao Xie, *Living with the Dragon* (New York: Columbia University Press, 2010), pp. 69–87.

13. Ramon Myers, Michel Oksenberg, and David Shambaugh (eds.), *Making China Policy: Lessons from the Bush and Clinton Administrations* (Lanham, MD: Rowman & Littlefield, 2001), pp. 201–222.

14. Robert Sutter, *U.S. Policy Toward China: An Introduction to the Role of Interest Groups* (Lanham, MD: Rowman & Littlefield, 1998), pp. 10–25.

15. Myers, Oksenberg, and Shambaugh, *Making China Policy,* pp. 79–222.

16. Robert Sutter, "The Bush Administration and U.S. China Policy Debate," *Issues and Studies* Vol. 38, No. 2 (June 2002), pp. 14–22.

17. Robert Sutter, "U.S. Domestic Debate over Policy toward Mainland China and Taiwan: Key Findings, Outlook, and Lessons," *The American Journal of Chinese Studies* Vol. 8, No. 2 (October 2011), pp. 133–144.

18. Sutter, "The Bush Administration and U.S. China Policy Debate," p. 16.

19. Thomas Friedman, "Will Congress View China as Scapegoat or Sputnik?" *New York Times,* November 10, 2006.

20. *New Study Reveals Most Americans Remain Committed to Steady Internationalism Despite Frustration Over Iraq War* (Chicago Council on Global Affairs Media Advisory, October 11, 2006).

21. Robert Sutter, "The Democratic-Led 110th Congress: Implications for Asia," *Asia Policy* No. 3 (January 2007), pp. 125–150.

22. Gordon Silverstein, "The Law: Bush, Cheney, and the Separation of Powers: A Lasting Legal Legacy?" *Presidential Studies Quarterly* Vol. 39 (December 2009), pp. 878–895.

23. Norman J. Ornstein and Thomas E. Mann, "When Congress Checks Out," *Foreign Affairs* Vol. 85, No. 6 (November/December 2006), pp. 67–82.

24. Sutter, *U.S.-Chinese Relations*, pp. 153, 166.

25. Sutter, *U.S.-Chinese Relations*, pp. 79–81, 97–146.

26. James Thurber, ed., *Rivals for Power* (Lanham, MD: Rowman & Littlefield, 2009), pp. 285–350.

27. The following examples are taken from Bates Gill and Melissa Murphy, *Meeting the Challenges and Opportunities of China's Rise* (Washington, D.C.: CSIS, 2006), pp. 9–11.

28. "U.S.-China Relations," *Comparative Connections* Vol. 13, No. 3 (January 2012), www.csis.org/pacfor; "Romney Would Be Tougher on China," *Washington Post*, October 14, 2011, available at: www.washingtonpost.com; "Barack Obama Accused China of Gaming International Trade," *Reuters*, October 7, 2011.

29. Jake Chung, "Perry Says Taiwan Would Be His First Visit as U.S. Leader," *Taipei Times*, December 2, 2011, available at: http://www.taipeitimes.com/News/taiwan/archives/2011/12/02/2003519745.

30. "U.S. Speaker Boehner Opposes China Currency Bill," *Strait Times*, October 13, 2011, available at: http://www.straitstimes.com/BreakingNews/Money/Story/STIStory_722815.html.

31. *Pivot to the Pacific? The Obama Administration's "Rebalancing" Toward Asia* (Washington, D.C.: Congressional Research Service Report R42448,March 28, 2012).

32. Page and Xie, *Living with the Dragon*.

33. Xiuli Wang and Pamela J. Shoemaker, "What Shapes Americans' Opinion of China? Country Characteristics, Public Relations and Mass Media," *Chinese Journal of Communication* Vol. 4, No. 1 (March 2011), pp. 1–20.

34. See coverage of the Sanya Initiative available at http://cusef.org.hk/eng/program_index.asp?id=High-Level+Dialogues.

35. Jim Wolf, "Lockheed Lobbies Anew for New Taiwan F-16s," *Reuters*, September 28, 2011, available at: http://in.reuters.com/article/2011/09/29/idINIndia-59608520110929.

36. Committee of 100, *American Attitudes toward China, Phase II* (2005), available at: http://www.committee100.org/publications/survey/phase2/Executive_Summary.pdf.

37. For background on various lobbying and interest group activities, see Sutter, *U.S. Policy Toward China*.

38. Interview with Chinese embassy official, in Xiaoning Wu, "The Congressional Exchanges," Georgetown University seminar paper, May 2011, pp. 4, 6.

39. Robert Sutter, "Taiwan's Future: Narrowing Straits," *NBR Analysis* (May 2011), pp. 19–22.

40. See the websites of the Committee of 100 at http://www.committee100.org and of the Formosan Association for Public Affairs at www.fapa.org.

41. Sutter, *U.S. Policy Toward China*, pp. 109–110.

6

Domestic Chinese Influences on U.S.-China Relations

Yufan Hao

U.S.-China relations have become increasingly complicated by Chinese domestic influences. Not only have the number of actors participating in the policy making process proliferated, but there is also a diversity of interests and ideas within Chinese society that are reflected in China's policy towards the United States.[1] This chapter addresses China's domestic influences on U.S.-China relations by examining the institutional actors within this more diffuse policy process and the impact of societal factors such as netizens, mass media, think tanks, public opinion, and the business community.

STRUCTURAL CHANGES IN DOMESTIC DETERMINANTS

Since Chinese foreign policy has historically been elite-driven and free from public scrutiny, most attention before the mid-1990s was devoted to trying to peer inside the "black box" of the Chinese foreign policy process. This research relied largely on a state-centered approach, and it paid special emphasis to the foreign policy making structure, processes, and bureaucratic politics. A. Doak Barnett's ground-breaking work in 1984 revealed the role of various domestic institutions and their interaction within China's foreign policy making process.[2] David Shambaugh examined, through in-depth interviews of scholars and officials, the Chinese foreign policy bureaucracy and foreign policy analysts at various institutions regarding their perceptions and approaches to international affairs (first the United States and later Asia and Europe).[3] Some scholars attempt to understand Chinese foreign policy making through examining institutions, structures, and processes from various perspectives.[4] Others try to provide a deeper understanding of the policy making milieu via the relationship between the external environment and domestic politics.[5] These approaches provide useful information and understanding—yet, until recently, less attention has been paid to domestic societal constraints and influences. The new sources of information that have become available have triggered a more vigorous and diverse study of Chinese foreign policy. Since the mid-1990s, there has been an increasing number of studies concerning the relationship between domestic determinants and China's external behavior.

Since 1979 Chinese foreign policy has undergone significant changes. It has become less personalized, radical, and ideological, while becoming increasingly pragmatic and sophisticated. China's national interests are more specifically defined, and the pursuit of those interests has become more realistic and flexible. Accordingly, more efforts have been made to explore the role of various domestic factors in the Chinese foreign policy making process in the age of globalization. This domestic-centered approach, however, still emphasizes ideological preferences, objectives of key players, factional politics, and bureaucratic cleavages as an extension of domestic politics.[6] Only recently has attention been given to social factors that have long been held as insignificant such as public opinion, media, think tanks, NGOs and local governments, and other social forces.[7] Scholars have begun to recognize that Beijing's leaders are under increasing social pressure when formulating their foreign policies. Yet the complexity of the leaders' responses to social pressures remains largely obscure.

CHANGES IN DOMESTIC INSTITUTIONAL ACTORS

In general, there are two types of domestic factors that influence Sino-American relations: (1) a multitude of institutional actors with a more diffuse process and (2) societal forces. The institutional actors are related official entities and institutions with foreign policy making capabilities defined by the state and governmental structure of China. Here, the Chinese Communist Party (CCP) and its Politburo and Standing Committee, the CCP Central Committee Foreign Affairs Leading Small Group (FALSG), the Central Committee Foreign Affairs Office, the CCP International Department, the State Council ministries closely related to foreign affairs, and the People's Liberation Army (PLA) are still the main players affecting Sino-U.S. relations. Bonnie Glaser's and Wu Xinbo's chapters in this volume discuss these actors, as have a number of other recent studies.[8]

Yet Chinese foreign policy making actors have undergone several interesting changes since the late 1970s. These changes can be characterized as pluralization, institutionalization, and professionalization.[9] In terms of pluralization, the number and variety of actors involved in decision making have expanded rapidly and now include even non-government (or quasi-government) actors. China's growing economic, political, and military interaction with the world has created an environment in which many ministries at the national level, most Chinese provinces, and many large military and civilian corporations are engaged in foreign affairs through their direct dealings with foreign entities. Foreign policy is no longer the exclusive domain of the Ministry of Foreign Affairs (MFA), Ministry of Defense, and State Council officials (Premier and State Councilors). It has begun to involve ministries dealing with industry, commerce, trade, agriculture, banking, and even publicity (propaganda). One example of the latter was the decision made by the CCP Publicity Department (still the Propaganda Department, or *Xuanchuan Bu*, in Chinese) to censor a *Southern Daily* newspaper interview with U.S. President Obama during his state visit to China in November 2009, largely because the White House officials only obtained the approval from the MFA, but did not consult with the Publicity Department regarding the matter. [10]

The National Development and Reform Commission's (NDRC) influence in China's foreign affairs is most apparent lately over Chinese climate change policy and its role in ensuring China's access to critical resources abroad. One of the NDRC's responsibilities is "to draft strategic, regulations and policy plans concerning climate change, participate in international negotiations on climate change with related government bodies, and implement the work China promised under the United Nations Framework Convention on Climate Change (UNFCCC)." [11] In fact, the NDRC's Department of Climate Change team, led by Xie Zhenhua, takes the policy lead and holds the main positions of the Chinese delegation during many international climate negotiation summits, while the MFA only plays a secondary role. It was NDRC official Xie Zhenhua who argued with President Obama in Copenhagen.

The Ministry of Commerce (MOFCOM) is also a major actor affecting Sino-U.S. relations, given the centrality of bilateral trade and investment in bilateral relations. MOFCOM plays a key role in coordinating the trade, intellectual property rights, investments, anti-dumping cases, WTO filings, and other commercial issues. While outside its portfolio, MOFCOM held a hardline attitude toward the *renminbi* valuation issue as China's export enterprises may suffer from any currency appreciation. Benefiting from the knowledge-based economy, the United States has used the issue of intellectual property rights to protect the commercial interests of U.S. corporations, making it a powerful weapon in dealing with China. In charge of the negotiation of intellectual property rights, MOFCOM is responsible for drafting regulations to protect the interests of Chinese enterprises in line with the WTO's related provisions. MOFCOM is also at the center of a variety of U.S.-China trade cases involving dumping duties, countervailing tariffs, and WTO disputes.

The People's Liberation Army (PLA) has been increasingly involved in Sino-U.S. relations lately, even though the professionalization of the armed forces aims to distance it from the civilian leadership. In addition to defense policy and military strategy, the military gets involved in foreign policy making relating to arms control, non-proliferation, and other national security related areas. The PLA's stance and attitude obviously have certain effects regarding Taiwan, as it still remains a critical issue involving China's American policy. The military's role increased after the 1996 Taiwan Strait crisis, when the PLA's military exercises were used as an instrument to achieve political objectives. The voice of the PLA has grown louder in recent years as territorial disputes in the East China Sea and South China Sea have intensified and as the U.S. insists it has national interests in the free access to sea lanes in this high-profile region.

The policy making process has thus become much more fragmented and decentralized with an increasing number of agencies becoming active players. Internal institutional actors can have influence on Sino-U.S. relations by both formal and informal channels. Officials can take advantage of their position in China's power structure and foreign policy decision-making process to exert their influence. Every ministry also needs to offer internal and international information affecting the decisions made at the top. Heads of some ministries are even in the core circle of foreign policy decision making. Besides, they can also conduct campaigns to guide public opinion on certain issues relating to China-U.S. relations. For example, the PLA officers often express their hawkish opinions in the media either through television interviews or by participating in public debates at civilian research institutions. Their hardline stance, which always arouses nationalistic public sentiment, can exert stronger pressures on the decision makers.

In terms of institutionalization, various inter-agency organizations have been set up in recent years to shift power and influence from individuals to institutions involved in foreign policy making. Some formerly symbolic institutions such as the National People's Congress have started to assume a greater role in Chinese foreign affairs. In addition, there have been attempts to create horizontal linkages among institutions in the Chinese foreign policy community, the economic community, and various agencies in the national security community to enhance policy coordination and consensus building in the policy making process. The fact that a wide range of ministers are represented on the Foreign Affairs Leading Small Group (FALSG) is one effort to institutionalize and improve inter-agency coordination.

There has also been a growing trend of professionalization in China's foreign policy-making apparatus. Many mid-level officials have received extensive training in both international affairs and foreign languages at China's top universities. Many of them were sent overseas as students or visiting scholars in order to give them international exposure. They have an internationally oriented outlook and are generally supportive of China's integration with the world. The decision makers are increasingly reliant on the information provided by specialized bureaucracies.[12]

The decision making style of the Beijing leadership has also changed profoundly as the charismatic appeal of the revolutionary leaders of the first and second generation is long gone. Both Jiang Zemin and Hu Jintao had to participate in a collective leadership that requires internal consensus building when making major policy decisions. The "paramount leader" in China is no longer so paramount. This fact, taken together with the structural changes mentioned above, has provided opportunities for various unconventional factors to influence Chinese foreign policy making process in a way that was unimaginable two decades ago. Largely due to these changes, societal factors began to influence the Chinese decision making process.

SOCIETAL FORCES

Societal forces refer to a host of factors and actors outside of the official realm, which increasingly contend for influence and crowd the foreign policy making process. This includes netizens on the internet, the mass media, opinion makers both in the media and in the academic community, technocrats within the bureaucratic apparatus, random public opinion, think tanks and research institutes, the business community, and other sub-national entities within Chinese society—that *all* seek to influence, directly or indirectly, intentionally or unintentionally, final foreign policy outcomes.[13] These societal forces operate as a loose conglomeration of individual actors and uncoordinated groups with different interests and goals. Each perceives different problems and acts independently, but together they represent forces that are often powerful enough to make an impact on decision makers even in an authoritarian state like China.

Jurgen Habermas argued in his book *The Structural Transformation of the Public Sphere* that rational-critical debate about public issues conducted by private citizens may contribute to determining final decisions by the state.[14] Although the sociability he referred to was primarily from the experience of seventeenth- and eighteenth-century Europe, the concept is relevant to what is happening today in China as exemplified on the internet and the dense web of media, chat forums, and scholarly publications. All sorts of topics concerning foreign relations (over which state authorities have previously exercised a virtual monopoly of interpretation) have gradually opened to discussion, inasmuch as the public defines its discourse as patriotic.

The media and think tanks in China have exerted increasing influence on the foreign policy process.[15] The distribution of information is no longer limited to ranking officials in the party and government hierarchies. Media sources have already begun to shape and influence public opinion and their support for government policies. The internet has allowed rising numbers of Chinese to access the global media, influencing public opinion and the way the Chinese decision makers formulate their foreign policy ideas. Although the government has recently attempted to censor internet material, technical innovation has made it possible for many Chinese to breach governmental internet and social media controls.

Even governmental officials rely more and more on the opinions of non-government experts. For example, the Ministry of Foreign Affairs Policy Planning Department has a regularized biweekly consultation process with academics. Many Chinese scholars utilize their own personal connections to individually access policymakers. Although Chinese think tanks have not reached the level of independence and influence of their American counterparts, their new roles have challenged the monopoly of the government in conducting foreign policy.

It is within this changing context that Chinese domestic and societal forces are examined as a new variable affecting U.S.-China relations. So far, the societal pressures as domestic determinants have been largely neglected as a meaningful inquiry by foreign scholars studying Chinese foreign relations because of the traditional view of government's autonomy in public policy making in an authoritarian society.

The Role of the Internet

The swift development of the internet in China bears a much more important socio-political significance than in many other societies, not only because the internet in China has developed at an exponential rate and has the largest number of users in the world, but also because of China's unique political and social contexts. Since China built up the first domestic internet e-mail node in September 1987, the internet has grown explosively. By the end of 2010, the total number of internet users in China had reached 457 million, comprising 23.2 percent of the global share of internet users, and 55.4 percent of total internet users in Asia.[16] The ways people access the internet are more various, with 78.4 percent of users using desktop computers; mobile phones and laptop computers of web users are 66.2 percent and 45.7 percent respectively. Blog users in China have reached 63.11 million, constituting 13.8 percent of total internet users.[17] The Chinese government allows this rapid development of the internet under the assumption that the market operates more efficiently when people are better informed.

Considering China's unique social and political contexts, probably the most significant internet development is the emergence of cyber chat forums that provide public access to online discussion. Cyber forums refer to the on-line chatting, instant messages, bulletin boards (BBS), micro blogs, and other online discussion forums. Among them, online chatting is the fourth most frequently used online activity with 77.1 percent of internet users, and BBS postings are twelfth with 32.4 percent of users.[18] These figures indicate that online discussion and opinion-exchange have become a major social activity in China and have become an important part of people's daily life.

According to Hong Junbao, a scholar who studies China's internet activity, the online forum is effectively functional in four ways, especially for "public participation" or "civic involvement." Firstly, it is a *publishing medium*, as post-ings and news texts on the online forums can be read by any visitor. Secondly, it is a *distribution medium* as the information posted on the forums can be instantly spread to other online communities throughout the entire nation and the whole world. Thirdly, it is a *participatory medium* as the posted informa-tion and comments can elicit further responses, promote replies, and encour-age various kinds of views from the public—thus facilitating civic participation on a large scale that is impossible by any other means. Fourthly, it is also an *action-oriented medium* as cyber forums can be a platform for organizing off-line campaigns and social movements. In addition, cyber forums have more significant and unique functions in a society like China, as the availability of cyber forums has inevitably become a new force to yield an unprecedented impact on the social structure and political system.[19]

For more than half a century, even in the reform period, foreign policy had always been a forbidden area for public discussion and all foreign policies were made at the top level of the Chinese Communist Party and government. Common people were completely excluded from any kind of participation in foreign policy discussions, let alone the policy making process. This situation started to change in recent years, thanks to the internet. Many ordinary Chi-nese began to use the internet to express their views on various foreign policy issues, especially when major international events or crises involved China. A number of specialized cyber forums on foreign policy issues have been estab-lished. Since the internet has been more loosely controlled than the traditional media, the government seems to take a slightly more tolerant attitude toward the internet, allowing it to be a channel where ordinary people can vent and more or less voice their opinions, criticize some components of foreign poli-cies, and make suggestions.[20] The public's cyber discussions have thus begun to exert direct and indirect, subtle and salient, influences on China's foreign policy making.

For example, the *People's Daily*, the most important state-owned national newspaper and the political organ and mouthpiece of the CCP, runs a very popular BBS known as "Strong Nation Forum" (*Qiangguo Luntan*). This

website offers a platform for the public to vent their emotions and to publish
their voices on sensitive social and political issues, many of which would have
been forbidden in the past. The Strong Nation Forum has more than 2.17 million registered users, with the highest number of browsers (3.5 million people
per day).²¹ The main reason for this kind of online forum to emerge and exist
is that while China is moving toward a more open society, the party and government have, willingly or unwillingly, come to want to know what issues the
public reactions are concerned with. As a result, in order to more easily collect
the public's views online, over the past several years the Chinese government
at various levels has been working on an e-government plan, which utilizes
advanced information technologies to improve communications and relations
with citizens and to make the government work more efficiently. The central
government has vigorously promoted the e-government project. Although officials never cite public opinion as reference for their foreign policy making,
they obviously want to know how the public thinks and feels about the policies
they make. Many government agencies have come to regard the internet as a
useful tool that can help them make better decisions.

Despite the fact that chat rooms and many other online forums are mainly used for discussing people's daily life, many of the discussions do contain
bursts of frustration with the political system and other political or policy issues as well. For example, in regard to U.S.-China relations, the U.S. bombing
of the Chinese Embassy in Yugoslavia in 1999, the collision of a U.S. spy plane
with a Chinese jet fighter in 2001, and the assault on Chinese businesswoman
Zhao Yan by a U.S. immigration officer in 2004, all led to heated discussions
and fierce criticisms of the United States in chat rooms and other types of
cyber forums. Recent U.S. arms sales to Taiwan, President Obama's meeting
with the Dalai Lama, and the U.S. Asia-Pacific strategic adjustment ("America's 'pivot' to Asia") are among the hottest topics. In August 2011, before Vice
President Joe Biden visited China, *Huanqiuwang* (Global Net) took an online
survey with a question of: "What would you most want to say to Biden?" The
result was revealing as the top five answers to the question from netizens were:
(1) "do not intervene in the South China Sea issue"; (2) "stop selling arms
to Taiwan"; (3) "cut the fiscal deficit"; (4) "abrogate the export restrictions of
high-tech products to China"; and (5) "stop supporting the Dalai Group and
other ethnic division forces."²²

The Role of the Media

In examining societal forces, no one can downplay the importance of the media in shaping public opinion and influencing the social environment in which
officials formulate policy. Conventional wisdom says that mass media in mod-

ern societies is powerful and omnipotent. Since media can sway public opinion on fashion, automobiles, pop music, movie stars, and political candidates, it can certainly influence public opinion on the image of a particular country and foreign policies.

Obviously the media is good at "selecting and highlighting some facets of events or issues and making connections among them so as to promote a particular interpretation, evaluation, or solution."[23] Historically, the Chinese government's propaganda system has played a significant role in shaping public opinion about a particular country by sketching a general frame and allowing scholars and government-controlled media to fill in the details. The government would usually provide a basic guideline to be circulated among TV, newspapers, and the press, specifying what could be covered and where the borderlines were. Today they are presenting diverse voices in their coverage. The pattern is that the government influences the media, and through the media it thus influences public opinion. However, since most of the party-controlled newspapers and publishing houses have become profit-making operations, many began to create lively mass-appeal papers and sensational tabloids and have published a variety of books that have flourished on urban newsstands and in bookstores. The commercialization of mass media changed the relationships among government, media, and public audiences.

Media and audience can influence each other. On the one hand, as the content that media can cover expands, the impact of Chinese media on public opinion has grown. A new pattern has gradually emerged that as the government's monopoly on information and opinions has weakened, the media sometimes presents views different from those of the government, to attract public attention and therefore help to set the agenda which may influence the government by influencing the public.[24] The content and pattern in which the media reports international events affects how the public views those events. On the other hand, the mass media has the tendency to try to please the public so as to get more public attention and thus broaden their market share. For this purpose, the mass media have to learn about what the public likes and even what the public wants. The media naturally tries to appeal to the tastes of its potential audiences. Editors make choices about which stories to cover based on their judgments about what will resonate best with audiences.[25]

The explosion of information made available to the public though profit-making and internet-based news sources have changed the way leaders and the public interact in the process of making foreign policy.[26] In order to guide public opinion and even get public support, the government often tries hard to explain its position through mass media. For example, the Foreign Ministry held media briefings before each U.S.-China Strategic and Economic Dialogue to explain the background, the main content, and the significance of the dialogue.[27] In addition, all local media are supposed to base their coverage of international events on reports from the official Xinhua News Agency. However, this rule is often not followed by commercial media when they frequently plagiarize translation of foreign news reports or add some new flavor from local experts' understanding to make it more appealing to local audiences.[28] By way of reporting each event, the media can help shape public opinion, therefore increasing or constraining the policy maneuvering room for the government. Mass media provides the stage on which China and the U.S. communicate with each other. The media do much to construct the public image of America in China. At the end of the 2009 China-U.S. Strategy and Economic Dialogue, Dai Bingguo and Wang Qishan personally thanked the media at the press conference when Dai Bingguo acknowledged the important role played by the media. He hoped that the media's reporting would continue to promote a better understanding on China side and the development of China-U.S. relations.[29]

The Role of the Sub-elite

Joseph Fewsmith and Stanley Rosen once categorized three levels of opinion that may have impact on Chinese foreign relations: elite, sub-elite, and popular.[30] At the elite level, it seems that there are fewer policy differences among the top leadership concerning whether or not China should continue its opening-up policy and the policy of integration into the international economy. However, regarding China's policy of "peaceful rise," how to view the role of the United States in the world and in Asia, and the strategy of coping with the United States, there seem to be policy differences among the sub-elites.

Sub-elites are largely academics, intelligence analysts, and policy analysts working within the governmental institutions and universities. Some are public intellectuals whose opinions influence the public via their participation in public discourse and may impact decision makers on a range of issues relating to foreign relations. Such intellectuals exist across a broad range of fields, including economics, politics, and culture.[31] While the boundaries of these sub-elites are indistinct, generally they include think tanks affiliated with the government, research institutes of the universities, and some unofficial think tanks. In terms of the role played by think tanks, David Shambaugh argues that over the past two decades China's foreign policy think tanks have come to play increasingly important roles in Chinese foreign policy making and intelligence analysis.[32] Indeed, after two decades of reform and opening up, an "epistemic community" of professionals with recognized expertise in a particular domain and issue area has been created and is playing an increasingly important role in the Chinese foreign policy making process. These intellectuals influence China's foreign policy through direct or indirect means. Some researchers write papers for decision makers within the internal government channels.[33] Intelligence analysts working in think tanks like the China Institutes of Contemporary International Relations (CICIR) or the China Institute of International Studies (CIIS) spend almost all their time writing briefing papers for government officials. Because of the complex and technical nature of the issues involving China's foreign policy, leaders in Beijing have increasingly relied on the advice offered by specialists in governmental institutions and/or within the academic community. The impact of scholars and experts in those think tanks on Chinese foreign policy making under Jiang Zemin and Hu Jintao has been increasing and multi-layered channels between the center and the periphery have been created. The difference between the Jiang-Hu era and Deng era is that intellectuals now have greater freedom in voicing their opinions on foreign policy issues.

Second, they can influence public opinion by writing articles for magazines, newspapers, websites, or airing their views on national and local television. Chinese academics are playing, together with the media, the role of opinion-shapers in China. More and more academics have been consulted by CCTV and local TV stations, radio talk shows, and have written for local newspapers about international events, resulting in more informed and less biased reporting. They have begun to influence public views on international affairs. It also provides a lucrative private income for these scholars. Unfortunately, a large number of scholars are spending the majority of their time on such media consulting, or traveling overseas to attend conferences, with the result that they are not producing new research and original scholarship.

Finally, they influence the elites and public opinion through their participation in policy debates on some special issues. In the first decade of the twenty-first century, when the international community is pondering what kind of world power China will be, there are intense internal debates among Chinese intellectuals about how to understand "the distinctive feature of our times," "changes in the international distribution of power (*guoji geju*)," "whether China should pursue the goal of being a global power," "what it means to be a 'responsible power'," "whether China should pursue the policy of peaceful rise," "is the United States in decline?," "should China pursue the goal of being number two in world power following the United States?" and "whether China should develop a grand strategy to compete with the United States."[34]

The outbreak of the financial crisis in 2008 brought forth further debate on America's decline. Most scholars consider that the power of the U.S. has been significantly weakened and wounded by the financial crisis. However, they have different views on the extent to which the U.S. can recover from the crisis. Some scholars argue that the financial crisis is rooted in the "monopoly-finance capitalism" which results in American politics becoming more and more conservative and centralized, and leads to the decline of American hegemony.[35] Others think that the U.S. has the ability of self-correction and may still remain the most powerful country in the world.[36]

Some believe that China's interests would be better served by acting as a traditional power, therefore China should change the strategy of keeping a low profile (*taoguang yanghui*). This strategy was formulated by Deng Xiaoping in the early 1990s and has guided China's diplomacy ever since. Others believe the strategy of keeping a low profile goes against improving the international image of China, as China is becoming more powerful and its national interests expand naturally around the world.[37] Some argue that China should not adopt the policy of self-protection by "hiding its capabilities and biding its time," and they argue China should keep the balance between maintaining a low profile and doing something (*yousuo zuowei*).[38]

As America is perceived to have adjusted its global strategy with more focus on the Asia-Pacific, some scholars believe that the American aim is to preserve its hegemony in Asia by containing China, the only country that can challenge America's primacy. Others argue that China should face reality and invest more resources into military and defensive infrastructure to consolidate China's power across the Asia-Pacific region. They argue that China's rise must include a military dimension by building a first-rate military and developing state-of-the-art military forces.[39] In order to protect national security, some argue China must abandon wishful thinking, face reality, and consider its national security situation and strategy from the perspective of the worst case.[40] Others even put forward more aggressive opinions by paraphrasing Mao Zedong that "political power grows out of the barrel of gun," and that only after China relies on itself to develop its strategic power will it be able to reach a certain international status.[41]

It may be difficult to discern the extent to which these debates among the community of scholars and experts influences the foreign policy establishment. It is safe to say that it may not only have some indirect impact on mid-level bureaucrats within the government and party circles, but also has an influence on the bigger social environment in which any major policy is made. Chinese officials within the foreign policy making apparatus tend to be divided into two groups with fundamantally different outlooks towards the United States: a pro-America group who generally favor a better relationship with the United States, and an anti-America group who are highly suspicious of America's intentions towards China and advocate a confrontational position. It is fair to say that those working in the foreign policy apparatus, particularly those with overseas studying experience like Yang Jiechi, Cui Tiankai, Wang Yi, Wang Guangya, among others, tend to hold a pacifist view and see the benefit of maintaining a stable relationship with Washington. Those working in the national security and military apparatus tend to hold more hawkish views.

Chinese officials are not only influenced by the public, but are increasingly engaging in "public diplomacy" (*gonggong waijiao*) to influence public opinion concerning foreign policy. The Ministry of Foreign Affairs now has an Office of Public Diplomacy, which states that it performs a dual mission of external and internal media guidance.

Meanwhile, Chinese civil society is also under construction. More enterprises and institutional units that were traditionally subordinated to the state increasingly act independently, and the pluralization of interest groups has enlivened the political environment. According to Suzanne Ogden, there are more than 200,000 interest groups and professional associations at the county, prefectural, and provincial levels, and some 1,800 national level and interprovincial groups. She divides them into three types: those that assist state policies by providing consultation and by regulating their membership to conform to state policies; those that represent their member's interests in a way that challenges state policies or state control; and those that do both.[42] Although Beijing has prohibited the formation of competing political parties, it has tolerated interest groups and associations that represent narrow concerns or localized issues. In terms of Sino-American relations, the largest NGO of the first group is the China American Studies Association. Members of this association actively participate in various policy debates regarding the domestic politics, history, culture, economy, and foreign policy of the United States.

One may anticipate that as civil society continues to develop in China, there will be a further demand for policy input and increasing professionalism in both governmental agencies and think tanks. It is likely that this will push intellectuals and scholars to play an even greater role in the years to come.

There are still limitations in terms of policy inputs. This is particularly true when comparing China with Western countries or comparing China with other East Asian societies that have been deeply influenced by the West (such as Japan, South Korea, and Taiwan). One major difference is the degree to which official lines of foreign policy can be openly criticized or challenged. There remain many "no go zones." The true policy debates over key foreign policy decisions are still not open to the public in contemporary Chinese society, despite the significant progress that has been made.

When dealing with the increasing influence of intellectuals and think tanks on Chinese foreign policy, Beijing clearly has to calculate the advantages and disadvantages. On the one hand, more policy input from intellectuals and think tanks will improve the quality of decision making, and it may also provide bargaining chips when acting in the international community, that is, Chinese officials can hide behind the rationale that the public demands them to take a certain (tough) policy position. On the other hand, as an authoritarian state, the Communist Party has been careful to protect its monopoly of power when making major decisions, including foreign policy decisions. With this kind of cost-benefit analysis, there will be inevitable ups and downs in terms of Beijing's control over intellectual life. The degree of intellectual participation in foreign policy formation will correspond to the degree of party-state control over society.

The Role of Public Opinion

Because of the internet, a new force has recently emerged within China's foreign policy process: semi-autonomous (though still limited) public opinion. The spread of the internet, the rise of multiple media outlets in an emerging market economy, and the decreased ability of the Chinese government to control people's minds have opened China's intellectual door to the world. A better educated population has begun to look outward, and more forcefully express their opinions on international affairs. The most active social groups are academics, college students, professionals, white-collar employees, and off-duty bureaucrats at governmental agencies. The urban blue collar working class tends to be less interested in external affairs, and farmers in rural areas may be least interested in anything beyond their daily life.

Public opinion in China is apparent in two major ways. First, it is relevant to the extent that current Chinese leaders want to know what people think. Since the current generation of Chinese leadership lacks the charismatic appeal that its predecessors Mao Zedong and Deng Xiaoping enjoyed, they must listen to the public to show that they care about their interests. It is also important for the objective of achieving a "harmonious society" as advocated by the leadership. Lately, the government has even made efforts to commission various kinds of opinion polls and solicit public thinking on various issues.

Secondly, public opinion matters in that the elite within policy circles mobilize public support so as to strengthen their policy positions, especially when there is an internal struggle over policy preferences. For example, there is disagreement regarding China's America policies; some feel pessimistic about the prospect of Sino-American relations and want to be prepared for the worst, while others believe that Sino-American confrontation can be avoided by building trust through cooperation and by interaction between the two countries in all areas. It is in this case that public opinion can be extremely valuable. The change of the Chinese position in Sino-American negotiations over China's entrance into the WTO reflected the role of public opinion. It is reported that China's chief negotiator, Vice Minister of Foreign Trade Long Yongtu, said that his greatest pressure during the negotiation came not from his foreign counterparts—but from domestic opinion that cursed him as a "traitor."[43]

Chinese interest in the United States is not new.[44] But the role of Chinese public opinion is. This increasingly assertive public is contributing to the evolution of Chinese-American relations. Overall, those relations have dramatically improved over the last thirty years. Still, the relationship remains a fragile one. Chinese have different perceptions of America in different periods. Before 1989, the United States enjoyed a positive image among the Chinese. During the 1990s, there has been rising anti-American sentiment among the Chinese public because of the Taiwan issue, the Yinhe incident, human rights issues, and the bombing of the Chinese embassy in Yugoslavia by NATO and the United States in 1999. In the twenty-first century, China's better-educated younger generation is gaining a more objective, balanced, and reasonable understanding of the United States. However many Chinese disapprove of American double standards in international affairs as the American government constantly condemns other nations for repressive and violent actions even though America displays similar international behavior.[45]

During June and August 2010, the Chinese Academy of Social Sciences conducted a survey of "Chinese perceptions of America" in eight Chinese cities. The results of the survey demonstrated that 90.7 percent of respondents regarded China-U.S. relations as "very important" or "more important." Among the respondents, only 15.8 percent thought current China-U.S. relations were "very good" or "good," 73.5 percent of responders think they are "not very good," and 10.7 percent of responders think they are "bad" or "very bad." This survey indicates that most Chinese believe that America is still the most influential country in the world.[46]

On December 2010, the *China Daily* cooperated with the Horizon Group to conduct a different survey of "Chinese perceptions of America." The results show that 90.9 percent of the respondents regard Sino-American relations as very important, and over half of the respondents believe that Sino-American relations will remain stable. Educated Chinese seem to have a more objective understanding of America as more information regarding the United States is available. But 53 percent of respondents attribute the political, economic, and trade disputes between the two countries to the American side. Sixty-nine percent of respondents think China-U.S. economic relations include competition and cooperation. Seventy percent of respondents believe China's economy will transcend America's, and 53.5 percent think this will be realized within 20 years. According to the survey, compared to the last century, the favorable Chinese perception of America is now at its highest level. Around 86.7 percent of respondents oppose American military action on the Korean peninsula, and 81.7 percent are against America's military stationing troops in East Asia.[47]

According to these surveys, we can reach some conclusions about China's public opinion about America. Firstly, most Chinese think that China-U.S. relations are the most important bilateral relationship for China. This is consistent with the official government position. Secondly, Chinese have different attitudes about economic and military issues. Many believe that China and America can deal with the economic issue through consultation and cooperation, but oppose America's military commitment in East Asia. Thirdly, they oppose America utilizing China's internal issues to undermine China's development and internal stability. On November 2011, after the Republican presidential candidate (and former U.S. ambassador to China) Jon Huntsman expressed that America should utilize China's internet users to "take China down," *Huanqiuwang* (the online version of *Huanqiu* newspaper) conducted a survey with the result showing that most Chinese netizens felt disgusted about this suggestion.[48]

The traumatic recollection of long suffering in China's modern history has understandably generated anger and indignation, which has also been directed at the United States. This is reflected in books like *China Can Say No* (1996) and *Behind the Demonization of China* (1997), as well as mass demonstrations after the U.S. bombing of China's embassy in 1999. One aspect of Chinese nationalism is a sense of national pride and dignity, which is generally understood as the need to overcome national humiliation and oppression.[49]

Thus, there definitely seems to have been a shift in Chinese public opinion of the United States during the 1990s and 2000s. Previously, the U.S. was seen as a role model—the shining city on the hill—but over the past two decades Chinese opinion of, and respect for, the United States has declined precipitously. The question is how this anti-American nationalism in Chinese society could gain such a great momentum in such a relatively short period of time? The answer seems to lie, to a large extent, in the role of the internet and media in the wake of the gradual opening of Chinese society to the world. The recent rise of anti-American sentiments were made possible by the emergence of public opinion resulting from easier access to national and international news, less government control over some areas of public expression, and greater skills acquired by Chinese students and intellectuals in taking advantage of the available information and limited freedom of speech. Some even describe recent anti-American and anti-Japanese nationalism as internet nationalism (*wangluo minzuzhuyi*). It is true that anti-American sentiments, as expressions of nationalism, were generally tolerated and sometimes used by the government, but the Chinese government has taken steps to ensure that anti-American sentiments would not spin out of control and impede the implementation of its policy toward the United States or challenge its rule in China.

Institutional Lobbying Groups

After China started the reform and opening policy, China's corporations and business circles expanded rapidly and became an active actor trying to affect China's domestic and foreign policy. China's "going out" strategy has created a powerful interest group as the Chinese business community went abroad. According to the statistics of the Ministry of Commerce (MOFCOM), China's outward FDI net flows in 2010 reached US$68.81 billion, increasing by 21.7 percent compared to the past year, and by the end of 2010, more than 13,000 domestic investing entities had established about 16,000 overseas enterprises, spreading in 178 countries (regions) globally.[50]

This expansion increased the influence of these business corporations on China's government and on its foreign relations. Stable and rapid economic development is one of the important bases on which the Chinese government bases its legitimacy. Corporations and businesses can offer not only employment opportunities, but also generate tax revenues. China's large SOEs also undertake the responsibility to gain resources for domestic economic development, so they have great influence on the Chinese government on certain policies—particularly toward those countries where China has substantial commercial interests. For example, where the SOEs go abroad, China's leaders soon follow. Over half of Hu Jintao's foreign visits between January 2005 and July 2010 were to countries in which at least one of the three companies (China National Petroleum Corporation, China National Offshore Oil Corporation, and the China Petroleum & Chemical Corporation) had oil or natural gas interests.[51]

Large SOEs in strategic industries such as oil, minerals, nuclear power, defense, and banking may have a larger say when dealing with the United States. Since the People's Bank of China and its affiliate the State Administration of Foreign Exchange (SAFE) participate in policy making relating to currency exchange rate and the management of huge Chinese foreign reserves, their voices count greatly in deciding whether to reduce or increase purchasing American bonds. On some occasions, the government relies on these large SOEs to pursue Beijing's broader foreign policy and security agendas.[52] For example, China's government often utilizes the SOEs to provide aid to some countries. In April 2011, China released the Foreign Aid White Paper, showing that the funds China allocated to foreign aid keeps quickly increasing at an average annual growth rate of 29.4 percent. The main form of China's foreign aid is to provide some economic or construction projects—with Chinese companies executing the aid project with complete design, construction, and post-delivery maintenance.[53]

Corporations and businesses have many ways to influence China's policy making.[54] To lobby relevant government departments is the most common way. While the United States blames China for underestimating its currency value and pressures China, officials in the Ministry of Commerce went to Guangdong Province to learn the opinions of these manufacturers. These trade-related businessmen showed their difficulty at the time of the global financial crisis in order to influence the monetary and currency policy of the central government. As a result, it was reported that the Ministry of Commerce became a forceful lobbying institution against any rapid appreciation of the *renminbi*.

Corporations can also lobby local governments. Developing the economy is the most important responsibility of every level of government in China, so local governments have close relationships with corporations and often lobby higher-level government to protect the interests of those corporations. In China, some companies are owned by the government, but their executives are often appointed by the Communist Party's Organization Department. Some big SOEs' executives circulate in and out of the central government. In this situation, they have direct connection with the policy makers.

Business interest groups play an important role in China-U.S. relations. In general, they tend to be proponents of a better relationship between China and the United States. Business activities are the binding ligament of the interdependent relationship between the two countries. Close economic ties between China and the U.S. cannot only reduce the likelihood of conflict, but can expand cooperative interests. Chinese corporations may lobby their government to share some international responsibility with America in order to safeguard their interests overseas. However, corporations' overseas activities may also lead to differences and frictions between China and the United States.[55] The U.S. believes that Chinese companies' investment in "rogue states"—such as Iran, Libya, Myanmar, Syria, and Zimbabwe—weakened the effect of the U.S. sanctions against these countries. On the contrary, China advocates settling differences through negotiation and suspects America's real purpose is to limit China's overseas activities, and to prevent the rise of China by undermining its economic development.

CONCLUSION

Along with China's rapid integration with the outside world and the pluralization of its society, domestic influences have become an important factor affecting China's relationship with the United States. As a result, the leadership must consider a variety of sub-elite ideas and public opinion relating to America and occasionally have to accommodate competing agendas. The emerging collective leadership requires consensus building, which also complicates the policy making process and provides porous opportunities for societal forces to influence China's policy toward the United States. All internal institutional actors and societal forces claim to act in the name of national interests, but in fact many evince narrow parochial interests. Nonetheless, decision makers have to take into account the interests and concerns of these actors when trying to formulate a coherent foreign policy, while considering the demand and concerns from Washington at the same time.

This chapter illustrates that societal forces have become one of the increasingly important variables among domestic determinants in China's relations with the United States. These forces have been largely accommodating and positive for decades, but are now pulling in different directions. There are a growing variety of views among scholars, opinion makers, and officials regarding the degree to which China should abandon its non-alignment policy, whether China should pursue the goal of global power, and, above all, how to cope with the United States. All of these have clear implications for Sino-American relations.

Among the new variables, the most prominent ones are the netizens and the internet, which have fundamentally transformed the way government and society interacts. Although civil society in China remains weak, it is developing in the age of the internet. The internet facilitates civil society activities by offering new possibilities for citizen participation, and civil society facilitates the development of the internet by providing the necessary social basis—citizen and citizen groups—for communication and interaction. This makes it more challenging for the Chinese government to monopolize Chinese policy towards the United States, as there is growing demand in Chinese society for participation in the policy making process. Chinese policy towards the United States has been constrained by societal pressures especially during the external crises, despite the fact that decision makers in China have a much wider degree of latitude for action than their American counterparts. Within the society, there are voices urging China to take a stronger stance against American demands and to defend China's "core national interests" in Taiwan, Tibet, Xinjiang, and the South China Sea. More and more people believe that China deserves equal international status and equal treatment on trade, human rights, and many other issues. There will be strong popular reactions whenever people in China feel that China is treated unfairly by the United States. This will have direct impact on the Chinese leadership when they make decisions regarding the United States.

The deeper China integrates with the world, the more rapid the growth of societal forces will be in China. This change will force the Beijing leadership to increasingly consider a variety of interests reflected by a growing number of institutional actors and societal forces, and thus will further complicate Sino-American relations.

NOTES

I would like to thank David Shambaugh for his insightful comments and constructive suggestions on previous drafts. I would also like to thank Li Baolin for her assistance in collecting data and in preparing this chapter.

1. See Linda Jakobson and Dean Knox, *New Foreign Policy Actors in China* (Stockholm: SIPRI Policy Paper, 2010); Yufan Hao and Lin Su (eds.), *China's Foreign Policy Making: Societal Force and Chinese American Policy* (London: Ashgate, 2005).

2. A. Doak Barnett, *The Making of Foreign Policy in China: Structure and Process* (Boulder: Westview Press, 1985).

3. David Shambaugh, *Beautiful Imperialist: China Perceives America* (Princeton: Princeton University Press, 1989).

4. Lu Ning, *The Dynamics of Foreign-Policy Decisionmaking in China* (Boulder, CO: Westview Press, 1997); Michael Swaine, *The Role of the Chinese Military in National Security Policymaking* (Santa Monica, CA: Rand Corporation, 1998); Carol Lee Hamrin and Suisheng Zhao (eds.), *Decision-making in Deng's China: Perspectives from Insiders* (Armonk, NY: M. E. Sharpe, 1995).

5. Yufan Hao and Guocang Huan (eds.), *The Chinese View of the World* (New York: Pantheon Books, 1989); Thomas Robinson and David Shambaugh (eds.), *Chinese Foreign Policy, Theory and Practice* (Oxford: Oxford University Press, 1994); Thomas Christensen, *Useful Adversaries: Grand Strategy, Domestic Mobilization and Sino-American Conflict, 1947–1958* (Princeton: Princeton University Press, 1996); Robert Ross and Andrew Nathan, *The Great Wall and the Empty Fortress: China's Search for Security* (New York: W.W. Norton, 1997); Samuel Kim (ed.), *China and the World: Chinese Foreign Policy Faces the New Millennium* (Boulder, CO: Westview Press, 1999).

6. Alastair Iain Johnston, "Learning versus Adaptation: Explaining Change in Chinese Arms Control Policy in the 1980s and 1990s," *The China Quarterly*, No. 35 (January 1996), pp. 27–61; Allen S. Whiting, "Chinese Nationalism and Foreign Policy after Deng," *The China Quarterly*, No. 142 (June 1995), pp. 295–316; Quansheng Zhao, *Interpreting Chinese Foreign Policy: The Micro-Macro Linkage Approach* (Oxford: Oxford University Press, 1996); Yong Deng and Feiling Wang (eds.), *China Rising: Power and Motivation in Chinese Foreign Policy* (Lanham, MD: Rowman & Littlefield, 2005).

7. David M. Lampton (ed.), *The Making of Chinese Foreign and Security Policy in the Era of Reform: 1978–2000* (Stanford: Stanford University Press, 2001); Yufan Hao and Lin Su (eds.), *China's Foreign Policy Making: Societal Force and Chinese American Policy*, op cit; Linda Jakobson and Dean Knox, *New Foreign Policy Actors in China*, op cit; Xu Wu, *Chinese Cyber Nationalism: Evolution, Characteristics, and Implications* (Lanham, MD: Lexington Books, 2007).

8. Among the more important studies, see A. Doak Barnett, *The Making of Foreign Policy in China: Structure and Process*, op cit ; Michael D. Swaine, *The Role of the Military in National Security Policymaking*, op cit; David M. Lampton (ed.), *The Making of Chinese Foreign and Security Policy in the Era of Reform*, op cit; Lu Ning, *The Dynamics of Foreign-Policy Decisionmaking in China*, op cit; Hongyi Lai, *The Domestic Sources of China's Foreign Policy: Regimes, Leadership, Priorities and Process* (London: Routledge, 2010); Yufan Hao and Lin Su (eds.), *China's Foreign Policy Making: Societal Force and Chinese American Policy*, op cit; Richard Bush, *The Perils of Proximity: China-Japan Security Relations* (Washington, D.C.: Brookings Press, 2010), chapter 8; Linda Jako-

bson and Dean Knox, *New Foreign Policy Actors in China*, op cit; John Wilson Lewis and Xue Litai, *Imagined Enemies: China Prepares for Uncertain War* (Stanford: Stanford University Press, 2006); Susan V. Lawrence, *Perspectives on Chinese Foreign Policy* (Washington, D.C.: Congressional Research Service, 2011); Bonnie S. Glaser and Phillip C. Saunders, "Chinese Civilian Foreign Policy Research Institutes: Evolving Roles and Increasing Influence," *China Quarterly* No. 171 (September 2002); David Shambaugh, "China's International Relations Think Tanks: Evolving Structure and Process," ibid; David Shambaugh, "China's Quiet Diplomacy: The International Department of the Chinese Communist Party," *China: An International Journal*, No. 5 (2007); Wei Li, *The Chinese Staff System: A Mechanism for Bureaucratic Control and Integration* (Berkeley: Institute for East Asian Studies, 1994); Alice Lyman Miller, "The Central Committee Departments under Hu Jintao," *China Leadership Monitor*, No. 27 (Winter 2009), available at: http://media.hoover.org/sites/default/files/documents/CLM27AM.pdf; Alice Lyman Miller, "The CCP Central Committee's Leading Small Groups," *China Leadership Monitor*, No. 26 (Fall 2008), available at: http://media.hoover.org/sites/default/files/documents/CLM26AM.pdf; Michael D. Swaine, "China's Assertive Behavior, Part III: The Role of the Military in Foreign Policy," *China Leadership Monitor*, No. 36 (2012), available at: http://media.hoover.org/sites/default/files/documents/CLM36MS.pdf.

9. David M. Lampton (ed.), *The Making of Chinese Foreign and Security Policy in the Era of Reform*, op cit.

10. Linda Jakobson and Dean Knox, *New Foreign Policy Actors in China*, op cit, p. 49.

11. "Fazhan gaigewei zhuyao zhize"(The main duties of NDRC), available at: http://www.sdpc.gov.cn/jj/default.htm.

12. David M. Lampton (ed.), *The Making of Chinese Foreign and Security Policy in the Era of Reform, 1979–2000*, op cit.

13. Yufan Hao and Lin Su (eds.), *China's Foreign Policy Making: An Analysis of Societal Forces*, op cit, p. 15.

14. Jurgen Habermas, *The Structural Transformation of the Public Sphere*, trans. T. Burger and F. Lawrence (Oxford, UK: Polity Press, 1999).

15. For further discussion of China's international relations "think tanks," see David Shambaugh, "China's International Relations Think Tanks: Evolving Structure and Process," and Bonnie Glaser and Phillip Saunders, "Chinese Civilian Foreign Policy Research Institutes: Evolving Roles and Increasing Influence," op cit. For a Chinese assessment, see Song Xufeng, *Zhongguo Sixiang Ku: Zhengce Guochengzhong de Yingxiangli Yanjiu* [Chinese Think Tanks: Research on Their Influence in the Policy Process] (Beijing: Qinghua University Press, 2009).

16. The Statistical Survey Report on the Internet Development in China 2010, by China Internet Information Center, p. 13.

17. Ibid, pp. 17–18.

18. Ibid, p. 33.

19. Hong Junhao, "The Internet and China's Foreign Policy Making: The Impact of Online Public Opinions as a New Societal Force," in Yufan Hao & Lin Su (eds.), *China's Foreign Policy Making*, op cit, pp. 93–109.

20. Yu Yanmin, "The Role of the Media: A Case Study of China's Media Coverage of the U.S. War in Iraq," in ibid, p. 84.

21. "Jiemi Qiangguo Luntan: Sicheng Wangmin Zuiai Lunzheng, Banzhu Rikan Jishiwanzi" (Reveal the Strong Nation Forum: Forty percent of Internet users like to

discuss politics, The forum moderators read hundreds of thousands of words every day), available at: http://politics.people.com.cn/GB/1026/11146828.html.

22. "Zhongguo wangmin xiang meiguo tichu wuda yaoqiu baideng fanghua zhuangshang wangluo minyi"(Chinese netizens put forward five requirements to the U.S. Biden's visit clash with network public opinion), available at: http://world.huanqiu.com/roll/2011-08/1916713.html.

23. R. M. Entman, "Framing US Coverage of International News," *Journal of Communication*, Vol. 41, No. 4 (1991), pp. 6–27, cited in Jian Wang, "Politics of Goods: A Case Study of Consumer Nationalism and Media Discourse in Contemporary China," *Asian Journal of Communication*, Vol. 16, No. 2 (June 2006), p. 192.

24. Yu Yanmin, "The Role of the Media: A Case Study of China's Media Coverage of the U.S. War in Iraq," in Yufan Hao and Lin Su (eds.), *China's Foreign Policy Making: Societal Force and Chinese American Policy*, op cit, p. 84.

25. Susan L. Shirk, "Changing Media, Changing Foreign Policy in China," *Japanese Journal of Political Science*, Vol. 8, No. 1 (April 2007), pp. 43–70.

26. Ibid, p. 47; Susan L. Shirk (ed.), *Changing Media, Changing China* (Oxford: Oxford University Press, 2011), p. 2.

27. "Waijiaogbu jiu disanlun zhongmei zhanlueyujingjiduihua juxing meiti chuifenghui"(Foreign Ministry Takes Media Briefing for Chinese and Foreign Media on the Third China-U.S. Strategic and Economic Dialogue), available at: http://www.fmprc.gov.cn/chn/pds/wjdt/cfhsl/t820597.htm.

28. Susan L. Shirk (ed.), *Changing Media, Changing China* op cit, pp. 225–231.

29. "Shoulun zhongmei jingji duihua: chule shangyueqiuwai zhuyao wenti junyi tanji" (The First China-U.S. Strategic and Economy Dialogue: Except landing on the moon, the dialogue includes all main issues), available at: http://www.chinanews.com/gn/news/2009/07-29/1794984.shtml.

30. Joseph Fewsmith and Stanley Rosen, "The Domestic Context of Chinese Foreign Policy: Does Public Opinion Matter?" in David M. Lampton (ed.), *The Making of Chinese Foreign and Security Policy in the Era of Reform*, op cit, p. 152.

31. Ibid, p. 153.

32. David Shambaugh, "China's International Relations Think Tanks: Evolving Structure and Process," op cit, pp. 575–596.

33. Quansheng Zhao, "Impact of Intellectuals and Think Tanks on Chinese Foreign Policy," in Yufan Hao and Su Lin (eds.), *China's Foreign Policy Making: Societal Force and Chinese American Policy*, op cit, p. 127.

34. Zhu Liqun, *China's Foreign Policy Debates* (Paris: European Union Center for Security Studies, Chaillot Papers, 2010), available at: http://www.iss.europa.eu; Zhao Kejin, "Zhongguo jueqi duiwai zhanlue tiaozheng" (The rise of China and the adjustment of foreign strategy), *Social Science*, No. 9 (2010); Yufan Hao, "Grand Strategy is Needed in Chinese Foreign Policy," *Nanfeng Chuang*, March 20, 2011.

35. Chen Zhouwang, "Meiguo Baquan Shuailuo Lema?"(Is U.S. Hegemony Declining?) *Zhejiang Shengwei Dangxiao Xuebao* (Journal of Zhejiang Provincial Party School), No. 5 (2011); Pang Zhongying, "Baquan Zhili yu Quanqiu Zhili"(Hegemonic governance and global governance), *Waijiao Pinglun* (Foreign Affairs Review), No. 4 (2009); Chen Yugang, "Jinrong Weiji, Meiguo Shuailuo yu Guoji Guanxi Geju Bianpinghua," (The Global Financial Crisis, the Decline of U.S. and the Flattening of the International Order) *Shijie Jingji yu Zhengzhi* (World Economics and Politics), No. 5 (2009).

36. Sun Zhe, "Meiguo Baquan de Fazhan Weidu-Aobama Zhengfu Quanqiu Fazhan Zhanlue Pingxi" (A Developmental Perspective on American Hegemony: A Critique of the Obama Administration's Strategy for Global Development) *Shijie Jingji yu Zhengzhi* (World Economics and Politics), No. 11 (2009); Shang Hong, "Jinrong Weiji dui Meiguo Baquan Diwei de Chongji" (The Impact of the Financial Crisis on America's Hegemonic Status), *Xiandai Guoji Guanxi* (Contemporary International Relations), No. 4 (2009); Zi Zhongyun, "Zhongguo Fazhan Moshi Buke Chixu, Meiguo Zaicha ye Yuanchao Renhe Lao'er" (China's Development Model is Not Sustainable, America Far Exceeds Any Number Two), available at: http://finance.ifeng.com/opin ion/hqgc/20111217/5286976.shtml.

37. Gao Fei, Cong taoguang yanghui dao heping jueqi-Ping zhongguo Waijiao de Celue Tiaozheng" (From "Taoguang Yanghui" to "Peaceful Rise": Comments on China's Readjustment of Foreign Policy) *Taipingyang Xuebao*, No. 1 (2006), p. 8.

38. Zhu Feng, "Zai taoguangyanghui yu yousuozuowei zhijian qiupingheng" (Seeking Balance Between "Taoguang Yanghui" and "Yousuo Zuowei"), *Xiandai Guoji Guanxi* (Contemporary International Relations), No. 9 (2008), p. 20.

39. Liu Mingfu, *Zhongguo Meng: Hou Meiguo Shidai de Daguo Siwei he Zhanlue Dingwei* (China Dream: The Great Power Thinking and Strategy Positioning in the Post-American Age) (Beijing: Zhongguo youyi chuban gongsi, 2010).

40. Zhou Jianming, "Guanyu Woguo Duiwai Zhanlue de Jige Wenti" (The Issues of Our Country's Foreign Strategy) *Guoji Guancha* (International Survey), No. 3, (2001).

41. Zhang Wen Mu, *Shijie diyuan zhengzhi zhong de zhongguo guojia anquan liyi* (The Geopolitical Perspective of China's Security Interests) (Jinan: Shandong Renmin chubanshe, 2004); Zhang Wenmu, *Lun Zhongguo Haiquan* (On China's Seapower) (Beijing: Haiyang chubanshe, 2009).

42. Suzanne Ogden, *Inklings of Democracy in China* (Cambridge, MA: Harvard University Press, 2002), pp. 265–275.

43. Ma Licheng, "New Thinking," in Yufan Hao nad Lin Su (eds.), *China's Foreign Policy Making: Societal Force and Chinese American Policy*, op cit, pp. 1–15.

44. See Harold R. Issacs, *Scratches on Our Minds* (New York: John Day, 1958); David Shambaugh, *Beautiful Imperialist: China Perceives America, 1972–1990*, op cit; Tu Wei-ming, "Chinese Perceptions of America," in Robert C. Oxnam and Michel C. Oksenberg (eds.), *Dragon and Eagle* (New York: Basic Books, 1978); R. David Arkush and Leo O. Lee (eds.), *Land Without Ghosts: Chinese Impressions of America from the Mid-Nineteenth Century to the Present* (Berkeley: University of California Press, 1989).

45. Yufan Hao and Lin Su, "Beautiful Imperialist or Warmongering Hegemon: Contemporary Chinese Views of the United States?" in Hao Yufan and Lin Su (eds.), *China's Foreign Policy Making*, op cit, p. 82.

46. "Zhongguoren yanzhong de meiguo yu zhongmei guanxi" (The Chinese perception of America and China-U.S. relations), in *Liaowang dongfang zhoukan*, available at: http://news.sina.com.cn/c/sd/2011-09-13/115323147530_3.shtml.

47. "2010 Zhongguoren yanzhong de meiguo xilie diaocha" (Chinese perceptions of America 2010), available at: http://www.chinadaily.com.cn/hqjs/2011-01/17 /content_11866720.htm.

48. "Diaochaxianshi zhognguo wangyou jujue ti meiguo 'bandaozhognguo'" (the survey shows China's internet users refuse to "take China down" for America), available at: http://china.huanqiu.com/roll/2011-11/2209641_3.html.

49. A. D. Smith, *Nationalism: Theory, Ideology, History* (Cambridge: Polity Press, 2001).

50. *2010 Statistical Bulletin of China's Outward Foreign Direct Investment*, Ministry of Commerce of the People's Republic of China Department of Outward Investment and Economic Cooperation, available at: http://hzs.mofcom.gov.cn/aarticle/date/201109/20110907741156.html.

51. Linda Jakobson and Dean Knox, *New Foreign Policy Actors in China*, op cit, p. 27.

52. Ibid, p. 24.

53. "The release of China's Foreign Aid White Paper," available at: http://www.chinanews.com/gn/2011/04-21/2989430_2.shtml.

54. Scott Kennedy, "Comparing Formal and Informal Lobbying Practices in China: The Capitals Ambivalent Embrace of Capitalists," *China Information*, Vol. 23, No. 2 (2009), pp. 199–212.

55. David Zweig and Bi Fianbai, "China's Global Hunt for Energy," *Foreign Affairs*, Vol. 84, No. 5 (September/October, 2005), p. 32.

Part V

The Bilateral Context

7

The Diplomatic Relationship
Substance and Process

Bonnie S. Glaser

Prior to normalization of relations in 1972, interactions between the United States and China were held sporadically in a series of ambassadorial-level talks held in Geneva and Warsaw that focused on a limited number of issues of practical concern, beginning with the repatriation of American and Chinese nationals after the Korean War.[1] Under the guidance of President Richard Nixon and his interlocutors Chairman Mao and Premier Zhou Enlai, U.S.-China discussions were elevated to senior levels and tackled the strategic challenge of countering the Soviet Union and reaching a modus vivendi on Taiwan. After China's return to the United Nations in 1971, working level coordination and bilateral dialogue increased through diplomats and senior officials. Direct exchanges provided new opportunities for discussions that advanced bilateral ties from the normalization of relations in 1979 until the Tiananmen crackdown a decade later. The brutal suppression of demonstrators by Beijing led to a pronouncement of a temporary suspension of high-level exchanges, although President George W. Bush sent envoys secretly. Regular dialogue and exchanges gradually resumed in the 1990s, with primary concentration on bilateral issues, including human rights and trade.

As the decade progressed, Beijing, traditionally suspicious of international institutions and their potential to harm Chinese interests, began to participate more actively in multilateral forums and coordinate with major players on economic and security issues[2]—a change which the United States encouraged. China joined Asia-Pacific Economic Cooperation (APEC) in 1991 and acceded to the nuclear Non-Proliferation Treaty (NPT) in 1992. Under the Clinton administration, the groundwork was laid for China to join the World Trade Organization. U.S.-China coordination in these institutions flourished. With the spread of China's national interests, the bilateral U.S.-China agenda expanded as well and high-level dialogue became more frequent and intense. A U.S.-China presidential hotline was established in 1998.

Early in the George W. Bush administration, U.S. recognition that China was acquiring the capacity to influence other countries regionally and globally, creating both challenges and opportunities for U.S. interests, prompted an active effort to shape China's foreign policy behavior. Communication between U.S. and Chinese presidents assumed greater importance on key security issues, especially the nuclear weapons programs of Iran and North Korea. Motivated by a desire to ease the burden of global responsibilities and by concerns about the negative impact on global governance of Chinese behavior abroad, the Bush administration urged China to abandon its free-rider approach and "strengthen the international system that has enabled its success," thereby becoming a "responsible stakeholder."[3] Toward this end, two dialogue mechanisms were established: the Strategic Economic Dialogue and the Senior Dialogue. The Senior Dialogue, launched in August 2005, provided an opportunity for in-depth discussion of a host of strategic issues as well as exploration of ways to narrow differences and enhance cooperation on matters of mutual concern. The Obama administration combined and upgraded these two mechanisms in July 2009 to form the Strategic and Economic Dialogue.

As the U.S.-China bilateral relationship has evolved, and with China's emergence as an important regional and global player, the depth and breadth of the diplomatic agenda has expanded dramatically. Today U.S.-China discussions cover all four corners of the globe and address a panoply of issues that encompass virtually all the twenty-first century's regional and global challenges. Moreover, U.S.-China coordination in multilateral institutions has increased and a web of bilateral dialogue mechanisms was established as part of a common strategy to institutionalize the relationship in pursuit of enhanced understanding, deeper trust, and greater cooperation.

This chapter describes the increasingly diverse, globalized and institutionalized U.S.-China diplomatic agenda.[4] It presents and analyzes the two countries' respective goals, the roles of their bureaucracies, the bilateral mechanisms for dialogue, and the array of topics discussed. In addition, the chapter assesses the efficacy of bilateral dialogue mechanisms in managing the U.S.-China relationship, advancing U.S. and Chinese interests, and promoting cooperation.

RESPECTIVE GOALS

Eight consecutive U.S. presidents, beginning with President Nixon, have pursued engagement with China. As an approach, engagement has evolved to include interaction at the highest levels and across the various bureaucracies of both the U.S. and Chinese governments. In an increasingly globalized world in which the U.S. and China have a great deal at stake and have both overlapping and divergent interests, engagement serves three main U.S. objectives: (1) to promote greater Chinese acceptance of Western norms and practices, constrain China's policy choices and behaviors, and enmesh China into the prevailing international system; (2) to persuade China to contribute more actively to addressing regional and global problems (essentially to become a "responsible stakeholder," although use of the phrase lapsed with the end of the George W. Bush administration); and (3) to increase mutual understanding, reduce mutual distrust, and avoid miscalculation. These goals are pursued to advance American interests in developing a cooperative relationship with China. At the same time, the U.S. is hedging against a possible shift in Chinese policy toward undermining the international system and military aggression through its own military modernization and sustained presence in Asia and strengthening U.S. relationships with countries in the region.

China's objectives in its dealings with the U.S. focus on protecting Chinese interests and promoting the overall bilateral relationship, which remains extremely consequential for Chinese national security. China's goals can be enumerated as: (1) preserving a peaceful and stable security environment to ensure continued Chinese development and security; (2) maintaining a positive, productive, and stable relationship with the United States; and (3) defending and gaining U.S. respect for Chinese "core interests."[5] Beijing has placed a premium on managing differences with the U.S. and sustaining cooperation through dialogue and negotiation. It seeks to avoid a zero-sum rivalry with the U.S. while maximizing China's freedom of action and reducing constraints on Chinese behavior. In addition, Beijing strives to limit U.S. interference in China's internal affairs. Like the U.S., Beijing is also hedging against a potential U.S. effort to thwart the expansion of China's capabilities, status, and influence. This is especially necessary as China remains suspicious about U.S. long-term intentions and willingness to accept China's rise as a global power and competitor.

THE ROLE OF BUREAUCRACIES

In the U.S. government, the president's National Security Council (NSC) is the primary agency of the executive branch responsible for coordinating policies among various departments and advising the president on national security and foreign policy matters. The statutory members of the NSC are the president, vice president, and the secretaries of state, energy, and defense. The chairman of the Joint Chiefs of Staff and the director of national intelligence are statutory advisers to the NSC. Other senior U.S. officials can be invited to participate in NSC meetings as needed. The National Security Council Staff is responsible for running the interagency policy process, which consists of Interagency Policy

Committees (IPCs), Deputies Committees (DCs) and Principals Committees (PCs). All these mechanisms can make decisions, but must do so by consensus of their interagency members. IPCs "conduct the day-to-day interagency analysis, generation of courses of action, policy development, coordination, resource determination, and policy implementation planning."[6] The East Asia regional IPC is headed by the Assistant Secretary of State for East Asia and the Pacific. The DC is chaired by the Deputy National Security Advisor and consists primarily of interagency deputy secretaries. It is the task of the DC to ensure that the issues are thoroughly analyzed and all views and options are considered. The majority of policy decisions are made in the DC and then provided to the PC for review and subsequently to the president for a final decision.

The Principals Committee (PC), whose membership is in essence the same as the NSC without the president and vice president, acts as the president's senior level policy review and coordination group. On China policy, as with all other foreign policy and national security issues, the primary task of the PC is to forge a consensus among various departments and provide policy recommendations to the president. When differences among PC members cannot be resolved, the president becomes involved and makes a decision. PC meetings are usually convened once or twice per week, though this varies based on how many issues require deliberation. On average, more than a dozen PC meetings are held annually that concern policy toward China.[7] In 2010, for example, there were meetings convened to discuss policy on U.S.-China strategic and economic relations and to approve an arms package for Taiwan. In addition to these formal mechanisms, the China policymaking process contains its own informal, small working groups that meet irregularly and consist of lower-level officials from NSC, State, and DoD responsible for China.[8]

The Department of State is the lead U.S. foreign affairs agency and the secretary of state is the president's principal foreign policy adviser. The Department develops, represents, and implements the president's foreign policy. In practice, the power of the secretary of state varies depending on his or her relationship to the president and the extent to which he or she is supported by other key members of the Cabinet. A secretary of state may also be more influential on some issues than others.

Specific policy proposals toward China are usually coordinated between the Department of State and the NSC, but there are exceptions. When Deputy Secretary of State James Steinberg proposed a policy of "strategic reassurance" toward China in September 2009, it had not been approved in the interagency process, although it had been introduced conceptually at a DC.[9] In addition, the numerous policy speeches delivered by the secretary of state and other officials from the Department on Asia and other issues are not necessarily reviewed and approved by the NSC.

In China, the Chinese Communist Party (CCP) and the Government of the People's Republic of China (PRC) have separate decision making structures, although the two parallel structures overlap in function, authority, and even personnel. Although the National People's Congress (NPC) is the highest organ of state power according to the Constitution, the Standing Committee of the Politburo (PBSC) of the CCP Central Committee—which is derived from the larger Politburo—issues strategic guidelines, principles, and policies which are then implemented by the various ministries.[10] The members of the PBSC serve concurrently as directors of the Central Committee's eight leading small groups (LSGs) that coordinate and supervise policy. LSGs are not decision making bodies, but rather are intended as communication and coordination mechanisms that ensure the flow of information and forge consensus across various parts of the Chinese system. They also make policy recommendations that are forwarded to the PBSC for deliberation. In the vast majority of cases, policy proposals that are agreed upon within an LSG by its membership of relevant CCP officials are subsequently endorsed by the top leadership.[11]

The two LSGs that discuss policy toward the United States are the Foreign Affairs Leading Small Group (FALSG, established in 1958) and the National Security Leading Small Group (NSLSG, established in 2000), which have overlapping but not identical memberships. Both LSGs are headed by the secretary general of the CCP, who is also president of the PRC. The PBSC meets weekly and always convenes in advance of a major summit meeting between the presidents of China and the United States. Decisions are reached through consensus building and are based on recommendations from relevant government, party and military organs. The deliberations of the PBSC are tightly held, but, in practice many foreign policy decisions are made by a small subset of PBSC members.

Three other bodies associated with the CCP Central Committee play important roles in the foreign policy making process: the Policy Research Office, the General Office, and the International Department. The Policy Research Office conducts research, provides advice and drafts policy documents for the top leadership. The General Office provides administration and logistical support to the Politburo. Its primary function is to control the distribution of documents to decision makers. The respective heads of the Policy Research Office and the General Office frequently accompany the Party General Secretary on overseas trips. The International Department is in charge of managing the CCP's relations with all foreign political parties and movements, including the Democratic and Republican parties in the U.S. It plays a special role in formulating policy toward socialist countries such as North Korea and Vietnam.

The Ministry of Foreign Affairs (MFA), situated under the State Council, which functions as the cabinet of the government, is tasked with the implementation of

Chinese foreign policy. The MFA and its minister are far less powerful than their nominal U.S. counterparts, the Department of State and the secretary of state. Moreover, the clout of the MFA has declined over the past decade, in part due to the growing complexity of foreign policy and the resulting rise in influence of entities with an interest in shaping foreign policy decisions, such as the ministries of commerce, finance, and state security, the People's Bank of China, the National Development and Reform Commission, and the military.

The Minister of Foreign Affairs is neither a member of the PBSC nor a member of the expanded Politburo and does not have regular access to China's president and the other members of the PBSC. Due to the importance of the United States in Chinese foreign policy, the bilateral relationship is mostly handled by the state councilor in charge of foreign policy, who, since 2008 is concomitantly director of the Central Committee's Foreign Affairs Office (FAO), which conducts research and coordinates activities for the FASLG and the NSLSG. When tasked by the top leadership, the FAO takes the lead in coordinating the various ministries and government think tanks to conduct research and analysis on a specific issue and provide policy recommendations or manage a crisis. For example, the MFA was initially assigned the lead role in handling the EP-3 crisis in April 2001, but on the third day—after the PBSC had set principles for the resolution of the crisis—President Jiang Zemin put the NSLG in charge with then Vice President Hu Jintao as its acting head.[12]

BILATERAL MECHANISMS

Even more than in other bilateral relationships, direct communication between top leaders is essential to advancing bilateral cooperation and solving problems in the U.S.-China relationship. China's top-down flow of authority and reliance on party leadership directives to guide the system require securing its president's imprimatur on something consequential before the bureaucracy will take action. Once an agreement is struck at the highest level, bureaucracies get engaged and are motivated to implement the high-level understanding. A good personal rapport between top leaders has proven critical in securing agreement on sensitive issues and resolving problems.

The U.S. especially uses presidential meetings to "set priorities, send messages, and elicit commitments."[13] Only the most pressing issues are included on the agenda of presidential meetings. In recent years the U.S. has prioritized such issues as North Korea, Iran, Sudan, China's currency and trade practices, economic rebalancing, human rights, maritime security, and the importance of sustaining military-to-military dialogue. Chinese presidents have repeatedly raised concerns about U.S. policy toward Taiwan and restrictions on U.S. exports to China.

Presidential discussions were critical in coordinating policies to respond to the 2008 financial crisis and in support of the referendum on independence that took place in Southern Sudan in January 2011. After a spate of diplomatic clashes involving the U.S. and China in the Yellow Sea and the South China Sea in 2010, as well as heightened friction over trade and cyber security, Presidents Obama and Hu used the opportunity afforded by their January 2011 summit to refocus the relationship on shared interests and reassure each other about their respective intentions.

Other high-level interactions are also important in advancing coordination and cooperation on diplomatic issues. Exchanges of visits by American and Chinese vice presidents are especially important in anticipation of a change in leadership in China because they provide important opportunities for the U.S. to engage with China's incoming leader and influence his worldview and perspectives on the United States. Meetings between the U.S. secretary of state and China's state councilor in charge of foreign affairs (who are co-chairs of the U.S.-China Strategic and Economic Dialogue, discussed below) are viewed by both governments as useful to increase understanding of each other's policies and identify areas of common interest where joint action can be undertaken.

The importance of interactions between lower level officials, such as the U.S. deputy secretary of state and assistant secretary of state for East Asia and Pacific affairs and their counterparts in the Chinese foreign ministry varies based in part on the personalities and relative influence of these officials, especially on the U.S. side. Also important, but less widely publicized, are contacts between the Chinese officials and U.S. NSC staffers, which, due to the latter's proximity to and frequent contact with the president, are highly influential in shaping the policy agenda and strategies. One important channel of communication is between the senior director for Asia, who is also a senior adviser to the president, and China's ambassador to the United States. NSC officials at various levels, including the president's national security adviser, occasionally travel to China at key junctures for consultations.

Solving problems or making headway on specific issues in U.S.-China relations is often facilitated by the existence of a "go to" person on both sides. That individual is able to dispense with talking points and engage in candid discussion with his or her counterpart, including the domestic political context of issues, and explain what is achievable. Such an official usually highly values the bilateral relationship and drives the agenda to create positive outcomes. When a "go to" person does not exist on either the U.S. or Chinese side, the bilateral relationship works less smoothly and efficiently.

Embassies and consulates play a valuable role in the bilateral relationship through their reporting on developments inside each country, handling visiting delegations from their own country, and promoting overall friendly relations. Regular contacts between the ambassadors posted to the U.S. and China and senior officials in the capitals where they serve provide an important conduit for exchanging information and promoting understanding, especially if they have earned the trust of the host government.

In addition to the frequent exchanges of official visits, over 60 bilateral dialogue mechanisms have been created (see textbox 7.1) to discuss issues of shared interest as well as differences, coordinate policies, and promote bilateral, regional, and global cooperation.[14] These mechanisms are a testament to the institutionalization of the U.S.-China relationship and demonstrate the growing importance that both countries attach to it.

The Strategic and Economic Dialogue

The relationship's highest-level and highest-profile regularly scheduled dialogue is the annual Strategic and Economic Dialogue (S&ED), created in 2009 by combining the Strategic Economic Dialogue (SED) and the Senior Dialogue (SD), both of which were established in the George W. Bush administration. The S&ED is composed of a strategic track and an economic track, respectively headed by the U.S. secretary of state and China's state councilor for foreign affairs, and the secretary of the treasury and China's vice premier for foreign trade. All four co-chairs are special representatives appointed by their presidents. Meetings are held annually and alternate between the two countries' capitols. The S&ED includes high-level representation from multiple other agencies and ministries in the U.S. and Chinese governments and serves as an umbrella for numerous sub-dialogues, most of which existed prior to the establishment of the S&ED.

The S&ED provides an invaluable opportunity for in-depth discussion of a broad range of immediate and long-term issues at a very high level. Meetings are structured to allow for a large inclusive plenary session to address cross-cutting issues of both strategic and economic import, as well as smaller meetings to focus on sensitive concerns. Between 15 and 30 agency heads and cabinet-level officials and a total of more than 150 officials from each country participate. The agenda of the plenary sessions has included global economic issues, climate change, proliferation, and overseas development assistance.

Although the S&ED and its predecessors the SED and SD have produced some concrete agreements, the most significant achievement of these mechanisms has been facilitating the development of closer relationships between key high-level U.S. and Chinese officials that have enabled these individuals to more effectively address problems in the bilateral relationship when they arise. According to a former Obama administration official, "These relationships would not have been as intense if they had not been anointed as key counter-parts. This is not trivial."[15] For example, at the onset of the 2008 financial crisis, then-U.S. Treasury Secretary Paulson was able to quickly contact his Chinese counterpart to discuss potential responses.

The S&ED has also made headway in breaking down the stove-piped system that exists in China and to some extent in the U.S. Chinese officials who normally focus on narrow issues such as food safety or forestry are able to gain an understanding of the broader strategic context of the relationship and have an opportunity to meet other individuals from China's system whom they would otherwise not have a chance to become acquainted with. Chinese officials acknowledge that the S&ED has improved coordination among agencies in China and between the central government and provinces on specific issues.[16]

Interagency linkages among U.S. and Chinese officials have been strengthened through the S&ED and new areas of common interest have been identified. For example, discussions initiated at one round on conservation management opened up a new arena of bilateral cooperation. Other dialogues have sprung from the S&ED framework, such as the U.S.-China discussions on law of the sea and polar issues which first met in 2010, the U.S.-China Consultations on the Asia-Pacific and the U.S.-China Strategic Security Dialogue (SSD), both established in 2011.

The S&ED has also enabled the two sides to surmount challenges posed by bureaucratic misalignment. Responsibility for development assistance resides in the U.S. Department of State, while in China the Ministry of Commerce is in charge. Through the S&ED process, discussions have begun on U.S. and Chinese approaches to development assistance and opportunities for coordination are being explored. The S&ED has undoubtedly strengthened the overall U.S.-China relationship. By bringing together such large delegations with many senior participants, both sides demonstrate to their respective publics and to other nations the importance of the bilateral relationship and that the U.S. and China can work together in support of shared goals. Over time, the potential exists for habits of cooperation to be built, misperceptions eliminated, and mutual understanding enhanced.[17]

A major challenge for U.S. and Chinese officials in preparing for S&ED meetings is structuring the interactions and events to satisfy the needs of both countries. For the Chinese side, large banquets and cultural displays are necessary to demonstrate to the domestic audience that the highly important Sino-U.S. relationship is cooperative and is being well managed by Beijing. The U.S. attaches greater significance to producing "deliverables," which are viewed as evidence that the many hours spent are worth the investment of the time of the many principals who participate. Since its inception, modifications have been made to the structure of the Dialogue's strategic track to improve its efficiency and effectiveness. In the first two meetings, according to one U.S. official, lengthy plenary sessions were held in which the senior representatives largely exchanged talking points on a few targeted issues, leaving insufficient time to discuss other topics. In the third meeting, the plenary was shortened and smaller split sessions were held that focused on specific issues. Maximizing opportunities for interaction between the U.S. secretary of state and China's state councilor is a key objective to enable discussion on pressing issues.[18]

The S&ED has been lauded for its achievements, but has also drawn criticism, especially in the U.S. Some American experts were skeptical of the Dialogue's efficacy from the start, arguing that the deficit of bilateral cooperation and trust was not due to failure of the U.S. and Chinese governments, but rather was due to "mismatched interests, values, and capabilities" and that "elevating the bilateral relationship [was] not the solution."[19] Others warned that holding the S&ED annually instead of biannually, which had been the practice of the S&ED's forerunner, the Senior Dialogue, could reduce the effectiveness of the interactions, unless the subordinate working groups are able to maintain momentum.[20] Some critics charged that the creation of a unique dialogue mechanism that the U.S. doesn't even have with its close allies could cause anxiety of a "G-2" condominium among U.S. allies and partners. Within the U.S. bureaucracy, there are complaints about infighting and lack of effective coordination between the Departments of State and Treasury. Another criticism is that the Dialogue involves excessive pomp and circumstance and occupies two days (and another two travel days when held in China) of many senior U.S. officials.[21] One expert cautioned that the U.S. must guard against the Dialogue becoming "an end to itself" that could result in reduced incentives for the Chinese to work toward tangible outcomes.[22]

S&ED Sub-Dialogues

As part of a broader U.S. strategy to engage with China on a range of political and security matters at the global level, the two countries hold regular working-level dialogues that are subsumed under the S&ED. Regional sub-dialogues are held on Africa, Latin America, South Asia, Central Asia, and the Asia-Pacific. These mechanisms were created at the initiative of the United States and predated the establishment of the S&ED, with the exception of the Asia-Pacific Consultations which were proposed by Beijing and launched in June 2011. Most of the regional sub-dialogues are led by the U.S. Department of State's regional assistant secretaries of state and China's assistant foreign ministers, and are conducted annually. The Asia-Pacific Consultations are headed on the

Chinese side by a vice-foreign minister, and convened twice in the four-month period after they were inaugurated.

Other bilateral sub-dialogues that focus on security issues include: 1) the Strategic Security Dialogue (SSD), which is the first high-level joint civilian-military mechanism (discussed below); 2) the U.S.-China International Security and Non-Proliferation Dialogue, which has traditionally been headed on the U.S. side by the under secretary for Arms Control and International Security at the Department of State and on the Chinese side by a vice-minister from the MFA; 3) the U.S.-China Policy Planning Dialogue, headed by the director of the U.S. Department of State's policy planning office and the director-general of China's MFA policy research department; and 4) the U.S.-China Counterterrorism Security Consultation. Other bilateral mechanisms that address issues on the diplomatic agenda and promote cooperation are the Human Rights Dialogue (HRD) and its sub-dialogue the Legal Experts Dialogue (discussed below); the U.S.-China High-level Consultation on People-to-People Exchange; the U.S.-China Women's Leadership Exchange and Dialogue; and the U.S.-China Dialogue on Law of the Sea and Polar issues.

Strategic Security Dialogue

In May 2011, China and the United States launched the first joint civilian-military dialogue under the S&ED's strategic track, called the Strategic Security Dialogue. The U.S. goal in this mechanism is to build more understanding on issues in the bilateral relationship that have the potential for miscalculation and accident. Priority issues for the U.S. include nuclear strategy and doctrine, missile defense, outer space, and cyber security. China hopes to use the SSD to advance bilateral mutual strategic trust and seeks progress on its priority concerns of U.S. maritime surveillance in its 200-mile Exclusive Economic Zone (EEZ) and U.S. arms sales to Taiwan. Impetus for the new mechanism came from the slow progress in bilateral military-to-military relations and growing American concerns about lack of effective coordination between civilian and military actors in the Chinese system. The SSD is chaired by senior defense and civilian officials from both countries and includes representatives from the military, diplomatic, and intelligence communities.

The SSD was the brainchild of Deputy Secretary of State James Steinberg, who proposed the creation of a high-level civilian-military dialogue on security issues on a visit to China in February 2010. From the perspective of the U.S., an advantage of the SSD is that it includes a relatively small number of officials, which enables discussions to very quickly move away from talking points to "revealing discussions about intentions and mistrust."[23]

THE BILATERAL DIPLOMATIC AGENDA

The U.S.-China diplomatic agenda has expanded both in nature and scope over the past decade. Whereas the predominant focus in the 1980s and 1990s was on bilateral issues, in the twenty-first century bilateral dialogue has broadened to encompass a host of global topics. Geographically, as discussed above, Washington and Beijing engage in consultations on every major region in the world with the exception of the Middle East and Europe. The agenda of specific issue areas has also increased dramatically. Below is a partial list of topics that are currently included in U.S.-China diplomatic dialogues and multilateral venues for bilateral coordination.

Economics

As Charles Freeman's chapter in this volume illustrates, economic issues are increasingly prominent on the U.S.-China agenda, especially in presidential discussions. U.S. goals focus largely on integrating China into the global economic system and ensuring unhindered access to Chinese markets for American companies. Chinese objectives are to manage friction resulting from economic issues, and to persuade the U.S. to loosen export controls on high-tech transfer to China and create favorable conditions for Chinese companies to invest in the U.S. Specific economic issues discussed include global economic rebalancing, currency, trade protectionism, intellectual property rights (IPR), bilateral trade imbalance, unfair trade practices and trade disputes, and coordination at multilateral institutions such as the G-20.[24] Beijing has rhetorically agreed with many U.S. goals, but the pace of implementation of its promises has been slow. For example, China has been reluctant to rapidly appreciate its currency due to domestic concerns,[25] and has resisted entering into trade agreements that would compel it to open its economy further because doing so would put added pressure on its state-owned enterprises (SOEs). There is a close linkage between economic issues and the diplomatic agenda. According to a former Obama administration official, "Other issues can't be managed if the U.S. and China are having a low-level trade war. There are consequences for the diplomatic agenda if the economic relationship is deteriorating. A strong economic relationship underpins and bolsters the ability to make progress on the diplomatic agenda. There can't be trade-offs."[26]

Arms Control and Nonproliferation

Preventing proliferation of weapons of mass destruction (WMD), related materials, and their delivery methods, have been discussed bilaterally and multilaterally for several decades. The U.S. has focused attention primarily on gaining

Chinese support for sanctions, such as through the United Nations Security Council resolutions (UNSCR), stronger safeguards and export controls, and international institutions intended to regulate or stop the spread of WMD materials. Sino-U.S. cooperation on multilateral arms control and nonproliferation represents the most extensive area of policy convergence. Both countries are party to several international institutions pertaining to nonproliferation, namely the Nonproliferation Treaty (NPT), the Biological Weapons Convention, the Chemical Weapons Convention, the Geneva Protocol, the Nuclear Suppliers Group, and the Zangger Committee. Both are also signatories of the Comprehensive Nuclear Test Ban Treaty, but neither country has ratified the treaty. China remains outside of several other institutions, such as the Australia Group and the Missile Technology Control Regime, but has agreed to adhere to the 1987 guidelines and China's potential membership is under discussion. China tacitly supports the goals of the Proliferation Security Initiative, but has not joined due to concerns over the initiative's legality. Inspections under the Container Security Initiative are now underway at the major ports of Shenzhen, Shanghai, and Hong Kong. China participates in the Department of Energy's Megaports Initiative, a U.S. initiative to detect the flow of nuclear materials. Bilateral negotiations on arms control and nonproliferation issues have been contentious, especially over alleged Chinese WMD proliferation to Iran, North Korea, and Pakistan. Transfers to Iran of equipment and technology prohibited under U.S. export control rules by Chinese companies have resulted in repeated U.S. sanctions.

Counterterrorism

After 9/11, the U.S. intensified its efforts to combat terrorism at home and abroad, and sought to cooperate with a large number of countries, including China. A U.S.-China counterterrorism dialogue was established in which both sides seek to address terrorism with a whole-of-government approach. Cooperation has been strengthened on anti-money laundering and counter-financing of terrorism, including counterfeiting. Formally established in 2002, the FBI Legal Attaché Office in Beijing bolstered U.S.-Chinese cooperation on counterterrorism investigations. Tension persists over U.S. worries that the Chinese are using counterterrorism as a pretext to repress Uighur Muslims. In addition to bilateral consultations, the two countries have coordinated on counterterrorism multilaterally at the ASEAN Regional Forum and APEC.

Cybersecurity

Cybersecurity drew attention in January 2010 when the internet search provider Google announced that it had discovered highly sophisticated cyber attacks originating in China had stolen some of the company's source code and broke into the Gmail accounts of Chinese human rights advocates. Bilateral talks on cybersecurity got underway in May 2011 when the U.S. and China launched the first SSD. Issues to be addressed include ensuring supply chain security, protecting critical infrastructure, committing to freedom to find and disseminate online information, and promoting a culture of cyber security, capacity building, and international norm development. The U.S. has raised concerns about China's alleged practice of economic espionage. Both sides complain that they are targets of hackers from the other country. American and Chinese law enforcement agencies work closely to combat internet crime. The U.S. and China also interact on cyber issues in various U.N. committees and U.N. organizations.

Taiwan

Beijing raises concerns about U.S. policy toward Taiwan at virtually every level of bilateral interaction. As discussed by Shelly Rigger in her chapter in this volume, China views U.S. involvement in Taiwan and cross-Strait issues as meddling in its internal affairs and there is a widely held belief among Chinese officials that the U.S. relationship with Taiwan is part of a strategy to prevent reunification. The Chinese protest U.S. arms sales to Taiwan, visits by U.S. officials to the island, and U.S. actions in support of expanded participation for Taiwan in international organizations. China recurrently presses the United States to discuss ways of managing U.S. arms sales to Taiwan to minimize the negative impact on U.S.-China relations, but the U.S. has refused, in part due to concerns that doing so would violate its promise to not consult with Beijing on arms sales, which is one of "Six Assurances" that were made to Taipei by U.S. President Ronald Reagan.

Maritime Security

The U.S. and China differ over which activities are permitted in a country's 200-mile Exclusive Economic Zone (EEZ) under the U.N. Convention on the Law of the Sea (UNCLOS). Beijing strongly objects to U.S. surveillance, reconnaissance, and observation (SRO) activities in its EEZ, as Christopher Twomey details in his chapter in this volume. Aggressive Chinese intercepts of U.S. military surveillance ships and aircraft operating in its EEZ in 2009 took place in the South China Sea, which heightened U.S. concerns about the risk of another military accident similar to the 2001 collision of a Chinese fighter and a U.S. EP-3 reconnaissance plane. Rising tensions between China and other claimants of disputed land features and waters in the South China Sea resulted in greater attention to that body of water in 2010. The issue was included in U.S.-China discussions after Secretary of State Clinton broached the subject at the July 2010 ARF (ASEAN Regional Forum) meeting, expressing U.S. national interest in freedom of navigation and the peaceful settlement of disputes according to international law. Beijing insists that the territorial disputes be settled bilaterally and opposes U.S. involvement; Washington supports the demands of many regional states for a code of conduct and a multilateral dialogue to help maintain peace and reach a solution to quarrels over sovereignty and resources.

Afghanistan/Pakistan

Over the last decade, U.S.-China coordination on Afghanistan and Pakistan has focused largely on the fight against the Taliban as well as stabilization and rebuilding efforts in Afghanistan. During the operations by the NATO-led International Security Assistance Force (ISAF) in Afghanistan, the U.S. engaged in dialogue with Beijing about possible ways that China could contribute to the counterinsurgency campaign. In early 2009, the Obama administration appealed to China to open a supply route that could be used to deliver nonlethal items such as food and clothing through western China to coalition forces in Afghanistan.[27] The Chinese agreed to study the proposal, but reportedly never accepted it, despite a shared interest in stability in Afghanistan. Chinese hesitation to cooperate with the U.S. has likely been due to several reasons: 1) fear that opening their border with Afghanistan could cause a backlash from their Muslim population; 2) wariness of overtly supporting a NATO-led military operation; and 3) concern about causing friction with Pakistan. Beijing agreed to train Afghan police and deminers, however,[28] and contributed to stabilization efforts through humanitarian assistance and economic investment. Issues pertaining to Pakistan, including ensuring that Pakistan's nuclear weapons are secure and that the country remains stable, are also discussed between the two countries.[29]

Climate Change, Energy, and Environment

In the areas of climate, energy, and the environment, the U.S. and China hold multiple bilateral dialogues and exchanges at both the senior and working levels, such as at the Climate Change Policy Dialogue. In addition, they coordinate their participation in several multilateral fora, including the U.N. Climate Change Conference and the Major Economies Forum. At the July 2009 S&ED, China and the U.S. negotiated a memorandum of understanding (MOU) to enhance bilateral cooperation on climate, energy, and the environment. Progress on energy and the environment continues to be made on the Ten Year

Framework on Energy and Environment, established in 2008, and on the seven presidential clean energy initiatives agreed to in 2009.[30] Cooperation has proceeded on joint projects to develop new technologies and incentivizing practices that can reduce emissions, but fundamental disagreements persist on responsibility for environmental damage and burden sharing. Securing an international legally binding commitment to curbing carbon emissions has been elusive, and China has frequently stressed its developing nation status to fend off demands to more quickly reduce carbon emissions.

Development Assistance

As Chinese foreign aid has expanded dramatically over the past decade, the U.S. has sought to engage Beijing in discussions on official development assistance (ODA). China's reticence to coordinate its foreign assistance programs with other Western donor countries and to provide clear figures on its ODA are sources of tension with the U.S. To advance bilateral cooperation in this arena, the U.S. proposed several joint development projects in third countries. The first such project, announced in July 2011 at the ARF, seeks to promote agricultural development and food security in Timor Leste. Bilateral dialogue on foreign assistance ensued between China's Ministry of Commerce and the U.S. Agency of International Development. Progress has been slow, however, as U.S. and Chinese approaches to foreign aid differ radically. The Chinese are studying other countries' ODA policies, but Beijing seems more eager to cooperate in the development working group in the G-20 than with the Development Assistance Committee of the Organization for Economic Cooperation and Development (OECD), which China views as a club of rich nations.

Human Rights

The U.S. and China differ in their conceptual definitions of human rights, with the U.S. emphasizing civic rights such as freedom of speech, assembly, and religion and the right to vote, and China prioritizing economic well-being and social rights, while downplaying the freedom of the individual. Established in 1990, the Human Rights Dialogue (HRD) is led by the U.S. assistant secretary of Democracy, Human Rights, and Labor, and the Chinese director-general of the MFA's Department of International Organizations. Meetings are held irregularly, and have often been postponed by Beijing in retaliation for objectionable U.S. policies such as sponsoring resolutions at the U.N. Human Rights Commission criticizing Beijing, selling arms to Taiwan, and holding meetings between the U.S. president and the Dalai Lama. The mechanism provides a venue for candid dialogue on human rights that is framed within the context of international standards and norms. Issues addressed at the HRD include rule of law, religious freedom, freedom of expression, labor rights, minority issues, multilateral cooperation,[31] recent trends in the human rights field such as forced disappearances and extra-legal detentions, arrests, and convictions,[32] as well as individual cases of concern. Beijing is generally on the defensive in these discussions, with the U.S. side raising concerns about Chinese human rights practices and the Chinese side presenting its achievements in improving and safeguarding people's livelihood, advancing the construction of its legal system, and developing grassroots democracy. Subsumed under the HRD is the Legal Experts Dialogue, at which government and non-government experts from both countries discuss the rule of law and other legal matters of mutual concern in a broader context, including issues such as legal reform, new laws being proposed, implementation of existing laws, the role of lawyers in society and the legal system, and the role of the judiciary.[33]

Critics argue that the HRD and its legal experts' sub-dialogue, like China's human rights discussions with other countries, enable Beijing to keep uncomfortable issues like religious repression, extralegal detention, and the use of torture by the policy largely confined to periodic closed-door discussions that produce few concrete results. Supporters of the HRD, however, cite achievements such as discussions that paved the way for death penalty reforms that led to a sharp drop in the number of executions in China.[34] U.S. officials counter that a closed-door, government-to-government exchange, provides the opportunity to have constructive discussion in which the two sides can respectfully, but directly, disagree, and identify areas of potential agreement and cooperation.[35]

People-to-People Exchanges

The U.S.-China High-Level Consultation on People-to-People Exchange, as described in the chapter in this volume by Terry Lautz, was launched in May 2010 to expand opportunities for meaningful engagement between U.S. and Chinese citizens. Education is a major focus; the "100,000 Strong Initiative" is aimed at dramatically increasing the number of Americans studying in China. There is also the U.S.-China Fulbright Program and a Friendship Volunteers program. Promoting cultural and sports exchanges, and a bilateral Women's Leadership Exchange and Dialogue are additional cooperative endeavors. The U.S. secretary of state co-chairs the mechanism with China's state councilor responsible for education, science and technology, culture and sports.

The U.N. Security Council

As permanent members of the U.N. Security Council (UNSC), the U.S. and China consult and coordinate regularly on many issues. Iran and North Korea are at the top of the U.S.-China agenda at the U.N. Beginning in 2006, Beijing has supported a number of UNSC resolutions that impose sanctions on Iran and North Korea, despite its preference for non-interference in other nations' internal affairs. Negotiations have often been contentious, but in most cases compromises have been struck. Between 2006 and 2010, four UNSC resolutions were passed tightening sanctions against Iran for pursuing a nuclear weapons program. In addition to supporting the toughest sanctions so far against Tehe-ran in UNSCR Resolution 1929 in 2010, China informally agreed to slow its energy investments in Iran, and privately encouraged Iranians to address the concerns of the international community about alleged violations of the NPT.[36] Also between 2006 and mid-2012, three UNSC resolutions were passed and three UNSC Presidential Statements issued imposing sanctions against North Korea for its nuclear and ballistic missile activities and suspected human right violations, and condemning the attack that led to the sinking of the South Ko-rean naval ship *Cheonan* and a North Korean satellite launch in April 2012 in violation of prior UNSC resolutions.

The U.S. and China also successfully coordinated their policies toward Su-dan at the U.N. In the run up to Beijing's hosting of the Olympics in 2008, Chinese disregard for the human rights implications of their investments in Sudan and aid to Khartoum drew criticism from the U.S. and other nations. China's desire to avoid tarnishing its international image provided some lever-age. The U.S. helped persuade Beijing to accept the inevitability of the separa-tion of Southern Sudan and paved the way for a constructive Chinese role in encouraging a free and fair vote on independence for the south, including the dispatch of observers to Sudan for the referendum.

The U.S. and China continue to disagree on many issues at the U.N., in-cluding the use of international force, humanitarian intervention, and U.N. re-form. Although Beijing has historically rarely used its veto on the UNSC—and usually only on resolutions concerning Taiwan—China's growing economic and political clout have emboldened it to exercise that power somewhat more often in recent years, though rarely as the sole outlier. As one former U.S. of-ficial noted, "China now has the strength to pursue its own interests and will walk away from negotiations if it feels they are not in its interests; it now has the ability to say no."[37] Despite intense negotiations, the two countries failed to narrow their differences in January 2007 when China along with Russia vetoed a UNSC resolution that called on Myanmar's government to cease military at-tacks against civilians in ethnic minority regions and commence a substantive political dialogue that would lead to a genuine democratic transition. In Octo-ber 2011 and February 2012, China and Russia vetoed UNSC draft resolutions condemning Syria over its crackdown on anti-government protesters.

Other Global and Regional Institutions

U.S.-Chinese interactions in regional and global multilateral institutions continue to expand. Most importantly, officials from both countries coordinate closely in preparation for meetings both bilaterally and with other nations to promote positive outcomes. Regional institutions include APEC, the ASEAN Regional Forum, the East Asia Summit, and the Pacific Islands Forum; the G-20 is the most prominent global institution other than the U.N. in which the U.S. and China participate.

FRUSTRATIONS AND COMPROMISES

Diplomatic interaction between the U.S. and China has been replete with frustration, irritation, and anger on both sides. Difficulty in forging common strategies to manage diplomatic problems is only seldom due to diverging interests; more commonly it is a result of differences over the best approach to achieve shared objectives. Intense negotiations have more often than not led to compromise. Through many episodes of consuming and intensive deliberations on thorny issues, the U.S. and China have achieved a better understanding of each other's interests and perspectives, and developed strategies to advance their respective agendas.

The U.S. and China use different metrics to evaluate the overall quality of the U.S.-China ties, which engenders frustration on both sides. Beijing typically attaches great significance to the term that the U.S. employs to describe bilateral relationship and expends a lot of energy pressing various U.S. administrations to accept ever more positive language. For example, the Chinese were especially pleased that the Obama administration agreed through consultations with the Chinese that the two countries would pursue a "positive, cooperative, and comprehensive relationship." When China's President Hu Jintao visited the United States in January 2011, the most important phrase in the Joint Statement from China's perspective was that the two countries "committed to work together to build a cooperative partnership based on mutual respect and mutual benefit."[38] The Chinese also measure success in terms of quantity—the number of high-level visits, phone calls, letters, and meetings. From the American perspective, success is measured primarily in the form of concrete achievements such as U.N. Security Council resolutions and Chinese actions in support of U.S. policy agendas.

North Korea has been an especially discordant issue despite shared U.S. and Chinese interests in establishing a nuclear weapons–free Korean Peninsula. Beijing maintains that the "crux" of the problem lies between the U.S. and North Korea and therefore urges bilateral negotiations to find solutions to the concerns of both sides, even as it supports continuing Six Party Talks to ensure Chinese interests are protected. Washington considers that as the country that supplies 90 percent of North Korea's energy and more than half of its imported food, China has significant leverage over Pyongyang's behavior, which it should use to persuade North Korea to abandon its nuclear ambitions. Bilateral and multilateral negotiations over how to respond to North Korea's missile tests, nuclear detonations, and conventional attacks on South Korea have been fraught with friction.

For example, after four rounds of the Six Party Talks between August 2003 and July 2005, Chinese negotiator Wang Yi publicly pinned blame on U.S. policy as the "main obstacle" to reaching a breakthrough in negotiations.[39] A few months later, in September 2005, China brokered an agreement among all six parties that laid out a road map to denuclearization, which the U.S. subsequently praised. Following the sinking of a South Korean corvette, the *Cheonan*, in March 2010, U.S. officials urged China to review the findings of an international investigation that concluded North Korea was the perpetrator and join the U.S. and other countries in the U.N. Security Council in a condemnation of the attack. After being rebuffed by Chinese President Hu Jintao in a meeting on the margins of the June 2010 G-20 summit in Toronto, President Obama publicly charged China with "willful blindness to consistent problems."[40] The U.S. strategy of shaming China and appealing to Beijing's desire to enhance its image as a responsible player was only partly successful given China's overriding interest in maintaining stability on the Korean Peninsula and preserving its close ties with Pyongyang. Negotiations at the U.N. with the other players produced a compromise presidential statement in July that condemned the "attack" and referred to the findings of the Joint Civilian-Military Investigation Group, but did not pin blame on North Korea.

U.S. frustrations boiled over again when North Korea shelled the South's Yeonpyeong Island in November and Beijing refused to censure its belligerent action. A senior U.S. official told the *Washington Post* that China's "embrace of North Korea in the last eight months has served to convince North Korea that China has its back and has encouraged it to behave with impunity. . . . We think the Chinese have been enabling North Korea."[41] U.S.-Chinese differences were narrowed when Hu Jintao, on a state visit to the U.S. in January 2011, agreed to include a clause in the Joint Statement opposing "all activities inconsistent with the 2005 Joint Statement and relevant international obligations and commitments" and voicing concern about North Korea's uranium enrichment program. When Beijing refrained from condemning Pyongyang prior to its failed launch of a satellite in April 2012 in violation of UNSC resolutions, Obama accused China of "rewarding bad behavior." Following the launch, the

U.S. and China quickly led negotiations in the UNSC that resulted in yet another Presidential Statement criticizing North Korea.

Chinese frustrations have run high over the refusal of the U.S. to discuss its arms sales to Taiwan. Following the U.S. approval of large weapons packages for Taiwan in January 2010 and September 2011, Beijing pressed the Obama administration to open discussions on ways to manage differences over Taiwan to prevent further harm to the U.S.-China relationship, but Washington resisted. Another issue that riled the Chinese was U.S. unwillingness to reiterate language in the January 2011 Sino-U.S. Joint Statement that had been included in the November 2009 bilateral Joint Statement that referenced "respect for each other's core interests as extremely important to ensure steady progress in U.S.-Chinese relations." The U.S. side demurred because the concept of "core interests" had generated considerable controversy domestically, in Taiwan, and between Washington and Beijing. Seventy hours of arduous negotiations were required to finalize the 2011 Joint Statement. Knowing that signing a Joint Statement during Hu's visit to the U.S. was more important to Beijing than to Washington, the U.S. effectively employed leverage and China was compelled to yield on the inclusion of "core interests" and concur on the language on North Korea.

Other diplomatic issues that have caused U.S. frustration in recent years include China's resistance to revalue its currency, lack of progress in discussions about human rights, China's refusal to provide data on its ODA and coordinate with Western aid donors, and Beijing's decisions to veto several UNSC resolutions: 1) calling on Myanmar to release all political prisoners, initiate a wide-ranging dialogue, and end military attacks and human rights abuses (January 2007); 2) proposing sanctions against Zimbabwe for human rights violations (July 2008); and 3) condemning Syria for its military crackdown against civilians (October 2011 and February 2012). In the case of the four UNSC resolutions, the U.S. strategy of isolating China and calling into question its willingness to be a responsible global player failed in part because Russia provided cover by joining China in exercising its veto.

Apart from U.S. policy toward Taiwan, Chinese frustrations mainly arise on economic issues. China claims that the environment for Chinese companies to invest in the United States is not favorable and seeks U.S. government help to improve it. Moreover, Beijing has not been successful in its efforts to persuade the U.S. to ease restrictions on high-tech exports to China that have been in place since the violent Tiananmen Square crackdown in 1989. U.S. interference in matters that China considers domestic, such as human rights, or unsuitable for U.S. intervention, such as the South China Sea, continue to provoke objections, although Beijing appreciates that discussions with the U.S. on such issues is necessary to manage and improve the overall relationship.

EFFICACY OF U.S.-CHINA POLITICAL DIALOGUES

The U.S. and China have made headway in reducing misperceptions and mis-understanding, managing areas of competition and friction, improving policy coordination on a broad range of issues, and identifying new arenas of cooperation. Progress achieved so far is in large part due to increasingly frequent and intensive dialogue at all levels, most importantly between U.S. and Chinese presidents, but also between senior cabinet officials, diplomats, and working-level experts. Moreover, dialogue mechanisms have expanded, become more frequent and regular, and cover more issues than in the past.

Arguably most important among these institutionalized mechanisms is the S&ED, which has facilitated closer personal relationships between senior cabinet-level officials, promoted interagency coordination, and provided a platform to discuss an ever-broadening agenda of geographical and functional issues. The establishment of new sub-dialogues under the S&ED has enabled both sides to tackle emerging and pressing problems in the relationship. The Asia-Pacific Consultations were launched at Beijing's suggestion to discuss U.S. and Chinese strategies around China's periphery and avert the adoption of zero-sum approaches that could result in greater rivalry. The SSD was created at Washington's behest, to simultaneously engage civilian and defense officials on critical security matters that have the potential to cause a major crisis.

Bilateral dialogue mechanisms have played a positive role in enhancing exchange of information and increasing policy transparency and predictability. The extensive and varied structure of dialogue channels have been aimed at promoting mutual understanding and building habits of cooperation between the U.S. and China, a relationship which lacks the multitude of conduits and connections that exist in U.S. relations with its allies. They have also been intended to prevent miscalculation and build relationships between counterparts that could be activated in a crisis to defuse tensions.

Deliberate efforts to identify new arenas of cooperation and increase people-to-people exchanges have provided a critical balance to negative aspects of the bilateral relationship such as increased mutual suspicion and competition in the security realm. Successful cooperation on developing alternative energy sources and environmental protection aids, for example, have helped to offset mounting friction in other areas of the relationship such as the South China Sea. Cooperative endeavors serve to remind elites and domestic publics in both countries of the shared interests and potential for working together in pursuit of greater common prosperity and global stability. Coordination on a range of issues of importance to both countries has improved, including counterterrorism, non-proliferation, energy security, and environmental protection.

Despite the achievement of greater understanding of each others' policies and initiation of new forms of cooperation, it is nevertheless undeniable that strategic mistrust persists and is likely increasing. The absence of trust is driven in part by immediate policies but even more so by suspicions about the other country's long-term intentions. This is especially true in China where the leadership portrays the U.S. as engaged in a strategic plot to "westernize and divide" the country, and the media regularly maintains the U.S. intends to harm Chinese vital national interests and prevent the country from reemerging as a major power. China's arrival as a global economic power and its growing political influence and military capabilities has unleashed heretofore repressed nationalistic sentiment and created increased demands on Chinese leaders for the nation's interests to be respected that they ignore at their own peril. The lack of shared values or common political systems between the U.S. and China makes achieving greater strategic trust especially challenging.

U.S. concerns persist about a range of Chinese behavior along with worry that once China becomes more powerful it will seek to alter the international system in ways that could be damaging to American interests. Washington's goal of persuading China to become a "responsible stakeholder" in the international system has achieved only limited and uneven success. On the positive side of the ledger, China's nonproliferation record and policies have improved and Beijing has demonstrated a willingness to selectively use pressure and influence to promote changes in policy in Iran, North Korea, and Sudan. On the negative side, China has been reluctant to coordinate its ODA with other foreign donors to promote improved governance in developing countries and is disinclined to coordinate its policies with the U.S. toward Pakistan and other countries. The lack of progress toward convincing China to take on the role of "responsible stakeholder" is primarily a result of two factors: 1) Beijing does not fully share the Western definition of "responsible" and has its own views about how to address regional and global problems; and 2) China is still reluctant to assume leadership roles and the burdens that they entail due to its focus on domestic development.

The U.S. remains the main *demandeur* in the relationship. "China is still primarily reactive," noted one former U.S. official. "We seek to get China to do something and the Chinese are often trying to fend off pressure." The bulk of the initiatives are tabled by the U.S. side; the Chinese remain "very bureaucratic and not very creative."[42] U.S. strategies that have achieved a degree of success in persuading China to adopt specific policies include: 1) leverag-

ing upcoming international events and high-level bilateral meetings to enlist
Chinese cooperation; 2) engaging in direct dialogue at senior levels; 3) giving
China respect and "face"; 4) employing positive and negative inducements;
and 5) "shaming" China and appealing to Beijing's desire to have a positive
international reputation.[43] Often, however, the most effective strategy is convincing China that a different policy better serves its national interests.

To further strengthen the U.S.-China relationship, existing dialogue
mechanisms should be utilized to dispel strategic mistrust. Strategic dialogue must move beyond immediate challenges and focus on how to jointly
shape mutually beneficial outcomes. In particular, the American approach
that focuses on obtaining Chinese support for the U.S. agenda should instead center on identifying ways that the U.S. and China can work together
to address regional and global problems more effectively. As Michael Swaine
has argued, a genuine strategic dialogue "would need to connect separate
global, regional, and functional policy issues with a large discussion of
Chinese and American grand strategic objectives and interests over time,
in the context of several alternative possible changes in the structural environment facing both countries."[44] For example, discussion of North Korea
must include more in-depth consideration of long-term U.S. and Chinese
intentions in Northeast Asia and a road map developed for establishing permanent peace on the Korean Peninsula. On especially sensitive issues, such
as U.S. surveillance at the edges of China's 12-mile territorial waters, nuclear
weapons, cybersecurity, and military use of outer space, in-depth dialogue is
needed, but should also be complemented by actions: the United States and
China should pursue mutual restraint and reciprocal reassurance in these
areas to ease mistrust.[45]

In addition to deeper and more comprehensive dialogue, closer personal
relationships between U.S. officials and Chinese counterparts should be forged
through regular and sustained dialogue. It is especially critical for the U.S. and
Chinese presidents to establish a good personal rapport and a high level of
credibility. More concerted efforts are needed to identify potential areas of cooperation where interests overlap. Effective cooperation on concrete projects
and policies is essential to prevent rivalry from overwhelming the agenda and
the broader relationship. Finally, the U.S. and China should enhance coordination in multilateral forums to promote further integration of China into the
international system.

TEXTBOX 7.1. U.S.-Chinese Dialogue Mechanisms

U.S.-CHINA JOINT COMMISSION ON COMMERCE AND TRADE
Trade
1. Transparency Dialogue
2. Trade Remedies Working Groups
3. Anti-Monopoly Dialogue
4. Commercial Law Working Group
5. Structural Issues Working Group
6. Business Development and Industrial Cooperation Working Group
7. Telecommunications Dialogue
8. Insurance Dialogue
9. Industries and Competitiveness Dialogue
10. Broadband Wireless Internet Protocol Standard Group
11. Statistics Working Group
12. High-Technology and Strategic Trade Working Group
13. Industrial and Innovation Policies Dialogue

Intellectual Property Rights
14. Intellectual Property Rights Law Enforcement Group
15. Intellectual Property Rights Criminal Enforcement Working Group
16. Government and SOE Procurement Group
17. Intellectual Property Rights Working Group on Software Legalization

Sectors
18. Agricultural Trade Working Group
19. Textiles Consultative Group
20. Travel and Tourism Working Group
21. Information Industry Working Group
22. Steel Dialogue
23. Administration of Quality Supervision, Inspection and Quarantine (AQSIQ) Technical Group
24. U.S.-China Joint Liaison Group on Law Enforcement Cooperation

U.S.-CHINA STRATEGIC AND ECONOMIC DIALOGUE
Energy
25. Climate Change Policy Dialogue
26. Energy Policy Dialogue
27. Ten Year Framework (TYF) Joint Working Group (energy-related)
28. U.S.-China Energy Efficiency Forum
29. Oil and Gas Industry Forum
30. Renewable Energy Forum
31. Advanced Biofuels Forum

Diplomatic
32. U.S.-China Strategic Security Dialogue
33. U.S.-China Human Rights Dialogue
34. U.S.-China International Security and Non-Proliferation Dialogue
35. U.S.-China Discussions on Law of the Sea and Polar Issues
36. U.S.-China Policy Planning Dialogue
37. U.S.-China Counterterrorism and Security Consultation

TEXTBOX 7.1. U.S.-Chinese Dialogue Mechanisms (*continued*)

Diplomatic/Regional
38. Africa Dialogue
39. South and Central Asia Dialogue
40. Latin America Dialogue
41. Asia-Pacific Consultations

Sectors
42. Forum on Traditional Chinese Medicine
43. Transportation Forum
44. Railway Program Exchange
45. Joint Working Group of Agricultural Science and Technology Cooperation
46. Export Controls Dialogue
47. Legal Experts Dialogue
48. U.S.-China Bilateral Forum on Combating Illegal Logging and Associated Trade

OTHER
49. U.S.-China Anti-Corruption Working Group
50. U.S.-China Investment Forum
51. U.S.-China Initiative on City-Level Economic Cooperation
52. U.S.-China Governors Forum
53. U.S.-China High-Level Consultation on People-to-People Exchange
54. U.S.-China Women's Leadership Exchange and Dialogue

QUASI-INDEPENDENT
55. Joint Experts Dialogue on Rules of Origin
56. Annual Labor Dialogue
57. Sino-American Symposium on Health Care Reforms
58. Economic Development and Reform Dialogue
59. Joint Financial Committee
60. Joint Commission on Science and Technology

U.S.-CHINA MILITARY DIALOGUES
61. Defense Consultative Talks
62. Defense Policy Consultative Talks
63. Military Maritime Consultative Agreement
64. U.S.-China Nuclear Experts Dialogue

Sources: Nina Hachigan, "Looking Past the 'Orchestra Pit' on China," Blog Post, Democracy Arsenal, May 13, 2011, http://www.democracyarsenal.org/2011/05/looking-past-the-orchestra-pit-on-china .html; Derek Scissors, "Tools to Build the U.S.-China Economic Relationship," August 8, 2011, Heritage Foundation Backgrounder #2590, http://www.heritage.org/research/reports/2011/08/tools-to-build-the-us-china-economic-relationship; author interviews.

NOTES

The author is indebted to CSIS research associate and program manager Brittany Bill-ingsley for her invaluable research assistance in the preparation of this chapter.

1. Office of the Historian, U.S. Department of State, available at: http://history .state.gov/milestones/1953-1960/ChinaTalks.

2. Susan L. Shirk, "China's Multilateral Diplomacy in the Asia-Pacific," testimony before the U.S.-China Economic and Security Review Commission, February 12–13, 2004, available at: http://www.uscc.gov/hearings/2004hearings/written_testimonies/04_02_12wrts/shirk.htm.

3. Robert B. Zoellick, "Whither China: From Membership to Responsibility?" remarks to National Committee on U.S.-China Relations, September 21, 2005, available at: http://www.ncuscr.org/files/2005Gala_RobertZoellick_Whither_China1.pdf.

4. Writing in a volume published in 1981, Michel Oksenberg called for the U.S.-China relationship to be institutionalized so that it would survive the almost inevitable leadership struggles and political changes ahead. "The Dynamics of the Sino-American Relationship," in *The China Factor: Sino-American Relations and the Global Scene*, Richard H. Solomon (ed.) (Englewood Cliffs, NJ: Prentice-Hall, 1981). See also Chen Dongxiao, "Complexity and Transformational Structure of China-U.S. Relations," in *China-U.S. Relations Transformed: Perspectives and Strategic Interactions*," Zhao Suisheng (New York: Routledge, 2008), pp. 58–74.

5. China's core interests, as defined in the September 6, 2011 *White Paper on China's Peaceful Development*, include: state sovereignty, national security, territorial integrity and national reunification, China's political system established by the Constitution and overall social stability, and the basic safeguards for ensuring sustainable economic and social development. Available at: http://news.xinhuanet.com/english2010/china/2011-09/06/c_131102329.htm.

6. See Alan G. Whittaker, Frederick C. Smith, and Elizabeth McKune, *The National Security Policy Process: The National Security Council and Interagency System* (Washington, DC: Industrial College of the Armed Forces, National Defense University, October 8, 2010), available at: http://www.ndu.edu/icaf/outreach/publications/nspp/docs/icaf-nsc-policy-process-report-08-2011.pdf, p. 17.

7. Ibid., p. 32.

8. See Michael D. Swaine, *America's Challenge: Engaging a Rising China in the Twenty-First Century* (Washington, DC: Carnegie Endowment for International Peace, 2011), p. 610.

9. Interview with senior former Obama administration official, October 20, 2011, Washington, DC.

10. Alice L. Miller, "Hu Jintao and the Party Politburo," *China Leadership Monitor*, No. 9 (Winter 2004); and Jean-Pierre Cabestan, "China's Foreign and Security Policy Decision-Making Processes Under Hu Jintao," *Journal of Current Chinese Affairs*, Vol. 38, No. 3 (2009), pp. 63–97.

11. Linda Jacobson and Dean Knox, *New Foreign Policy Actors in China*, SIPRI (Stockholm International Peace Research Institute, Policy Paper No. 26, September 2010), p. 5.

12. Interview with Chinese military officer, February 14, 2003, Beijing.

13. Interview with U.S. NSC official, October 20, 2011, Washington, DC.

14. See textbox 7.1.

15. Interview with former U.S. NSC official, October 20, 2011, Washington, DC.

16. According to a PRC embassy official, in advance of S&ED sessions, interagency meetings are held in China to resolve differences and coordinate positions. The official cited progress in coordination on enforcement of intellectual property rights protection as an example. Interview with Chinese embassy official, October 26, 2011, Washington, DC.

17. Interviews with current and former U.S. officials, October 3 and 19–20, 2011, Washington, DC.

18. Ibid.

19. Elizabeth C. Economy and Adam Segal, "The G-2 Mirage," *Foreign Affairs*, Vol. 88, No. 3 (May/June 2009), pp. 14–23.

20. Dennis Wilder, "The U.S.-China Strategic and Economic Dialogue: Continuity and Change in Obama's China Policy," *China Brief*, Vol. 9, No. 10, May 15, 2009, available at: http://www.jamestown.org/uploads/media/cb_009_02.pdf.

21. Interviews with current and former U.S. government officials, October 19–20, 2011, Washington, DC.

22. Swaine, *America's Challenge*, p. 134.

23. Interview with U.S. State Department official, October 3, 2011, Washington, DC.

24. "U.S. China Joint Statement," The White House, Office of the Press Secretary, November 17, 2009, available at: http://www.whitehouse.gov/the-press-office/us-china-joint-statement; and "U.S. China Joint Statement," The White House, Office of the Press Secretary, January 19, 2011, available at: http://www.whitehouse.gov/the-press-office/2011/01/19/us-china-joint-statement.

25. Between 2005 and 2011, the *renminbi* appreciated 25 percent. See also Arthur R. Kroeber, "The Renminbi: The Political Economy of a Currency," *Shaping the Emerging Global Order*, No. 3 (September 2011), available at: http://www.brookings.edu/papers/2011/0907_renminbi_kroeber.aspx.

26. Interview with former Obama administration official, October 20, 2011.

27. Richard Weitz, "Is China Freeloading Off the U.S. Military's Work in Afghanistan and Iraq?" *The Diplomat*, August 15, 2011, available at: http://www.huffingtonpost.com/2011/08/15/china-military-afghanistan-iraq_n_927342.html.

28. "China Plays Nice in Afghanistan," October 21, 2009, available at: http://www.strategypage.com/htmw/htun/20091021.aspx.

29. Andrew Small, "China's Caution on Afghanistan-Pakistan," *The Washington Quarterly*, Vol. 33, No. 3 (2010), pp. 81–97.

30. "U.S.-China Clean Energy Cooperation," U.S. Department of Energy, January 2011, available at: http://www.us-china-cerc.org/pdfs/U.S._China_Clean_Energy_Progress_Report.pdf.

31. U.S. Department of State, Bureau of East Asian and Pacific Affairs, "Background Note: China," September 6, 2011, available at: http://www.state.gov/r/pa/ei/bgn/18902.htm.

32. U.S. Department of State, Office of the Spokesman, "United States and China to Hold Human Rights Dialogue," media note, April 21, 2011, available at: http://www.state.gov/r/pa/prs/ps/2011/04/161492.htm.

33. U.S. Department of State, "China: U.S.-China Legal Experts Dialogue," media note, June 6, 2011, Washington, DC, available at: http://www.state.gov/r/pa/prs/ps/2011/06/165160.htm.

34. Andrew Jacobs, "Always Awkward, New Rights Talks With China Now May Be Hopeless," *New York Times*, April 28, 2011.

35. U.S. Department of State, "Briefing on the U.S.-China Human Rights Dialogue," special briefing, May 14, 2010, Washington, DC, available at: http://www.state.gov/r/pa/prs/ps/2010/05/141899.htm.

36. Interviews with current and former U.S. government officials, October 19–20, 2011, Washington, DC.

37. Interview with former U.S. NSC official, October 19, 2011, Washington, DC.

38. U.S.-China Joint Statement, January 19, 2011.

39. Joseph Kahn, "Chinese Aide Says U.S. Is Obstacle in Korean Talks," *New York Times*, September 2, 2003.

40. Simon Martin, "N. Korea vows to bolster nuclear deterrent," AFP, June 27, 2010.

41. John Pomfret, "U.S. Raises Pressure on China to Rein in N. Korea," *Washington Post*, December 6, 2010.

42. Interview with U.S. NSC official, October 20, 2011, Washington, DC.

43. Swaine, *America's Challenge*, pp. 327–335.

44. Ibid., p. 354.

45. See, for example, David C. Gompert and Phillip C. Saunders, *The Paradox of Power* (Washington, DC: National Defense University Press, 2011).

8

The Commercial and Economic Relationship

Charles W. Freeman III

In the early 1970s, when the United States and China began the set of official exchanges that would attempt to map out the broad parameters of their
relationship, commercial relations were essentially an afterthought. The fundamental purpose of the early overtures was geo-strategic, and trade was far
from the minds of U.S. officials. Ambassador John Negroponte, who accompanied Dr. Kissinger to China in 1972, recalls colleagues at the State Department
asking one another incredulously during the early years before normalization,
"What are we going to buy from these people?"

In 1972, the first year the two countries resumed trade relations, the United
States imported $32.4 million in goods from China, and exported $63.5 million
in goods to China. In 2011, nearly 40 years later, U.S. imports from China were
$399.3 billion and exports were $103.9 billion. China was the United States'
second largest trading partner after Canada in 2011 and its largest source of
imports by nearly $83 billion. By December 2011 China held $3.2 trillion in
foreign exchange reserves, largely in U.S. dollar denominated assets.[1] U.S. negotiators no longer wonder what China can sell the United States. Rather, U.S.
officials are now confronted by a public that is increasingly alarmed at the
extent to which China is a primary source of consumer goods and a major
creditor of the United States.[2]

The explosion of China's importance as an import source and holder of
U.S. debt is not the whole story of U.S.-China economic relations. By 2011,
China had been the fastest growing export market for U.S. firms for some
15 years. Between 2000 and 2011, U.S. exports to China grew by 542 percent
compared to 80 percent export growth with the rest of the world.[3] U.S.-based
multinationals with operations in China were overwhelmingly focused not

TABLE 8.1. China's Trade with the United States, 2001–2011 ($ billion)

	2000	2001	2002	2003	2004	2005	2006	2007	2008	2009	2010	2011
U.S. exports	16.3	19.2	22.1	28.4	34.7	41.8	55.2	65.2	71.5	69.6	91.9	103.9
% change	23.9	18.3	14.7	28.9	22.2	20.5	32.0	18.1	9.5	-2.6	32.1	13.1
U.S. imports	100.1	102.3	125.2	152.4	196.7	243.5	287.8	321.5	337.8	296.4	364.9	399.3
% change	22.3	2.2	22.4	21.7	29.1	23.8	18.2	11.7	5.1	-12.3	23.1	9.4
U.S. balance	-83.8	-83.0	-103.1	-124.0	-162.0	-201.6	-232.5	-256.3	-266.3	-226.8	-273.1	-295.5

Source: U.S. International Trade Commission; U.S. Department of Commerce.

on using China as an export platform, but on serving the growing Chinese domestic market. Indeed, given the slowing opportunities for new growth in mature markets in North America and Europe, U.S. multinationals had become increasingly reliant on China's market to provide significant current and long-term revenue growth.

THE U.S. ECONOMY AS A MODEL

China's extraordinary rise from underachiever to become the world's second largest economy just over 30 years after Deng Xiaoping initiated the "reform and opening up" process parallels the expansion of relations with the United States. Indeed, while one would not want to overstate the enormity of importance the United States played in that rise as both a market and a mentor, the U.S. relationship has certainly been a critical factor. For one thing, net exports have been a significant contributor to China's gross domestic product (GDP) growth over that period (although characterizing China's economy as purely "export driven" is inaccurate), and demand from the United States has been a fundamental driver of positive export growth.[4] Furthermore, China's embrace of market principles and the norms of international trade were made with an eye to the United States as an economic model. While few Chinese officials have viewed the United States as an ideal for Chinese development, during the 30 years of reform and opening up between 1978 and 2007 the U.S. way was accorded tremendous deference among leading Chinese policy circles.[5]

During the run-up to and in the years immediately following China's 2001 accession to the World Trade Organization (WTO), PRC policymakers routinely studied U.S. economic systems with a view to their application to China's unique paradigm. The operation of U.S. banking, insurance, logistics, manufacturing, and other sectors were analyzed with almost devotional fervor. While Chinese policy professionals were always certain to warn that China's unique economic structure would make wholesale adoption of these systems impossible, the unspoken goal of the efforts to understand the U.S. economic structure was to seek to adopt as much of the underpinnings of this structure as possible while still maintaining the underlying socioeconomic oversight mandated by Communist Party control.[6]

China's drive to WTO accession is a useful example of the influence of the U.S. market and economic model on Chinese policymaking during the heyday of economic reform.[7] While the WTO accession process was fueled in part by a raw patriotic desire to achieve membership in a prestigious multilateral body, two practical economic rationales also animated the effort. First, then Premier Zhu Rongji and other reformers had decided that vested interests among Chinese state-owned enterprises and the economic bureaucracy were obstacles

TABLE 8.2. Selected Economic and Financial Indicators, 2000–2011

	2000	2001	2002	2003	2004	2005	2006	2007	2008	2009	2010	2011
GDP	9,921.5	10,965.5	12,033.3	13,582.3	15,987.8	18,493.7	21,631.4	26,581.0	31,404.5	34,090.3	40,120.2	47,156.4
% growth (real GDP growth)	8.4	8.3	9.1	10.0	10.1	10.4	11.6	13.0	9.0	8.7	10.4	9.2
Consumer price index	0.4	0.7	−0.8	1.2	3.9	1.8	1.5	4.8	5.9	−0.7	3.3	5.4
Industrial value-added output*	2,539.5	2,832.9	3,299.5	4,199.0	5,480.5	7,218.7	9,107.6	11,704.8	N/A	N/A	N/A	N/A
% growth	17.8	11.6	16.5	27.3	30.5	31.7	26.2	28.5	12.9	11.0	15.7	13.9
Fixed-asset investment**	3,291.8	3,721.3	4,350.0	5,556.7	7,047.4	8,877.4	10,999.8	13,732.4	17,282.8	22,459.9	27,812.2	N/A
% growth	10.3	13.0	16.9	27.7	26.8	26.0	23.9	24.8	25.9	30.0	23.8	N/A

Source: China National Bureau of Statistics. All GDP-related figures in billions of RMB.

*All state-owned industrial enterprises and all non-state industrial enterprises with revenue from principal business of more than RMB 5 million. Beginning in 2008, NBS releases listed only the growth rate, not the absolute figure.

**2011 overall fixed-asset statistics not available, though NBS has reported official fixed-asset investment statistics for China excluding rural areas, which came to RMB 30,193.3 and a growth rate of 23.8% over a similar figure from the year before. These are not comparable, however, with the overall fixed-asset investment figures reported previously.

to the development-through-reform agenda.[8] By seizing on the national goal of WTO membership, the reformers effectively deployed external pressures to overcome domestic intransigence to implementation of their agenda. Not surprisingly, the most active and forceful source of external pressure was the United States which, through the negotiating team led by the United States Trade Representative, sought to make China's commercial regulatory landscape as friendly to U.S. sectoral interests, and thus as similar to U.S. economic structures, as possible. This is not to suggest that the negotiations between the United States and other WTO members were not hard-fought and occasionally bare-knuckled. But the prevailing economic policymaking authorities in China were deeply enamored of the U.S. economic system, so a process that forced recalcitrant Chinese industries and bureaucracies to become more like U.S. counterparts was far from unwelcome to the architects of reform and WTO accession.[9]

A second major practical motivator behind China's WTO accession was a desire to overcome the embarrassment and uncertainty that was the annual "most favored nation" (MFN, also called "normal trade relations" or NTR) debate in the United States Congress.[10] The 1974 Jackson-Vanick amendment to U.S. trade law effectively allows the United States to treat as conditional the rights of certain, "non-market" economies to enjoy access to the United States market on terms no less favorable than any other economy with which the United States trades on a "normal" basis. While Jackson-Vanick is inconsistent with WTO rules, U.S. trade with China, as a non-member of WTO, was the subject of ferocious congressional debate each spring in the 1990s when representatives from the business and labor lobbies would descend on Capitol Hill, with representatives of religious freedom and human rights organizations and others joining the fray.[11] On one hand, that debate was deeply offensive to Chinese leaders that viewed the public criticism of China as an effort to interfere in Chinese internal affairs. On the other, and more alarming to the architects of Chinese economic policy, the annual debate and maintenance of China's "conditional" MFN or NTR status injected significant risk for investors into the Chinese export sector that the U.S. market was only temporarily open. Joining WTO would require the United States to accord China "permanent" NTR and thus allow greater certainty for investors in China's important export sector.

Clearly the United States was not the sole market of importance nor economic policy beacon for Beijing during the 30-year period of reform and opening up between 1978 and 2007. Chinese officials carefully studied Europe, Japan and the Asian tigers for policy elements that worked and might have application for Chinese development.[12] But in many respects, many Chinese economic thinkers viewed the United States economy as the gold standard, and policymakers took seriously the policy recommendations of U.S. coun-terparts. For the better part of the years leading up to WTO accession and the six years that followed, standard practice among U.S. trade negotiators when faced with Chinese trade policies they did not like was to negatively contrast those policies with U.S. standards. While this certainly did not guarantee a fix to the policies, it almost always guaranteed a respectful audience.[13]

Financial Crisis and Revelation

The post-2008 global economic crisis changed that dynamic dramatically. The rapid unraveling of the U.S. financial markets, the revelation of previously un-disclosed hazards, and the fragility of the U.S. economy to credit risks were deeply alarming to many Chinese that had staked their professional lives and reputations on aspirations to achieve American-style economic systems. As Vice Premier Wang Qishan noted in 2008 with both sarcasm and understate-ment: "The teachers now have some problems."[14] The public reaction among Chinese commentators to the crisis and the apparent humbling of the "teach-ers" was a hysterical mix of outraged betrayal, embarrassment at having been "hoodwinked," and nervousness at being set adrift in uncertain economic wa-ters. The crisis also sparked a furious debate about why China emerged from the crisis in relatively robust economic health, and an attempt to define and put forward China's unique economic model as having been successful *because* of the differences from U.S. and other Western economies, rather than because of the similarities or borrowed policies.[15]

In any case, the crisis effectively ended the automatic granting of a respect-ful audience to U.S. trade negotiators and economic policymakers who seek to counsel Chinese officials on the "correct" (i.e., American standard) way of doing things. Whether or not the "China model," loosely defined by some commentators as referring to "state directed capitalism," is an effective alter-native to U.S. and other Western models to deliver long-term sustainable and equitable development, Chinese officials are increasingly convinced that they no longer have much to learn from American counterparts on economic mat-ters.[16] At the same time, political interests in the United States increasingly view trade with suspicion and see China as a peer competitor in strategic, eco-nomic and normative terms; chipping away at the 60-year consensus that sup-ported a global liberalized trade agenda and viewed constructive engagement with China as a sine qua non of a successful Asia-Pacific diplomatic strategy.[17] As a result, the already testy trade relationship between the two countries, be-set by public suspicions of unfairness in both countries, has become that much less simple for the two governments to manage.[18]

Public Mistrust

The disconnect in perceptions between the two countries on their economic relationship is palpable. While many Americans believe that China is singularly responsible for the hollowing out of the U.S. manufacturing sector, many Chinese believe that U.S. policy is deliberately aimed at maintaining China as a low-value, labor-intensive economy. A common Chinese narrative portrays U.S. and other foreign interests as carefully constraining Chinese production to final processing of goods of which the lion's share of the value is owned and controlled by U.S. and other foreign interests. Both officials and members of the Chinese public frequently complain that foreigners are profiting excessively from China's export machine, either by hoarding rights to higher value components of Chinese-assembled goods, or by commanding retail prices from final consumers that represent dramatic mark-ups to the price paid to Chinese suppliers.[19] This sense that China needs to reassert control over a larger share of the value of goods that pass through the Chinese supply chain is reflected in a variety of policies that add to suspicions among Americans that China is seeking to undercut comparative advantages of the United States.[20] A 2010 American Chamber of Commerce survey indicated growing concerns among U.S. businesses in China about discriminatory government regulations that favor domestic companies and other policies that limit market access to sectors that had been open to foreign investment for the past 30 years.[21] A CNN poll in November 2010 revealed that 58 percent of American respondents saw "China's wealth and economic power" as a threat to the United States compared to 35 percent who saw it as an opportunity.[22]

A HAPPY INTERDEPENDENCE

The shifting paradigm and the rancorous political overtones of the U.S.-China economic relationship emanating from both Washington and Beijing tend to obscure the essential feature of that relationship: for most of the decade from 1998–2008 during which trade relations between the United States and China exploded in importance, the two economies have been intimately interdependent and remarkably complementary. While the prevailing political narrative in the United States is that China's economic success has been a result of U.S. manufacturers shifting jobs and production to China as imports from China displace goods made in the United States, that traditional story does not bear up under rigorous scrutiny.

For one thing, the story fails to account for the realities of the hyper-efficient global supply chain.[23] What we buy from China and what we sell to

China have been, for the great majority of the last 30 years, very different. We have been in large part buying products from China of which our manufacturers ceased final assembly years prior to China's arrival on the international trade scene. Final production of electronics, toys, garments, and other labor-intensive goods began migrating from Hong Kong, Japan, Taiwan and Korea to mainland China in the 1990s and, while those economies maintained footholds in the supply chain that led to China, the origin of U.S. imports of these goods began to be stamped "Made in China" at that time. This phenomenon has resulted in a relative (as a percentage of GDP) reduction of the trade deficit from other Asian markets even as the U.S. deficit with China has ballooned to compensate.[24] Taken together, however, the U.S. deficit with Asia has remained fairly constant relative to GDP, so discerning unique employment and manufacturing losses to China is hard to pinpoint by product category.

On the other hand, the United States primarily sells products to China that are not made competitively in China, such as higher-end technology and manufactured goods; branded products; and agricultural goods that China struggles to produce domestically to meet expanding consumer demands. For these sectors, the primary source of competition for the United States is not China or developing Asia. Rather, it is Japan and Western Europe. While some stages of goods production have shifted from the United States to China in the past 30 years, U.S. exports to China and production of higher-value inputs that are embodied in Chinese-assembled goods are an important part of the China trade story.[25]

A significant problem with identifying which imports from China might be displacing U.S. production is that the dynamic global supply chain has made bilateral and even regional trade statistics relatively meaningless.[26] Quite simply, the statistical methodology utilized to determine the origin of an import assigns the full value of an import to the country in which the good in question was finally assembled. An enormous number of products that Americans buy from China are *processing trade goods*. That is, the only value that China adds to the goods is the labor required to assemble a number of inputs exported to China from East Asia, primarily, but also other parts of the world, including the United States. In other words, a good assembled in China may contain technology produced in Taiwan, Japan, Korea or Thailand under license from a U.S. intellectual property owner. The value of the other inputs, particularly that of the U.S. intellectual property, may vastly exceed that of the Chinese value added, but the imported product is treated for statistical purposes as having been designed and built completely within China.

TABLE 8.3. U.S. Trade Deficit with China and Other Countries, 2000–2011

	2000	2001	2002	2003	2004	2005	2006	2007	2008	2009	2010	2011
China	-83,833.0	-83,096.1	-103,064.9	-124,068.2	-162,254.3	-202,278.1	-234,101.3	-258,506.0	-268,039.8	-226,877.2	-273,063.2	-295,456.5
% of trade deficit	19.2	20.2	22.0	23.3	24.8	26.2	28.3	32.0	32.8	45.1	43.0	40.7
Other East Asia	-142,763.6	-121,955.6	-126,258.0	-123,330.1	-141,534.7	-152,500.1	-162,109.5	-146,891.7	-126,677.9	-84,937.0	-94,220.9	-99,037.1
% of trade deficit	32.7	29.6	27.0	23.2	21.6	19.7	19.6	18.2	15.5	16.9	14.8	13.6
Brunei	-227.5	-295.0	-240.7	-385.0	-358.0	-513.1	-502.2	-264.9	-2.7	58.6	112.3	160.9
Burma	-453.8	-458.5	-346.1	-268.8	11.7	5.4	7.5	7.5	10.8	6.8	9.7	48.8
Cambodia	-793.9	-932.9	-1,041.8	-1,204.2	-1,438.5	-1,697.3	-2,113.9	-2,324.6	-2,257.3	-1,797.1	-2,147.0	-2,526.6
Hong Kong	3,133.0	4,381.4	3,266.2	4,699.3	6,513.5	7,459.3	9,795.5	12,875.7	15,015.2	17,479.6	22,274.1	32,214.8
Indonesia	-7,965.2	-7,583.0	-7,087.6	-6,998.7	-8,139.1	-8,960.4	-10,346.2	-10,331.6	-10,154.7	-7,831.6	-9,532.2	-11,696.4
Japan	-81,555.0	-69,021.6	-69,979.4	-66,032.4	-76,236.5	-83,323.1	-89,721.8	-84,303.8	-74,120.4	-44,669.5	-60,059.6	-62,643.0
Laos	-5.4	-0.1	1.4	0.6	2.5	5.6	-1.7	-14.5	-24.1	-23.1	-47.1	-32.8
Malaysia	-14,630.9	-12,962.6	-13,665.3	-14,526.1	-17,328.7	-23,224.3	-24,089.1	-20,948.3	-17,786.6	-12,879.3	-11,820.5	-11,553.9
Mongolia	-99.2	-131.8	-95.5	-162.6	-211.0	-121.8	-90.8	-57.5	4.5	25.7	103.9	302.3
North Korea	2.6	0.5	25.0	8.0	22.3	5.8	0.0	1.7	52.2	0.9	1.9	9.4
Singapore	-1,372.0	2,651.8	1,415.5	1,422.4	4,027.0	5,356.0	6,057.5	7,224.9	11,968.7	6,526.9	11,590.2	12,282.3
South Korea	-12,477.7	-13,000.8	-12,996.0	-13,156.8	-19,981.2	-16,209.8	-13,584.5	-13,160.6	-13,400.4	-10,603.7	-10,028.9	-13,130.5
Taiwan	-16,096.7	-15,252.6	-13,766.2	-14,151.5	-13,038.4	-13,211.3	-15,502.5	-12,448.9	-11,399.8	-9,876.5	-9,802.6	-15,429.4
Thailand	-9,768.1	-8,737.6	-9,932.7	-9,343.2	-11,210.5	-12,633.1	-14,550.9	-14,418.2	-14,471.7	-12,164.1	-13,716.2	-13,898.5
Vietnam	-453.8	-592.8	-1,814.8	-3,231.1	-4,169.8	-5,438.0	-7,466.4	-8,729.8	-10,111.6	-9,190.6	-11,158.9	-13,144.5
Overall U.S. Trade Deficit	-436,103.0	-411,899.0	-468,262.0	-532,350.0	-654,828.5	-772,374.2	-827,970.0	-808,765.0	-816,200.0	-503,582.0	-634,896.0	-726,714.0
U.S. GDP (U.S.$ trillion)	10.0	10.3	10.6	11.1	11.9	12.6	13.4	14.0	14.3	13.9	14.5	15.1

Source: U.S. Census Bureau. Figures listed are in millions of U.S. dollars unless otherwise listed.

SHIFTING SANDS AND THE REBALANCING AGENDA

The post-2008 global financial crisis was not only a psychological shock to those in China that believed in the fundamental health of the U.S. economy and the wisdom of U.S. economic policy, it was also an important turning point in assumptions about the long-term sustainability of the two countries' respective economic structures. As the investment bank Lehman Brothers collapsed in September 2008, household consumption in the United States as a percentage of GDP was over 70 percent, with real consumption having grown faster than GDP growth since 1980. Chinese household consumption, though growing in real terms, had fallen relative to GDP to around 35 percent of GDP by the fall of 2008.[27] The two economies were effectively mirror images of one another, with U.S. consumption reaching unsustainable excesses fueled in no small part by deficit spending enabled by cheap credit, while Chinese consumption was taking a backseat to investment and exports as the primary drivers of its economy. To U.S. and Chinese economic officials, the long-term sustainability of a system in which the appetite of U.S. consumers for imports above and beyond their ability to pay for them absent the willingness of exporters, China chief among them, to finance these consumption excesses, was clearly dubious.

The two governments have devoted much time and energy, independently and in consultations with each other, to the concept of economic rebalancing. President Obama pledged to double U.S. exports in five years and has initiated a series of programs designed to stimulate new, productive investment (including efforts to attract FDI from China).[28] China's 12th Five-Year Plan, unveiled in the spring of 2011, is almost completely focused on the concept of rebalancing, with the emphasis on boosting domestic consumption by reducing public concerns about the lack of a social safety net and shifting production to higher-value goods and services.[29]

Recognizing the unsustainability of and committing to reform the structural weight of various components of GDP is one thing. Implementing corrections to the relative imbalances by restructuring their respective economies is quite another. Any significant move to reduce long-term consumption in the United States and reduce excessive reliance on investment and exports in China will require both massive re-allocations of capital and enormous reserves of political will, neither of which would be in ample supply even in the best of times. With the global economy still beset by fragilities and with both the United States and China in the midst of difficult political transitions, acting to curb traditional sources of growth in either economy while hoping other sources will compensate is necessarily a leap of faith. Any move that acts to increase unemployment in either country would be an act of political suicide for that country's respective leadership.

TABLE 8.4. GDP by Expenditure Approach, 2000–2011

	2000	2001	2002	2003	2004	2005	2006	2007	2008	2009	2010	2011*
GDP (by expenditure approach)	9,874.9	10,902.8	12,047.6	13,663.5	16,080.0	18,713.1	22,224.0	26,583.4	31,490.1	34,631.7	39,430.8	N/A
Final Consumption Expenditures	6,151.6	6,693.4	7,181.7	7,768.6	8,755.3	9,905.1	11,263.2	13,151.0	15,234.7	16,682.0	18,690.5	N/A
% of total GDP	62.3	61.4	59.6	56.9	54.4	52.9	50.7	49.5	48.4	48.2	47.4	N/A
Household Consumption	4,585.5	4,943.6	5,305.7	5,765.0	6,251.9	7,265.3	8,210.4	9,651.0	11,059.5	12,113.0	13,329.1	N/A
Government Consumption	1,666.1	1,749.8	1,876.0	2,003.6	2,233.4	2,639.9	3,052.8	3,590.0	4,175.2	4,569.0	5,361.4	N/A
Gross Capital Formation	3,484.3	3,976.9	4,556.5	5,596.3	6,916.8	7,785.7	9,295.4	11,094.3	13,832.5	16,446.3	19,169.1	N/A
% of total GDP	35.3	36.5	37.8	41.0	43.0	41.6	41.8	41.7	43.9	47.5	48.6	N/A
Gross Fixed Capital Formation	3,384.4	3,775.5	4,363.2	5,349.1	6,511.8	7,423.3	8,795.4	10,394.9	12,808.4	15,668.0	18,234.0	N/A
Change in Inventories	99.8	201.5	193.3	247.2	405.1	362.4	500.0	699.5	1,024.1	778.3	935.1	N/A
Net Exports of Goods and Services	239.0	232.5	309.4	298.6	407.9	1,022.3	1,665.4	2,338.1	2,422.9	1,503.3	1,571.2	N/A
% of total GDP	2.4	2.1	2.6	2.2	2.5	5.5	7.5	8.8	7.7	4.3	4.0	N/A

Source: China National Bureau of Statistics. All GDP-related figures in billions of RMB.

*2011 statistics not yet available from the National Bureau of Statistics.

A grand bargain on rebalancing is therefore almost certainly unattainable. Instead, each side is left to its own independent efforts while attempting to cajole the other side into not making damaging moves. For China, that requires that the United States not limit access for Chinese exports (as China attempts to transition to lesser reliance on those exports) or restrict access for Chinese capital into U.S. assets that may be more productive in the long-term than sovereign U.S. debt instruments. For the United States, that means China's market to U.S. exports be increasingly welcoming; and Chinese policies and practices that act to reduce the United States' global competitiveness be reduced.

Rebalancing is not the only agenda item in U.S.-China economic policy: both sides are attempting to jockey for greater competitive positions in an economic world in which the United States (with Europe) has a reduced role; and China (along with India, Brazil, and other fast-growing large emerging economies) has increasing punching power. Since some of the policies designed to promote preferences for domestic growth can be said to create competitive barriers for non-domestic firms, these policies themselves have near term consequences for both the rebalancing agenda and for efforts to reduce economic frictions between the two sides.[30]

POINTS OF CONTENTION

Currency

In 2003, a group of American industrial firms and labor organizations first began to lobby Congress and the Bush administration on the fact that the Chinese currency, the *renminbi* or RMB, was undervalued relative to the U.S. dollar and offered an unfair competitive advantage for Chinese exporters to the United States. Senator Charles Schumer of New York and others took up their cause and began to push for legislation that would levy a 27.5 percent tariff on Chinese imports to correct for the undervaluation of the RMB.[31]

Most credible observers, while differing on the extent to which the RMB is undervalued, agree that the value of China's currency is systematically repressed by Chinese intervention in global currency markets on a massive scale.[32] Clearly, if the RMB is undervalued, it ensures that Chinese products will cost less on global markets than they otherwise would and that the RMB's value acts as a de facto export subsidy for Chinese manufacturers. For international economic purposes, the undervaluing of the currency of the world's second largest economy has an undeniable distortive effect, reducing the ability of some markets of comparable development and economic structure to compete with China. In this regard, many observers suggest the undervaluation of the RMB acts as a distinct drag on global growth.[33]

TABLE 8.5. RMB/USD Exchange Rate and U.S. Trade Deficit, 2000–2011

	2000	2001	2002	2003	2004	2005	2006	2007	2008	2009	2010	2011
Exchange Rate, RMB/USD	8.28	8.28	8.28	8.28	8.28	8.07	7.80	7.29	6.82	6.83	6.60	6.29
% Appreciation	0.0	0.0	0.0	0.0	0.0	2.5	3.3	6.5	6.5	0.0	3.3	4.6
U.S. Trade Deficit with China ($U.S. bn)	83.8	83.1	103.1	124.1	162.3	202.3	234.1	258.5	268.0	226.9	273.1	295.5

Sources: U.S. Federal Reserve Bank of New York, http://www.federalreserve.gov/releases/h10/hist/dat00_ch.htm; U.S. Census Bureau, http://www.census.gov/foreign-trade/balance/.

Note: RMB exchange rate listed is that at the closing of the last trading day of the calendar year. Calculation made by subtracting a given year's figure from the previous year's figure, then dividing by the previous year's figure.

Empirical evidence suggests, however, that even taking into account relatively high estimated values for the RMB, the landed U.S. costs of many products produced in China are still below those at which they can be competitively produced in the United States under similar conditions particularly since, as discussed above, most of the products imported from China into the United States have replaced products imported from other countries rather than supplanted U.S. produced goods. This suggests that even if China revalued the RMB to the extent that global trade patterns were altered, production in China would not revert to the United States but would instead go to third country markets and be exported to the United States from there. With this in mind, while some U.S. products may compete with Chinese imports, the overall effect for domestic U.S. economic purposes has been to repress consumer prices for goods and, on the margin, reduce the ability of Chinese firms to source goods from the United States.[34]

Against a backdrop of double-digit unemployment in the United States, the trade deficit with China is strong political brew, and the undervaluation of China's currency has emerged as the most potent issue.[35] Commentators from the left and right have made explicit linkages between the undervaluation of the RMB and lost American employment opportunities. Whether or not the undervaluation of the RMB is a significant bilateral trade issue between the United States and China, the issue continues to crowd out discussion of other issues in the relationship. Although by the summer of 2011 the RMB had appreciated against the dollar in real terms some 27.5 percent (the amount of undervaluation originally identified and the amount of the punitive tariff originally sought by Senator Schumer in his 2004 legislation), the United States Senate in October 2011 formally passed China-focused (though not country-specific) legislation seeking to apply punitive tariffs against currency manipulators. Although this particular legislation is unlikely to achieve bicameral passage, currency will continue to be a focus of political debate about the U.S. economic relationship with China.[36]

At times the politicization of the currency issue in the United States has frustrated members of Chinese officialdom who support a more liberalized exchange rate regime.[37] These officials have quietly complained to U.S. interlocutors that the perceived interference of U.S. officials in China's sovereign decisions with respect to currency management has limited the ability of institutions like the People's Bank of China (PBOC) to make changes in the exchange rate regime for Chinese domestic purposes for fear of criticism that they were kowtowing to American interests. Secretaries of Treasury Henry "Hank" Paulson in the George W. Bush administration and Timothy Geithner of the Obama administration have sought to publicly play down the issue with China in order to give the PBOC political space to make the case internally within China that a liberalized exchange rate regime would ease pressures on China's financial system and give the PRC government additional tools to manage inflation.[38] However, even absent express U.S. pressure to revalue the RMB, the PBOC has had its hands full with resistance from other parts of the Chinese bureaucracy.

In a late 2003 meeting with a then vice governor of the PBOC, the author raised the issue of China's currency valuation as having political implications in the United States because of the perceived impact on manufacturing job losses. The vice governor shook off an exasperated look and said, in essence, "In China we need to come up with 50,000 new jobs a day to keep ahead of new labor market entries and lay-offs at the State-Owned Industries. The domestic politics of that fact far outweigh international political factors for our government." Indeed, the currency issue is widely viewed outside of the PBOC, notably within the Ministry of Commerce (MOFCOM), as a jobs issue for China. MOFCOM officials and affiliated intellectuals privately suggest that the Chinese export sector, which continues to play an important role in ensuring new growth and has been a consistent source of employment among coastal firms, is heavily reliant on the de facto subsidy of the undervalued RMB. Economist Nicholas Lardy at the Peterson Institute of International Economics has tracked the rise in value of the RMB over the past eight years and showed that China's current account surplus has actually increased as the RMB has increased in value, suggesting that exporters have faced little or no hardship as a result of RMB appreciation.[39] However, many Chinese officials believe that the low margins generated by most Chinese export firms will not sustain those firms in the event of significant RMB appreciation absent a major downsizing by these firms.

In practice, rising wages among many coastal centers for export industries have put significant pressure on export firms to relocate to less costly areas in the past few years. The increased value of the RMB may be exacerbating these pressures, but Chinese economic policymakers are less focused these days on maintaining low margin, low value-added production in traditional export-intensive geographies and more focused on delivering strategies that improve margins and value for the firms in these geographies.[40]

Intellectual Property Rights and Technology Transfer

One of the most long-standing areas of contention between the United States and China is the concern over the extent to which U.S. intellectual property is misappropriated by Chinese businesses and individuals.[41] Starting as early as the 1980s copyrighted music, films and software along with branded garments with U.S.-origin trademarks began appearing in pirated form in larger Chinese cities. Copyright piracy and trademark infringement was already rampant at that time in Hong Kong, Taiwan, and other markets in Asia but after migrating to China it achieved a scale for which U.S. industry was unprepared. In the late 1990s and thereafter Chinese firms began to produce counterfeit versions of patented products as diverse as pharmaceuticals and industrial machines. On one level, the sheer moxie and remarkable duplicative skills of Chinese pirates and counterfeiters is astounding. On another, the losses to American innovators and manufacturers from IPR theft are unconscionable.

In any case, even before China joined the WTO and signed onto the Agreement on Trade-Related Aspects of Intellectual Property Rights, the practice of piracy and counterfeiting was illegal under Chinese law. Prior to WTO accession the U.S. and Chinese governments engaged in brinkmanship on the issue a number of times, with the United States coming close to invoking punitive tariffs on Chinese imports to compensate for the perceived losses to IPR violations.[42] After China joined the WTO and put in place a new and extensive regime to protect and enforce IPR, American negotiators were hopeful that the problem of IPR violation in China would be curbed once and for all. Nevertheless, enforcement of China's IPR laws has been distinctly lacking and U.S. rights-holders continue to experience dramatic losses due to Chinese piracy and counterfeiting.

A May 2011 U.S. International Trade Commission report estimated that losses to U.S. industry due to Chinese IPR theft were approximately $48 billion in 2009, a number that may be understated given that it was based solely on a survey of firms in the IP-intensive part of the U.S. economy.[43] These firms reported that an improvement in China's IPR protection and enforcement to levels comparable to the United States' would likely increase U.S. employment in their operations by approximately 923,000 jobs.

One of the primary challenges to those seeking to prevent the unopposed theft of their IPR is that China's extreme geographic and political decentralization makes it very difficult for rights-holders to pursue legal protection and enforcement of their rights without having to run a gamut of local and provincial officials and courts that are more likely to side with local violators with more local political clout.[44] When rights-holders are successful at seeking legal redress for their grievances in court, they are frequently awarded damages that are *de minimis*—barely adequate to cover legal costs let alone serve as a deterrent of future IPR theft. For many recidivist IPR pirates and counterfeiters, legal fines are an unfortunate but bearable cost of doing business: the rewards for piracy far outweigh the risks.

A primary complaint of Chinese economic policy officials is that China's economy, while it has grown exponentially in the past 30 years, remains on the low end of industrial input values. Searching for a means to bring Chinese industry up the value chain, some of these policymakers have seized on an effective IPR regime as an important means to an end. If China can better protect IPR, so the theory goes, China's domestic inventors and entrepreneurs will have a greater incentive to build Chinese technology companies and brands. There is thus a highly energized cadre of Chinese officials that understand the importance of IPR to an innovative economy and are seeking to establish a more effective system of IPR protection and enforcement not because of an interest in protecting foreign business interests, but promoting domestic Chinese innovation.[45]

This cadre of officials is bolstered somewhat by the increasing attention of China's most senior leadership to the importance of innovation to China's future growth plans. China's desire for technological advancement is a long-standing obsession. As early as the mid-1970s, China's Premier Zhou Enlai espoused the goal of "Four Modernizations," among which technological modernization was prominent. In the 1980s and 1990s, China sought to increase its technology base through technology transfer, attempting through incentives to encourage Western companies to incorporate higher technology platforms into their production bases.

But China's effort to seek technology transfer, through incentives or (occasional) coercion, has been less than successful. Some Chinese individuals and firms, not necessarily with state sponsorship, have on occasion attempted to access higher technologies from the United States and other Western economies through industrial espionage. But in most cases, U.S. companies have largely abstained from large-scale transfers of technology to China. Chinese officials in many cases suggest that the reason for such abstention is U.S. export control laws. In practice however, the reason for China's lack of success in encouraging technology transfer is not U.S. policy but rather a rational U.S. company approach to risks associated with exposure of technology to the Chinese market: intellectual property theft is so rampant that rational companies think long and hard before willingly exposing their first-line technologies to the Chinese marketplace.

Domestic Preferential Policies and Market Access

China today is a world leader in technology applied in communications, alternative energy, rail and other sectors. High-tech manufactured goods accounted for 35 percent of China's exports in 2011.[46] Year-on-year growth in Chinese patent filings is astronomical: in 2010 the number of Chinese-filed patents grew by 56.2 percent, while U.S.-filed patents dropped by 1.7 percent.[47] China graduated 10,000 Ph.D. engineers in 2010 while the United States graduated just 8,000 (and of those who are Chinese or of Chinese descent, many have plans to seek their professional fortunes in China).[48] China's drive to build an enterprise-led "indigenous innovation" capacity has set off alarm bells among multinational companies and the popular press.[49]

In 2006 China's State Council published an ambitious science and technology program to establish China as an innovative nation by 2020. The program outlines a planned expenditure of 2.5 percent of GDP on research and development, such that "by 2020, the progress of science and technology will contribute 60 percent or above to the country's development. Meanwhile, the country's reliance on foreign technology will decline to 30 percent or below. The number of patents granted to Chinese nationals and the introduction of their academic essays are expected to rank among the first five throughout the world."[50]

A national goal to increase technological innovation is laudable both for reasons of economic development and national pride. There are important reasons for China's leadership to focus on improving China's technological capabilities. President Hu Jintao and Premier Wen Jiabao recognized early in their tenure that the economic strategy of the past three decades, one that relies heavily on inputs of land, labor, capital and natural resources, is unsustainable for demographic, environmental and sociopolitical reasons.[51]

Although Chinese capacity to adopt and adapt existing technologies (itself a form of innovation) has been impressive, China's manufacturing prowess remains decidedly low-tech. Indeed, a World Bank study in 2008 suggested that the skill intensity of China's exports remains unchanged since 1992 after adjusting for Chinese processing trade, the business activity of importing all components and accessories from abroad and re-exporting the finished products after processing or assembly by enterprises in China.[52] Stories of remarkable Chinese innovators such as telecommunications giant Huawei aside, Chinese industry today is a combination of a small number of innovators together with a large number of non-innovating manufacturers, the vast majority of whom do not engage in continuous R&D activities.

Hu Jintao's 2005 articulation of the "scientific development strategy" has at its center the notion that China's long-term prosperity requires an economy based more on efficiency and knowledge than on primary inputs.[53] Challenging Chinese enterprises to become more competitive through innovation is therefore highly rational. For the enterprises to respond appropriately, however, their focus must be on serving the ultimate goal of sustaining Chinese economic development, and not simply innovating for innovation's sake.

The lessons to date of China's efforts to become an innovative economy are several. The first is that an unquestioning focus on innovation without linkage to genuine economic development may frustrate the ultimate goal of the effort. A broad definition of innovation that includes not only development of frontier technologies but also adaptive and adoptive technology may better serve the goals of long-term job and wealth creation. To that end, focusing on limiting reliance on foreign technology in pursuit of techno-nationalist goals may be to limit the growth of knowledge and efficiency in the country. The stated goal of reducing to 30 percent China's reliance on foreign technology looks an awful lot like the failed import substitution policies of the past, and is a rather marked departure from the open market policies that have fueled much of China's success to date.

The second lesson is that China's government must recognize where its efforts to promote innovation end, and where those of the market begin. To date, much of the innovation drive has concentrated on promoting research and development in large, state-owned enterprises (SOEs) that are less susceptible to incentives that have traditionally yielded invention and innovation. R&D effectiveness, that is, results for a given level of R&D expenditure and employment, is statistically much lower for SOEs than domestic private firms. Although a crude metric, private firms file more patent applications per million RMB of R&D expenditures, and own more patents per 100 scientists and engineers employed, than do their SOE counterparts. Relying on SOEs to innovate in a way that genuinely delivers economic growth is not an efficient proposition.

Finally, if private firms are likely to be better innovators than state-owned behemoths, China must improve its enforcement of IPR in order to reward them for their inventions. SOEs, with more political power, may be better positioned to protect their inventions from copycats and pirates, but the private companies that ultimately can be more globally competitive are not going to have the incentive to invent. Indeed, a 2007 study of the National Bureau of Statistics showed some 86 percent of medium-sized firms and 96 percent of small firms did not engage in any R&D at all.

Cross-Border Investment

The past decade has seen an unprecedented boom in Chinese investment flows to the United States. China has been using its massive dollar reserves to purchase U.S. Treasury bills and it is now the largest foreign holder of treasury securities. By February 2012, China held U.S.$1178.9 trillion in treasuries (Japan, the second largest holder, held U.S.$1095.9 billion).[54] Moreover, China's Outward Foreign Direct Investment (OFDI) to the U.S. has also soared in recent years. In both 2009 and 2010, the value of China's direct investment assets in the United States increased by 130 percent. The total OFDI flow in 2010 was in the vicinity of U.S.$5.3 billion, bringing accumulated Chinese direct investment in the U.S. to roughly U.S.$11.6 billion since 2003.[55]

With the growing amount of Chinese investment inflows, there is an increasing concern among some in the United States that China's investment in the United States is a strategic endeavor of the Chinese government, and one not made based on solely commercial merits, but rather as part of a larger government policy to secure access to natural resources and core technology for China's rapidly growing economy.[56] The subsequent conclusion is that the security of U.S. strategic assets and technology may be threatened by China's government-controlled investment. On the other hand, those who support increased investment from China assume that the United States is able to encourage further investment flows from China through lobbying the Chinese central leadership, operating under the perception that the investment is entirely government controlled.

China's investment flows to the United States are through: (1) The People's Bank of China (PBOC) using the majority of China's foreign reserves to invest in U.S. debt; (2) China's sovereign wealth funds using part of China's foreign reserves to invest in U.S. equities; and (3) China's outward foreign direct investment, in both greenfield transactions as well as mergers and acquisitions (M&A). Among them, the Chinese government exerts tight control over the first and second category of investment, while the third category is partly government controlled and partly market driven.

China's reserves, which have increased significantly since 2000, reached U.S.$3.2 trillion in June 2011 and now account for around one-third of the global total. Around 70 pecent of this is estimated to be denominated in U.S. dollars.[57] Between 2000 and 2005, the bulk of Chinese foreign reserves went to purchase U.S. treasury securities. In response to dollar volatility concerns, however, China's leadership has adopted a more risk-averse investment strategy that aims to diversify into commodities and other hard assets, including equities and OFDI, particularly in resources and technology.[58]

The United States is of two minds on the question of Chinese investment. On the one hand, there is widespread enthusiasm for any new source of investment capital. On the other hand, concerns that Chinese investment is largely driven by strategic Chinese national considerations that may not align with U.S. national security interests make many U.S. policymakers nervous about Chinese investment in "strategic" technology and resource assets. High-profile efforts by the Chinese National Overseas Oil Company to acquire Unocal and Huawei to acquire a division of 3COM failed after intensive scrutiny by the Committee on Foreign Investment in the United States (CFIUS) because of these considerations.[59]

Despite fears among American policymakers that the goal of China's external investment strategy is to put national security considerations ahead of firm-by-firm profitability, the evidence suggests that most companies, whether state owned or private, are typically driven by profit maximization ahead of any national strategy.[60] Bad overseas investments by state energy companies in particular have received scathing treatment in Chinese popular media, and their proponents within the Chinese government have been criticized for wastefulness. Therefore, it is unlikely that the Beijing authority has a free hand to push non-market-driven OFDI initiatives by fiat in support of narrow security interests. To the extent to which the OFDI strategy is driven by a desire to diversify foreign exchange holdings, channeling these funds to private Chinese firms to invest overseas may be more politically palatable and may be driven by more rational, market-oriented concerns than those of the larger SOEs.

Industrial Policy

As noted above, the return of industrial planning to the fore of Chinese economic policymaking is a major challenge to market-oriented businesses in China, including U.S. businesses. Policies that encourage the development of one business sector to the disadvantage of another have long been a factor in Chinese economic policy. Each year, China's central government has published an "investment catalogue" that lists businesses that qualify for "encouraged," "accepted" and "discouraged" status. This catalogue has been a guide for local and provincial officials in seeking foreign direct investment. "Encouraged" investments (typically in high-technology, high-employment businesses) have had preferences showered upon them. Subsidies in the form of tax, land and labor breaks as well as dramatically simplified regulatory processes and the easing of other legal burdens have made the process of favoring some businesses over others a fact of life in China's economic landscape.

The process of encouraging and discouraging different businesses has developed into a high art in recent years. Various national and sub-national official groups within China, especially those charged with working with various domestic constituency industries, have increasingly sought to develop new industrial groups in China. On a number of occasions, these groups have developed individual policies, not necessarily with the broad consensus of the Chinese government, that aim to encourage the development of industries in China in ways that challenge or disadvantage American companies and their workers. Certain Chinese companies, not necessarily state-owned companies, have in recent years found special favor as firms that may develop into distinctly Chinese multinational companies.[61] The advantages conferred on these "national champions" vary, but the rationale for their promotion by parts of the Chinese government is straightforward. Chinese government officials, largely for reasons of national pride, favor the existence of Chinese national companies that operate on a world stage with a stature comparable to U.S.,

Japanese and European multinationals. When the interests of these companies compete with those of American companies, the Chinese companies are generally accorded a "patriotic" advantage. An area of particular concern at this point is in green technology, which many Chinese officials perceive to be a competitive international commercial battleground that, given the dramatic scale of China's domestic market for wind and solar power in particular, Chinese companies will be uniquely poised to capture.

The challenge faced by many competitors to Chinese national champions in international markets is the perception that the Chinese state is prepared to subsidize these companies without regard to rational economic behavior. The sense of an unlimited subsidy for these company's efforts can skew the economic playing field and distort markets. This has particularly manifested in resource and commodities, but increasingly emerging Chinese technology companies are perceived to have the blank checkbook of the Chinese state at their disposal.

Technical standards are another area in which certain Chinese agencies have made an effort to carve out parts of the Chinese marketplace for domestic firms.[62] In some cases citing security concerns, in some cases citing safety, Chinese agencies involved in commercial areas as diverse as agriculture to wireless encryption technology have been active in promoting China-only standards, frequently in collusion with domestic Chinese firms seeking market advantages. Some of these standards issues have become significant sources of friction in the relationship, such as the WLAN Authentication and Privacy Infrastructure (WAPI), a unique wireless encryption standard that Chinese regulators originally insisted be mandatory for all wireless equipment providers.[63] That standard and its progeny, despite numerous high-level interventions at the Vice Premier and Secretary level, continue to percolate under the surface of international trade relations. Numerous other standards in various stages of development, some seemingly created purely to confound the ability of American and other companies to compete with Chinese rival firms in the marketplace, will almost certainly prove to be a major source of commercial friction in the years to come.

MECHANISMS FOR MANAGING THE ECONOMIC AND COMMERCIAL RELATIONSHIP

The two governments have since the early twenty-first century dramatically increased their official interaction on economic and trade matters. A range of sleepy dialogues among the various economic ministries and departments designed to promote dialogue and cooperation (and, in many cases, provide a platform for American "instruction" of Chinese counterparts on U.S.-style economic activities) have been repeatedly upgraded and formalized to the extent that by 2008 sizable percentages of the U.S. cabinet and China's ministerial cadre were traveling back and forth to their respective capitals to debate and negotiate economic and commercial matters.

In 2003, a long-standing annual bilateral mechanism, the Joint Commission on Commerce and Trade (JCCT), was elevated to Vice Premier representation on the Chinese side with two cabinet officials (the Secretary of Commerce and U.S. Trade Representative) representing the United States. What began as an exercise in promoting cooperation became an effort to solve trade and economic problems and demonstrate the effectiveness of official efforts to respond to public concerns about the state of that relationship. In 2006, incoming Treasury Secretary Henry "Hank" Paulson quietly shelved a dormant dialogue between the Department of the Treasury and Chinese Ministry of Finance (the "Joint Economic Commission") and replaced it with a Vice Premier-to-Treasury Secretary "Strategic Economic Dialogue" (SED or S&ED[64]) involving multiple U.S. cabinet officials and their Chinese counterparts. That effort—which sought to elevate the discussion from one of bilateral commercial friction to one of global economic strategy—included discussions of financial structure, environmental sustainability, and other matters in which the United States increasingly sought to draft China as a partner in global economic management, rather than a student of U.S. economic policy. Bonnie Glaser's chapter discusses this process in considerable detail.

The JCCT and S&ED have been important vehicles to both address concrete issues of economic concern in an atmosphere of cooperation. In addition to these very senior-level discussions, a wide range of cabinet and sub-cabinet exchanges on agriculture, energy, innovation and other matters are an important basis for managing and maintaining a positive basis for the commercial and economic relationship. The outcomes of these dialogues, released at their conclusion, reflect the efforts of both governments to simultaneously attack concrete problems and deflect public criticism in both countries of perceived inequities in the relationship.

CONCLUSION

Tension over trade issues has, of course, long been a feature of the U.S.-China bilateral relationship. Managing these issues and preserving a domestic consensus in support of open markets to China has been hard but not unrewarding work: despite all the gnashing of teeth and occasional hysteria, by any reasonable accounting the U.S.-China economic relationship is enormously successful and productive for both countries. China is a rare bright spot for U.S. multinationals these days, and many companies are doubling-down on their China businesses. Nevertheless, trade issues between the two countries are proliferating, and it is getting increasingly difficult to achieve meaningful progress on these issues, in part because Chinese officials don't seem to be taking American counterparts very seriously.

The efforts of China's reformers in the 1990s to use the external pressure of WTO accession and jurisprudence in order to enshrine market principles in the economy delivered remarkable gains for China's economy. Yet today, many Chinese believe the country lost more than it gained by joining the WTO and some privately wonder at the compatibility of the China economic model with the principles of WTO that were in large part shaped by U.S. leadership. At its heart, WTO membership is about two principles: market access (that a country's default position should be to keep its market open) and national treatment (that a country should accord foreign players in its market the same treatment it accords its own). WTO membership is a web spun of reciprocal commitments to openness as a matter of national self-interest. WTO members recognize the benefit of adherence to the two core principles outweighs the parochial benefits to domestic firms that may be lost. The WTO in some respects is an audacious creation: the cession by sovereign governments of some of their rights to restrict and control their own economy. By breaking down trade barriers, the WTO and the consensus among governments it represents stands for the proposition that a borderless commercial world is much bigger than the sum of its constituent parts. That consensus has delivered remarkable benefits and wealth to Americans and Chinese. But the consensus is fragile, and Americans and Chinese, among many others, seem to have forgotten what the alternatives look like.

For China, a more recent entrant into that consensus, this should be troubling: China is very dependent for its economic health and well-being on an effective rules-based system governing global trade. That the United States has wavered in its leadership of a more robust WTO liberalization process and has had trouble articulating much of a trade policy vision (other than one that is strikingly provincial in its approach) may have more to do with China's decreasing willingness to come to the table on substantive trade matters than anything else.

The realities of constituent politics in every political system inevitably claw away at international commitments to market access and national treatment. Domestic actors in every system can and will attempt to access (and sometimes manipulate) political processes to preserve or secure benefits in ways that run contrary to the essential spirit of WTO. It is not surprising that the United States and China both are facing resistance from vested interests to full embrace of the WTO's principles. But the danger is that, in rejecting WTO principles, both sides will reject an essential element of their individual economic success and thus make more difficult their long-term economic future, and eat away at a fundamental basis for constructive engagement. Dialogues like the S&ED and JCCT are useful mechanisms, but they are far from exercises in building the kind of sustainable win-win approach to trade that is required.

If the United States and China are going to have a relationship that allows both sides to protect their own national interests while affording space to the other side to protect their own, a successful economic relationship is paramount. Domestic political concerns are features of every mature trade relationship. But the two sides must agree, or at least reaffirm certain core principles. That does not mean that China must align itself completely with Washington's view of the world; nor does it require that the United States must sacrifice domestic economic interests in favor of some greater diplomatic good. But the relationship is increasingly defined by discord, rather than shared enterprise. Economic relations used to be the glue that held the two sides together. It is in danger of becoming a force that drives the two apart.

Forty years of commercial interaction has produced one of the most complex and dynamic economic relationships on the planet. The official interaction between governments grabs much of the headlines but increasingly many other stakeholders in both the United States and China drive the relationship. Official dialogues between the two governments are going to continue to be critical both to managing policy challenges and signaling respective publics about the commitment of both sides to an effective relationship. However, direct relationships and dialogue between the stakeholders in both economies are going to be increasingly important as well. Public discourse on the relationship fails to capture the dynamism and success that lies at the heart of that relationship. Interaction between stakeholders in both countries will need to evolve to reflect that dynamism if the relationship is to advance to reach its full potential.

NOTES

1. People's Bank of China, "Financial Statistics, H1 2011," July 12, 2011, available at: http://www.pbc.gov.cn/image_public/UserFiles/english/upload/File/Financial%20 statistics,%20h1%202011.pdf.

2. Eswar S. Prasad, "The U.S.-China Economic Relationship: Shifts and Twists in the Balance of Power," Testimony before the U.S.-China Economic and Security Review Commission, Hearing on "U.S. Debt to China: Implications and Repercussions," February 25, 2010.

3. U.S.-China Business Council, *U.S. Exports to China 2000–2011,* available at: https://www.uschina.org/public/exports/2000_2011/2000-11-us-exports-to-china .pdf.

4. Richard McGregor, "China's Economic Growth Passes Its Peak," *Financial Times,* February 7, 2008.

5. Lee Branstetter and Nicholas Lardy, "China's Embrace of Globalization," in Loren Brandt and Thomas Rawski, eds., *China's Great Economic Transformation* (New York, NY: Cambridge University Press, 2008).

6. Yingyi Qian and Jinglian Wu, "China's Transition to a Market Economy: How Far Across the River," in Nicholas C. Hope, Dennis Tao Yang and Mu Yang Li (eds)., *How Far Across the River: Chinese Policy Reform at the Millennium* (Stanford, CA: Stanford University Press, 2003), 31–63.

7. Nicholas Lardy, *Integrating China into the Global Economy* (Washington, DC: Brookings Institution Press, 2002).

8. Joseph Fewsmith, "China and the WTO: The Politics Behind the Agreement," *NBR Analysis: South Korea, China, and the Global Economy* (December 1999): 23–39.

9. "Zhu Rongji: China to Fulfill WTO Entry Promises," *People's Daily*, October 2000.

10. Wayne M. Morrison, "China and the World Trade Organization," *CRS Report for Congress*, Congressional Research Service, November 19, 2001.

11. "U.S.-China Trade Relations and Renewal of China's Most-Favored-Nation Status," Hearing before the Subcommittee on Trade of the Committee on Ways and Means, U.S. House of Representatives, June 17, 1998; and "PTNR Trade Status for China: Ten Key Considerations," U.S.-China Business Council, February 2000.

12. Jinglian Wu, "China's Economy: 60 Years of Progress," *Caijing*, September 2009.

13. Charan Deveraux, Robert Z. Lawrence and Michael D. Watkins, *Case Studies in US Trade Negotiation: Making the Rules*, Vol. 1 (Washington, D.C.: Peterson Institute for International Economics, September 2006): 241–300.

14. "When Fortune Frowned," *The Economist*, October 11, 2008.

15. Zhang Weiwei, "Eight Ideas Behind China's Success," *New York Times*, September 30, 2009; "China Model Can Absorb Best of the West, Discard Rest," *Global Times*, November 15, 2011; "The China Model: A Dialogue between Francis Fukuyama and Zhang Weiwei," *New Perspectives Quarterly*, Vol. 28, No. 4 (Fall 2011).

16. Liu Guoguang, "The Chinese Model Gives Us Hope That China Will Be the First to Recover," *Social Sciences Journal*, May 7, 2009; Zhang Leisheng, "The Financial Crisis Is a Necessary Result of the Movement of the Basic Contradictions of Capitalism," *Chinese Academy of Social Sciences Review* (November 2008).

17. Robert D. Hormats, "Addressing the Challenges of the China Model," Remarks at AmCham-China's Annual D.C. Dialogue, Washington, DC, May 3, 2011.

18. Joseph S. Nye, "American and Chinese Power After the Financial Crisis," *Washington Quarterly* Vol. 33, No. 4 (October 2010): 143–153; Henry Paulson, "The United States and China: Five Principles for Strengthening the Global Economy," Remarks at the School of Advanced International Studies, Johns Hopkins University, Washington, DC, October 25, 2011.

19. Chen Weihua, "China Bashing Is Bad Campaign Politics," *Xinhua*, October 21, 2011.

20. "2010 Special 301 Report," Office of the U.S. Trade Representative, April 2010, 19–27, http://www.ustr.gov/webfm_send/1906.

21. "2010 China Business Climate Survey," The American Chamber of Commerce in the People's Republic of China, 2010.

22. "CNN Poll: Americans See China as an Economic Threat," CNN.com, November 17, 2010.

23. Wayne Morrison, "China-U.S. Trade Issues," *CRS Report for Congress*, Congressional Research Service (September 2011): 8–10.

24. C. Fred Bergsten, Bates Gill, Nicholas R. Lardy, and Derek J. Mitchell, *China: The Balance Sheet* (New York, NY: Public Affairs, 2006), 89–91.

25. Nicholas R. Lardy, "China: The Great New Economic Challenge?" in C. Fred Bergsten, ed., *The United States and the World Economy: Foreign Economic Policy for the Next Decade* (Washington, D.C.: Peterson Institute for International Economics, 2005), pp. 131–134.

26. Michael J. Ferrantino, Robert B. Koopman, Zhi Wang, and Falan Yinug, "The Nature of US-China Trade in Advanced Technology Products," *Comparative Economic Studies* 52 (2010): 207–224; Robert Koopman, Zhi Whang, and Shang-jin Wei, "How Much of Chinese Exports Is Really Made in China? Assessing Foreign and Domestic Value-Added in Gross Exports," U.S. International Trade Commission Office of Economics Working Paper No. 2008-03-B (Washington, DC: March 2008).

27. World Bank, *World Development Indicators.*

28. Remarks by the President in State of the Union Address, January 27, 2010, http://www.whitehouse.gov/the-press-office/remarks-president-state-union-address; Report to the President on the National Export Initiative: The Export Promotion Cabinet's Plan for Doubling U.S. Exports in Five Years, September 2010, http://www.whitehouse.gov/sites/default/files/nei_report_9-16-10_full.pdf.

29. "Key Targets of China's 12th Five-Year Plan," *Xinhua*, March 5, 2011; *China's Great Rebalancing Act*, Eurasia Group Report, August 2011.

30. Eswar S. Prasad, "China's Approach to Economic Development and Industrial Policy," Testimony before the U.S.-China Economic and Security Review Commission, Hearing on "China's Twelfth Five-Year Plan, Indigenous Innovation and Technology Transfers, and Outsourcing," June 15, 2011; Joseph Casey and Katherine Koleski, "Backgrounder: China's 12th Five-Year Plan," U.S.-China Economic and Security Review Commission, June 24, 2011.

31. Edward Alden and Christopher Swann, "US Set to Get Tough Over Renminbi," *Financial Times*, April 7, 2005.

32. Morris Goldstein and Nicholas R. Lardy, eds., *Debating China's Exchange Rate Policy* (Washington, D.C.: Peterson Institute for International Economics, 2008).

33. Paul Krugman, "Taking on China," *New York Times*, March 14, 2010.

34. Ray C. Fair, "Estimated Macroeconomic Effects of a Chinese Yuan Appreciation," Cowles Foundation Discussion Paper No. 1755 (March 2010), http://cowles.econ.yale.edu/P/cd/d17b/d1755.pdf.

35. The Treasury Department's Report on International Economic and Exchange Rate Policies, September 16, 2010, http://www.gpo.gov/fdsys/pkg/CHRG-111shrg64995/html/CHRG-111shrg64995.htm.

36. Eric Lichtblau, "Senate Nears Approval of Measure to Punish China Over Currency Manipulation," *New York Times*, October 6, 2011; Tao Wenzhao, "Protectionism Will Not Create US Jobs," *China Daily*, October 15, 2011.

37. Zhou Xiaoyuan, "'RMB Undervaluation' Claims Defy Economic Logic," *People's Daily*, November 11, 2011; "China Calls for Firm Opposition to U.S. Legislation Scapegoating Yuan Policy," *Xinhua*, October 12, 2011.

38. Aaron Back, Dinny McMahon and Nathalie Boschat, "China Meeting Highlights Currency Conflict," *Wall Street Journal*, April 1, 2011; "Paulson Says It Is in 'China's Interest' to Have a More Flexible Currency," *Bloomberg*, April 9, 2010; "Paulson Pledges "Chinese Decision" on Currency, Joint Efforts on Climate Changes," *Xinhua*, July 30, 2007.

39. Morris Goldstein and Nicholas R. Lardy, "The Future of China's Exchange Rate Policy," *Policy Analyses in International Economics* 87 (Washington, DC: Peterson Institute of International Economics, July 2009).

40. Edward Wong, "China's Export Economy Begins Turning Inward," *New York Times*, June 24, 2010.

41. Wayne M. Morrison, "China-U.S. Trade Issues" (Washington, D.C.: *CRS Report for Congress*, Congressional Research Service, September 30, 2011), 29–32.

42. Marcus Noland, *U.S.-China Economic Relations* (Washington, D.C.: Peterson Institute for International Economics Working Paper 96–6, 1996).

43. U.S. International Trade Commission, *China; Effects of Intellectual Property Infringement and Indigenous Innovation Policies on the U.S. Economy* (Washington, D.C.: USITC Publication 4226, May 2011).

44. Cong Cao, Denis Fed Simon, and Richard P. Suttmeier, "Commentary: China's Innovation Challenge," *Innovation: Management, Policy & Practice* 11–2 (August 2009): 253–259; Andrew Yeh, "China's Piracy Problems 'Remain Severe,'" *Financial Times*, September 14, 2005.

45. "China Seeks to Add More Value to Domestic Products through Innovation," *Xinhua*, December 19, 2010; Ding Qingfen, "Crackdown on IPR Infringement Is Set to Continue," *Xinhua*, July 2, 2011.

46. National Bureau of Statistics of China, *China Statistical Yearbook* (Beijing: State Statistical Press, 2011).

47. "China's International Patent Filings on 56.2-pct Jump Last Year: WIPO," *Xinhua*, February 10, 2011.

48. Geoff Colvin, "Desperately Seeking Math and Science Majors," *CNN.com*, July 29, 2010.

49. Jamil Anderlini, "US Companies Find China Less Welcoming," *Financial Times*, March 22, 2010.

50. "China Issues Guidelines on Sci-Tech Development Program," *Xinhua*, February 9, 2006.

51. Joseph Fewsmith, "Promoting the Scientific Development Concept," *China Leadership Monitor* 11 (July 30, 2004).

52. "Mid-Term Evaluation of China's 11th Five Year Plan," World Bank Report No. 46355-CN, Poverty Reduction and Economic Management Unit, East Asia and Pacific Region, December 18, 2008, 28.

53. "Leadership to Adjust Growth Model," *China Daily*, October 10, 2005.

54. U.S. Department of the Treasury, "Major Foreign Holders of Treasury Securities," available at: http://www.treasury.gov/resource-center/data-chart-center/tic/Documents/mfh.txt

55. Daniel H. Rosen, "Regarding Chinese Investment in the United States," Testimony before the U.S.-China Economic and Security Review Commission, Hearing on Chinese State-Owned Enterprises and U.S.-China Bilateral Investment, March 30, 2011.

56. Michael Martin, "China's Sovereign Wealth Fund: Developments and Policy Implications," *CRS Report for Congress*, Congressional Research Service, September 23, 2010.

57. "Why China Slashed Its US Debt Holdings," *People's Daily*, October 25, 2011.

58. Wayne M. Morrison and Marc Labonte, "China's Holdings of U.S. Securities: Implications for the U.S. Economy," *CRS Report for Congress*, Congressional Research Service, September 26, 2011, 11–13.

59. These experiences have resulted in the apparent tit-for-tat Chinese creation of similar processes to oversee foreign investment in Chinese assets that U.S. multinationals are concerned will restrict their access to investment targets in China.

60. Nargiza Salidjanova, "Going Out: An Overview of China's Outward Foreign Direct Investment," U.S.-China Economic and Security Review Commission, March 30, 2011.

61. Bruce Dickson, "Updating the China Model," *The Washington Quarterly*, Vol. 34, No. 4 (Fall 2011), 39–58.

62. Richard P. Suttmeier, Xiangyu Yao and Alex Zixiang Tan, *Standards of Power? Technology, Institutions, and Politics in the Development of China's National Standards Strategy* (Seattle: National Bureau of Asian Research, June 2006).

63. "USBC Calls on China to Adopt Internationally Recognized 'Wi-Fi' Standard," U.S.-China Business Council Press Release, February 24, 2004.

64. The SED was further upgraded in 2009, when Secretary of State Hillary Clinton upgraded a Deputy Secretary-led discussion (the "Senior Dialogue") through her participation and integrated that dialogue with the SED, resulting in the "Strategic and Economic Dialogue" (S&ED).

9

The Cultural Relationship

Terry Lautz

— why is it important?

Culture has the potential to reduce tensions and enhance trust between nations and peoples. It can also be used to win hearts and minds for national and political purposes. Yet policy analysts tend to overlook the dual role of culture, both as a bridge for understanding and as an instrument of power. They focus instead on the "hard" security issues of state-to-state diplomatic, economic, and military relations, neglecting the ways that cultural exchange and cultural diplomacy can form images, shape opinions, and convey values.

This chapter surveys prevailing trends in the U.S.-China cultural relationship in recent years. I first examine how the two governments employ culture to improve their images and increase influence, and then review some emerging forms of interaction between China and American society—through universities, non-governmental organizations (NGOs), think tanks, foundations, and the arts—in response to greater wealth and opportunities in the PRC. The chapter raises three overarching questions: Is the United States losing the competition with China for cultural influence or even soft power? Is cultural exchange creating more trust and confidence than friction and anxiety? And what are the lessons, opportunities, and concerns looking ahead?

The history of Chinese and American mutual perceptions is complex and contradictory. China views the United States as model, partner, self-serving bully, and hegemonic power. The U.S. sees China either as weak and needy or as threatening and hostile. This volatile mix of positive and negative stereotypes haunts the relationship. Much of the problem is explained by the paternalism and exceptionalism that is deeply woven into the fabric of America's past. More foreign missionaries went to China than any other country, carrying the message that modernization would flow naturally from the adoption of Christianity and Western values. Many Chinese educators and leaders agreed and worked hand-in-hand with foreigners to establish colleges, hospitals, and famine relief programs. But the Communists viewed these institutions as evidence of cultural imperialism and shut them down after assuming power in 1949. As Nancy Tucker's chapter shows, efforts to remake China in America's image during the first half of the twentieth century ended in a dramatic failure.

A new era in U.S.-China relations began in 1971 with an exchange of ping-pong players, capped by President Richard Nixon's trip to China the following year. Then came panda bears, performing arts troupes, sports teams, and scholars, with the expectation that these goodwill efforts would help to create public support for official relations. Cold War isolation had produced dangerously distorted views about the other side's intentions. With rapprochement, Americans would no longer be labeled cultural imperialists, nor would Chinese be called Reds or Commies.

As the PRC reached out to the U.S., there seemed to be another chance for Americans to change China. The unspoken hope was that cultural and commercial engagement would lead China to evolve in the direction of a more open, liberal, and democratic system. This was a familiar idea, espoused by Secretary of State John Foster Dulles as a strategy of "peaceful evolution" in the early 1950s. Deng Xiaoping had opened the door to the West during the reform period of the 1980s, but China's leaders remained suspicious about the corrupting effects of Western values, which they labeled "spiritual pollution" or "bourgeois liberalism." They doubted American claims of universal values, arguing that cultural and historical differences must be taken into account.

Ideological debates over culture and values have continued. In 2011, President Hu Jintao warned of the need to strengthen China's "cultural security": "We must clearly see that international hostile forces are intensifying the strategic plot of westernizing and dividing China, and ideological and cultural fields are the focal areas of their long-term infiltration."[1] A follow-up campaign was launched in January 2012 to limit the number of "low taste" talent, game, and reality TV shows, and to air more news and educational programming.[2] On the U.S. side, American government officials regularly accuse China's Communist Party of human rights abuses and policies consciously designed to prevent Chinese citizens from achieving freedom and democracy.

Even the decision by Deng Xiaoping and Jimmy Carter to launch programs for student exchange in 1979 reflected competing agendas. A pragmatic Deng looked to American universities for training to compensate for the devastation of higher education during the Cultural Revolution. Thousands of Chinese graduate students were sent to the United States, mainly to study science and technology, while a handful of American students and teachers went to the PRC for Chinese studies. For the U.S., the arrival of Chinese students revived residual images of China as supplicant and Americans as generous benefactors. Both Carter and Deng agreed that the guiding principles should be equality, reciprocity, and mutual benefit—but the playing field was far from level.[3]

The results, however, have been far more positive than negative. As Cheng Li has written, China's foreign study movement has had a far-reaching impact on virtually all aspects of Chinese higher education. "New academic disciplines such as international finance, international law, constitutionalism, and public administration have been established. Courses on human rights, environment and climate change, religion, gender issues, and homosexuality are offered in China's universities." There are no guarantees that these U.S.-educated elites are "less nationalistic and more pro-American than other Chinese elites."[4] Conversely, it may be the case that the loyalty of returned students is suspect. Nonetheless, they have had a profound impact not only on U.S.-China cultural relations, but also on the massive social changes taking place in China.

Despite frictions and mistrust, the overall benefits of cultural interchange are numerous. Chinese citizens enjoy Hollywood films, NBA basketball, and McDonald's while Americans embrace acupuncture, art exhibitions, and martial arts. Tourism is booming in both directions, and American families adopted more than 65,000 children from China during the first decade of the twenty-first century. All Chinese students are required to study English, and more Americans are learning the Chinese language than ever before. Thousands of exchange programs animate and inform the relationship. There is good reason to celebrate these connections, which are crucial in overcoming misperceptions and explaining Americans and Chinese to one another. But there are also questions and risks involved as Sino-American relations are transformed and both nations compete to project soft power.

CULTURAL DIPLOMACY BETWEEN CHINA AND THE UNITED STATES

Officials in Washington and Beijing are giving more attention to the public diplomacy and cultural dimension of the relationship.[5] One prominent example is the U.S.-China Consultation on People-to-People Exchange (CPE) mechanism, launched in May 2010, which meets alternately in Beijing and Washington. The goal is to "enhance and strengthen ties between the citizens of the United States and China." As a complement to the U.S.-China Strategic and Economic Dialogue, Secretary of State Hillary Clinton views the Exchange as "the premier convening mechanism for building cooperation between our two governments."[6]

The CPE serves as a high-level forum for discussion, an umbrella for exchanging information, and a means to encourage increased interaction between the two countries. Culture, education, sports, science and technology, and women's issues have been designated as areas of shared interest. The culture category includes youth outreach in the performing and visual arts; a cultural forum jointly hosted by the National Endowment for the Humanities and the Chinese Ministry of Education; museum and library exchanges; and programs organized by organizations such as the Philadelphia Orchestra, Rodeo China (to introduce the American West to China), the American Council of Young Political Leaders, and the Ivy Council (Ivy League colleges that cooperate with the All-China Students' Federation). China's State Councilor Liu Yandong has endorsed the CPE as an effort that "will not only bring benefits to the people of the two countries, but will also contribute greatly to the world peace, stability, and the prosperity."[7]

China's Cultural Diplomacy

President Hu Jiatao announced a strategy to "enhance culture as part of the soft power of our country" in a speech to the national congress of China's Communist Party in 2007. Exporting Chinese culture, the leadership believes, will enhance the country's image, garner respect, and contribute to its greater acceptance throughout the world. It will also help to counter fears about China's rise. Hu's policy was very much in evidence during the 2008 Beijing Olympics and the 2010 Shanghai Expo, and is visible in a growing number of educational and cultural exchange programs sponsored by China's government.

In September 2011, Minister of Culture Cai Wu told an American audience about the "great openness and tolerance of Chinese culture, which is based on the importance of human ethics. . . . It reflects the Golden Mean and temperance, and a firm belief in harmony and balance, which is free from narrow-mindedness and paranoia. Furthermore, the Chinese culture is a compassionate culture centered on humanity." China has never colonized smaller countries, and it has long maintained a tradition of peaceful exchange for mutual benefit, said the Minister. In short, China "has a longstanding historical tradition of advocating culture rather than force." This culture of harmony, he added, is crucial to China's future development, which depends on "a peaceful, tranquil and stable international environment." He concluded, "We should deepen mutual understanding through communication, increase mutual trust through dialogue, and expand common ground through exchanges."[8]

The flagship for China's international soft power push is the Confucius Institute program, established to promote Chinese language and culture in foreign countries. There is considerable irony in the choice of Confucius as the namesake for this effort since Confucian values were anathema to the Communists during their revolutionary years. His legacy was rehabilitated after

Mao, but ambivalence about the sage remains: a massive 31-foot bronze statue of Confucius placed in Tiananmen Square in January 2011 was removed four months later in the dead of night.

Confucius Institutes are administered by Beijing's Office of Chinese Language Council International, a government-funded organization commonly known as the *Hanban*. The first Institute in the United States was established at the University of Maryland in 2004, and by 2011 the number had increased to about 75 in the U.S. and some 350 worldwide, for a total cost of at least $500 million. Over 500 Confucius Classrooms, usually affiliated with the Institutes, provide resources to elementary and secondary schools.[9] Most Institutes are based at universities, a different approach from the freestanding cultural centers sponsored by France, Germany, the United Kingdom, and other countries. Chinese partner universities provide language teachers and *Hanban* provides teaching materials—but does not require they be used—and convenes annual conferences in China. More than 2,000 delegates attended the December 2011 meeting in Beijing. Among the most active U.S. programs are the University of Pittsburgh (which assists teachers and high schools across Pennsylvania), University of Oklahoma, University of Utah, and the City of Chicago Public Schools. President Hu Jintao visited the Chicago program in January 2011.

Each Confucius Institute typically receives $100,000 per year from *Hanban*, and provides matching support, usually in the form of staff and office space. However, a two-tier system is emerging with considerably more money going to some elite universities, such as University of Chicago, Columbia, and Stanford. (Others, such as the University of Pennsylvania, have decided against applying.) Stanford University received and matched $1 million for conferences and other programs, $1 million for graduate fellowships, and $2 million for a Confucius Institute professorship in Chinese poetry, for a total of $4 million.[10]

There was considerable skepticism about Confucius Institutes at the outset. Would the Chinese government influence the curriculum, censor activities, and threaten academic freedom? Would the Institutes become outlets for communist propaganda? Would the funding be worth the effort and would it be sustained?[11] Given these concerns, what accounts for their rapid growth in the U.S. and other countries? There are several reasons for their success. Confucius Institutes have considerable autonomy, and there is little evidence that *Hanban* dictates or interferes with local agendas. There is flexibility in how the funds can be used: many concentrate on elementary, high school, and public education, while some focus on business and one even pursues Chinese opera. In most cases, PRC funding is a very small percentage of overall budgets. Another incentive is the way that Institutes create or reinforce relationships with universities in China, opening up opportunities for faculty research, exchange, and student recruitment. From the Chinese perspective, the Institutes are cost-effective and valuable in reaching new audiences.

There is a tacit understanding that certain topics (human rights, Taiwan, Tiananmen, for example) should be avoided. Although *Hanban* has become more relaxed about its guidelines, not poking your finger in the eye of a sponsor is just a matter of common sense, say some Confucius Institute directors. Critics argue that funding from China will lead to self-censorship, and point to Tibet as an especially prickly subject. It appears, for example, that Emory University's president did not receive a visa to China and renewal of the university's Confucius Institute was delayed for several months in 2011 because of Emory's close relations with the Dalai Lama. Stanford University declined an initial offer from *Hanban* when told that sensitive issues like Tibet could not be discussed, and negotiations led to the compromise of a professorship in traditional Chinese poetry.[12]

U.S. Cultural Diplomacy

The Senate Foreign Relations Committee published a detailed report on U.S. public diplomacy in China in February 2011, voicing concerns about China's burgeoning soft power campaign. Requested by Senator Richard Lugar, the report argues that China's vigorous and well-funded programs are not being matched by the United States. "We are being overtaken in this area of foreign policy by China, which is able to take advantage of America's open system to spread its message in many different ways, while using its fundamentally closed system to stymie U.S. efforts." Just as U.S. trade with China is out of balance, "when it comes to interacting directly with the other nation's public we are in another lop-sided contest."[13]

Despite increased economic interdependence, Beijing has blocked U.S. efforts to engage Chinese citizens, charged the Lugar report. While China has funded Confucius Institutes in the United States, the U.S. government has not been able to establish equivalent programs. Unlike other countries, the United States has no major cultural center—only five public diplomacy "spaces." "American Corners"—resource centers that are placed in many host-country libraries around the world—have not been allowed in China. The Fulbright Program is active, but shared funding is modest and discussions about a joint U.S.-China Fulbright Commission, common in other countries, have not been successful. The overall lack of reciprocity is all the more distressing, says the Lugar report, because Beijing "restricts its own population's access to information about the outside world" through state-control of the media, including censorship of the Internet.

The report also expresses concern that the U.S. is losing an information war with China. The official Xinhua news agency opened an office in Times Square in New York in May 2011 and China Central Television airs on many U.S. cable channels. *China Daily*, the national English-language newspaper in China, is printed in nine cities in the United States (whether this growing footprint actually influences American public opinion is another question). By comparison, the Voice of America (VOA), which has only two correspondents in Beijing, has cut back on its Mandarin language radio and TV broadcasting, eliminated its Cantonese service, and is shifting its resources toward the Internet and social media. Radio Free Asia (RFA), which is more critical of China than VOA, has taken over shortwave broadcasts.[14]

Not only is the playing field uneven, contends the Lugar report, but China's motives are suspect. Harking back to a distant, unchanging past, China does not present an honest portrait of its culture and society today. The report concludes that China is doing everything it can to "obstruct, limit and blunt" American public diplomacy, and use its soft power efforts to enhance its prestige and regain its rightful position as a world power. "While some of their efforts are more effective than others, China currently has the resources and determination needed to drive this policy forward."[15]

To get around some of these restrictions, the U.S. Embassy in Beijing made ten awards to American institutions for a total of nearly $1 million in October 2011 to establish American cultural centers in tandem with Chinese universities, an approach that mirrors the structure of Confucius Institutes. Their purpose is to explain U.S. history and culture. The test case for this initiative was a project of Arizona State University and Sichuan University who jointly launched a Center for American Culture with State Department funding in December 2010; the two universities have various ties, including a Confucius Institute partnership.

It should be noted that U.S. public diplomacy in China has been circumscribed not only by China's policies, but also due to congressional budget cuts, security concerns (which limit access to the U.S. embassy and consulates), and a preoccupation with diplomacy in the Muslim world. After the Cold War, the Bureau of Educational and Cultural Affairs (ECA) at the U.S. Department of State replaced U.S. Information Service in 1999, signaling a lower priority for public diplomacy. In the final analysis, however, the most effective expressions of American culture and values are not conveyed by U.S. government agencies. The diversity and vitality of American life is conveyed by individuals and institutions in the private sector, through media, films and television, corporate advertising, non-governmental organizations, and many other forms of interaction.

PATHWAYS FOR CULTURAL UNDERSTANDING

Education

Teaching and learning is the single most important means of cultural exchange between China and the U.S. It is also big business. China sends more students to the United States than any other nation, with 157,558 (nearly 22 percent of all international students) studying in American universities in 2010–2011. Undergraduates from China have soared to more than one-third of the total, an increase of 43 percent over the previous year.[16] Most of them are paying the full cost of tuition, room and board. Many also pay substantial fees to recruiting agents, and there are serious complaints about unqualified students who use forged documents.[17]

By contrast, about 14,000 American students went to China in 2010–2011 as compared with 3,000 ten years earlier. This makes China the fifth most popular destination for study abroad, but represents only 5.1 percent of the U.S. total.[18] (The top four countries are the United Kingdom, Italy, Spain and France.) An additional 1,666 Americans are enrolled in various degree programs in China, according to the Institute of International Education.

On his trip to China in 2009, President Obama called for expanding these numbers. Secretary of State Clinton subsequently announced the "100,000 Strong Initiative" with the goal of doubling the number of American college and high school students going to the PRC by 2014. A related objective is to increase opportunities for underrepresented students "so that a broader cross-section of Americans can gain a deeper understanding of China, and will be better equipped to engage in the global economy."[19] This includes community colleges, middle and high school students, African Americans and Hispanics, students from lower economic backgrounds, and public schools. To help meet the $68 million goal for the program, Caterpillar, Motorola, Citigroup, and Coca-Cola have made major gifts to various schools and study abroad programs, and the Department of State has approached major U.S. foundations for support. For its part, China provides major support for the "100,000 Strong Initiative." For example, *Hanban* provides 10,000 Chinese Bridge scholarships for American high school students as well as school principals and American Chinese language teachers for short trips to China. In April 2011, the China Scholarship Council (CSC) announced another 10,000 scholarships, over a four-year period, for U.S. undergraduate and graduate students to study in China. Each of China's six consulates in the United States awards 50 scholarships to American colleges and universities annually, and local Chinese governments also offer money to foreign students.

The U.S. government funds various programs for American undergraduate and graduate students, postdoctoral students, and faculty to do research, language training, and cultural study in China and other countries. These include the Fulbright Program, Benjamin A. Gilman Scholarships, Boren Awards for International Study, National Security Education Program, National Security Language Initiative for Youth (for high school students), and programs of the National Science Foundation. However, funding for Title IX National Resource Centers, which support area studies training (including Chinese studies) at various American universities, was slashed by nearly 47 percent, from $34 million to $18 million, for the 2011 fiscal year. Another setback was the cancellation of the Fulbright-Hays Doctoral Dissertation Research Abroad program.[20]

Despite the fact that far fewer Americans study in China than Chinese in the United States, the academic study of China in the U.S. has considerable strength while American studies in China remains underdeveloped, although it is true that Chinese generally know more about American popular culture.[21] Scholars in China are eager for a more nuanced understanding of the United States, but immediate policy issues (such as Taiwan) as well as a concentration on English language and literature, rather than a broad appreciation of history and culture, have preempted deeper investigations of American society. "We need to look beyond what the U.S. president said yesterday," says one Chinese analyst, "and investigate the cultural, ethnic, and religious factors that help to explain America's behavior and its foreign-policy decisions."

The American Studies Association, Hong Kong-America Center, National Committee on U.S.-China Relations, U.S.-China Education Trust (USCET), and the China Fulbright Scholar Program are active in explaining American history and culture, but more collaborative research and institutional exchanges are needed. U.S. foundations, think tanks, and universities provide only modest support for American studies in China. In addition, Americans tend to take their own culture for granted, assuming their interests and values are easily accessible and widely understood.

Language Teaching and Learning

English language training has been central to China's modernization strategy, and the demand for foreign English teachers remains high. The U.S. government responds in different ways. The State Department's Bureau of Educational and Cultural Affairs (ECA) manages an Office of English Language Programs for teacher training and curriculum development, and the Regional English Language Office at the U.S. Embassy in Beijing helps to coordinate these efforts. The Peace Corps has 138 volunteers teaching English in China.

Many young Americans encounter China as English teachers with nonprofit organizations such as the Colorado China Council, Oberlin Shansi

Association, Princeton-in-Asia, VIA (formerly Volunteers in Asia at Stanford), World Teach (founded by Harvard students), and the Yale-China Association. All of them provide well-organized opportunities for in-depth cross-cultural learning.

Teach for China (TFC)—previously called the China Education Initiative—is an especially ambitious new venture. Founded in 2008, it is a U.S. non-profit with offices in Beijing, affiliated with the highly successful Teach for America program. After receiving start-up grants from the Lingnan Foundation and Luce Foundation, TFC secured major funding from Goldman Sachs and the Li Ka Shing Foundation in Hong Kong. Bright and able graduates from universities both in the U.S. and China make two-year commitments to teach in cities and towns where there is a shortage of qualified teachers. The Americans primarily teach English and the Chinese teach science and math. The Chinese schools provide housing and 50 percent of the salaries for the teaching fellows; TFC requires that all teachers have access to showers and the Internet. About 60 fellows taught in 20 middle schools in Yunnan Province during 2010, and 180 will participate in 2011 when the program expands to Guangdong Province. The goal is to have 1,000 teachers by 2016.[22]

In the U.S., nearly 61,000 American college students were enrolled in Chinese language classes in 2009, according to the Modern Language Association, and the emergence of dual language and two-way immersion programs in the U.S. suggests that studying Chinese is more than a passing fad.[23] Despite its small Asian population, the state of Utah has made an unusual commitment with 17 immersion programs at the elementary school level. (Jon M. Huntsman, who was a Mormon missionary in Taiwan and U.S. ambassador to Singapore and China, was influential in establishing these intensive language programs when he was Governor of Utah.) Students have a half-day in Chinese and the other half in English. "The demand is huge, and every school has waiting lists to get in," reports Eric Chipman at the University of Utah. During 2011–2012, 30 language teachers were sent to Utah by China's *Hanban*, six of them to teach in immersion programs and the remaining 24 in middle and secondary schools. Taiwan's Ministry of Education provides another eight or ten guest teachers annually. While business appears to be the primary explanation for the state's language programs—China is Utah's second largest trading partner—there is interest in Eastern culture, philosophy, and spirituality as well as the influence of the Morman church. "Most non-native Chinese immersion teachers are former missionaries and many parents of immersion students are also former missionaries, so they have seen the value of fluency in Mandarin Chinese and want their children to learn it as well," says Chipman.[24]

A number of non-profit organizations promote K–12 education on China. Some 1,200 participants attended the National Chinese Language Conference in San Francisco in 2011. The College Board, which administers the Advanced Placement exam in Mandarin, assists administrators and teachers through its Chinese Language and Culture Initiative, and collaborates with China's Confucius Institute headquarters to work with school districts and independent schools throughout the United States. The National Consortium for Teaching about Asia offers seminars and other resources for Asian studies at the elementary and secondary levels in the United States. The U.S.-China Teachers Education Exchange Program, based at the National Committee on U.S.-China Relations and funded by the Freeman Foundation, has sent about 400 teachers in both directions during the past five years.

American Universities in China

Propelled by a confluence of factors, American universities are flocking to China to set up ventures that go beyond conventional study abroad and language training. China offers physical safety and political stability for foreign students, not to mention the delights of Chinese food, the excitement of living in a different society, and the prospect of jobs. Chinese universities, for their part, see increased numbers of foreign students and scholars as a catalyst for world-class institutions and a means to counter the brain drain of talented Chinese students who choose to go overseas. To circumvent Internet censorship, some American university programs get beyond the "Great Firewall" by providing direct links to their home websites.

In addition, China has become a big revenue source for American higher education at a time when U.S. universities face fiscal problems. Thomas George, chancellor of the University of Missouri–St. Louis (UMSL), did not mince his words in announcing the formation of Sichuan Missouri University in Chengdu. "This is a money maker for us," he said. Under the agreement, UMSL, the Missouri University of Science and Technology, and China's Tianfu College will collaborate. The two American schools will help design the curriculum and Chinese students will spend their final two years in Missouri. The American universities could receive up to $4 million annually through the partnership.[25]

It is not surprising that the opening wedge for many joint projects is business management and executive education since these fields cater to China's desire to move up the economic value chain. Harvard Business School offers a Senior Executive Program taught in English and Chinese in cooperation with Tsinghua University's School of Economics and Management and the China Europe International Business School; a total of three weeks of training in China and Cambridge costs $45,000. Harvard's Global CEO Program for China, also three one-week modules, charges about $70,000.

New American university centers are springing up to coordinate large-scale overseas studies, faculty research, and exchange programs. The University of Chicago Center in Beijing, which opened in September 2011, focuses on three areas: business, economics, and policy; science, medicine, and public health; and culture, society, and the arts. Stanford University opened a center at Peking University in 2012 "as a base of operations for anyone in the Stanford community seeking to advance research or education by spending time in China." A Stanford alumnus in Hong Kong contributed $5 million for the project.[26] The University of Michigan and Shanghai Jiaotong University have collaborative research projects in biotechnology and renewable energy, and the University of California Berkeley is planning a program in engineering, also in Shanghai.

Nine American institutions had branch campuses in China and Hong Kong in 2009, based on a survey by the Observatory on Borderless Higher Education in London. The Hopkins-Nanjing Center, the earliest Sino-American joint academic venture, co-founded by Johns Hopkins University and Nanjing University in 1986, offers a one-year certificate and a two-year master's degree. A recent $10 million gift to Hopkins from Benjamin Yeung, an automotive industrialist who emigrated from China to the U.S., will build on the relationship to create new opportunities for research and exchange between the two universities.[27]

New York University is building a new campus in Shanghai's Pudong district which is due to open in 2013, in partnership with East China Normal University. NYU Shanghai will be a "completely independent comprehensive research university with a liberal arts and science college," according to the university, similar to NYU's first international campus in Abu Dhabi. With English as the primary language of instruction, it will offer both undergraduate and graduate programs to students from China, the U.S., and other countries. The initial financing will come from the government of Shanghai.[28]

Meanwhile, Duke University has partnered with Jiangsu Province to build a 200-acre campus in Kunshan, about 40 miles west of Shanghai. Due to open in 2013, the project has stirred controversy among Duke's faculty, who fault the decision-making process, are concerned about academic freedom, and worry about the project's financial implications, which will cost Duke about $40 million. While the stated goal is to establish a comprehensive university, Duke Kunshan University will start with master's programs in business administration. Students will divide their time between Kunshan and North Carolina.[29]

Nongovernmental Organizations (NGOs)

Private American organizations play a vital role in promoting cultural interaction with China. They foster education, dialogue, advocacy, and exchange between China and the U.S. They provide training and technical assistance on issues such as healthcare, humanitarian aid, law and human rights, and the environment. A closely related goal of such programs is to stimulate the development of civil society in China, a small but growing sector.

International NGOs typically work with Chinese government ministries to implement programs. One example is Mercy Corps, headquartered in Portland, Oregon, which assists ethnic minorities, migrant workers and rural farmers, and provided relief after the 2008 Sichuan earthquake. World Resources Institute, World Wildlife Fund (WWF), and National Resources Defense Council share best practices and sponsor activities with partners in China on biodiversity, climate change, energy, and other issues. WWF, which uses the giant panda as its international logo, has an office in Beijing and six field offices in China with about 80 staff working on renewable energy, sustainable forest management, and better regulation of trade in medicinal plants and animals, with the aim to "offer solutions that will simultaneously reduce China's global impact and improve livelihoods."[30]

Faith-based NGOs have considerable latitude to operate in China. American organizations such as World Vision, Adventist Development Relief Agency, American Friends Service Committee, and Habitat for Humanity have large staffs and large budgets. While proselytizing by foreign missionaries is illegal, other religious activities are permitted. East Gates International, headquartered in Sumner, Washington, has distributed millions of Bibles, and has built 50 churches and over 200 small libraries in China.[31]

Numerous organizations foster education and exchange. The National Committee on U.S.-China Relations, which dates from 1966, promotes "understanding and cooperation between the United States and Greater China in the belief that sound and productive Sino-American relations serve vital American and world interests." The Committee provides forums for American and Chinese leaders to present their views; training for teachers, congressional staff members, and young academics; and programs to increase public understanding. Another noteworthy organization is the Committee of 100, a nonpartisan group that offers "a collective voice for Chinese American leaders to speak to both U.S. and international issues."[32] The Carter Center in Atlanta offers voter education and monitors elections at the village level in cooperation with China's Ministry of Civil Affairs. Other groups, such as Human Rights Watch and Human Rights in China, are banned from mainland China but operate from Hong Kong or the U.S.

Chinese government officials have been ambivalent about the expansion of the private sector, concerned that independent organizations might become rallying points for political opposition. Civil society is emerging in China but faces many challenges, including restrictive laws, weak internal management and governance structure, lack of full-time professional staff, and unstable funding sources. Despite these limitations, the trend is toward greater acceptance of organizations that help to increase China's capacity to provide training and social services.

Think Tanks

All the major American think tanks have resident China specialists who analyze U.S.-China relations and China's domestic, regional, and global capabilities. These organizations inform the public and the media through lectures, conferences, and publications making the case for policy positions, testifying before Congress, and meeting with U.S. government agencies. Some sponsor unofficial Track II diplomacy meetings for off-the-record discussions on topics such as Taiwan or North Korea. Funding comes from individuals, corporations, and foundations as well as fees for briefings, seminars, and courses.

The American Enterprise Institute, Brookings Institution, Carnegie Endowment for International Peace, Center for Strategic and International Studies (CSIS), Council on Foreign Relations, Heritage Foundation, Peterson Institute of International Economics, National Bureau of Asian Research (NBR), National Committee on American Foreign Policy, and the Woodrow Wilson International Center for Scholars all deal with domestic, bilateral, regional, and transnational issues involving China. Their agendas cover health, energy and climate change, trade, economics, political, strategic, and other issues.

American policy specialists also spend time exchanging information and ideas with their counterparts in China. Two think tanks have established satellite operations in Beijing. In 2006, Brookings opened the Brookings-Tsinghua Center for Public Policy at Tsinghua University to facilitate "joint and individual research projects by Chinese and American scholars focusing on economic and social issues in China's development."[33] In 2010, the Carnegie Endowment set up a center in Beijing, also at Tsinghua University following the launch of offices in Moscow, Beirut, and Brussels. It brings together senior scholars and experts for collaborative research "on common global challenges that face the United States and China, including issues related to: nonproliferation and arms control; international economics and trade; climate change and energy; and other global and regional security issues such as North Korea, Afghanistan, and Iran."[34] It seems that an additional unspoken objective in having a presence in Beijing is to tap into Chinese funding.

While Chinese graduate students and policy specialists regularly have fellowships at U.S. think tanks and university research centers, only a handful of American scholars spend significant periods of time in China. Senior China specialists generally have weak Chinese language skills, although many younger policy specialists, some of them originally from China, are fluent in Chinese. Various PRC institutions welcome foreign scholars, but most of them lack well-organized programs for this purpose. Collaborative policy research between Americans and Chinese is fairly uncommon.

Foundations and Philanthropy

In concert with non-profit institutions and organizations, private foundations have several overlapping areas of concern: education and cultural exchange; poverty alleviation and healthcare; the development of civil society and philanthropy in China; and China's role in regional and global issues.

The Freeman, Luce, and Starr foundations support education and exchange aimed at increasing America's capacity to engage with China. It is not coincidental that the founders of these three philanthropies—Houghton ("Buck") Freeman, Henry R. Luce, and C.V. Starr, respectively—had formative personal experiences as young men in Asia. Other foundations pursue transnational themes. For example, the MacArthur and the Smith Richardson foundations concentrate on security issues in the Asian region. The Blue Moon Fund works on environmental issues. The Bill and Melinda Gates Foundation has committed $50 million to fighting HIV/AIDS in China.

The development of civil society and cultivation of local organizations in China has been a consistent theme of the Ford Foundation's Beijing office, which makes $12 million in grants annually. Ford gives particular attention to helping poor communities, women, migrants, minorities, and other groups. The Asia Foundation (TAF), an operating foundation with a Beijing office, concentrates on legal development, governance, women's empowerment, disaster management, environmental protection, and international relations. Both Ford and TAF have been unable to renew their registrations with the Chinese government, which has made banking and payrolls for local staff more complicated but has not otherwise impinged on their operations.

The Rockefeller Brothers Fund (RBF) supports environmental work in southern China where it funds U.S.-China partnerships. One is a project on carbon reduction jointly directed by the Global Environmental Institute in Beijing and the Center for Climate Strategies in Washington, D.C. Program Director Shenyu Belsky divides her time between New York and Guangzhou, working to "incubate" local Chinese foundations and help NGOs increase their ability to make grants. At present, she says, China's emerging philanthropic sector "has more money than they know how to give," and the ability to manage and absorb large grants can be a problem.[35]

Various American groups work with their Chinese counterparts to share best practices in order to increase transparency and accountability. According

to the China Foundation Center in Beijing, there were 1,186 private foundations in 2011, a dramatic increase since regulations were liberalized in 2004.
Public response to the 2008 Sichuan earthquake—which left 70,000 dead and
some five million homeless—marked a turning point for philanthropy and
volunteerism in China, although the majority of giving still comes from the
corporate sector.

The Foundation Center in New York shares information and databases
with the China Foundation Center in Beijing, which opened its doors in 2010.
The Center on Philanthropy at Indiana University has signed agreements with
new philanthropy centers and institutes in China, including the Beijing Normal University Philanthropy Research Center and the Institute for Civil Society at Sun Yat-sen University in Guangzhou. Another effort is the China-U.S.
Strategic Philanthropy Partnership (CUSP), launched by the East-West Center
in August 2011, which aims to build "a network of U.S. and Chinese leaders working together to promote innovative philanthropy." Joint committees
have been established for five areas: legal issues, including tax policy; capacity
building; social enterprise investment and innovation; the non-profit sector;
and transparency and accountability.[36]

American foundations face opportunities as well as challenges in responding to China's growing wealth. Two key questions are, first, how can the rise of
organized philanthropy in China be encouraged and how can U.S. foundations
contribute to the relationship in ways that will complement Chinese efforts?
And, second, can Americans reconcile their agendas with China's realities, especially in sensitive areas such as law and human rights?

Arts Organizations

Exchange in the arts is sometimes expressed in surprising ways. The new Martin
Luther King Jr. Memorial on the National Mall in Washington, D.C., was carved
out of granite from China's Fujian Province by Chinese sculptor Lei Yixin, who
was selected through an international competition. Unprecedented joint concerts took place in Washington, D.C., Philadelphia, and New York in 2011.

Numerous new collaborations are emerging. The U.S.-China Forum on the
Arts and Culture is a high-profile venture organized by the Asia Society and
the Aspen Institute. Its inaugural event in Beijing in November 2011—a $1
million production—featured film-screenings, dialogues, and performances
with prominent American and Chinese actors, musicians, directors, and writers such as Meryl Streep, Yo-Yo Ma, Joel Cohen, and Amy Tan. A reciprocal
delegation of Chinese cultural figures is expected to visit the U.S. in 2012.[37]

As China ramps up investment in its domestic cultural offerings, a partnership has emerged between New York's Lincoln Center for the Performing Arts

and a Chinese state-owned company to help develop a new performing arts complex in the city of Tianjin, China's fifth largest city. The Americans will "recommend the content of artistic programming, propose an economic model for the performing arts center's operations, establish a design and construction process, and provide staff training." A spokesperson for Lincoln Center hopes the joint venture "will foster greater artistic exchanges between Chinese artists and organizations and their American counterparts."[38]

Museums play an active role in shaping and informing cultural perceptions. *Art in America: 300 Years of Innovation,* which appeared in Beijing and Shanghai in 2007, was the first survey exhibition of its kind. In 2010, the Asian Art Museum of San Francisco featured an exhibition about life and culture in Shanghai co-organized with the Shanghai Museum. Exhibitions of traditional Chinese art draw big audiences in the U.S., and the Asia Society, China Institute, and International Center of Photography have organized shows of contemporary Chinese art and photography in New York, works that are hugely popular on the international art market but not always acceptable in China.

Even the ancient past can be controversial. In early 2011, an exhibition organized by the University of Pennsylvania Museum featuring 4,000-year-old mummies and cultural objects from China's Xinjiang Province. When "Secrets of the Silk Road" was due to open, Chinese authorities almost cancelled and then cut back the dates for the show. They claimed the shortened schedule was unrelated to politics, but the fact that the mummies have Caucasian faces, suggesting that Xinjiang's earliest inhabitants were not Chinese, may have contributed to the decision. Protests by Uyghur separatists in Xinjiang have been a thorn in Beijing's side.[39]

The exchange of individual artists is fostered by organizations like the New York–based Asian Cultural Council. The resulting cross-pollination leads some Chinese to create hybrids that appeal mainly to Western aesthetics. The fact that these artists are better known outside China—satire of socialist realism is one persistent theme—raises questions about audience, taste, and identity, not to mention money and politics. The most visible example is Ai Weiwei, who lived in New York City from 1981 to 1993, and whose use of art to protest China's human rights abuses led to his highly publicized arrest in Beijing in April 2011.

Ai's case may help to explain why China's contemporary popular culture has not penetrated the U.S. very deeply. When the Hollywood movie *Kung Fu Panda* was hugely successful in China, it led some Chinese critics to ask why their country has not produced its own version of such a film for foreigners. Robert Daly believes the fundamental reason is censorship, which leads American audiences to boredom and suspicion about China's true motives. Culture is mandated or at least monitored in a top-down system managed by the Ministry of Culture; the State Administration of Radio, Film and Television; State Council Information Office; and the General Administration of Press and Publication. Artistic productions designed for export are stifled in this environment. "In an attempt to skirt this problem," writes Daly, "Chinese cultural diplomacy focuses on spectacle, decoration, the politically safe past, or vague discussion of values. But song and dance troupes, acrobats, photo exhibits, and lectures on Confucianism cannot wholly compensate for the absence of free Chinese artists and entertainers."[40]

CONCLUSION

In education, policy studies, philanthropy, the arts, and many other realms Chinese and American partnerships and collaborations have opened minds and imaginations on both sides of the Pacific. They are public and private, formal and informal, institutional and individual. Thirty years ago, China was impoverished and its own traditions were only beginning to recover from the devastation of the Cultural Revolution. For the sake of modernization Deng Xiaoping was willing to send the best and brightest abroad for education, realizing that not all of them would return. Playing catch-up, China's relations with the U.S. were one-sided because Americans did the teaching while Chinese did the learning. Now that China has arrived on the world stage, Beijing is bankrolling its cultural diplomacy on a major scale, sending out the message that Chinese soft power should be taken seriously.

Have the tables been turned because of China's wealth and a relative decline of U.S. power? Is the United States losing a competition with China for cultural influence, as the 2011 Senate Foreign Relations Committee report charges? U.S. diplomats do face obstacles from Chinese authorities in telling America's story, and it is true that Beijing is investing more money in its cultural power than Washington. Congressional budget cuts for international education at American universities are worrisome. However, there is no evidence that the growing number of Confucius Institutes in the U.S. represents a sinister plot to undermine the American way of life, despite some frictions over the Dalai Lama and Tibet. The fact that more Americans are studying Chinese language and culture is widely recognized as a good thing for the United States. Similarly, the State Department's support for American culture centers at universities in China is a positive development for Chinese citizens.

Overall, the balance sheet remains very uneven. There are, for instance, almost nine times more Chinese students and scholars coming to the U.S. than Americans going to China, a ratio that both governments are trying to improve. Because Chinese focus heavily on science and business, their understanding of U.S. history and culture lacks depth. By contrast, American scholarly expertise in Chinese studies has considerable strength. On the other hand, while Chinese people are quite familiar with American movies, music, and TV shows, Americans have almost no appreciation for Chinese popular culture. The most important disparity, however, is the fact China relies heavily on government, while the United States has a huge range of private organizations to convey its cultural values and norms. Chinese culture therefore has the appearance of being packaged and managed, and by contrast American culture seems open and fluid.

These disparities have not dampened the energy and enthusiasm for new relationships between the two societies. As we see from the case studies highlighted in this chapter, the overall trends are encouraging. There is a greater volume of cultural connections, increased reciprocity and mutual benefit, more partnerships and collaborations, experimentation with new forms of exchange, and the transfer of best practices from the U.S. to China in the NGO and philanthropic sectors.

Nonetheless, there are significant hazards in U.S.-China cultural relations beyond other measurements or comparisons. One danger is to imagine that institutions in China and the United States are equivalent. The gaps are usually explained in terms of a history of misperceptions and a need for mutual respect. This line of thinking holds that people-to-people exchange will inevitably demolish stereotypes and will inspire empathy and understanding. Yet increased engagement may produce dashed hopes if Chinese and Americans fail to closely examine their distinctive assumptions, motives, objectives, professional and educational standards, laws, and regulations.

Another risk is the commercialization and monetization of cultural relations. Flush with cash, Beijing has launched a campaign to buy influence that has produced a gold-rush mentality for American institutions, no matter how wealthy or prestigious they may be. The lure of Chinese students who are able to pay full tuition, but may lack English language and critical thinking skills, can lead to opportunism. As with Japan in the 1980s, the scramble to set up joint and dual degree programs and branch campuses in China may lead to diluted standards and disillusion. Regrettably, there is very little to show for U.S.-Japan joint educational ventures today.[41]

A third problem is China's restrictions on free expression, including censorship; crackdowns on artists, lawyers and writers; and the denial of visas for foreign scholars. The latitude for free speech in China has grown dramatically, but arrests and detentions of dissidents have also increased. Some prominent China specialists in the U.S. have been prevented from traveling to the PRC because of their support for human rights issues; various scholars who study Tibet have had visa problems; and a group of specialists on Xinjiang's history and politics has been banned because of their participation in a book project.[42] Such cases can lead to self-censorship on the part of other American scholars.

Until China's government allows open discussion and debate of social, cultural, and political issues with unfettered access to the Internet, any aspirations for world-class universities or other institutions will be hampered. Corruption and a lack of transparency are related problems, which are disincentives for foreign entities to join forces with Chinese partners. It is unlikely that major U.S. production companies will back films that offend China; the downside of doing so was made clear to Disney in 1997 when it released *Kundun*, a movie about the life of the Dalai Lama. But threats and coercion, subtle or not, only diminish a nation's soft power.

Public and cultural diplomacy need not be viewed as a zero-sum game or a blunt instrument for Cold War–type propaganda, and cultural power is, of course, not just a matter of numbers, money, and politics. To be credible the content must be interesting, useful, and reliable. American culture has enormous appeal because it emerges from individual expression and innovation. These values are certainly not absent in Chinese society, which has seen a vibrant cultural renaissance in the past three decades, but China's message will be muted so long as the ruling Communist Party insists on playing it safe— imposing censorship, buying influence, and resorting to the trope of China as a refined, peaceful, superior civilization.

Polls by the Chicago Council on Global Affairs in 2008 and BBC in 2010 show that U.S. soft power remains far greater than China's, much of it is residing within civil society rather than government. As Joseph Nye notes, "American soft power rests on a variety of resources that range from Hollywood to Harvard; from Madonna to the Gates Foundation; from Martin Luther King's speeches to Barack Obama's election. It is not easy for governments to sell their country's charm if their narrative is inconsistent with domestic realities."[43] In short, there is a disconnect between China's rhetoric about peace and harmony, and the realities of an authoritarian system that actually undermines China's cultural power.

Americans and Chinese have long been fascinated by one another; admiration and emulation have alternated with envy and hostility depending on needs, opportunities, and political circumstances. Broader and deeper cultural engagement between the U.S. and China has helped to reduce misunderstanding, but culture also continues to be an arena for competition. The U.S. asserts the universality of democracy, and the PRC proclaims the virtues of Confucian values. Yet until China comes to terms with its own recent past and can celebrate its diversity without fear, the openness and freedom of American culture will continue to lure Chinese into thinking that the moon shines brighter in the United States.

NOTES

I am grateful to Helena Kolenda, Cheng Li, Carola McGiffert, Kathryn Mohrman, and David Shambaugh for their comments on earlier drafts of this chapter.

1. Quoted in Edward Wong, "China Must Raise Cultural Influence, Leader Says," *New York Times*, January 4, 2012.

2. Gillian Wong, "Hu: Hostile Forces Seek to Westernize, Split China," *Associated Press*, January 3, 2012; Carlos Tejada, "China Culls 'Low Taste' Shows," *Wall Street Journal*, January 4, 2012.

3. See Cheng Li (ed.), *Bridging Minds Across the Pacific: U.S.-China Educational Exchanges, 1978–2003* (Lanham, MD: Lexington Books, 2005).

4. Communication with Cheng Li, December 16, 2011.

5. Cultural diplomacy, as one aspect of public diplomacy, is the use of cultural resources by governments to communicate with and influence citizens of another country. It becomes propaganda when audiences doubt the motives or truthfulness of the message.

6. http://www.state.gov/secretary/rm/2010/05/142181.htm.

7. http://www.state.gov/secretary/rm/2011/04/160631.htm.

8. See "Culture a Common Thread Throughout the World," *China Daily,* September 21, 2011, available at: http://www.chinadaily.com.cn/usa/201109/21/content_13752499.htm, for the full text for Cai Wu's speech at the Woodrow Wilson International Center for Scholars.

9. Chen Jia, "Making a World of Difference," *China Daily,* December 14, 2011; available at: http://english.hanban.org. The first Confucius Institute at a historically black school opened at Xavier University in New Orleans in 2011.

10. Daniel Golden, "China Says No Talking Tibet as Confucius Funds U.S. Universities," *Bloomberg*, November 1, 2011, available at: http://www.bloomberg.com/news/2011-11-01/china-says-no-talking-tibet-as-confucius-funds-u-s-universities.html.

11. Peter Schmidt, "At U.S. Colleges, Chinese-Financed Centers Prompt Worries About Academic Freedom," *Chronicle of Higher Education*, October 17, 2010.

12. Telephone interviews; Golden, "China Says No Talking Tibet."

13. "Another U.S. Deficit—China and America—Public Diplomacy in the Age of the Internet," authored by Paul Foldi, Committee on Foreign Relations, United States Senate, February 11, 2011, v, available at: http://www.lugar.senate.gov/issues/foreign/diplomacy/ChinaInternet.pdf.

14. L. Gordon Crovitz, "The VOA Is Losing Its Voice," *Wall Street Journal*, April 20, 2011. VOA and RFA also broadcast in Tibetan, and RFA has a Uyghur service.

15. "Another U.S. Deficit," p. 3.

16. *Open Doors Report on International Educational Exchange* (Institute of International Education, New York, 2011), available at: http://www.iie.org/opendoors. Business and management accounts for 28 percent, followed by 19 percent in engineering. Women represent 53 percent of the undergraduate total. An additional 7,000 Chinese students study at the secondary level in the U.S., mainly in private schools.

17. Daniel Golden, "China Rush to U.S. Colleges Reveals Predatory Fees for Recruits," *Bloomberg*, May 22, 2011, available at: http://www.bloomberg.com/news/2011-05-22/china-rush-to-u-s-colleges-reveals-predatory-fees.html.

18. *Open Doors Report*, op. cit. Fifty-four percent of the 270,604 U.S. students who studied abroad in 2009/2010 went to Europe.

19. Carola McGiffert, "100,000 Strong: Building Strategic Trust in U.S.-China Relations through Education," in *IIE Passport: Study Abroad in China 2011*, 5–6; telephone interview with Carola McGiffert, July 13, 2011.

20. Seteney Shami and Holly Danzeisen, "Midnight Surprise: Preliminary Reactions to the Federal International Education Budget Cuts," *Items and Issues* (Social Science Research Council), July 20, 2011, available at: http://itemsandissues.ssrc.org/midnight-surprise-preliminary-reactions-to-the-federal-international-education-budget-cuts. The Andrew W. Mellon Foundation stepped into the breach with a one-time $3.16 million grant to IIE for doctoral students in the humanities who had lost their funding.

21. See Terrill E. Lautz, "China's Deficit in American Studies," *Chronicle of Higher Education*, August 12, 2010.

22. Telephone interview with Andrea Pasinetti and Rachel Wasser, June 9, 2011.

23. *Enrollments in Languages Other Than English in United States Institutions of Higher Education* (New York: Modern Language Association, Fall 2009). Enrollments in Chinese increased by 18.2 percent since 2006, but the number of students was behind those for Spanish, French, German, Italian, and Japanese.

24. E-mail exchanges with Eric Chipman, July 18 and 19, 2011.

25. "UMSL joins plan for university in China," *St. Louis Post Dispatch*, September 22, 2011, available at: http://www.stltoday.com/news/local/education/article_6ba5719c-a047-5ec8-8588-0d66de5800e5.html.

26. Stanford Center, available at: http://scpku.stanford.edu/about.

27. The University of Nottingham in the U.K. opened the first Sino-foreign university in Ningbo, Zhejiang Province in 2005.

28. NYU Shanghai, available at: http://www.nyu.edu/about/news-publications/news/2011/03/27/nyu-and-shanghai-partner-to-create-nyu-shanghai.htm. Yale University is setting up a liberal arts college with National University of Singapore.

29. Lauren Carroll, "Kunshan Campus Takes Shape Amid Doubts," *The Chronicle of Higher Education*, April 6, 2011; Ian Wilhelm, "Duke Faculty Question the University's Global Ambitions," *Chronicle of Higher Education*, November 4, 2011.

30. http://www.wwfchina.org/english/loca.php?loca=60.

31. Xu Yihua, "Religion in Current Sino-U.S. Relations," in Douglas Spelman (ed.), *The United States and China: Mutual Public Perceptions* (Washington, D.C.: Woodrow Wilson International Center for Scholars, Washington, D.C., 2011), p. 114.

32. Committee of 100, available at: http://www.committee100.org.

33. http://www.brookings.edu/brookings-tsinghua.aspx.

34. http://carnegieendowment.org/about/index.cfm?fa=beijing.

35. Telephone interview with Shenyu Belsky, June 28, 2011.

36. Stephan Finsterbusch, "Nurturing the Germ of Philanthropy," *South China Morning Post*, September 21, 2010; telephone interview with Peter Geithner, September 23, 2011.

37. www.asiasociety.org/uschinaforum.

38. Robin Pogrebin, "Lincoln Center to Venture Into China as Adviser for a Performing Arts Project," *New York Times*, April 28, 2011; *China Daily*, June 21, 2011, available at: http://www.chinadaily.com.cn/usa/epaper/2011-05/31/content_12612478.htm.

39. James Cuno, "When Millennia-Old Mummies Threaten National Identity," *Yale-Global*, February 23, 2011, available at: http://yaleglobal.yale.edu/content/when-millennia-old-mummies-threaten-national-identity; Philip Kennicott, "Following Controversy, Mummies at Penn Museum Remain Objects of Mystery," *Washington Post*, March 3, 2011.

40. Robert Daly, "A Rise Without Shine: The Global Weakness of Chinese Culture," in Spelman (ed.), *The United States and China: Mutual Public Perceptions*, op cit, p. 85.

41. See Gail Chambers and William Cummings, "Profiting from Education: Japan-United States International Educational Ventures in the 1980s" (New York: Institute of International Education, 1990); and Beth McMurtrie, "Culture and Unrealistic Expectations Challenge American Campuses in Japan," *Chronicle of Higher Education*, June 2, 2000.

42. Daniel Golden and Oliver Staley, "China Banning U.S. Professors Elicits Silence from Colleges Employing Them," *Bloomberg*, August 10, 2011, available at: http://www.bloomberg.com/news/2011-08-11/china-banning-u-s-professors-elicits-silence-from-colleges.html.

43. Joseph S. Nye, "American and Chinese Power after the Financial Crisis," *The Washington Quarterly*, October 2010, 146.

10

The Military-Security Relationship

Christopher P. Twomey

Until rather recently it was easy to conclude that Sino-American security tensions did not dominate the countries' relationship. Today, such a judgment remains accurate, but the uncertainties loom much larger. The focus of this chapter will be on these dynamics; as such, it presents a generally bleak picture. That does not, however, reflect a fully accurate appraisal of the overall relationship. As the other chapters in this volume illustrate there are a wide range of institutional, economic, cultural, and international factors that will tend to reduce these tensions. Most stabilizing is the massive amount of bilateral trade and China's broader incorporation within the global economy, and the global institutional infrastructure that facilitate its operation, as emphasized in John Ikenberry's chapter. These phenomena will have a much greater positive influence on the relationship, likely overwhelming the negative elements in the security domain.

It is important to avoid the most pessimistic assumptions in evaluating the relationship. Contrary to offensive realist views (e.g., see the chapter by Ashley Tellis), zero-sum competition does not dominate in the relationship, even if security dilemmas (by their nature, mitigable) are important drivers of the competitive elements in the relationship. There are some conflicts of national interest, as they are currently defined. But such interests do evolve over time, and such conflicts do not overwhelm the relationship today. There remains room for adroit statecraft to reduce the prospects of worst-case outcomes.

NEW SECURITY CONSIDERATIONS

China is increasingly emphasizing "global" interests for its military. In 2004, Hu Jintao proclaimed the People's Liberation Army's (PLA) "New Historic Missions."[1] This strategic guidance retains the PRC's longstanding generally benign view of the international environment, the centrality of the military's role to support the Communist Party, the reform era's emphasis on economic development, and the need to defend China's territorial integrity. However, notable in Hu's instructions was an expectation that the military "play an important role in safeguarding world peace and promoting common development."

The United States has long had such global security interests. As the American involvement in Iraq and Afghanistan draws to a close, issues such as nonproliferation and the protection of "global commons"—international waters, outer space, among others—rise in relative importance and require multilateral cooperation. America's strategic "pivot to Asia" is another shift in emphasis. Still, U.S. policy explicitly renounces "containment" of China, instead, calling for "strategic stability."[2]

Nevertheless, it is critical to recognize that security interests are predominantly viewed through a military lens. This is shown definitively by the priority each country gives to its military in budgetary terms. For Beijing, real defense spending in the past 15 years has averaged approximately 12 percent per year, significantly outpacing overall GDP growth rates.[3] For the United States, total annual military spending of some $700 billion amounts to 15 times the spending on foreign aid and diplomacy and represents nearly half of global military spending.

The areas of interaction on security issues between the United States and China are numerous. As a way of organizing the consideration of these, the bulk of this chapter will consider different geographies, working outward from China. Beginning with the "littoral and immediate periphery," progressing through the "intermediate periphery," and finally to global issues, this chapter details a broad range of security issues in the U.S.-China relationship. In each of the subsequent geographic sections, this chapter discusses the security interests at stake for the two before turning to an assessment of the relevant military balance of power that might come into play there.

Across these zones it is clear that the balance of power has shifted toward Beijing; however, this is predominately the case in the geography nearest to China's shores. Given that, the diverging interests within this nearest geographic zone pose serious potential problems for strategic relations between the two nations. Further afield, the conflicts are less divisive, and the balance favors the United States. In all cases, it is important to recognize that there are both elements of traditional security dilemmas and conventional conflicts of interest in Sino-American relations.

THE LITTORAL AND IMMEDIATE PERIPHERY

It is in the seas nearest to China where Beijing's security interests are strongest and most sensitive. China is a continental power blessed with natural barriers on most land borders whose main concerns lie a few score miles off its shores. Taiwan and, increasingly, U.S. reconnaissance in nearby waters are the most important of these, but the troubled Korean Peninsula is only slighter further afield.

The Taiwan Strait

Taiwan remains the most likely source of conflict between Washington and Beijing, despite very promising improvements in cross-Strait relations in recent years.[4] Both sides have a shared interest in avoidance of military conflict across the Taiwan Strait, but they also have diverging secondary preferences between reunification and ensuring Taiwan possesses adequate defensive capabilities. Politically, President Hu Jintao led a more moderate political tone on reunification (such as a relaxed approach toward reunification timetables and a toleration of pragmatic engagement with Taipei). Nevertheless, for his entire tenure, military modernization has enhanced China's capabilities to threaten Taiwan. Most importantly, the increase in short-range missiles that are relevant (essentially) only for Taiwan scenarios has been rapid over the past decade, although promisingly it has tailed off in the last few years as shown in figure 10.1.

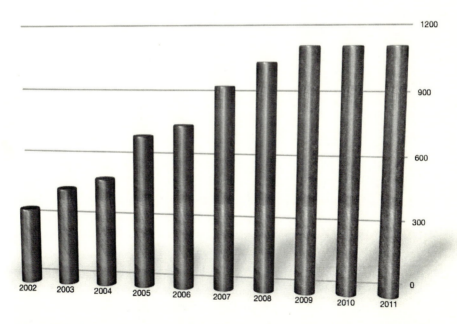

Figure 10.1. Chinese Short-Range Ballistic Missiles. Average values drawn from specified years of *Military and Security Developments Involving the People's Republic of China: Annual Report to Congress* (Washington, DC: Department of Defense, 2011).

Beginning under President Bush and continuing in the Obama administration, the United States worked to strengthen its unofficial relationship with
Taiwan. The "regularization" of U.S.-Taiwan interactions remains anathema
to Beijing. There has been a strengthening of policy language on U.S.-Taiwan
relations that goes back over a decade now, with increased emphasis on the
Taiwan Relations Act (TRA) alongside the traditional "three communiqués" in
describing U.S. policy toward Taiwan.[5] But the purest measure of this is arms
sales, which have become more "normal" and are accompanied by greater
military-to-military contact between the U.S. and the island's defense communities. The large arms sales of recent years were about all that Taiwan's military (or defense budget) could absorb at the time. In addition to high profile
weapons sales, there is notable cooperation on doctrinal and other "software"
reforms to Taiwanese defense capabilities.[6] While high-level political contacts
are still frozen, a variety of other bilateral initiatives have flourished. One area
that remains particularly disconcerting to Beijing is Taiwan's purchase of missile defense systems from the United States. Such systems address (minimally)
the main coercive weapon China has against Taiwan, but more than that, imply a degree of operational cooperation between Washington and Taipei that
is deeply disturbing to Beijing.[7]

As Shelley Rigger's chapter discusses, nationalism—among the most powerful forces in international affairs—is strengthening in Taiwan. This does not
bode well for cross-Strait relations, and therefore for Sino-American relations.

EEZs and Local Reconnaissance

The United States routinely engages in reconnaissance and "freedom of navigation" patrols near Chinese sovereign territory, raising two issues. First, as China rises it is chaffing at prevailing norms that had been shaped by the United
States. These include close-in reconnaissance, the treatment of "international
waters" (a term without legal standing that the United States regularly refers
to), and the United Nations Convention on the Law of the Sea, or UNCLOS
(which the United States generally adheres to as a representation of "custom-
ary law" despite not ratifying it). Washington is following its own decades-long
practices, and generally acting in accordance with widely, although not universally, accepted international norms.[8] But these are norms that the United States,
following the practices of the previous global maritime hegemon, Britain, has
played the lead role in establishing. Beijing did not have a major voice in any of
them, and now as power ratios have shifted, there is bound to be some contestation of those rules.[9]

Most critically, China claims a higher degree of sovereign rights over its
Exclusive Economic Zone (EEZ) than is generally accepted. Specifically, China

has called for a cessation of military transits there (which could be viewed as patrols and espionage). The status of such transits in international law is not perfectly clear on this point, although United States' practices engaging in such transits and viewing them as consistent with UNCLOS are aligned with normal international behavior. These conflicting views were an important source of the EP-3 incident (2001) and the USNS *Impeccable* incident (2009), both incidents where China bristled at reconnaissance dozens of miles from its coastline.

Second, the United States will be continually, indeed increasingly, interested in monitoring Chinese military modernization through precisely such missions. The operating tempo of offshore reconnaissance apparently increased in the late Clinton administration, as modern Chinese naval vessels began plying the nearby waters.[10] That interest level has remained substantial, then, through several presidential administrations and numerous military commanders. As the People's Liberation Army Navy (PLAN) continues to deploy new ships and submarines at sea, particularly nuclear-armed submarines in the near term, U.S. intelligence gathering on them will likely intensify, and the means of gathering it, will diversify.[11] For the United States, gathering such intelligence is critical to maintaining its military advantages should conflict erupt.

Korean Contingencies

The Kim dynasty has made North Korea an erratic actor in the Northeast Asian security environment that complicates Sino-American relations. More fundamentally, however, the United States and China have conflicting interests about the future of Korea. While both would like to see North Korea denuclearized, that goal is a much higher priority for the United States. China has other competing goals: avoiding a North Korean collapse that would lead to economic and migration pressures on China's northeast provinces. Furthermore, regardless of how smoothly a reunification might occur, China would have a very strong interest in reducing the U.S. role on the entire peninsula and certainly in the north. The United States cannot credibly commit to avoiding such temptations, and indeed has remained studiously silent on the issue. For China, even a problematic North Korean buffer is preferable to a unified Korea that is under the sway of Washington.

A number of mechanisms have emerged to help deal with the problems posed by North Korean nuclear weapons. The diplomatic framework that the United States encouraged China to develop, the Six Party Talks, is not likely to resolve these Korean problems, but it has reduced the tensions in the Sino-American relationship and provided a degree of regional consensus in facing North Korea over the nuclear program.[12] The Proliferation Security Initiative, a broader U.S.-led program aimed to prevent proliferation beyond North Korea, has been viewed cautiously in Beijing. These may help bound the dangers of North Korean proliferation, but cannot address the broader differences over North Korea itself between China and the United States.

The dangers of inadvertent conflict between China and the United States in future Korean contingencies are large. Future provocations from the North are likely to be met with a firm response by the allied South Korean and United States militaries. China's reactions to their previous modest responses was shrill; larger and more kinetic engagement by those allies will bring potent military capabilities into waters and airspace very close to Chinese territories and threaten an important interest of the sustainability of a buffer state. Were a North Korean provocation or collapse to result in a ground conflict, the inevitable combined command offensive north, manned by South Korean and U.S. troops, would soon press toward Chinese borders. There have been no significant discussions between the United States and China about how such a scenario could be managed. Given that such a situation led to massive misperceptions in 1950,[13] and the stakes remain high today, similar catastrophes are possible.

Key Military Considerations in the Littoral and Immediate Periphery

Chinese military assets densely populate the immediate periphery in which the above three security issues reside. Although ranges vary, many relevant systems have capabilities out to a few hundred kilometers, thus affecting the aforementioned littoral cases and those alone.

Today, China's military activities in its home waters are often summarized in the term "anti-access/area denial (A2/AD)."[14] Such capabilities seek to deny the use of nearby waters to opposing forces, forestalling their ability to project power.

A first layer to consider is China's very modern diesel submarine fleet.[15] Numbering some 30 boats and counting, this is a potent but short-range force. These remain primarily useful for nearby contingencies given their small size, slow deployment, and limited—if expanded—endurance.

Land-based air assets flying from numerous Chinese airbases are a second element. Increasingly, the People's Liberation Army Air Force (PLAAF) and the PLAN's air wings, are flying modern strike aircraft that can be equipped with standoff cruise missiles that are varied in their flight profiles and potent in their capabilities. Such aircraft, while certainly at risk from attack from other aircraft, would be more secure as they fly within a hundred miles of the Chinese coastline where advanced surface to air missiles (SAMs) would complicate the tactics of attackers.[16]

Numerous Chinese naval vessels would also ply such waters. China currently fields approximately 80 small fast attack boats that are armed with advanced surface-to-ship missiles. These lethal boats and other expendable craft would pose grave dangers to any navy operating near Chinese waters.[17] Other more capable ships have comparative advantage further afield.

Most problematic inside the few hundred kilometer range are the short-range ballistic missiles (SRBMs) in China's possession. As figure 10.1 illustrates, those that can reach Taiwan number well over 1,000 (although Okinawa and Guam are beyond the reach of the brunt of China's arsenal). There is increasing agreement that these missiles put in grave jeopardy the ability of Taiwan's air force to play a meaningful role in intense conflict.[18]

The newest system of relevance in this strategic terrain is the anti-ship ballistic missile (ASBM) that is approaching operational capability.[19] This DF-21 variant had range that far exceeds the narrow confines of China's home waters, but it is most relevant for such conflicts; the farther one gets from Chinese waters, the more complicated the targeting of such a missile becomes.[20]

To date, Chinese effectiveness with all these capabilities has been marred by a lack of integration and "jointness." This may change and improve over time.

The Pentagon is responding to these Chinese improvements by emphasizing synergies between naval and air forces and more dispersed platforms to complicate the Chinese calculus.[21] Today, the United States maintains selected assets that can penetrate through the A2/AD zone from positions of relative security, such as stealthy bombers, submarines, and standoff cruise missiles. Still, operating in close proximity to Chinese territory during intense military conflict has become increasingly dangerous for U.S. forces. U.S. anti-submarine warfare capabilities (ASW) have atrophied substantially from their Cold War peaks. Naval patrol planes would be vulnerable in contested airspace. Absent corvettes in large numbers, there is no credible way for the United States to insert surface naval assets into the littoral region in wartime. On the other hand, American nuclear-powered attack submarines (SSNs) are extremely quiet, have tremendous endurance, and a range of advanced sensors and weaponry.

Tactical attack aircraft, a mainstay of contemporary U.S. military operations, will also face challenges. The dangers of Chinese submarines and other elements of A2/AD complicate the deployment of carriers in areas near Chinese shores. Similarly, given vulnerabilities of Okinawa and Guam to attack by Chinese land-based missiles, ground based tactical aircraft would face challenges.[22]

Beyond military weaponry, Taiwan's role and geography shape the contours of any potential conflict. While Taiwan's location in range of more than a thousand short-range ballistic missiles puts it under grave threat, Taiwan has the great advantage of a wide moat. Taiwan is increasingly arming itself with a mirror image of Chinese capabilities: small anti-ship missile boats, surface-to-surface missiles, advanced mobile SAM systems, among others, that take advantage of this terrain.[23]

A Dangerous Cauldron

In the area of China's immediate periphery, China's security interests are robust and her military capabilities to defend them are potent and growing. U.S. security interests there are also substantial, and in some cases potentially conflictual. The ability of the United States to project power through these seas into China proper is much reduced from a decade ago. Furthermore, given the substantial A2/AD capabilities, the ability of the United States to even operate in such areas during a period of intense combat is also reduced. This is not to say that the United States does not have other options to compete militarily were conflict to break out in China's immediate periphery. However, it does mean that such options shift, and generally escalate, the conflict beyond this geography.

Thus, a second important aspect of this geography is its propensity towards escalatory conflict. Surface ships in the littoral will present attractive targets. Even absent intent to escalate, the presence of significant numbers of vulnerable but offensively potent systems is a recipe for instability, both at the strategic level (security dilemma) but more narrowly as military commanders on both sides press for authority to take the first shot for force protection reasons.

Finally, given the current prevalence of accurate and lethal anti-ship cruise missiles, what was referred to as "an empty ocean" is likely to prevail.[24] The goal of "sea control" in this environment is moot, but that is the case for both sides: China's navy too faces small missile boats, lethal submarines, and a blizzard of threats from the air. Should a conflict erupt, something of a no-man's land or wasteland will characterize those waters, challenging either side's ability to project power, but giving each an opportunity to wreak such havoc in that area.

THE INTERMEDIATE PERIPHERY

Moving somewhat further afield, other potential areas of contestation lie many hundred miles from China. Most prominent among these in the 2009–2011 period has been the South China Sea, although tensions have flared with Japan intermittently in the East China Sea as well.

The South China Sea

The South China Sea (SCS) is a stew of multiple tensions. One of the main sources of contention are the Spratly Islands, claimed in entirety or part by

China, Taiwan, Vietnam, the Philippines, Malaysia, and Brunei. Were "owner-ship" of the entire archipelago of islands, reefs, and shoals to be acknowledged by the international community, their owner would have commercial rights to substantial fisheries and potentially lush oil and natural gas fields. As deadlines regarding claims under the UNCLOS loomed in 2009, many regional players, including China, laid theirs out explicitly regarding archipelagic baselines, ter-ritorial waters, and exclusive economic zones. This has led to a greater percep-tion of Chinese assertiveness given the very expansive nature of Chinese claims (essentially, all of the South China Sea).[25]

Beyond that, given Chinese restrictive views on rights in EEZs, the issue takes on greater implications. The Straits of Malacca carry 40 percent of all global trade.[26] Any threat to these vital sea-lanes of communication has both economic and security implications. Also, since the United States regularly deploys air and naval assets through and routinely exercises in the region, this could be a major area of contention.

Third, the U.S. has a number of longstanding relationships near the South China Sea.[27] Washington maintains an alliance with the Philippines whose sa-lience is resurgent for Manila, in part due to increased threat perceptions of China. Alliances with Australia and New Zealand represent partnerships of global importance for the United States. Singapore is an important strategic partner. Washington is building a newly normalized relationship with Vietnam and deepening cooperation with Indonesia. There are even signs of warming Burmese-U.S. relations. Each of these represents U.S. reputational commit-ments, and several are overlain on deep historical and cultural friendships.

Finally, there is an emerging strategic nuclear element to the importance of the SCS. China has constructed a submarine base and seems to be basing its nuclear-powered, ballistic missile carrying submarines (SSBNs) on Hain-an Island. This has the potential to further intensify security competition in that region: China may be viewing the SCS as something of a SSBN bastion, if not for launching purposes (its missiles would not reach most targets in the United States from there) but as a place from which to deploy securely. Because it will be an area where Chinese naval and land-based air power can easily patrol, the U.S. Navy will struggle to conduct anti-submarine warfare (ASW) operations safely there.[28] As such, it will draw increased military at-tention from both sides.

The Security of Japan

The second major area of intersection between Chinese and American secu-rity interests is over Japan. The U.S.-Japan alliance has long been viewed as the linchpin in the hub and spokes system of the American pattern of bilateral alliances in East Asia. The U.S. interest in Japanese security and the robust status of the alliance is hard to overstate. American bases in Japan are the foundation of America's military presence in the region. The alliance includes extremely close coordination and integration of capabilities that also serves a global role. The two economies are deeply tied, and the social linkages between the countries are substantial. All of these factors, important in and of themselves, elevate the reputational stakes still further.

As discussed elsewhere in this volume, Japan's sense of threat from China has risen significantly in the past five years. As Japan has pointed out with increasing frequency and directness, Chinese overall military modernization poses threats to Japanese security. A long-simmering nationalist enmity between the two complicates two specific additional problems.

As Chinese naval forces are developing "blue water" capabilities, they have increasingly deployed past the "first island chain" that includes Japan. In order to do so, China's northern fleet essentially has to cross through Japan's EEZ and often near its territorial waters. As the Chinese fleet has grown, however, these deployments have been viewed more provocatively by Tokyo. At least seven such surface deployments have occurred since 2004,[29] and submarine passages predate these.[30] The deployments of increasingly diverse "surface action groups" show both increased tactical facility and more dangerous offensive capability. As in the case of U.S. offshore reconnaissance, what appears "natural" to the deploying navy provokes the nearby coastal power. (Here again, there is an element of intrinsic security dilemma dynamics, with Chinese buildups not centrally being aimed at Japan, but provoking Japan.)

Japan and China also have their own territorial disputes over the Senkaku Islands. Possessed by Japan, the minuscule islands have served as a spark for popular extremism on both sides, with spats over fishing boat violations becoming increasingly common. These culminated in the 2010 arrest of a Chinese boat captain by local authorities in Japan and a major diplomatic incident.[31] The United States has become increasingly involved as its commitment to the defense of the Senkakus expanded somewhat over the past decade.[32]

Finally, U.S. involvement in nuclear extended deterrence commitments to Japan has risen in importance. Publicly, Japanese concerns with regard to the reliability of the American nuclear umbrella point to increased threats from North Korea. However, these conceal deeper concerns about Chinese nuclear capabilities. Over the past several years, the Japanese and Americans have formalized an official bilateral process on extended deterrence policy to consider ways to bolster this commitment, and senior American officials have reiterated nuclear guarantees on Japanese soil. Missile defense cooperation supports that guarantee, but is also threatening to China.[33]

Key Considerations in the Intermediate Periphery Military Balance

The bulk of Chinese A2/AD capabilities are capable within a hundred miles or so of the Chinese coastline. The Spratly Islands are 800 miles and Kyushu is 500 miles from China. Conflict in these regions would bring into play different, and fewer, Chinese forces than in the home waters environment discussed above. Chinese forces operating in these areas would be vulnerable to attack from the air. They would be far out of range of their own land-based SAMs, and they would rely on ground-based aircraft at the edge of their combat radii.[34] The newest Chinese diesel submarines have enough range to patrol these areas, but only if they are willing to sacrifice much of their stealth by transiting closer to the surface where they would be vulnerable to maritime patrol aircraft. Chinese missile boats and most of the Chinese missile force will be out of range.

There are certainly some Chinese weapons platforms that would still be relevant, although each has limitations in these theaters. China's relevant missile force is small. The Pentagon estimates there are no more than 100 DF-21s, with several hundred more of the slower moving, less destructive DH-10 cruise missiles.[35] Both could be used against U.S. or allied bases, and some variants might be useful against ships at sea, but it will take more than a few missiles to keep any large base closed. Furthermore, increasingly capable theater or tactical missile defense systems are useful in these scenarios.[36]

Another relevant platform are China's strategic attack submarines (SSNs), which have begun to patrol further from Chinese shores, ranging the Japanese islands and joining in combined fleet operations, an impressive tactical improvement for the PLAN.[37] However, the current generation of SSNs is quite noisy relative to modern standards.[38] Additionally, patrol rates for the entire fleet are very low compared to those of the U.S. Navy.[39] With only six in the fleet, maintaining continual patrols will be a challenge.

Finally, Chinese surface flotillas are beginning to exercise beyond the littorals, but the risks to Chinese capital ships doing so in times of conflict are great.[40] The historically acute vulnerabilities to air attack have been reduced, but this remains a concern for Chinese ships. Worse for China, its ASW capabilities and propulsion systems remain backward.[41] Thus, Beijing's flotillas, while potentially powerful relative to smaller navies, would be gravely at risk to U.S. SSNs and carrier-borne aircraft.

U.S. naval forces, while no longer as numerous as in the Cold War, are still dominant in comparison. Eleven carrier battle groups can be supplemented with another 11 amphibious assault groups that would be called carrier groups in any other navy. U.S. SSNs and Aegis air defense ships are generations ahead of the rest of other navies.

Beyond weapons capabilities, there are a number of security relationships that greatly advantage the United States in competition in these farther seas. Increasingly tight alliances with Japan and South Korea are among the strongest known in world history. The U.S. holds annual naval exercises with most of the original six ASEAN nations. Two modern corvettes will be based in Singapore, a deployment of Marines is now based in Australia, and the relationships with the Philippines, Indonesia, and Vietnam have each been reinvigorated. Each of these facilitate broad competition with China for regional influence in security cooperation in Southeast Asia and further diversify the U.S. force posture.[42]

This proliferation of relationships greatly increases the number of potential forward operating bases that might be used in a conflict by the United States. It also complicates the political calculus in Beijing, posing an increasingly *regional* response to any aggression.[43]

THE GLOBAL ARENA

China in the twenty-first century has both global security interests and growing capabilities to defend them. Here, the issues are eclectic and less uniformly tense than those in nearer geographic regions. Additionally, the military tools that might be brought to bear are also different.

The most important of these interests is access to resources and markets. As China deepens its direct involvement in resource extraction in Latin America and Africa, its national interests in those regions rise accordingly, with some inherent security element. Ensuring access to those regions is an important security issue that interacts with the United States, as is discussed in the chapter by David Shambaugh and Dawn Murphy.

China depends on extended "lines of communication" beyond "the first island chain" ranging across the Pacific and through the Straits of Malacca to the Indian Ocean and beyond. China and the rest of northeast Asia are heavily dependent on these. China imported 53.5 percent of its total oil consumption in 2009, and 85 percent of its imported oil and petroleum products come through the Straits.[44] Accordingly, Chinese President Hu Jintao has voiced concern regarding China's "Malacca dilemma,"[45] and top PLAN admirals write in official journals: "Maritime transport and strategic passageways for energy resources have already become lifelines for the development of the national economy and society. . . . [We must] fully recognize the security threats our country faces at sea, and fully recognize the special status and utility of our navy in preparing for military conflict."[46]

However, energy security is not narrowly a military issue.[47] Indeed, as discussed in the Goldstein and Shambaugh/Murphy chapters, China has rather broad interests in this regard that are not necessarily amenable to military solutions: for instance, only 10 percent of Chinese oil is carried by Chinese flagged ships.[48] What would it mean for China to "defend" the oil on other vessels? Recognizing these challenges, by the mid-2000s Chinese leaders emphasized viewing this issue through less of a military lens. Thus, one Chinese scholar now concludes, "Hence, Beijing primarily relies on the non-military means to alleviate its concern of the 'Malacca dilemma.'"[49]

Certainly beyond the local waters of the South China Sea, there is a degree of shared interest between the United States and China with regard to ensuring that non-traditional threats do not challenge the free flow of goods. Antipiracy operations has generally been the most positive area with regard to non-traditional security, perhaps because here the implications for each side's well-being is most clear. Chinese participation in antipiracy patrols in the Gulf of Aden has brought the U.S. Navy and the PLAN into close proximity, working towards a common goal.[50] While China has not fully integrated into the combined NATO command and control mechanisms for these patrols, China has coordinated extensively. With a ninth flotilla on station at the outset of 2012, this has been a major commitment for a navy not accustomed to such long-range deployments. While in the region, the United States and China have exchanged reciprocal visits and exchanges between operational elements in the area. That said, bilateral anti-piracy exercises have been agreed to, but have not yet occurred.

India also plays some role in Sino-American security competition. India is relevant to China's contemplation of this Malacca dilemma, and Sino-Indian border relations remain tense, precisely half a century after their war.[51] The border negotiations have not made substantial progress, in contrast to Beijing's ability to resolve literally all its other land-based border disputes—often on favorable conditions to its neighbor.[52] Recent signs of military buildups along the border, coupled with the latent nuclear rivalry between the two are also inauspicious. While this has not been a central issue in Sino-American relations, it has been (yet another) source of moderate tension. The development of U.S.-Indian relations, as well as nascent arms sales, suggests this will continue to be a problem area.

Key Considerations in the Global Military Balance

In these extra-regional venues of potential combat, the military balance favors the United States in lopsided fashion. (Indeed, even against small powers, China can bring little to bear when far from home.) The United States benefits from a substantial global basing structure. It dominates the oceans of the globe with large self-sustaining battle fleets that are capable of underway replenishment and contain many vessels with endurance measured in months. As discussed earlier and shown in many wars over the past twenty years, bombers based in the continental United States can provide sustained firepower anywhere on the planet.

Were China to face off against the United States or an ally anywhere outside Asia, there is little the PLA can offer. Its submarines have no experience on such long patrols. Its flotillas have no experience of combat deployments at such range. (That said, the anti-piracy patrols off the Gulf of Aden are beginning to shift that situation.[53]) Furthermore, those surface fleets would be acutely vulnerable to attack from above or below the water's surface.

China's new aircraft carrier might play a role in the waters of Asia just outside those "home seas," but its primary comparative advantage is further afield.[54] While trite, it bears stating explicitly: the small Chinese carrier's only value is its ability to provide air power where no land-based Chinese air assets can reach. While still some years away from becoming operational, we might hazard an estimate that it will be eventually equipped with some 15–20 or so SU-33/J-15 fighters.[55] However, as the British discovered in the Falklands, with such small numbers of short-ranged fighters such as these, nearly all the sorties are taken up in defensive combat air patrols to protect the carrier. This is particularly the case in the absence of integrated intelligence, surveillance, and reconnaissance (ISR) systems and without capable air defense escorts, conditions that would face the Chinese carrier as well. Thus, China's carrier, were it to deploy far afield, would have its attention centered on self-protection.

Because both the military balance heavily favors the United States and the nature of the two sides' interests are not fundamentally opposed (indeed often are aligned), the prospects for dangerous global-oriented conflict are low.

The Strategic Level

Transcending all these geographically delineated issues discussed above hover "strategic" weapons. Consideration of the nuclear balance played a major role in shaping the context of the Cold War, and that is likely to remain the case today. However, today, the "strategic" situation is more complex with multiple actors, missile defenses, and new arenas.[56]

China is engaged in a modernization and modest buildup of its nuclear forces. Ten years ago, China depended on an arsenal of a few dozen vulnerable missiles that could reach the continental United States. Today, Beijing can rely on a growing arsenal that includes survivable, land-based missiles. In five years, China may also deploy operational SSBNs, thereby diversifying China's strategic assets but complicating her command and control concerns.

Lined up to deter what is emerging as several score Chinese missiles, the United States maintains 1,500 warheads under the provisions of a new strategic arms reduction agreement with Russia. (Additionally, the United States maintains another 5,000 "non-deployed" warheads.) These can be delivered from a variety of advanced bombers, submarines, and intercontinental ballistic missiles (ICBMs).

U.S. ballistic missile defenses are increasingly reliable and capable, complicating China's calculations. However, while greatly improved, these systems remain very much unproven in combat and likely highly susceptible to "countermeasures." Indeed, Chinese security analysts occasionally hint at possessing such countermeasures for their offensive arsenal (which are certainly within their technical means). Nevertheless, they are clearly unnerved by these missile defense systems, and their role in tightening U.S. alliances in the region.

The United States is also developing a range of "conventional prompt global strike" weapons. Some, such as the converted SSBNs that now carry 154 conventional long-range cruise missiles each, already ply the waters of Asia.[57] These and future systems raise the prospect that Beijing might lose its nuclear ICBMs without America having to cross the nuclear threshold. Thus, these programs deepen threat perceptions in China.

Space has increasingly become another zone of U.S.-Chinese strategic competition. Washington criticized China's 2007 anti-satellite test that shattered a defunct weather satellite. Still, U.S. capabilities in this arena are diverse. Recently, the United States has tested a robotic space plane, destroyed a satellite, and planned a new very-heavy lift rocket. Given the fragile nature of the orbital environment, it is unfortunate that the mutual restraint that eventually characterized Soviet and American behavior in this area is so far lacking in the Chinese case.[58] As China increasingly depends on space-based information/surveillance/reconnaissance (ISR) capacity for its own military and its commercial interests develop,[59] that situation may well change. However, the intrinsic difficulty in "verification" in any space weapons arms control regimes, and the intertwining of missile defense and space weapon capabilities, ensures this area will remain contentious.

Cyber security is an increasingly important issue between the United States and China, but it is important to differentiate espionage from attacks. Cyber attack can circumvent traditional military defenses to target things of value to states in the same way nuclear weapons do—thus some elevate it to the "strategic" level. China is certainly engaged in preparations for cyber war; undoubtedly the United States is as well. While there is a cottage industry predicting dire outcomes, more sober analysis is more persuasive.[60] Indeed, to date the physical effects of cyber attacks have been very small. Espionage, a commonplace activity in international politics, increasingly utilizes cyber tools. While both the U.S. and China avail themselves of cyber tools to conduct military espionage, China is extremely aggressive in industrial espionage.[61] This issue will remain a major concern, in part because of vastly different treatments of intellectual property in the two countries (see Charles Freeman's chapter). More generally, both sides point fingers regarding low-level hacking and espionage. China is also singled out as particularly aggressive in this regard by a number of third countries and large technology firms such as Google.

In terms of U.S.-China diplomacy on the strategic (nuclear) level, the United States has tried to signal that it accepts the existence of a vague if stable "strategic balance" between Beijing and Washington.[62] While eschewing "mutual vulnerability" (a term laden with Cold War baggage and politically sensitive in the United States), the Pentagon explicitly denies attempting to undermine that balance or "strategic stability" through nuclear weapons, conventional weapons, or missile defenses. Beijing is not entirely convinced by such statements, but has welcomed shifts in U.S. declaratory policy on the role of nuclear weapons.[63] The two sides are engaging in discussions on the nature of such commitments, and there is unofficial engagement about the parameters of future confidence building measures.[64] Nevertheless, it must be noted that these discussions are far less substantive than discussions were with the Soviet Union during the Cold War. Given that both Beijing and Washington assert there is no such conflictual relationship today, it is unfortunate that Beijing is not willing to engage more deeply on these vital issues.

INSTITUTIONAL RESTRAINTS ON MILITARY COMPETITION?

The previous sections of this chapter have focused on the central areas of competition between the two and evaluated the evolving military balance in those. Substantial evidence shows that institutions and norms can temper the excesses of such narrow security competition, as John Ikenberry (in his chapter in this volume) and others argue.[65] Unfortunately, while there are a number of such institutions in Sino-American security relations, they remain generally underdeveloped and thin in substantive terms.

There is a substantial bilateral military-to-military diplomacy agenda between the two countries.

- Most years, either the Chairman of the Joint Chiefs or the Defense Secretary meets his counterpart from China in a formal bilateral visit.
- The Defense Consultative Talks (DCTs) have brought together the U.S. Undersecretary of Defense and Chinese Deputy Chief of the General Staff level nearly every year since 1997.
- Following an inaugural session in 2005, the Defense Policy Coordination Talks (DPCTs) bring together the U.S. Deputy Assistant Secretary of Defense with the PLA Deputy Chief of Staff.
- The Military Maritime Cooperation Agreement (MMCA) talks are long-standing working level discussions that address "rules of the road" during peacetime for the militaries, and navies in particular (similar to the U.S.-Soviet Incidents at Sea Agreement of 1973).

- Senior military commander visits are common.
- There are occasional National Defense University delegations by new flag and general officers to tour selected sites in each other's country.
- The annual Strategic and Economic Dialogue (S&ED), traditionally a civilian-dominated meeting that had centered on economic and political issues, has increasingly considered security issues, and beginning in 2011 included a Strategic Security Dialogue linked to the S&ED. These are intended to integrate discussions between the civilian and militarily leaders on security topics.

Thus, across this range of regular dialogues, there is substantial opportunity for senior leaders to engage on issues of broad threat perceptions, statecraft, and geo-political influence. As discussed in Bonnie Glaser's chapter, there is generally an increase in the substantive engagement in such meetings, rather than a recitation of prepared talking points (particularly on Taiwan). In many of these exchanges, there are some signs of increased transparency by the Chinese side, long a U.S. concern.

Beyond such diplomatic contacts, there are only a few tangible steps the two sides have taken to reduce dangers. After much delay, a military hotline was set up between Washington and Beijing in 2008. Port visits by major combatant vessels peaked in the mid-2000s, as shown in figure 10.2. To date,

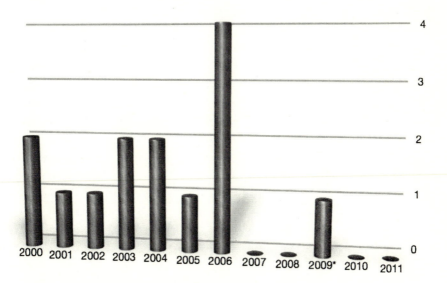

Figure 10.2. Naval Port Calls. Data primarily collected from Shirley Kan, "US-China Military Contacts: Issues for Congress" (Washington, D.C.: Congressional Research Service, 2011). Visits do not include Hong Kong, but only to China and the United States. *2009 visit was part of an international fleet week, not a bilateral visit as the others are.

only two joint naval exercises have occurred (a communications exercise off of San Diego and a search and rescue exercise near southern China in 2006). Although agreements to hold humanitarian aid/disaster relief (HA/DR) and anti-piracy exercises were reached (in 2008 and 2011, respectively), those have yet to occur.

Expanding outward, the record is similar in multilateral arenas. The United States leads a large number of multilateral exercises and military dialogues. China participates in several such dialogues. However, and despite U.S. attempts to encourage Chinese participation, the PLA has not participated in many military exercises, even when those exercises are centered on HA/DR or search and rescue practice. Table 10.1 highlights several of these events, noting the wide breadth of participation from the region.

There has been some limited operational cooperation between the two on global "non-traditional security" issues. Disaster relief, in the region and globally, is an area where the two sides' militaries interact with no significant grounds for rancor. (While hard power may be "zero-sum," soft power is decidedly not.) Thus, American military aircraft provided aid to China in

TABLE 10.1. Selected Multilateral Military Exercises and Dialogues

Exercises	Purpose	Countries participating	Years in existence	Notes
RIMPAC	Military Exercise	14 (+ 3 observers)	40	China does not participate (declined to observe in '10)
Pacific Airlift Rally	HA/DR airlift exercise	25	16	China declined to participate
Pacific Endeavor	HA/DR exercise	20	8	China declined to participate
Pacific Reach	Submarine search and rescue exercise	5 (+13 observers)	5	China observed but declined to participate
Military Dialogues				
Western Pacific Naval Symposium	Naval affairs dialogue	20 (+4 observers)	23	China participates
Pacific Armies Chiefs Conference/Pacific Armies Management Seminar	Multilateral security dialogue	22	35	China participates
Chiefs of Defense	Senior dialogue	36	14	China declined to participate

Source: Author's research of various sources.

2008. China's military cooperation in aid provision to Haiti in January 2010 occurred under the U.N.'s auspices and has yet to be repeated.

China is playing an increasing role in U.N. peacekeeping operations (UN-PKO) and emphasizes that is the largest contributor to such among permanent U.N. Security Council members.[66] That said, it contributes little financial support and has yet to deploy combat troops, preferring instead to send "support" elements (which certainly can be in high demand[67]). There has been little interaction between U.S. forces supporting PKOs and Chinese forces doing the same; that said, the primary case of such, again in Haiti, in 2008 went smoothly.

In the absence of more routine direct interaction, any positive implication of such Chinese involvement in UNPKO depends on such participation shifting Chinese security identities and norms. This is certainly a possibility in the future, but the conclusions of a recent study emphasize other rationales: "China's peacekeeping behavior is motivated by diverse interests, from multilateralism and image building to more traditional concerns such as isolating Taiwan and securing its investments."[68] Note that each of these, with the possible exception of "image building," suggests that normative or identity shifts have yet to occur. Still, this is an emerging area, and such changes should be expected to occur over decades, not years.[69] China's very participation in UNPKOs is already a sign of shifting norms to some extent, as noted in Rosemary Foot's chapter.

Similarly, as discussed in Avery Goldstein's chapter, the Chinese leadership of the Six Party Talks has shown an activist and constructive engagement with a set of security topics that are problematic for both. In this case, the Chinese pursued a range of initiatives that were supportive of U.S. interests in the aggregate and did so through a multilateral forum that institutionalized a strong voice for U.S. partners such as Japan and South Korea.

In the nuclear arena, there are limited bilateral contacts, but more broadly, some signs of convergent interests and practices. In the area of global nonproliferation institutions, again the conclusions have to be measured, but there are a few positive signs. At the United Nations Conference on Disarmament, China has been advocating its selective proposal on restricting militarization of outer space, and holding up discussions of the Fissile Material Cutoff Treaty (with support from Pakistan). On the other hand, its recent acquiescence to P-5 discussions on transparency in nuclear issues and its position on the Comprehensive Test Ban Treaty (which it has signed but not ratified, similar to the U.S.) have been more positive. However, as progress on the global non-proliferation and denuclearization agenda has become an important priority for the United States, this area is unlikely to provide solace from the Sino-American relationship's other tensions.

While these contacts are positive and should be continued, they have not yet had a dramatic effect. Part of the challenge is that all of these are routinely held hostage to "political" concerns. American arms sales to Taiwan have served as the largest excuse to "freeze" ties in the military-to-military relationship, leading to a temporary discontinuation of all of the bilateral elements discussed above. Over the longer term, incidents such as the bombing of the Chinese embassy in Belgrade and U.S. reconnaissance (and, to a degree, the 1995–1996 Taiwan Strait crisis) have all been grounds to put the military-to-military relationship on hold. With such breaks in discussions, expectations have to be lowered.

More fundamentally, the discussions themselves have only made slow substantive progress. The Military Maritime Cooperation Accord talks bog down on issues of sovereignty in the EEZ. Reciprocity of similarly open visits with modern ships has been an issue in port calls. China is reluctant to engage in discussions on strategic issues given its position of military inferiority. Although some analysts suggest this is somehow part of China's "strategic culture," comparative analysis would note that the Soviets had the same concerns. Nevertheless, whatever the sources and despite recent progress in this regard, there is only limited concrete discussion of how military capabilities serve national strategic goals. This deeper discussion is vital to reducing the sorts of misperceptions that can exacerbate the existing differences in national interests.

Still, it is likely that halting progress will continue to be made. In particular, on issues such as humanitarian work and anti-piracy—both global commons issues—the two great powers find themselves working alongside each other with increasing frequency. This will create a functional demand for further direct engagement between the militaries, in both bilateral and multilateral fora and exercises.

CONCLUSION

This survey of the security dimension in the Sino-American relationship belies summary. Still, a few overarching themes emerge.

First, while the balance of power has shifted, that effect is most pronounced near China's shores. The further from China's territory one looks, however, the less relevant Beijing's 12 percent per year military budgetary increases are. Indeed, beyond the second island chain, they have only a modest effect on the U.S.-China balance.

Second, because of that, the security challenges within the nearest geographic area discussed are quite dangerous. The military dynamics in that area are inflammatory. The propensity for inadvertent escalation as forces angle for a first strike or rush to activate mobilization and deployment plans are major concerns were political tensions to escalate.

Third, further afield the issues that divide the two are more surmount-able. In part because China cannot defend its sea lines of communications (SLOCs) beyond the Straits of Malacca, it has to—and has begun to—think more broadly about multilateral energy security and protection of shipping. Similar factors will likely influence Chinese behavior as other aspects of its "global activism" begin to have security implications.[70]

Fourth, the changes in the balance of power and in the shifting nature of technology on the strategic level greatly complicate matters. Redlines, thresh-olds, signaling, all are complicated when technology is changing and the two sides are facing off with different sets of military tools. This has proven prob-lematic before in the Sino-American relationship, and it threatens to do so now again.[71]

Finally, there are both elements of traditional security dilemmas and con-ventional conflicts of interest in Sino-American relations. It is not the case that the entire security dynamic is one or the other. Both are present. Security di-lemmas are surmountable through adroit diplomacy. Conflicts of interests are more problematic. However, *interests* are not fixed nor solely given by the inter-national system (contrary to the severe view of realist writings such as Ashley Tellis's chapter). Instead, interests evolve in response to shifting international systemic structures (see John Ikenberry's chapter), evolving political coalitions and shifting cultures, and the changing nature of interdependencies in this era of globalization. Those factors will gradually temper the degree to which Sino-American global interests are conflictual, although the nearby geographic areas will continue to present zero-sum conceptions of China's security.

NOTES

This chapter represents the author's views and does not necessarily represent any of-ficial U.S. government policy. I would also particularly like to thank Jonathan Pollack and David Shambaugh for their helpful suggestions on previous drafts.

1. See James Mulvenon, "Chairman Hu and the PLA's 'New Historic Missions,'" *China Leadership Monitor*, Vol. 27 (2009), pp. 1–11.

2. *Nuclear Posture Review* (Washington, DC: Department of Defense, April, 2010).

3. To be sure, that follows a period of some stagnation in such budgets in the ear-ly reform era. Separately, such growth figures refer to official budgets; those budgets clearly understate China's defense spending. See "SIPRI Military Expenditure Data-base," available at: http://www.sipri.org/databases/milex.

4. See the chapter by Shelley Rigger in this volume, as well as Robert Ross, "Taiwan's Fading Independence Movement," *Foreign Affairs* Vol. 85, No. 2 (2006), pp. 141–148.

5. Christopher Twomey, "Limits of Coercion: Compellence, Deterrence, and Cross-Strait Political-Military Affairs," in Roger Cliff, Scott Harold and Phillip Saun-ders (eds.), *Cross-Strait Relations: New Opportunities and Challenges for Taiwan's Secu-rity* (Santa Monica: The RAND Corporation, 2011).

6. Michael Chase, "Defense Reform in Taiwan: Problems and Prospects," *Asian Survey*, Vol. XVL, No. 3 (2005), p. 363.

7. That said, there is no evidence that such operational coordination exists.

8. The legal niceties are somewhat more complex, involving delineation of baselines, determination of archipelagic status, and interpretation of rights in EEZ. Peter Dutton, "Carving Up the East China Sea," *Naval War College Review*, Vol. 60, No. 2 (2007), pp. 45–68. For a more critical view of U.S. interpretations, see Mark Valencia, "The *Impeccable* Incident: Truth and Consequences," *China Security*, Vol. 5, No. 2 (2009), pp. 22–28.

9. Amitai Etzioni, "Is China a Responsible Stakeholder?" *International Affairs*, Vol. 87, No. 3 (2011), pp. 539–553.

10. Shirley Kan et al., *China-US Aircraft Collision Incident of April 2001: Assessments and Policy Implications* (Washington, DC: Congressional Research Service, 2001), p. 15.

11. See, for instance, the recent decision to permanently station very high altitude Global Hawk reconnaissance UAVs to Guam.

12. Drew Thompson and Natalie Matthews, "Six Party Talks and China's Goldilocks Strategy: Getting North Korea Just Right," in *Tomorrow's Northeast Asia*, Joint U.S.-Korea Academic Studies (Seoul: KEI, 2011); and Christopher Twomey, "Explaining Chinese Foreign Policy Toward North Korea: Navigating Between the Scylla and Charybdis of Proliferation and Instability," *Journal of Contemporary China*, Vol. 17, No. 56 (2008), pp. 401–423.

13. Christopher Twomey, *The Military Lens: Doctrinal Differences and Deterrence Failure in Sino-American Relations* (Ithaca, NY: Cornell University Press, 2010).

14. While China does not use that term, it is an accurate assessment of these capabilities. Thomas Mahnken, "China's Anti-Access Strategy in Historical and Theoretical Perspective," *Journal of Strategic Studies*, Vol. 34, No. 3 (2011).

15. For excellent discussions of the sub-ASW balance, see Owen Cote, "Assessing the Undersea Balance between the U.S. and China" (Cambridge: Security Studies Program, MIT, February, 2011) and Michael Glosny, "Strangulation From the Sea? A PRC Submarine Blockade of Taiwan," *International Security*, Vol. 28, No. 4 (2006), pp. 125–160.

16. Often referred to as "two-digit SAMs" systems such as the SA-10 and -20 have nominal intercept ranges of 93 and 122 miles, respectively. China currently fields approximately 1,000 of these Russian missiles spread across dozens of units. "S-300P," in *Jane's Land-Based Air Defence, Online* (March 30, 2011), available at: http://www.jlad.janes.com.

17. For a discussion of the large-scale coast guard like paramilitary patrol organizations in China, see Lyle Goldstein, *Five Dragons Stirring Up the Sea: Challenges and Opportunities in China's Improving Maritime Enforcement Capabilities* (Newport, RI: China Maritime Studies Institute, 2010).

18. David Shlapak et al., *A Question of Balance: Political Context and Military Aspects of the China-Taiwan Dispute* (Santa Monica: RAND, 2009). On the role that China conceives for these weapons, see my "The People's Liberation Army's Selective Learning: Lessons of the Iran-Iraq 'War of the Cities' Missile Duels and Uses of Missiles in Other Conflicts," in *Chinese Lessons From Other Peoples' Wars*, in Andrew Scobell, David Lai and Roy Kamphausen (eds.) (Carlisle, PA: U.S. Army War College Strategic Studies Institute, 2011).

19. See discussion in Andrew Erickson and Gabge Collins, "China Deploys World's First Long-Range, Land-Based 'Carrier Killer': DF-21D Anti-Ship Ballistic Missile (ASBM)," *China SignPost*, No. 14 (2010), pp. 1–27.

20. The challenges of a many stepped "kill chain" are immense, ranging from initial cueing from a wide area sensor, to a narrower high-resolution satellite, then communicating to the missile through timely command and control systems, then updating the missile during flight to account for ship movement. See interview of Roger Cliff in Roger Kazianis, "Beyond the Missile Hype," *The Diplomat*, January 20, 2012, available at: http://the-diplomat.com/. Related, see Cote, "Assessing the Undersea Balance."

21. Jim Garamone, "Pentagon Office to Coordinate New Air-Sea Strategy," *American Forces Press Service* (November 10, 2011); Eleni Ekmektsioglou, "AirSea Battle and Escalation" *The Diplomat* (July 28, 2011), available at: http://the-diplomat.com/new-leaders-forum/.

22. Shlapak, *A Question of Balance*.

23. For a sketch of a strategy incorporating these, see William Murray, "Revisiting Taiwan's Defense Strategy," *Naval War College Review*, Vol. 61, No. 3 (2008). Taiwan's military, through its "Hard ROC" initiative, is moving in many such directions.

24. John Keegan, *The Price of Admiralty: The Evolution of Naval Warfare* (New York: Viking, 1989). For a good discussion of the centrality of missiles to contemporary naval combat, see Wayne Hughes, *Fleet Tactics and Coastal Combat*, 2nd Edition (Annapolis, MD: Naval Institute Press, 2010).

25. For a detailed parsing of the spiral of tensions in the past few years there, see Michael Swaine's "China's Assertive Behavior, Part One: On 'Core Interests.'" *China Leadership Monitor*, No. 34 (2011), pp. 1–25.

26. Robert Kaplan, "Center Stage for the 21st Century: Power Plays in the Indian Ocean," *Foreign Affairs*, Vol. 88, No. 2 (2009), p. 20.

27. Victor Cha, "Complex Patchworks: US Alliances as Part of Asia's Regional Architecture," *Asia Policy*, Vol. 11 (2011), pp. 27–50.

28. Modern ASW relied on combined forces working together: patrol aircraft, helicopters with dipping sonars, SSNs, and some surface ships with a large active sonar (and to serve as a platform for the helicopter). Only U.S. SSNs would safely operate there in intense combat against China.

29. Toshi Yoshihara and James Holmes, "The Japanese Archipelago Through Chinese Eyes," *China Brief*, Vol.10, No. 16 (2010).

30. Joseph Ferguson, "Submarine Incursion Sets Sino-Japanese Relations on Edge," *China Brief*, Vol. 4, No. 23 (2004).

31. For good discussion on this, see Taylor Fravel, "Explaining Stability in the Senkaku (Diaoyu) Islands Dispute," in *Getting the Triangle Straight: Managing China—Japan—US Relations* (Washington, DC: Brookings Institution, 2010).

32. While the U.S. government would not characterize it so, it is hard not to come to that conclusion. Prior to 2004, there was no explicit public commitment to the inclusion of the islands under the treaty; in the latest 2010 incident, such assertions were common and routine. Ibid., 148–149. See also Peter Ennis, "Japan Blinked? Look Again," *Dispatch Japan* (September 26, 2010).

33. Eben Lindsey, Michael Glosny and Christopher Twomey, "Conference Report: U.S.-China Strategic Dialogue, Phase VI" (Monterey, CA: Naval Postgraduate School, January, 2012).

34. The radius for the longer ranged SU-27 variants (the SU-30MKK in particular) is approximately 700 miles. Note this range might be extendable by air-to-air refueling,

but: (1) it is unclear how many of Chinese J-11/SU-27/Su-30s have this capability; (2) the Chinese are just starting to practice this; and (3) China has a trivial number of refueling tankers. See "SAC (Sukhoi Su-27) J11," in *Jane's All the World's Aircraft, Online* (June 9, 2011).

35. *Military and Security Developments Involving the PRC*, p. 78.

36. Craig Hooper and Christopher Albon, "'Get Off the Fainting Couch,'" *Proceedings*, Vol. 136, No. 4 (2010).

37. Bernard Cole, *The Great Wall at Sea: China's Navy in the Twenty-First Century* (Annapolis, MD: Naval Institute Press, 2010, 2nd ed.); Edward Wong, "As Chinese Navy Extends Reach, Pacific Governments Grow Uneasy," *New York Times* (June 14, 2011).

38. Hans Kristensen has a declassified chart from the Office of Naval Intelligence showing relative acoustic signature of Chinese submarines compares unfavorably to 1970s era Soviet boats in "China's Noisy Nuclear Submarines," *FAS Strategic Security Blog* (November 21, 2009).

39. Ibid. In this case, Kristensen is relying on separately declassified ONI data.

40. Cole, *The Great Wall at Sea*; Toshi Yoshihara and James Holmes, *Red Star Over the Pacific: China's Rise and the Challenge to U.S. Maritime Strategy* (Annapolis, MD: Naval Institute Press, 2010).

41. Gabriel Collins and Michael Grubb, *A Comprehensive Survey of China's Dynamic Shipbuilding Industry: Commercial Development and Strategic Implications* (Newport, RI: China Maritime Studies Institute, 2008).

42. On the corvettes' role in a broader strategic competition with China, David Axe, "How the Navy's Warship of the Future Ran Aground," *Wired.com* (August 3, 2011), available at: http://www.wired.com/dangerroom/2011/08/future-warship-ran-aground/all/1.

43. Thus it is notable that there were widespread critiques of Chinese behavior at recent ARF meetings. Robert Sutter and Chin-Hao Huang, "Managing Rising Tensions in the South China Sea," *Comparative Connections*, Vol. 13, No. 2 (2011). More generally, see Cha, "Complex Patchworks."

44. On the former, see Guy Leung, "China's Energy Security: Perception and Reality," *Energy Policy*, Vol. 39, No. 3 (2011). On the latter, see Kaplan, "Center Stage for the 21st Century."

45. Marc Lanteigne, "China's Maritime Security and the 'Malacca Dilemma,'" *Asian Security*, Vol. 4, No. 2 (2008).

46. Cited in Andrew B. Kennedy, "China's New Energy-Security Debate," *Survival*, Vol. 52, No. 3 (2010), p. 142.

47. Daniel Yergin, "Ensuring Energy Security," *Foreign Affairs* (2006), pp. 69–82.

48. Erica Downs, "China's Energy Rise," in Brantly Womack (ed.), *China's Rise in Historical Perspective* (Lanham, MD: Rowman and Littlefield, 2010), p. 179.

49. Shaofeng Chen, "China's Self-Extrication from the "Malacca Dilemma" and Implication," *International Journal of China Studies*, Vol. 1, No. 1 (2010), pp. 1–24. Reflecting this more complex view of energy writ large, see Bernard Cole, *Sea Lanes and Pipelines: Energy Security in Asia* (Westport, CT: Praeger Security International, 2008).

50. Andrew S. Erickson, "Chinese Sea Power in Action: The Counterpiracy Mission in the Gulf of Aden and Beyond," in Roy Kamphausen, David Lai, and Andrew Scobell (eds.), *The PLA at Home and Abroad: Assessing the Operational Capabilities of China's Military* (Carlisle, PA: U.S. Army War College Strategic Studies Institute, 2010), p. 329.

51. Jonathan Holslag, *China and India: Prospects for Peace* (New York: Columbia University Press, 2010).

52. Taylor Fravel, *Strong Borders, Secure Nation: Cooperation and Conflict in China's Territorial Disputes* (Princeton: Princeton University Press, 2008).

53. Erickson, "Chinese Sea Power in Action."

54. Only somewhat more optimistic than this author is Andrew Erickson, Abe Denmark and Gabriel Collins, "Beijing's 'Starter Carrier' and Future Steps: Alternatives and Implications," *Naval War College Review*, Vol. 65, No. 1 (2012), pp. 14–54.

55. The SU-33 is a large airframe, and the Varag is a smaller ship than American carriers that routinely deploy with 76 fixed wing aircraft. David Axe, "The Limits of China's Fighter," FIX (July 15, 2011).

56. Christopher Twomey, "Asia's Complex Strategic Environment: Nuclear Multipolarity and Other Dangers," *Asia Policy*, No. 11 (2011), pp. 51–78.

57. Greg Torode, "US Submarines Emerge in Show of Military Might: Message Unlikely to Be Lost on Beijing as 3 Vessels Turn Up in Asian Ports," *South China Morning Post*, July 4, 2010.

58. James Clay Moltz, *The Politics of Space Security: Strategic Restraint and the Pursuit of National Interests* (Stanford: Stanford University Press, 2008).

59. James Clay Moltz, *Asia's Space Race: National Motivations, Regional Dynamics, and Global Implications* (New York: Columbia University Press, 2011).

60. David Betz and Tim Stevens, *Cyberspace and War* (London: International Institute of Strategic Studies *Adelphi Paper* No. 424, 2011); Martin C Libicki, *Cyberdeterrence and Cyberwar* (Santa Monica: Rand Corporation, 2009).

61. *Foreign Spies Stealing US Economic Secrets in Cyberspace: Report to Congress on Foreign Economic Collection and Industrial Espionage, 2009–2011* (Washington, D.C.: Office of the National Counterintelligence Executive, October, 2011); Dmitri Alperovitch, "Revealed: Operation Shady RAT" (McAfee, August 3, 2011).

62. *Ballistic Missile Defense Review Report* (Washington, D.C.: Department of Defense, 2010). See also *Nuclear Posture Review*.

63. Thomas Fingar, "Worrying About Washington: China's Views on the US Nuclear Posture," *The Nonproliferation Review*, Vol. 18, No. 1 (2011), pp. 51–68.

64. Eben Lindsey et al., "Conference Report."

65. E.g., Bruce Russett and John Oneal, *Triangulating Peace: Democracy, Interdependence, and International Organizations* (New York: Norton, 2001).

66. Note its numbers overall are not particularly high, ranking well below Ghana and Ethiopia, for instance. International Crisis Group, *China's Growing Role in UN Peacekeeping* (Brussels and Beijing: Asia Report No. 166, 2009).

67. Courtney Richardson, "A Responsible Power? China and the UN Peacekeeping Regime," *International Peacekeeping*, Vol. 18, No. 3 (2011).

68. International Crisis Group, *China's Growing Role*, p. 11.

69. Miwa Hirono and Marc Lanteigne, "Introduction: China and UN Peacekeeping," *International Peacekeeping*, Vol. 18, No. 3 (2011).

70. Phillip Saunders, *China's Global Activism: Strategy, Drivers, and Tools* (Washington, D.C.: National Defesnse University Institute for National Strategic Studies, 2006).

71. Twomey, *The Military Lens*.

Part VI

The Regional Context

11

U.S.-China Interactions in Asia

Avery Goldstein

Since the turn of the century the context for Asian, especially East Asian, international relations has been most importantly defined by the roles played by the two largest actors in the region—China and the United States. Yet, the effects of U.S.-China interactions across Asia have varied. Variety should not be surprising, since the region is as nationally diverse as it is geographically sprawling. Thus, the implications of changing U.S.-China relations for East Asia (from Korea to Myanmar) have differed from those for South Asia (India and Pakistan) and Central Asia (Afghanistan and the former Soviet republics bordering China). Even within East Asia one sees variation, presenting important exceptions to any generalizations about broad regional trends. Obviously, within the limits of a single chapter it is impossible to do full justice to such regional complexity. Instead, I identify several broad trends in U.S.-China relations and suggest connections between them and some of the key recent developments across the region. This approach aims not only to underscore some common themes, but also to take note of important variations on and exceptions to these themes.

In addition to its regional focus, this chapter (like others in the volume), has a temporal focus, examining the effects of U.S.-China dynamics on Asian international relations since 2008. Inasmuch as it was the last year of a period in which a relatively stable working relationship between the U.S. and China seemed to have taken root, 2008 is an especially useful starting point. At that point, the relationship looked like it would help foster stability in regional affairs going forward. After 2008, however, an increasingly problematic U.S.-China relationship and a spike in tensions in East Asia have raised questions both about stability and predictability. Some have interpreted these tensions as the cause for a major change, even a turning point, in relations between the U.S. and China, and for each in their relations with other key countries in the region. Others, however, view the recent difficulties as no more than the usual sorts for complications that occasionally roil relations among diverse states with diverse and sometimes competing interests—simply part of a familiar cycle of tension and relaxation in the region and between Beijing and Washington that has played out since the end of the Cold War and that does not herald the advent of a new, more confrontational era in Asian international relations.

The chapter begins with a brief look at the context within which regional changes unfolded. It then examines the way interactions between the "tangled titans" has affected and been affected by events across Asia. As the subregion where the most dramatic shifts occurred, much of the focus is on East Asia. But the chapter also looks at relevant developments in Australia, South and Central Asia, and selected Asian multilateral organizations. I conclude by suggesting implications for the region's future, identifying key questions more than offering definitive answers.

THE U.S.-CHINA CONTEXT FOR REGIONAL RELATIONS

As the U.S. election season unfolded during 2008, U.S.-China relations in Asia appeared to be firmly set on a path defined mainly by cooperation, despite persistent differences over the best approach to resolving many international problems. At the time, it seemed reasonable to anticipate continuity in U.S.-China bilateral relations and in their attempts to manage or avoid sharp conflict over their disagreements in Asia. Continuity seemed likely because a solid working relationship had not only benefited both the U.S. and China but most other Asian states as well. Continuity also seemed likely because there were few indications that the leadership in either China or the U.S. had any interest in changing course. China's top leaders seemed committed to a grand strategy of "peaceful development" manifest in improved relations with its regional neighbors, as well as constructive and cooperative ties with the U.S. This grand strategy had been openly embraced early in the twenty-first century, and the cohort of CCP leaders who embraced it were slated to remain in place for another five years. Moreover, during the 2008 U.S. presidential campaign the logic of encouraging and welcoming China's larger international role as a responsible great power was one of the few foreign policy issues on which candidate Barack Obama expressed broad agreement with President Bush, whom he would replace in 2009. And during the first year of the Obama administration, U.S.-China relations and most areas of Asian regional relations were indeed characterized by continuity.

Thereafter, however, the expectation of continuity was confounded. From late 2009 through late 2010, regional stability was challenged on many fronts. In most instances, the surprising changes were closely linked with uncertainty about the course of U.S.-China relations. By the summer of 2010, observers wondered whether these newly unsettling developments in the region marked the beginning of a fundamentally different era in Asian international relations. But even if the unsettling events of 2010 did not herald a dramatic transformation in the region, it was clear that they at least partly reflected important shifts in the perception of the capabilities, behavior, and intentions of China and the U.S. For many in the region, these three dimensions shaped their interpretation of the most central questions for ensuring their national interests: What were the implications of China's rise? And what role would the U.S. play in Asia's future?

After 2008, American foreign policy was constrained by overriding concerns about recovery from the great recession and coping with threats to the foundation of the country's long-term economic health. This reality added urgency to the plans for completing a drawdown of the U.S. military deployment in Iraq and for explicitly limiting the duration of the large-scale military deployment in Afghanistan. The U.S. willingness and ability to shoulder international burdens that had quickly expanded after the attacks of September 11, 2001 was quickly contracting by the end of the decade as combat operations in Iraq and Afghanistan proved more daunting and less decisive than anticipated, while economic challenges at home loomed ever larger.

As Washington began scaling back its overseas deployments and no longer evinced the same enthusiasm for the weighty demands of international leadership, it reviewed plans for U.S. military modernization to identify funding priorities in an era of scarcer resources. The review had important implications for U.S.-China relations and for their effect on the security landscape in Asia. As Secretaries of Defense Robert Gates, and then Leon Panetta, outlined future military procurement needs, the implicit justification for investing in systems geared to major power conflict (as opposed to counterinsurgency and counterproliferation) clearly rested on the expectation that the contingencies for which the U.S. must prepare are those that would involve a more capable China.[1] Proposed adjustments in U.S. military strategy pointed in the same direction. In particular, plans for modernizing the U.S. air and naval forces reflected a redirection of U.S. attention to a concern that a rising China might be poised to play a role in Asia that could infringe on vital American interests. In this context, the U.S. initiated a discussion about development of a newly framed "AirSea Battle concept," whose details remain ill-defined and whose budgetary implications may determine whether it ultimately serves as the basis for U.S. military modernization geared towards the renewed focus on China-related contingencies.[2]

Complementing this clarification of military priorities going forward, Washington also clarified its diplomatic priorities early in the Obama administration emphasizing a focus on Pacific Asia.[3] The initial rhetorical shift was followed by a more activist American diplomacy. The U.S. worked on strengthening relations with Asian countries who comprised the longstanding, American-designed "hub and spokes" regional security architecture. In addition to carrying forward the Bush administration's deepening of U.S. alliances with South Korea and Japan, the Obama administration also worked to reinforce spokes that had weakened after the Cold War, especially U.S. military ties to the Philippines, and nurtured potentially significant new security spokes that might be built on the budding partnership with India and, somewhat ironically, with Vietnam. The point of this diplomatic activity was eventually detailed by Secretary of State Hillary Clinton in an essay published in October 2011.[4] Clinton asserted a grand strategic vision that informed an American "pivot" from its recent focus on the Middle East and Afghanistan to Pacific Asia.

Neither the U.S. plan for its future military modernization nor the reemphasis on allies and partners in Asia were portrayed as a new strategy to contain China. But American policy did clearly reflect worries about the challenges that a stronger China posed, and especially worries about its likely capabilities and intentions in a murky future, even as the U.S., like its Asian partners, retained an interest in continued cooperation with China. After all, on important matters of immediate concern all shared overlapping, if not identical, interests—including preventing open conflict on the Korean Peninsula, reinvigorating the global economy, and avoiding the escalation of periodic maritime conflicts. Nevertheless, from late 2009 U.S.-China relations grew more fractious partly as a result of bilateral disagreements (detailed by others in this volume), and partly as a result of changes in China's relations with its regional neighbors. For much of the preceding decade, China had experienced a period of generally improving ties with South Korea, Japan, and the member states of the Association of Southeast Asian Nations (ASEAN). Indeed, this regional trend had led to speculation after 2001 that China's gains in East Asia might be coming at the expense of a U.S. distracted by its "global war on terror."[5] By the end of the decade, however, China's relations in the region had taken a turn for the worse, undermining Beijing's recently impressive diplomatic accomplishments and leading its neighbors to strengthen their ties with Washington.

What was seen as China's more direct pursuit of its own interests in East Asia prompted renewed concerns in Japan, South Korea, the Philippines, and Vietnam about Beijing's intentions in the region, especially as a feistier China's wealth and power grew apace. Its economic rise continued despite the global financial crisis and recession that set in during 2008.[6] And its military was realizing the returns from nearly two decades of steep increases in funding, as it tested, displayed, or began to deploy a range of advanced weapons (notably including an anti-satellite system, a stealth aircraft, an anti-ship ballistic missile with a maneuverable warhead, larger numbers of quiet diesel submarines, more capable ships, a second generation nuclear missile submarine, and China's first aircraft carrier). Although the near term military significance of most of these new systems (other than the diesel submarines and new destroyers) was marginal, they were seen as a portent whose effect on the regional balance of power was only a matter of time.

To be sure, regional concerns about the possible implications of China's growing economic and military capabilities existed before 2009. But Beijing had been remarkably successful in reassuring others that its greater power would not pose a threat. Policies aimed at offsetting inevitable anxiety about China's rise had been a central thread in the grand strategy Beijing's leaders embraced during the 1990s.[7] Even if not fully convincing, China's reassurances had at least facilitated a widespread view that its longer term intentions remained unclear, might be shaped through cooperation, and did not require an immediate counterbalance. China's neighbors had been comfortable with simultaneously improving relations with Beijing in order to give it a stake in sticking with a cooperative stance even as it grew more powerful, while also maintaining traditionally good ties to Washington as a hedge against the possibility that a stronger China abandoned cooperation. Because China's longer term role in shaping the future of East Asia remained unclear, for most of the first ~~ of the twenty-first century it was neither necessary nor sensib~~ choose between cultivating closer relations with either China o~~

After 2009, however, China's regional behavior fostered a perception that Beijing was shifting to a foreign policy that more clearly asserted its own interests even where they conflicted with others.' This interpretation led several of Beijing's East Asian neighbors to view the implications of a rising China's future role as ominous rather than uncertain.[8] The ultimate purposes of China's military modernization and, more immediately, its vigorous defense of its interests in the South and East China Seas, and its response to elevated tensions on the Korean Peninsula fostered a less forgiving perception. Instead of welcoming signs of reassurance about the future of regional relations, Seoul, Tokyo, Manila, and Hanoi saw what they feared was an alarming preview of Beijing's long-term intentions. Their interest in maintaining a relatively even-handed approach to relations with Beijing and Washington gradually gave way to attempts to shore up or, in the case of Vietnam, build ties to the U.S. as the most feasible approach for coping with the pressures they expected to face from a more powerful and active China. And after late 2009, renewed friction in U.S.-China relations increased Washington's readiness to cooperate with Beijing's nervous neighbors in East Asia.

At the end of 2010, however, China's leaders began to respond to this adverse trend in regional relations as they tacitly acknowledged the risks their foreign policy over the preceding year had generated. In a landmark statement that was initially designed for consumption by the policy elite within China but was later broadly publicized at home and abroad, Beijing's senior State Councilor for foreign affairs, Dai Bingguo, reiterated China's commitment to the approach of peaceful development that had guided relations in Asia and beyond since the mid-1990s.[9] Thereafter, a shift in Beijing's rhetoric was matched by efforts at engaging its Asian neighbors to mitigate the disruptive effects of disputes, described below, that had flared in 2009–2010. While partly effective in stopping the deterioration of regional relations—most notably with Japan, the Philippines, and Vietnam—Beijing's return to a heavy emphasis on reassurance at the end of 2010 did not bear the fruit that similar efforts had yielded after the mid-1990s. Perhaps because fifteen years later China was so much richer and more powerful, or perhaps because others had seen what they understood to be actions that belied Beijing's self-proclaimed unalterable commitment to being a good neighbor eschewing power politics, it had become much more difficult for China to persuasively allay nagging doubts about the sincerity or durability of its welcome policy readjustment in late 2010.

REGIONAL DEVELOPMENTS

Japan

In 2008, Tokyo seemed set to enter a period in which it would be able to enjoy good ties to both China and the U.S. By the end of the Bush administration, the U.S. and Japan had negotiated an agreement to redeploy some of the American forces stationed in Japan, an agreement that would bolster the stability of the decades-long U.S.-Japan security alliance. In 2008 and 2009, Japan's relations with China had also been relatively smooth. And the electoral victory of Japan's Democratic Party in September 2009 seemed to bode well for further progress in addressing longstanding disagreements that had periodically plagued bilateral relations since the administration of Junichiro Koizumi. As elsewhere in the region, however, events in 2009 and 2010 had a profound effect on Japan's relations with both the U.S. and China.

When President Obama began his term as president, the U.S. and Japan were on track to implement an agreed relocation of U.S. military forces on Okinawa that had been negotiated during the Bush administration. But Japan's new prime minister, the Democratic Party's Yukio Hatoyama, had made an electoral campaign promise to reconsider the agreement his predecessor had approved. He also indicated he might seek other changes in the terms of the U.S. military presence in Japan under the alliance and revisit Tokyo's role in supporting U.S. operations in Afghanistan.[10] Hatoyama's initiatives cast a shadow over visits to Japan by U.S. Secretary of Defense Robert Gates and President Obama in October and November 2009 respectively. Moreover, as part of a rebalancing of Japan's foreign policy, Hatoyama sought to further the improvement of Japan's relations with China that had marked the years since Prime Minister Koizumi left office. Such an improvement would parallel increasingly robust Sino-Japanese economic ties. Two developments, however, soon led Hatoyama, and later his successor, Naoto Kan, to tack back to strengthening Japan's ties with Washington.

First, North Korea's attack on the South Korean ship *Cheonan* in March 2010 dramatically increased Japan's persistent concerns about the threat that the North's nuclear weapons capability represented (a capability made ever more tangible by Pyongyang's missile and warhead tests in spring 2009). North Korea's unrepentant stance after the sinking of the *Cheonan* in March (and the subsequent artillery shelling of Yeonpyeong Island in November) deepened Japan's concern about this near term security challenge, against which Tokyo's best protection was its alliance with the U.S. In this context, China's decision not to join in the broad international condemnation of North Korea's provocative actions raised worrisome questions about Hatoyama's original intention to rebalance Japan's regional position more evenly between Beijing and Washington.

Second, in September 2010 a Japanese coast guard vessel collided with a Chinese fishing boat that it was ordering out of waters in the East China Sea in which Beijing and Tokyo have competing claims. The arrest of the Chinese captain triggered a diplomatic confrontation as Beijing insisted on his release and Japanese authorities insisted that he be held for trial. As tensions rose, China's exports of critical rare earth minerals were interrupted, threatening key high-tech industries in Japan. Beijing insisted that the interruption did not reflect a policy decision to use its economic leverage over Japan in order to pressure Tokyo to release the Chinese captain. Nevertheless, the supply disruption highlighted for Japan the potential risks that growing economic interdependence with China entailed. Japanese public opinion turned sharply against China, reciprocating hostility being expressed among Chinese who questioned Tokyo's account of the maritime incident and the legitimacy of the captain's arrest.

In short, over the course of a year, Japan's foreign policy had shifted from managing tensions with the U.S. that threatened to weaken the alliance even as Tokyo pursued closer ties with Beijing, to a determination to counter China (and the unpredictable dangers its North Korean ally posed) by shoring up relations with Washington. As Richard Samuels aptly put it: "The Hatoyama tilt toward China was abandoned in favor of a hug with the United States."[11] The basing issue was put on the back burner and under Hatoyama's successors, Naoto Kan and then Yoshihiko Noda, the allies agreed to work towards a solution that would take into account local objections to American plans for relocating military forces on Okinawa.

By 2011, U.S.-Japan relations were back on track, whereas relations with China had returned to the condition once described as "economically warm, politically cool" that had characterized the more strained period during the Koizumi administration. The extensiveness of Sino-Japanese economic relations continued to provide reason enough to avoid a serious rupture of bilateral ties. The events of 2010, however, meant that the vulnerability economic dependence denotes was more clearly understood in Tokyo to be a double-edged sword, potentially exacerbating political friction with Beijing and serving as a reminder of the enduring importance of Japan's alliance with the U.S.

Korea

For the most part, in 2008 and 2009 China and the U.S. seemed to be on the same page in supporting a negotiated end to North Korea's nuclear weapons program within the framework of the Six Party Talks. Disruptions to the talks triggered by Pyongyang's nuclear warhead and missile tests in 2009 had seemed to further cement what was one of the most significant areas of U.S.-China diplomatic cooperation. But in 2010, tensions on the peninsula rose and U.S.-China cooperation on the North Korean nuclear issue frayed. In March, North Korea sank the South Korean ship *Cheonan* and in November it fired artillery shells at Yeonpyeong Island, both attacks resulting in South Korean casualties. The U.S. and China reacted in starkly different ways to these incidents. The U.S. backed its South Korean ally's claims (and, in the case of the *Cheonan* attack, the findings of a multinational investigation) about the North's culpability, restated its treaty commitment to the South's security, and moved forward with plans for high-profile joint military exercises as a strong signal of alliance solidarity. China, however, refrained from directly criticizing the North and instead urged all parties to exercise restraint.

While Beijing and Washington both continued to profess their interest in resuming the Six Party Talks, they disagreed about whether as a precondition North Korea needed to account for its actions since 2008 that raised doubts about the sincerity of its commitment to peace and nuclear disarmament. China was eager to bring North Korea back to the negotiating table, and saw that as the venue where the broader issue of escalating tensions could be discussed.[12] The U.S. supported the South in its demand that a resumption of the nuclear talks depended on Pyongyang entering a dialogue with Seoul to satisfactorily address the two deadly attacks. Moreover, the U.S. insisted that North Korea must first take steps demonstrating that it was ready to resume talks whose goal would require it to fully dismantle its nuclear weapons capability.

In 2010, this became even harder when Pyongyang revealed that it was operating a uranium enrichment program, a potential alternative to its plutonium reactor/reprocessing path for amassing weapons-grade nuclear materials.

The divergence of the American and Chinese approaches to rising tension on the Korean Peninsula in 2010 in part reflected a longstanding disagreement about the usefulness of publicly pressuring North Korea while trying to rely on diplomacy to negotiate a denuclearization deal. The significance of this divergence increased along with the generally adverse trend in U.S.-China relations during 2010. To Beijing's consternation, Washington had been lending stronger support to East Asian states whose disputes with China re-intensified.[13] Faced with this deteriorating strategic and diplomatic position in the East and South China Seas, it seemed that China was about to add instability along its northeastern border with Korea to its list of challenges. Beijing's enduring interest in working with the U.S. to restart the Six Party Talks and encourage North Korea's nuclear disarmament were now balanced against the worry that siding with the U.S. and its allies against Pyongyang might increase the risk of turmoil on the peninsula that could ultimately enhance American influence in yet another theater near China.[14] China's criticisms of U.S.-South Korean naval exercises during the summer and fall of 2010 reflected Beijing's concern that instability in Korea was already being used as a pretext for the U.S. and its allies to make the peninsula and its surrounding seas another venue near China where they would be ramping up military cooperation. The U.S. refuted this interpretation, arguing instead that it was China's reluctance to pressure North Korea that increased the risk Pyongyang would repeat its provocations and elicit a response from the U.S. and its allies that could alter the northeast Asian security environment in precisely the ways that Beijing feared.

However, as in other areas of East Asia where tensions increased and then eased, in 2011 all parties backed away from their most unyielding positions and the prospects for a resumption of the Six Party Talks improved. North Korea, South Korea, China, and the U.S. all began searching for face-saving ways to satisfy the conditions each had set for restarting the negotiations. The death of North Korea's Kim Jong-il on December 17, 2011 and the transition of leadership to his son, Kim Jong-un, at least temporarily froze progress on this front. It remains unclear whether this transition will fundamentally alter North Korea's position on resuming talks. What is clear is that the events of 2010 had underscored important disagreements between the U.S. and China about how best to deal with North Korea, despite their shared interest in seeking its denuclearization. At best, the lessons the U.S. and China draw from the events of 2009–2010 will complicate the Six Party Talks; at worst they increase the prospect of continued stalemate that yields the outcome both Beijing and Washington want to avoid—an unrestrained North Korean nuclear weapons program.

The Philippines and Vietnam

Since the 1990s, shared economic interests reflected in thickening trade and investment ties with China had facilitated better political relations between Beijing and its ASEAN neighbors. Beijing's interest in sustaining this improvement and cultivating a strategic partnership with ASEAN had resulted in a China-ASEAN free-trade pact that provided generous "early harvest" concessions to ASEAN states even before the agreement was scheduled to come into effect in 2010.[15] Beijing had also shown a new flexibility by agreeing to work towards a "Code of Conduct" whose purpose would be to buffer regional relations from conflicts rooted in remaining disputes about sovereignty claims to territory and adjacent portions of the South China Sea. Progress on both the economic and political fronts, as noted above, was taken as evidence of China's remarkably successful ASEAN policy. After 2008, however, Vietnam and especially the Philippines grew increasingly apprehensive about what they perceived to be a rising China's stronger assertion of its regional interests. As for Japan and Korea, but arguably even more dramatically, the result was an adjustment in their relations both with China and the U.S.

Sovereignty disputes between China and its southeastern neighbors over claims in the South China Sea were proving intractable. Progress towards realizing the goal they had declared in 2002, to sign and implement a Code of Conduct, was halting.[16] And then, in 2009–2010, China's relations with both the Philippines and Vietnam deteriorated sharply as the lingering maritime disputes re-intensified. In reaction, both more actively cultivated their ties with the U.S. to reduce the risk that they would be on their own in defending their claims against an ever more powerful China.

Analysts have debated whether the sharpening of these disputes in the South China Sea resulted from a decision by Beijing to adopt a more confrontational posture with the Philippines and Vietnam. Those who saw a change in China's approach as the cause for increased tensions suggested that leaders in Beijing believed their country's accelerated economic and military ascent, together with America's focus on its continuing military operations in the Persian Gulf and Afghanistan as well as its debilitating economic crisis at home, created a strategic opening for China.[17] Others, however, did not see enough evidence to convince them that Beijing had made a strategic decision to seize the moment and advance its sovereignty claims.[18] Instead, they suggested that all three claimants had been more clearly asserting their overlapping positions not only because plans for economic development were moving forward, but also because they needed to meet deadlines for submitting clarifications of relevant maritime claims to the relevant U.N. agencies. Absent a resolution of their differences prior to this deadline, all three countries unsurprisingly asserted their traditional "indisputable" sovereignty claims. None could afford to allow the others' statements to go unchallenged since that might affect the viability of their claims under international law in future efforts to resolve the disputes.[19]

During 2009 and 2010, rhetoric heated up and incidents in contested parts of the South China Sea became more salient. Some of the incidents allegedly resulted from Chinese ships acting to enforce Beijing's claims, though the extent to which their actions were directed or even authorized by Chinese leaders was not clear.[20] Confusion about culpability and the triggers for the renewed turn to confrontation notwithstanding, the consequences for China's strategic position in maritime Southeast Asia were soon clear. The Philippines looked to the U.S., its best hope for support in the event of a direct challenge from China, for a re-affirmation of America's alliance obligations under the U.S.-Philippine security treaty. Vietnam also accelerated what had been a gradual warming of diplomatic ties to the U.S., and surprisingly quickly added a degree of bilateral military co-operation whose ultimate dimensions were not immediately apparent.[21]

The decision early in the Obama administration to more actively partici-pate in East Asian multilateral forums also created opportunities for the U.S. to signal its position. With maritime tensions high, such an opportunity was dramatically seized by Secretary of State Hillary Clinton at the August 2010 ARF meeting in Hanoi. The meeting's Vietnamese venue and the broad, coor-dinated support among ASEAN states for the position Clinton outlined (re-stating the U.S. interest in ensuring freedom of passage through international waters and peaceful resolution of sovereignty disputes about which the U.S. otherwise does not take a position, and indicating an American willingness, if asked, to assist with regional efforts to resolve the outstanding disagreements) was taken as a warning to China that it should not assume its material advan-tages over smaller ASEAN states would enable it to get its way in settling the disputes bilaterally.

Public perceptions of the speech, along with China's initially harsh reac-tion delivered at the Hanoi meetings by Chinese Foreign Minister Yang Jiechi, underscored the new challenges confronting China in Southeast Asia. Beijing faced a choice between ramping up its confrontations in the South China Sea or trying to revive the spirit of cooperation with its ASEAN neighbors that had seemed firmly in place earlier in the decade. By late 2010, Beijing clearly signaled that it had opted for the latter course.[22] During 2011, China stepped up its diplomacy and economic cooperation with both the Philippines and Vi-etnam and reiterated its interest in finalizing a Code of Conduct to reduce the risks of conflicts over remaining territorial and maritime disputes.[23] Neverthe-less, as with South Korea and Japan, China was able to moderate tensions with Vietnam and the Philippines but could not erase the twin lessons that these neighbors had learned from their recent experience—the risks they faced in ensuring their own interests if China's intentions changed as its capabilities grew, and the irreplaceable benefits they derived from the leverage an attentive, powerful, and present American partner could provide.

The difficulty China faced in restoring confidence about its professions of regional goodwill was most clearly manifest in the Philippines' persistent efforts to elicit ever stronger indications of support from the U.S. The zenith of these efforts occurred just prior to the November 2011 East Asia Summit (EAS) in Bali. While Secretary of State Clinton was in Manila to commemorate the 60th anniversary of the U.S.-Philippine alliance, she signed the Manila Declaration aboard the U.S.S. *Fitzgerald* in Manila Harbor. And in remarks afterward, Clinton pledged continued bilateral cooperation with the Philippines, reaffirmed the broader U.S. position on maritime security, seemed to offer a more explicit endorsement of multilateral approaches to resolving sovereignty claims in the South China Sea than she had the previous year in Hanoi, and echoed her Philippine counterpart by referring to the disputed waters of the South China Sea with the neologism, "the West Philippine Sea."[24]

In addition to cultivating support from its ally in Washington, Manila also sought to build solidarity among its ASEAN partners. This effort was less successful, however, and the Philippines failed to win regional backing for presenting a united front openly opposing China's maritime claims at the 2011 EAS.[25] Although other ASEAN countries had their own concerns about China's maritime ambitions, welcomed America's growing engagement with ASEAN and the EAS, and had already made maritime security a major issue on the agenda in Bali, they (perhaps most importantly ASEAN's largest member, Indonesia) resisted what would have amounted to a decision to stand with Washington and its ally against China.[26] Other ASEAN states did not face the pressing challenges from China that Vietnam and especially the Philippines thought they saw at the end of the decade. For most, their priority was coping with domestic rather than international challenges.[27] And with a vital stake in preserving a peaceful regional environment that facilitated extensive economic relations with China, they were not inclined to adopt a stance on maritime disputes that would exacerbate tensions with Beijing. At least outside of the Philippines and Vietnam, ASEAN countries instead sought to refrain from steps that would provoke China and risk the sort of Sino-American confrontation that could force smaller countries to choose sides.[28] China's growing economic role in the region was clearly tempering the reaction of some of its southeast Asian neighbors. Indeed, even as Vietnam and the Philippines acted on their concerns about China by turning to Washington, they also sought to sustain their engagement with Beijing.[29] Still, events in 2009–2010 had confounded the expectations of those who had been suggesting that China's economic clout would soon enable it to edge the U.S. out of this subregion. The undeniably strong economic interest in ties with China was not leading ASEAN states to discount the advantages of also preserving a substantial American role in their region.

Perhaps tellingly, even Myanmar, an ASEAN state with exceptionally close ties to China, in 2011 sought to improve relations with the U.S., a turn which might enable it to offset the disadvantages of what had become a heavy dependence on Beijing.[30] As disputes between Rangoon and Beijing over development projects surfaced, and protests in Myanmar about China unfairly exploiting Burmese resources were reported, the military junta simultaneously pressed for revision of agreements with China and announced domestic political reforms in part designed to meet American conditions for improving bilateral relations.[31] The U.S. took note, indicated it would meet "action with action" and, following the East Asian Summit, announced that Secretary Clinton would visit Myanmar in December 2011, the first visit by such a high-ranking American official since 1955.[32] Progress was rapid. On January 13, 2012, the U.S. announced it would restore full diplomatic relations with Myanmar. Although the ultimate strategic significance of this opening remained unclear, it suggested that henceforth Myanmar, like most other countries in the region, would pursue its interests with an eye to the opportunities and constraints provided by the inextricably entangled regional relations of China and the U.S.

Australia

Australia's relations with China, like those of many of China's neighbors, have grown economically stronger but remained prone to recurrent political tension. When Kevin Rudd became Australia's prime minister in 2007, some speculated that his personal familiarity with Chinese culture, including his fluency in Mandarin, might usher in a golden age of relations between China and Australia. That did not happen. Instead, familiar disputes with Beijing about China's human rights record and new disagreements about Beijing's handling of dissent in Tibet and Xinjiang flared. And in 2009, ties were more seriously strained by a diplomatic row over Chinese charges of economic espionage leveled at the Australian mining firm Rio Tinto, including the arrest of an Australian national in China. Whether or not the arrest was, as some speculated, related to the failed attempt by a Chinese firm that sought to increase its stake in Rio Tinto, it badly soured Sino-Australian political relations. Nevertheless, as with other political disagreements between Canberra and Beijing, the case did not fundamentally affect the robust bilateral economic relationship that had taken root. In 2007, a booming China had become Australia's largest trade partner.[33] And as its main destination for exports after 2009 (especially iron, coal, and liquefied natural gas), the economic relationship with China was a key reason why Australia escaped the worst effects of the global recession.

In what was a familiar pattern throughout the region, close economic relations with China did not fundamentally alter Australia's traditionally strong political and military alliance with the U.S. Julia Gillard, who replaced Rudd as the Labor Party's leader and became prime minister in July 2010, staked out a position that underscored the importance of, but differences between, Australia's interests in good relations with both the U.S. and China.[34] She called for her government to develop an updated strategic posture consistent with these dual interests and more fully accounting for the dramatic changes that have been unfolding in the region and the world economy during the twenty-first century—specifically the rising role of emerging powers, and especially China.[35]

Gillard's statements signaled that, like many states in neighboring East Asia, Australia remained hopeful that Sino-American rivalry would not require others to "choose sides." On the one hand, economic realities provide a compelling reason to avoid conflict with a China that seemed certain to remain an attractive partner for trade and investment. On the other hand, Australia's need to hedge against the unpredictable security challenges an increasingly powerful China might pose, provides a compelling reason to preserve a robust alliance with the U.S. to complement Australia's own military modernization. Australia's actions have reflected both considerations. It has repeatedly reassured China about the importance it attaches to bilateral ties,[36] and it has been deeply engaged with Asia's multilateral organizations even as American interest has varied.[37] At the same time, Australia has re-strengthened bilateral security ties to the U.S., most tangibly with the announcement during President Obama's visit in November 2011 that up to 2,500 U.S. marines would regularly rotate through bases in Australia's Northern Territory.[38]

This widely noted new military arrangement is not the first time regional and international changes have prompted action that reaffirms the U.S.-Australia alliance. But the context for the announcement had changed in two respects. First the previous updating of the alliance in 1996 had occurred just after the end of the Cold War, a time when China's economic rise was in its earliest stages and its military modernization had not yet gotten very far. The difference in 2011 was that China had emerged as a key economic actor and, after two decades of heavy investment in military modernization, was beginning to deploy an array of advanced forces to be reckoned with. Second, in a climate of fiscal austerity the U.S. was expected to reduce its military personnel and equipment deployed overseas. Given this context, the new American military foothold in Australia was not only a signal of Washington's continuing commitment to its ally in Canberra. It was also a tangible manifestation of President Obama's broader promise that the U.S. was in Asia to stay, and that there would be no reduction in U.S. military forces deployed in Pacific Asia (a point also underscored by the U.S. agreement with Singapore to base

American littoral combat ships at Changyi, a modest military step but one that symbolized the U.S. commitment to its presence in Southeast Asia).[39] China's reaction echoed its response to other U.S. initiatives in Asia after 2009. Even though Australia (and the U.S.) explicitly denied that the new military arrangement was motivated by concerns about Beijing, China's statements ranged from measured skepticism to harsh criticism of a deal labeled another reflection of "obsolete Cold War thinking" and part of the ever more visible American plan to encircle and "contain" China.[40]

Central and South Asia

In South, and especially Central, Asia after 2008, the interests of the U.S. and China, while certainly not identical, have proven more compatible than in other parts of the region examined here. Re-intensification of the U.S. military effort in Afghanistan after late 2009 that had been initiated along with a publicly stated plan to draw down the effort beginning in late 2011, provided the overarching context. This latest turn in America's war strategy merely confirmed for many in the region the longstanding expectation that, like its Russian and British predecessors, the U.S. would recoil from the heavy burden of protracted involvement in Afghanistan's complex and inhospitable polity.

As Evan Feigenbaum has persuasively argued, in Central Asia, even without formal attempts at coordination, overlapping interests in economic development and trade as well as opposition to religious extremism and subnational terrorist groups with cross-border connections allow the U.S. and China to work in parallel rather than in opposition.[41] In Central Asia, the U.S. and China share a political interest in limiting instability that could fuel international criminal and terrorist activity, and share an economic interest in fostering conditions that will unleash the resource rich and geographically central region's full potential. In addition, they both have strategic interests that are modest and negatively construed—ensuring that the other does not dominate the region.[42] The U.S. has a strategic interest in preventing a highly capable adversary from controlling the Eurasian heartland. This concern, previously fueled by fears of Soviet power, is now linked with uncertainty about China's future capabilities and intentions. China's strategic interest is of more recent vintage—the fear of American sponsored geopolitical encirclement, in which Central Asia completes a ring of daunting U.S. influence and power in Asia that already extends from the Korean Peninsula in the Northeast to India in the South.[43] Although these mirror image strategic concerns suggest a basis for conflict, at least since 2008 trends in Central Asia have neither reflected nor exacerbated U.S.-China rivalry in the ways that were evident in East Asia.

For three reasons Central Asia did not provide fertile soil for Sino-American rivalry. First, after 2009 China's security concerns about the possibility of a significant long-term U.S. military presence to its west diminished. The projected drawdown of U.S. military operations in Afghanistan would soon reduce the American need for the kind of logistical cooperation with Central Asian states (the use of Central Asian airfields) that had been vital after 2001. Second, American disillusionment with the prospects for its nation-building effort in Afghanistan eased China's concern that a U.S. campaign to promote Western liberal democratic values across Central Asia—an American aim in the region ever since the collapse of the Soviet Union—would pose yet another political-ideological challenge to the authoritarian rulers in Beijing.[44] Third, in contrast with East Asia, the legacy of Soviet rule and geopolitics mean that Russia continues to play an important role in Central Asia that mitigates concerns either the Americans or Chinese might harbor about the other achieving a dangerous degree of unchallenged dominance.[45] Moreover, this de facto Russia-China-U.S. triangle in a setting where the U.S. and China also share important common interests, creates distinctive opportunities for the Central Asia states to exploit the great powers' limited rivalry that are not as readily available to most states in the more hotly contested and conflict ridden East Asia.

With the departure of U.S. and other NATO forces from Afghanistan scheduled to begin in late 2011, Pakistan and India faced the prospect of increased uncertainty in their part of Asia. As they did, each worried about the other exploiting a fluid situation in Afghanistan to its advantage. Pakistan's strategic interest predated the American war initiated in 2001. It has been to prevent the emergence of a strong national government in Afghanistan that is too closely aligned with India. A pro-Indian Afghan regime would confront contingency planners in Islamabad with the daunting prospect that a military conflict with India could escalate horizontally to a western front. And India's strategic interest in Afghanistan is partly defined by a desire for precisely the sort of relationship with Kabul that makes it too risky for Pakistan's military to focus solely on its eastern front with India. But New Delhi's arguably greater strategic interest is in preventing Afghanistan, with or without Pakistani complicity, from serving as yet another regional incubator of Islamic extremism. This would exacerbate two major challenges Delhi already faces—the traditional security threat of interstate conflict over Kashmir and the related nontraditional security threat of lethal terrorist attacks against the Indian homeland.

While these South Asian considerations are seemingly unrelated to the changing interaction between the U.S. and China, two links exist. First, the Obama administration's announced "pivot" of the American security focus, including a shift away from its largely continental concerns in South and

Southwest Asia to largely maritime concerns in East Asia that bear on China's role, provides increased incentives for India and Pakistan to think about alternatives to U.S. support for their regional interests. Second, the increase in Sino-American friction which developed after late 2009, just as the time horizon for U.S. involvement in Afghanistan shortened, reshaped the strategic context within which Pakistan and India adjusted their policies.

Pakistan's formal cooperation with the U.S. war effort, already plagued by disputes over American strikes against insurgents based on its side of the border with Afghanistan, frayed badly following the U.S. special forces raid in May 2011 that killed Osama Bin Laden.[46] As ties with Washington soured, Pakistan's leaders turned to China in an effort to demonstrate that it had an option for strategic support other than the U.S. While Beijing invoked ostensibly supportive rhetoric about Islamabad being its "all weather friend," the tangible results of high level meetings between the countries' leaders were minimal. China's realpolitik interest in complicating India's strategic environment had long provided a solid foundation for Sino-Pakistani partnership. But this traditional security concern increasingly competed with Beijing's nontraditional security concerns about Islamic extremist groups operating out of Pakistan and Afghanistan, which it believes exacerbate ethnic tensions and separatist impulses in Xinjiang. China's interest, like that of the U.S., is to ensure that Pakistan's government presses the fight against extremists in its border regions. Moreover, China has developed a much greater economic stake in its relations with India than with Pakistan (which promises to be more an economic liability than an economic asset), establishing a new constraint on Beijing's willingness to closely align with and strongly support Islamabad.[47] Finally, and perhaps most importantly, any temptation for China to exploit trouble between Washington and Islamabad was limited by the reality that after 2009 Beijing's principal strategic focus turned to the challenges it saw in East Asia, where turbulence in relations with the U.S. and its regional allies became a more salient and pressing concern.

India's worries about Islamic extremism put it on the same page as the U.S. and China. Still, New Delhi's longer term national interest in coping with an increasingly capable Chinese neighbor provided incentives to look beyond the immediate dangers posed by nonstate actors, their state supporters in Pakistan, and their connection with Afghanistan's future strategic status. The territorial dispute along the China-India border that sparked war in 1962 has so far proved manageable. And India's economic interests have not yet come into sharp conflict with China's (as two of the BRICs, their positions on international economic governance often overlap). But India's concerns about the ultimate implications of China's economic and military ascent sustain an interest in furthering the improvement in ties with the U.S. that began at the end of the Clinton administration and accelerated under President Bush. While it was initially unclear whether the Obama administration shared its predecessors' enthusiasm for cultivating India as a strategic partner, difficulties in Afghanistan, frustrations with Pakistan, and the turbulence of America's relations with China soon led Washington to reaffirm the importance of its ties with New Delhi.[48]

Multilateralism

In the latter years of the century's first decade, China had difficulty matching its initial string of successes in working through multilateral organizations to deepen economic cooperation in the region and reduce anxiety over its growing military power. Some friction was a predicable by-product of more extensive economic interactions that followed from greater trade and investment flows. These sorts of routine challenges, however, do not explain recent changes in the region's multilateral diplomacy. These changes were more clearly a consequence of China's intensifying disagreements with its Southeast Asian neighbors over disputed territories and their adjacent seas, recurrent tensions with Japan in the East China Sea, and the deterioration of relations with South Korea that followed Beijing's unnerving neutrality after provocative attacks by North Korea. More suspicious about the "good neighbor" policy of an increasingly powerful China, China's East Asian neighbors welcomed a renewed American interest in regional organizations.

Fairly or not, during the Bush administration the U.S. had been seen as insufficiently interested in Asia's regional architecture beyond the hub-and-spokes arrangement that defined the American alliance network, and insufficiently attentive to issues other than those relevant to the "global war on terrorism."[49] The U.S. alleged disinterest in or skepticism about other aspects of Asian international relations (such as ASEAN sponsored meetings and the effort to establish an East Asia Summit in 2005) and the absence of high-level American representation at major regional meetings may simply have reflected the massive demands on U.S. time and resources that accompanied its costly efforts in Iraq and Afghanistan.[50] Whatever its basis, this legacy of the Bush administration created an opportunity for President Obama to draw a clear contrast with his predecessor. Trumpeting a shift from an emphasis on unilateralism to multilateralism, determined to bring American military operations in Iraq and Afghanistan to an early conclusion, and asserting the growing importance of Pacific Asia for the U.S., his administration seized this opportunity and did so in a highly visible fashion.

Under President Obama, the U.S. adopted a more visible and more activist posture within the ASEAN Regional Forum of which it had long been a member. It was at the aforementioned July 2010 Hanoi session of the ARF that Secretary Clinton made her comments about maritime security in the South China Sea that were welcomed by ASEAN countries and criticized by China. But even before this, the Obama administration had strongly signaled its intention to more closely engage the region's organizations. In July 2009, the U.S. acted to remove what had been a key stumbling block to U.S. participation in the East Asia Summit by signing the Treaty of Amity and Cooperation (TAC).[51] This announcement predated perceptions of China's new assertiveness in 2010, and may have been motivated by broader U.S. concerns about the risks of not having its voice heard in a regional institution that could have important implications for American interests. But as disagreements between China and the U.S. as well as between China and its East Asian neighbors flared in 2010, Washington's embrace of the EAS (especially President Obama's active role at the 2011 summit in Bali) and the welcome it met with in the region were seen as a manifestation of the concern that other Asian-only ASEAN spinoffs (such as the ASEAN+3, which included China, Japan, and South Korea) could become vehicles for China to limit American influence in the region.

The changing environment for regional multilateralism was also reflected in the evolution of a proposal first vetted in 2005 to set up a Trans-Pacific Partnership (TPP), a Pacific Rim multilateral free-trade regime whose membership was expected to include several of Asia's leading economies. During President Obama's November 2009 trip to China, Japan, and South Korea, and on the heels of Washington's decision in July to sign the TAC, the U.S. announced that it would join the negotiations to set up the TPP.[52] In 2009, this announcement was viewed simply as part of a broader American free-trade policy that aimed to ensure U.S. economic interests in the region. But when American support for realizing the TPP was given a high priority two years later in conjunction with the November 2011 Asia-Pacific Economic Cooperation (APEC) meetings in Honolulu, the prominence accorded the initiative was widely viewed as having a new political significance related to the turbulence in U.S.-China relations during the years following Obama's 2009 trip to China. This interpretation was reinforced by Japan's announcement, on the eve of the 2011 APEC session, that it intended to join the TPP. Although it was widely recognized that Tokyo would first have to overcome stiff domestic opposition to the conditions of membership, it was also recognized that the hurdles Japan would need to clear were less daunting than those that would face China if it chose to participate.[53] While Beijing was welcome to join the TPP, it would have to make changes in its economic policies governing foreign business and investment in China that it had long resisted. It was widely understood that the requirements for TPP membership meant that China was unlikely to be able to join in the near future. The upshot was the perception that the TPP had become a multilateral project whose design, if not intent, would make it a counterweight to regional economic groupings that included China but excluded the U.S. (e.g., ASEAN+3). Especially in the view of Chinese skeptical about the reason for the renewed American enthusiasm for multilateralism in Asia, the TPP was seen as yet another element in Washington's effort together with its regional partners to parry Beijing's growing influence in Pacific Asia.[54]

Suspicious of U.S. intentions, China might have been expected to reconsider the usefulness of regional organizations that, since the mid-1990s, it had seen as venues for reassuring nervous neighbors. If they were instead becoming settings in which others could gang up on China or act as fronts for American efforts to check China's rise (as Beijing had feared in the early 1990s), their appeal would diminish. Indeed, that sort of reassessment might have seemed plausible in the wake of the harsh Chinese reaction to Secretary Clinton's speech at the July 2010 ARF. But by late 2010 Beijing signaled that it believed maintaining China's position as a constructive partner in regional organizations would better serve the country's interests, and that they were a useful multilateral complement to renewed bilateral efforts at reassuring neighbors that China would remain a responsible power, a position consistent with the expectations for enduring cooperation that John Ikenberry identifies in his chapter.[55] It was unclear, however, whether China's moderation and continued support for regional multilateralism after late 2010 reflected a broad consensus in Beijing, or only the temporary resolution of an ongoing debate. If the latter, then the evolution of the U.S. position on the TPP and its support for the ASEAN countries' decision to put maritime security issues on the agenda of the 2011 EAS summit in Bali could well reopen that debate in Beijing—a debate likely to be shaped by the complex domestic forces affecting China's foreign policy.

CONCLUSION

After 2008, international relations in Asia took an unexpected turn. For nearly a quarter of a century the region had experienced a general trend towards expanding cooperation built upon a broadly shared interest in preserving regional peace and facilitating economic development. More recently, however, conflicting interests have surfaced that cast doubt on the expectation that regional relations in the coming years will be as smooth as they were early in the century. Also surprising, perhaps, new and renewed tensions had not emerged in what were viewed early in the century as the two settings where conflicting Chinese and American interests were most likely to become dangerously engaged—the Taiwan Strait and Central Asia. After 2008, the risks of a Sino-American clash over their still unresolved disagreements about Taiwan's future diminished. And even though American military involvement in Afghanistan temporarily spiked, the planned U.S. withdrawal meant that this theater was not likely to become a new front for U.S.-China rivalry. Instead it was events elsewhere across the region that fed new worries about stability.

An ever more capable China had already begun to play a larger regional role. But as it responded to developments from Korea through the South China Sea in ways that its neighbors found unsettling, American allies and states with whom the U.S. was fostering closer ties (such as India and Vietnam) acted to ensure their own interests. To the extent they worried about bilateral disagreements with China, they cultivated the kind of leverage that only their American partner could provide. And as U.S.-China relations took a turn for the worse after November 2009, Washington was increasingly inclined to offer the support others sought. Beijing, seeing its own policies as no more than a necessary defense of its own interests, rejected the rationale offered for the alarmed reaction (especially claims about China's increased assertiveness) and labeled it a thinly veiled pretext offered by those determined to check China's rise.

Some realist scholars may not find these developments surprising, seeing them as no more than a reflection of the security dilemma that inevitably arises among self-regarding states with potentially conflicting interests who are constrained to coexist and cope with uncertainty about one another's intentions in an anarchic international realm. But the logic of the security dilemma, while clearly important, leaves unanswered important questions about variations in its intensity. As power shifts, states face new challenges to which leaders respond according to perceptions of their interests. Among most states, in Asia as elsewhere, neither peaceful cooperation nor intractable conflict is inevitable. The choices states make, which in turn affect the perceptions and choices of others, determine whether the security dilemma they face is mitigated or exacerbated. Asian international relations since 2008 demonstrate that such choices have consequences, and that among the most significant are the consequences for managing inevitable disagreements that reflect states' differing interests.

In 2010, managing these differences at a moment when power seemed to be shifting in significant ways became a particularly salient challenge. As it did, some concluded that China's relations with the others in the region and with the U.S. had reached a turning point. In this view, polarization and confrontation in Asia would henceforth reflect an intensifying rivalry between a beleaguered U.S. and a rising China, a rivalry that would define the context for Asian international relations, much as Soviet-American rivalry had defined the Cold War.[56] Others, however, discounted the notion that such a turning point had been reached. In this view, tensions were temporary and likely to give way to a resumption of the relatively cooperative relations among China, its regional neighbors, and the U.S. that had prevailed earlier in the decade. The benefits from economic exchange, the constraining logic of interdependence, the costs of military conflict, and the multiplicity of international institutions that provided venues for diplomacy to head off polarization and instead facilitate "win-win" approaches to managing differences would define a context for Asian international relations.

It is, of course, too soon to know whether the new turbulence in Asia after 2008 represents a turning point or a brief detour. China's recommitment to a policy of peaceful development following the strongly negative reaction it had sparked in 2009–2010 could be invoked to support the latter interpretation. And yet, the enthusiasm with which some of China's neighbors welcomed the more visible U.S. "return to Asia" in 2011, the frequency with which the Western media repeated the claim that President Obama's Asian trip in November was designed to demonstrate the determination of the U.S. to resist a more assertive and powerful China, and the harsh reaction to this interpretation from Beijing, all suggest that the period of turbulence has not ended. It also suggests a third interpretation of its meaning.

The year 2011 proved to be one that was not consistently defined by the benign trends that had prevailed earlier in the decade or by the worrisome tensions that had unfolded after late 2009. Instead, 2011 was a mixed bag, and this may be the new normal. If so, regional relations in Asia will be neither as frightening as feared by those who see the advent of a new era in Asia defined by U.S.-China confrontation, nor as reassuring as hoped by those who expect a return to a trajectory defined by growing cooperation. Much as Harry Harding suggested two decades ago, the new normal for Asia may finally reflect a more realistic and potentially healthier relationship between the tangled titans than one that fluctuates between overstated hostility and naïve professions of friendship.[57] Avoiding unreasonable hopes and fears focuses greater attention on managing genuine conflicts of interest to minimize their disruptive effect on cooperation where common interests exist.

Though Asia's future direction remains uncertain, it will be shaped by the answers to questions whose significance had become clearer than ever at the end of the twenty-first century's first decade. Are key states in Asia, along with the U.S., shifting from "cooperation while hedging" to "balancing" China? Or do recently shifting policies merely reflect tactical adjustments as hedging continues? Is China responding, as it did in the mid-1990s, with a more convincing effort to reassure others about its benign intentions? Or does its response reflect its own hedge against the possibility that a deteriorating strategic environment could transform the trellis of security cooperation among the U.S. and its regional partners into a coalition aimed at countering and containing China? If China's capabilities continue to grow, what sort of regional role will Beijing find acceptable? And what sort of increased influence for a more powerful China will Washington, its allies, and others in Asia find acceptable? If differences over acceptable regional roles prove irreconcilable, what strategies might states embrace to ensure their interests? In a region where extensive economic exchange complicates political calculations, and in which the enduring specter of nuclear weapons constrains military calculations, are traditional strategic choices implausible or unattractive? If so, will the region's states, including China and the U.S., be able to devise new alternatives that satisfy their interests as power shifts, or will they simply embrace old familiar options even if they are ill-suited to the realities of twenty-first-century Asia?

NOTES

1. See Robert M. Gates, "A Balanced Strategy: Reprogramming the Pentagon for a New Age," *Foreign Affairs*, Vol. 88, No. 1 (Jan/Feb 2009), pp. 28–40; "Opening Summary—Senate Appropriations Committee—Defense (Budget Request)," Dirksen Senate Office Building, Washington, DC, June 15, 2011, available at: http://www.defense.gov/speeches/speech.aspx?speechid=1585; David Alexander, "Asia-Pacific Head of U.S. Forces Confident of Funding," *Reuters*, September 23, 2011, available at: http://www.reuters.com/article/2011/09/24/us-usa-defense-pacific-idU.S.TRE78N03I20110924; "Media Availability with Secretary Panetta in Bali, Indonesia," October 23, 2011, U.S. Department of Defense, Office of the Assistant Secretary of Defense (Public Affairs), available at: http://www.defense.gov/transcripts/transcript.aspx?transcriptid=4909.

2. On the AirSea Battle concept, see Eric Sayers and Fan Gaoyue, "AirSea Battle: An Exchange," *PacNet*, March 17, 2011, available at: http://csis.org/files/publication/pac1117.pdf; Jan van Tol, with Mark Gunzinger, Andrew F. Krepinevich, and Jim Thomas, *AirSea Battle: A Point-of-Departure Operational Concept* (Washington, DC: Center for Strategic and Budgetary Assessments [CSBA], 2010), available at: http://www.csbaonline.org/wp-content/uploads/2010/05/2010.05.18-AirSea-Battle.pdf; "Background Briefing on Air-Sea Battle by Defense Officials from the Pentagon," U.S. Department of Defense, Office of the Assistant Secretary of Defense (Public Affairs), November 9, 2011, available at: https://mail.google.com/mail/u/0/?shva=1#search/air+sea+battle/133940d7a507572a.

3. See Hillary Rodham Clinton, "Remarks on Regional Architecture in Asia: Principles and Priorities," January 12, 2010, available at: http://www.state.gov/secretary/rm/2010/01/135090.htm.

4. Hillary Clinton, "America's Pacific Century," *Foreign Policy*, No. 189 (November 2011), pp. 56–63.

5. See Joshua Kurlantzick, *Charm Offensive: How China's Soft Power Is Transforming the World* (New Haven: Yale University Press, 2007).

6. See François Godement, "The United States and Asia in 2009: Public Diplomacy and Strategic Continuity," *Asian Survey*, Vol. 50, No. 1 (January/February 2010), pp. 8–24; Wu Xinbo, "Understanding the Geopolitical Implications of the Global Financial Crisis," *The Washington Quarterly*, Vol. 33, No. 4 (October 2010), pp. 155–163.

7. M. Taylor Fravel and Evan S. Medeiros, "China's New Diplomacy," *Foreign Affairs*, Vol. 82, No. 6 (November-December 2003), pp. 22–35; Avery Goldstein, *Rising to the Challenge: China's Grand Strategy and International Security* (Stanford: Stanford University Press, 2005); David L. Shambaugh, "China Engages Asia: Reshaping the Regional Order," *International Security* Vol. 29, No. 3 (Winter 2004/05), pp. 64–99.

8. See David Shambaugh, "Coping with a Conflicted China," *The Washington Quarterly*, Vol. 34, No. 1 (Winter 2011), pp. 7–27; Zhu Feng, "China's Trouble with the Neighbors," *Project Syndicate*, October 31, 2011, available at: http://www.project-syndicate.org/commentary/fzhu3/English; Robert S. Ross, "Chinese Nationalism and Its Discontents," *The National Interest*, No.116 (November–December 2011), pp. 45–51.

9. See Dai Bingguo, "We Must Stick to the Path of Peaceful Development," Ministry of Foreign Affairs of the People's Republic of China, December 6, 2010, available at: http://www.fmprc.gov.cn/eng/zxxx/t777704.htm.

10. Helene Cooper, "Japan Cools to America as It Prepares for Obama Visit," *New York Times*, November 12, 2009, available at: http://www.nytimes.com/2009/11/12/world/asia/12prexy.html.

11. Chris Acheson, "Japan after Kan: Implications for the DPJ's Political Future, an Interview with Richard J. Samuels," *The National Bureau of Asian Research*, August 19, 2011, available at: http://www.nbr.org/research/activity.aspx?id=168.

12. Qin Jize, "PRC's Li Keqiang Ends D.P.R.K. Visit Amid 'Renewed Sense of Optimism,'" *China Daily*, October 26, 2011, available at: http://www.chinadaily.com.cn/china/2011-10/26/content_13976188.htm.

13. At the July 2010 ASEAN Regional Forum meetings in Hanoi, China's Yang Jiechi had testily reacted to Secretary of State Clinton's statement about peaceful resolution of disputes in the South China Sea. And in September, Washington reiterated that its security treaty with Japan applied to territories under the administrative control of Japan, implicitly including disputed areas of the East China Sea where the arrest of the Chinese fishing captain had sparked tensions. See Sun-won Park, "The East China Sea Dispute: Short-Term Victory and Long-Term Loss for China?" The Brookings Institution, November 1, 2010, available at: http://www.brookings.edu/papers/2010/1101_east_china_sea_park.aspx.

14. Aside from concerns about the dangers of unpredictable military conflict, the potential for larger refugee flows across the border into China easily anticipated pressures on China's leaders to respond to events on its doorstep in a way that preserved its reputation at home and abroad, and a strengthening of the U.S.-Japan alliance, if the endpoint of instability on the peninsula were a unified Korea allied with the U.S., then China would lose the buffer against American military deployments that North Korea provided.

15. For the Chinese Foreign Ministry's recapitulation of China-ASEAN relations since 1991, see "China-ASEAN Cooperation: 1991–2011," *China Daily*, November 16, 2011, p. 9, available at: http://www.chinadaily.com.cn/cndy/2011-11/16/content_14101968.htm.

16. The intention to devise "rules of the road" to avoid conflict was formalized by China and ASEAN in November 2002 in the "Declaration on the Conduct of Parties in the South China Sea (DOC)." Almost nine years would pass before China and ASEAN in July 2011 agreed to guidelines for implementing the declaration in a code of conduct.

17. See Bonnie S. Glaser and Lyle Morris: "Chinese Perceptions of U.S. Decline and Power," *China Brief*, Vol. 9, No. 14 (July 9 2009), pp. 1–6. On China's claims in the South China Sea, see Li Jinming and Li Dexia, "The Dotted Line on the Chinese Map of the South China Sea: A Note," *Ocean Development & International Law*, Vol. 34 (2003), pp. 287–295. Confusion reigned, as well, about whether China was defining its maximal claims delimited by the nine-dashed line as a "core interest," a vital interest that Beijing would defend as it would defend no less vigorously than the rest of China's national territory. Despite their repetition as a claim conveyed in meetings to American officials, none of those officials have confirmed such reports, and there are no officially authorized Chinese statements defining the area a core interest.

18. Michael D. Swaine and M. Taylor Fravel, "China's Assertive Behavior, Part Two: The Maritime Periphery," *China Leadership Monitor*, No. 35 (September 2011), available at: http://www.hoover.org/publications/china-leadership-monitor.

19. Ibid., pp. 3–4.

20. Chinese interlocutors have frequently commented on the unusually large number of poorly coordinated maritime agents and agencies (coast guard, military, Chinese Fisheries Administration, State Oceanographic Administration, independent fisherman, local authorities) that Beijing says it is unable to fully control. See ibid., pp. 5–6.

21. Ross, "Chinese Nationalism and Its Discontents," op. cit.

22. See Dai, "We Must Stick to the Path of Peaceful Development," op. cit.

23. See Ziphora Robina, "ASEAN and China Agree on South China Guidelines," July 20, 2011, available at: http://www.dw-world.de/dw/article/0,,6575680,00.html; A. S. O. Alegado, "ASEAN, China to Start Talks on Conduct in South China Sea," *Business World*, November 28, 2011, available at: http://www.bworldonline.com/content .php?section=Nation&title=ASEAN,-China-to-start-talks-on-conduct-in-South-China-Sea&id=42380.

24. See "Signing of the Manila Declaration on Board the U.S.S. *Fitzgerald* in Manila Bay, Manila, Philippines," U.S. Department of State, November 16, 2011; http://www .state.gov/r/pa/prs/ps/2011/11/177226.htm; "Presentation of the Order of Lakandula, Signing of the Partnership for Growth and Joint Press Availability with Philippines Foreign Secretary Albert Del Rosario," November 16, 2011, available at: http://www .state.gov/secretary/rm/2011/11/177234.htm.

25. See "South China Sea Dispute: ASEAN Backs Away From Maritime Stand Against China," *Economic Times,* November 15, 2011, available at: http://economic times.indiatimes.com/news/politics/nation/south-china-sea-dispute-asean-backs-away-from-maritime-stand-against-china/articleshow/10742729.cms. See also Renato Cruz De Castro, "Exploring a 21st-Century Japan-Philippine Security Relationship: Linking Two Spokes Together?"*Asian Survey*, Vol. 49, No. 4 (July/August 2009), pp. 691–715.

26. On the evolution of China-Indonesia relations, see Rizal Sukma, "Indonesia-China Relations: The Politics of Re-engagement," *Asian Survey*, Vol. 49, No. 4 (July/August 2009), pp. 591–608.

27. See especially, Catharine Dalpino, *The United States–Thailand Alliance: Issues for a New Dialogue* (Seattle: The National Bureau of Asian Research, NBR Special Report #33, October 2011).

28. Indonesia and other ASEAN states agreed that maritime security should be included on the agenda for the East Asia Summit, something China had opposed

but resisted, giving it the priority that would have required directly confronting an isolated China. See "South China Sea Dispute: ASEAN Backs Away From Maritime Stand Against China," *The Economic Times,* November 15, 2011, available at: http://economictimes.indiatimes.com/news/politics/nation/south-china-sea-dispute-asean-backs-away-from-maritime-stand-against-china/articleshow/10742729.cms; Leonard C. Sebastian, "Indonesia and EAS: Search for a 'Dynamic Equilibrium,'" *RSIS Commentaries,* No. 168/2011, November 16, 2011.

29. See "Aquino Arrives Home from a Very Successful State Visit to the People's Republic of China," *Presidential Communications Operations Office (PCOO),* September 3, 2011, available at: http://www.pcoo.gov.ph/china2011/news.htm#home; also Chris Buckley, "China and Vietnam Sign Agreement to Cool Sea Dispute," *Reuters,* October 11, 2011, available at: http://www.reuters.com/article/2011/10/11/china-vietnam-idU.S.L3E7LB4D420111011.

30. See Edward Wong, "U.S. Motives in Myanmar Are on China's Radar," *New York Times,* November 29, 2011, available at: http://www.nytimes.com/2011/11/30/world/asia/hillary-rodham-clintons-trip-to-myanmar-on-chinas-radar.html?scp=7&sq=myanmar&st=cse; "In Myanmar, Government Reforms Win Over Some Skeptics," *New York Times,* November 29, 2011, available at: http://www.nytimes.com/2011/11/30/world/asia/in-myanmar-government-reforms-win-over-countrys-skeptics.html?scp=6&sq=myanmar&st=cse. Another reason for Myanmar's domestic relaxation was also its desire to break out of an international ostracism that had not only retarded its economic development but also complicated its aspiration to take its turn as chairman of ASEAN in 2014.

31. See Zha Daojiong, "China and Its Southern Neighbours: Issues in Power Connectivity," *RSIS Commentaries,* No. 147/2011, October 14, 2011. For historical perspective, see also John W. Garver, "China's Influence in Central and South Asia: Is It Increasing?" in *Power Shift: China and Asia's New Dynamics,* David Shambaugh (ed.) (Berkeley: University of California Press, 2005), pp. 218–220.

32. See Ben Bland and Geoff Dyer, "Clinton Warning over Aid from China," *Financial Times,* November 30, 2011, available at: http://www.ft.com/intl/cms/s/0/33efc23c-1b35-11e1-85f8-00144feabdc0.html#axzz1fIMw09oq.

33. See "Trade and Investment," Australian Embassy, China, available at: http://www.china.embassy.gov.au/bjng/relations2.html.

34. A lively public debate had emerged in Australia following a 2010 essay by Hugh White in which he argued that shifting regional power and interests required Australia to decide whether its interests would be best served by accommodating a rising China or siding with a declining U.S. See analysis in Carlyle A. Thayer, "China's Rise and the Passing of U.S. Primacy: Australia Debates Its Future," *Asia Policy,* No. 12 (July 2011), pp. 20–26.

35. See Julia Gillard, "Speech to the AsiaLink and Asia Society Lunch, Melbourne," September 28, 2011, available at: http://www.pm.gov.au/press-office/speech-asialink-and-asia-society-lunch-melbourne; Stephen Smith, "Australian Defence Force Posture Review," Australian Department of Defence, MR 177/11, June 22, 2011, available at: http://www.defence.gov.au/oscdf/adf-posture-review/docs/mr_110622.pdf; Australian Government Department of Defence, *Defence Capability Plan (Public Version):* Defence Materiel Organisation, 2011, available at: http://www.defence.gov.au/dmo/id/dcp/html_aug11/wp-content/uploads/2011/07/Defence-Capability-Plan-2011.

pdf.; Australian Government, *Defending Australia in the Asia Pacific Century: Force 2030*: Department of Defence, 2009, available at: http://apo.org.au/sites/default/files/defence_white_paper_2009.pdf.

36. Peter Smith, "See Gillard Visits China as Boom Times Roll On," April 25, 2011, *Financial Times*, available at: http://www.ft.com/intl/cms/s/0/7453bcd8-6f60-11e0-952c-00144feabdc0.html#axzz1fZs1Ovv4.

37. Australia was a founding member of APEC as well as the EAS, and identifies the TPP as the "government's highest regional trade negotiation priority." See "Asia Pacific Economic Cooperation," available at: http://www.dfat.gov.au/apec/index.html; "The East Asia Summit," available at: http://www.dfat.gov.au/asean/eas/index.html; and "Trans-Pacific Partnership Agreement Negotiations," available at: http://www.dfat.gov.au/fta/tpp/index.html, Department of Foreign Affairs and Trade, Australian Government.

38. "Obama Visit: Australia Agrees U.S. Marine Deployment Plan," *BBC News*, November 16, 2011, available at: http://www.bbc.co.uk/news/world-asia-15739995; Jackie Calmes, "A Marine Base for Australia Irritates China," *New York Times*, November 17, 2011, available at: http://www.nytimes.com/2011/11/18/world/asia/obama-addresses-troops-at-final-stop-in-australia.html?_r=1&hp.

39. See Craig Whitlock, "Navy's Next Stop in Asia Will Set China on Edge," *Washington Post*, November 18, 2011, available at: http://www.washingtonpost.com/blogs/checkpoint-washington/post/navys-next-stop-in-asia-will-set-china-on-edge/2011/11/18/gIQAzY7wYN_blog.html?tid=wp_ipad.

40. See especially "Remarks by President Obama and Prime Minister Gillard of Australia in Joint Press Conference Parliament House," Canberra, Australia, November 16, 2011, available at: http://www.whitehouse.gov/the-press-office/2011/11/16/remarks-president-obama-and-prime-minister-gillard-australia-joint-press; "Gillard Keen to Reassure China on U.S. Presence," *Sydney Morning Herald*, November 19, 2011, available at: http://www.smh.com.au/national/gillard-keen-to-reassure-china-on-us-presence-20111119-1noaa.html. For the initial Chinese government response, see, "Foreign Ministry Spokesperson Liu Weimin's Regular Press Conference on November 17, 2011," Ministry of Foreign Affairs, the People's Republic of China, available at: http://www.fmprc.gov.cn/eng/xwfw/s2510/2511/t879769.htm. For gradually escalating Chinese criticism of the move, see Chris Buckley, "China Looks Across Asia and Sees New Threats," *Reuters*, November 10, 2011, available at: http://www.reuters.com/article/2011/11/10/us-china-asia-idU.S.TRE7A91CY20111110; Keith B. Richburg, "U.S. Pivot to Asia Makes China Nervous," *Washington Post*, November 16, 2011, available at: http://www.washingtonpost.com/world/asia_pacific/us-pivot-to-asia-makes-china-nervous/2011/11/15/gIQAsQpVRN_story.html?; Barbara Demick, "China's Fury Building over Obama's New Asia Policy," *Los Angeles Times*, November 21, 2011, available at: http://latimesblogs.latimes.com/world_now/2011/11/china-obama-asia-policy.html; "Chinese Spokesman Rebukes U.S.-Australian Military Alliance," *Xinhua*, November 30, 2011, available at: http://news.xinhuanet.com/english2010/china/2011-11/30/c_131280105.htm.

41. See Evan A. Feigenbaum, "Central Asia Contingencies," in Paul B. Stares, Scott A. Snyder, Joshua Kurlantzick, Daniel Markey, and Evan A. Feigenbaum, *Managing Instability on China's Periphery* (New York: Council on Foreign Relations, 2011), pp. 60–70; also Evan A. Feigenbaum, "Does U.S.-China Strategic Cooperation Have to Be So Hard?" September 27, 2011, available at: http://blogs.cfr.org/asia/2011/09/27/does-u-s-china-strategic-cooperation-have-to-be-so-hard/.

42. See Zalmay Khalilzad, "The United States and China in Central and South Asia: Prospects for Cooperation and Conflict," paper prepared for the Fifth Symposium on U.S.-China Relations in a Global Context, Beijing, China, June 1–3, 2011.

43. See Chris Buckley, "PLA Researcher Says U.S. Aims To Encircle China," *Reuters*, November 28, 2011, available at: http://www.reuters.com/article/2011/11/28/us-china-usa-pla-idU.S.TRE7AR07Q20111128.

44. China's political concern about U.S. intentions in the region deepened after the color revolutions and the populist, anti-authoritarian movements in the Middle East during 2011, in China's view political upheavals supported by a meddlesome U.S. See Shambaugh, "Coping with a Conflicted China," op. cit.

45. See Martha Brill Olcott, "Central Asia: Carving and Independent Identity among Peripheral Powers," in *International Relations of Asia,* David Shambaugh and Michael Yahuda, eds. (Lanham, MD: Rowman and Littlefield Publishers, Inc., 2008), pp. 234–257. See also Garver, "China's Influence in Central and South Asia," in Shambaugh (ed.), *Power Shift: China and Asia's New Dynamics*, pp. 205–227.

46. Tensions that seemed to grow even worse after an American airstrike in Pakistan in November 2011 killed 24 Pakistani soldiers. See John H. Cushman, "Obama Offers 'Condolences' in Deaths of Pakistanis," *New York Times*, December 4, 2011, available at: http://www.nytimes.com/2011/12/05/world/asia/obama-offers-condolences-in-deaths-of-pakistani-troops.html?hp.

47. See Daniel Markey, "Pakistan Contingencies," in Stares, Snyder, Kurlantzick, Markey, and Feigenbaum, *Managing Instability on China's Periphery*, pp. 41–59.

48. Vikas Bajaj and Heather Timmons, "Obama to Visit India, and Both Sides Hope to Expand Ties," *New York Times*, November 4, 2010, available at: http://www.nytimes.com/2010/11/05/business/global/05indiabiz.html?pagewanted=all.

49. For a more benign view of recent developments in regional multilateralism, see Victor Cha, "Complex Patchworks: U.S. Alliances as Part of Asia's Regional Architecture," *Asia Policy*, No. 11 (January 2011).

50. See Ralf Emmers, "U.S. in East Asia Summit: Implications for U.S.-ASEAN Relations," *RSIS Commentaries,* No. 163/2011, November 9, 2011.

51. Hillary Rodham Clinton, Secretary of State, "Remarks From the Signing Ceremony of the Treaty of Amity and Cooperation Accession," July 22, 2009, available at: http://www.state.gov/secretary/rm/2009a/july/126334.htm.

52. See "The United States in the Trans-Pacific Partnership," Office of the United States Trade Representative, available at: http://www.ustr.gov/about-us/press-office/fact-sheets/2011/november/united-states-trans-pacific-partnership. This intention had been foreshadowed in the closing months of the Bush administration. See Deborah Elms, "U.S. Trade Policy in Asia: Going for the Trans-Pacific Partnership?" *East Asia Forum,* November 26, 2009, available at: http://www.eastasiaforum.org/2009/11/26/u-s-trade-policy-in-asia-going-for-the-trans-pacific-partnership/.

53. Hiroko Tabuchi, "Premier Says Japan Will Join Pacific Free Trade Talks," *New York Times*, November 11, 2011, http://www.nytimes.com/2011/11/12/world/asia/japan-to-join-talks-on-pacific-trade-pact.html?_r=1&adxnnl=1&pagewanted=print&adxnnlx=1322740900-vj/dro5gBp5RAPUvOd5MUA.

54. The official reaction from China was measured, but the unofficial reactions reflected the perception that the move was aimed at undercutting China's regional economic clout. See "China Holds an Open Attitude to Trans-Pacific Partnership Pact: Official," Xinhua report, *People's Daily Online*, November 16, 2011, available

at: http://english.people.com.cn/90883/7646382.html; Xue Litai, "The Role That U.S. Plays in Asia," *China Daily*, November 24, 2011, available at: http://www.chinadaily .com.cn/opinion/2011-11/24/content_14151883.htm; John Ross, "Realities behind the TransPacific Partnership," *China.org.cn*, November 18, 2011, available at: http://www .china.org.cn/opinion/2011-11/18/content_23953374_2.htm; Zhou Luxi, "A Meeting of Minds, or U.S.-China Faceoff?" *China.org.cn*, November 11, 2011, available at: http://www.china.org.cn/opinion/2011-11/11/content_23889056.htm.

55. Ikenberry, "The Rise of China, the United States, and the Future of the Liberal International Order," this volume.

56. All analysts recognize important differences between the world in the twenty-first century and in the twentieth century, and between today's China and the now defunct Soviet Union, that make any such parallels imprecise.

57. Harry Harding, *A Fragile Relationship: The United States and China Since 1972* (Washington, DC: Brookings Institution, 1992).

12

Taiwan in U.S.-China Relations

Shelley Rigger

The agenda of U.S.-China relations includes many disputed items, but the quarrel over Taiwan has bedeviled the relationship as long and as fiercely as any. The two powers' views on the issue are firmly held and hard to reconcile, but what makes this knotty problem especially vexing is Taiwan's capacity to influence developments in Beijing and Washington. While their broad strategic goals are largely fixed, the details of U.S. and PRC policy toward Taiwan are driven by a combination of strategic considerations and domestic political pressures; however, Taiwan's capacity to deliver game-changing initiatives keeps American and Chinese policy makers in a reactive mode much of the time. Thus, Taiwan's domestic politics has become an important driver, not only of Taipei's relationships with Beijing and Washington, but of Sino-U.S. relations as well. These dynamics were especially evident in the early decades of the twenty-first century as Taiwan politics whiplashed between the Sinophobic leadership of Chen Shui-bian and the pro-engagement presidency of Ma Ying-jeou, but they are not new, and they are unlikely to change soon.

The origin of today's "Taiwan problem" lies in the Chinese Civil War. As Nancy Bernkopf Tucker's chapter details, the People's Republic of China was founded on the rubble of the previous Chinese state, the Republic of China (ROC). After 1949, all that was left under ROC control was the island of Taiwan, to which the remnants of Chiang Kai-shek's government and military forces evacuated as the Communist victory loomed. From its inception, the PRC leadership has viewed Taiwan's separation from the mainland as unfinished business.

Since its victory over the KMT in 1949 the CCP's position has never wavered: Taiwan is part of China, and China's sole legal government is the PRC state headquartered in Beijing. The island's ability to evade PRC control is thus a historical anomaly that must be rectified. It is also, importantly, an anomaly that is possible only because of the U.S.'s continuing interference—including military interference—in China's internal affairs. Accomplishing the unification of Taiwan with the mainland under a single flag thus represents the restoration of China's sovereignty, the realization of her territorial integrity, and the fulfillment of her national destiny.

In the early years of the People's Republic the Chinese Communist Party set its sights on attaining national unification through the liberation of Taiwan. By "liberation" the CCP meant that Taiwan would be forcibly incorporated as a province of the PRC. The liberation discourse constructed Taiwanese "compatriots" as the last remnant of the Chinese proletariat still oppressed by the Nationalists and their foreign overlords; its goal was as much to free Taiwanese from the Nationalists' authoritarian capitalism as to unite it with the mainland. As Civil War passions cooled and nationalism came to play a more important role in PRC ideology, Beijing shifted its rhetoric from liberation to peaceful unification. "Peaceful unification" envisions Taiwan's incorporation into China not through armed force but via a negotiating process in which the Nationalists accommodate themselves to China's new political reality. Exactly what the endpoint of such a process would look like is a matter of ongoing debate.

TAIWAN IN U.S.-CHINA RELATIONS, 1949–2000

Taiwan's position in Sino-American relations has changed over the decades since the PRC was founded, but it has remained a central concern. In the '50s and '60s, it made little sense to think of Taiwan as an issue in the relationship because in those decades Sino-American relations meant relations between the U.S. and the Republic of China. There was no "Taiwan problem," just a "Red China problem." Still, from the moment Washington and Beijing initiated diplomatic contact in the early 1970s, the U.S.'s relationship with Taiwan has been a stumbling block in the development of closer Sino-American ties.

When Kissinger and Nixon visited China in the early '70s they found PRC officials determined to use Sino-U.S. rapprochement to press for unification. In the view of Mao Zedong, Zhou Enlai and their colleagues, U.S. political and military support was the lynchpin that allowed the Nationalists to hold out against unification and to hold up the ROC as a challenger to the PRC. Thus, Beijing expected that normalizing relations with the U.S. would end American support for Taiwan and open the door for unification.

In Beijing Nixon and Kissinger encouraged those expectations, but back in the U.S., trading Taiwan for a deal with China was not a popular idea. "Free China" had powerful friends, including anti-Communists in Congress and a well-heeled lobby. In the end, the Nixon administration decided to finesse the issue. The result was language in the Shanghai Communiqué—a statement of

principles jointly issued by Beijing and Washington—that nodded toward unification without actually endorsing it as a goal:

> The United States acknowledges that all Chinese on either side of the Taiwan
> Strait maintain there is but one China and that Taiwan is a part of China.
> The United States Government does not challenge that position. It reaffirms
> its interest in a peaceful settlement of the Taiwan question by the Chinese
> themselves.[1]

At the time it was signed, the Communiqué was an accurate description of
the preferences of politicians on both sides of the Strait, making it an effective
and clever solution to a knotty diplomatic problem. Indeed, it may have been
too clever: to Chinese, it read as an endorsement of unification, but Americans
understood it was no such thing. The document that opened the door for all
that followed in Sino-American relations was thus not a statement of shared
values or principles, but an artfully worded refusal to take a position—one
guaranteed to produce misunderstanding in the future.

The normalization process that culminated in a second communiqué in
1979 likewise sidestepped the fundamental issue of how the U.S. would view
Taiwan's status vis-à-vis the PRC. The Normalization Communiqué reaffirmed
the Shanghai Communiqué as the basis on which Washington and Beijing
would establish formal diplomatic ties—but, back in the U.S., Taiwan's congressional allies remained determined to protect the island's interests in the face
of what looked to be abandonment by the United States. Congress passed the
Taiwan Relations Act, domestic legislation that required the U.S. government to
treat Taiwan *as if* it were a state, even as it ended formal recognition of the ROC.
The TRA also stated that it was U.S. policy "to consider any effort to determine
the future of Taiwan by other than peaceful means . . . a threat to the peace and
security of the Western Pacific area and of grave concern to the United States."
Furthermore, the act mandated that the U.S. "maintain the capacity . . . to resist
any resort to force or other forms of coercion that would jeopardize the security, or the social or economic system, of the people on Taiwan."[2]

Throughout the normalization process one of Beijing's central goals was to
sever the security relationship between the U.S. and Taiwan. The U.S. agreed
to abrogate its Mutual Security Treaty with the ROC and remove troops from
the island, but ending arms sales was a different matter. Many Americans opposed leaving Taiwan defenseless against what they viewed as an aggressive
Communist regime. Their convictions were embodied in a provision of the
TRA that stated it was U.S. policy "to provide Taiwan with arms of a defensive
character."[3] The TRA did not commit the United States to defend Taiwan in the
event of a cross-Strait conflict, but it did require that successive U.S. adminis-

trations "maintain the capacity of the United States to resist any resort to force or other forms of coercion that would jeopardize the security, or the social or economic system, of the people on Taiwan."[4]

Not surprisingly, PRC officials were bitterly disappointed by their failure to incorporate an arms sales cut-off into the normalization agreement, but they were not prepared to walk away from the normalization talks. Still, they kept the pressure on the U.S. side to do something about the "Taiwan problem," and in 1982 the Reagan administration signed a third Joint Communiqué stating: "the United States Government states that it does not seek to carry out a long-term policy of arms sales to Taiwan, that its arms sales to Taiwan will not exceed, either in qualitative or in quantitative terms, the level of those supplied in recent years since the establishment of diplomatic relations between the United States and China, and that it intends to reduce gradually its sales of arms to Taiwan, leading over a period of time to a final resolution."[5]

The Chinese interpret the 1982 Communiqué as a promise to end arms sales, but the U.S. has refused to meet that expectation. On the contrary, Washington has approved the sale of vast amounts of weapons and other defense equipment to Taiwan, including items that significantly upgraded its systems. To Beijing (and many American analysts) this is a clear violation of the 1982 agreement. U.S. policymakers, for their part, justify arms sales on the grounds that the 1982 Communiqué was predicated on a reduction in military tensions in the Strait that has not occurred.[6]

The 1982 Communiqué has been a source of friction between the U.S. and China for three decades. U.S. actions stretched the letter and spirit of the agreement, and Washington further undermined its commitment to Beijing by making a contradictory promise to Taipei. Fearing the effect on Taiwan of the soon-to-be-signed Communiqué, President Reagan asked his representative in Taipei to deliver an oral message to President Chiang Ching-kuo. His "Six Assurances" stated that Washington would not consult with Beijing on arms sales or set a date for ending arms sales to Taiwan, and promised the U.S. would not mediate between the two sides or pressure Taiwan to enter into negotiations. Reagan's consolation gesture reassured Taipei, but it reinforced PRC leaders' conviction that the U.S. was negotiating in bad faith.

In sum, Sino-American relations are built on a foundation of ambiguously worded documents that allowed the relationship to move forward, but injected into it a hefty measure of distrust.[7] The ambiguous wording in the three communiqués led PRC officials to expect the U.S. would cut political and military ties to Taiwan—a move they believed would guarantee unification on Beijing's terms. Meanwhile, whatever Nixon and Kissinger might have been willing to promise, the U.S. government as a whole never was prepared to hand Taiwan over to Beijing.

This tortuous history made the Taiwan issue a source of contention in U.S.-China relations, and Taiwan's democratization in the 1980s and '90s exacerbated the trend. The island's democratic transition gave it a powerful new claim on Americans' affection and loyalty. At the same time, it changed Taiwan's relationship with the PRC in ways that destabilized the static (albeit prickly) equilibrium that had prevailed for decades.

From the end of the Chinese Civil War until 1987, Taiwan followed a policy of no contact with the mainland or its "Communist bandit" leaders. Taiwan's job was to prepare itself for the day when legitimate authority—that of the Republic of China and its Nationalist Party–led regime—would be restored to the mainland. Inevitably, some contacts did occur, but they were minimal. Because each side claimed for itself the mantle of the sole legal government of China, actual progress toward unification was nil. Nonetheless, the fact that both governments understood unification to be China's national destiny gave a certain symmetry to their positions, even as they rattled their swords and promised to cut one another down.

Taiwan's democratic transformation broke this stalemate. To begin with, it allowed Taiwanese to pressure their leaders to open people-to-people exchanges across the Strait. When Taiwanese were permitted to travel to the PRC in 1987 they quickly learned two things: mainland China was very different from Taiwan, and some of those differences made it an ideal site for investment. In short order, Taiwanese entrepreneurs were pouring into the mainland to give their manufacturing businesses—many of which were bumping up against high wage and land bills in Taiwan—a new lease on life. The idea of the mainland as an implacable enemy, a dangerous, alien place Taiwanese dared not go, evaporated almost overnight.

Democratization opened the door to the mainland and transformed Taiwan people's views of the PRC for the better, but it also awakened contrary forces. Political reform ended restrictions on freedom of speech; the result was a flourishing debate over what Taiwan's relationship with the mainland should be—a debate that soon included calls for formal independence.[8] The reforms also made electoral politics more competitive and politicians more responsive to voters' preferences. Unification was not a mainstream preference (neither was independence), so Taiwan's politicians began speaking less—and less enthusiastically—about unification.

Lee Teng-hui, the ROC's president from 1988 to 2000, embodied the ambivalence of the era. On the one hand, he presided over the creation of the National Unification Guidelines and Council and he instigated Taiwan's participation in the first series of cross-Strait negotiations, the Koo-Wang Talks. On the other hand, Lee cultivated a distinctive Taiwanese identity and appealed to the international community to shelter the ROC as it made its first tentative steps toward the mainland.

The changes in Taiwan between 1987 and 1994 destabilized the cross-Strait relationship. Some changes were positive: there was actual cooperation and interaction across the Strait for the first time in decades. Lee Teng-hui even declared an end to hostilities between the Nationalists and Communists. PRC leaders failed to recognize the signs of progress, however, because they were focused on the negative changes: given freedom of speech, Taiwanese said things PRC leaders did not want to hear, and Lee Teng-hui's idea of unification was not what the Beijing elite had in mind.

At first, PRC leaders tried to influence Taiwan's political process directly. In the run-up to the island's first direct presidential election in 1996 Chinese leaders loudly proclaimed their opposition to the "splittist" incumbent, Lee Teng-hui. They backed up their rhetoric with displays of military might. Instead of driving Taiwanese voters toward pro-unification candidates, however, China's bullying increased support for Lee, who won the four-way race with 54 percent of the vote. It also sparked a sobering reaction from the U.S., which moved naval forces into the region. Incidents like these ultimately persuaded Beijing that overt intimidation would backfire. Instead, Chinese leaders increasingly looked to the U.S. to rein in Taiwan's most unwelcome tendencies.

Most U.S. officials cheered Taiwan's democratization. The island's traditional anti-Communist political protagonists were joined by a new set of advocates whose pro-Taiwan sentiment was inspired by its turn-around on democracy and human rights. President Bill Clinton was expressing those sentiments when he said, "We'll continue to reject the use of force as a means to resolve the Taiwan question. We'll also continue to make absolutely clear that the issues between Beijing and Taiwan must be resolved peacefully and with the assent of the people of Taiwan."[9] Clinton's insistence on the "assent" of the Taiwan people to a cross-Strait deal was a new element in U.S. Taiwan policy, one necessitated by Taiwan's democratization.

When Lee Teng-hui asked for a visa to give a speech at Cornell University in 1995, the left-right alliance of pro-Taiwan congressmen overruled the Clinton administration's decision to deny his request. For Beijing, this was another betrayal: the White House had promised to keep relations between Taiwan and the U.S. unofficial, yet it granted Lee a visa. The missile tests and military exercises that followed the decision made it clear that Taipei and Washington would pay a price for continuing their close (albeit unofficial) relationship.

CROSS-STRAIT RELATIONS, 2000–2008

Taiwan's second direct presidential election in March 2000 surprised Taiwanese almost as much as it shocked PRC leaders. Support for the opposition Democratic Progressive Party seemed stuck at just over 40 percent, well short of a majority. In 2000, however, an overconfident KMT miscalculated. Its presidential nomination divided the party and the disgruntled faction put forth its own candidate. The DPP captured its usual vote share, but with the KMT's majority split, the DPP's Chen Shui-bian was elected.

Chen's moderate inaugural address was calculated to reassure the Chinese leadership (as well as Taiwan's voters and officials in Washington), but the CCP remained suspicious of Chen and his party, both of which Beijing believed were committed to Taiwan independence. Beijing initially promised to "watch what he does, listen to what he says," but there was little common ground between the DPP and CCP, and cross-Strait relations slowed to a crawl. Chen also faced intense resistance from the KMT-led legislature. In August 2002, Chen pivoted away from moderation when he described the relationship between Taiwan and the mainland as "one country on each side" (*yibian, yiguo*). The remainder of his presidency was dominated by efforts to strengthen Taiwan's resistance to unification, including educational reforms aimed at inculcating a Taiwanese identity and political mobilization aimed at pushing through a new constitution.

President Ma Ying-jeou's election in 2008 ushered in a new era in cross-Strait relations. Under Chen Shui-bian economic ties and people-to-people contacts skyrocketed but negotiations between the two governments' semi-official representatives stagnated because Chen refused to accept Beijing's precondition for talks—acknowledgment that Taiwan is Chinese territory. Even a vague, watered-down formulation of that idea worked out during the Lee Teng-hui era—the so-called "'92 Consensus"—was too much for the Sinophobic Chen and his party to swallow. Talks that had enabled an orderly relationship between the two sides languished and political tensions swelled.

In his campaign, Ma promised to reinvigorate cross-Strait ties, both to reduce the tension and make economic interactions more efficient and profitable. He was happy to endorse the '92 Consensus as the basis for a new round of talks. From Beijing's perspective, Ma's election in 2008 was a huge relief. It removed the threat of a sudden lunge toward independence and opened the possibility of progress on economic and even political issues.

After eight years of glowering, Chinese leaders found themselves—if not smiling, exactly—relaxing a bit in 2008. The worst-case scenarios they had feared during the Chen years were off the table, and while there was little chance that Ma would move quickly toward anything remotely resembling unification, the prospects for cooperation and engagement were better than at any time in history. And in the long run, PRC leaders believe, cooperation and engagement will set the stage for unification.

Within a month of Ma's inauguration the two sides' semiofficial representatives—Taiwan's Straits Exchange Foundation (SEF) and the PRC's Association for Relations Across the Taiwan Strait (ARATS)—broke their long stalemate and reached agreements on issues that had bedeviled the two sides for eight years. They institutionalized a regular schedule of meetings, while regular CCP-KMT party-to-party talks functioned as a parallel channel. Together SEF and ARATS pumped out signed agreements faster than their respective governments could implement them. The climax came on June 29, 2010 when representatives from Taipei and Beijing signed the Economic Cooperation Framework Agreement (ECFA). ECFA loosened investment and market restrictions, reduced tariffs, and created dispute resolution mechanisms and other economic coordination measures in ways economists agree benefit Taiwan more than the PRC.

Cross-Strait negotiations and economic cooperation surged between 2008 and 2012. But while those gains are real and significant, there still were worrisome undertones in the relationship. Many Taiwanese citizens were skeptical about the pace and direction of cross-Strait developments. They wanted peaceful relations with the mainland and they recognized the benefits of economic engagement, but they had little interest in moving beyond economic and other practical issues to consider political topics. The violent protests that greeted Beijing's top Taiwan policy maker when he visited in 2009 revealed just how thin the political ice under the cross-Strait rapprochement really was.

The mixed record on cross-Strait development since 2000 underscores the challenges facing the PRC in its Taiwan policy. PRC leaders want to take advantage of opportunities, but they do not want to be taken advantage of; they worry that Taiwan's leaders—including Ma—will pocket concessions without returning China's favors. As a result, their accommodations have been limited almost entirely to economics, in part because political concessions would be hard to revoke.

Beijing's reticence also reflects its determination to achieve its long-term goals. It is willing to make economic deals that are advantageous to Taiwan so long as they lock Taiwan in and give Beijing political leverage. If the plan succeeds, the PRC won't need to make political concessions. This strategy may take time to bear fruit, but with 1,500-plus missiles ready to punish any move toward formal independence, Beijing can be patient.

TAIWAN IN U.S.-CHINA RELATIONS, 2000–2011

The sources of tension between Washington and Beijing regarding Taiwan have changed very little since the early '70s. First, the PRC wants the U.S. to respect its sovereignty claim. It grudgingly accepts unofficial ties between Washington and Taipei but protests any action that might imply an upgrade in Taiwan's status. The U.S. is willing to forgo the trappings of officiality in its relations with Taiwan but is not prepared to deny the island the substantive benefits it affords to other international friends. Chief among those substantive benefits is defense assistance—the second source of Sino-U.S. tension. As CCP leaders see it, Nixon, Carter, and Reagan all made promises on arms sales that the U.S. later broke. A fundamental contradiction undergirds both disagreements: Beijing believes unification is a moral and political imperative, while U.S. officials stress Taiwan people's right not to be coerced into unification.

Chen Shui-bian's policies challenged both Beijing and Washington on each of these dimensions. After mid-2002 Chen undertook a series of initiatives aimed at raising Taiwan's international status: promoting a new constitution, pressing for referendums on issues related to Taiwan's sovereignty, filing an application for United Nations membership for "Taiwan," and many others. Not surprisingly, the PRC found these moves unacceptable and threatening; in April 2005 the National People's Congress passed "anti-secession" legislation authorizing the People's Liberation Army to use force to stop Taiwan from asserting formal independence.

Washington, too, judged many of Chen's moves risky, destabilizing, and gratuitous. After beginning his term with the strongest pro-Taiwan outlook of any president in decades, George W. Bush was pushed to the breaking point by Chen's provocations in late 2003. During a visit to Washington by PRC premier Wen Jiabao Bush told reporters, ". . . comments and actions made by the leader of Taiwan indicate that he may be willing to make decisions unilaterally to change the status quo—which we oppose."[10]

Chen's policies were not the only reason U.S.-Taiwan relations soured. Between 2000 and 2008 the ballyhooed Taiwan lobby's effectiveness declined sharply. After playing political football with China policy throughout the Clinton administration, Congress lost interest in the game after George W. Bush was elected. This happened both for political reasons and in response to the PRC's rise. Legislators' inattention reduced Taiwan's salience on Capitol Hill, a trend executive-branch officials encouraged. After the Lee Teng-hui visa fiasco, they urged Taiwan to bring its concerns to them rather than using Congress to press its case. That strategy left Taiwan no one to turn to when the White House lost patience with Chen.

Taiwan's declining influence in Washington was partially self-inflicted. Lee Teng-hui had outsourced much of the diplomatic effort in the U.S. to private lobbying firms. Chen's government outsourced diplomacy in another way. Chen and his DPP colleagues distrusted the professional diplomats on loan from the Ministry of Foreign Affairs who staffed Taiwan's quasi-official representative office in Washington, so they sent envoys from Taipei to communicate directly with U.S. officials. Inevitably, different messengers' messages conflicted, leaving U.S. officials confused and frustrated—especially because so many of Chen's envoys showed little interest in hearing what U.S. officials

had to say. Non-governmental organizations claiming to speak for Taiwan, including Taiwanese-American groups, only added to the cacophony.

Even arms sales became a source of tension between Washington and Taipei during the Chen years. In the spring of 2001 President Bush approved a
long list of military systems Taiwan had requested during the Clinton administration. The decision brought the expected reaction from Beijing—a storm
of criticism—but the reaction from Taipei was entirely unexpected. Instead
of welcoming the long-awaited defense package, Taiwanese politicians politi-
cized it. For seven years, the KMT-dominated Legislative Yuan refused to appropriate funds to purchase most of what the United States was willing to sell.

Opponents of the package used the issue to drum up electoral support,
even accusing Washington of exploiting Taiwan for economic gain. Their goal
was to deny Chen Shui-bian a political victory, but their actions damaged
U.S.-Taiwan relations. U.S. officials lost confidence in both political parties in
Taiwan. Most galling of all, U.S. officials endured Beijing's wrath when they
approved the arms package, but America received no political or economic
payoff for its trouble.

The first two years of Chen's presidency were something of a missed opportunity, as the PRC overlooked chances to encourage his moderate side, and
the last two years were a scandal-driven death spiral, but Chen spent 2002 to
2006 entrenching his Sinophobic outlook in Taiwan's policy and politics. For
decades, the PRC had stressed that cross-Strait relations was China's business
and the U.S. should stay out of it, but during those four years the PRC came
to rely on the U.S. to restrain Taiwan. PRC efforts to pressure Taiwan directly
backfired; Taiwanese voters did not always agree with Chen, but they invariably preferred him to finger-wagging PRC officials. It thus fell to American
officials to chastise Chen. As Zhao Quansheng has written, Washington and
Beijing began to "co-manage" Taiwan.[11]

After the tension and uncertainty of the Chen years, Ma Ying-jeou's election relieved both U.S. and PRC officials; his reelection in 2012 was equally
welcome. Still, leaders in all three capitals recognized that their divergent goals
and preferences would continue to create daunting challenges. Beijing welcomed Ma's anti-independence stance, but it continued to build up its missile
forces opposite Taiwan and did little to ease the island's international isolation.
U.S. officials welcomed the resumption of cross-Strait talks and cooperation,
but they made it clear that arms sales would continue so long as the military threat remained. The Ma administration pressed simultaneously for trade
deals with Beijing and arms deals with Washington.

The U.S. signaled its intentions for the new administration in October 2008
when the White House notified Congress that it intended to offer Taipei a
$6.5 billion arms package. A statement from then-candidate Barack Obama's

campaign suggested a new administration would follow Bush's lead: "Senator Obama strongly supports the reduction of tensions between China and Taiwan, and commends China's President Hu Jintao and Taiwan's President Ma Ying-jeou for their efforts in that regard. A strengthening of Taiwan's defenses will not undermine the process of reduction of tensions and can actually promote it."[12]

Beijing denounced the decision and suspended a variety of interactions with the U.S. It did not, however, lash out at Taiwan. Instead, Chinese officials blamed the U.S. alone, a pattern it followed throughout Ma's first term. No matter how hard Taipei pushed for weapons, the PRC ignored its role in the arms sales process and directed its rhetorical fire exclusively at the U.S. As an editorial in the *Taipei Times* put it:

> A close reading of Chinese Foreign Ministry spokesman Liu Jianchao's comments on the most recent sale . . . reveals a subtle change in Beijing's expression of anger. This time, in addition to the usual rhetoric, China argued that "nobody could stop" the "warming" relations between Taipei and Beijing. All of a sudden, Beijing was casting the US not as an ally of Taiwan, but rather as an enemy common to both Taipei and Beijing, one that sought to hammer a wedge between the two sides of the Taiwan Strait.[13]

The PRC stepped up its efforts to roll back U.S. arms sales in Ma's first term. In June 2009 Chinese military officials attending defense talks in the U.S. reiterated their government's demand that Washington end arms sales. Arms sales were a key talking point in Taiwan Affairs Office head Wang Yi's conversations with diplomats in Washington in mid-2009, while Admiral Guan Youfei unleashed a tirade against U.S. arms sales during the Security and Economic Dialogue in May 2010. That summer, the People's Liberation Army (PLA) declined to invite Secretary of Defense Robert Gates to Beijing when he was traveling in Asia. When Gates suggested the PLA was over-emphasizing arms sales PLA General Ma Xiaotian replied that "arms sales show that the U.S. considers China to be an enemy."[14]

The pace of congressional notifications on arms sales to Taiwan remained measured through the end of the Bush administration and into the Obama administration, but Beijing did not acknowledge the deliberate pacing, choosing instead to react strongly to each new development. When media reported the U.S. government was contracting with firms to produce PAC-III anti-missile defense equipment for Taiwan Beijing lashed out, threatening sanctions against the companies involved. The strength of the reaction and the unprecedented threat to punish private firms led some U.S. observers to conclude the PRC was escalating its anti-arms sales campaign.

In January 2010 the Obama administration notified Congress of a pending arms sale worth $6.4 billion. As before, Beijing lashed out at the U.S., not Taiwan. It cut military-to-military exchanges and threatened sanctions on American firms; Beijing's spokesman blamed the arms sales for China's inability to achieve good relations with the United States. In October 2011 Washington approved an upfit to Taiwan's existing F-16A/B fighters.[15] The decision to upgrade existing jets instead of supplying new aircraft disappointed Taiwan—which was hoping for new, more capable F-16C/Ds—and its congressional allies, but it evoked the standard reaction from Beijing. Taipei's failure to appropriate sufficient funds to complete many approved sales added to Washington's discomfort.

In sum, the arms sale issue took on new complexities in the Ma era. Beijing ratcheted up its opposition and added new arguments to its rhetorical arsenal. In addition to the standard line—arms sales constitute interference in China's internal affairs and violate the 1982 Communiqué—Chinese leaders now used the cross-Strait warming trend to justify ending the sales. They argued, now that all is well between Taipei and Beijing the only troublemaker is the U.S.

Ma's reelection in January 2012 affirmed Chinese president Hu Jintao's approach to cross-Strait relations. Under Hu, the PRC provided generous economic concessions to Taiwan in the hope of tightening the island's reliance on the mainland, while it refrained from pressuring Ma for political breakthroughs that could backfire in Taiwan's volatile domestic environment. At the same time, the PRC continued to expand its military capacity, both as a deterrent to Taiwan independence and as a way of expanding China's long-term options across the Strait.

During the Chen years Beijing openly sought American assistance in reining in actions it opposed. With Ma in office, that strategy changed. Instead of asking the U.S. to check Taipei, Beijing worked to drive a wedge between Taipei and Washington. Chinese officials lashed out at the U.S. for selling weapons to Taiwan, but they raised no parallel objection to Taipei. When Taiwan did not complete arms purchases, U.S. officials hardly could be blamed for wondering why they should incur punishment when Taiwan seemed to be pocketing the political benefits of arms sales without following through. Chinese officials also pointed to congenial relations in the Strait as evidence that the U.S. was out of step with regional developments. They were reluctant to dismantle the "co-management" arrangement entirely, however, since U.S. assistance might again be needed if "unfriendly elements" returned to power in Taipei.

TIME FOR SOMETHING NEW?

The policy approach Washington has followed since normalizing relations with the PRC has allowed the U.S. to maintain generally good relations with both sides of the Taiwan Strait. That approach, known as "strategic ambiguity," does not endorse unification or independence; instead, it emphasizes that whatever relationship develops in the Strait, it must come about through a peaceful process in which the interests of the Taiwan people are protected. According to this policy, the purpose of U.S. defense assistance to Taiwan is to enable that non-coercive, peaceful process. The policy is ambiguous in that Washington has made no firm commitment as to whether and under what circumstances it would defend Taiwan in the event the peaceful process breaks down. Its proponents maintain that ambiguity serves the goal of dual deterrence: it deters the PRC from attacking Taiwan, and it deters Taipei from provoking Beijing.

Strategic ambiguity has critics. Some would like the U.S. to support Taiwan more robustly; others argue the U.S. should prioritize good relations with Beijing, even if that means reducing or eliminating support for Taiwan. Early in Ma's presidency this debate heated up. The Obama administration continued to follow the long-standing U.S. approach, but the pressure to rethink Taiwan policy was growing. The critics made many different recommendations, most of which grew out of two distinct analytical judgments, one about the direction of Sino-American ties, and one about cross-Strait relations.

China policy was a bit of a political football in 1990s America, but after 2000, American politicians became much more sober about the PRC's rising power. U.S.-China economic cooperation reached a massive scale, and after September 11, 2001 the U.S. was more eager than ever to cultivate China's support. President George W. Bush established the goal of encouraging China to become a "responsible stakeholder" in global economic and political institutions. With Chen Shui-bian in office, even Taiwan policy became an area of tacit cooperation—or co-management—for Beijing and Washington.

At the end of the decade, analysts found themselves divided about what those developments signified. Some experts emphasized the potential for cooperation between the U.S. and China, while others worried that China's rise would drive a strategic rivalry between the two great powers. On the Taiwan issue, observers were divided between those who believed that Taiwan was and would continue to be a disruptive factor in China's domestic politics and external relations, and those who believed Taiwan's challenge to Beijing would ease in the coming years.

In 2011 veteran China hand Chas W. Freeman Jr. gave a speech at the U.S. Naval War College in which he argued that growing strategic competition between the U.S. and China combined with Taiwan's negative role in Chinese politics made it imperative that the U.S. withdraw its military support to Taiwan. According to former Ambassador Freeman, America's power is in freefall while China's is rising. He concluded, "In this context . . . it would seem wise to minimize activities that increase rather than diminish China's perceived need to prepare itself for future combat with the United States." One such activity, he argued, was U.S. defense support for Taiwan:

> The Taiwan issue is the only one with the potential to ignite a war between China and the United States. To the [People's Liberation Army], U.S. programs with Taiwan signal fundamental American hostility to the return of China to the status of a great power under the People's Republic. America's continuing arms sales, training, and military counsel to Taiwan's armed forces represent potent challenges to China's pride, nationalism, and rising power, as well as to its military planners.[16]

Freeman implied that arms sales prevent Taiwan from accepting what he characterized as reasonable unification terms. He said, "China sees the policies of the United States as the last effective barrier to the arrival of a ripe moment for the achievement of national unity under a single, internationally respected sovereignty. Dignity and unity have been and remain the core ambitions of the Chinese revolution. . . . the political dynamics of national honor will sooner or later force Beijing to adopt less risk-averse policies than it now espouses."[17] Military assistance to Taipei, in other words, puts a flagging U.S. on a collision course with a rising China.

Similar assessments led Nancy Bernkopf Tucker and Bonnie Glaser to a very different conclusion. Tucker and Glaser agree with Freeman that there is strong potential for strategic competition between the U.S. and China, and that Taiwan is a challenging issue for Beijing, but they reject his claim that accommodating Beijing on the Taiwan issue would mitigate those problems. On the contrary, they maintain, "A decision to jettison Taiwan, or even cut back significantly on U.S. support, would prove to an increasingly confident China that Washington has become weak, vacillating, and unreliable."[18] Meanwhile, strong nationalism within the PRC ensures that "a U.S. sacrifice of Taiwan, while gratifying, could not thoroughly slake a continuing need for Beijing to demonstrate its power."[19] Thus, they conclude, withdrawing defense assistance to Taiwan would destabilize the cross-Strait situation while yielding little or no benefit to the U.S.

In his contribution to the debate over Taiwan policy Robert Sutter concurs with these authors that strategic rivalry is building between the U.S. and China, but where they see the potential for the Taiwan issue to challenge the PRC more and more, he wonders whether the risk to the U.S. is that Taiwan itself may be accommodating the PRC. In his view, Taiwan has been irresolute in pursuing its own interests against Beijing's pressure. As a result, "cross-Strait power realities and trends also pose a broader challenge to the longstanding U.S. policy goal of maintaining a balance of power and influence in the

Taiwan area favorable to Taiwan and U.S. interests and influenced by the United States."[20] Sutter's goal is not so much to recommend a course of action as to call attention to developments that could make America's long-standing policy ineffective. Still, he hints that if Taiwan is allowed (and allows itself) to be absorbed by the PRC, the U.S. will face serious problems.

Another scholar who sees Taiwan moving toward the PRC is Bruce Gilley. Unlike Sutter, however, Gilley believes this development, which he calls "Finlandization," is one the U.S. should welcome. Finlandization means that "Taiwan would reposition itself as a neutral power, rather than a U.S. strategic ally, in order to mollify Beijing's fears about the island's becoming an obstacle to China's military and commercial ambitions in the region. It would also refrain from undermining the [Chinese Communist Party's] rule in China. In return, Beijing would back down on its military threats, grant Taipei expanded participation in international organizations, and extend the island favorable economic and social benefits." [21]

In Gilley's view, Washington's strategic ambiguity policy complicates the Finlandization process. If Taiwanese knew they could not turn to the U.S. for help, they would be less ambivalent, and Finlandization could proceed more quickly. Getting out of the way and letting the process unfold is the right U.S. policy, he argues, because Taiwan need not be a troublesome issue. Gilley criticizes those who (like Chas Freeman) believe "that Beijing is motivated by nationalism and that the PRC's irredentist claims to Taiwan stem from a broader national discourse of humiliation and weakness . . . [and that it is] striving to reincorporate Taiwan into China in order to avert a domestic nationalist backlash and a crisis of legitimacy." On the contrary, he says, "both sides have embraced a view of security that is premised on high-level contact, trust, and reduced threats of force."[22]

In Gilley's view, Finlandization is good for the PRC, Taiwan, and the U.S. It is good for the U.S. because Beijing's fundamental interest in Taiwan is not ideological, but geostrategic: it wants to ensure that Taiwan cannot be used to encircle and threaten China. In fact, he says, the "tragic result" of existing U.S. policy is, "that it has played into Beijing's fears of encirclement and naval inferiority, which in turn has prompted China's own military buildup."[23]

In contrast to Freeman, Tucker, Bonnie Glaser and Sutter, Gilley stresses the potential for cooperation and win-win interactions between the U.S. and China. Getting Taiwan "out of the way" is a prerequisite to realizing those mutual gains. In fact, he says, "Taipei's decision to chart a new course is a godsend for a U.S. administration that increasingly needs China's cooperation in achieving its highest priority: maintaining the peaceful international liberal order."[24]

Gilley's sanguine view of U.S.-China relations is echoed by two other contributors to the Taiwan policy debate, Bill Owens and Charles Glaser. As

Charles Glaser wrote in *Foreign Affairs*, "China's rise need not be nearly as competitive and dangerous as the standard realist argument suggests, because the structural forces driving major powers into conflict will be relatively weak."[25] However, on the second dimension at issue in this debate—the role of the Taiwan issue in PRC politics—Owens and Glaser are anything but sanguine.

Charles Glaser observes that the PRC devotes much of its military spending to preparing for a war over Taiwan and concludes, "Given such risks, the United States should consider backing away from its commitment to Taiwan. This would remove the most obvious and contentious flashpoint between the United States and China and smooth the way for better relations between them in the decades to come."[26] Owens made a similar point in an essay urging the U.S. to revise or repeal the Taiwan Relations Act. "A thoughtful review of this outdated legislation," Owens wrote, "is warranted and would be viewed by China as a genuine attempt to set a new course for a relationship that can develop into openness, trust and even friendship."[27]

A fifth school of thought on the Taiwan issue advocated retaining the status quo policy of strategic ambiguity, not out of any particular optimism or pessimism about the future of U.S.-PRC relations or cross-Strait relations, but out of a sense that given an uncertain future, changing policy now carries more risk than benefit. In a rejoinder to Robert Sutter, Richard Bush and Alan Romberg insist that the U.S.'s interest is in peace and stability, not maintaining a balance of power across the Taiwan Strait.

Given that objective, they say, Sutter need not worry about Taiwan's direction, as the island's robust democracy protects it from succumbing to pressure or intimidation. They endorse Taiwan's current strategy of engaging the mainland: "Reassurance of the mainland has its risks, but it also has the advantage of reducing the probability of war, and of laying a foundation for a cross-Strait relationship on terms acceptable to both sides, which is the goal not just of the United States but Taiwan and the PRC as well."[28] I have weighed in on the Taiwan policy debate from this same direction. In my view, Taiwan is not yet ready to accept unification, so ending U.S. defense assistance to Taiwan would raise hopes in Beijing (and increase nationalistic pressure to "do something" about Taiwan) without making successful unification more likely. In the end, "Such a change would indeed delight Beijing, but it would create new problems just as intractable as the old ones, but less familiar and therefore potentially even more challenging."[29]

EPILOGUE

The global recession in 2008 hit the U.S., Japan, and Europe hard. In China, the recession led some to speculate that the world's economic and political center of gravity was turning away from traditional power centers, toward China. China's increasing confidence was evident in public statements by intellectuals and officials and in a series of assertive actions in areas close to its borders. In the U.S., some commentators viewed these developments as evidence that a strategic rivalry was underway. President Barack Obama's "pivot to Asia" policy in 2011 was widely interpreted—including in Beijing—as a move to counter China's new assertiveness.

If the future of U.S.-China relations is, in fact, a great power rivalry, Taiwan's position in the relationship also is likely to change. Instead of a stand-alone issue in U.S.-China relations, Taiwan could become a pawn in a great power game. Beijing insists that Taiwan is different from other issues; its determination to unify with Taiwan should not be construed as aggressiveness toward others, because Taiwan is Chinese territory, and the Taiwan issue is a domestic issue. Despite Chinese leaders' protestations, however, observers have long been tempted to draw inferences about China's regional ambitions from its behavior toward the island.

As Chinese policies in the South China Sea and elsewhere became more assertive, some observers, including Richard Bush and former U.S. representative to Taiwan Stephen Young, began referring to Taiwan as a "canary in the coal mine" of China's rise. As they see it, how the PRC treats Taiwan is an indicator of how it will behave toward other neighbors. So far, the mainstream position among American policy makers is that Taiwan is unique, but that logic was easier to accept when the PRC limited its ambitions to Taiwan. Now that China is leaning outward on other issues—the South China Sea, the East China Sea, the Indian border—policy makers may wonder whether Taiwan is not the end of China's ambition, but the beginning.

From China's point of view, U.S. intentions are critical. It is one thing for the U.S. to maintain, as it has for decades, that it is agnostic on the unification issue, that it can accept any outcome so long as it is peacefully achieved. It is something else, however, for the U.S. to supply arms and other support to Taiwan in the context of a broader, regional advance. As with China, the jury is still out. Some Americans are ready to accommodate China's demands in the hope of avoiding an escalating conflict. Others believe the U.S. must block China's ambitions—even if that means opposing Taiwan's efforts to engage China.[30]

For Taiwan, the situation is even less certain. What are Beijing's intentions? Can the status quo—political autonomy within a framework of positive engagement—endure? Or will the PRC ratchet up the pressure for unification? If the latter, how can Taipei leverage its relationship with Washington to fend off that pressure? And what about the United States? Is it motivated by a desire to help Taiwan accomplish its own goals, or is it determined, finally, to block

China's rise? If the latter, how can Taiwan avoid been trapped between warring superpowers? These are only some of the difficult questions Taiwan's policy makers must grapple with in the years to come.

NOTES

1. Joint Communiqué of the United States of America and the People's Republic of China (Shanghai Communiqué), February 28, 1972, available at: http://www.china .org.cn/english/china-us/26012.htm.
2. Taiwan Relations Act, January 1, 1979, available at: http://www.ait.org.tw/en/ taiwan-relations-act.html.
3. Ibid.
4. Ibid.
5. Sino-U.S. Joint Communiqué, August 17, 1982, available at: http://www.nti.org/ db/china/engdocs/commk82.htm.
6. President Reagan placed a memorandum in the files of the National Security Council clarifying his intention that the 1982 Communiqué should be implemented only insofar as the PRC was committed to solving the cross-Strait conflict peacefully. The memorandum read, in part, "Taiwan's defense capability relative to that of the PRC will be maintained." See Shirley A. Kan, "China/Taiwan: Evolution of the 'One China' Policy-Key Statements from Washington, Beijing and Taipei," Congressional Research Service *Report for Congress*, September 7, 2006, p. 43.
7. This argument is worked out in detail in: Nancy Bernkopf Tucker, *Strait Talk: United States-Taiwan Relations and the Crisis with China* (Cambridge: Harvard University Press, 2009).
8. The reader may wonder why Taiwan—a self-governing democracy—is not already independent? In Taiwan, though, "Taiwan independence" (*Taidu*) has a specific meaning: the permanent separation of Taiwan not only from the PRC, but from the very idea of China. Taiwan independence would require new national symbols that made no reference to Taiwan as part of a larger Chinese entity, past, present or future. To true partisans of Taiwan independence, the Republic of China is a quasi-colonial government; it can never authentically represent the Taiwanese people because it defines Taiwan as a Chinese place. Islanders may think of Taiwan as independent of mainland Chinese authority in the present, but "Taiwan independence" means something else. The ROC label preserves a vestigial Chinese identity for Taiwan that cannot be reconciled with true Taiwan independence.
9. Quoted in Shirley A. Kan, "China/Taiwan: Evolution of the 'One China' Policy—Key Statements from Washington, Beijing, and Taipei," Congressional Research Service, June 24, 2011, p. 64, available at: http://www.fas.org/sgp/crs/row/RL30341.pdf.
10. John King, "Blunt Bush Message for Taiwan," CNN.com, December 10, 2003, available at: http://edition.cnn.com/2003/ALLPOLITICS/12/09/bush.china.taiwan/ index.html.
11. Quansheng Zhao, "Moving Toward a Co-Management Approach: China's Policy toward North Korea and Taiwan," *Asian Perspective*, Vol. 30, No. 1 (2006), pp. 39–78.
12. Charles Snyder, "Obama Welcomes Arms Package," *Taipei Times*, October 10, 2008, p. 3, available at: http://www.taipeitimes.com/News/taiwan/archives/2008 /10/10/2003425462.

13. "Beijing's New Tune on Arms Sales," *Taipei Times,* October 7, 2008, p. 8, available at: http://www.taipeitimes.com/News/editorials/archives/2008/10/07/2003425221.

14. David G. Brown, "China-Taiwan Relations: Economic Cooperation Framework Agreement Signed," *Comparative Connections* (July 2010), available at: http://csis.org/files/publication/1002qchina_taiwan.pdf.

15. Associated Press, "US-Taiwan F-16 Deal Aims at Compromise," *The Economic Times,* September 20, 2011, available at: http://economictimes.indiatimes.com/news/international-business/us-taiwan-f-16-sale-aims-at-compromise/articleshow/10049871.cms.

16. Chas W. Freeman, Jr., "Beijing, Washington and the Shifting Balance of Prestige: Remarks to the China Maritime Studies Institute," May 10, 2011, available at: http://www.mepc.org/articles-commentary/speeches/beijing-washington-and-shifting-balance-prestige.

17. Freeman, "Beijing, Washington."

18. Nancy Bernkopf Tucker and Bonnie Glaser, "Should the U.S. Abandon Taiwan?" *The Washington Quarterly* Vol. 34, No. 4 (2011), pp. 23–24, available at: http://www.twq.com/11autumn/docs/11autumn_tucker_glaser.pdf.

19. Tucker and Glaser, "Should the U.S. Abandon Taiwan?," p. 25.

20. Robert Sutter, "Cross-Strait Moderation and the United States—Policy Adjustments Needed," *Pacnet* Vol. 17, No. 1 (2009), available at http://csis.org/files/media/csis/pubs/pac0917.pdf.

21. Bruce Gilley, "Not So Dire Straits: How the Finlandization of Taiwan Benefits U.S. Security," *Foreign Affairs* Vol. 89 (2010), pp. 44–60, available at: http://www.foreignaffairs.com/articles/65901/bruce-gilley/not-so-dire-straits.

22. Ibid.

23. Ibid.

24. Ibid.

25. Charles Glaser, "Will China's Rise Lead to War?: Why Realism Does Not Mean Pessimism," *Foreign Affairs* Vol. 90, No. 2 (2011), available at: http://www.foreignaffairs.com/articles/67479/charles-glaser/will-chinas-rise-lead-to-war.

26. Ibid.

27. Bill Owens, "America Must Start Treating China as a Friend," *Financial Times,* November 17, 2009, available at: http://www.ft.com/intl/cms/s/0/69241506-d3b2-11de-8caf-00144feabdc0.html#axzz1RXebUtOH.

28. Richard Bush and Alan D. Romberg, "Cross-Strait Moderation and the United States—A Response to Robert Sutter," *Pacnet,* Vol. 17A (2009), available at: http://csis.org/files/media/csis/pubs/pac0917a.pdf.

29. Shelley Rigger, "Why Giving Up on Taiwan Will Not Help Us with China," *Asian Outlook* (2011), available at: http://www.aei.org/article/foreign-and-defense-policy/regional/asia/why-giving-up-taiwan-will-not-help-us-with-china/.

30. U.S. Representative Dana Rohrabacher's decision to withdraw from the Congressional Taiwan Caucus in 2009 on the grounds that Taiwan had given up resisting the PRC is an example of this outlook. Rohrabacher said supporting the caucus was "pointless" because Taiwan was working with China instead of fighting against it. See Nadia Tsao, "Rohrabacher to leave Taiwan Caucus position," *Taipei Times,* March 15, 2009, p. 3.

Part VII

The Global Context

13

U.S.-China Interactions in the Middle East, Africa, Europe, and Latin America

David Shambaugh and Dawn Murphy

The most distinguishing new dimension of the U.S.-China relationship is that it has gone global. Since the rapprochement of 1971–1972, the relationship has always had bilateral and (Asian) regional dimensions of interaction, but it was primarily restricted to these two spheres. Although the two governments always *discussed* global issues—dating back to the Kissinger and Nixon geostrategic *tours d'horizon* with Zhou and Mao—actual *interaction* between the two nations was really restricted to the Asia-Pacific region (except during the 1970s when China supported insurgent movements in Africa against the Soviet and Cuban presence). The Chinese side appreciated being included in the geostrategic dialogues across seven consecutive U.S. administrations (Nixon to Obama), and the American side indulged this identity, but in reality it was the United States that was the global superpower with China's influence being restricted to Asia (at best).

This is no longer the case. Today and increasingly into the future, the Sino-American relationship will be characterized as a *global* relationship.[1] This is because *China* now has a global presence. Since the 1990s, China has substantially broadened its global footprint in several dimensions. While 22 nations in Central America and West Africa still diplomatically recognize Taiwan, the People's Republic of China has essentially completed its global quest for diplomatic recognition. In various regions of the world—Asia, the Middle East, Africa, and the Americas—China has become deeply integrated into regional intergovernmental organizations (IGOs) as either a full member or observer (in some regions it has created new inter-regional dialogue groupings). China is now a full member of virtually all important IGOs (except the OECD and International Energy Agency). China engages in military exchanges with foreign militaries worldwide. It has educational and cultural exchanges all over the world and has prioritized its "external publicity" (对外宣传) and cultural exchange (文化交流) work. China's economic footprint is also truly global—not only in terms of trade, but also in services and overseas direct investment and as an increasingly significant aid donor in Asia and Africa. China has also become increasingly involved in transnational global governance issues.

In all of these and other dimensions, China's global impact is being felt. Yet, it can be argued that China remains a global *actor* without yet becoming a true global *power*. That is, despite its increasing *presence* in each of these domains—diplomatic, institutional, military/security, cultural, and economic—China is not yet really *influencing* regional or global trends in any of these dimensions (except in the economic domain). If power is defined as the ability to influence others and the outcome of events,[2] then Beijing does not yet possess or wield it on a global basis.[3] Other than the realm of trade and commodity prices, it remains far from being able to do so. China thus should be thought of as a "partial power" rather than a global power.[4] Chinese diplomacy still remains rather passive and reactive—Beijing is not actively involved in addressing regional or global issues or shaping outcomes in contentious issues. The positions it takes on a wide range of sensitive global issues in the UN Security Council are often a kind of "lowest common denominator." Other than the North Korea nuclear issue and perhaps climate change, Beijing is not in the middle of trying to address or resolve *any* global issue. Even on these two issues—North Korea and climate change—Beijing often acts slowly and stubbornly. China sits on the periphery of the Iran nuclear issue, backed the repressive regimes in Myanmar and Zimbabwe, and was a significant impediment to alleviating human suffering in Syria and Sudan. This diplomatic passivity and obstinacy often frustrates Washington—which would often prefer a more activist and cooperative Chinese diplomacy,[5] and for Beijing to become a "responsible [international] stakeholder" (in the famous words of Robert Zoellick). Apart from ballistic missiles, space program, and cyber warfare capabilities, China's military has no global reach as its power projection capacities remain very much limited to the Asia-Pacific region. While it is a new government priority to build soft power and improve China's global image, by a number of measures China's soft power remains weak and its global image (as measured by public opinion surveys) is mixed-to-negative in most regions of the world. China is truly a global trading giant, but its outbound direct investment (ODI) only ranked fifth in the world in 2010 ($58 billion), a long way behind the United States' $240 billion invested abroad in the same year.

Thus, by a number of measures, China is *active* but not yet *influential* globally. The American presence remains both broad and deep (albeit shrinking relatively), while China's presence is increasingly broad but not (yet) deep.

While China may be a "shallow" power internationally, it is certainly an increasingly consequential power. To recall the late Gerald Segal's famous 1999 article "Does China Matter?"[6] the answer today (as then) is definitely "yes." Yet Segal was correct to caution analysts not to inflate or overestimate China's capabilities (although he did not address the question of influence).

Nonetheless, China's growing presence on every continent in each of these spheres has contributed to a redefinition of the U.S.-China relationship. The U.S. and China are bumping up against each other in parts the planet where they never have before. Yet, the essential argument of this chapter is that, to date, the two countries are really acting in *parallel* with each other around the world. That is, the two pursue their interests and policies in an autonomous— rather than interactive—fashion with each other. To be sure, U.S. officials and intelligence agencies are keeping an eye on China's activities in the western hemisphere, and to a lesser extent in Africa and the Middle East, but Washington is not yet setting its priorities or policies in *reaction* to China. For its part, China is very conscious of America's strategic sensitivities and Beijing has gone out of its way not to irritate Washington or get itself in America's "strategic headlights" (China's ties with rogue regimes such as Iran and Syria are perhaps the exception to this rule).

Thus, this chapter argues that while a global Sino-American relationship now truly exists for the first time, it is not (yet) an intrinsically strategically competitive *or* interactive relationship—as was the case during the Cold War between the United States and former Soviet Union. This may change over time as China's global footprint deepens, if it maintains close ties with "rogue" regimes that are hostile to the United States, directly challenges longstanding U.S. alliances or partnerships, begins to establish a naval presence in or near the Persian Gulf, works to undermine U.S. regional security arrangements, supports anti-American terrorism, or undercuts U.S. economic or energy interests. To date, Beijing has done some of these things, but not others. It has rhetorically challenged American alliances, it has sought to counter-balance U.S. security arrangements throughout Asia, and has supported some rogue states that are hostile to the U.S. Thus, there does exist a nascent strategic competition—but it has not yet become fully manifest on a global basis.

While not directly competitive, neither are the two nations acting *in tandem* or working in a truly coordinated fashion with each other in any region—thus dispelling any operative notion of a "G-2."[7] This is not to suggest that bilateral *consultation* does not exist on a broad range of global issues and regions. The Joint Statements issued in the wake of the 2009 and 2011 U.S.-China presidential summits or the annual Strategic and Economic Dialogues are clear indications of the truly globalized nature of the bilateral dialogue.[8] As Bonnie Glaser's chapter illustrates, there are more than 60 other intergovernmental mechanisms to try and build tangible cooperation. These bilateral dialogues include annual ones on four separate regions of the world: Asia-Pacific; South and Central Asia; Africa; and Latin America. These were created for the specific purpose of exchanging views on priorities, policies, and equities of the two governments in each region—to serve simultaneously as an "early warning indicator" of possible competitive frictions, but also to try and identify areas of practical Sino-American cooperation in third regions. These official exchanges are backstopped by non-official "Track II" dialogues.[9]

The global U.S.-China relationship is thus neither fully competitive nor cooperative. Rather, as argued in the introductory chapter to this volume, it is a mixture of "coopetition." Internationally, it operates like an awkward modern dance—with both sides moving around each other on the dance floor without coming into contact or dancing in unison, both wary of stepping on the other's toes, and each "doing their own thing." In the remainder of this chapter, we will survey the respective U.S.-China positions in four important regions of the world: the Middle East, Africa, Europe, and Latin America. Avery Goldstein's contribution to this volume does the same for the Asian region (his chapter clearly indicates there is a clear competitive dynamic that exists in this region). Taken together, readers should be able to grasp the totality of the Sino-American global relationship.

EUROPE

While the United States and China both enjoy strong ties with Europe, transatlantic ties are much deeper and stronger. The United States and Europe share many bonds—rooted in common values, civics, democracy, religion, languages, immigration and inter-marriage, economies, mutual security, and many other dimensions. These ties date to the eighteenth century, have been strengthened by generations of interactions, tested by wars and built in peace, institutionalized by governments and built through a plethora of societal linkages.

China and Europe, on the other hand, have much more ambivalent histories also dating to the eighteenth century when European traders, missionaries, and colonial powers established footholds along the China coast. The Sino-European experience over the next century was shaped by this commercial and colonial experience, reinforced through "gunboat diplomacy" and humiliating wars and territorial dismemberment. While some imperial Chinese officials and intellectuals looked to Europe for the keys to "wealth and power" (福强), Chinese generally came to view Europe with disdain for its imperialist ways. This negative legacy became embedded in the Chinese Communists' revolutionary identity and mission, culminating in the seizure of power in 1949. Thereafter, for several decades, the Sino-European relationship was attenuated. China established diplomatic relations and ties with the eastern communist bloc and the Scandinavian countries, but its links to Western Europe were weak owing to the Cold War. Although China and Britain established trade relations following the Geneva Conference in 1954, Beijing established official relations with France in 1964 and the other West European nations in the early 1970s, the continuing Cold War cast a long shadow over the practical development of exchanges. It was only in the post–Cold War era that China and Europe began to establish relations autonomous from Washington and Moscow.[10] In the wake of the collapse of the Soviet Union, both individual European nations and the European Union began to build more comprehensive ties with China and to work out a strategy for relations with China.[11] This led to a certain "honeymoon" between 2000 and 2006, but since then relations have become strained and complex as the two sides entered the "marriage" phase of their relationship.[12]

China's ties with Europe today have a number of features. The most notable is commercial. The EU is now China's largest (collective) trading partner, export market, and leading source of high-technology imports. Conversely, China is the EU's second largest trading partner and export destination. Total bilateral trade volume in goods and services in 2010 reached €431.5 billion.[13] Trade in goods surged 35 percent from 2009 to 2010, with the EU now taking 23 percent of China's global exports while China has become the fastest growing market for European exports worldwide. Foreign investment also flows in both directions. The EU invested €4.9 billion into China in 2010, and a cumulative total of €73.3 billion into 33,361 projects over time, ranking it the fourth largest foreign investor (after Hong Kong, Taiwan, Japan, and United States).[14] For their part, Chinese companies only invested €0.9 billion into Europe in 2010, accounting for only 1.7 percent of total inflows. Europe absorbs 7 percent of China's total outbound direct investment (ODI), ranking it third worldwide behind Asia/Oceania (65 percent) and Latin America (17 percent).[15]

Sino-European commercial ties are not without frictions. Trade remains very unbalanced, with China running a surplus of €168.8 billion in 2010. European companies and chambers of commerce regularly complain about a host of market access barriers they face in China, while the Chinese government is constantly badgering the EU to grant it "market economy status" (MES). This is a designation under the WTO (but granted by sovereign states) that exempts exporting nations from anti-dumping duties. As of 2009, 97 nations had granted China MES—but not the major developed economies. China has been the target of dozens of anti-dumping cases filed against it every year (largely by the European Union and United States). In 2009 China was the object of 40 percent of total anti-dumping investigations and 75 percent of countervailing duties in the world.[16] According to the WTO, China was subject to 119 anti-dumping cases in just the first six months of 2010.[17] Without MES, Chinese products are calculated based on the market prices of a "substitute country"—often with much higher production costs than China—as the benchmark instead of its real costs, making Chinese companies vulnerable to anti-dumping and anti-subsidy investigations.

So anxious is Beijing to win MES from the European Union that Premier Wen Jiabao argued during a visit to Europe in September 2011 that China's willingness to buy European debt to help stabilize European economies mired in the sovereign debt crisis was contingent on China being granted MES by the EU. By some estimates, China already holds as much as 45 percent of its $2.3 trillion in foreign exchange reserves in Euro-denominated assets (much of it in German government bonds).[18] Chinese government authorities believe that even this amount is overexposure at a time when the Eurozone was poised on the precipice of multiple defaults by several European nations (Greece, Italy, Ireland, Spain, Portugal, and possibly France). For this reason, the Chinese government was reluctant to pour additional monies down a black hole by contributing more to the European bailout fund through sovereign bond purchases, which would evaporate if European nations defaulted on their debts. China's $400 billion sovereign wealth fund, the China Investment Corporation (CIC), was equally hesitant to contribute to Europe's financial rescue—arguing instead that it was prepared to invest in fixed assets. In particular, CIC Chairman Lou Jiwei indicated an interest in investing in projects to upgrade decaying European hard infrastructure (roads, rails, bridges, ports), but on one condition: ownership was coupled with investment.[19] As in the United States, this conditionality makes Europeans nervous, that is, for China to own and operate core national infrastructure.

Another significant irritant in relations is the so-called "arms embargo" that the EU has maintained on China since 1989. While it was a voluntary restriction adopted by the EU in the aftermath of the "June 4th Incident," and has now been replaced by a much more systematic and comprehensive "Code of Conduct" binding all 27 member states, the stigma of the arms sales ban still annoys Beijing. Any change would require all 27 states to agree to lift the embargo, something that is very unlikely. The vast majority of governments still support maintaining it.

This issue is symptomatic of the fact that Europe remains very divided on China. While all governments seek to maintain positive diplomatic ties and productive trade and investment relations, tensions have risen over a number of issues. China's impact on European economies—particularly in central and southern Europe—has been devastating. European companies, while enjoying a strong presence in China, are among the most vocal critics of Chinese protectionist practices. China's human rights record remains highly contentious and is harshly criticized in many European societies and parliaments. China's heavy-handed policies in Tibet are a particularly neuralgic issue for Europeans (more so than Americans). For these and other reasons, China's popularity ratings among European publics—as measured by a variety of public opinion polls—have been the *lowest* in the world and in steady decline from 2007–2010. But in 2011, the secular trend seemed to temporarily reverse, as all European countries surveyed in the Pew Global Attitudes survey demonstrated an improved view of China (see table 13.1). It is not certain if this recent turnaround in European public opinion towards China will be sustained or will return to the negativity of recent years. The 2011 spike seems to be part of a more general global improvement in China's image—with only Brazil, Turkey, Jordan, Pakistan, and Kenya showing year-on-year declines (albeit from very positive numbers in the latter two cases).

U.S.-Europe relations, for their part, show stability and strength in recent years. Following the difficulties in the aftermath of the U.S.-led invasion and occupation of Iraq in 2003, transatlantic ties have steadily improved. In 2011

TABLE 13.1. China Favorability Ratings (2002–2011)

	2002 %	2005 %	2006 %	2007 %	2008 %	2009 %	2010 %	2011 %	2010–2011 *Change*
U.S.	—	43	52	42	39	50	49	51	+2
Britain	—	65	65	49	47	52	46	59	+13
France	—	58	60	47	28	41	41	51	+10
Germany	—	46	56	34	26	29	30	34	+4
Spain	—	57	45	39	31	40	47	55	+8
Lithuania	—	—	—	—	—	—	—	52	—
Poland	—	37	—	39	33	43	46	51	+5
Russia	71	60	63	60	60	58	60	63	+3
Ukraine	—	—	—	64	—	—	—	63	—
Turkey	—	40	33	25	24	16	20	18	-2
Egypt	—	—	63	65	59	52	52	57	+5
Jordan	—	43	49	46	44	50	53	44	-9
Lebanon	—	66	—	46	50	53	56	59	+3
Palest. ter.	—	—	—	46	—	43	—	62	—
Israel	—	—	—	45	—	56	—	49	—
India	—	—	—	—	—	—	—	25	—
Indonesia	68	73	62	65	58	59	58	67	+9
Japan	55	—	27	29	14	26	26	34	+8
Pakistan	—	79	69	79	76	84	85	82	-3
Brazil	—	—	—	—	—	—	52	49	-3
Mexico	—	—	—	43	38	39	39	39	0
Kenya	—	—	—	81	—	73	86	71	-15

Source: Pew Global Attitudes Project, July 13, 2011, http://www.pewglobal.org/2011/07/13/china-seen-overtaking-us-as-global-superpower/5/#chapter-4-views-of-china.

only 4 percent of European publics polled by the German Marshall Fund of the United States indicated that U.S.-Europe relations were poor, with a strong majority judging them to be "good" or "mixed."[20] While the war in Afghanistan has grown increasingly unpopular on both sides of the Atlantic and the campaign is being wound down, it was nonetheless a NATO-led mission (International Security Assistance Force or ISAF) that included forces from 12 European nations plus Turkey. Similarly, the military effort to support rebel forces seeking to overthrow Libya's Colonel Muammar Gaddafi was similarly led by NATO. While there are serious fiscal concerns about NATO's future, as a result of Europe-wide government cutbacks on defense spending, the alliance has been retooled and substantially strengthened since the end of the Cold War. China and Russia do not like this fact at all, and both view NATO as a new interventionist tool of the West. Despite sustained efforts, NATO has failed to establish a modus vivendi with Moscow—while only a perfunctory dialogue mechanism exists between NATO and Beijing.

The post-2008 global financial crisis and post-2010 European sovereign debt crisis have hit both the American and European economies hard, but it has also given both sides of the Atlantic common resolve.[21] In 2010 transatlantic trade between the U.S. and EU totaled a staggering €667.8 ($889.9 bn.). In the same year, Europe invested €79.2 bn. in the United States, while U.S. investment flows to Europe were $129.6 billion (€97.3 bn.).[22] Commercial ties across the Atlantic remain robust.

While there was some discussion of a new "strategic triangle" among the United States, Europe, and China a few years ago,[23] since 2007–2008 the three sides tend to interact relatively autonomously from one another. There exist no regularized consultations among government officials from the three sides. While non-official consultations do occur periodically in an effort to build mutual understanding and common cooperation to address global governance challenges,[24] the principal bond remains across the Atlantic between Americans and Europeans. Since 2005 U.S. Government officials meet their European Commission counterparts annually for official (but private) consultations concerning China, rotating between Brussels and Washington, D.C. Less formalized official interactions take place on a regular basis in Washington, D.C. and European capitals. Since 2008, China has figured prominently on the annual U.S.-EU presidential summit agenda, reaching a "Camp David Consensus" at the 2008 summit that discussions of respective relations with China would always be on the agenda.[25] Meanwhile, American and European experts continue to hold regular private discussions about China and managing Western relations with China.[26] All of this reflects the basic fact that China remains much more of an *object* of Western policy than a *partner* in common cooperation.

THE MIDDLE EAST

The Middle East is an area of increasing Sino-American interests and inter-actions. For the United States, it has been of central strategic importance for more than half a century. Its current interests in the region include promoting energy security, combating terrorism, preventing Iran from acquiring nuclear weapons, and supporting Israel.[27] In contrast with the United States, China's interests in the Middle East are relatively new and limited in scope. China's pri-mary interests are protecting energy security, developing markets for Chinese goods and services, and preventing support for Muslim insurgency activities in China, especially in Xinjiang.[28]

Over the last 20 years China's interactions with the Middle East have grown dramatically.[29] Increased involvement with this region includes:

- deepening economic relations (see figures 13.1 and 13.2);
- the establishment of the China-Arab States Cooperation Forum (CASCF) in 2004;[30]
- the appointment of a Special Envoy for Middle East Issues in 2002;
- contribution of troops to United Nations peacekeeping operations (UNPKO) in Lebanon, Sudan and Darfur;[31]
- the deployment of People's Liberation Army-Navy ships to the waters off Somalia to participate in multilateral anti-piracy operations in 2008;[32]

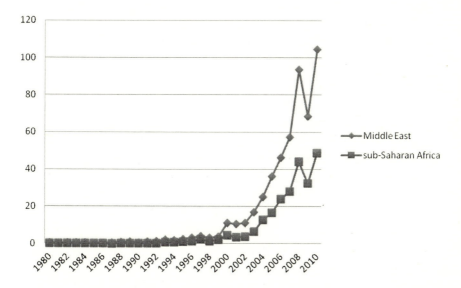

Figure 13.1. China's Imports from the Middle East and Sub-Saharan Africa, 1980–2010 (U.S.$ bn.). International Monetary Fund (IMF). *Direction of Trade Statistics Database,* 2011.

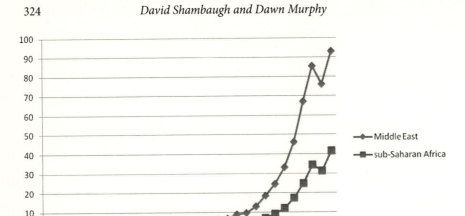

Figure 13.2. China's Exports to the Middle East and Sub-Saharan Africa, 1980–2010 (U.S.$ bn.). International Monetary Fund, *Direction of Trade Statistics Database* (2011).

- the development of strategic partnerships with Egypt (1999), Saudi Arabia (1999), and Algeria (2004);
- free trade agreement negotiations with the Gulf Cooperation Council (GCC);
- the launching of special economic zones (SEZ) in Algeria and Egypt;
- and the opening of Confucius Institutes in Egypt, Iran, Israel, Jordan, Lebanon, Morocco, Sudan, Turkey, and the United Arab Emirates.

Energy Security

As figure 13.3 indicates, the United States is the world's largest oil importer (9.6 mn. bb/d) and China is the second largest (4.8 mn. bb/d).[33]

Both countries have a vested interest in the uninterrupted flow of oil and gas from the Middle East and stability in global energy markets to ensure the affordability of these key resources.

China's global energy security concerns are relatively new. China became a net oil importer in 1993. As a result, its global oil imports since the late 1990s have skyrocketed. In 2010, 52 percent of China's crude oil imports (2.5 million barrels per day) originated in the Middle East.[34] The U.S. Energy Information Administration estimates that China will import 72 percent of its crude oil by 2035, as compared to 50 percent in 2010.[35] China's top crude oil suppliers from the Middle East are Saudi Arabia (19%), Iran (9%), Oman (7%), Sudan (5%), Iraq (5%), Kuwait (4%), and Libya (3%).[36] By comparison, only 25 percent of

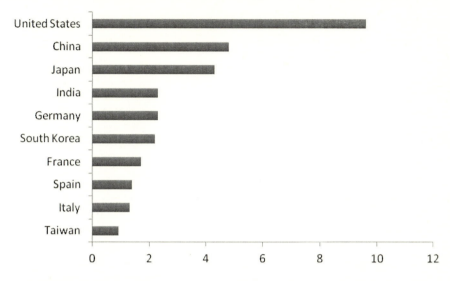

Figure 13.3. Top Ten Oil Importers, 2010 (millions of barrels per day). U.S. Energy Information Administration, *Country Analysis Briefs: China.*

the United States' worldwide oil imports (2.4 mn. bb/d) are from the region.[37] Top United States crude oil suppliers in the region are Saudi Arabia (10%), Iraq (5%) and Algeria (5%).[38]

In light of these projections and the size of available reserves in the Middle East, China's reliance on Middle Eastern oil will likely grow. Due to the importance of Middle Eastern energy resources to both the United States and China, energy security is the most likely long term area of tension for these two powers in the region.[39] That said, conflict over energy security is not predestined. Through its participation in anti-piracy operations near Somalia, China has demonstrated its willingness to cooperate in maritime security when its economic interests are threatened. Since both countries have a vested interest in the continued transportation of energy resources from the Middle East, one potential area of cooperation could be working together to protect the flow of energy resources from the region. For example, they could combine efforts to ensure the free flow of tankers and other commercial ships through oil transit chokepoints such as the Straits of Hormuz, the Suez Canal, and the Strait of Bab el-Mandab.[40]

Export Markets

After energy security, China's second largest interest in the Middle East is developing markets for its goods and services.[41] By 2010, China's exports to the Middle

East had risen to $93 billion (see figure 13.4).[42] China's top five export destinations in 2010 were the United Arab Emirates ($21.24 bn.), Turkey ($11.96 bn.), Iran ($11.1 bn.), Saudi Arabia ($10.37 bn.), and Egypt ($6.04 bn.).[43] China's primary exports were light industrial products (including consumer electronics and appliances), textiles, clothing, machinery, and automobiles.[44]

Searching for markets includes not only goods, but also services. China's primary service sector export markets in the Middle East are construction, telecommunications, and finance. Contract services by construction firms are a particularly important segment of these services.[45] By 2009, China's construction services in the Middle East had risen to $24.4 billion. China's 2009 top construction service markets in the Middle East were Algeria ($5.9 bn.), Saudi Arabia ($3.6 bn.), United Arab Emirates ($3.5 bn.), Iran ($2.1 bn.), and Sudan ($2.1 bn.).[46]

Foreign direct investment is not a major interest for China in the Middle East. Compared to its exports of goods and services, China's outbound direct investment (ODI) in the region is minimal. In 2009, it was merely $973.03 million.[47]

In contrast to China, export opportunities (products or services) in the Middle East do not appear to be a major interest for the United States. In 2010, United States exports to the Middle East were only $60 billion (see figure 13.4).[48] That said, in light of the United States' recent economic recession,

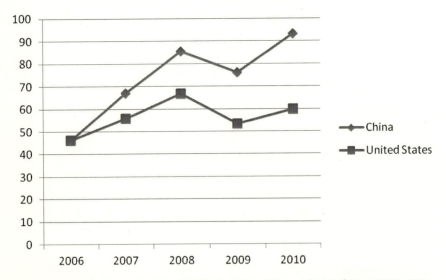

Figure 13.4. Product Exports to the Middle East from China and United States 2006–2010 (U.S.$ bn.). International Monetary Fund, *Direction of Trade Statistics Database* (2011); and United States International Trade Commission, *U.S. Trade by Geographic Regions.*

export promotion to the Middle East may increase in future years to encourage the creation of jobs in the United States.

In the aftermath of the Arab Spring, many Middle Eastern states may require assistance in reforming their economies to promote economic growth and prosperity for their populations. This political development could provide opportunities for cooperation between the United States and China. As Middle Eastern states economically develop, both China and the United States are likely to benefit from increased export opportunities to the region. As a result, the two states could potentially pool their economic development expertise and jointly advise governments on how to restructure and grow their economies.

Terrorism

Combating terrorism in a post-9/11 world is a vital national interest of the United States.[49] In a much more limited way, China shares a concern over terrorism emanating from the Middle East. Although official Chinese statistics likely underreport the population of Muslims in China, it is widely believed to be between 20 and 100 million (mostly composed of Hui, Uighurs, and Kazakhs).[50] Fifty percent of China's Muslim population are Uighurs, who primarily reside in the western Xinjiang Autonomous Region. Uighurs share an ethic heritage with the Turks of Turkey. For many years the Uighurs have been engaged in a series of attacks against Han Chinese (both in Xinjiang but also eastern provinces). The main insurgent movement for the Uighurs is known as the East Turkestan Islamic Movement (ETIM), which has been officially designated as a terrorist organization by the U.S. State Department and INTERPOL. ETIM receives a substantial portion of funding from citizens in Turkey, and has cells in a number of countries where Uighurs live in exile.

China's concerns about home-grown and cross-border terrorism have markedly increased in the aftermath of July 2009 riots in Xinjiang.[51] There are some indications that al-Qaeda support for Uighurs is increasing as a result of the 2009 riots combined with China's expanding economic presence in Muslim countries.[52] As China's economic interaction with Middle Eastern countries grows, its foreign operations may increasingly become al-Qaeda targets.

China has already demonstrated its willingness to participate in multilateral security initiatives in the Middle East (e.g., participation in anti-piracy operations off the coast of Somalia and contributions to United Nations peacekeeping troops in Lebanon, Sudan and Darfur). Therefore, if a threat from al-Qaeda toward China's global economic interests emerges, it may be increasingly willing to actively cooperate with the United States and other nations in coordinated anti-terrorism operations. That said, due to human rights concerns and U.S. domestic political constituencies, it is unlikely that the United

States will become involved in China's efforts to suppress Uighur insurgency activities in Xinjiang.

Supporting "Rogue" States

China's support for what the United States describes as "states of concern" (a.k.a. "rogue regimes") in the Middle East could cause future tensions with the United States. Over the last several years, the United States' preoccupation with preventing Iran from developing nuclear weapons has escalated. Although China has voted in favor of a number of UN Security Council resolutions imposing sanctions on Iran, it has generally been supportive of Iran and has repeatedly attempted to shield Iran from United Nations sanctions pursued by the United States and other members of the international community.[53] China is also Iran's main trading partner and is deeply engaged in a wide variety of state-to-state and non-governmental interactions with the Iranian regime. Indeed, China has become Iran's main international benefactor. Moreover, given Iran's role as a major oil supplier for China and China's philosophical opposition to both sanctions and interfering in the domestic politics of other states, it is highly unlikely that China will become substantially more supportive of the United States' actions towards Iran over time. The Iran issue has significant potential for strategic strife between Beijing and Washington.

Sudan is another recent example of a rogue state supported by China due to its oil interests. China repeatedly used its position on the UN Security Council to shield Sudan from sanctions for human rights violations.[54] However, around the time of the 2008 Olympics, China's stance on Darfur did change as a result of U.S. and international pressure. Since then China has participated in peacekeeping operations in southern Sudan, and appointed a Special Envoy for China-Africa Issues to deal with Darfur related issues.

In the post–Arab Spring environment, China's support of states such as Syria, Sudan, and Iran may increase tensions with the United States. In March 2011, although China abstained rather than veto the United Nations' resolution which resulted in NATO military action in Libya, it subsequently vocally criticized the use of force.[55] Also, the moribund Qaddafi regime attempted to buy weapons from China during the nation's civil conflict.[56] China's United Nations Security Council vetoes (together with Russia) in November 2011 and February 2012 of resolutions condemning Syria for its crackdown on antigovernment protestors are another example of China's opposition to the United States' action in the Middle East and increasing concerns over U.S. meddling in the region.[57]

There also appears to be a high probability that, in a post–Arab Spring environment, United States democracy and human rights promotion activities in the Middle East will increase. As a result, the United States may pressure more authoritarian regimes to step down in response to local protests. If the United States continues to attempt to influence the domestic political situation of Middle Eastern countries and China seeks to protect those targeted regimes, tensions between the United States and China in the Middle East could escalate. Conversely, if U.S. influence in the Middle East declines and China's influence rises due to the Arab Spring, this could also cause future tensions.[58]

Israel

Finally, in addition to ensuring energy security, combating terrorism, and preventing Iran from acquiring nuclear weapons, a major interest of the United States in the Middle East is supporting Israel. China has achieved the difficult diplomatic feat of having a relatively balanced relationship with both Israel and the Arab States.[59] That said, before 1992 (when it established diplomatic relations with Israel), China was a strong supporter of the Palestinian Liberation Organization. In 2002, at the urging of Arab States, China established a Special Envoy for Middle East issues focused on the Middle East Peace Process. Despite this move, China's involvement in the Middle East peace process has been minimal—although Arab States are currently encouraging China to play a larger role due to the perception that it is a less biased actor than the United States. Despite these entreaties, China appears reluctant to challenge the United States' interests in the peace process and wants to maintain its own good bilateral relations with Israel. In the future, if China succumbs to Arab pressure or for other reasons attempts to more assertively influence the peace process on the side of the Arab States, this could cause significant tensions with the United States.

SUB-SAHARAN AFRICA

Similar to the Middle East, China's involvement with Sub-Saharan Africa has grown rapidly over the last two decades. But, unlike the Middle East, China has maintained deep ties to the region for more than six decades.[60] China's primary interests in sub-Saharan Africa are energy security, natural resource acquisition and market development for its goods and services. Particularly striking developments include:

- substantially increased economic relations (see figures 13.1 and 13.2);
- the emergence of China as a major foreign aid donor;[61]
- the establishment of the Forum on China-Africa Cooperation (FOCAC) in 2000,[62] and Forum for Economic and Trade Cooperation between China and Portuguese Speaking Countries in 2006;[63]

- the appointment of a Special Envoy for China-Africa Issues in 2007;
- contributions of peacekeeping troops to United Nations (UN) missions in Congo, Liberia, Cote d'Ivoire, and southern Sudan;
- the initiation of strategic partnerships with South Africa (2000), Nigeria (2004), and Angola (2010);
- negotiations for a free trade agreement with the Southern African Customs Union;
- the launch of special economic zones (SEZ) in Ethiopia, Mauritius, Nigeria, and Zambia;
- and the establishment of Confucius Institutes in Benin, Botswana, Cameroon, Ethiopia, Kenya, Liberia, Madagascar, Nigeria, Rwanda, South Africa, Togo, Zambia, and Zimbabwe.[64]

The United States' interests in the region are more limited. To the degree that the United States does have strategic interests in Sub-Saharan Africa, they are energy security, preventing the spread of terrorism (due to failed states and residual al-Qaeda cells), and public health concerns.[65] The United States also has a key policy goal of promoting democracy and human rights in the region.[66]

Energy Security, Natural Resources and Export Markets

Sub-Saharan Africa is important for both China and the United States due to current oil imports from the region and the potential to diversify away from dependency on Middle Eastern oil.

While China has diverse commercial, political, and cultural interests in Africa, energy security remains Beijing's top interest. As of 2011, 25 percent of China's crude oil imports (1.2 mn. bb/d) originate in Sub-Saharan Africa.[67] As of 2010, China's top crude oil suppliers in the region were Angola, Republic of Congo, Nigeria, and Equatorial Guinea.[68] By contrast, 14 percent of United States' oil imports (1.3 mn. bb/d) come from Sub-Saharan Africa.[69] Top suppliers for the United States are Nigeria and Angola. As discussed above, in relation to the Middle East, China's energy needs are growing rapidly. As a result, competition between the United States and China for oil resources in Sub-Saharan Africa may develop over time.

China's second most important interest in sub-Saharan Africa (after energy security) is acquiring non-energy natural resources. In contrast to the Middle East, Chinese imports from Sub-Saharan Africa represent a more diverse set of natural resources, including not only energy, but also minerals and agriculture. China's key natural resource imports from Sub-Saharan Africa include iron ore, copper, chromium, cobalt, zinc, tin, gold, diamonds and agricultural products. The United States also imports natural resources from Sub-Saharan Africa. Nonetheless, 80 percent of U.S. imports from Sub-Saharan Africa are energy products. Outside of energy, primary U.S. imports include minerals, metals, chemicals and agricultural products.

Similar to the Middle East, China views Sub-Saharan Africa as a region brimming with opportunities for Chinese product and service exports. This is China's third most important interest in the region. In 2010, China's product exports to Sub-Saharan Africa were $41.5 billion (see figure 13.5).[70] China's top five export destinations in 2010 were: South Africa ($10.8 bn.), Nigeria ($6.69 bn.), Liberia ($4.39 bn.), Benin ($2.27 bn.), and Angola ($2 bn.).[71] Most of China's exports to Sub-Saharan Africa are electronics, mechanical products, textile products, and transportation equipment. In comparison to China, U.S. exports to sub-Saharan Africa are $17 billion (see figure 13.5).[72]

As in the Middle East, Sub-Saharan Africa is a major market for Chinese services, particularly construction, telecommunications, and finance. For example, in 2009, China's construction services in Sub-Saharan Africa were valued at $16.6 billion.[73] The top markets for these services were Angola ($4.9 bn.), Nigeria ($2 bn.), Equatorial Guinea ($1.3 bn.), Ethiopia ($1.2 bn.) and Republic of Congo ($0.9 bn.).[74] In contrast to trade, outbound investment (ODI) is not currently a major interest for China in Sub-Saharan Africa. In 2009, China's FDI into Sub-Saharan Africa was only $1.07 billion.[75]

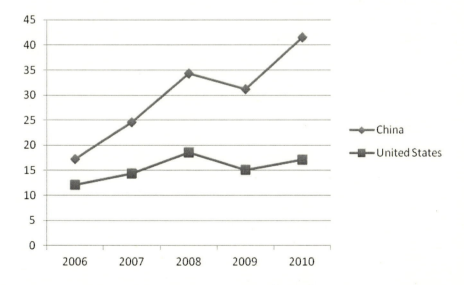

Figure 13.5. Exports to Sub-Saharan Africa from China and the United States 2006–2010 (U.S.$ bn.). International Monetary Fund (IMF), *Direction of Trade Statistics Database*, 2011.

To date, exports to Africa (product or services) do not appear to have been a priority for the United States, but this is changing. Promoting sub-Saharan African exports (both natural resources and manufactured goods) may be a future area of cooperation for the United States and China.

Chinese and American economic interests in Sub-Saharan Africa described above may provide further opportunities for collaboration. Both countries have a vested interest in the free flow of commercial goods to and from the region. In recent years, African coastal waters—particularly along the Gulf of Guinea, the Gulf of Aden, and the western Indian Ocean—have been plagued with piracy. As discussed above, China is already participating in anti-piracy operations off the coast of Somalia. Perhaps similar joint operations with the United States and China would be possible in parts of Sub-Saharan Africa.

Terrorism

After energy security, the United States' second most important interest in Sub-Saharan Africa is preventing the emergence of terrorist threats towards the United States as a result of weak and failed states. This concern began with the terrorist attacks on Dar es Salaam, Tanzania, and Nairobi, Kenya in 1998 and continued to grow after 9/11. In 2008 the United States launched AFRICOM in response to these concerns. In contrast to the Middle East, terrorism per se is not a concern for China in Sub-Saharan Africa (although Chinese workers have been kidnapped in a number of African countries in recent years). In recent years China has demonstrated a concern for stability in African states by deploying United Nations peacekeeping troops to Congo, Liberia, Cote d'Ivoire, and southern Sudan. As a result, the United States and China could potentially work together to train local African militaries with the objective of preventing failed states and terrorist elements from operating in weak states.

Public Health

A final potential area of cooperation for the United States and China in Sub-Saharan Africa is public health. The United States has a strong interest in fighting HIV/AIDS and other health issues in the region. During the administrations of George W. Bush and Barack Obama, U.S. federal funding in these areas has increased significantly. China is also heavily involved in sub-Saharan Africa health initiatives including providing Chinese doctors to work in Africa and training African doctors in China. China's anti-malarial work is particularly impressive. Coordination between China and the United States on these health initiatives would both benefit Sub-Saharan Africa and could build goodwill and understanding between the U.S. and China.

Clash of Values?

One key policy objective of the United States in Sub-Saharan Africa is promoting democracy and human rights.[76] China's support for rogue states and provision of foreign aid to countries without political "strings attached" directly contradicts this U.S. policy objective (as well as the European Union, World Bank, and other donors).[77] China provides condition-free aid to sub-Saharan African countries regardless of their regime type, and this has become a significant concern to other donors. It is unlikely that China will change its philosophical stance on non-interference in the internal affairs of other countries, so these issues will likely continue to cause friction with the United States in the future.

LATIN AMERICA AND THE CARIBBEAN

The western hemisphere is another region of the world where the United States and China dance around each other, with both keeping a careful eye on the other. It is China's emergence as a regional actor that has begun to change the strategic equation in the western hemisphere. While the Monroe Doctrine has been consigned to history, Washington continues to view the region as its "backyard" and keeps a close eye on China's multi-dimensional thrust into the region. Beijing is aware of this and has gone out of its way not to stray into America's "strategic headlights." For example, it has kept its distance from the Hugo Chavez regime in Venezuela; has not been directly involved in supporting insurgencies, socialist movements, or far left-leaning governments; has maintained very low levels of arms sales in the region; has not established any kind of military presence in the region; and, while being supportive of Havana, has kept its ties with Cuba at a relatively low profile.

While Beijing has been careful not to provoke Washington's nascent fears about its "backyard," it has nonetheless established broad-gauged linkages across the region since the 1990s.[78] If one examines four dimensions of China's presence in the region—diplomatic, commercial, cultural, and security—one sees both similarities and differences to the other regions noted above and in Avery Goldstein's chapter.

Diplomatically, it must first be noted that Central America, the Caribbean, and Latin America still represent an area of diplomatic competition with Taiwan. Eleven of the 23 nation-states in the world that still diplomatically recognize Taiwan are in the region. While Beijing and Taipei have declared an unofficial "truce" in their diplomatic competition over the last few years—as relations across the Taiwan Strait have improved—it is still an essential element of Beijing's regional strategy. The other element to bear in mind is that—like its ties in Africa and the Middle East—the Latin American region represents simultaneously China's solidarity with developing countries as well as its desire to foster a multipolar world—so both sides advance so-called "South-South" cooperation. Brazil is a key actor for Beijing in both respects. For their part, it is evident that Latin countries are increasingly trying to pursue "omnidirectional" foreign policies of their own—reaching out more to Europe and Asia, as well as to each other, while trying to reduce dependence on the United States. Thus China fits in their strategies well.

China has forged a variety of diplomatic "strategic partnerships" (no fewer than eight different types!) with most countries in the region, and this designation provides an overarching framework to develop bilateral ties. Brazil's ties with China are particularly strong—perhaps the strongest of all Latin countries—yet Beijing has managed to build sound relations with most other regional states—notably Argentina, Chile, Peru, Venezuela, Mexico, and Cuba. High-level bilateral diplomacy is surprisingly active (if not always reported in the international media). During 1997–2010, over 110 Latin American heads of state and government leaders visited China—while China's president visited the region five times and a steady stream of Politburo-level leaders tour various Latin countries.

Multilaterally, Beijing is also active in a range of organizations in the region. In 2008 China became a full member of the Inter-American Development Bank, it joined the Caribbean Development Bank in 1997, and has held permanent Observer status in the Organization of American States (OAS) since 2004. China has held numerous rounds of dialogues with the Rio Group since 1990, has established a dialogue mechanism with the MERCOSUR common market group, as well as the Caribbean Community and Latin American Conference. China is a full member of APEC, and Beijing has initiated a series of separate forums with the region—including the China-Latin America Forum, the China-Caribbean Economic and Trade Cooperation Forum, the China-Latin America Common Market Dialogue, the China-Andean Community Consultation Forum, and the China-Latin American Business Summit. With all of these multilateral mechanisms, China is now extensively linked multilaterally to the region. Thus, both bilaterally and multilaterally, China has built strong diplomatic and political ties throughout the western hemisphere.

In addition to state-to-state diplomacy, the Chinese Communist Party's (CCP) International Department is also extremely—albeit quietly—active in exchanges with a wide range of political parties across the region (including in countries that diplomatically recognize Taiwan). The CCP now has working relations with more than 80 political parties in almost all 33 countries in the region. This ties China not only to ruling parties, but perhaps more importantly to opposition parties and politicians in waiting—so when they come to

power Beijing is already familiar with them (and vice versa). Party-to-party exchanges also provide Beijing with a good mechanism of intelligence collection.
China also engages in parliamentary exchanges with a number of Latin countries, although this is not nearly as widespread as party-to-party diplomacy.

China's cultural presence is also rising in the region. Chinese tourists are
beginning to flow into the region in large numbers—a result of Beijing having signed group tourism accords with 19 countries. There also exist over 100
pairs of sister province and city relationships between Chinese and Latin localities. Immigration is also growing. There are now, for example, 30,000 ethnic
Chinese living in Argentina, and large numbers in Peru. Another element in
China's attempts to increase its cultural exchanges in the region has been the
establishment of 24 "Confucius Institutes" across the region (out of 350 worldwide), while the Chinese government provides 1,000 university scholarships
for Latin students to study in China every year.[79] Numerous government-
to-government cultural exchange accords have been agreed, and a variety of
universities are beginning to sign their own MOUs as well. Nonetheless, the
level of understanding in the academic world and throughout Latin societies
remains abysmally low.[80]

China's military-security presence in the Latin American region is not
great, but it is expanding. Beijing is very aware that there are already concerns in Washington concerning China's growing presence in the region,
and the military dimension is particularly sensitive. There are several levels
of the Chinese military-security presence in the region. The first are professional military exchanges. Some of these are very high-level. For example, four
members of China's Central Military Commission visited the region between
2008–2010—more than any other region of the world—while a steady stream
of Latin defense ministers and service chiefs visit Beijing annually. China also
trains Latin officers in its staff academies. China's arms sales to, and imports
from, the region are a second type.[81] China sells a relatively small amount of
weaponry and military equipment to Latin America—approximately $150
million per year of helicopters, artillery, armored personnel carriers, vehicles,
K-8 trainer aircraft, radars and command and control equipment, anti-ship
missiles, and light assault weapons—while buying avionics, anti-tank and
anti-air missiles from Brazil. Some of the Sino-Brazilian aerospace cooperation is also military-related. A third type is China's contribution to the multinational UN peacekeeping forces in Haiti. It has also been alleged that China
may have some access to former Soviet built military intelligence communications facilities in Cuba, but this has not been established. All in all, China's
military-security footprint in Latin America is not large, but it is gradually
growing.[82] But it has certainly not yet reached a level where Washington needs
to be seriously concerned.

Commerce is by far the most important dimension of China's presence in Latin America. Trade has been growing at an almost exponential rate, reaching $178.9 billion in 2010. This is a dramatic increase of more than 15 times since 2000 and 160 percent from 2006–2010, and the growth rate seems to be accelerating. China is now the No. 1 trading partner of many Latin nations, having supplanted the United States. Brazil dominates regional trade with China, accounting for almost 40 percent of the total. While two-way trade has grown dramatically in recent years, Latin America still only accounts for about 4 percent of China's total foreign trade. While Brazil is China's largest export market in Latin America, it only ranks as China's No. 20 trading partner.

In terms of trade composition, though, it is heavily concentrated and non-diversified. It is dominated by Chinese purchases of raw materials and agricultural commodities; fully 70 percent of Brazil's exports to China are in two commodities (iron ore and soybeans). China imports large amounts and a wide range of minerals, energy supplies, and raw materials from Latin America. In 2008 this included $16.8 billion in iron ore; $7.4 billion in copper ores; $5.8 billion in refined copper; $9.4 billion in crude and refined oil; and lesser (but still significant) amounts of aluminum, nickel, lead ores, zinc, manganese, and molybdenum. China's purchases of oil (refined and unrefined) from the region are also growing: Venezuelan President Hugo Chavez promised in Beijing in April 2009 to quintuple his country's daily deliveries from 200,000 to 1 million barrels per day. Brazil's oil exports to China increased to 200,000 barrels per day in 2010. China's voracious appetite for raw materials has contributed to the high global price levels for these commodities (and has provided a significant revenue stream for Argentina, Brazil, Chile, and Peru). Today China consumes about 40 percent of the world's coal, 25 percent of the nickel, 25 percent of iron ores, 20 percent of copper ores, and 14 percent of aluminum. China is the No. 1 and 2 leading importer of iron ore and copper in the world.

China also buys large amounts of agricultural products, fish, and wine from the region. Soybeans and soy oil are the second largest category of China's regional imports. China accounts for 40 percent of global soybean imports. About 80 percent of China's imported fish meal comes from Peru and Chile, while 80 percent of its sugar comes from Cuba. Argentina is also a significant source of meats and leather goods for the Chinese market.

In return, Latin countries purchase a range of electronics (largely cell phones and computers) and manufactures. Large volumes of Chinese exports of textiles, footwear and other low-end consumer goods have hit several Latin economies hard—particularly Mexico and Argentina. There is also evidence of China's dumping these goods on Latin markets, taking advantage of the "market economy status" accords China has managed to sign with fifteen Latin countries. Many of these countries signed these accords unwittingly, as Chinese diplomats told them they were "normal" parts of bilateral "strategic partnerships." In fact, MES exempts China from countervailing dumping duties. As a result, Mexico and Argentina have had to institute unilateral safeguards against the flood of Chinese goods since 2007. Fully 50 percent of all Argentine antidumping and counter-trade measures were directed against China that year, and it rose to 90 percent in 2008. Gradually, China is beginning to move up the technological ladder in its regional trade—beginning to trade in autos, motorcycles, aircraft and aircraft parts, electronics, and agro-, bio-, nano-, and information technologies. As it does so, it may begin to alleviate the competitive dynamic in low-end manufactured goods.

To facilitate trade, China has signed bilateral FTAs with Chile, Peru, and Costa Rica. Creative trade financing is also an interesting new area. Beijing struck a $10 billion arrangement with Buenos Aires that permits Argentina reliable access to Chinese currency to pay for its imports from China. This deal follows similar ones Beijing has struck with South Korea, Indonesia, and Belarus.

China is also increasing its direct investment in the region, becoming the second largest destination for Chinese ODI after Asia ($7.3 billion in 2009), according to MOFCOM. However, the vast majority of these financial flows are into the British Virgin Islands ($1.61 bn.) and the Grand Cayman Islands ($5.36 bn.) tax havens.[83] MOFCOM estimates that the total stock of Chinese ODI in the region at the end of 2009 was $30.5 billion.[84] The Economic Commission for Latin America and the Caribbean (ECLAC) provides higher figures, however. ECLAC reports that Chinese ODI into the region was $15 billion in 2010.[85] This represents approximately 10 percent of the total foreign investment into the region.

China also provides some aid to Latin countries. Exact figures are hard to come by, but one study reported that Beijing contributed $26.7 billion between 2002 and 2007.[86] This figure seems high, however, and no doubt partially involves Chinese commercial investments in the region. While no official figures have been released by the Chinese government, the Director General of Latin American and Caribbean Affairs in the Foreign Ministry observed that the real figure is "less than $2 billion per year."[87]

In all these dimensions, China's footprint in Latin America and the Caribbean is growing, and growing quickly. Despite this, the American footprint remains significant. Consider some indicators:

- Bilateral trade totaled $523 billion in 2009—more than three times that of China in the same year.[88]
- The U.S. enjoys eleven Free Trade Agreements (FTAs) in the region—China has two.

- The U.S. is a founding member of the Organization of American States (OAS), Inter-American Development Bank (IADB), and many other regional organizations.
- U.S. direct investment in Latin America and the Caribbean during 2010 totaled $51.9 billion—20 times as much as China and nearly as much as China invested globally in the same year![89] From 2003–2010 the U.S. invested $147 billion in the region.[90]
- In 2010 the United States transferred $627 million in weapons to the region—more than three times China's sales in the same year.[91]
- The United States is bound to the hemisphere's "mutual security assistance and common defense" via the Inter-American Treaty of Reciprocal Assistance (Rio Treaty) of 1947.
- The United States trains around 15,000 military and police personnel per year (based on 2009 figures).[92]

The United States is more broadly engaged in a wide range of aid and training programs throughout the hemisphere. This includes significant drug eradication and counter-trafficking programs in Mexico and Colombia. The Department of State identifies four broad policy priorities in the region: promoting democracy, expanding trade, sustainable economic development, and fostering cooperation.[93]

Thus, both China and the United States are actively engaged in Latin America and the Caribbean region—but America's ties run much longer and deeper. As is the case in transatlantic relations between Europe and the United States, the U.S. has been bonded to Latin countries and societies for more than two centuries. Common values, languages, democratic political systems, market economies, common security, extensive trade and investment, and generations of Latin immigrants settling in the U.S. are all elements that China will never be able to match.

CONCLUSION

This chapter has surveyed the respective presence and policies of the United States and China in Europe, the Middle East, Africa, Latin America and the Caribbean. We have shown that China's presence is growing—often dramatically—in each region, but that (perhaps with the exception of Africa), both the breadth and depth of American presence and influence still dwarfs that of China. As noted at the outset, China's footprint is increasingly broad, but not particularly deep.

We have also demonstrated that the two nations operate quite autonomously from each other in these regions. They are *not* (yet) locked into a geostrategic competitive dynamic, as was the case (to some extent) between the United and former Soviet Union during the Cold War. Each nation's governmental and private sector actors pursue their respective activities in these regions, but not (yet) in *reaction* to the other. This is not to say, however, that the two do not keep a close and sometimes wary eye on each other. The U.S. Government, in particular, is carefully monitoring China's diplomatic, military, cultural, and commercial activities in each of these regions. We have also noted that, for its part, Beijing is conscious of and careful about not impinging on U.S. interests and equities—particularly in the Middle East and Latin America. While not competitive, neither have we discovered much—if any—bilateral cooperation in these third regions. Thus, as noted at the outset, the two nations seem to be "dancing" around, rather than with, each other. This may change over time, as China continues to ramp up its presence globally or if the U.S.-China relationship assumes a more competitive or adversarial geostrategic dynamic in Asia. But, for the time being, the United States and China are operating rather independently of one another on the global stage.

NOTES

1. See Kenneth Lieberthal, "The China-U.S. Relationship Goes Global," *Current History* (September 2009), pp. 243–249; Evan Mederios, "Beijing: The Ambivalent Power," *Current History* (September 2009), pp. 250–256; David Shambaugh, "A New China Requires a New U.S. Strategy," *Current History* (September 2010), pp. 219–226.

2. See, for example, Joseph Nye, *The Future of Power* (New York: Public Affairs, 2011).

3. See Joseph Nye, "The Premature Superpower," *Aspenia* No. 49–50 (2011), pp. 92–97.

4. See David Shambaugh, *China Goes Global: The Partial Power* (Oxford and New York: Oxford University Press, 2013).

5. See, for example, Thomas J. Christensen, "The Advantages of an Assertive China," *Foreign Affairs* (March/April 2011).

6. See Gerald Segal, "Does China Matter?" *Foreign Affairs*, Vol. 78, No. 5 (September/October 1999), pp. 24–36; Also see the essays in Barry Buzan and Rosemary Foot (eds.), *Does China Matter? A Reassessment (Essays in Memory of Gerald Segal)* (London and New York: Routledge, 2004).

7. Also see Elizabeth C. Economy and Adam Segal, "The G-2 Mirage: Why the United States and China Are Not Ready to Upgrade Ties," *Foreign Affairs* (May/June 2009).

8. See: http://www.whitehouse.gov/the-press-office/2011/01/19/us-china-joint-statement; http://www.whitehouse.gov/the-press-office/us-china-joint-statement; http://www.state.gov/r/pa/prs/ps/2011/05/162967.htm.

9. For example, since 2001 the China Policy Program of the Elliott School of International Affairs at George Washington University has partnered with the China Institute of International Studies on a series of conferences on "The U.S.-China Relationship in Global Context."

10. See David Shambaugh, *China and Europe, 1949–1995* (London: SOAS Contemporary China Institute *Research Notes and Studies* No. 11, 1996).

11. See European Commission, *A Long-Term Policy for China-Europe Relations*, COM (95), 279 final, Brussels, July 1995.

12. See David Shambaugh, Eberhard Sandschneider, and Zhou Hong, "From Honeymoon to Marriage: Prospects for the China-Europe Relationship," in Shambaugh, Sandschneider, and Zhou (eds.), *China-Europe Relations: Perceptions, Policies, and Prospects* (London: Routledge, 2008); David Shambaugh, "China-Europe Relations Get Complicated," available at: http://www.brookings.edu/opinions/2007/05china_shambaugh.aspx.

13. European Commission, "Trade: China (2010)," available at: http://ec.europa.eu/trade/creating-opportunities/bilateral-relations/countries/china/.

14. Wei Jianguo, "Partnership Can Prosper," *China Daily*, November 15, 2011. While not an insignificant amount of investment, this contrasts with an accumulated stock of $1.1 trillion of European investment in the United States.

15. Source: Ministry of Commerce (China).

16. Wang Chao, "China Investments Meet Bottleneck Overseas," *China Daily*, December 21, 2010.

17. World Trade Organization, "China," available at: http://stat.wto.org/CountryProfile/WSDBCountryPFView.aspx?Language=E&Country=CN.

18. Keith Bradsher, "China Says It's Unable to Easily Aid Europe," *New York Times*, December 5, 2011.

19. Lou Jiwei, "China Can Help West Build Economic Growth," *Financial Times*, November 27, 2011.

20. See German Marshall Fund of the United States, *Transatlantic Trends 2011*, available at: http://www.gmfus.org/publications_/TT/TTS2011Toplines.pdf.

21. The sovereign debt crisis also has a China dimension, as an estimated 60 percent of China's foreign currency holdings are denominated in U.S. dollars (treasury bills) while 25 percent are denominated in Euros.

22. Source: European Commission, "Trade: the United States (2010)," available at: http://ec.europa.eu/trade/creating-opportunities/bilateral-relations/countries/united-states/.

23. David Shambaugh, "The New Strategic Triangle: U.S. and European Reactions to China's Rise," *The Washington Quarterly* (Summer 2005), pp. 7–25.

24. The most notable examples are: the Stockholm China Forum, co-sponsored by the German Marshall Fund of the United States, Swedish Ministry of Foreign Affairs, and Riksbankens Jubileumsfond; the U.S.-EU-China "Trialogue," co-sponsored by the Aspen Institute, Aspen Italia, and the Central Party School.

25. Discussion with EU official, November 18, 2011, Paris.

26. See, for example, David Shambaugh and Gudrun Wacker (eds.), *American and European Relations with China: Advancing Common Agendas* (Berlin: Stiftung Wissenschaft und Politik, 2008), available at: http://www.swp-berlin.org/fileadmin/contents/products/research_papers/2008_RP03_shambaugh_wkr_ks.pdf.

27. President of the United States, "The National Security Strategy of the United States," available at: http://www.whitehouse.gov/sites/default/files/rss_viewer/national_security_strategy.pdf.

28. Notable studies of contemporary China-Middle East relations include Geoffrey Kemp, *The East Moves West: India, China and Asia's Growing Presence in the Middle*

East (Washington, D.C.: Brookings Institution Press, 2010); Ben Simpfendorfer, *The New Silk Road: How a Rising Arab World Is Turning Away from the West and Rediscovering China* (Basingstoke: Palgrave Macmillan, 2009); Jon B. Alterman and John W. Garver, *The Vital Triangle: China, the United States, and the Middle East* (Washington, D.C.: CSIS Press, 2008); John W. Garver, *China and Iran: Ancient Partners in a Post-Imperial World* (Seattle: University of Washington Press, 2006).

29. For the purposes of this chapter, the region of the Middle East is defined as all League of Arab States members (except Comoros) located both in the Gulf and North Africa plus Iran, Israel, and Turkey.

30. See China Arab States Cooperation Forum website at: http://www.cascf.org/chn/.

31. As of the end of 2011, China had 1,936 personnel deployed worldwide in UN-PKO Missions. This includes personnel in Liberia, Democratic Republic of the Congo, Cote d'Ivoire, southern Sudan (and Darfur region), and Lebanon. Source: United Nations Peacekeeping Operations, available at: http://www.un.org/en/peacekeeping/contributors/2011/oct11_5.pdf.

32. For a detailed discussion of China's anti-piracy operations, see Alison A. Kaufman, *China's Participation in Anti-Piracy Operations Off the Horn of Africa* (Alexandria, VA: CNA Corporation, 2009), available at: http://www.cna.org/sites/default/files/Piracy%20conference%20report.pdf.

33. U.S. Energy Information Administration, *Country Analysis Briefs: China,* available at: www.eia.doe.gov/countries/cab.cfm?fips=CH.

34. Data from U.S. Energy Information Administration, *Country Analysis Briefs: China,* available at: www.eia.doe.gov/countries/cab.cfm?fips=CH.

35. U.S. Energy Information Administration, *Country Analysis Briefs: China,* available at: http://www.eia.doe.gov/countries/cab.cfm?fips=CH.

36. Ibid.

37. U.S. Department of Energy, *Crude Oil and Total Petroleum Imports Top 15 Countries* (2010), available at: http//www.ftp.eia.doe.gov/pub/oil_gas/petroleum/data_publications/company_level_imports/current/import.html.

38. Ibid.

39. It could be argued that the source of China's oil supply (e.g., from Saudi Arabia or Iran) is not especially important because China buys its oil on the international oil market. As a result, source of supply would only be relevant in the case of oil embargo or war. That said, due to the percentage of proven world oil reserves in the Middle East (and the percentage of China's current and future oil originating from the Middle East), we assert that China is particularly dependent on the Middle East as a supplier. Combined with the fact that the Middle East is firmly within the United States' sphere of influence, this oil dependence could result in long term energy security competition in the Middle East between these two powers.

40. U.S. Energy Information Administration, *World Oil Transit Chokepoints,* available at: http://www.eia.gov/countries/regions-topics.cfm?fips=WOTC.

41. For a detailed discussion of China's economic interests in the Middle East, see Geoffrey Kemp, *The East Moves West,* op cit; and Ben Simpfendorfer, *The New Silk Road,* op cit.

42. Statistics calculated by authors from International Monetary Fund (IMF), *Direction of Trade Statistics Database* (2011), available at: http://www.imfstatistics.org.

43. Ibid.

44. See Wang Lian, "Economic and Trade Relations Between China and Middle Eastern Countries," *International Studies*, No. 4 (2008), p. 26; and Jon B.Alterman and John W. Garver, *The Vital Triangle: China, the United States, and the Middle East,* op cit, p. 57.

45. Data compiled by authors from *China Statistical Yearbooks* 2000–2010.

46. Ibid.

47. Data compiled from *Statistical Bulletin of China's Outward Foreign Direct Investment* (Beijing: China Ministry of Commerce, 2009), available at: http://chinainvests .files.wordpress.com/2010/12/2009-mofcom-investment-report1.pdf.

48. United States International Trade Commission, *US Trade by Geographic Regions,* available at: http://dataweb.usitc.gov/scripts/Regions.asp.

49. See President of the United States, "National Security Strategy of the United States," op cit.

50. See Dru Gladney, *Muslim Chinese: Ethnic Nationalism in the People's Republic* (Cambridge: Harvard University Press, 1996, 2nd ed.). For further discussion of the demographics of the Muslim population in China, see United Nations High Commissioner for Refugees, *2010 Report on International Religious Freedom—China*, available at: http://www.unhcr.org/refworld/docid/4cf2d0a85c.html.

51. In July 2009, there was large scale violence between ethnic Han Chinese and Uigurs in Xinjiang. According to Chinese authorities, 137 of those killed were Han, 46 were Uighur and 1 was from the Hui ethnic group. See Edward Wong, "China Raises Death Toll in Ethnic Clashes to 184," *New York Times*, July 10, 2009, available at: http:// www.nytimes.com/2009/07/11/world/asia/11china.html.

52. For a detailed discussion of al-Qaeda's evolving approach to China see Brian Fishman, "Al-Qaeda and the Rise of China Jihadi Geopolitics in a Post-Hegemonic World," *The Washington Quarterly* (Summer 2011), pp. 47–62.

53. See John W. Garver, "Is China Playing a Dual Game in Iran?" *The Washington Quarterly* (Winter 2011), pp. 75–78; Willem van Kemenade, *Iran's Relations with China and the West: Cooperation and Confrontation in Asia* (The Hague: Netherland Institute of International Relations (Clingendael), November 2009; Sanam Vakil, "Iran: Balancing East Against West," *The Washington Quarterly* (Autumn 2006), pp. 51–65; Shen Dingli, "Iran's Nuclear Ambitions Test China's Wisdom," *The Washington Quarterly* (Spring 2006), pp. 55–66.

54. See David H. Shinn, "China and the Conflict in Darfur," *Brown Journal of World Affairs* (Fall/ Winter 2009), pp. 85–99.

55. UN Security Council Resolution 1973 (2011). See press release for China's concerns about the resolution: United Nations Department of Public Information, "Security Council Approves 'No-Fly' Zone over Libya, Authorizing 'All Necessary Measures' to Protect Civilians, By Vote of 10 in Favor and 5 Abstentions," New York, March 17, 2011, available at: http://www.un.org/News/Press/docs//2011/sc10200.doc.htm.

56. See Michael Wines, "China Says It Will Tighten Arms Sales Procedures," *New York Times*, September 6, 2011.

57. See United Nations Department of Public Information, "Security Council Fails to Adopt Draft Resolution Condemning Syria's Crackdown on Anti-Goverment Protestors, Owing to Veto by Russian Federation, China," available at: http://www.un.org/ News/Press/docs//2011/sc10403.doc.htm; Neil MacFarquhar and Michael Schwirtz, "With Rare Double UN Veto on Syria, Russia and China Try to Shield Friend," *New York Times*, October 6, 2011; and Michael Schwirtz, "Russia Rejects Criticism of Its UN Veto on Syria," *New York Times*, February 7, 2012.

58. See Bruce W. Jentleson, "Beware of the Duck Test," *Washington Quarterly* (Summer 2011), pp. 137–149; Lee Smith, "Weakening Washington's Middle East Influence," *Middle East Quarterly* (Summer 2011), pp. 3–10.

59. In the past, China-Israel relations have caused tension in U.S.-China relations. One important aspect of China-Israel relations is China's desire to purchase military technology from Israel. U.S. concerns over these relations began in the late 1990s and on numerous occasions forced Israel to halt weapon sales to China. Since 2005, under U.S. pressure, Israeli military technology sales to China have ceased. For a detailed discussion of this aspect of U.S.-Israel-China relations, see Alterman and Garver, *The Vital Triangle*, op cit. pp. 71–72.

60. In this chapter, Sub-Saharan Africa is defined as all non-Arab League Member states in Africa plus Comoros. Notable studies of contemporary China-Africa relations include Deborah Brautigam, *The Dragon's Gift: The Real Story of China in Africa* (New York and Oxford: Oxford University Press, 2009); Sarah Raine, *China's African Challenges* (London: International Institute of Strategic Studies, 2009); Serge Michel and Michel Beuret, *China Safari: On the Trail of Beijing's Expansion in Africa* (New York: Nation Books, 2009); Ian Taylor, *China's New Role in Africa* (Boulder: Lynne Rienner, 2009); Chris Alden, Daniel Large, and Ricardo Soares de Oliveira, *China Returns to Africa: A Rising Power and a Continent Embrace* (London: Hurst and Company, 2008); Kweku Ampiah and Sanusha Naidu (eds.), *Crouching Tiger, Hidden Dragon? Africa and China* (Scottsville, South Africa: University of KwaZulu-Natal Press, 2008); Robert I. Rotberg (ed.), *China into Africa: Trade, Aid, and Influence* (Washington, D.C.: Brookings Institution Press, 2008); Arthur Waldron (ed.), *China in Africa* (Washington, D.C.: Jamestown Foundation, 2008); Chris Alden, *China in Africa* (London: Palgrave Macmillan, 2007); Firoze Manji and Stephen Marks, *African Perspectives on China in Africa* (Capetown, South Africa: Fahamu, 2007); and Ian Taylor, *China and Africa: Engagement and Compromise* (London and New York: Routledge, 2006).

61. For example, in 2007 China's Official Development Assistance (ODA) to Africa (including North Africa) was estimated at $1.4 bn. That same year, ODA from other traditional bilateral donors were United States $7.6 bn., France $4.9 bn., United Kingdom $2.8 bn., Japan $2.7 bn., and Germany $2.5 bn. ODA includes grants, zero-interest loans and concessional loans. See Deborah Brautigam, *The Dragon's Gift*, ibid, pp. 162–188.

62. See Forum on China-Africa Cooperation website: http://www.focac.org/eng/.

63. See website on Forum for Economic and Trade Cooperation between China and Portuguese Speaking Countries: http://english.mofcom.gov.cn/subject/chinaportuguese/index.shtml.

64. As of December 31, 2010, these include: Benin 1, Botswana 1, Cameroon 1, Ethiopia 1, Kenya 2, Liberia 1, Madagascar 1, Nigeria 2, Rwanda 1, South Africa 4, Togo 1, Zambia 1, and Zimbabwe 1. For full listing of Confucius Institutes worldwide, see Han Ban website: http://english.hanban.org/.

65. See Lauren Ploch, *Africa Command: U.S. Strategic Interests and the Role of the U.S. Military in Africa* (Washington, D.C.: Congressional Research Service, 2011), pp. 13–19.

66. See President of the United States, "National Security Strategy of the United States," op cit.

67. U.S. Energy Information Administration, *Country Analysis Briefs: China*, op cit.

68. Ibid.

69. U.S. Department of Energy, *Crude Oil and Total Petroleum Imports Top 15 Countries* (2010) (Washington, D.C.: U.S. Department of Energy, 2011).

70. International Monetary Fund (IMF), *Direction of Trade Statistics Database*.

71. Ibid.

72. United States International Trade Commission, *U.S. Trade by Geographic Regions*.

73. Data compiled by authors from *China Statistical Yearbooks* 2000–2010.

74. Ibid.

75. Data compiled from *Statistical Bulletin of China's Outward Foreign Direct Investment* (Beijing: China Ministry of Commerce, 2009).

76. See President of the United States, "National Security Strategy of the United States," op cit.

77. For a detailed discussion of China's foreign aid, see Deborah Brautigam, *The Dragon's Gift*, op cit.

78. For studies of China-Latin America relations, see "Latin America's Response to China's Rise," special issue of the *Journal of Current Chinese Affairs (China Aktuell)* Vol. 41, No. 1 (2012); Adrian Hearn and José Luis León-Manríquez (eds.), *China Engages Latin America: Tracing the Trajectory* (Boulder, CO: Lynne Rienner, 2011); Riordan Roett and Guadalupe Paz (eds.), *China's Expansion into the Western Hemisphere* (Washington, D.C.: Brookings Institution Press, 2008); R. Evan Ellis, *China in Latin America: The Whats & Wherefores* (Boulder, CO: Lynne Rienner, 2009); Javier Santiso (ed.), *The Visible Hand of China in Latin America* (Paris: OECD, 2007); Kevin P. Gallagher and Roberto Porzecanski, *The Dragon in the Room: China & The Future of Latin American Industrialization* (Stanford: Stanford University Press, 2010); Robert Devlin et al. (eds.), *The Emergence of China: Opportunities and Challenges for Latin America and the Caribbean* (Washington, D.C.: Inter-American Development Bank, 2006); Alex E. Fernández Jilberto and Barbara Hogenboom (eds.), *Latin America Facing China: South-South Relations Beyond the Washington Consensus* (New York and Oxford: Berghan Books, 2010); R. Evan Ellis, *The Expanding Chinese Footprint in Latin America* (Paris: IFRI Center for Asian Studies, 2012).

79. Statement by Yang Wanming, Director General, Latin American and Caribbean Affairs Department, Ministry of Foreign Affairs, Inter-American Dialogue, Washington, D.C., March 9, 2012. Wu Hongying, "China and the U.S. in Latin America: Cooperation or Competition?" paper presented to the Fifth Dialogue on U.S.-China Relations in Global Context, June 2, 2011, Beijing.

80. For further discussion, see David Shambaugh, "Foreword," in Adrian H. Hearn and José Luis León-Manríquez (eds.), *China Engages Latin America: Tracing the Trajectory* (Boulder: Lynne Rienner, 2011), pp. ix–xviii.

81. See Cynthia Watson, "China's Arms Sales to Latin America: Another Arrow in the Quiver," *China Brief*, Vol. 10, No. 4 (2010), available at: http://www.jamestown.org/single/?no_cache=1&tx_ttnews[tt_news]=36053.

82. See R. Evan Ellis, *China-Latin America Military Engagement: Good Will, Good Business, and Strategic Position* (Carlisle Barracks, PA: U.S. Army War College Strategic Studies Institute, 2011).

83. 2009 Statistical Bulletin of China's Outward Foreign Direct Investment, op cit.

84. Ibid.

85. See Economic Commission for Latin America and the Caribbean, *Foreign Direct Investment in Latin America and the Caribbean* (Santiago, Chile: 2011).

86. See Jörn Dosch and David S.G. Goodman, "China and Latin America: Complementarities, Competition, and Globalization," *Journal of Current Chinese Affairs*, Vol. 41, No. 1 (2012), p. 12.

87. Yang Wanming, statement at Inter-American Dialogue, March 9, 2012, Washington, D.C.

88. Source: Congressional Research Service, *U.S.-Latin American Trade: Recent Trends and Policy Issues* (Washington, D.C.: Congressional Research Service, 2010), Appendices A & B.

89. Source: U.S. Department of Commerce Bureau of Economic Analysis, *U.S. Direct Investment Abroad: Financial Outflows without Current Cost Adjustment (2010)*, available at: http://www.bea.gov/international/di1usdbal.htm.

90. Cited in William J. Burns, "Asia, the Americas, and U.S. Strategy for a New Century," available at: http://www.state.gov/s/d/2011/176667.htm.

91. Source: Center for International Policy Washington Office on Latin America (WOLA), available at: http://justf.org/taxonomy/term/31.

92. Source: U.S. Department of State, *Foreign Military Training and DoD Engagement Activities of Interest* (2009–2010), available at: http://www.state.gov/t/pm/rls/rpt/fmtrpt/.

93. U.S. Department of State, Bureau of West Hemisphere Affairs, available at: http://www.state.gov/p/wha/.

14

U.S.-China Interactions in Global Governance and International Organizations

Rosemary Foot

The People's Republic of China and the United States have been interacting in international organizations and other associated global governance mechanisms[1] in a few cases for about four decades and in many others since Vice-Premier Deng Xiaoping, the architect of China's "Reform and Opening" policy, determined in the early 1980s that Beijing's integration into global mechanisms would help maintain regional and global peace and stability. Peace and stability were critical, he believed, to successful attainment of the Chinese leadership's policy priorities: economic development, national unity, social stability, and maintenance of the socialist system led by the Chinese Communist Party.[2] Whereas the United States was actively "present at the creation"[3] of these crucial post–World War II institutions, Beijing only joined Washington as one of the Permanent Members of the U.N. Security Council in 1971, as well as other core organizations such as the International Monetary Fund (IMF), the World Bank and the Conference on Disarmament in 1980, and the U.N. Commission on Human Rights in 1982 (now the U.N. Human Rights Council). When the G-20 mechanism was created in the late 1990s, China soon emerged alongside the United States as a key member, and has become especially central to the discussions since the Global Financial Crisis (GFC) of 2008.

Academic analysis of China's record of participation in these organizations over three decades largely has been appraised positively, though few analysts would describe China as having contributed directly or creatively to the provision of global public goods. In 2003, for example, Alastair Iain Johnston argued that "The People's Republic of China (PRC) is more integrated into, and more cooperative within, regional and global political and economic systems than ever in its history."[4] Others writing after this date often concurred (as I discuss below).

However, exceptions to this generally positive appraisal have begun to cluster in the period since 2008. From that date, China's multilateral diplomacy has sometimes been described as challenging, disturbing or disrupting the various global governance arrangements with which we have become familiar.[5] Few have yet matched Elizabeth Economy's position, but it may not be long before the unease associated with determining the nature and quality of China's participation in global governance leads to a wider acceptance of her argument. As Economy pointedly puts its: "Beijing has launched a 'go out' strategy designed to remake global norms and institutions. China is transforming the world as it transforms itself." In her view, we need to put aside any notion of China as a status quo actor, and had better recognize instead that "China has become a revolutionary power."[6]

Explanations for both the degree of Chinese integration into international organizations as well as this perceived negative change in its behavior often connect quite closely with the state of the Sino-American relationship. In the former case, the United States has regularly used incentives and disincentives of a political and economic nature to induce cooperation.[7] More recently, increases in China's relative power compared with the United States are said to have fueled conservative and nationalist voices in China calling for the tangible realization of benefits from this increase in power.[8] China emerged in 2010 with the world's second largest economy and the world's second largest defense budget and, for some among this group of Chinese nationalists, this should result in something more tangible than a diffuse increase in status.

Moreover, these increases in China's material power have occurred at the same time as the U.S. government has struggled to deal convincingly with the aftermath of the global financial crisis amid a widespread perception that all shreds of bipartisanship in policymaking have broken down, resulting in an unproductive stasis. This is disturbing for some because we had become used to operating in a world in which the United States has been the hegemonic power, central to the construction and maintenance of global order.[9] In the post–Cold War era, Washington had appeared to enjoy increased latitude deriving from its unrivaled resources and the implosion of its major strategic enemy, the former Soviet Union.[10] However, now a multipolar system appears to beckon at a rate that makes adaption difficult and challenging and a change in the "rules of the game" more possible.

Since a resurgent China is seen as the new, pivotal, actor in a number of international venues, and more able than other of the so-called emerging powers to effect a change in the rules, this suggests it is necessary in this chapter to give somewhat more attention to Beijing rather than to Washington's behavior, assessing the relative "newcomer's" quality of international institutional participation. In addition, as Kerry Brown has aptly put it, the world "will increasingly see itself as a stakeholder in China just as China has been encouraged to be a stakeholder in the international system,"[11] a statement that reinforces the sense that the central analytical and political challenge is to understand what China is doing both externally and internally. Nevertheless, it is important to remember that China's external actions over a long period have often been conditioned by its perception of what it, together with the United States, may stand to gain or lose in a material and social sense from arrangements worked out in multilateral settings, or what U.S. behavior indicates about the strength and autonomous legitimacy of a particular international organizational or governance arrangement. In more recent years, the United States finds itself in a somewhat similar position. American officials, analysts and commentators have shown increasing awareness of how quickly global events and the processes of globalization have served to reshape the global power hierarchy, greatly raising the importance of its bilateral relationship with China.[12] Thus Washington, too, more often assesses the merits of its global governance-related behavior in terms of the actual and potential impact this has on the Sino-American relationship itself, as well as on its own relative standing in the hierarchy of global power.

I argue, then, that an interactive Sino-American relationship requires attention to these relativities and to *both* states' behavior and perceptions. Discussion of China's actions in the absence of consideration of U.S. behavior in the same or other multilateral organizational settings would seriously compromise our understanding of Beijing's participation in such organizations. Increasingly, this is also the case with respect to the United States. Neither should we assume on the basis of a recent rise in bilateral tensions and of China's relative power that the interactive processes and outcomes lack nuance or should be perceived solely in zero-sum terms.[13] Indeed, we should think of this as a range of possible interactions where there are clearly issues of global governance over which China and the U.S. have an antagonistic relationship with zero-sum positioning; where they have ostensibly disagreed, but have both derived satisfaction from the resultant stasis that they have created because it constrains an international agreement that neither likes; where there is a compatibility in their positions (but often on the basis of different values or interests); and where their positions may differ in approach but, in combination, and in ways that may not always be directly intended, may be beneficial for global governance.

In uncovering this range of activities I therefore challenge the argument that China is deliberately setting out to remake global norms and institutions, arguing instead that its often self-regarding strategy sometimes facilitates co-operation and on other occasions constrains or promotes reform of existing international organizations. I also use the empirical evidence in what follows to question whether 2008 should be regarded as a fundamental turning away from a Chinese strategy of re-emergence from within international institu-tions, a strategy followed quite closely for over three decades. However, I do acknowledge that increases in relative power have made Chinese officials more willing to speak out in support of their objectives. These officials also show a higher level of responsiveness to the broader range of Chinese interests that have emerged and have to be accommodated within a more pluralist domestic political setting.

I begin first with brief reflection on the problems of assessing and gener-alizing about state behavior in relation to global governance before offering broad descriptions of U.S. and Chinese attitudes towards the multilateral ar-rangements that are the substance of governance, including their perceptions of each others' behavior within such bodies. Next, I provide some representa-tive examples of the various types of interactions that have been occurring across the range referred to in the previous paragraph. In particular, I focus on interactions involving the U.N. Security Council because, as Ian Hurd has argued, it has the potential to be the most powerful of all the world's organiza-tions involved in global governance.[14] However, I also use illustrations from other key global organizations, some of which are subsidiaries of the Unit-ed Nations, such as the IMF, and U.N. Framework Convention on Climate Change (UNFCCC), as well as the informal G-20 grouping.[15] These examples more often show persistent trends in Chinese and U.S. behavior rather than highlighting 2008 as a significant turning point in China's approach. Finally, I briefly assess the implications of U.S.-China interactions for the future of global governance.

THE PROBLEMS OF EVALUATING BEHAVIOR

There are recognized difficulties in measuring a state's behavior with respect to the various international norms, treaties and other multilateral arrangements that have been created in order to help us with governing the globe. For exam-ple, global governance mechanisms may be made up of a range of broad prin-ciples or may be associated with more detailed rules and behavioral standards. This matters because, in general, the more specific are the requirements, the less willing states may be to conform. Global regimes may also contain several different components, some of which are in tension with each other, and can attract varying levels of compliance.[16] This gives states the option of "cherry-picking" among the requirements of a global normative framework thereby opening opportunities for a government to argue that it is indeed in compliance with that framework.

States may also participate passively or more actively in different eras. They may be minimally compliant or may engage in behavior that is more beneficial to the core values of a particular organization or global mechanism.[17] Distinguishing between minimal compliance and deeper examples of cooperation and assessing whether such patterns of behavior are consistent over time is a major analytical challenge. Then there are questions of domestic capacity: a government may want to comply but be unable to implement certain of the obligations because of a lack of institutional and legal capability—a point that has often been made about China in reference to its early years of involvement with the nuclear non-proliferation norm and the climate change regime. Indeed, for these and other similar reasons, it is difficult to think of any state that has a perfect record of compliance with international organizational requirements.[18] Finally, when we evaluate behavior with respect to global governance we are dealing with more than one form of multilateralism. That concept can have both minimalist and maximalist understandings attached to it. Minimalist forms refer to coordination among three or more political actors. Maximalist ones imply that actors are willing to constrict their areas of policy autonomy in order to adhere to agreed rules, norms and standards that apply to all. They may also result in a multilateral arrangement having supranational authority.[19]

These analytical, measurement and definitional issues need to be borne in mind when we give summary assessments of a state's behavior encouraging us to treat the idea of "status quo" versus "revolutionary power" as an axis rather than an either/or framework of analysis.

THE UNITED STATES, CHINA, AND GLOBAL GOVERNANCE

The United States

Despite these complexities, there is something of a consensus in the academic literature on U.S. behavior in reference to global governance and multilateral organizational arrangements. It has long been argued that the U.S. relationship with international organizations or multilateralism more broadly is at best ambivalent. In summary form, the United States has been described as an "instrumental multilateralist"—a state that within both regional and global organizations and in both the security and economic fields "picks and chooses from a range of possible approaches, depending on the issue, its interests, and changing international and domestic conditions."[20] Writing in 2002, Stewart Patrick and Shepard Forman noted the "deepening of global interdependence" and expansion of "transnational problems that no one country can resolve on its own." Yet, they went on to lament that the United States nevertheless has been "deeply ambivalent about multilateral engagement and highly selective in assuming new international commitments."[21] Moreover, even while we should acknowledge that the U.S. government has played a leading role in establishing several of the key global governance arrangements of the modern era, it has exhibited a persistent tendency to depart from these arrangements when it believed it necessary to do so.

The U.S. position at the peak of the global hierarchy is an important factor in explaining this tendency. U.S. hegemony has afforded it broad discretion to use a variety of means—from unilateral to multilateral—to obtain its objectives. But this selectivity also derives from America's exceptionalist impulse that has led it to presume close correspondence between its ideals and the needs of other external actors, wedded to a related self-perception as the "ultimate custodian of international order." As Edward C. Luck has written, the United States has assumed "its national values and practices are universally valid and its policy positions are moral and proper, not just expedient."[22] This amalgam of beliefs has encouraged U.S. policymakers sometimes to ignore multilateral venues, and on occasion to attempt to reform or revise certain collective arrangements when these are seen as being incompatible with both U.S. needs and the perceived needs of global order.[23] Thus, both relative power and America's sense of uniqueness have made it willing to stand aside from a global consensus with respect to global governance arrangements when need be and sometimes to attempt to reshape these frameworks entirely. At a time, for example, when other members of the P-5 have eschewed regular use of the veto, the United States has continued to wield it quite frequently, between 1990 and 2007 casting some 15 out of the 22 cases of use.[24] When it comes to determining the use of force, its view of U.N. prerogatives is also robust and distinctive. As Joseph R. Biden, now Vice-President in the Obama administration, put it to the Senate Foreign Relations Committee when responding to U.N. Secretary General Kofi Annan's statement that the U.N. Security Council was the "sole source of legitimacy" on the use of force: "nobody in the Senate agrees with that. . . . [Annan] is dead, flat, unequivocally wrong."[25]

It is hardly surprising, therefore, given these U.S. perceptions that as China became more engaged internationally, U.S. officials and other commentators would choose to put much emphasis on the need for China to become a responsible participant in a world order that the United States believed it had shaped to good effect, largely on its own, and would continue to shape. Robert Zoellick's "China as a Responsible Stakeholder" speech of 2005 has been given the greatest attention in this regard, but there have been many similar exhortations in the past, including President Nixon's call in 1971 to draw China "into a constructive relationship with the world community," to Michel Oksenberg's statement of 1989: "Our strategy toward China since 1971 has been to draw it out of its isolation and to integrate it in the international community. . . . Our expectation was that a forthcoming posture toward China would prompt its leaders gradually to accept and abide by international standards of behavior."[26]

China

China entered international organizations and other global arrangements aware of this U.S role in creating many core global institutions and also its occasional selectivity in behavior. Added to this awareness are two related if somewhat contradictory positions: that the U.S. bends many international organizations and global norms to its will, but that China's strong adherence to some of these bodies and the norms that they embody can be used as ways of undermining U.S. legitimacy and therefore power, and as a useful means of illustrating that China is a more reliable global actor clearly engaged in a peaceful rise. Despite China's own patchy record, especially in the Maoist era, in the area of nuclear non-proliferation, China's nuclear weapons experts have described the U.S.-Indian nuclear deal, first negotiated in 2005 during the George W. Bush era, in ways that underline both the role of treaties and the selectivity in U.S. behavior. The agreement, they write, "weakens an important plank in the N[on] P[roliferation] T[reaty] . . . effectively condones [India's] nuclear weapons program . . . demonstrates that America's nuclear policy is selective and biased . . . [and shows that d]ouble standards are everywhere: some countries are demonized and sanctioned for their nuclear weapons programs, others are given tacit consent and even cooperation."[27]

Nevertheless, despite this underlying skepticism about the relationship between international organizations and powerful states, China's behavior in these venues—with some important exceptions—has shown many of the co-operative characteristics that Johnston alluded to in his study of 2003. From a low starting point associated with the Maoist era, China has broadly become more integrated and involved in global governance in ways that have not posed deep challenges to global order, at least so far.[28] As Ann Kent concluded on the basis of her 2007 study of China's levels of compliance with four global regimes: "China may be judged to have complied reasonably with the constituent instruments of international organizations and with the norms, principles, and rules of their associated treaties. Indeed, when measured against the base level of its compliance and cooperation in 1980, its progress has been remarkable."[29] Thomas J. Christensen, while noting negative developments in 2009 and 2010, nevertheless praised China's creative and proactive global governance actions between 2006 and 2008—his period as an official in the Bush administration.[30] Evan Medeiros describes specific Chinese policies towards

nuclear non-proliferation over a longer period and concluded broadly positively: "China has joined numerous non-proliferation treaties and agreements,
narrowed the scope and content of its sensitive exports, institutionalized its
commitments in national laws and regulations, and built a cadre of non-proliferation specialists both within and outside government circles."[31] Moreover, it
has made some effort to promote that particular normative framework beyond
its own territory—a particular kind of commitment that brings the policy into
direct competition with its other state-to-state interests. In the area of global
finance, despite clearly being a "norm-taker" rather than a "norm-maker" in
the banking regulatory system (the so-called Basel rules), again China has
largely conformed to these regulatory requirements and in 2003 set up its own
China Banking Regulatory Commission. Since that time, China has accepted
the G-20 consensus that the Basel framework remains vital but needs to be re-
formed along the lines laid out in the G-20 summits since November 2008. In
March 2009 it joined the Basel Committee on Banking Standards and agreed
to engage in an ongoing process of peer review aimed at promoting the implementation of these standards.[32]

Of course, there are critical exceptions to this generally cooperative trend,
exceptions that can be explained quite frequently by the liberal values at the
root of most global governance arrangements (values that are outlined in G.
John Ikenberry's chapter), and the perceived negative domestic outcomes that
would result from full adherence. For example, since 2004 Beijing has become
less accommodating to IMF demands that it revalue the *renminbi* (discussed
in more detail below). Although it has been staunchly supportive of the nuclear non-proliferation norm in terms of its rhetoric, improved domestic regulations, and treaty adherence, it remains reluctant consistently to impose tough
sanctions on either North Korea or Iran for their nuclear-weapons related activity.[33] In such cases, its stances can partly be explained by its perception that
accommodation will have negative consequences for China's domestic priorities of development and social stability. Where global and domestic needs
come into alignment, however, as in the case of the Basel regulations which
domestic reformers used to try to effect reform of China's fragile banking sector, then we have seen behavior in Beijing that is broadly supportive of global
voluntary rules, even those initially determined entirely by others.

However, where there is evidence of positive Chinese behavior in multilateral settings, this is not meant to imply that China is a committed multilateralist
in the strongest meaning of multilateralism as defined earlier. Beijing generally
remains ambivalent about the liberal international order and uncomfortable in
bodies that act too independently of the states that make up their membership.
This is manifested in its preferences at the regional level for organizations with
weak secretariats and with decision-making rules based on consensus, and at

the global level for a U.N. Security Council that retains veto power for the five permanent members. Moreover, these types of preferences may more recently have grown stronger: with increases in its relative power, it has come to see these bodies sometimes as venues for demanding more of China, rather than arrangements from which all peoples and states can derive absolute gains. As Shi Yinhong has put it: "Among the primary enduring concerns determining China's external posture and foreign policy, there has been what could be described as an overwhelming concern: the Chinese government often feels that the west's demands, in terms of shouldering international responsibility, will surpass what China can do and thereby hurt its economic and other interests."[34]

Thus, China like the United States wishes to retain as much autonomy over its policy decisions as possible. However, unlike Washington, Beijing has neither played a dominant role in constructing global governance mechanisms, nor operated a kind of custodial role in their operation. That role has led the United States into a patterned history of picking and choosing among multilateral organizations and among unilateral, bilateral and multilateral means in reference to global order issues. On balance, China has perceived benefits from involvement in some international organizations and global governance mechanisms especially where they align with its domestic goals. Important, too, is that engagement in these multilateral mechanisms has been perceived as useful reinforcement for its rhetoric of "peaceful rise" and "peaceful development," and sometimes can serve to differentiate its behavior in positive ways from its major strategic competitor.

SINO-AMERICAN INTERACTION TYPES

U.S.-Chinese interactions at the global level fall into four main categories: (1) those that are antagonistic with zero-sum outcomes; (2) those where there is explicit disagreement but joint satisfaction with the outcome; (3) those that demonstrate the two states' coincidences of interest; (4) and those where their approaches may differ, but when combined may be of overall benefit to global order.

Antagonistic and Zero-Sum Interactions

A major example of the first type relates to global economic imbalances, now a major feature of G-20 deliberations, and of a longer standing concern within the IMF, as well as in Sino-American bilateral discussions (for detail on the latter, see Bonnie Glaser's chapter in this volume). The November 2010 meeting of the G-20 in Seoul was particularly prickly, with one report describing the proceedings as "stormy" and another quoting the spokesperson for the Republic of Korea's G-20 presidential committee as noting that in the preliminary discussions among deputy finance ministers "voices were raised. . . . They wouldn't compromise. They actually had to keep the door open because the debate was so heated and we were lacking oxygen."[35] President Barack Obama criticized the Chinese leadership openly and directly at the time of that 2010 gathering, stating that the Chinese *yuan* was "undervalued and China spends enormous amounts of money intervening in the market to keep it undervalued." President Hu Jintao countered with a call for the debt-burdened United States to adopt "responsible policies," and maintain a stable dollar, and China's Vice-Minister of Finance demanded that Washington be more attentive to the negative impact of its policies of "quantitative easing."[36] There have also been several Chinese statements at the highest official levels indicating that *renminbi* revaluation is not a matter for discussion within international forums, that the matter of currency appreciation has serious domestic consequences for China, and that these need to be taken into account by outside actors like the IMF and G-20 as well as the United States.[37]

U.S.-Chinese relations over this matter deteriorated further—at least rhetorically—after the U.S. Congress finally voted to raise the U.S. debt ceiling in August 2011, a move followed by the rating agency Standard and Poor's decision to downgrade America's long-term debt. As Xinhua News Agency put it, the U.S. had to "cure its addiction to debts" and "live within its means." This meant cutting its "gigantic military expenditure" and "bloated social welfare" programs. Meanwhile Chinese bloggers criticized their government for being so foolish as to invest about half the country's foreign exchange reserves in U.S. treasuries.[38] According to the Chinese scholar, Zhu Feng, officials at the Chinese Ministry of Finance sat in their offices "wringing their hands."[39]

There is little doubt that these polarized positions have absorbed much of the G-20's attention, stymieing its ability over the longer term to deal effectively with the serious consequences of the global financial crisis. China has also become more vocal in its criticisms of U.S. policy and more determined than ever to keep the matter of currency revaluation off the global agenda. Nevertheless, the explanation for this polarity and increasing vitriol are complex and go beyond the argument that increased tension over the matter relates solely to increases in China's relative economic power dating especially from 2008. This is an issue that emerged in a more significant way in U.S.-China relations since 2005 when Chinese surpluses grew suddenly, making it by 2006 the world's major surplus country at a time when the U.S. was by far the largest deficit country.[40]

More important to any understanding of the Chinese perspective than 2008 increases in relative power is that the original IMF norm dating from the establishment of the Bretton Woods institutions required mutual adjustment by surplus and deficit countries, a requirement that the U.S.-China joint statement of November 2009 seemed to recognize. As that measured statement put it:

China will continue to implement the policies to adjust economic structure, raise household incomes, expand domestic demand to increase contribution of consumption to G[ross] D[omestic] P[roduct] growth and reform its social security system. The United States will take measures to increase national saving as a share of GDP and promote sustainable non-inflationary growth. To achieve this, the United States is committed to returning the federal budget deficit to a sustainable path and pursuing measures to encourage private saving.[41]

Unfortunately, however, this symmetrical and sensible approach was not a deeply embedded idea either within the IMF or within these two countries and there was a reversion to what had been the dominant U.S. policy from the late 1970s: an IMF focus on surplus country reserve accumulation and a weakening of IMF constraints on U.S. monetary and fiscal policies. Indeed, as Chinese officials argued in 2005 in ways that are reminiscent of language used in the late 2000s, "[A] resolution to the problem of global imbalances required a concerted effort by all major countries, led first by credible action in the United States to reduce its fiscal deficit and increase national savings."[42] Frustrated with China in the mid-2000s, the U.S. sought further refinement of the IMF surveillance rules. The resulting 2007 *Decision on Bilateral Surveillance over Members' Policies* tightened IMF surveillance over exchange rate movements, a policy that China saw as targeting it and that irritated Beijing because it prompted further speculative capital flows into the country. Most unusually for a board that normally operates by consensus, China voted against the proposal. It withdrew from the bilateral surveillance process during 2007–2008, only returning to it in 2009, though it remains wary of surveillance. For China, then, from the mid-2000s onwards, it has come to see the rules as unfair, the institutions too responsive to U.S. interests and in need of reform, and the multilateral venues as unsympathetic to the domestic costs of exchange rate adjustment. China has increased its voting weight within the IMF's Executive Board, but it is worth noting that this has only raised it to 3.81 percent in 2010, smaller than that of France and the U.K. combined and far less than the U.S. at 16.73 percent.[43] China will remain suspicious, therefore, of an IMF that appears unresponsive to its domestic concerns and the prospects for the resolution of the matter of global imbalances via the G-20 are not good either.

Antagonism with Joint Satisfaction over Outcomes

There have been occasions, however, when U.S.-Chinese interactions are overtly antagonistic—either because of a valid assumption about an incompatibility in values or because of the tone of official statements—but in fact implicitly promote an underlying and actual coincidence of interest in terms of the outcome.

Much of the relevant discussion in this section coincides with a U.S. administration under George W. Bush that, as Johnston noted, converged with China in its preference for a more traditional definition of state sovereignty.[44] However, given the continuing power of conservative Republicans in the United States, many of these coincidences of interest remain in place, even at a time of an administration under President Obama that is more multilateralist and less nationalist in its approach.

Global climate change negotiations, particularly in the period after 1997 and the signature of the Kyoto Protocol, as well as during the George W. Bush era, provide illustration of this type of interaction. In these negotiations, there has been strong U.S. and Chinese disagreement over what it means to promote the central norm associated with preventing further anthropogenic harm, that of accepting "common but differentiated responsibilities." Relations at the Copenhagen conference in December 2009 were particularly strained and unproductive.

China has long been seen in the United States as the source of many of the difficulties of enacting policy in this area. U.S. commentators, especially in the U.S. Congress, have argued strongly that the 1997 Kyoto Protocol is unfair in placing all the adjustment costs on the developed world leaving leading-emitting countries like China required to do little or nothing. China, on the other hand has argued that developed countries like the United States caused the problem in the first place, are profligate in terms of energy usage, and have been through their emissions-intensive phase of urban and industrial development. They also point out that many of the goods produced in China and that lead to emissions are consumed elsewhere, especially in the U.S. market. These antagonistic positions have seriously constrained the unlocking of a climate protection deal and a suitable successor to the Kyoto arrangements.

However, many in both the United States and China would applaud that lack of movement in the climate protection legislation associated with the UNFCCC process. A reluctance to make progress in this issue area may even have led to forms of collusion between the two governments. Ann Kent reports that both appeared to work together at negotiations in 2005 to weaken attempts to work out post-Kyoto arrangements.[45] That year, some four years after the U.S. left the Kyoto process, the Bush administration launched the Asia Pacific Partnership on Clean Development and Climate, which China joined and no doubt supported in part because of its voluntary rather than mandatory requirements. China also joined the Major Economies Forum on Energy Security and Climate Change (MEF), initiated by the U.S. in 2007 again in part to deal with global criticism of Washington's failure to participate in the UNFCCC deliberations. Beijing welcomed the link that the Forum established between climate change and energy security. Even so, the MEF achieved very little.[46] President Obama's environmental policy up to and since the Copenhagen conference has also been difficult to advance, with Congress refusing to stump up the funding for various international mitigation efforts, and other political groups in the United States hostile to the idea of emissions restraint on economic grounds, often directing their ire at the U.S. Environmental Protection Agency.[47] China's long period of reluctance to agree to mandatory abatement measures offers a vital plank in the argument of those in the United States critical of Obama's efforts to advance climate protection goals.

Coincidences of Interest

Within the United Nations, China and the United States have also worked in ways that show they share certain limited coincidences of interest. As Michael Fullilove has put it, in broad terms, "China has developed a good working relationship in the [Security] Council with the United States."[48] For example, in the run-up to the World Summit in 2005, and debate of the U.N. Secretary General's document *In Larger Freedom*, the concept of "the Responsibility to Protect" (R2P) in reference to how the global community should respond to gross violations of human rights came to be shaped in ways that suited both Chinese and U.S. requirements. Both Beijing and Washington opposed Kofi Annan's preference for developing guidelines on intervention for humanitarian purposes. China (and Russia) insisted that any intervention must be authorized by the U.N. Security Council—and therefore subject to possible veto. Washington, too, opposed criteria that might restrict its freedom to decide when it would be involved in the use of force, not wanting to be drawn into actions that did not engage its interests. John Bolton, when he was the U.S. Permanent Representative to the United Nations, was insistent that the obligations and responsibilities contained within the concept of R2P were "not of a legal character," adding "we do not accept that either the United Nations as a whole, or the Security Council, or individual states, have an obligation to intervene under international law. We also believe that what the United Nations does in a particular situation should depend on the specific circumstances." There is nothing here that sparked Beijing's agreement; indeed there was much that it applauded, even if its main underlying concerns related more to the rights of states over individuals and any potential breach of non-intervention rules, rather than strategic autonomy, as is the case for the United States.[49]

The United States under President Obama is sympathetic to the concept of R2P and the protection of individual human rights, but its caution with respect to the Sudan where its approach has been to promise "frank dialogue" and various incentives and disincentives, its use of economic rather than threatened military pressure on the Sri Lankan armed forces even as their actions against the Tamil Tigers resulted in the large-scale loss of civilian life, and its carefully circumscribed responses with respect to atrocities committed during "the Arab Spring" illustrate that it does not wish to lose policy autonomy to the United Nations in this area. China's approach to the concept of R2P as it has been elaborated and in some cases (such as the Libyan intervention) actually applied also shows a desire to narrow its application. But there is no evidence that China is blocking outright the development of this norm.[50]

China and the United States have also had broadly compatible positions on the question of U.N. Security Council reform, even if Beijing has worked hard to prevent Japan becoming a permanent member of the Security Council and Washington has endorsed Tokyo's candidature. Where their preferences have come into alignment is in privileging "no reform" over "unacceptable reform." They have come together in insisting that international divisiveness over the issue is to be avoided—a recipe for a stalled outcome. As China's Ambassador to the U.N., Wang Guangya, reported to the world's press during debate over the issue in 2005, he had reached an agreement on the matter with Bolton because "both believe the proposal by the so-called Group of 4 [Brazil, Germany, India, and Japan] would divide the U.N.'s 191 member states."[51] Although there have been expressions of concern in the Obama administration about the need to enhance the representative legitimacy of the Security Council, the process of reform has not advanced much. Considerable weight continues to be put in Washington on the idea that reform should not reduce the Council's "effectiveness or its efficiency,"[52] again an argument that can be found in Chinese official statements.[53]

Differing Approaches of Potential Benefit to Global Order

The examples of U.S.-Chinese interaction in this previous section can either be viewed as detrimental to the solution of global governance challenges, or at best as ambiguous in their results. The two cases I draw on in this next section are more positive in their implications for global order, although in neither case do the examples represent a direct or intentional form of interaction between the United States and China. I discuss here the unintended consequences of their respective behavior.

The first, U.N. peacekeeping, represents an area where China has filled an important vacuum that the West, and the United States in particular, has chosen to create. Since the Brahimi report of 2000—paradoxically, a document that "endorsed a primarily Western vision of what peace operations were for"—western personnel in U.N. peace operations have decreased by about a half "in both relative and absolute terms." This was particularly so for the United States after the failed Somalia operation of the early 1990s, and with the passage in 2002 of the "American Service-Members Protection Act" which expressly forbids U.S. personnel from participation in U.N. operations unless the host state guarantees immunity from prosecution by the International Criminal Court.[54]

Some of the slack has been taken up by China which now supplies the largest number of U.N. forces out of all the P-5, and it has been the twelfth to fifteenth largest contributor among all U.N. member states since May 2004—a good record in absolute terms, although not on a per capita basis of course. It has also become the seventh-largest supplier of peacekeeping funding. In Miwa Hirono and Marc Lanteigne's view, "China is now an enthusiastic supporter of UN Peacekeeping Operations (UNPKO) and is seeking to deepen and widen its engagement with that institution."[55] Its contributing methods in these operations focus mainly on the building and repairing of infrastructure in post-conflict countries. Beijing also places greater emphasis on conflict prevention, and the political mediation of disputes than on the use of coercion to protect those suffering from abuse.[56] Hostility to intervention and fear of breaches in state sovereignty mean, then, that they are not "first-responders" in a humanitarian crisis and tend to try to stall a military response. This contrasts with what Bellamy and Williams describe as a Western preference for a "'fire-fighting' role and saving lives that are immediately endangered."[57]

However, although these approaches differ, and at their root rest on values that in important ways are not in alignment, this western tendency to adopt short-term roles in U.N. operations is, to a degree, complemented by China, a state that prefers to concentrate on approaches that have the potential to build long-term peace based on the provision of projects that relate directly to development. Hirono and Lanteigne conclude: "Irrespective of whether the Chinese government intends to do so, China's peacekeeping contribution facilitates the host country's economic development and modernization trajectories that the Chinese government and investment corporations have tended to support."[58]

There is one other way to think about complementarity in relation to the U.S.-China relationship in the U.N. Their behavior may help to sustain some degree of legitimacy for the U.N. Security Council in global politics and in this sense contribute to the stability of global order. As Ian Clark and others have argued,[59] mutual engagement between the U.N. Security Council and the United States is beneficial to both because "when they fall out—as over Iraq" this can generate a mutual crisis of legitimacy that diminishes both U.S. power and U.N. authority.[60] China's actions can sometimes help to sustain this mutuality. Beijing's frequent abstention on votes in the Security Council (as with its abstention on U.N. Security Council Resolution 1973 in March 2011 on the U.N. intervention in Libya[61]) and infrequent use of its veto make it less likely that on issues where U.S. interests are strongly engaged Washington will bypass the Security Council. A Chinese veto (as in the case of Syria in

February 2012) encourages U.S. unilateralist behavior, or leads it to search for a "coalition of the willing" resulting in a legitimacy crisis for the U.N.—a body that China states it wishes to sustain and that many perceive as vital to sustaining some sense of an international community. Clark notes that actions that block U.S. involvement would risk U.S. unilateralism, and this would damage the very institution that gives China (and other P-5 members) special status.[62] It would also damage an organization that has frequently been described by Chinese officials in positive terms. As China's 2005 position paper on U.N. reform put it: "the U.N. plays an indispensable role in international affairs. As the most universal, representative, authoritative inter-governmental international organization, the U.N. is the best venue to practice multilateralism, and an effective platform for collective actions to cope with various threats and challenges."[63] When China holds back from using its veto, one effect is to help sustain U.S. engagement with the U.N., which in turn helps to maintain the U.N.'s relevance as a governance mechanism.

CONCLUSION

The full scope of U.S.-Chinese interactions in global governance is too vast to cover in a single chapter. Moreover, my illustrations do not help us to determine which of the four interaction-types predominate in the relationship. However, uncovering these forms of interaction does prompt reflection on the viability of the term "revisionist" versus "status quo" power, and the assumption that declining and rising powers—especially those based on very different political systems—will necessarily have an unproductive relationship in all international organizations. Such multilateral bodies and their structural rules can facilitate compromise and encourage pragmatic behavior. Everyday diplomacy can have the effect of dampening the damaging fallout from strategic distrust. Even where tensions are high, unintended outcomes may be positive for global and domestic governance. As Elizabeth Economy has written, "China's efforts to move the international financial system away from the dollar as the world's reserve currency, although potentially costly if done abruptly, might nevertheless be advantageous for Washington over the long run" should it impose "a potentially helpful fiscal discipline on the U.S. economy."[64] Moreover, as G. John Ikenberry explicates in his chapter, it is not easy (for China) to overturn global governance arrangements that are reasonably well established. Norms, rules and their associated standards, embedded in global institutions can be difficult for any single actor to change or dislodge which creates an element of inertia in global order and a perceived need for states, and especially for rising states, to justify behavior that can be labelled as "revisionist."[65]

China's reasonably productive involvement in international organizations has been important to it materially but has also been perceived as a way for it to signal that it is a responsible great power engaged in a peaceful rise and vital domestic reform. International organizations have also sometimes been the welcome source of ideas about how best to reform its domestic laws, and respond to its economic and social development needs in areas where these ideas are perceived likely to contribute to its dominant domestic values. However, the problem is that China's preoccupation with its domestic needs has led to a form of parochialism in its behavior and a preference for conservative incrementalism in order to test out the implications of international organizational decisions for its own domestic political-economic system. It has shown a much shallower concern for the needs of a wider global society. Thus, while it seeks better representation in global governance arrangements and regards certain of these institutions as unfair in terms of their procedural and substantive outcomes (such as the IMF), a weightier Chinese voice might not lead to anything other than an improvement in its ability to protect its own interests.

The United States, on the other hand, has played a leading role in the creation of the liberal international order. Many in the global system still look to it to provide leadership in sustaining and developing this order. Yet, in this promotion of a more universalistic vision, the United States has frequently exhibited an unhelpful tendency to assume a strong resonance between its domestic values and those of global society. This has often made it inattentive to the validity of the positions of others—a tendency that matters more within a global system where power has been diffusing. At a time of recession and general economic and political uncertainty, questioning of this resonance has been amplified in global society. Within the United States itself, however, there has been reinforcement of the sentiment that international organizations often represent an undemocratic and hostile space that are designed to allow others to free-ride on the American provision of public goods which it can no longer afford to supply.

This heightened attention to domestic needs in the United States together with the continuing focus in China on sustaining a level of development that ensures social stability and one-party rule presages a mixed and potentially impoverished period for global governance over the next several years. As both Harry Harding and Wu Xinbo argue in this volume, there will be instances where these two states interact cooperatively to obtain particular benefits for themselves. Moreover, many of the examples of cooperation given in this chapter favor inaction rather than action in search of solutions to some of the complex collective problems with which we are confronted. In addition, there will also be areas of contention where the needs of global society are neglected. Given the centrality of the relationship between these two states, global governance is entering a challenging and less predictable era.

NOTES

I am grateful to Professors Michael B. Yahuda and David Shambaugh for valuable comments on an earlier version of this chapter. I would also like to record my thanks to Amy King for her excellent research assistance.

1. Global governance generally refers to the formal and informal institutions and their associated regulatory frameworks that have been designed to assist states and other significant political actors resolve or manage collective action problems. In the absence of world government, international organizations and other forms of global governance have rapidly expanded in number and scope since the start of the twentieth century.

2. The State Councillor for External Relations, Dai Bingguo, issued a statement on December 6, 2010, entitled "Adhere to the Path of Peaceful Development." He gives China's core interests as follows: "First, China's form of government and political system and stability, namely the leadership of the Communist Party of China, the socialist system and socialism with Chinese characteristics. Second, China's sovereignty, territorial integrity and national unity. Third, the basic guarantee for sustainable economic and social development of China." Available at: http://china.usc.edu/ShowArticle .aspx?articleID=2325. See also Wang Jisi, "China's Search for a Grand Strategy: A Rising Great Power Finds Its Way," *Foreign Affairs*, Vol. 90, No. 2 (March/April 2011), pp. 68–79.

3. Dean Acheson, *Present at the Creation: My Years in the State Department* (London: W.W. Norton, 1969); Stewart Patrick, *The Best Laid Plans: The Origins of American Multilateralism and the Dawn of the Cold War* (Lanham, MD: Rowman & Littlefield, 2009).

4. Alastair Iain Johnston, "Is China a Status Quo Power?" *International Security*, Vol. 27, No. 4 (2003), pp. 5–56. Johnston's figures show steady increases in China's international organizational memberships especially from the mid-1980s. Using GDP per capita as a proxy indicator of expected levels of involvement, he demonstrates that "during the 1990s China became overinvolved in international organizations." See pp. 12–13.

5. See, for example, Thomas J. Christensen, "The Advantages of an Assertive China: Responding to Beijing's Abrasive Diplomacy," *Foreign Affairs*, Vol. 90, No. 2 (March/April 2011), pp. 54–67; David Shambaugh, "Coping with a Conflicted China," *The Washington Quarterly*, Vol. 34, No. 1 (2011), pp. 7–27. See too the Wikileaks cable dated 4 December 2010 written by the U.S. ambassador in Beijing. He writes of China's "newly pugnacious foreign policy," its "muscle-flexing, triumphalism and assertiveness" which is "losing [it] friends worldwide" available at: http://www.guardian .co.uk/world/2010/dec/04/. For a Chinese perspective see Da Wei, "Has China Become 'Tough'?" *China Security*, Vol. 6, No. 3 (2010), pp. 97–104.

6. Economy, "The Game Changer: Coping with China's Foreign Policy Revolution," *Foreign Affairs*, Vol. 89, No. 6 (Nov./Dec. 2010), p. 142.

7. An argument made in, for example, Evan S. Medeiros, *Reluctant Restraint: The Evolution of China's Nonproliferation Policies and Practices, 1980–2004* (Stanford, CA: Stanford University Press, 2007).

8. David Shambaugh quotes China's "offensive realists" as arguing that China should "leverage its holdings of U.S. treasury bonds to get Washington to stop selling arms to Taiwan" and for China to "establish a much broader military (particularly

naval) presence in the western Pacific to force the United States to stop operating close to China's coastline." See Shambaugh, "Coping with a Conflicted Power," op cit, p. 12.

9. A useful discussion of the concept of hegemony and of forms of U.S. hegemony in particular are contained in Ian Clark, *Hegemony in International Society* (Oxford: Oxford University Press, 2011).

10. Stephen G. Brooks and William C. Wohlforth, *World Out of Balance: International Relations and the Challenge of American Primacy* (Princeton, NJ: Princeton University Press, 2008).

11. Kerry Brown, "China's Normative Challenge," Australian Strategic Policy Institute (22 June 2011), available at http://www.aspi.org.au/research/.

12. A pithy example is contained in Hillary Clinton's remarks to Australian Foreign Minister Kevin Rudd as reported in a Wikileaks cable. She asked Rudd, "How do you deal toughly with your banker?" Available at: http://www.guardian.co.uk/world/2010/dec/04/wikileaks-cables-hillary-clinton-beijing (4 December 2010).

13. For a study text that suggests that the Chinese side tends to think in terms of a "long-term zero-sum game" between the United States and China, see Kenneth Lieberthal and Wang Jisi, *Addressing U.S.-China Strategic Distrust* (Washington, D.C.: John L. Thornton China Center, Brookings Institution, Washington D.C.: March 2012), p. ix.

14. Ian Hurd is quoted in Clark, *Hegemony,* p. 152.

15. In Li Mingjiang's view, "China is likely to treat the UN as the most important multilateral institution to deal with international political and security issues and regard the G-20 as the most important multilateral arrangement to cope with international financial and economic problems." "Rising from Within: China's Search for a Multilateral World and Its Implications for Sino-US Relations," *Global Governance,* Vol. 17 (2011), p. 346.

16. Robert Falkner writes of the climate change norm as being dynamic and multi-layered. See his "The United States and the Global Climate Norm: Who's Influencing Whom?" paper presented at the Annual Convention of the International Studies Association, New York City (15–18 February 2009).

17. A point made in Ann Kent, *Beyond Compliance: China, International Organizations, and Global Security* (Stanford, CA: Stanford University Press, 2007).

18. See Johnston, "Is China a Status Quo Power" for useful discussion of some of these points, as well as Rosemary Foot and Andrew Walter, *China, the United States, and Global Order* (New York: Cambridge University Press, 2011), pp. 12–15.

19. John G. Ruggie, "Multilateralism: the Anatomy of an Institution," in Ruggie (ed.), *Multilateralism Matters: The Theory and Praxis of an Institutional Form* (New York: Columbia University Press, 1993), pp. 3–47.

20. Rosemary Foot, S. Neil MacFarlane and Michael Mastanduno (eds.), *U.S. Hegemony and International Organizations* (Oxford: Oxford University Press, 2003), p. 266 and p. 272.

21. Stewart Patrick and Shepard Forman (eds.), *Multilateralism and U.S. Foreign Policy: Ambivalent Engagement* (Boulder, CO: Lynne Rienner Publishers, 2002), p. 2.

22. Luck, "American Exceptionalism and International Organization: Lessons from the 1990s," in Foot, et al. (eds.), *US Hegemony and International Organizations,* p. 27.

23. Michael Ignatieff (ed.), *American Exceptionalism and Human Rights* (Princeton, NJ: Princeton University Press, 2005); Walter McDougall, *Promised Land, Crusader State* (New York: Houghton Mifflin, 1997); W. Michael Reisman, "The United States and International Institutions," *Survival,* Vol. 41, No. 4 (1999–2000), pp. 63–64; Tim J.

Dunne, "'The Rules of the Game Are Changing': Fundamental Human Rights in Crisis after 9/11," *International Politics*, Vol. 44, Nos. 2/3 (2007), p. 720.

24. Clark, *Hegemony*, p. 155.

25. Quoted in Clark, *Hegemony*, p. 152. U.S. Ambassador to the U.N. Jeane Kirkpatrick said something similar during the Reagan era, describing the U.N. Charter position on the use of force as broadly sensible, but "hardly in itself a sound basis for either U.S. policy or for international peace and security." Quoted in Christine Gray, *International Law and the Use of Force* (Oxford: Oxford University Press, 2008, 3rd ed.), p. 29.

26. Nixon and Oksenberg (and John K. Fairbank in 1966) are quoted in Foot, *The Practice of Power: U.S. Relations with China since 1949* (Oxford: Oxford University Press, 1995), pp. 223–227. Johnston, "Is China a Status Quo Power?" pp. 6–7 covers similar statements for the years 1995–2001. Zoellick was, of course, assuming China was integrated but now needed to develop a more "responsible" approach.

27. *Renmin Ribao*, Overseas Edition (September 15, 2008), available at: http://news.xinhuanet.com:80/world/2008-09/15/content_10003743.htm.

28. This is a conclusion my co-author and I arrived at having considered Chinese (and U.S.) behavior in relation to five issue areas. See in particular "Conclusion" in Foot and Walter, *China, the United States and Global Order*.

29. Kent, *Beyond Compliance*, p. 230.

30. Christensen, "The Advantages of an Assertive China," pp. 54–67.

31. Medeiros, *Reluctant Restraint*, p. 240.

32. Foot and Walter, *China, the United States, and Global Order*, pp. 255–264.

33. In the case of North Korea, Beijing has major concerns about the collapse of a regime on its borders—concerns that have been heightened as Pyongyang has tried to ensure a smooth succession from Kim Jong-il to his son; and with respect to Iran it has important commercial and energy-related interests. Relations with North Korea are also discussed in Avery Goldstein's chapter in this volume, and that with Iran in the chapter by Dawn Murphy and David Shambaugh.

34. Shi Yinhong, "China, 'Global Challenges' and the Complexities of International Cooperation," *Global Policy*, Vol. 2, No. 1 (2011), p. 90. David Shambaugh records even more negative sentiment. He has argued that, especially in the period since 2008 when various international commentators have called on the Chinese to do more with respect to the provision of public goods, "Most Chinese analysts believe (and there is virtual consensus across the spectrum) that the whole concept of global governance is a Western trap which tries to undermine China's sovereignty and lure it into a variety of foreign entanglements where China does not belong." Shambaugh also quotes one Chinese scholar as stating: "For Chinese, multilateralism is a *tool* and a *tactic*." See his "Coping with a Conflicted China," pp. 17–19.

35. Agence France-Presse (AFP), November 10 and 12, 2010.

36. AFP, November 12, 2010; China Xinhua News Network Corporation, November 10, 2010.

37. As China's Vice Foreign Minister, Cui Tiankai, put it in June 2010, "The *renminbi* is China's currency, and it is not an issue for international discussion." *Xinhua*, June 18, 2010. Premier Wen Jiabao said much the same thing in 2009. For further detail see Foot and Walter, *China, the United States, and Global Order*, pp. 118–123. It is worth remembering that China did adopt a revaluation strategy from 2005–2008 and that the currency has appreciated somewhat since 2010. In April 2012, the People's Bank of

China announced that from April 16, it would widen the currency's daily trading band against the US dollar to 1.0%, up from 0.5%.

38. *New York Times*, "China Tells U.S. It Must 'Cure Its Addiction to Debt,'" August 6, 2011 and "Chinese Fault Beijing over Foreign Reserves," August 8, 2011, available at: http://www.nytimes.com/2011/08/07/business/global/ and www.nytimes.com/2011/08/09/business/global.

39. *New York Times*, "U.S. Economic Woes Loom over Biden visit to China," August 13, 2011, available at: http://www.nytimes.com/2011/08/14/world/asia/14china.html.

40. See Foot and Walter, *China, the United States, and Global Order*, p. 124.

41. U.S.-China Joint Statement, November 17, 2009, Beijing, available at http://beijing.usembassy-china.org.cn/111709.html. This statement came at the conclusion of President Obama's official visit to China.

42. International Monetary Fund, "People's Republic of China: 2005 Article IV Consultation—Staff Report," *Country Report No. 05/411,* November 17, 2005, p. 15.

43. China's voting power is due to increase again in 2012.

44. Johnston, "Is China a Status Quo Power?" p. 15, note 26.

45. Kent, *Beyond Compliance*, p. 196.

46. Foot and Walter, *China, the United States, and Global Order,* p. 208.

47. "Obama Administration Encounters Opposition to International Climate Agenda," *Washington Post*, August 15, 2011, available at: http://www.washingtonpost.com/national/health-science/.

48. Michael Fullilove, "China and the United Nations: The Stakeholder Spectrum," *The Washington Quarterly* (Summer 2011), p. 73.

49. Edward C. Luck, "Sovereignty, Choice, and the Responsibility to Protect," *Global Responsibility to Protect*, Vol. 1 (2009), pp. 10–21 (Bolton quoted at p. 19); Nicholas J. Wheeler and Frazer Egerton, "The Responsibility to Protect: 'Precious Commitment' or a Promise Unfulfilled?" *Global Responsibility to Protect*, Vol. 1 (2009), pp. 114–132, esp. pp. 120–123.

50. Foot, "The Responsibility to Protect (R2P) and Its Evolution: Beijing's Influence on Norm Creation in Humanitarian Areas," *St Antony's International Review*, Vol. 6, No. 2 (Feb. 2011); Sarah Teitt, "The Responsibility to Protect and China's Peacekeeping Policy," *International Peacekeeping*, Vol. 18, No. 3 (June 2011), pp. 298–312.

51. Edith M. Lederer, "U.S. and China Unite to Block G4 Plan," *Associated Press*, August 4, 2005; Clark, *Hegemony*, p. 162. Wang spoke of the U.S. and China "working in parallel rather than together in the coming weeks 'because we have different friends in different parts of the world.'" BBC News, "China and U.S. 'Unite' over UN Bid," available at: http://news.bbc.co.uk/go/pr/fr/-/1hi/world/americas/4746459.htm, August 4, 2005.

52. Clark, *Hegemony,* pp. 158–165.

53. China's Position Paper on UN reform of June 2005 states: "Reforms should be in the interest of multilateralism, and enhance authority and efficiency, as well as its capacity to deal with new threats and challenges." Available at: http://na.china-embassy.org/eng/xwdt/t199361.htm.

54. Alex J. Bellamy and Paul D. Williams, "The West and Contemporary Peace Operations," *Journal of Peace Research*, Vol. 46, No. 1 (2009), pp. 39–57, esp. pp. 43–45.

55. Miwa Hirono and Marc Lanteigne, "Introduction: China and UN Peacekeeping," *International Peacekeeping*, Vol. 81, No. 3 (June 2011), p. 243.

56. Teitt, "The Responsibility to Protect and China's Peacekeeping Policy," pp. 307–309.

57. Bellamy and Williams, "Peace Operations," p. 54. They describe this activity as being "broadly positive."

58. Hirono and Lanteigne, "China and UN Peacekeeping," p. 249.

59. Clark, *Hegemon*, chap. 7; Ian Hurd, *After Anarchy: Legitimacy and Power in the United Nations Security Council* (Princeton, NJ: Princeton University Press, 2007); Ramesh Thakur, *The United Nations, Peace and Security: From Collective Security to the Responsibility to Protect* (Cambridge: Cambridge University Press, 2006).

60. Clark, *Hegemony*, p. 152.

61. China's explanation of its abstention is available at: http://www.un.org/News/Press/docs/2011/sc10200.doc.htm.

62. Clark, *Hegemony*, pp. 167–68.

63. China's Position Paper on UN Reform, June 9, 2005.

64. Economy, "The Game Changer," p. 152.

65. This latter point is explained well in Randall L. Schweller and Xiaoyu Pu, "After Unipolarity: China's Visions of International Order in an Era of U.S. Decline," *International Security*, Vol. 36, No. 1 (Summer 2011), pp. 41–72.

Part VIII

Visions for the Future

15

Chinese Visions of the Future of U.S.-China Relations

Wu Xinbo

Chinese scholars and experts tend to believe that since the normalization of the Sino-American relationship in 1979, it invariably undergoes a major transformation every 10 years, as is manifested in both the agenda and trajectory of bilateral ties. From 1979 to 1989, against the background of the Cold War and China's pursuit of opening-up and reform, Sino-U.S. relations were characterized by cooperation in a wide range of areas and relative smooth development. During the following 10 years, however, with the end of the Cold War and the United States standing as the only remaining superpower, the relationship witnessed constant disputes and tensions over China's human rights situation, economic relations, Taiwan, non-proliferation, among other issues, moving on a bumpy and zigzag path. In the first decade of the twenty-first century, as the United States was preoccupied with Afghanistan and Iraq wars and China rapidly expanded its economic power, bilateral ties were characterized by deepening economic interdependence and widening cooperation in regional, international affairs and on global issues.

What, then, will the Sino-U.S. relationship look like by 2020? A U.S. consensus does not seem to exist on this question among policy and academic elite in China. The mainstream view within the Chinese government appears to be optimistic. In early 2011, China's Vice Foreign Minister Cui Tiankai, who oversees ties with the United States, delivered a speech on Sino-U.S. relations. After mentioning the troubles in Sino-U.S. relations in 2010, he raised a question: "Can the ship of China-U.S. relations stay on the course of cooperation and sail through the storms toward a brighter future?" His answer was an unequivocal and emphatic "yes." He went on to explain the following rationale: the historical trend of China-U.S. cooperation is irreversible; the pace of China-

U.S. cooperation is unstoppable; China-U.S. cooperation and the rejuvenation of the Asia-Pacific region are complementary to each other; and there are high expectations on the prospect of China and the United States working together to address global challenges.[1] President Hu Jintao, during his state visit to the U.S. in January 2011, noted that "we are fully confident about the prospects of China-U.S. relations."[2] In the Joint Statement released during this visit, Presidents Hu and Obama agreed that both sides should work together to build "a cooperative partnership based on mutual respect and mutual benefit."[3]

On the other hand, however, both civilian leaders and the Chinese military publicly aired their complaints about U.S. policy towards China. Dai Bingguo, Chinese State Councilor in charge of foreign affairs, criticized the United States in an article for its attempts "to team up to counter or contain China" and its practices of "sowing discords between countries in the region and conducting joint military exercises in China's adjacent waters," as well as its arms sales to Taiwan "out of Cold War mentality and geo-political needs."[4] China's Defense White Paper released in 2011 also expressed concern over U.S. efforts to reinforce its military alliances and to step up its involvement in security affairs in the Asia-Pacific region, and deemed U.S. weapons sale to Taiwan as "severely impeding Sino-U.S. relations and impairing the peaceful development of cross-Strait relations."[5]

Chinese academic circles are even more sharply divided over the nature of Sino-U.S. relations. The optimistic view argues that against the background of the multipolarization of the international system, the development of globalization, and the constructive tendencies in China's foreign policy, China and the U.S. are more likely than not to become real partners.[6] The pessimistic view, however, contends that the structural contradiction between China and the U.S. produces the strategic competition, and predicts that they will have more conflicting and confronting interests than common and complementary ones, and therefore it is difficult to develop real strategic friendship between them.[7]

Amid the different views among Chinese policy and academic circles of Sino-U.S. relations, this chapter tries to provide a Chinese vision of its future. It starts with an analysis of the new landscape in bilateral relationship and its importance to China, followed by an in-depth study of major factors affecting Sino-U.S. ties. Then the chapter will examine the merits of Chinese approaches to bilateral relations, and finally it will present an overall analysis of the future of Sino-U.S. ties.

THE NEW LANDSCAPE OF RELATIONS

After the rapid developments in the first decade of the twenty-first century, Sino-U.S. relations are taking on new features. The previous chapters in this volume elaborate this new landscape in considerable detail, and it is true that all of these complex factors now shape the U.S.-China relationship. But, in this chapter I wish to focus on a few key elements that will help us better understand the orientation of bilateral ties in the years ahead.

The first is the deepening of economic interdependence and the enhancement of symmetry between China and the United States. Along with China's further reform and opening up, the symmetric economic interdependence between China and the United States has been strengthened. Since the 1980s, the United States has been a major economic partner for China, and China's economic development has benefited a lot from the United States in terms of exports, foreign direct investment (FDI) and introduction of new technologies. Yet for quite some time, China was not that important to the United States' economy. Thanks to the rapid growth of Sino-U.S. trade and economic relations in the early twenty-first century, the economic interdependence between China and the United States has remarkably increased and today the United States is also relying heavily on China for its economic growth. China has now become the second largest trading partner and the third largest export market of the United States with the fastest growth among America's overseas markets. The United States is China's second largest trading partner and export market, as well as its fourth largest FDI source. In addition, China is the largest sovereign creditor of the United States. China has played a pivotal role in helping the U.S. government to mobilize capital for dealing with its substantial financial deficits and international payment deficits. In this sense, China plays a huge role in balancing the huge deficits of the U.S. government. Besides, China is contributing to the economic growth of the United States as China is holding a large amount of U.S. dollar-denominated assets, giving the American government the ability to maintain a low interest rate, thus making a great contribution to the American economy. The present economic and trade relations between China and the United States have painted a picture in which the world's largest developed country and the largest developing country have formed an unprecedented level of economic interdependence and structurally have created a multifaceted and growing symmetry.

The second factor is the internationalization of Sino-American relations. Relations between the two countries initially became internationalized in 1972 when President Nixon visited China and kicked off the formation of the international strategic triangle among China, the United States and the Soviet Union. As a result, Sino-American relations took on global strategic significance. However, with the end of the Cold War and the collapse of the Soviet Union, the strategic triangle disappeared and the interactions between China and the United States centered mostly on bilateral issues and only occasionally on regional and international ones. As globalization picked up its pace in the post–Cold War era, it has created more and more transnational problems that have to be addressed through international cooperation. The United States, weakened by the war on terror and the Iraq war, has become more aware of its limited power. During George W. Bush's second term, American policymakers came to realize that the United States, though powerful, is not omnipotent. It has to seek coordination and cooperation from the global community, in particular, from other major international powers. Under such circumstances, Sino-American interactions have broadened the scope and are covering more and more international and regional problems. Just as President Hu Jintao pointed out in 2005, China-U.S. relations have gone far beyond the bilateral context and have increasingly taken on global significance.[8] Nowadays, when Chinese and U.S. presidents meet, they usually spend more time on international and global issues than on bilateral ones.

The third is the increasingly complicated decision-making process on the Chinese side. China's U.S. policy used to be made by a very few senior leaders. However, as Chinese politics evolved from the phase of "strongman" to one of collective leadership over the past decade, more actors in and out of the leadership have joined in the policy process. Meanwhile, as the scope of Sino-U.S. interactions broadened to cover more areas, a growing number of government agencies have been involved in the handling of Sino-U.S. relations, while the influence of the Foreign Ministry has relatively declined. As a result, the making of U.S. policy is always characterized by difficult internal coordination (or, in some cases, the lack of internal coordination) and hard bargaining, causing from time to time low efficiency and even self-contradiction. Moreover, as Hao Yufan's chapter illustrates, due to some important developments brought about by economic growth and information technology, Chinese society has become more pluralistic in terms of the existence of different thinking and interests, the internet is widely accessed, an educated public is becoming more interested in and vocal on China's foreign relations and relations with the United States in particular. As policymakers invariably care about their domestic image and popularity in the information era, they are paying more attention to the public mood, particularly on "high-profile" issues in relations with the U.S. (such as Taiwan, Tibet, trade frictions, etc.). This has rendered China's U.S. policy both more uncertain and generally tougher than before.

Last, but not the least, is the shifting balance of power between China and the United States. In 2001, China's Gross Domestic Product (GDP) was around $1.18 trillion, only about 11.6 percent of U.S. GDP. In 2010, however, China surpassed Japan as the world's second largest economy with a GDP of $5.88 trillion, about 40.5 percent of the U.S. GDP.[9] Although still far behind the U.S., China is confident about further narrowing the gap in this decade. Meanwhile, the global financial crisis originated in the U.S., the slow economic recovery in the developed world and the sovereign debt crisis confronting the U.S. and the European Union all highlighted China's economic vigor. Moreover, China's international influence also expanded as a result of its growing economic power and expanding business activities across the globe. All these served to promote China's position and confidence in dealing with the U.S. For a long time since the end of the Cold War, Washington has taken the initiative in agenda-setting in bilateral relations while Beijing has been in a reactive position. In recent years, however, Beijing has become more active in setting the agenda. China's growing economic power and international clout give it more leverage vis-à-vis the U.S. As a result, compared with the past two decades, China is now playing a more active and important role in shaping Sino-U.S. relations.

Since normalization of formal diplomatic relations in 1979, particularly after the end of the Cold War, ties with the U.S. have been regarded as China's single most important foreign relationship—as it affects a wide range of China's key national objectives, from the Taiwan issue to economic development, and from the security environment to domestic stability. Under the new circumstances, relations with the U.S. will remain the top priority on China's diplomatic agenda due to its evolving importance to China.

Economically, the U.S. will remain China's indispensable partner. As China's second largest export market, it makes important contributions to China's economic growth and employment. Even though China has been making efforts in recent years to boost domestic demand, it takes time to reduce reliance on exports. The value of the United States as a major source of FDI gradually declines as China is no longer short of capital, yet it remains a major source of technology transfer to China. In fact, as China strives to undertake economic restructuring, trying to lift its labor-intensive industries to become technology driven ones, it more than ever needs technology transfer from other countries. This explains why in recent years China has been pushing the U.S. to relax its technology export control policy. Moreover, as the Chinese government encourages its enterprises to go abroad, the U.S. is a major destination of investment, and China has been calling on the U.S. to improve its environment for Chinese investors. Finally, as the largest international holder of U.S. federal bonds, a serious depreciation of the U.S. dollar or failure by Washington to pay back its federal debt would cause China to suffer from big financial losses. Therefore Beijing expects Washington to maintain its financial stability and sovereign credit so as to ensure the safety of China's dollar-denominated assets.

Taiwan remains an issue on which China will always expect U.S. cooperation. Although cross-Strait relations have been on a path of steady improvement since May 2008 when the Kuomintang (KMT, or the Nationalist Party) regained power in Taiwan, the internal politics on the island are very fluid and pro-independence forces in the form of the Democratic Progressive Party

(DPP) are struggling to return to power. Beijing hopes that when the KMT holds the power, Washington would encourage the improvement of cross-Strait ties—and when the DPP is in office Washington would exercise its influence to constrain its push for Taiwan independence. Meanwhile, China also expects the U.S. to gradually reduce and finally stop its arms sales to Taiwan, no matter which party is in power on the island.

The United States, with its numerous security assets in the Asia-Pacific, stands as the most significant external actor affecting China's security environment. Since President Obama came into office, the U.S. has been working to actively strengthen security cooperation with its regional allies as well as other regional actors who are concerned about China's growing military capability, security policy and strategic intention. Washington also now takes a hands-on approach to the South China Sea disputes. All these actions are regarded by China as complicating its security environment and building up the security pressure that it has to bear. Since a stable and peaceful security environment in the Asia-Pacific is deemed essential to China, which is in a critical phase of building a moderately prosperous society in an all-round way, Beijing hopes that Washington will not go too far in adjusting its security policy towards China. For instance, Chinese State Councilor Dai Bingguo laid out China's expectations on U.S. security policies in the region as follows, "[w]e hope that what other countries do in Asia is not aimed to keep off, contain or harm China. We hope that what they say and do at our gate or in this region where the Chinese people have lived for thousands of years is also well intentioned and transparent."[10]

As China emerges as a major power with growing overseas interests, it has developed a stake in securing a peaceful global environment and sustaining a workable international system. In this regard, Beijing views Washington as a key player and values its role in helping provide this public good. As China becomes more active in shouldering international responsibilities,[11] it counts on the U.S. to be a responsible and active partner. President Hu told a U.S. audience during his visit to Washington in January 2011, "China and the United States should pursue global cooperation as partners to fulfill common responsibilities and meet common challenges. We should enhance consultation and coordination on global issues such as the Doha Round trade negotiations, climate change, energy and resources security, food security and public health security through bilateral and multilateral channels, maintain dialogue and exchanges on regional security, regional cooperation and hotspot issues, and work together for a more equitable, just, inclusive and better-managed international system."[12] Rosemary Foot's chapter discusses U.S.-China views on many of these global issues in more depth. China certainly does not want to see a U.S. paralyzed by its polarized domestic politics and unable to meet its international obligations, or a U.S. suffering from the syndrome of the post-Afghanistan and Iraq wars to turn isolationist, unwilling to contribute to addressing international and global challenges.

Last, but not the least, Beijing would expect Washington's cooperation when it endeavors to expand its international clout. Over the last three decades, China has been a major beneficiary of the international system that the U.S. helped establish and leads. As a result, China does not intend to challenge it as its power grows, but rather seeks to increase its influence within the system. With a louder voice in the international system, China hopes to better protect and promote its national interests and reform the system so that it becomes more equitable, just, inclusive and better managed. To realize this goal, understanding and support from the U.S. is important. For example, during the global financial crisis, both the World Bank and International Monetary Fund (IMF) agreed to shift more power to emerging and developing nations, as a result of which, China is now the third largest bloc in the World Bank and IMF in terms of voting shares. Given Washington's influence within both institutions, such adjustments would have been unlikely had the U.S. not endorsed the position of the emerging and developing countries and pressured some European countries to curtail their voting power. This is, however, just the beginning of the reform of international institutions which have long been dominated by developed countries. With the rise of both economic power and political ambition of the developing countries, further adjustments are inevitable. Looking into the future, as China and other developing countries push for a bigger voice in international affairs, especially when it inevitably comes at the expense of U.S. influence, Beijing would expect Washington to respond in an enlightened and accommodating manner.

MAJOR FACTORS SHAPING THE FUTURE
OF BILATERAL RELATIONS

So, how will these factors affect the future development of Sino-American relations? To be sure, there is unpredictability of the future, but let us consider the most likely impact of the aforementioned variables.

Economic ties will continue to be a major factor contributing to a stable and cooperative bilateral relationship. As China's economy continues to grow, interdependence between the two countries will deepen and become more symmetric. China, currently standing as America's third largest export market (the fastest growing one) and second largest trading partner, will likely become the largest trading partner and export market of the United States by the end of this decade. China is also going to be a major source of FDI for the U.S. while remaining one of the largest foreign holders of U.S. federal bonds.

Frictions over trade and investment will surely occur from time to time, sometimes causing retaliations and counter measures, but these should be controllable, as neither side wants to seriously damage economic ties that are so important to both countries. In addition, as has been seen in recent years, the World Trade Organization stands as a useful dispute settlement mechanism and provides a buffer zone for bilateral economic frictions.[13] Overall, benefits of being each other's major trading and investment partners will help keep bilateral relations on a stable track.

Cooperation and coordination on international and global issues will also spur the development of Sino-U.S. relations. In this decade, U.S. ability to dominate international affairs will further decline as compared with the last two decades in the post–Cold War era. Multipolarization will further increase in the international power structure. Yet, this does not mean a return to a nineteenth-century world of major power competition. Rather, in an era of globalization and interdependence, major players are required to cooperate to improve global governance, which is in the interests of everybody. As China is expected to play a more active international role, both for the pursuit of its own interests and the quest for the reputation of being a responsible major power, Beijing will be an indispensable partner to the U.S. in world affairs. There is a long list of areas of cooperation, but the most prominent include the Korean Peninsula issue (both the denuclearization of the DPRK and the establishment of peace mechanism on the peninsula); stability of Afghanistan after a U.S. withdrawal; the Iranian nuclear issue; promotion of strong, sustainable and balanced global economic growth; mitigation of climate change; conclusion of WTO Doha round negotiations, among others. Robust Sino-U.S. cooperation in world affairs, while promoting each other's national interests in economic, security, environmental and other fields, will also cultivate habits of cooperation between the two countries, substantiate the partnership to address common challenges that both sides pledge to develop, and underscore the positive trends in bilateral relations.

On the negative side, the shifting balance of power between China and the U.S. may turn out to be a major source of instability in bilateral relations. The current decade is likely to witness a significant narrowing of the gap in Chinese and American economic power. In China this may result in more confidence in its diplomacy and more vocal nationalism among its populace. On old or newly emerged differences with U.S., China may become more assertive in defending its interests and less willing to compromise. In the United States an anxiety over the rise of China and the relative decline of America and a fatalist notion that a shifting power balance is inevitably accompanied by conflict may cause Washington to overreact to China's growing power and influence. Under these circumstances, where elements of both cooperation and competition exist, the competitive trend will grow and may overwhelm the cooperative trend, generating more tensions in the entire relationship.

In this scenario, a strategic rivalry between China and the U.S. is likely to take place in the Asia-Pacific region. Developments in the Asia-Pacific have the most direct impact on China's political, economic and security interests, while the region is also the primary platform for China to expand its overseas interests. The United States—with huge political, economic and security assets embedded in the Asia-Pacific—seeks to maintain its central or dominant role in regional affairs and make sure that developments there will not undermine that role.[14] As Washington tries to check and counterbalance China's growing influence through its active diplomacy, strong military presence and security cooperation with regional allies and partners, Beijing will make all kinds of efforts to resist the perceived encirclement and even containment. Such zero-sum interactions between China and the U.S. may polarize regional political-security order, causing a return of geo-political competition to the Asia-Pacific. If this occurs, Sino-U.S. relations will be characterized by a bifurcation—economic cooperation vis-à-vis strategic and security competition—a situation David Shambaugh interestingly refers to in his introductory chapter as "coopetition." Should strategic and security competition become fierce overtime, it may even undermine the incentives for economic cooperation.

Although global governance is an area where cooperation between two countries is desirable, frictions will also arise therein. As China becomes more actively involved in promoting good governance of world affairs, it will not be content with mere demonstration of participation, but will seek to exercise its influence by making its voice heard and proposals adopted. On more and more issues—from the reform of the international system to the making and revision of the rules of the game—China will develop its own position and stick to it. As is shown by recent experiences with UN conferences on climate change and G-20 summits, where Sino-U.S. interactions demonstrated both cooperation and competition, differences between them could lead to harsh diplomatic frictions. Competition and friction arising from multilateral settings will have a negative impact on bilateral ties, poisoning the atmosphere and undermining mutual trust.

As a result of the fast economic growth of the past three decades and remarkable increase of its comprehensive national power, China has emerged as a successful developing country. Its model of development has received broad attention and won wide recognition in the developing world. While Beijing has been very cautious with promoting its development model, some in the U.S. feel very concerned and upset about the growing sway of the Chinese model. For some Americans, the so-called "Beijing Consensus" undermined the universal applicability of the "Washington Consensus," which also suffered from the global financial crisis of 2008. Alarmists in the United States believe that competition between these two models not only stirs up a rivalry for soft power by Beijing and Washington, but also gives rise to a tug-of-war between "authoritarian capitalism" or "state capitalism" versus "liberal capitalism."[15] Should this line of thinking gain more influence with U.S.-China policy in the future, it will cast a Cold War shadow of ideological rivalry onto bilateral relations.

MERITS OF CHINESE APPROACHES TO BILATERAL RELATIONS

The "China-U.S. Joint Statement" released during Chinese President Hu's visit to the U.S. in January 2011 noted that "[t]he two leaders recognize that the relationship between China and the United States is both vital and complex."[16] The complexity lies in differences in their respective political systems and ideologies, history and cultural traditions, stages of social-economic development, and postures of rising power vis-à-vis status-quo power. These differences, along with a high degree of economic interdependence between two countries, make Sino-U.S. relations different from any other kind of major power relationship that has been seen in world history.

The approaches that China adopts to Sino-U.S. relations further contribute to this uniqueness. As in any inter-state relationship, what matters is not only divergence and convergence of respective national interests, but also the strategies, policies and tactics that each side employs. Since the end of the Cold War, Washington has taken more initiatives in bilateral relations and largely controlled the setting of the bilateral agenda—hence its strategies and policies have had more weight in shaping China-U.S. relations. Yet, as China's power rises, so does its capability to shape bilateral ties. Looking into the future, China's approaches to bilateral relations will have growing impact on their orientation.

As a country with a long history, China attaches importance to learning from the past and drawing on the wisdom of history. As China's material power grows, one key concern among its policy and academic community is how to avoid the so-called "tragedy of major power politics," that is, the conflict between a rising power and the status quo power, that has been frequently witnessed in history. Over the past decade, China has developed its theory of "peaceful development" as the overarching conceptual framework of its grand strategy, which contains the following major elements: "Striving for a peaceful international environment to develop itself, and promoting world peace through its own development; achieving development by relying on itself, together with reform and innovation, while persisting in the policy of opening-up; conforming to the trend of economic globalization, and striving to achieve mutually beneficial common development with other countries; sticking to peace, development and cooperation, and, together with all other countries, devoting itself to building a harmonious world marked by sustained peace and common prosperity."[17] "Peace, opening-up, cooperation, harmony and win-win are our policy, our idea, our principle and our pursuit," the theory states.

The enunciation of the "peaceful development" theory was not only intended to reassure the outside world about China's intention, but also served to build domestic consensus and guide China's overall foreign policy. By so doing, China believes that it can choose a development path different from what other major powers took in the past, featured by wars and conflicts, thus avoiding the "tragedy of major power politics." It is fair to say that China is the first major power in modern history that has seriously and thoroughly thought about its peaceful development and is eager to evade the footsteps of the violent rise of other major powers in the past. In addition to the conceptual framework of "peaceful development," some important policies that China pursues will certainly contribute to the evolution of Sino-U.S. relations.

First and foremost, China refrains from challenging U.S. core national interests. China has never challenged U.S. sovereignty and territorial integrity, nor has it posed a threat to U.S. internal stability. China is also sensitive to major U.S. national security concerns. In the 1990s, non-proliferation was a priority concern on U.S. national security agenda; under U.S. pressure, China made a series of efforts to improve its nuclear and missile export control policies. After the "9/11" incident, anti-terrorism topped the U.S. national security agenda, and China extended a wide range of cooperation with the U.S. in curtailing terrorist threats. During President Obama's visit to China in November 2009, the two countries issued a Joint Statement which held that "[t]he two sides agreed that respecting each other's core interests is extremely important to ensure steady progress in China-U.S. relations."[18] This should not just be interpreted as Beijing's attempt to gain Washington's respect for China's core national interests, but it also demonstrates a Chinese commitment to respecting vital U.S. national interests.

Secondly, China does not attempt to build an exclusive sphere of influence in the Asia-Pacific. As China has stated on many occasions, it "welcomes the United States as an Asia-Pacific nation that contributes to peace, stability and prosperity in the region."[19] While China has been actively promoting East Asian cooperation, the government has pledged to "adhere to open regionalism and respects the presence and interests of countries outside the region in Asia."[20] China understands that the U.S. has profound political, security and economic interests in East Asia and feels concerned about China's intention of turning the region into its own sphere of influence, as Japan did before World War II or the U.S. did in the Western hemisphere under the Monroe Doctrine. To mitigate U.S. concern Beijing not only keeps reassuring Washington rhetorically, but also accepted U.S. participation in the East Asia Summit. Beijing's efforts should help constrain the U.S. impulse of engaging a geopolitical rivalry with China in the Asia-Pacific and reduce the risk of bipolarization of the region.

Thirdly, China is not interested in engaging in an arms race with the U.S. While U.S. defense policy is characterized by "offensive realism" which stresses military superiority, China's defense policy has been in line with "defensive realism" that puts a premium on reliable deterrence. This is not only determined by its relatively limited material power, but also informed by Chinese strategic culture. Even though China has been able to afford more defense spending with its booming economy, it is unlikely that Beijing will seek to catch up with or surpass U.S. military capability, even in a time when U.S. military assets may shrink due to defense budget cuts. In the context of Sino-U.S. security relations, the central tenet of China's ongoing defense modernization efforts is to gain reliable deterrence vis-à-vis the U.S., not to seek preponderance over it. While China cleverly evades an arms race with the U.S. as its defense modernization proceeds, it should make serious efforts to help check the alarmist tendency on the part of the U.S. and avoid a replay of U.S.-Soviet military rivalry during the Cold War.

Last but not the least, unlike the former Soviet Union or the United States, China does not seek to export its ideology or development model. In fact, the spiritual world in today's China is more characterized by pragmatism, not by ideology. Moreover, in the post-Mao era, China is no longer interested in changing the outside world by exporting its ideology, but intent on changing itself through economic development. Even though China's rapid development over the past three decades has won international recognition, Beijing has generally been very low-key with its experiences—while some in China discuss the "Chinese model" or "Beijing Consensus," the government has been careful not to export it to the outside world. It is true that China values its path of development which seems to be working well—on the other hand, it believes that the development model a country chooses should keep in line with its own national conditions.[21] China's lack of interest in exporting its ideology or development model should help dampen a Sino-U.S. ideological competition.

From a tactical viewpoint, some of China's approaches also work to stabilize and improve bilateral ties. For instance, China always adopts a long-term view of Sino-U.S. relations and is not preoccupied with short-term gains and losses (this attitude helps release the pressure that may arise from short-term losses). In interacting with the U.S., China also plays a positive-sum rather than a zero-sum game, which helps build up momentum for bilateral relations and maintain a positive trend. Moreover, over the last decade, China has become more enthusiastic in establishing all kinds of dialogue mechanisms with the U.S., not necessarily to seek immediate solution of problems as the U.S. does, but to enhance mutual understanding that, over time, will facilitate the solution of problems or reduce troubles.

Finally, in most cases where disputes arise, except for the Taiwan issue, China refrains from resorting to confrontational measures, such as exerting military pressure or imposing sanctions. The U.S. is usually inclined to draw on its military advantages based on its superior military power, forward military deployments and security alliances in the region, to exert pressure on China from time to time. It also frequently takes advantage of the asymmetrical market reliance between the two countries to sanction Chinese companies or launch anti-dumping measures against them. For China, such measures not only undermine mutual trust, but also raise the level of confrontation—projecting a negative impact on overall bilateral relations.

In addition to the above merits in China's strategy, policies and tactics that contribute to the management of bilateral relations, China's political system also ensures continuity and stability in its foreign policy, including U.S. policy. American foreign policy lacks continuity and credibility due to political cycles arising out of election politics and the interplay of interest group politics, while China policy in particular has fallen victim to internal politics in the U.S. from time to time.[22] Chinese leaders always emphasize the need to adopt strategic and long-term perspectives on bilateral relations—whereas U.S. leaders, driven by political cycles, invariably pay more attention to tactical and short-term gains in dealing with China. It is true that China's domestic politics also increasingly work to complicate its handling of relations with the U.S., but such impact is largely manageable and has caused much less volatility to bilateral ties than vice versa. Compared with their U.S. counterparts, Chinese leaders are more willing to spend their political capital on bilateral relations, partly because they face much less policy controversy and political risk at home than U.S. leaders do in an environment featured by partisanship and interest group politics.

POSSIBLE FUTURE SCENARIOS FOR SINO-U.S. RELATIONS

Theoretically, there exist three scenarios regarding the future of bilateral relations: partners, competitors, and enemies. Let us think about how each of these three "ideal types" may play out in the future.

As partners, China and the U.S. would engage each other in a generally cooperative mode. In this scenario, the two sides not only trust each other with their respective strategic intentions, but also hold the same or similar views on most regional and global developments—thus providing a strategic and conceptual framework, and practical foundation, for their cooperation. Bilaterally,

growing economic interdependence will cause the world's two largest economies to develop a mode of cooperative coexistence, expanding areas of common interests while effectively overcoming or managing differences. In the
Asia-Pacific region, the two countries will work together to shape a new regional order featured by Sino-U.S. coordination in regional institutions. On
international and global issues, China will play a more active role while the
U.S. will be more willing to listen to other major players, including China, thus
developing a pattern of burden- and power-sharing among the major powers.

As competitors, both China and the U.S. would harbor a certain level of
suspicion towards each other and frequently hold diverging views on—and
pursue different approaches to—major regional and global issues. As a result,
competition instead of cooperation would characterize the overall relationship.[23] In bilateral interactions, economic frictions over trade, currency and
investment and political quarrels over human rights occur from time to time.
In the Asia-Pacific region, as China's influence expands, the U.S. will actively
pursue a strategy of counterbalance vis-à-vis China so as to maintain its al-
pha position in regional affairs. While they can get along with each other and
sometimes cooperate and coordinate, their competition for influence and interests invariably complicates the handling of regional economic and security
issues. On international and global issues, the two countries are often on different pages regarding principles or approaches or both. Their concern over
relative gains makes cooperation always a tough bargaining process.

In an antagonistic relationship (enemies), China and the U.S. view each
other as major threats to their respective core national interests, and they hold
not just diverging but conflicting views on regional and international issues.
Unlike in a competitive relationship where each side seeks to gain more and
cooperation is still possible after hard bargaining, in the antagonistic mode
each side tries to prevent the other side from gaining and cooperation is rare
(if at all). In bilateral interactions, economic ties drastically decrease, trade
wars and sanctions occur frequently, while intensified political disputes increase. In the Asia-Pacific, each side plays the geopolitical card and actively
seeks to form and expand its own sphere of influence, in a competition for allies and partners in the region. As a result, a polarization of the regional order
is inevitable. On international and global issues, rivalry and antagonism prevail over cooperation and coordination, efforts to promote global governance
always run into deadlock due to disputes.

In reality, the nature of a future Sino-U.S. relationship is most likely to be
one of a blend of cooperation, competition, and limited conflict. They are both
partners and competitors at the same time and even in the same issue area, but
not enemies. This is what David Shambaugh describes in his chapter as "competitive coexistence." Harry Harding's (following) chapter seems to agree with

this overall assessment. In this situation, economic ties constitute the most important pillar for bilateral relations, even though more frictions may occur in trade, investment, currency, intellectual property rights, and so forth. Cooperation and coordination between Beijing and Washington on regional, international and global issues are another pillar. Disputes over human rights, military development and activities, and approaches to regional and international issues will continue to exist and may intensify at some point, but will be unlikely to cause a major setback in bilateral relations. For both sides, the challenge is how to secure more cooperation than competition while reducing and avoiding the risk of conflict.

Recognizing this, one should not be blind to possibilities of bilateral relations derailing under certain circumstances. If the U.S. economy remains sluggish while the Chinese economy continues its robust growth, it will not only speed up the narrowing of the power gap between the two countries, but also contribute to a further decline of national self-confidence and rising resentment against China in the U.S., as is seen currently.[24] Endured China-bashing by the U.S. will certainly poison the atmosphere of bilateral ties and undermine any positive momentum behind Sino-U.S. relations. On the other hand, should the Chinese economy lose its strong momentum of growth, it will not only slow down the expansion of Sino-U.S. economic ties, but also adversely affect China's willingness and capability to play an active role in international affairs, thus damaging the two major pillars for bilateral relations.

Things may go wrong in other areas as well. On the Korean Peninsula, as North Korea enters an uncertain period with the sudden passing away of Kim Jong-il and the ill-prepared succession of Kim Jong-un, China and the U.S. may enter a head-on collision in a contingency on the Korean Peninsula. Beijing wants to maintain the stability there while Washington may take advantage of the contingency and push for the collapse of the regime. In the South China Sea disputes, both the Philippines and Vietnam are trying to make use of U.S. support in standing up against China—while the U.S. is also more and more interested in getting involved in the South China Sea. Should Manila or Hanoi, out of their calculated purpose of further dragging Washington into the disputes, create a crisis and even a conflict with China in the South China Sea, a Sino-U.S. confrontation there is likely to occur.

Looking into the future, the pattern of Sino-U.S. relations will bear other features as well. First, China's growing self-confidence will make it more active in agenda-setting and tougher in bargaining; as a result, Washington should be prepared to deal with China in a more equal and reciprocal mode. Second, more domestic actors will try to influence bilateral relations, such as the media and the public in China and the state and local governments in the U.S. This will make the management of bilateral ties even more complicated. Third, the "third-party factor" will project more influence on bilateral relations than it did in the past, further expanding a bilateral agenda and calling for the creation of new mechanisms governing bilateral interactions.

CONCLUSION

Since the end of the Cold War, Sino-U.S. relations have been confronted with different challenges in each decade. In the 1990s, the challenge was how to establish a new mode for bilateral relations in the post–Cold War era. Economic cooperation became the main focus of bilateral interactions, while Washington avoided challenging China's domestic political stability and China sought to participate in an international system. In the first decade of the twenty-first century, the challenge was how to manage bilateral ties against the background of China's rapid development and the explosion of global issues. The fast growth of bilateral economic ties were maintained, while the U.S. addressed China's concern on the Taiwan issue and China acted to take up more international responsibilities. For the current decade, the challenge is how to manage bilateral relations as the power gap between China and the U.S. narrows while the mission for global governance expands. As the power balance rapidly shifts, Beijing and Washington need to build a decent level of strategic trust and keep economic frictions under control so as to maintain stability of the overall relationship. On the other hand, in the face of more complicated global challenges, China and the U.S. should forge a genuine partnership so as to effectively address them and enhance global governance for the common interests of humankind.

NOTES

1. "On the Theme of China-U.S. Relations in the New Era," address by Vice Foreign Minister Cui Tiankai at the Second Lanting Forum, January 14, 2011, available at: http://www.fmprc.gov.cn/eng/wjdt/zyjh/t786020.htm.

2. "Building a China-U.S. Cooperative Partnership Based on Mutual Respect and Mutual Benefit," speech by President Hu Jintao at the welcoming luncheon hosted by friendly organizations in the United States, Washington, D.C., January 20, 2011, available at: http://www.fmprc.gov.cn/eng/wjdt/zyjh/t789956.htm.

3. "China-U.S. Joint Statement," January 19, 2011, Washington, D.C., available at: http://www.fmprc.gov.cn/eng/wjdt/2649/t788173.htm.

4. Dai Bingguo, "Stick to the Path of Peaceful Development," *Beijing Review*, No. 51, December 23, 2010, available at: http://www.bjreview.com.cn/quotes/txt/2010-12/27/content_320120.htm.

5. Information Office of the State Council, The People's Republic of China, *China's National Defense in 2010,* March 2011, Beijing, available at: http://www.gov.cn/english/official/2011-03/31/content_1835499.htm.

6. Wu Xinbo, "The Re-internationalization of Sino-American Relations," *World Economics and Politics*, No. 8 (2009).

7. Yan Xuetong, "The Instability of China-U.S. Relations," *World Economics and Politics*, No. 12 (2010).

8. Department of Policy Planning, Ministry of Foreign Affairs, People's Republic of China, *China's Foreign Affairs 2006* (English Edition) (Beijing: World Affairs Press, 2006), p. 351.

9. The Chinese data are drawn from National Bureau of Statistics of China, available at: http://www.stats.gov.cn/english/statisticaldata/yearlydata/YB2002e/ml/indexE .htm. The U.S. data are drawn from Bureau of Economic Analysis, U.S. Department of Commerce, available at: http://www.bea.gov/national/xls/gdplev.xls.

10. Dai Bingguo, "Stick to the Path of Peaceful Development," op cit.

11. The White Paper that China released in September 2011 suggested that "China will assume more international responsibility as its comprehensive strength increases." See State Council Information Office, China, *China's Peaceful Development*, September 6, 2011, available at: http://english.gov.cn/official/2011-09/06/content_1941354.htm.

12. Hu Jintao, "Building a China-U.S. Cooperative Partnership Based on Mutual Respect and Mutual Benefit," op cit.

13. As of April 18, 2012, the United States has brought 13 cases against China to WTO, while China has brought six cases against the U.S., available at: http://www.wto .org/english/tratop_e/dispu_e/dispu_by_country_e.htm.

14. See, for example, Michael D. Swaine, *America's Challenge: Engaging a Rising China in the Twenty-First Century* (Washington, D.C.: Carnegie Endowment for International Peace, 2011), p. 341.

15. See, for instances, Azar Gat, "The Return of Authoritarian Great Powers," *Foreign Affairs*, Vol. 86, No. 4 (July/August 2007), pp. 59–69; Robert Kagan, "The World Divides . . . and Democracy Is at Bay," *Sunday Times*, September 2, 2007; Harry Harding, "Blazing a New Trail," *China Security*, Vol. 4, No. 2, (Spring), pp. 7–8; Condoleezza Rice, "Rethinking the National Interest," *Foreign Affairs*, Vol. 87, No. 4 (July/August 2008), pp. 2–26.

16. "China-U.S. Joint Statement," January 19, 2011, op cit.

17. State Council Information Office, China, *China's Peaceful Development Road*, December 22, 2005, available at: http://www.china.org.cn/english/2005/Dec/152669 .htm.

18. "China-U.S. Joint Statement," November 17, 2009, Beijing, available at: http:// www.fmprc.gov.cn/eng/wjb/zzjg/bmdyzs/xwlb/t629497.htm; "China-U.S. Joint Statement," January 19, 2011, op cit.

19. "China-U.S. Joint Statement," January 19, 2011, ibid.

20. Hu Jintao, "Towards Common Development and a Harmonious Asia," speech delivered at Boao Forum for Asia, April 15, 2011, available at: http://www.fmprc.gov .cn/eng/wjdt/zyjh/t816535.html.

21. As the White Paper of *China's Peaceful Development* argues, "In the ever-changing world of today, all doctrines, systems, models and paths are subject to the test of the times and practice. As national conditions vary from country to country, there is no such thing as a fixed mode of development which claims to be the only effective one and applicable to all. A path of development is viable only when it suits the national conditions of a country." State Council Information Office, *China's Peaceful Development*, op cit.

22. For a narrative of how U.S. presidential successions had caused a cyclical pattern of ups and downs in Sino–U.S. relations since normalization, see Suisheng Zhao,

"Shaping the Regional Context of China's Rise: How the Obama Administration Brought Back Hedge in Its Engagement with China," *Journal of Contemporary China* Vol. 21, No. 75 (June 2012), available at: http://dx.doi.org/10.1080/10670564.2011.64 7428.

23. See Aaron L. Friedberg, *A Contest for Supremacy: China, America, and the Struggle for the Mastery of Asia* (New York: W.W. Norton, 2011).

24. Ted Galen Carpenter, "An Insecure America Scapegoats China," January 9, 2012, available at: http://nationalinterests.org/blog/the-skeptics/insecure-america-scapegoats-china-6349.

16

American Visions of the Future of U.S.-China Relations
Competition, Cooperation, and Conflict

Harry Harding

The future of U.S.-China relations has all too often been portrayed in overly stark, mutually exclusive scenarios. Will China and the U.S. become "friends" or "foes, partners or rivals?"[1] Will they become close collaborators, working together in addressing a growing number of regional and global issues on which they increasingly share common interests? Will the two countries become economic or strategic competitors, not necessarily engaged in direct confrontation, but vying for power and influence on the international stage?[2] Or will the remaining differences in their interests and values be so great as to make their relationship antagonistic, with a significant risk of open conflict?[3]

While some observers believe that competition, even conflict between the U.S. and China is inevitable, and others predict that the two countries will be forced by common interests and a shared fate to cooperate with each other, however reluctantly,[4] an increasingly common view is that their future relationship will be characterized by a blend of cooperation, competition, and discord, with the balance among these three outcomes depending on the two countries' definition and prioritization of their national interests, their ability to identify common goals and to work together to advance them, and their skill at managing the differences in interests and values that could foster competition or conflict.[5]

Many of the contributors to this volume agree that this more balanced assessment of the future of U.S.-China relations—characterized by a combination of cooperation, competition, and discord—is more likely to be accurate than either of the two categorical scenarios (conflict or partnership) that have often dominated commentary on the relationship.[6] But that assessment still needs to be taken one step further. Each of these three possible outcomes—cooperation, competition, and conflict—contains a further range of possibilities that should be more carefully identified and examined. Rather than simply predicting that there will be competition between the two countries, we need to explore the *kind* of competition there is likely to be: the aspects of the relationship where competition is evident, the ways in which competition is conducted, and the consequences of those competitive interactions for the overall relationship. Similar questions can also be asked about the cooperative and antagonistic dimensions of the relationship.

In this chapter, I argue that different forms of competition, cooperation, and antagonism will have different effects on the overall tone of U.S.-China relations. Looking further ahead, that tone will then shape the probable balance among these three types of relationship, in that a relationship primarily characterized by fruitful cooperation and rules-based competition will likely become more trustful and less discordant, whereas one characterized more by unsatisfying efforts at cooperation, and by unregulated competition that either or both parties regard as unfair, will become more prone to mistrust and conflict. In other words, the future of U.S.-China relations may not only be a complex amalgam of competition, conflict, and cooperation, but each element in that amalgam, and the nature of that blend among them, may change over time, depending on how the two countries manage those different aspects of their relationship.

COMPETITION

China and the U.S. already see themselves as competitors in many arenas, ranging from their rivalry for gold medals in the Olympics to their competition for votes in the U.N. Security Council. But the issue is not just whether the two countries are engaged in competition, but rather the *form* that their competition takes: the arenas in which it occurs, the degree to which it is effectively governed by rules (tacit or institutionalized) that both countries accept, and whether the competition produces outcomes that both of them regard as reasonable. The problem for China and the United States is not only that their relationship has become increasingly competitive—although it has—but that aspects of their competition are perceived by either or both parties to be costly, unfair, and risky—a perception that can produce mistrust and eventually give rise to an even more contentious relationship.

One of the most important tasks in assessing a competitive relationship is to identify the arenas in which it occurs. In economics, for example, fair and open competition, whether between countries or among firms, is the defining characteristic of a well-functioning market, where it is seen as a mechanism that improves the quality, increases the availability, and lowers the prices of the goods and services on offer. Therefore, most advanced market economies have policies to *promote* competition and to prevent the emergence of monopolies and other commercial practices that restrict it. Similarly, in a globalized economy the competitive benefits of trade and cross-border investment are also increasingly recognized, and are promoted through various bilateral and multilateral agreements. In the economic arena, in short, competition is to be welcomed, not avoided, even though some actors may benefit more from that competition than others.

Competition is also regarded as a necessary and beneficial feature of democratic political systems, where political candidates engage in competitive elections for public office, political parties and non-governmental organizations compete for membership and financial contributions, and policies and ideologies compete for support from both political leaders and ordinary citizens. In fact, the concept of the "marketplace of ideas" draws an implicit analogy between the benefits of competition for an economy and the benefits of ideological or political competition for a society.

Conversely, in other arenas, competition may be a less positive phenomenon, either for the parties engaged in it or for the system as a whole. In the realm of international security, competition can lead to costly arms races and can foster the well-known "security dilemma," in which one country's attempts to enhance its own security lead to reactive measures by other parties that feel threatened, ultimately making all sides feel less secure and, even worse, prone to engage in preemptive action or to escalate a confrontation once it has begun. In the security arena, competition may increase the chances of miscalculation, accident, and the risk of war.[7]

A second dimension along which competitive relationships vary is the extent to which they are governed by rules that limit the negative consequences of competition, promote more beneficial outcomes, and are accepted and honored by the participants. In Anatol Rapoport's classic trichotomy of competitive relationships,[8] both "games," and "debates" are normally regulated by rules that restrict the means and methods that the competitors may use. Thus domestic economic competition may be governed by regulations outlawing false advertising, discouraging monopoly, and ensuring the quality of goods and services. International competition is also promoted by a growing number of rules that reduce barriers to the flow of goods, services and investment capital while simultaneously prohibiting unfair practices such as dumping (subsidizing exports so that they can be sold below their domestic market prices). Many of these measures have been codified in bilateral and multilateral free trade agreements and in the various rounds of the World Trade Organization

(WTO), with a dispute resolution mechanism established within the WTO to adjudicate disagreements over the application of those rules. Domestic political campaigns may also be governed by campaign laws intended to promote "fair" competition. And even if there are no formal laws or regulations, competition may be governed by a commonly shared normative understanding of what constitutes "fair play."

Even "fights"—Rapoport's third and most adversarial type of competitive relationship—may also be regulated in analogous ways: virtually all sports that involve physical contact (wrestling, soccer, boxing, football, etc.) have rules intended to reduce the risks of physical injury. The development of the laws of war, the creation of arms control regimes, and the development of confidence-building measures can also be seen as efforts to reduce some of the costs and risks of competitive relationships in the international security realm.

Finally, a third aspect of variation among competitive relationships is the outcomes that they generate. All competitions produce winners and losers. But they can differ, often significantly, with regard to relative gains and losses: how much the winners win, how much the losers lose, and whether the outcomes are zero-sum, negative-sum, or positive-sum. They can also differ with regard to whether the competing parties regard those outcomes as reasonable or unreasonable, just or unjust.

From this perspective, it is clear not only that the U.S. and China are engaged in competitive relationships, but also that some of the arenas in which they are competing are more costly and risky than others, that the mechanisms regulating their competitive relationship are only partially effective, and that some observers in both countries have come to regard the outcomes of that competition as imbalanced and unfair.

Economic Aspects of U.S.-China Competition

In the immediate post-normalization period, China and the United States saw themselves as highly complementary economies, given their different factor endowments and their different levels of development. One of the most familiar ways of describing their economic relationship at the time was as involving the world's largest developed economy and the world's largest developing economy, implying that their economic ties would be mutually beneficial and far more complementary than competitive. As the Cold War wound down, Richard Nixon often remarked that while the common security threat from the Soviet Union had brought the U.S. and China together, it would be the economic relationship between their two complementary economies that would keep them together.[9]

But the U.S.-China economic relationship has become far more competitive than it was in the 1980s and early 1990s when Nixon made that prediction.

With its rapid modernization, China has moved into areas of manufacturing that are less labor-intensive, more capital- and technology-intensive, and that involve the production of higher-value-added goods—in other words, into areas of economic activity that had once been regarded as the preserve of the United States. As that has occurred, the sphere of complementarity between the two countries has shrunk and the sphere of competition has increased, with Chinese and American firms competing for market share both domestically and globally, and with the competition gradually extending into sectors that both governments see as highly strategic, such as automobiles, supercomputers, commercial aircraft, solar panels, and the like.[10] Chinese and American scientists and engineers are competing to make new achievements in such areas as supercomputing, biotechnology, and manned space flight, and Chinese and American companies are competing with each other (as well as with firms from third countries) to win contracts to exploit energy and mineral resources around the world. To the extent that China's currency becomes convertible, the two countries' financial centers (New York and Shanghai) may start to vie for listings on their stock exchanges, and the two economies may increasingly compete to attract both direct and portfolio investment from abroad.

To some degree, this competition has had, and will continue to have, the kinds of beneficial consequences that neo-classical economic theory would predict. The growing productivity of Chinese manufacturing, for example, while doubtless displacing manufacturing industries in other countries, including the United States, has also helped limit inflationary pressures around the world, as well as contributing significantly to China's economic growth. It has also opened up new or larger markets to foreign companies producing the equipment, materials, and components needed by Chinese manufacturing firms. The inventions created by Chinese engineers and the new discoveries made by Chinese scientists will ultimately add to the world's storehouse of knowledge.

Increasingly, however, observers in both China and the U.S. are complaining that the economic competition between the two countries is not only intensifying, but is also unfair and, additionally, inadequately regulated. Some Chinese believe that their country is the target of discriminatory treatment by the U.S., particularly when proposed Chinese investment projects in the U.S. are scrutinized and blocked on the grounds that they involve access to advanced technology or ownership of critical infrastructure. Beijing also complains about continuing American controls on the export of advanced technologies to China, and the fact that China is not yet regarded as a market economy with regard to the application of anti-dumping regulations. Conversely, there have been many complaints, first in the U.S. and now increasingly in the

EU and Japan, that Chinese firms benefit from government regulations that discourage the purchase of foreign products and imported technology, restrict foreign ownership in strategic sectors of the Chinese economy, and promote the emergence of strong Chinese "national champions" that can compete more effectively with their foreign counterparts both at home and abroad. Chinese firms are also alleged to take advantage of a deliberately undervalued Chinese currency to gain advantage on international markets. They are accused of pirating software and other proprietary technology, and engaging in industrial espionage. Some foreign critics charge that China is engaged in unfair competition with the U.S. and other countries to gain access to energy supplies and natural resources abroad, in part by providing large unconditional foreign aid "packages" to acquire influence over the foreign governments that are letting the exploration and production contracts, with the aim not only of seeking the revenues and profits that would come from selling those resources on an open international market, but also of trying to "lock up" those resources for China's exclusive benefit.

To some degree, the two countries have sought to utilize or develop mechanisms that can alleviate these complaints by regulating this economic competition between them. In order to join the WTO, China was required to agree to a variety of market-opening measures and to accept rules aimed at ensuring fair cross-border competition. The WTO has also provided a dispute resolution mechanism to adjudicate alleged violations of those rules. In addition, the two countries have engaged in a variety of bilateral negotiations and dialogues to address other issues that have emerged in the course of their competition. But China has increasingly been perceived as failing to honor many of the commitments to increase market access and to protect intellectual property rights that it made during its accession to the WTO and during subsequent negotiations with the U.S. Moreover, some aspects of the competition remain unregulated; in particular, the two countries lack a bilateral investment treaty that could provide rules for the flow of direct investment between them.

Chinese officials and analysts often insist that China's economic relations with the U.S., as with other countries, produce "win-win" outcomes that are beneficial to both sides, at least in overall terms. While there may be winners and losers in each country, they say, both economies benefit from their economic relationship. While that may be true to some degree, the relationship is increasingly burdened by the perception that the relative gains favor China and are costing Americans jobs, market share, and comparative advantage in key economic sectors. Accurate or not, these perceptions of unfair competition complicate the economic ties between China and the U.S, and create a legacy of mistrust that can spill over into other aspects of the relationship.

Normative Aspects of U.S.-China Competition

In addition to their economic competition, China and the U.S. have been also engaged in a competition in the normative arena. This is sometimes portrayed as a debate over the virtues of two competing models of economic and political development: a "Washington Consensus" favored by the U.S., and a "Beijing Consensus," promoted by China. The Washington Consensus prescribes rapid movement toward private ownership and free markets, whereas the Beijing Consensus advocates a strong continuing role for the state in managing (and, to some degree, protecting) the economy, including a significant degree of state ownership (and, in the Chinese case, Party control) in strategic sectors, as well as a gradual and experimental approach to economic reform. With regard to human rights, the U.S. pays particular attention to the protection of civil and political rights and the promotion of democracy, whereas China focuses more on economic and social rights and is willing to sacrifice or postpone the promotion of civil and political rights and democracy for the sake of economic development and political stability.

While the idea of a "Beijing Consensus" has attracted considerable attention in recent years, it has more often been foreign observers, rather than the Chinese themselves, who have suggested a competition between these two models of economic development. Chinese analysts—especially official spokesmen—are more likely to deny that there is a distinctive "Chinese model" of development, and assert instead that the Chinese experience simply teaches that each country should find its own way, based on an independent assessment of its factor endowment and its international environment, and should take a gradual and experimental approach to economic reform and development. Moreover, there is considerable debate among Chinese analysts over the degree to which the Chinese experience significantly departs from the prescriptions embodied in the "Washington Consensus." Some Chinese observers acknowledge that their country's recent development experience has embodied many of them, including deep integration into the global economy, a shift from planning to markets, and a greater tolerance for both private and foreign ownership in economic life. Moreover, technical advice from the World Bank did play a major role in influencing some aspects of China's economic reforms.

In a real sense, therefore, the "Chinese model" is less a model than an "anti-model": a rejection of the claims to universality that are part of the "Washington Consensus," rather than the presentation of the "Beijing Consensus" as a clear, commonly applicable alternative. In this way there may actually be less competition between Chinese and American models of development than has been assumed. Still, there are evident competitive overtones between the American belief in the universality of the liberal model of reform and development embodied in the "Washington Consensus" and the Chinese insistence that there is no universal model that all other countries should be urged to follow.[11]

Moreover, there may be a clearer competition between the American and Chinese approaches in other areas, particularly the two countries' diverging views on the norms that should govern international relations. To a large degree, China still embraces what John Ikenberry describes in his chapter as the "Westphalian project": an international order based on long-standing principles of national sovereignty, non-interference in internal affairs, and territorial integrity. By comparison, the U.S. has adopted what Ikenberry calls a "liberal" conception of international politics, in which the more recent concept of self-determination may trump territorial integrity, and the promotion of human rights and other humanitarian considerations may justify outside intervention in the affairs of other states, up to and including the use of force. Those liberal norms also hold that the international community may try to prevent the proliferation of mass destruction and their associated delivery systems, despite the older principles of national sovereignty and the right of self-defense that might justify them. Although Beijing has expressed strong reservations about these new liberal norms, one can well argue that the U.S., sometimes working together with its allies, has challenged the "Westphalian project" more effectively than China has, at least so far, posed a fundamental threat to what Ikenberry calls the "liberal order building project."[12]

Relatedly, China and the U.S. have different views of the norms governing foreign aid. The U.S. is more likely to believe that conditions, including adhering to norms of good governance and human rights, can appropriately be imposed on developing countries via official development assistance programs (ODA). So far, at least, Beijing has been more willing to grant foreign aid unconditionally—or, at least without reference to the recipients' respect for human rights or their practices of domestic governance. To the extent that Beijing imposes conditions, tacitly or explicitly, they are more likely to be related to the recipient's position on issues of great salience to China, such as its relationship to Taiwan or its views on Tibet, than to involve conditions similar to those of greatest concern to the U.S.—at least until the Chinese government and Chinese firms have direct experience with the political risks engendered by poor governance and violations of human rights.

These diverging models and norms—the "Beijing Consensus" and the "Washington Consensus," the "Westphalian project" and the "liberal order building project," and unconditional and conditional approaches to the provision of foreign assistance—limit the two countries' ability to cooperate on a range of international issues, since those differences sometimes lead them to support different solutions to the same problems. Moreover, these differences may also introduce an element of competition into the U.S.-China relationship, if Beijing and Washington begin to seek endorsement of their competing visions from other countries.

Looking ahead, China and the U.S. may begin to compete in other cultural areas as well—competing, in effect, in the arena of developing national "soft power."[13] Chinese intellectuals appear eager to identify values that they regard as unique to China, or at least different from those dominant in the West. The recent emphasis on "harmonizing" divergent views in society is one possible example, standing in alleged contrast to the American tendency to celebrate differences as a reflection of cultural diversity, even at the cost (some Chinese would argue) of domestic instability. Similarly, some Chinese social scientists are keen to create "Chinese schools" of scholarship in various areas of inquiry, including international relations theory. The specific features of these "Chinese schools" remain to be determined, and many scholars (including some Chinese) believe that since science is universal in character, an attempt to create national "schools" in the natural and social sciences is no longer practical, in that any important differences in methodology, or conclusions that emerge in the course of scientific inquiry are unlikely to fall along national lines. What may be somewhat more realistic is China's effort to create first-rate institutions for research and higher learning to compete with those abroad, drawing in particular on the talent of Chinese trained overseas. Here, the model China is following, at least in form, is very much an American one—with an emphasis on hiring world-class faculty, the promotion of cutting-edge, peer-reviewed research, with success measured through institutional ranking systems virtually identical to those presently used in the U.S. and the West. There are many constraints that will hinder Chinese success in this area, including an environment that is relatively unattractive to many first-rate scholars, a continued insistence on political orthodoxy, and widespread plagiarism. But one must acknowledge the determination of China (as well as other countries) to engage successfully in this competition. This attempt to build world-class institutions of higher education parallels, and is integrated with, the competition in scientific and technological discovery discussed above.

Strategic Aspects of U.S.-China Competition

The biggest danger is that the U.S. and China increasingly regard themselves not only as economic or normative competitors, but as *strategic* competitors. Unfortunately, the two countries' militaries have begun to perceive each other in this way, each deploying weapons systems and devising military tactics to counter the other, especially with an eye to contingencies involving Taiwan. The Chinese are seeking to develop the capacity both to apply military pressure to the island and to deter and defend against any American intervention in support of Taiwan. In addition, the competition is also increasingly focusing on the South China Sea, where China asserts sovereignty over islands that are also claimed by countries that are friends or allies of the U.S. With an eye toward advancing both sets of territorial interests, the People's Liberation Army (PLA) is developing strategies (e.g., anti-ship ballistic missiles) to deny the U.S. unfettered access to the Western Pacific, while the U.S. is engaged in a parallel effort (e.g., the "air sea battle" concept) to maintain that access.

As noted above, this kind of competition produces both significant risks and economic costs. There have already been incidents in which American reconnaissance and patrol missions off the coast of China have literally collided with Chinese military units seeking to push them further away from Chinese territorial waters, with the risk that these incidents could, at a period of high tension, escalate into open conflict. This is related to another normative difference between the two countries: their differing interpretations of whether China has the right to restrict or prohibit the passage of foreign naval forces through its exclusive economic zones, a right that China asserts but the U.S. rejects.[14] The EP-3 incident of 2001 has been the most dramatic of these, but it has not been the only one. The risks that such episodes can escalate are not trivial, and are likely to increase the more that similar incidents occur.

There is also the growing perception that the two countries' diplomatic and security initiatives in Asia reflect the competition between them, with China's "good neighborly" policy and Beijing's criticism of American alliances and deployments in the region viewed by some Americans as an attempt to undermine the hitherto dominant American position in Asia. Conversely, the American "pivot back to Asia" after its withdrawal from Iraq, its efforts to further develop its security relations with countries like Australia, Japan, India, the Philippines, and Vietnam, its exclusion of China from the Trans-Pacific Partnership free trade group, and its construction of diplomatic links with former pariah states like Myanmar, have been perceived by many in Beijing as a renewed effort to encircle and contain China.[15]

In an effort to manage this emerging strategic competition, the U.S. and China have engaged in military-to-military exchanges to increase transparency and build trust, in high-level strategic dialogues to gain better mutual understanding of each other's interests and intentions, and in discussions of arms control measures that might limit the two countries' deployment of nuclear weapons and weapons in space. So far, however, the results have been disappointing. There have been few concrete agreements, the Chinese have not exhibited high levels of transparency in the exchanges, and the military-to-military dialogue has been frequently interrupted, particularly by the Chinese, as a way of expressing displeasure with other tensions in the broader relationship (especially American arms sales to Taiwan). This failure to find ways of mitigating the strategic competition between the two countries increases the danger that the costs and risks of that competition will continue to mount.[16] As in the economic sphere, the mechanisms that might reduce the costs and risks of competition in the strategic realm fall far short of the need.

Sino-American Cooperation

The existence of a competitive relationship between the U.S. and China, even in the strategic realm, does not preclude the possibility of cooperative behavior to advance common goals. Indeed, there is a long list of issues on which the two countries have had common or overlapping interests and have therefore tried to cooperate: balancing the rise of the former Soviet Union in Asia, encouraging the denuclearization of North Korea, preventing the nuclearization of Iran, ensuring the prosperity of the international economy, suppressing piracy off the African coast, supporting counter-terrorist activities in Central and Southwest Asia, discouraging Taiwanese independence, promoting the security of energy supplies, developing alternative sources of energy, and limiting climate change, to name a few.

The two countries' common interest in maintaining the vitality of the international economy was reflected in the parallel stimulus policies that they implemented after the post-2008 Global Financial Crisis. Both countries have supported the creation of regional security and economic architecture in the Asia-Pacific region. Doubtless they would also cooperate if there were crises in other areas that threatened both of them, such as a pandemic such as SARS or avian flu. And they have agreed to work together on still other issues—including enhancing energy security, developing alternative sources of energy, and promoting the more efficient use of energy.

As with competition, however, the issue is not just whether the two countries engage in cooperation, but also the form that cooperation takes, the outcomes it generates, and especially how the results are perceived. Predictably, the most basic problem in U.S.-China cooperation has been the distribution of costs and benefits, disagreement over which can make collaboration far more difficult. For example, the American and Chinese governments have agreed that climate change is a problem that would pose significant costs and risks to both their countries. But they have not been able to agree on the allocation of the burdens of reducing carbon emissions between the developed and developing countries, or even on whether an international undertaking on this issue should be legally binding. Similarly, both Washington and Beijing may also agree on the desirability of creating a more robust regional economic and security architecture in Asia, but they do not necessarily agree on the membership or agendas of those organizations. They have a common interest in the denuclearization of North Korea, but they differ over their willingness to impose such severe sanctions on the country as to threaten the collapse of its government, since such a collapse would impose far higher potential costs on China than on the United States. In the case of Iran, China's interest in the oil imports from that country reinforces its underlying skepticism about both the legitimacy and the effectiveness of economic sanctions.

These differences over burden-sharing have often reflected the more competitive aspects of the relationship that run counter to the common interests. The two countries' differences over how to allocate the burdens of dealing with climate change are related to their underlying economic competition, just as their differences over how to deal with North Korea may be related to their strategic competition in Asia and to their different definitions of human rights. Those differences make it difficult for Washington and Beijing to agree on a common approach to problems, and complicate the development of a fully cooperative relationship.

The distribution of costs and benefits is only one issue that may complicate a cooperative relationship between two countries. Another is the quality of that cooperation. At one end of the spectrum is what might be called "passive consent," given by a party that might otherwise be able to block an action that its counterpart might wish to take. In many votes taken by the UN Security Council, especially those involving the imposition of sanctions or military action against third countries, the Chinese "cooperation" that the U.S. has been able to obtain is simply Beijing's willingness to abstain, rather than to exercise its veto power. In that process, Beijing may be able to water down the resolution under consideration, removing some of what it regards as the most objectionable passages, as the price for its consent. And sometimes China's willingness to abstain simply reflects the fact that it is reluctant to be the only member of the P-5 to veto the resolution. But securing even this modest form of cooperation is important to Washington if it permits the adoption of a Security Council resolution that authorizes the United States to undertake the sanctions or military activity it seeks.

A stronger type of cooperative interaction would entail the ability of two countries to acknowledge common goals, either tacitly or openly, and then to take independent actions to promote those goals, without necessarily working closely together. True collaboration would go even further: not just identifying common interests and taking individual actions to advance them, but jointly designing and implementing similar or coordinated measures to achieve those shared goals, along with a commitment to continue that collaboration until the common purpose has been achieved. The distinction between these stronger and weaker forms of cooperation is similar to the difference between working in tandem and working in parallel, or between a formal alliance and a looser "united front." In the former, each party sacrifices far more autonomy and room for maneuver than in the latter, where each undertakes a greater commitment and accepts greater constraints for the sake of their cooperation.

Over the years many Americans have perceived that even when China cooperates with the U.S. on issues of common interest, it often does so in a relatively passive or remote manner. In some areas, it may consent to American initiatives, but not commit its own resources to supporting those initiatives, and may simultaneously express reservations about their wisdom or appropriateness.[17] In others, it may cooperate by more actively adopting and implementing its own policies to advance the interests it shares with the U.S., but it does not more actively and openly collaborate with Washington in formulating a joint response, largely because it does not want to be perceived by either domestic or foreign audiences as working too closely with the United States, and because it wants to preserve its autonomy. As Henry Kissinger has emphasized in *On China*, this was already apparent in the two countries' opposition to Soviet expansion in Asia, where both countries shared an interest in resisting Soviet hegemony, but did not collaborate as closely or openly as did the United States and its NATO allies. Kissinger summarizes a conversation with Mao in 1971 on this point as follows: "How would global coordination between the United States and China be implemented? Mao suggested that each side develop a clear concept of its national interest and cooperate [with its own means] and out of its own necessity."[18]

Mao described this as acting "hand-in-hand," but his comments strongly implied that in reality the two countries' "coordination" would be conducted more at arm's length. As Kissinger summarized this and other exchanges on U.S.-China American cooperation against Soviet hegemonism:

> [A]t every stage of the dialogue about cooperation, Mao and other Chinese leaders insisted on a proposition designed to preserve Chinese freedom of maneuver and self-respect: that they did not need protection and that China was able to handle all foreseeable crises, alone if necessary. They used the rhetoric of collective security but reserved the right to prescribe its content.[19]

Obviously much has changed since 1971, and China may not any longer be able to "handle all foreseeable crises, alone if necessary." But China's preference for tacit, rather than overt, cooperation with the U.S. remains on many issues. On North Korea, Beijing has subsequently wanted to maintain a clear difference between its position and that of the United States, perhaps seeking to play a mediating role between Washington and Pyongyang in a way that neither Seoul nor Tokyo would be able to do. To a degree, Beijing seems to believe that high-level consultations with the United States on major issues is, in itself, a form of cooperation, even if the result is more the mutual understanding of differences rather than the formulation of a common program for advancing common goals. It is the gap between these more nominal or passive forms of cooperation and the more collaborative and active forms that the U.S. would like to see that makes even the cooperative aspects of the U.S.-China relationship so unsatisfying to many American observers, and even contributes to the mistrust between the two countries.

AN ANTAGONISTIC RELATIONSHIP

The third possible outcome in U.S.-China relations is discord and conflict, up to and including what some call a "New Cold War," or even open military confrontation. An antagonistic relationship implies the existence of sharply different objectives that outweigh common or overlapping interests, and the possibility of using various kinds of pressure, ranging from diplomatic initiatives and economic sanctions to the use or threat of force, to try to force the other side to accommodate. This differs significantly from the competitive relationships we have discussed above. A competitive relationship is not necessarily a zero-sum game, in that competition may create overall benefits for the arena in which it occurs—economic competition may make the society in which it occurs better off—and may even be positive for the actors involved in that they may all gain from the competition, albeit to different degrees. In contrast, an antagonistic relationship is more likely to be a zero-sum game, in which one side wins while the other side loses, or, even worse, a negative-sum game, in which both sides lose, although again possibly to different degrees.

China and the United States are no strangers to confrontation, having engaged in several confrontational periods, including several instances of armed conflict, since the establishment of the People's Republic in 1949. These have included the Korean and Vietnamese Wars, several crises in the Taiwan Strait, the American imposition of sanctions against China following the Tiananmen crisis of 1989, the mistaken U.S. bombing of the Chinese embassy in Belgrade in 1999, and the EP-3 incident of 2001. Of these, the most enduring cause of confrontation—and the problem that China portrays as the central problem in its relationship with the U.S.—has been Taiwan: with the American interest in a peaceful future for the island contradicting China's insistence that it retains the right to use force to achieve unification. Since 1989, however, human rights has been a second major source of contention, and there is the possibility that economic and trade issues may join this list in the near future.

As with cooperation, however, we need to probe more deeply to understand that the relationships produced by divergent interests are not all alike, but can take different forms. Just as earlier in this chapter we distinguished among several forms of cooperative relationships; here we can distinguish among disagreement, confrontation, and open conflict as distinct points on a spectrum of antagonistic relationships.

Disagreement implies a situation in which China and the United States have divergent interests that they openly acknowledge, but that do not lead to confrontational behavior and therefore may not disrupt the broader relationship. This pattern of behavior is frequently described by the Chinese as "reserving differences," and by Americans as "agreeing to disagree." For example, the United States continues to criticize China for what Americans regard as violations of human rights and as retrogression in China's domestic affairs. But other than those statements, issued both publicly and privately in various forums, the United States no longer takes significant action to sanction China for its alleged human rights violations. China frequently describes the American military base structure in Asia as a relic left over from the Cold War, but does not actively encourage the host countries to expel the American bases (or the U.S. government to close them). The open statement of these disagreements may be irritating to the party being criticized, and may contribute to mistrust between the two countries, but it does not inflict immediate significant damage on the broader relationship.

Conversely, at other times, the two countries have engaged in a more confrontational approach to their differences. China has not only criticized the United States for selling arms to Taiwan—an action that it regards as the most objectionable example of American intervention in what it regards as a domestic issue—but it has periodically restricted military-to-military relations with the United States in retaliation for those arms sales, even though those military exchanges were presumably in the interests of both countries. And for some time after the Tiananmen crisis of 1989, for example, the United States imposed a series of sanctions on China because of its concerns about human rights, including the threat (never implemented) to remove China's most-favored-nation status unless its human rights situation improved. Even if such sanctions or threatened sanctions do not lead to a tit-for-tat pattern of escalatory retaliation—a common danger in this kind of situation—they can be difficult to reverse, if the sanctioning party insists upon a reversal, cessation, or repudiation of the behavior that led to the sanction, and if the target of the sanctions refuses to do so, perhaps on the grounds, often invoked by Beijing, that it never yields to pressure. This more confrontational relationship therefore does more damage to a relationship than simple disagreements, however bluntly stated.

The most dangerous and severe form of antagonistic international relationship is clearly the use or threat of force. The United States and China have already experienced such conflict in Korea, (to a lesser degree) in the Taiwan

Strait, and through a proxy war in Vietnam. There is the possibility that armed conflict could recur if either the Korean Peninsula or the Taiwan Strait exploded again. The most commonly acknowledged danger would be one of two developments in the Taiwan Strait: a unilateral declaration of independence by Taiwan that China sought to reverse through military means, or the unilateral use of force by the mainland to compel Taiwan to accept unification. In either scenario, the United States would have to decide whether or not to use force or the threat of force to uphold its residual commitments to Taiwan's security as contained in the Taiwan Relations Act. If it decided to do so, then the risk of military conflict between the United States and China would be extremely high. Moreover, although the scenario is less frequently discussed, the Korean Peninsula could once again become the occasion for armed conflict between China and the United States. The most worrying possibility would be the collapse of the North Korean regime, followed by a competitive intervention by outside powers to promote their interests, whether the installation of a friendly successor government, the securing of North Korea's nuclear weapons and fissile materials, or simply the restoration of order. Such competitive intervention would not necessarily involve the United States immediately. But if South Korea were to cross the DMZ in this situation, to be countered by Chinese forces crossing the Yalu, or if China were to intervene in the North, without a prior agreement with the U.S. and South Korea, the chances for conflict would be significant.

Other confrontational scenarios are also conceivable. These might include a crisis in the South China Sea or East China Sea involving China and an American ally, or an incident between American and Chinese military forces, similar to the EP-3 incident of 2001. The possibility that either of these scenarios would escalate to a point that involved actual armed conflict between Chinese and American military forces is quite low, but cannot be entirely ruled out.

Of additional concern is the fact that the mechanisms for managing these confrontational scenarios are poorly developed. There is little evidence that the various security dialogues have discussed what the two countries would do if any of these situations emerged.[20] In particular, China and the U.S. have thus far not been able to discuss what their governments would do in the event of the collapse of the North Korean regime, making it impossible to rule out the possibility of a competitive intervention as described above. Nor do there appear to have been serious discussions of how to manage another crisis in the Taiwan Strait. Although there is a hotline between the two capitals, there is little confidence that the top leaders of the two countries would be able to use this communication channel effectively to manage a crisis. Thus far, the possibility of confrontation between China and the U.S. has been reduced more by the clarification of each other's "red lines" than by the development of mechanisms that can defuse a situation in which those red lines have been crossed. The former is helpful, but cannot substitute for effective communication in the event of a crisis.

CONCLUSION

This chapter has argued that the U.S.-China relationship has, in recent decades, been perceived in both countries as having become more competitive, in the economic, normative, and security spheres. Moreover, both sides have increasingly come to view their economic relationship as unfairly imbalanced in favor of the other. Although there have been numerous efforts to develop rules to govern that competition—either through bilateral negotiations or by bringing China into international regimes governing competition—neither country is satisfied, either with the rules themselves or with the other party's faithfulness in abiding by them. In the strategic sphere, the mechanisms for managing competition, and for preventing discordant interests from being transformed into confrontation and conflict, are far weaker than would be desirable. And although the two countries have talked about becoming cooperative "partners" and have engaged in numerous dialogues to promote such cooperation,[21] China's preference to act autonomously, rather than in open collaboration with Washington, as well as its reluctance to "interfere" in the internal affairs of other countries or to endorse American attempts to do so, has produced considerable dissatisfaction in the U.S. In short, despite efforts to regulate competition, reduce discord, and promote cooperation, the main outcome has been to increase the mutual perception that the U.S.-China relationship is essentially competitive, and in so doing to generate considerable mistrust on both sides of the Pacific.[22]

Leaders in both countries have recognized the problem of mutual mistrust, but they have not devised effective methods for reducing it. They have not been able to resolve most of the issues where they have major disagreements. The level of transparency on sensitive issues has not been adequate. And the reassurances that each has offered the other have not, in the absence of other measures, been regarded as credible.[23]

What are the relative probabilities that any of these broad categories of interaction—competition, cooperation, and confrontation—will dominate the U.S.-China relationship in the years ahead? Under what circumstances would such a dominant pattern emerge? And if none of these patterns dominates, what blend of the three types of relationship will the two countries experience?

It appears highly unlikely for the relationship between the U.S. and China to be primarily cooperative, at least in the short to medium term. The differences in values, political systems, interests, levels of development, and perceptions of the existing international order are simply too great for the two countries to find common ground on all issues, or even to find a mutually agreeable allocation of costs and benefits when they try to pursue common interests. Only a common interest that was massively compelling—say a widespread pandemic, another financial crisis, a global outbreak of terrorist activity targeted at both countries, or increasingly severe consequences of climate change—might produce a predominantly cooperative relationship. Even if such common interests were to emerge, the two countries might not be able to agree on how to share the burdens of protecting them.

Fortunately, an essentially confrontational relationship is also unlikely, especially in the sense of a direct military conflict. The high degree of economic interdependence between the two countries has already created a relatively resilient relationship, since the costs of a fundamental break between the two countries would be very high for each of them.[24] Equally important, the cost of military conflict, especially given the fact that both China and the U.S. are nuclear powers, will be a significant deterrent against military conflict. Although China and the U.S. may not be compelled to cooperate, in other words, they may be compelled to avoid confrontation. Moreover, the probability of the most worrying of the trigger events identified above—a unilateral declaration of independence by Taiwan—is presently quite low, as is the risk that China would try to compel unification through the use of force. In this case a system of mutual deterrence prevents any party from crossing any of the other's "red lines," which have been clearly identified and communicated. Another possible trigger event, the collapse of the North Korean regime, has a somewhat higher probability, and the two countries' red lines are less clear, but their ability to communicate quickly and avoid open conflict over that issue, while worth bolstering, is probably adequate, unless the overall relationship had deteriorated further prior to the event. Here again, mutual deterrence will play an important role in preventing the descent into military confrontation.

If the above analysis is correct, then the most likely future for the U.S.-China relationship will be largely competitive, although combined with elements of cooperation and discord—a mixed condition that David Shambaugh aptly describes in his introductory chapter as "coopetition." But the nature of that blend still to be determined by the actions of the two parties. The balance will be tilted toward greater cooperation and less discord if the two countries are able to:

- Identify and acknowledge additional common interests.
- Transform their cooperative interactions in pursuit of those common interests from the relatively passive (unproductive "dialogues," efforts to "reserve differences," or unenthusiastic consent for each other's ini-

tiatives) to more active, more openly acknowledged, and more fruitful collaboration).

- Ensure that the competitive aspects of the relationship are governed by rules and norms that are regarded as fair by both sides, with each side abiding by those rules and norms, and acknowledging that the other is doing so as well.
- Minimize the introduction of strategic elements into the two countries' competitive relationship, especially in Asia. Unilateral restraint, or negotiated limits, with regard to military acquisitions and deployments will be particularly important in this regard.
- Anticipate, and attempt to preempt, controversial issues that could threaten the stability of the relationship.
- In managing the discordant aspects of the relationship, identify clear "red lines" that the other should not cross, and yet draw those red lines sufficiently conservatively such that the other party is unlikely to cross them.
- While expressing differences plainly, seek mutual accommodation, without engaging in an escalating pattern of sanction and counter-sanction.

In short, the familiar formula that the U.S.-China relationship will be characterized by a combination of competition and cooperation is not wrong, but is incomplete. Some of the competition will be healthy and constructive, even though possibly intense. Some of the cooperation will be grudging or strained, and thus disappointing. While open conflict is unlikely, there will also almost certainly be disagreements, and possibly even elements of confrontation, in the relationship, and the relationship between China and the U.S. will be plagued by a high level of mistrust, particularly regarding the issues where competition or discord is the greatest.

The U.S. and China are not necessarily doomed to an antagonistic relationship, if they can learn how to manage their competition, increase their collaboration, and limit the differences in how they define their interests—a responsibility and challenge that both of them share. Some progress has already been achieved in that regard and, moreover, the relationship between the two countries is highly interdependent in ways that should increase its resilience. In light of those developments, it is no longer appropriate to describe the Sino-American relationship as "fragile."[25] But given the levels of the mistrust between them, their divergent values and interests, and their differences over the norms of the international system, the U.S.-China relationship will still be vulnerable to shocks that neither country can control or prevent. The ability to anticipate, prevent or manage those shocks will test the wisdom of their leaders, and ultimately the resilience of their relationship.

NOTES

1. I addressed this question in 1989, in the aftermath of the Tiananmen crisis, and provided the answer I still believe to be correct, in "Neither Friend nor Foe: A China Policy for the Nineties," *Brookings Review* (Spring 1992), pp. 6–11.

2. In his chapter in his volume, Ashley Tellis argues that a realist perspective on the U.S-China relationship would forecast a competitive relationship between the two countries. Richard Bernstein and Ross Munro go even further, and foresee conflict in their *The Coming Conflict with China* (New York: A. A. Knopf, 1997).

3. This possibility is discussed in Charles Glaser, "Will China's Rise Lead to War?" *Foreign Affairs*, Vol. 90, No. 2 (March-April 2011), pp. 80–91; and Aaron Friedberg, "The Future of U.S.-China Relations: Is Conflict Inevitable?" *International Security*, Vol. 30, No. 2 (Fall 2005), pp. 7–45.

4. Henry Kissinger argues that, by the beginning of the twenty-first century, China and the U.S. had entered an enduring period of "cooperative coexistence." Kissinger, *On China* (New York: Penguin Press, 2011), p. 487.

5. This conclusion, that none of these scenarios is inevitable, but will depend on decisions made by Chinese and American leaders, parallels Avery Goldstein's assessment in this volume that "In Asia as elsewhere, neither peaceful cooperation nor intractable conflict is inevitable."

6. This is one of the principal conclusions of Wu Xinbo's contribution to this volume.

7. Christopher Twomey's chapter in this volume emphasizes the particular role of the deployment of "significant numbers of vulnerable but offensively potent systems" in creating this dilemma, and argues that the maritime deployments by China and the U.S. can be described in these terms.

8. Anatol Rapoport, *Fights, Games, and Debates* (Ann Arbor: University of Michigan Press, 1960).

9. The author recalls Mr. Nixon making comments to this effect at a reception at the Chinese Embassy in Washington in the early 1980s.

10. Charles Freeman's contribution to this volume stresses the degree to which the Chinese and American economies are, in fact, still more complementary than competitive. But he acknowledges that many domestic actors in both countries no longer regard the U.S.-China economic relationship in this way.

11. This conclusion is echoed in Wu Xinbo's chapter in this volume.

12. In her contribution to this volume, Rosemary Foot makes this same point with specific regard to the "responsibility to protect: while Beijing is skeptical about this principle, and often seeks to "narrow its application . . . , there is no evidence that China is blocking outright the development of this norm."

13. See the discussion in Terry Lautz's chapter in this volume.

14. This issue is discussed further in Christopher Twomey's contribution to this volume. Twomey notes that the U.S. is invoking norms that, "following the practices of the previous global maritime hegemon, Britain, has played the lead role in establishing," but that "now as power ratios have shifted, there is bound to be some contestation of those rules."

15. These trends are further analyzed in the chapters by Avery Goldstein and Ashley Tellis.

16. Twomey argues that "substantial evidence shows that institutions and norms can temper the excesses that narrow security competition can lead to," but "while there are a number of such institutions in Sino-American relations, they remain generally underdeveloped and thin in substantive terms."

17. China's passivity in this regard is related to a broader phenomenon. As Rosemary Foot has put it in her chapter in this volume, "few analysts would describe China as having contributed directly or creatively to the provision of global public goods."

18. Kissinger, *On China*, p. 283.

19. Kissinger, *On China*, p. 287.

20. Christopher Twomey's chapter reaches the same conclusion.

21. These dialogues, and their uneven results, are catalogued in Bonnie Glaser's contribution to this volume.

22. See Kenneth Lieberthal and Wang Jisi, *Addressing U.S.-China Strategic Distrust* (Washington, D.C.: The Brookings Institution John L. Thornton China Center, 2012).

23. When they perceive American mistrust, Chinese tend to attribute it to a "Cold War" mentality or to ideological "bias." These factors may play a role. But the mistrust cannot be attributed solely to misunderstanding or bias. Because of the competitive and discordant aspects of their relationship each country has some reason to mistrust the other. The best analysis of mistrust in international affairs, Andrew H. Kydd, *Trust and Mistrust in International Relations* (Princeton: Princeton University Press, 2005), concludes that the best way of overcoming mistrust is not to offer empty reassurances, or to raise accusations of bias, but rather to provide "costly reassurances" to the other, as a way of demonstrating a level of goodwill that the other party did not expect.

24. Christopher Twomey reaches a similar conclusion in his chapter in this volume, where he argues that the two countries' economic interdependence, along with "China's broader incorporation within the global economy," will "likely overwhelm" the negative aspects of their security competition.

25. Harry Harding, *A Fragile Relationship: The United States and China Since 1972* (Washington: Brookings Institution Press, 1992).

Index

Note: Page numbers of figures (tables, charts, etc.) are italicized.

A2/AD. *See* anti-access/area denial
accord, on spectrum of U.S.-China relations, *22*
Acheson, Dean, 31
Afghanistan, 37, 165, 244, 263, 277–80, 378; U.S. war in, x, 105, 110, 112, 236, 265–66, 268, 283, 322, 371, 377–78
Africa, Sub-Saharan. *See* Sub-Saharan Africa
AFRICOM, 332
AIDS/HIV, 225
"AirSea Battle concept," 265
Ai Weiwei, 227
Algeria, 324–26
"alliance making/breaking," 92
al-Qaeda, 22, 327, 330, 342n52
ambiguity, strategic, 305, 307–8
America. *See* United States
American Enterprise Institute (AEI), 122, 224
"American Model," ix–x, 395
anarchy, 10, 14–15, 61, 72, 76–77, 96n9, 283
Annan, Kofi, 352, 359
antagonism; antagonistic interactions, 31, 44, 54, 349, 384, 389–90, 402–5, 407; with joint satisfaction over outcomes, 355, 357–59; and zero-sum interactions, 355–57
anti-access/area denial (A2/AD), 87–88, 240–42, 245
anti-Americanism, x, 31–33, 136, 139–40, 317
anti-communism, 8, 16, 32, 36, 44, 294, 298

anti-satellite programs, 12, 249, 257n20, 266
APEC, 151, 163, 169, 281, 289n37, 334
Arab Spring, 327–29, 360
Arab States, 323, 329, 341n29
Argentina, 334–37
arms control, 18, 128, 161–63, 224, 249, 392, 398
"arms embargo," 320
Art in America: 300 Years of Innovation, 227
arts organizations, 226–28
ASEAN, 246, 266, 272–75, 280–82, 286n16, 287n28; ASEAN Regional Forum (ARF), 69, 163, 169, 280–81, 286n13
Asia, 86–87, 90, 99n37, 263–91; multilateralism, 280–82; regional developments/power transitions, 57–58, 268–82; U.S.-China context for regional relations, 264–68
Asia Foundation, The (TAF), 225
Asian Cultural Council, 227
Asia-Pacific Consultations, 159–60, 172, 176
Asia Pacific Economic Cooperation. *See* APEC
Asia-Pacific region, 3, 9, 117, 136, 186, 315–16, 318; and the future, 372, 376, 379, 381–82, 384, 399. *See also* "pivot to Asia" policy
Association of Southeast Asian Nations. *See* ASEAN
Augustine of Hippo, 76
austerity, 276

Australia, 44, 58, 92, 243, 246, 275–77,
    288n34, 289n37
authoritarian capitalism, 67, 294, 380
authoritarianism, 230, 278, 329; anti-
    authoritarian movements, 290n44;
    Chinese, and U.S.-China relations,
    129–30, 138; the Chinese political
    system, 11, 17, 30, 39, 66–68, 79, 91,
    117; Leninist, 7, 15

Balkan War, 41
Barnett, A. Doak, 35, 125
Basel Committee on Banking Standards;
    Basel rules, 354
Baucus, Max, 111
Behind the Demonization of China, 140
Beijing Consensus, 67, 379, 382, 395–96
"Beijing Model," 57, 67
Beijing Olympics, 168, 214, 328
Belgrade. *See under* Chinese Embassy: U.S.
    bombing of
Bellamy, Alex, 361
Belsky, Shenyu, 225
Biden, Joseph R., 24n11, 132, 352
bilateral relations/mechanisms, 156–69;
    major factors shaping future of, 377–80;
    merits of Chinese approaches to, 380–83.
    See also future of U.S.-China relations
Bin Laden, Osama, 279
biotechnology, 85, 222, 393
bipolarity, 4, 10, 13, 94–95, 382
Bolton, John, 359–60
"bourgeois liberalism," 212
Brazil, 57, 64–65, 68, 192, 321, 334–36, 360
Bretton Woods institutions, 16, 62, 64, 356
Britain, 12, 61–62, 80, 238, 319, *321*, 404n14
British Embassy in Beijing, 35
Brookings Institution, 121, 224
Brown, Kerry, 349
Brzezinski, Zbigniew, 36, 44
bureaucracies, role of, 153–56
Burma. *See* Myanmar
Bush, George H. W., 39–40, 109–10
Bush, George W., 151, 194, 238, 264,
    279–80, 302, 305, 358; administration
    of, 110–13; and congressional dialogues
    with China, 112–13
Bush, Richard, 308–9

Cai Wu, 214
Cambodia, 37, *189*
Canada, 83, 181
capitalism, 6, 35, 54, 56, 60, 65, 67;
    authoritarian, 67, 294, 380; liberal, 380;
    "monopoly-finance," 136–37; "state
    directed," 186; Taiwan and, 294
carbon emissions, 166, 399
the Caribbean, 333–39
Carnegie Endowment for International
    Peace, 122, 224
Carter, Jimmy, 36–37, 104, 108, 212–13,
    223, 301
CATO Institute, 122
CCP. *See* Chinese Communist Party
censorship, 43, 127, 130, 215–16, 221, 227,
    229–30
Center for Strategic and International
    Studies (CSIS), 121–22, 224
Central America, 315, 333
Central Asia, 160, 176, 263–64, 277–80,
    282, 318, 399
Central Committee, CCP. *See* CCP Central
    Committee
Chamber of Commerce, American, x, 187
Chavez, Hugo, 333, 336
Cheng Li, 213
Chen Shui-bian, 293, 299, 301–2, 304–5
Cheonan (South Korean ship), 43, 168, 170,
    269–70
Chiang Ching-kuo, 296
Chiang Kai-shek, 30–35, 105, 293
Chile, 334, 336–37
"Chimerica," 42
Chin, Gregory, 17
China, 6, 9–10, 125–48; core interests
    of, 153, 171, 177n5, 287n17, 364n2,
    381; demographic trends, 48n44, 81;
    favorability ratings, *321*; and global
    governance, 353–55; goals of, 68, 135,
    143, 153, 183, 185, 187, 197–200. *See
    also* People's Republic of China; *specific
    topics*, e.g., domestic politics; exports;
    foreign policy; gross domestic product;
    labor; modernization; trade
China, Republic of. *See* Republic of China;
    Taiwan
China, rise of. *See* rise of China

China, the United States, and Global Order (Foot), 17
China American Studies Association, 137
China Can Say No, 140
"China collapse school," 49n55
China Daily, 139, 217
China Institute of International Studies (CIIS), 135, 339n9
China Institutes of Contemporary International Relations (CICIR), 135
China Investment Corporation (CIC), 320
"China Model," ix–x, 67, 186
Chinese Civil War, 31–33, 293–394, 297
Chinese Communist Party (CCP), 6–7, 15, 105, 126–27, 131, 264, 334, 347; CCP Central Committee, 7, 126, 155–56; historical context, 30–32; and Taiwan, 293–94, 299–301, 307
Chinese Embassy, 117, 120, 408; U.S. bombing of (Belgrade), 41, 115, 132, 139–40, 140, 254, 402
Chinese language, 3, 213–15, 218, 220–21, 224, 228, 232n23
"Chinese schools" of scholarship, 397
Chipman, Eric, 220
Christianity, 211
Churchill, Winston, 30
C4ISR system, U.S., 88
civil society, 14, 137, 143, 223–26, 230
Clark, Ian, 361–62
climate change, x, 3, 114, 158, 175, 213, 223–25; bilateral diplomatic agenda and, 165–66; and the future, 376, 378–79, 399–400, 406; global context, 316, 350–51, 358–59, 365n16; U.N. Framework Convention on Climate Change (U.N.F.C.C.C.), 127, 350, 358. *See also* Copenhagen Conference
Clinton, Bill, 40–41, 109, 279–80, 298
Clinton, Hillary, x, 165, 209n64, 213, 218, 266, 273–75, 281–82, 286n13
"co-evolution," 22
coincidences of interest, 359–60
Cold War, 4, 7, 18, 104–5, 108–10; "Cold War mentality," 409n23; and evolution of U.S.-China relations, 31, 37, 39, 44; factors shaping, 248; and the future, 371–75, 378, 380, 382, 386, 392, 402–3,
409n23; global context, 317, 319, 322, 339, 347–48; the military-security relationship, 241, 245, 250; "New Cold War," 402; public diplomacy after, 217; theoretical context, 57, 62–63, 79, 91, 94; and U.S.-China interactions in Asia, 264, 266, 276–77, 283
Colombia, 338
colonialism, 6, 62, 310n8, 318
"commercial liberalism," 16
commercial relationship. *See* economic relations
communism, 31–32, 39, 79; U.S. anti-communism, 44. *See also* Chinese Communist Party (CCP)
competition, 390–402; and China's rise, 78–81; economic, 86, 392–94; increasing, areas of, 83; military/security, institutional restraints on, 250–54; normative aspects of, 395–97; security competition, 81–93, 172; on spectrum of U.S.-China relations, 22; strategic aspects of, 397–99. *See also* "competitive coexistence"; "coopetition"
"competitive coexistence," 4–5, 20–22, 384
Comprehensive Nuclear-Test-Ban Treaty (CTBT), 69, 163
compromises, diplomatic relationship and, 169–71
"concert" of multiple states, 4
conflict, on spectrum of U.S.-China relations, 22
confrontation, 33, 43, 45, 92, 136, 264, 383, 385; and American public opinion, 117; avoiding, 13, 138; concerns regarding, 31, 391, 402–7; disagreement vs., 403; past (U.S.-China), 402–3; and saving/losing "face," 8–9
Confucius Institutes, 214–17, 221, 228, 230, 231n9, 324, 330, 335
"congagement," 4
Congress, National People's (China), 128, 155, 301
Congress, U.S., 103–24, 185, 224, 228, 237, 251, 294; Bush administration, 112–13; and climate protection, 358–59; congressional dialogues with China, 112–13; debt ceiling vote, 356; lobbyists,

192, 294–95; and Taiwan, 294–95, 298, 301–4, 311n30

Congressional-Executive Commission on China, 119

constructivism, 5, 10, 18–20

containment, strategy of, 4, 11, 33, 49n51, 79, 87, 91, 236, 379; "without isolation," 35

cooperation, 399–402; arenas of, 172; on spectrum of U.S.-China relations, *22*; "cooperative coexistence," 384, 408n4

"coopetition," 4–5, 19–22, 318, 379, 406–7

Copenhagen Conference, x, 127, 358–59

copyright piracy, 195–96, 199

core interests, 153, 171, 177n5, 287n17, 364n2, 381

counterterrorism, 161, 163, 173, 175

crime, transnational, 17, 164

crisis, financial. *See* global economic crisis

crisis of legitimacy, 307, 361–62

cross-border investment, 199–201

"crossover point," 11

CTBT. *See* Comprehensive Nuclear-Test-Ban Treaty

Cuba, 34, 315, 333–36

Cui Taikai, 9, 136, 366n37, 371

cultural relations/diplomacy, 5–10, 211–33; American universities in China, 221–22; arts organizations, 226–28; education, 218–19; foundations and philanthropy, 225–26; language teaching and learning, 219–21; nongovernmental organizations (NGOs), 222–24; think tanks, 224–25

Cultural Revolution. *See* Great Proletarian Cultural Revolution

currency, 192, 194–95; manipulation, 114, 116, 118; revaluation, 142, 171, 194–95, 354, 356, 366n37; the yuan, 356. *See also* dollar, U.S.; *renminbi* (RMB)

cyber attacks, x, 12, 118–19, 249, 316

cyber forums. *See* online forums

cyber security, 157, 161, 163–64, 249

Dai Bingguo, 134, 268, 364n2, 372, 376

Dalai Lama, x, 132, 166, 216, 228, 230

Daly, Robert, 227–28

Darfur, 323, 327–28, 341n31

Darwinism, 15

death penalty, 167

debt: European, 320, 322, 340n21, 375; U.S., 42, 115–16, 181, 192, 200, 322, 340n21, 356, 375

Decision on Bilateral Surveillance over Members' Policies (2007), 357

decline of America, 41, 79, 94, 115, 228, 288n34, 305, 378; global financial crisis and, 135–36. *See also* power transitions; *specific topics*, e.g., realism

decolonization, 62

"defensive realism," 96n11, 382

deindustrialization, 83–85

democracy, 8, 11–12, 14–15, 30, 167, 212, 318, 328; and the liberal international order, 54, 56, 63–65, 67–68, 70; promoting, U.S. goal of, 330, 333, 338, 395; universality of, 230

Democracy Wall movement, 37

Democratic Party, Japan's, 268

Democratic Party, U.S., 110–11, 116

"democratic peace theory," 12, 14

Democratic People's Republic of Korea. *See* North Korea

Democratic Progressive Party (DPP), 121, 298–99, 301, 375–76

demographic trends, 48n44, 81

Deng Xiaoping, 36–39, 43, 75, 135–36, 138, 183, 212–13, 228, 347

denuclearization, 170, 239, 253, 271, 378, 399–400

Department of Homeland Security, 42, 118

Deputies Committees (DCs), 153–54

détente, 18, 106

development assistance, 158–59, 166, 396

dialogues; dialogue mechanisms, 172–76. *See also* sub-dialogues; *specific topics*, e.g., Strategic and Economic Dialogue (S&ED)

diplomacy; diplomatic relationship, 151–79; bilateral diplomatic agenda, 162–69; bilateral mechanisms, 156–61; bureaucracies, role of, 153–56; dialogues, political, 172–74; and economic issues, 162; frustrations and compromises, 169–71; goals, respective, 152–53; symbols of diplomacy, 8. *See*

also normalization; *specific topics*,
e.g., cultural diplomacy; Strategic and
Economic Dialogue (S&ED)
disagreements, 40, 166, 264, 266, 271, 273,
280–83, 405; confrontation vs., 403,
407; and joint satisfaction, 355
disarmament, 253, 270–71, 347
disaster relief/management, 225, 252
dissidents, x, 16, 229
"Does China Matter?" (Segal), 317
Doha Round trade negotiations, 376, 378
dollar, U.S., 42, 181, 192, 194, 199–200, 356,
362, 366n37; and the future, 373, 375
domestic influences on U.S.-China
relations: China, 125–48; U.S., 103–24
domestic politics, 14, 32, 45, 79, 328;
China's, 125–26, 195, 305, 383; Taiwan's,
293; U.S., 137, 376–77
domestic preferential policies, and market
access, 197–99
DPP. *See* Democratic Progressive Party
DPRK. *See* North Korea
Dulles, John Foster, 34, 212
dumping, 84, 127, 319–20, 336–37, 383,
393; definition of, 391

Eagleburger, Lawrence, 39
earthquake, Sichuan (2008), 223, 226
East Asia Summit (EAS), 69, 169, 274,
280–82, 287n28, 289n37, 382
East China Sea, 43, 88, 128, 256n8, 267,
269, 271, 280, 286n13, 309, 404
Economic Cooperation Framework
Agreement (ECFA), 300
economic crisis. *See* global economic crisis
(post-2008)
economics; economic relationship, 83–86,
181–209; and bilateral diplomatic
agenda, 162; competition, 86, 390–94;
cross-border investment, 199–201;
currency, 192, 194–95; dialogue,
158–60, 175–76; domestic preferential
policies and market access, 197–99;
industrial policy, 201–2; intellectual
property rights and technology transfer,
195–97; interdependence, 187–88;
mechanisms for managing, 202–3;
points of contention, 192, 194–202;

public mistrust, 187; rebalancing, 156,
162, 190–92; RMB/USD exchange
rate and U.S. trade deficit, *193*; U.S.
economy as a model, 183, 185–87. *See
also* investments; trade; *specific topics*,
e.g., global financial crisis; institutional
lobbying groups; Strategic and
Economic Dialogue
Economy, Elizabeth, 348, 362
education, 167; American universities in
China, 221–22; Chinese students in
the U.S., 229; and cultural relations,
5, 218–19. *See also specific topics*, e.g.,
Confucius institutes; science
EEZ. *See* Exclusive Economic Zone
Egypt, 321, *321*, 324, 326
Eisenhower, Dwight D., 33–34
elites; elite opinion, 106, 108, 119, 134–35,
138, 172, 213
"end of history" thesis, 15
energy, 3, 17, 43, 86, 201, 224, 376;
alternative/renewable, 172, 197, 202,
222–23, 399; bilateral diplomatic
agenda, 165–66; Chinese interests,
366n33; dialogues, 175, 203; energy
security, 173, 246, 255, 323–25, 329–32,
341n39, 358, 399; supplies/resources,
331, 336, 393–94, 399; U.S. interests,
317; usage by developed countries, 358
English language, 3, 213, 217, 219–22, 229
Enlightenment, 14
entitlement programs, 115–16
environment, 17, 223; bilateral diplomatic
agenda and, 165–66; environmental
protection, 172–73, 225, 359; Obama
administration's approach, 358–59
EP-3 incident, 31, 115, 132, 156, 164, 239,
398, 402, 404
"epistemic communities," 18–19, 134
espionage, x, 40, 85–86, 118–19, 239;
economic, 164, 275; industrial, 197,
249, 394
ethnic minorities, x, 6, 167–68, 223, 225
Europe, Western, 46, 61–62, 65, 79, 188,
315–22, 338–39
European Union (EU), 319–20, 322, 333,
340n24, 375, 393–94. *See also specific
topics*, e.g., debt

Eurozone, 320
evolution of U.S.-China relations, 29–49.
  See also historical context
exceptionalism: American, 6–8, 211, 352;
  Chinese, 7–8
exchange rates, 84, 141, *193–95*, 357
Exclusive Economic Zone (EEZ), 161,
  164; and local reconnaissance, 238–39,
  243–44, 254, 256n8
exports; export markets, 83, 190, 319, *323–*
  27, 330–32, 336; China to U.S., 187–88,
  373, 375; U.S. to China, 83, 85, 156, 181,
  188, 373, 377

"face," giving/saving/losing, 8–9, 174
"faggot vote," 30
Falkland Islands, 248
Falkner, Robert, 365n16
fascism, 32
FDI. *See* foreign direct investment
Feigenbaum, Evan, 277
Ferguson, Niall, 42
Fewsmith, Joseph, 134
financial collapse of 2008. *See* global
  economic crisis
"Finlandization," 307
Finnemore, Martha, 18
fishing boat clashes, 69, 244, 269,
  286n13
Five Year Plan, China's, 190
F-16 jet fighters, 114, 116, 122, 304
food safety/security, 159, 166, 376
Foot, Rosemary, 17, 19, 30, 69, 347–68,
  408n12, 409n17
Forbes, Randy, 113
Ford Foundation, 19, 225
Foreign Affairs, 308
Foreign Affairs Leading Small Group
  (FALSG), 126, 128
Foreign Affairs Office (FAO), 126, 156
foreign aid, differing approaches to, 166,
  396; China's, 141, 166, 329, 333, 394;
  U.S., 236
foreign direct investment (FDI), 3, 85, 141,
  201, 326, 373. *See also* Outward Foreign
  Direct Investment
foreign policy, China's, 8, 35, 69, 125–48,
  216, 267–68, 355, 364n5; and the

diplomatic relationship, 152, 155–56;
  and the future, 372, 381, 383
foreign policy, U.S., 79, 103–24, 153–54,
  216, 219, 224, 264–65, 383
Formosan Association for Public Affairs
  (FAPA), 121
forums, online, 131–32. *See also* internet;
  "Strong Nation Forum"
foundations and philanthropy, 225–26
"Four Modernizations," 197
"Four Policemen," 30
France, 215, 218, 232n23, 319–*21*, 343n61,
  357
Frankfurt School of critical social theory,
  18
"Free China," 15, 30. *See also* Taiwan
freedom of expression, 167
freedom of religion. *See under* religion:
  freedom of
Freeman, Charles W., III, 20, 112, 181–209
Freeman, Chas W., Jr., 305–7
Freeman, Houghton ("Buck") ; Freeman
  Foundation, 221, 225
Friedberg, Aaron, 11–12, 16, 26, 44
Friedman, Thomas, 110
Fullilove, Michael, 359
future of U.S.-China relations, 21–22,
  93–95; American visions of,
  389–409; antagonistic relationship,
  402–5; Chinese visions of, 371–88;
  competition, 390–402; cooperation,
  399–402; major factors shaping,
  377–80; merits of Chinese approaches,
  380–83; possible scenarios, 383–86

G-20, 162, 166, 169–70, 347, 350, 354–57,
  365n15, 379
Gaddafi, Muammar, 322, 328
Gang of Four, 36
Gates, Robert, 265, 269, 303
Gates Foundation, 225, 230
GDP. *See* gross domestic product
Geithner, Tim, 68, 194–95
Geneva, Switzerland; the Geneva
  Conference, 33, 151, 319; the Geneva
  Protocol, 163
geopolitics, 11, 14, 21, 35; and the
  future, 382, 384; regional, 83, 89–93;

theoretical context, 53–54, 58–59, 67–68, 71, 75, 80, 82–83, 94; and U.S.-China interactions in Asia, 277–78

German Marshall Fund, 322, 340n24, 343n61, 360

Germany, 12, 80, 215, 232n23, 320–*21*, 360

Gillard, Julia, 276

Gilley, Bruce, 307

Gilpin, Robert, 11, 58–59

Glaser, Bonnie, 48n46, 112, 151–79, 306–7

Glaser, Charles, 12, 307–8

global capitalism, 56

"global co-dependency," 80

"global commons," 236, 254

global economic crisis (post-2008), x, 41, 46, 67, 157, 159; China's rise despite, 266; consequences of, 356; domestic context, 114, 135–37, 142; and the future, 374–75, 377, 379–80; global context, 322, 347–48; and "monopoly-finance" capitalism, 136–37; policies implemented after, 399; and rebalancing agenda, 190; regional context, 272, 308–9; revelation, 186. *See also* recession

global governance, 14, 347–68; definition of, 364n1

globalization, 15, 126, 255, 349, 372–74, 378, 380, 391

global order, 17, 56, 58, 63, 69–70, 95, 348, 352–53, 355; differing approaches of potential benefit to, 360–62

"global partnership," x, 92

global warming. *See* climate change

GNP. *See* gross national product

goals, respective, 152–53. *See also under* China.: goals of; U.S.: goals of

"Goddess of Democracy," 39

Goldstein, Avery, 24n17, 246–47, 263–91

Google, x, 163–64, 250

Gorbachev, Mikhail, 38

government. *See specific topics*, e.g., bureaucracies

Great Britain. *See* Britain

Great Leap Forward, 34

great power war. *See under* war: great power war

Great Proletarian Cultural Revolution (GPCR), 34–35, 212, 228

Great Wall, 6, 46

Greece, 10, 320

green technology, 202

gross domestic product (GDP), 183–*84*, 188–*91*, 198, 236, 357, 364n4, 374

gross national product (GNP), 75, 81–82, 84, 93

"Group of 4," 360

Guam, 88, 241, 256n11

Guangdong province, 142, 220

guangfu dalu ("retake the mainland") , 33

Guan Youfei, 303

"gunboat diplomacy," 318

guoji geju (international distribution of power), 135

Habermas, Jurgen, 129

Haiti, 253, 335

Hanban, 215–16, 218, 343n64

Han Chinese, 327, 342n51

Han Feizi, 10

Hao, Yufan, 125–48, 374

Harding, Harry, 284, 363, 389–409

"harmonious society," achieving, 138

Hatoyama, Yukio, 268–69

hegemony, 408n14; China and, 67–68, 75, 88–90, 95; Soviet (cooperation against), 401; theories of, 11–12, 58–59, 70, 76; U.S., 9, 44, 56, 58, 60, 62–63, 78, 82–83, 87–89, 136, 211, 238, 348, 352

Heritage Foundation, 122, 176, 224

hierarchical order, 60, 63, 130, 349, 352

Hirono, Miwa, 361

historical approach/context, 5–10, 29–49; 1949–1969, 30–35; 1969–1979, 35–37; 1980–1989, 37–38; 1989–2001, 38–41; 2001 and after, 41–44

HIV/AIDS, 225

Hobbes, Thomas, 14, 78, 82, 91

Ho Chi Minh, 33

"holding the ring," strategy of, 86–87

Hong Junbao, 131

Hong Kong, 85, 163, 188–*89*, 196, 219–20, 222–223, *251*, 319

House of Representatives, U.S., 113–114, 116, 119

HRD. *See* Human Rights Dialogue

Huanqiuwang (Global Net), 132, 140

Hui ethnic group, 327, 342n51
Hu Jintao, 7–8, 113, 129, 135, 141, 303–4,
    356; the cultural relationship, 212,
    215; the diplomatic relationship, 156,
    169–70, 198; and the future, 372, 374;
    the military-security relationship, 235,
    237, 246
humanitarian issues, 66, 165, 168, 223, 252,
    254, 359, 361, 396
human rights, 8–9, 15–17, 39, 63, 68, 185;
    Carter as "human rights president,"
    37; and the cultural relationship,
    212–13, 216, 223, 226–27, 229; different
    definitions of, 395–96, 400; and the
    diplomatic relationship, 151, 156, 164,
    166–68, 171; domestic context, 109,
    111–12, 117, 119–20, 139, 143; and the
    future, 371, 384–85, 395–96, 400; global
    context, 320–21, 327–28, 330, 333, 347,
    359; regional context, 275, 298; and
    "reserving differences," 403; as source of
    contention, 402–3
Human Rights Dialogue (HRD), 161,
    166–67, 175
Hundred Flowers campaign, 34
Hunt, Michael, 29–30
Huntsman, Jon, 140, 220
Hurd, Ian, 18, 350

Ikenberry, G. John, 16–17, 20, 53–73,
    97n15, 235, 250, 255, 282, 354, 362, 396
immigration, 318, 335, 338
imperialism, 29–31, 34, 41, 62, 212, 318
imports; import markets: to and from Latin
    America, 335, 337; from the Middle
    East and Sub-Saharan Africa, *323*,
    330–31, 400; to U.S. from China, 84,
    181, 187–88, *323*
India, 57–58, 64–65, 89–90, 92, 94, 192,
    263, 277–80; China Favorability Ratings
    (2002-2011), *321*; "Group of 4," 360; the
    Indian border, 309; Sino-Indian war, 34;
    US-Indian nuclear deal, 353; US-Indian
    relations, 247, 266, 283. *See also* South
    Asia
Indian-Americans, 121
Indian Ocean, 89, 246, 332
Indonesia, *189*, 243, 246, 274, 287–88, *321*,
    337

Indo-Pacific region, 86–87, 89–91
industrial policy, 201–2
In Larger Freedom (U.N. Secretary
    General's document), 359
innovation, 203, 226; American culture
    and, 230; China's focus on, 43, 60, 64,
    78, 81, 85, 130, 175, 197–99, 380
institutionalization, 20, 126, 128, 158
institutional lobbying groups, Chinese,
    141–42
intellectual property rights (IPR), 43, 114,
    118, 127, 162, 175, 177n16, 199; and
    the future, 385, 394; and technology
    transfer, 195–97
intellectuals, 6–7, 134–35, 137, 140, 195,
    309, 318, 397
interaction types, Sino-American, 355–62
Interagency Policy Committees (IPCs),
    153–54
Inter-American Development Bank
    (IADB), 334, 338
Inter-American Treaty of Reciprocal
    Assistance (Rio Treaty), 338
interdependence, 12, 30, 45, 71–72, 78–82,
    112, 142, 284; concept of, 15; economic,
    54, 81, 91, 216, 269; and the future, 371,
    373, 377–78, 380, 384, 406–7, 409n24;
    "happy," 187–*89*; peace through, 79;
    structuralism and, 20
"internal disorder, external pressure," 6
international law, 165, 213, 239, 273,
    287n17, 359, 366n25
International Monetary Fund (IMF), 64,
    323–24, 326, 331, 347, 350, 354–57, 363,
    377
international order, 10, 57, 75, 81, 352,
    406; distribution of power, 135.
    See also liberal international order;
    "Westphalian project"
international organizations, 347–68;
    evaluating behavior, problems of,
    350–51
international relations theories, three
    principal, 5
international security, 12, 20, 391–92.
    See also specific topics, e.g., "security
    dilemmas"
International Security and Non-
    Proliferation Dialogue, 161, 175

International Security Assistance Force
(ISAF), 165, 322
international structures, 20
"international waters," 236, 238, 273
internet: in China, 130–32. *See also* media;
specific topics, e.g., cyber security
internet nationalism (*wangluo
minzuzhuyi*), 140
investments, 17, 43, 53, 56–58, 64, 66, 79,
176; China and (worldwide), 165, 168,
190, 253, 272, 276, 280–81, 319–20, 361;
China's in U.S., 85, 117, 190, 199–201,
320, 375, 393; cross-border, 199–201,
391, 393–94; Economic Cooperation
Framework Agreement (ECFA), 300;
"encouraged," 201; fixed asset, *184*;
frictions over, 378, 384–85; "investment
catalogue," 201; MOFCOM and, 127;
Taiwan in mainland China, 297; U.S.
and (worldwide), 320, 322, 338, 340n14;
U.S. in China, 3, 30, 112, 187, 209n59.
See also foreign direct investment
IPR. *See* intellectual property rights
Iran, 114, 142, 167–68, 173, 224, 345,
366n33, 399–400; alleged Chinese
WMD proliferation to, 163; China's
support of, 328–29; Iranian revolution,
36; nuclear weapons, 105, 152, 168, 316,
323, 328–29, 354, 378, 399; oil supply,
341n36; sanctions against, 167–68, 328,
354; "Silkworm" missiles, 38; "Stuxnet"
cyberattack, 249; U.S. as prioritizing,
156; the *Yin He*, 40. *See also* Middle East
Iran-Iraq War, 38
Iraq, 324–25; Iran-Iraq War, 38; U.S. war
in, 42, 105, 109–10, 112, 236, 265, 280,
321, 361, 371, 374, 377; U.S. withdrawal
from, 398
Islam, 42, 278–79, 327. *See also* Muslims
Israel, 329
ISR systems. *See* reconnaissance (ISR)
systems
Italy, 218, 232n23, 320

Jackson-Vanick amendment, 185
Japan, 6, 43, 65, 79, 85, 88–90, 319;
anti-Japanese nationalism, 140; and
China favorability ratings, *321*; and

commercial/economic relationship,
185, 188–*89*, 199, 201–2; cultural
context, 229, 232n23; fishing boat
clash, 69, 244, 269, 286n13; the future,
374, 381, 394, 398, 401; global context,
343n61, 360; and history/evolution of
U.S.-China relations, 30–32, 39; and the
military-security relationship, 242, 244–
45; recession's impact on, 308; regional
developments, 268–70; security of, 243–
44; U.S. alliance with, 35, 92, 107, 246,
253, 266, 270, 286n14; and U.S.-China
interactions in Asia, 266–70, 272–74,
280–81; Western influence, 137
Jervis, Robert, 12–13
jet fighter, U.S. collision with. *See* EP-3
incident
Jiang Zemin, 129, 135, 156
Jiwei, Lou, 320
jobs. *See* labor
Johnson, Bennett, 120–21
Johnson, Lyndon, 35
Johnston, Alastair Iain, 19, 44, 347–48, 353,
358, 364n4
Joint Commission on Commerce and
Trade (JCCT), 203, 205
Joint Communiqué (1982), 37, 296
"June 4th Incident," 320

Kan, Naoto, 269–70
Kang-Mei, Yuan Chao ("Resist America,
Aid Korea") campaign, 32–33
Kant, Immanuel, 14
Kautilya, 76
Kennan, George, 31
Kennedy, John F., 35
Kennedy, Paul, 54
Kent, Ann, 17, 19, 353, 358
Kenya, 321, 330, 332, 343n64
Keohane, Robert, 15
Khalilizad, Zalmay, 4
Khartoum, 168
Khrushchev, Nikita, 34
Kim dynasty (North Korea), 239
Kim Jong-il, 271, 366n33, 385
Kim Jong-un, 271, 385
King, Martin Luther, Jr., 226, 230
Kirk, Mark, 113

Kirkpatrick, Jeane, 366n25

Kissinger, Henry, 13, 21–22, 36, 105–6, 181, 294, 296, 315, 401; "cooperative coexistence," 408n4

knowledge, sociology of, 18

Koizumi, Junichiro, 268–70

Koo-Wang Talks, 297

Korea, 270–71, 286n14. *See also* North Korea; South Korea; *specific topics*, e.g., Yeonpyeong Island

Korean Armistice, 33

Korean Peninsula, 32, 139, 169–70, 237, 266–67, 271, 277; establishing peace on, 174; and the future, 378, 385, 404

Korean War, 32–33, 105, 151, 402

Kristensen, Hans, 258n38

Kugler, Jacek, 11

Kundun (movie), 230

Kung Fu Panda, 227

Kuomintang (KMT) Party, 31–33, 121, 293, 299–300, 302, 375–76

Kuwait, 38, 109, 324

Kyoto Protocol, 358

labor: American, 83–84, 122, 192; Annual Labor Dialogue, 176; Chinese, 43, 48n44, 81, 83–84, 187–88, 195, 198, 201, 375, 393–94; and human rights, 166–67, 185; jobs/loss of jobs, American, 83–84, 187, 194–96, 327, 394. *See also* economics

Lakatos, Imre, 76

language teaching and learning (and cultural understanding), 219–21

Lanteigne, Marc, 361

Lardy, Nicholas, 195

Larsen, Rick, 113

Latin America, 315–18, 333–39

Lautz, Terry, 7, 20, 167, 211–33

leading small groups (LSGs), 155

Lebanon, *321*, 323–24, 327, 341n31

Lee Teng-hui, 40–41, 48n38, 297–99, 301

legal system, 38, 167

legitimacy crisis, 307, 361–62

Lehman Brothers, 190

Lei Yixin, 226

Leninist authoritarianism, 7, 15

Leviathan (Hobbes). *See* Hobbes, Thomas

"liberal ascendency," 56, 60–67

liberal capitalism, 380

"liberal institutionalism," 16

liberal international order, 16–17, 94, 354, 363; ascendancy of, 60–63; future of, 53–73. *See also* power transitions

liberalism, 5, 10, 14–20, 212

Libya, 142, 324, 328, 360–61

Li Mingjiang, 365n15

Liu Jianchao, 303

Liu Xiaobo, 16

Liu Yandong, 214

lobbying groups, institutional (Chinese), 141–42

Locke, John, 14

Long Yongtu, 138–39

Lou Jiwei, 320

low profile (*taoguang yanghui*), 136

Luce, Henry R., 225

Luck, Edward C., 352

Lugar, Richard, 216–17

Machiavelli, Niccolo, 76–78, 82

Mahbubani, Kishore, 68

Major Economies Forum on Energy Security and Climate Change (MEF), 358–59

Malacca, Straits of; "Malacca dilemma," 243, 246–47, 255

The Manchurian Candidate, 32

Mandarin language, 217, 220–21, 275

"Manifest Destiny," 9

Mann, Catherine, 80

manufacturing, 80, 83–86, 183, 187–88, 195, 198, 393; Taiwan and, 297

Manzullo, Donald, 113

Mao Zedong, 29–35, 105, 136, 138, 151, 214–15, 294, 315, 401; post-Mao era, 107, 382

maritime security, 114, 156, 164–65, 274, 281–82, 287n28, 325. *See also specific topics*, e.g., piracy

market access, 114, 118, 187, 197–99, 204, 319, 394

"market economy status" (MES), 319–20, 336–37

"marketplace of ideas" concept, 391

Marshall Plan, 46

Marxism, 7, 9, 15, 19

mass media. *See* media

Ma Xiaotian, 303

Ma Ying-jeou, 42, 121, 293, 299, 302–3

McCarthy, Joseph, 32

Mearsheimer, John, 11–12, 96n10

Medeiros, Evan, 353–54

media, xiin3, 284, 303, 334; American, 39, 103, 105–9, 115, 118–19, 122, 217, 224; Chinese, ix–x, 38, 125–26, 128–35, 137–38, 140, 173, 201, 216–17, 385. *See also specific topics*, e.g., internet; Xinhua news agency

memorandum of understanding (MOU), 165, 335

MERCOSUR, 334

Mercy Corps, 223

Mexico, *321*, 334, 336–38

MFA (Ministry of Foreign Affairs, China's), 127, 155–56, 161, 166, 301

Middle East, 290n44, 315–18, 323–29, 338–39, 341n29

military; military operations, 86–89

military dialogues, 176

"military-industrial complex," 119

Military Maritime Cooperation Accord (MMCA), 250, 254

military modernization (China), 9, 12, 40, 91, 153, 237, 239, 244, 248, 265–67, 276, 382

military-security relationship, 235–59; American military-security community, 118–19; competition, institutional restraints on, 250–54; EEZs and local reconnaissance, 238–39; global arena, 246–50; intermediate periphery, 242–46; Korean contingencies, 239–40; littoral and immediate periphery, 236–42; naval port calls, *251*; new security considerations, 235–36; selected multilateral military exercises and dialogues, *252*; the strategic level, 248–50; Taiwan Strait, 237–38

military spending, 236, 308

military-to-military dialogues/exchanges, 156, 161, 238, 250, 254, 304, 398, 403

Ministry of Commerce (MOFCOM), China's, 127, 141–42, 159, 166, 195, 337

Ministry of Foreign Affairs, China's. *See* MFA

minorities. *See* ethnic minorities

missionaries, 31, 211, 220, 223, 318

"missionary impulse" (U.S.), 6–7

mistrust, public, 187

Modelski, George, 76–77

modernization, China's, 6, 45, 75, 211, 219, 228, 361, 393; "Four Modernizations," 197; technological, 197. *See also* military modernization

MOFCOM. *See* Ministry of Commerce, China's

Mondale, Walter, 29

"monopoly-finance capitalism," 136–37

Monroe Doctrine, 9, 333, 381

Morgenthau, Hans J., 76

most-favored-nation status, 109, 403

MOU (memorandum of understanding), 165, 335

multilateralism, 253, 280–82, 350–51, 354, 362, 366n34, 367n53

multipolarity, 10, 57–58, 62, 94, 334, 348, 372, 378; return to, 57, 72n1

Murphy, Dawn, 315–45, 366n33

Muslims, 163, 165, 217, 323, 327

Myanmar, 142, 168, 171, 189, 243, 263, 275, 288n30, 316, 398

National Committee on U.S.-China Relations, 120, 219, 221, 223, 224

National Development and Reform Commission (NDRC), 127, 156

nationalism, Chinese, ix, 91, 238, 294, 306–7, 378; internet, 140

Nationalist Party. *See* Kuomintang (KMT) Party

National People's Congress (NPC), 128, 155, 301

national security, 13, 81, 86; China, 122, 128, 136–37, 153, 177n5; education programs, 219; U.S., 113, 115, 118–20, 153–57, 200, 381

National Security Council (NSC), U.S., 153–57, 310n6

National Security Leading Small Group (NSLSG), 155–56

NATO, 139, 165, 247, 278, 322, 328, 401

naval port calls, *251*
Negroponte, John, 181
neo-classical economic theory, 81, 393
neoconservatives, 16
neoliberalism, 14, 19, 67
netizens, 125, 129, 132, 140, 143
New Deal period, 62
new normal, 4, 284
New York, N.Y., 393
NGOs. *See* nongovernmental
    organizations
Niebuhr, Reinhold, 76
Nietzsche, Friedrich, 76
Nixon, Richard, 22, 104–7, 151–52, 294,
    296, 301, 315, 352, 373, 392; Nixon
    Doctrine, 36; trip to China, 106, 212
Nobel Peace Prize, 16
Noda, Yoshihiko, 269–70
non-alignment policy, China's, 143
nongovernmental organizations (NGOs),
    126, 137, 211, 222–25, 229
non-intervention, principle of, 56, 61, 65,
    396
nonproliferation, 40, 173, 236, 253,
    351, 353–54, 371, 381; and arms
    control, 128, 162–63, 224; U.S.-China
    International Security and Non-
    Proliferation Dialogue, 161, 175
Nonproliferation Treaty (NPT), 69, 151,
    163, 168
normalization, 18, 35–36, 105, 120, 151,
    181, 294–96, 304; and the future, 371,
    375, 392
"normal trade relations" (NTR), 185
Northeast Asia, 174, 239, 246, 271
North Korea, 43, 114–15, *189*, 224, 244,
    280, 286n14, 366n33; alleged Chinese
    WMD proliferation to, 163; China's
    exports to, 170; and the diplomatic
    relationship, 155, 167–71, 173–74; and
    the future, 399–401, 404, 406; the Kim
    dynasty and, 239, 385; and the military-
    security relationship, 239–40; nuclear
    weapons program, 105, 112, 152, 168–
    70, 239, 269–71, 316, 354, 399–400, 404;
    sanctions against, 167–68, 354, 400;
    satellite launch, 168; U.S. as prioritizing,
    156

nuclear weapons, 12, 17, 34–35, 44, 85, 87,
    114, 165, 247; Comprehensive Nuclear
    Test Ban Treaty, 163, 253; deterrence,
    70, 89, 93, 244, 406; dialogue, 176, 398;
    espionage, 40; and the future, 381, 406;
    nuclear technology, 85; Sino-Soviet
    nuclear cooperation, 34; strategy, 161,
    248–50, 285; and "ultimate" weapons, 95.
    See also denuclearization; disarmament;
    nonproliferation; weapons of mass
    destruction; *specific countries*, e.g., Iran;
    specific topics, e.g., submarines
Nye, Joseph, 15, 230

Obama, Barack, 44, 113–14, 116, 122, 124,
    238; Asia, interactions in, 264–66, 268–
    69, 273, 276, 280–81, 284; commercial/
    economic relationship, 190, 194;
    diplomatic relationship, 152, 157–59,
    162, 165, 169–71; election of, 230; and
    the future, 372, 376; global context,
    315, 332, 352, 356, 360; multilateralist
    approach, 358; and Taiwan, 302–5;
    trip to China, ix–x, 127, 132, 218,
    281, 381. *See also specific topics*, e.g.,
    environment; "pivot to Asia" policy
ODA. *See* Official Development Assistance
OECD, 64, 166, 315
OFDI. *See* Outward Foreign Direct
    Investment
"offensive realism," 96n10, 382
Official Development Assistance (ODA),
    166, 171, 173, 343n61, 396
"offshore active defense," doctrine of, 88
Ogden, Suzanne, 137
oil, 3, 175, 243, 246–47, 324–25, 328,
    330, 336; China National Offshore Oil
    Corporation, 86, 141, 200; China's oil
    supply, 341n39; top ten oil importers
    (2010), *325*
Okinawa, Japan, 241, 268, 270
Oksenberg, Michel, 177n4, 352–53
Olympics, 168, 214, 328, 390
"one child" policy, 81
one China policy, 36–37, 41, 43, 295
"one world" vision of nation-states, 62
open trading system. *See under* trade: open
    system

opinion, three levels of, 134
Organization for Economic Cooperation and Development. *See* OECD
Organization of American States (OAS), 334, 338
Organski, A.F.K., 11, 76–77
Outward Foreign Direct Investment (OFDI), 141, 199–200
overseas/outbound direct investment (ODI), 316, 319, 326, 331, 337
Owens, Bill, 307–8

P-5, 253, 352, 361–62, 400
Pakistan, 40, 163, 173, 253, 263, 278–80, 321; American airstrike in, 290n46; and diplomatic relations, 165. *See also* South Asia
Panama Canal Treaties, 36
Panetta, Leon, 265
paradigm shift, x, 187
partisanship, 103, 115–16, 348, 383
paternalism, American, 6–8, 15, 211
Paulson, Henry, 159, 203
PBOC. *See* People's Bank of China
PBSC. *See* Standing Committee of the Politburo
peace, 79. *See also specific topics*, e.g., "democratic peace theory"
Peace Corps, 219
"peaceful development" concept, 264, 380–81
"peaceful evolution" strategy, 212
"peaceful rise" policy. *See under* China, rise of: "peaceful rise" policy
peacekeeping, 42, 253. *See also* U.N. peacekeeping operations (UNPKO)
Peloponnesian War, 10
Pelosi, Nancy, 110
People's Bank of China (PBOC), 141, 156, 194, 200, 366n37
People's Daily, 131–32, 290n54
People's Liberation Army (PLA), 86, 126, 128, 301, 303, 306, 323, 398
People's Republic of China (PRC), ix, 105–6, 119, 155, 306, 347–48; diplomatic recognition of, 315; establishment of, 29, 293–94, 402; Taiwan people's view of, 297. *See also* China; *specific topics*, e.g., "reform and opening" period

people-to-people exchanges, 161, 167, 172, 176, 213, 229, 297, 299
Permanent Normal Trade Relations (PNTR) status, 39, 79, 112
Persian Gulf War, 38, 40, 272, 317
Peru, 334–37
Peterson Institute for International Economics, 122, 195, 224
Pew Global Attitudes Project, 46, *321*
philanthropy and cultural understanding, 225–26
the Philippines, 42, 92, 243, 246, 266–68, 272–75, 385, 398
ping-pong diplomacy, 36
piracy (of intellectual property), 195–96, 199
piracy (on the seas), 247–48, 252, 254, 323, 325, 327, 332, 399
"pivot to Asia" policy, 9, 44, 132, 236, 266, 278–79, 309, 398
plagiarism, 397
pluralization, 126–27, 137, 142
PNTR (Permanent Normal Trade Relations) status, 39, 79, 112
political dialogues. *See* dialogues, political
"political formation," 16, 58, 67
political realism. *See under* realism: political
politics. *See* domestic influences on U.S.-China relations; domestic politics; *specific topics*, e.g., bureaucracies; partisanship
Pollack, Jonathan, 86–87
pollution, 46
Pol Pot regime, 37
popular culture, 227
popular opinion. *See* public opinion
postwar settlements, 62
postwar years. *See under* World War II: postwar years
power, wealth and. *See* wealth and power
power transitions; power transition theory, 4, 10–13, 71, 75–76, 81–83, 85–86, 89, 283; and liberal international order, 57–60; realist and liberal points of view, 54–56. *See also* decline of America; rise of China
power war. *See under* war: great power war

Principals Committees (PCs), 153–54
professionalization, 126, 128
propaganda, 127, 133, 215, 230, 231n5
protectionism, 16, 65, 84, 110–11, 162, 320
"public diplomacy," 137
public health, 222, 330, 332, 376
public mistrust. *See under* mistrust: public
public/popular opinion, 134; Chinese, ix, 6–8, 30, 138–40, 211; U.S., 8, 106, 108, 117, 211, 217

Qaddafi, Muammar, 322, 328
Qiangguo Luntan (Strong Nation Forum), 131–32

racism, 32
Radio Free Asia (RFA), 217
Rangel, Charles, 111
Rapoport, Anatol, 391–92
Reagan, Ronald, 37–38, 104–7, 116, 164, 296, 301, 310n6, 366n25
realism, 5, 10–14, 18–20, 75–100; "defensive," 96n11, 382; "offensive," 96n10, 382; political, 75–76, 96n9; socialist, 227; traditional, 76–78, 96n9
rebalancing, economic. *See* economic rebalancing
recession, global, 43, 114–15, 265–66, 275, 308–9, 326, 363. *See* global economic crisis
reconnaissance, 88–89, 164, 237–38; EEZs and local, 238–39, 256n11; ISR systems, 88, 248–49. *See also* EP-3 incident
"Red China," 15, 30, 294
"red lines," 405–7
"reform and opening" period/policy, 6–7, 134, 141, 183, 185, 347, 373
regional geopolitics, 89–93
Reid, Harry, 110
Relations across the Taiwan Strait (ARATS), 299–300
religion, 61, 76, 213, 219, 223, 318; extremism, 277; freedom of, 166–67, 185
renminbi (RMB), 127, 142, 178n25, *184, 191*–95, 199, 366n37. *See also under* currency: revaluation
"republican liberalism," 15

Republican (Nationalist) era (China), 6
Republican party, U.S., 16, 36, 110, 114, 116–17, 122, 155, 358
Republic of China (ROC), 6, 33, 293–95, 297. *See also* Taiwan
"Resist America, Aid Korea" campaign, 32–33
Responsibility to Protect (R2P), 359–60
"responsible stakeholder," role of, 42, 152–53, 173, 305, 352
reverse engineering, 85–86
"revisionist," the term, 162
Rigger, Shelley, 164, 293–311
rise of China, 53–73, 94–95, 228, 288n34, 305; implications for competition, 78–81; indeterminacy of, 81–83; "peaceful rise" policy, 11, 69, 134–35, 353, 355, 363. *See also* power transitions
RMB. *See renminbi*
Rockefeller Brothers Fund (RBF), 225
"rogue" states, 317, 328–29, 333
Rohrabacher, Dana, 311n30
Romberg, Alan, 308
Romney, Mitt, 114
Roosevelt, Franklin Delano, 30, 62
Roosevelt, Teddy, 29
Rosen, Stanley, 134
Ross, Robert, 13
Rousseff, Dilma, 68
R2P (Responsibility to Protect), 359–60
Rudd, Kevin, 275–76, 365n12
Russia, 6, 89–90, 168, 171, 248, 256n16, 277–78, *321*–22, 328, 359

Samuels, Richard, 269
sanctions: U.S. against China, 402–3, 407. *See also under specific countries*, e.g., Iran; North Korea
satellite launch, North Korean, 168, 170
Saudi Arabia, 324–26, 341n36
Schumer, Charles, 192, 194
science, 18, 64, 167, 176, 198, 212–14, 219–22, 228, 397
"scientific development strategy," 198
Scowcroft, Brent, 39
security: security competition, 81–93. *See also* international security; military-security relationship; national security

"security dilemmas," 4, 77, 91, 99n37, 235–36, 244, 255, 283, 391; concept of, 12–13

S&ED. *See* Strategic and Economic Dialogue

Segal, Gerald, 317

Senate, U.S., 110–11, 113–14, 116, 118, 194; Senate Foreign Relations Committee, 216, 228, 352

Senior Dialogue (SD), 152, 160, 209n64, *252*

separatist movements, 42, 227, 279

September 11, 2001, 42, 110, 112, 163, 265, 305, 327, 332, 381

Serbia. *See under* Chinese Embassy: U.S. bombing of

Shambaugh, David, 3–26, 44, 125, 134, 246–47, 315–45, 364n8, 366nn33–34, 379, 384, 406–7

Shanghai, ix, 41, 163, 222, 227, 393

Shanghai Communiqué, 36–37, 294–95

Shanghai Expo, 214

Shi Yinhong, 355

Shultz, George, 107

Sichuan earthquake (2008), 223, 226

"Silkworm" missiles, 38

Singapore, 68, 92, *189*, 220, 243, 246, 276–77

Sino-American relations. *See* U.S.-China relations; *specific topics*

"Sinocentric" world order, 9

Sino-Indian war, 34

Sino-Soviet bloc, 33–35, 39

Six Party Talks, 170, 239, 253, 259, 270–71

Skelton, Ike, 113

Smith, Adam, 14

socialism, 7–8, 38, 155, 227, 333, 347, 364n2

societal forces, 126, 129–30, 132, 143

SOEs. *See* state-owned enterprises

"soft power," 41–42, 211, 213–14, 216–17, 228, 230, 252, 316, 380, 397

Somalia, 323, 325, 327, 332, 360

South Asia, 160, 176, 263–64, 277–80, 318

South China Sea, 43, 69, 88, 128, 143, 267, 271–74, 286nn16–17, 309; bilateral context, 157, 164–65, 171–72, 242–43, 247; disputes, 272, 286n13, 287n28, 376,

385; and the future, 398, 404; rules to avoid conflict, 286n16

Southeast Asia, 280–81

South Korea, 32, 69, 79, *189*, 240, 266–67, 270–71, 273, 280–81, 337; and the future, 401, 404; G20 meeting in Seoul, 355; U.S. alliance with, 92, 246, 253, 266; Western influence, 137. *See also* *Cheonan*

Southwest Asia, 111, 278–79, 399

sovereign debt crisis, 320, 322, 340n21, 375

sovereignty, 61, 65, 396; state, 61, 177n5, 358, 361

Soviet Union, 106–7, 401; Afghanistan invasion, 37; China's support against, 107; former Soviet republics, 263; Sino-Soviet bloc, 33–35, 39. *See also* Cold War

space, outer, 161, 174, 236, 249, 253, 398

Spain, 218, 232n23, 320–*21*

"spiritual pollution," 39, 212

sports exchanges, 167, 212–14

SSD. *See* Strategic Security Dialogue

SSNs. *See* submarines

Standing Committee of the Politburo (PBSC), 126, 155–56

Starr, C. V., 225

State Administration of Foreign Exchange (SAFE), 141

"state directed capitalism," 186

state-owned enterprises (SOEs), 141–42, 162, 175, 199, 201

state sovereignty, 61, 177n5, 358, 361

Steinberg, James, 154, 161

stimulus policies, 399

Straits Exchange Foundation (SEF), 299–300

Straits of Malacca. *See* Malacca, Straits of

strategic ambiguity, policy of, 305, 307–8

Strategic and Economic Dialogue (S&ED), 17, 44, 133–34, 209n64, 213, 251, 317; and diplomatic relationship, 152, 157–60, 175, 177n16; sub-dialogues, 160–61

strategic and economic differences, 46

strategic and economic relations, 154

strategic dialogues, 158–60, 175–76. *See also* Strategic Security Dialogue

"strategic reassurance" policy, 154

Strategic Security Dialogue (SSD), 159, 161, 164, 172, 175, 251

"strategic shocks," 20

"strategic triangle," 322

"strategic trust," 21, 161, 173, 386

"Strong Nation Forum," 131–32, 145n21

structural interdependence, 5

structuralism, 20, 76

The Structural Transformation of the Public Sphere (Habermas), 129

"Stuxnet" cyberattack, 249

sub-dialogues, 112, 158, 160–61, 167, 172

sub-elite, Chinese, 134–38, 142

submarines; SSNs, 119, 239–45, 248, *252*, 257n28, 258n38, 267

Sub-Saharan Africa, 315–18, 329–33, 338–39

Sudan, 156–57, 168, 173, 316, 323–24, 326–28, 330, 332, 341n31, 359

SU-33/J-15 fighters, 248, 259n55

supercomputing, 393

surveillance, reconnaissance, and observation (SRO), 164

Sutter, Robert, 103–24, 306–8

Swaine, Michael, 13, 41, 174

Syria, 142, 168, 171, 316–17, 328, 361–62

Taiwan, 293–311; arms sales to, 114, 132, 164, 166, 296, 364n8, 403; bilateral diplomatic agenda and, 164; China's "core national interests" in, 143; "co-management of," 302; defense treaty, U.S.-Taiwan, 33, 107–8; democracy, impact of, 108–10, 298, 308, 310n8; and independence, 36, 41, 43, 80, 297, 299–302, 304–5, 310n8, 375–76, 399, 404, 406; military ("Hard ROC" initiative), 257n23; and unification, 35, 164, 177n5, 237, 239, 294–99, 301, 305–6, 308–9, 402, 404, 406; U.S. visa granted to Lee Teng-hui, 40, 109, 121, 298, 301; Western influence, 137. *See also specific topics*, e.g., Kuomintang Party

Taiwan Relations Act (TRA), 111, 238, 295, 308

Taiwan Strait, 32–33, 37, 43, 88, 333, 402, 404; 1996 crisis, 128, 254; military-

security relationship and, 237–38, 282, 295; and Taiwan in U.S.-China relations, 299–300, 303, 305, 308

Taliban, 42, 165

taoguang yanghui (keeping a low profile), 136

taxes; tax policies, 115, 141, 201, 226, 337

technology, 167, 195–97, 213–14; high/advanced, 83, 85–86, 175, 201, 319, 393. *See also* innovation; modernization

Tellis, Ashley, 10, 12, 75–100, 235, 255, 408n2

Ten Year Framework (TYF) Joint Working Group (energy-related), 165–66, 175

territorial integrity, 61, 83, 177n5, 236, 294, 364n2, 381, 396

terrorism, 22, 44, 105, 114, 161, 277–78, 317, 323, 327–30; and the future, 381, 399, 406; Middle East and, 327–28; sub-Saharan Africa, 332; "war on," 42, 112, 266, 280, 374. *See also* Counterterrorism; September 11, 2001

The Asia Foundation (TAF), 225

think tanks, 103, 109, 115, 121–22, 125–26, 129–30, 134–35, 137, 156; cultural context, 211, 219, 224–25

"third world," 33–34

Thucydides, 10, 76–78, 82–83

Tiananmen Square; the Tiananmen crackdown, 15, 38–40, 97n19, 122, 151, 215–16; and American public opinion, 117; and mainstream American media, 118; and U.S. policy toward China, 104, 108–10, 171, 402–3

Tibet, 109, 120, 143, 216, 228–29, 275, 321, 324, 396

Timor-Leste, 166

tourism, 175, 213, 335

trade, 83, 117, 181–82; dialogue, 175; Joint Commission on Commerce and Trade (JCCT), 175, 203; open system, 17, 62, 79, 85–86; RMB/USD exchange rate and U.S. trade deficit, *193*. *See also* economics; exports; imports; labor

trade deficit, 9, 110, 120, 188–*89*, *193*–94

trademark infringement, 196

traditional realism. *See under* realism: traditional

The Tragedy of Great Power Politics (Mearsheimer), 11–12, 96n10
Trans-Pacific Partnership (TPP), 281–82, 290n54, 398
Treaty of Amity and Cooperation (TAC), 281
triangle, strategic, 322
"tribute system," 9
tripolarity, 10, 94
Truman, Harry, 31–32
Tucker, Nancy Bernkopf, 5–6, 15, 29–49, 212, 293, 306–7
Turkey, 324, 326–27, 341n29
Tu Wei-ming, 30
two China policy, 34–36, 41
Twomey, Christopher P., 164, 235–59, 408n14, 409n16, 409n24

Uighur/Uyghur separatists, 163, 227, 327–28, 342n51
UNCLOS, 164, 238–39, 243
unemployment, 190, 194
unilateralism, 87, 116, 280, 301, 337, 352, 355, 362
unipolarity, 10, 13, 57–58, 70
United Kingdom, 215, 218, 232n27, 343n61, 357
United Nations (UN), 359–62, 365n15, 366n25, 367n53; China's admission to, 35–36
United Nations Convention on the Law of the Sea. *See* UNCLOS
United Nations Framework Convention on Climate Change(UNFCCC), 127, 350, 358
United Nations peacekeeping operations (UNPKO), 253, 323, 327–28, 330, 332, 335, 341n31, 360–61
United Nations Security Council (UNSC), 56, 163, 169–70, 253, 316, 347, 350, 355, 359–61; bilateral diplomatic agenda and, 167–68; China's use of veto, 66, 168, 171, 328, 354–55, 361–62, 400; and Chinese "cooperation," 400; competition for votes in, 390; U.S. use of veto, 352
United States, 30, 58, 103–24, 136, 351–53; goals of, 29, 152–53, 173, 305–6, 330;

tasks of, 90–91. *See also under specific topics*, e.g., Congress, U.S.; labor; national security; public opinion
United States–China relationship, 3–26, 29–49. *See also* future of U.S.-China relations; *specific topics*, e.g., diplomatic relationship
United States Embassy, ix, 41, 217, 219
United States House of Representatives. *See* House of Representatives, U.S. United States Senate. *See* Senate, U.S. Universal Declaration of Human Rights, 63
universities, 221–22. *See also* education
UNOCAL, 86, 200
USSR. *See* Soviet Union
Utah, state of, 220

Venezuela, 333, 334, 336
Vietnam, 42, 92, *189*, 266–68, 281, 286n13, 385, 404; China's relationship with, 155, 267, 272–75, 385; U.S. relationship with, 243, 246, 266–67, 273, 283, 385, 398
Vietnam War, 33–37, 111, 402
visas, 216, 229; granted to Taiwan president, 40, 109, 121, 298, 301
Voice of America (VOA), 217

Waltz, Kenneth, 76, 96n9
Wang Guangya, 136, 360
Wang Jisi, 67
wangluo minzuzhuyi (internet nationalism), 140
Wang Qishan, 134, 186
Wang Yi, 136, 170, 303
war on terror. *See under* terrorism: "war on"
Warring States period (China), 10
wars: great power war, 16, 58, 67, 69–70; and postwar settlements, 62. *See also specific wars*, e.g., Vietnam War; World War II
Warsaw, Poland, 33, 151
Washington Consensus, 379, 395–96
"watchful waiting" policy, 91
wealth and power, 6, 57, 266, 318
weapons of mass destruction (WMD), 40, 109, 120, 162–63
Wendt, Alexander, 18
Wen Jiabao, 198, 301, 320, 366n37

Western influence/values, 67, 137,
    211–12
Westphalian state system; "Westphalian
    project," 55–57, 60–71, 396
White, Hugh, 288n34
White Paper, 141, 177n5, 372, 387n11,
    387n21
Williams, Paul D., 361
Wilson, Woodrow, 62
"win-win" outcomes, 205, 284, 307, 394
WLAN Authentication and Privacy
    Infrastructure (WAPI), 202
women's issues/dialogues, 161, 167, 176,
    214, 225, 231n16
Woodrow Wilson International Center for
    Scholars, 224
Woon, Eden, 38
World Bank, 198, 333, 347, 377, 395
world politics, 53–54, 58, 63, 71–72
World Summit (2005), 69, 359
World Trade Organization (WTO), 16, 39,
    56, 112, 127, 138, 185–86, 196, 319–20;
    China joining, 64–65, 79, 151, 183, 204,
    394; and the future, 378, 387n13, 391–
    92; two principles of membership, 204
World War I, 62, 80
World War II, 9, 30–31, 46, 53, 56, 61–63,
    69, 79, 347, 381
Wu Xinbo, 363, 371–88

Xie Zhenhua, 127
Xi Jinping, 24n11

Xinhua news agency, 44, 134, 217, 356
Xinjiang province, 36, 120, 143, 227, 229–
    30, 275, 279, 323, 327, 328
Xuanchuan Bu (Propaganda Department),
    127

Yalu River, 32
Yang Jiechi, x, 136, 273, 286n13
Yellow Sea, 88, 157
Yeonpyeong Island, 170, 269, 270, 283
Yeung, Benjamin, 222
Yin He (Chinese ship), 40, 139
Young, Stephen, 309
yousuo zuowei, 136
yuan (currency), 356
Yugoslavia. *See under* Chinese Embassy:
    U.S. bombing of

zero-sum interactions, 7, 10, 14, 21, 53,
    71–72, 77, 153, 172, 230, 235, 255, 349,
    365n13; antagonism and, 355–57, 402;
    and the future, 379, 382, 392, 402
Zhao Quansheng, 302
Zhao Yan, 132
Zhou Enlai, 151, 197, 294, 315
Zhu Feng, 13, 356
Zhu Min, 64
Zhu Rongji, 183
Zimbabwe, 142, 171, 316, 330,
    343n64
Zoellick, Robert, 42, 316, 352,
    366n26

About the Editor and Contributors

EDITOR

David Shambaugh is professor of political science and international affairs and director of the China Policy Program in the Elliott School of International Affairs at The George Washington University. He is also a nonresident senior fellow in the Foreign Policy Studies Program and Center for Northeast Asian Policy Studies at The Brookings Institution. Before joining the faculty at George Washington, he held the position of Reader in Chinese Politics at the University of London's School of Oriental & African Studies (SOAS) and simultaneously served as editor of *The China Quarterly*. Professor Shambaugh has published widely on China's domestic politics, foreign relations, military and security, and the international relations of Asia. His most recent books are *China Goes Global: The Partial Power* (2013), *Charting China's Future: Domestic & International Challenges* (2011), *China's Communist Party: Atrophy & Adaptation* (2008), *China-Europe Relations: Perspectives, Policies, and Prospects* (2007), *China Watching: Perspectives from Europe, Japan, and the United States* (2007); *Power Shift: China and Asia's New Dynamics* (2005); *The Odyssey of China's Imperial Art Treasures* (2005); *Modernizing China's Military* (2002). He is a frequent commentator on Chinese and Asian affairs in the international media, sits on the editorial boards of a number of scholarly journals, and has served as a consultant to various governments, research institutes, philanthropic foundations, and private corporations. He holds a B.A. from George Washington University, an M.A. from Johns Hopkins University (SAIS), and a Ph.D. from the University of Michigan. He has been a visiting scholar or professor at institutions in Australia, Brazil, China, Germany, Hong Kong, Italy, Japan, Russia, and Singapore.

CONTRIBUTORS

Rosemary Foot is professor of international relations and the John Swire Senior Research Fellow in the International Relations of East Asia, St Antony's College, University of Oxford, where she teaches predominantly on the International Relations postgraduate program. She has also held visiting fellowships at

People's University, Beijing; Princeton University; the Belfer Center at Harvard's Kennedy School of Government; as well as at IDSS in Singapore. Professor Foot holds an M.A. from the University of London's School of Oriental and African Studies (SOAS), and a Ph.D. from the London School of Economics and Political Science. She has been elected a Fellow of the British Academy. She is the author or editor of several books, including *The Practice of Power: U.S.-China Relations Since 1949* (1997), *Rights Beyond Borders: The Global Community and the Struggle over Human Rights in China* (2001), *U.S. Hegemony and International Organizations* (2003), and *Does China Matter? A Reassessment* (2004). Her latest book, with Andrew Walter, is *China, the United States, and Global Order* (2011). Her research interests cover the international relations of the Asia-Pacific, including U.S.-China relations, human rights, and Asian regional institutions.

Charles W. Freeman III is vice president for Asia, Middle East and Africa at PepsiCo. He is also a nonresident senior adviser for economic and trade affairs at the Center for Strategic and International Studies (CSIS). Previously, he held the CSIS Freeman Chair in China Studies from 2004 to 2011. A second-generation "China hand," he has lived and worked between Asia and the United States for his entire life. During his government career, he served as assistant U.S. trade representative (USTR) for China affairs. In this capacity, he was the United States' chief China trade negotiator and played a primary role in shaping overall trade policy with respect to China, Taiwan, Hong Kong, Macao, and Mongolia, and oversaw U.S. efforts to integrate China into the global trading architecture of the World Trade Organization. He currently is a senior adviser to McLarty Associates, the global strategic advisory firm based in Washington, D.C., and serves on the Boards of Directors of the National Committee of U.S.-China Relations and the Harding-Loevner Emerging Market Fund Group. Freeman received his J.D. from Boston University School of Law, where he was an editor of the *Law Review* and graduated with honors. He earned a B.A. from Tufts University in Asian Studies, concentrating in economics, also with honors. He also studied Chinese economic policymaking at Fudan University in Shanghai and Mandarin Chinese at the Taipei Language Institute.

Bonnie S. Glaser is a senior fellow with the Freeman Chair in China Studies at the Center for Strategic and International Studies (CSIS), where she works on issues related to Chinese foreign and security policy. She is concomitantly a senior associate with CSIS Pacific Forum and a consultant for the U.S. government on East Asia. From 2003 to mid-2008, Ms. Glaser was a senior associate in the CSIS International Security Program. Ms. Glaser has written extensively on various aspects of Chinese foreign and security policy and international relations in the Asia-Pacific, including Sino-U.S. relations, cross-Strait relations, the role of think tanks and the PLA in Chinese foreign policy decision making, Chinese assessments of American power, China-Korea relations, and Chinese perspectives on missile defense and multilateral security in Asia. Her writings have been published in the *Washington Quarterly, China Quarterly, Asian Survey, International Security, Problems of Communism, Contemporary Southeast Asia, American Foreign Policy Interests, Far Eastern Economic Review, Korean Journal of Defense Analysis, New York Times,* and *International Herald Tribune,* as well as various edited volumes on Asian security. Ms. Glaser has been a regular contributor to the Pacific Forum quarterly Web journal *Comparative Connections* since its inception in 1999. She is currently a board member of the U.S. Committee of the Council for Security Cooperation in the Asia Pacific (USCSCAP), a member of the Council on Foreign Relations and the Institute of International Strategic Studies (IISS). Ms. Glaser received her B.A. from Boston University and her M.A. from Johns Hopkins School of Advanced International Studies (SAIS).

Avery Goldstein is the David M. Knott Professor of Global Politics and International Relations in the political science department, and associate director of the Christopher Browne Center for International Politics at the University of Pennsylvania. His research focuses on international relations, security studies, and Chinese politics. He is the author of *Rising to the Challenge: China's Grand Strategy and International Security* (2005), *Deterrence and Security in the 21st Century: China, Britain, France and the Enduring Legacy of the Nuclear Revolution* (2000), and *From Bandwagon to Balance of Power Politics: Structural Constraints and Politics in China, 1949–1978* (1991). Among his other publications are articles in the journals *International Security, International Organization, Journal of Strategic Studies, Security Studies, China Quarterly, Asian Survey, Comparative Politics, Orbis,* and *Polity,* as well as chapters in a variety of edited volumes. Professor Goldstein is also a Senior Fellow at the Foreign Policy Research Institute in Philadelphia.

Yufan Hao is professor of political science and dean of the Faculty of Social Sciences and Humanities at the University of Macau. His areas of expertise are U.S.-China relations, Chinese foreign policy-making, Chinese politics, and Macau politics. He previously was on the faculty at Colgate University, Tsinghua University, and Peking University. He was also formerly a MacArthur Fellow at the Belfer Center for International Affairs at Harvard University, a Luce Fellow at the East Asian Institute in Seoul, and a Visiting Fellow at the Center for Northeast Asia Policy Studies at the Brookings Institution in Washington,

D.C. He received his Ph.D. from Johns Hopkins University (SAIS). His book publications include: *Macao and Sino-U.S Relations* (2011), *China's Policies on Its Borderlands and the International Implications* (2010), *Sino-American Relations: Challenges Ahead* (2010), *Challenges to Chinese Foreign Policy: Diplomacy, Globalization, and the Next World Power* (2009), *Chinese Social Sciences and Humanities Since 1978: Retrospective and Prospective* (2008), and *Chinese Foreign Policy Making: An Analysis of Societal Forces* (2006).

Harry Harding is dean of the Frank Batten School of Leadership and Public Policy and professor of public policy and politics at the University of Virginia. Among other positions, he is also vice chairman of the Asia Foundation, a member of the Board of Governors of the Rajaratnam School of International Studies (Singapore), a member of the Board of Directors of the National Committee on U.S.-China Relations, and a member of the Committee on International Security Studies of the American Academy of Arts and Sciences. His previous positions include faculty appointments at Swarthmore College and Stanford University, senior fellow in the Foreign Policy Studies Program at the Brookings Institution, dean of the Elliott School of International Affairs at George Washington University, director of research and analysis at Eurasia Group, and university professor of international affairs at George Washington University (2005–2009). A specialist on Asia, his major publications include *The India-China Relationship: What the United States Needs to Know* (2004), *A Fragile Relationship: The United States and China Since 1972* (1992), *Sino-American Relations, 1945–1955: A Joint Reassessment of a Critical Decade* (1989), *China's Second Revolution: Reform After Mao* (1987), *China's Foreign Relations in the 1980s* (1984), and *Organizing China: The Problem of Bureaucracy, 1949–1976* (1981). Dr. Harding received his B.A. from Princeton University, and his M.A. and Ph.D. from Stanford University.

G. John Ikenberry is the Albert G. Milbank Professor of Politics and International Affairs at Princeton University in the Department of Politics and the Woodrow Wilson School of Public and International Affairs, where he is co-director of Princeton's Center for International Security Studies. Ikenberry is also a Global Eminence Scholar at Kyung Hee University in Seoul, Korea. He is the author of *After Victory: Institutions, Strategic Restraint, and the Rebuilding of Order after Major Wars* (2001), which won the 2002 Schroeder-Jervis Award presented by the American Political Science Association for the best book in international history and politics. Professor Ikenberry's books include *Liberal Order and Imperial Ambition: American Power and International Order* (2006); *End of the West? Crisis and Change in Atlantic Order* (2008); *Crisis of American Foreign Policy: Wilsonianism in the 21st Century* (2009), and *Liberal Leviathan:*

The Origins, Crisis, and Transformation of the American World Order (2011). Professor Ikenberry is the co-director of the Princeton Project on National Security, and he co-authored with Anne-Marie Slaughter the final report *Forging a World of Liberty Under Law*. Among his many activities, Professor Ikenberry served as a member of an advisory group at the State Department in 2003–2004 and was a member of the Council on Foreign Relations Task Force on U.S.-European relations.

Terry Lautz is a visiting professor at Syracuse University and was a public policy scholar at the Woodrow Wilson International Center for Scholars in 2010. Previously, he was vice president of the Luce Foundation, where he directed the Asia and Henry R. Luce Programs. Dr. Lautz is a director of the National Committee on U.S.-China Relations and has served as a trustee and board chair of the Lingnan Foundation and the Yale-China Association. He holds degrees from Harvard and Stanford University and is a Vietnam veteran. His recent research and writing deals with Sino-American mutual perceptions, the history of Christianity in China, and the study of the United States in China. Currently, he is working on a book about John Birch, who was an American missionary and soldier in China.

Dawn Murphy is a postdoctoral fellow in the Princeton-Harvard China and the World Program. She received her Ph.D. in political science from The George Washington University, where her dissertation examined China's relations with the Middle East and sub-Saharan Africa in the post–Cold War era. In support of her dissertation, she conducted field research as visiting scholar with the Chinese Academy of Social Sciences, Institute of World Economics and Politics, in Beijing, China, and as a visiting research fellow with the American University in Cairo, Egypt. She also conducted research at Stellenbosch University's Center for Chinese Studies in Stellenbosch, South Africa. Before pursuing her Ph.D., Ms. Murphy established an extensive private-sector career in the United States and China. She possesses an M.A. from Columbia University and a B.A. from Cornell University.

Shelley Rigger is the Brown Professor of East Asian Politics and chair of the political science department at Davidson College. She has a Ph.D. in government from Harvard University and a B.A. in public and international affairs from Princeton University. She has been a visiting researcher at National Chengchi University in Taiwan (2005) and a visiting professor at Fudan University in Shanghai (2006). Professor Rigger is the author of two books on Taiwan's domestic politics, *Politics in Taiwan: Voting for Democracy* (1999) and *From Opposition to Power: Taiwan's Democratic Progressive Party* (2001). Her other volumes include *Why Taiwan Matters: Small Island, Global Powerhouse* (2011) and *Taiwan's Rising Rationalism: Generations, Politics and "Taiwan Nationalism"* (2006). She has published articles on Taiwan's domestic politics, the national identity issue in Taiwan-China relations and related topics. Her current research studies the effects of cross-Strait economic interactions on Taiwan and Mainland China.

Robert Sutter is professor of practice of international affairs at the Elliott School of George Washington University. He previously served as visiting professor of Asian Studies in the School of Foreign Service, Georgetown University (2001–2011), and has taught part-time for forty years at Georgetown, George Washington, and Johns Hopkins Universities, and at the University of Virginia. Sutter holds a Ph.D. in History and East Asian Languages from Harvard University. He has published numerous books, articles, chapters, and government reports dealing with contemporary East Asian and Pacific countries and their relations with the United States. His most recent books are *Chinese Foreign Relations: Power and Policy Since the Cold War* (2012, 3rd ed.), *Historical Dictionary of Chinese Foreign Policy* (2011), *U.S.-Chinese Relations: Perilous Past, Pragmatic Present* (2010), *The United States in Asia* (2008), and *China's Rise in Asia: Promises & Perils* (2005). Sutter's government career (1968–2001) involved work on Asian and Pacific affairs and U.S. foreign policy for the Congressional Research Service of the Library of Congress, the Central Intelligence Agency, the Department of State, and the Senate Foreign Relations Committee. For many years he was the senior specialist and director of the Foreign Affairs and National Defense Division of the Congressional Research Service. He also was the National Intelligence Officer for East Asia and the Pacific at the U.S. Government's National Intelligence Council, and the China Division Director at the Department of State's Bureau of Intelligence and Research.

Ashley J. Tellis is a senior associate at the Carnegie Endowment for International Peace, specializing in international security, defense, and Asian strategic issues. While on assignment to the U.S. Department of State as senior adviser to the Undersecretary of State for Political Affairs, he was intimately involved in negotiating the civil nuclear agreement with India. Previously he was commissioned into the Foreign Service and served as senior adviser to the ambassador at the U.S. Embassy in New Delhi. He also served on the National Security Council staff as Special Assistant to the President and senior director for Strategic Planning and Southwest Asia. Prior to his government service, Dr. Tellis was senior policy analyst at the RAND Corporation and professor of Policy Analysis at the RAND Graduate School. He is the author of *India's Emerging Nuclear Posture* (2001) and co-author of *Interpreting China's Grand Strategy: Past, Present,* *and Future* (2000). He is the research director of the Strategic Asia program at the National Bureau of Asian Research (NBR) and co-editor of its eight most recent annual volumes, including *Strategic Asia 2011–12: Asia Responds to Its Rising Powers—China and India*. In addition to numerous Carnegie and RAND reports, his academic publications have appeared in many edited volumes and journals. Tellis received his Ph.D. from the University of Chicago.

Nancy Bernkopf Tucker is professor of history at Georgetown University and at the Edmund A. Walsh School of Foreign Service. She also holds an appointment as a senior scholar at the Woodrow Wilson International Center for Scholars. Her Ph.D. is from Columbia University, and she is an American diplomatic historian who specializes in American–East Asian relations, particularly United States relations with China, Taiwan and Hong Kong. She has been a member of the U.S. Department of State Advisory Committee on Historical Diplomatic Documentation, and the boards of the Institute for the Study of Diplomacy, the National Committee on U.S.-China Relations, and is a member of the Council on Foreign Relations. In 2007 she received a National Intelligence Medal of Achievement for distinguished meritorious service as the first Assistant Deputy Director of National Intelligence for Analytic Integrity and Standards and Analytic Ombudsman in the Office of the Director of National Intelligence. She is the author of *The China Threat: Memories, Myths and Realities in the 1950s*; *Strait Talk: United States–Taiwan Relations and the Crisis with China*; *Uncertain Friendships: Taiwan, Hong Kong and the United States*—winner of a Bernath Book Prize of the Society for Historians of American Foreign Relations; *Patterns in the Dust: Chinese-American Relations and the Recognition Controversy, 1949–1950*. She also co-edited *Lyndon Johnson Confronts the World*, annotated and edited *China Confidential*, and edited *Dangerous Strait*. Her essays have appeared in more than a dozen books and various journals including *Foreign Affairs, Journal of American History, American Historical Review, Survival, Political Science Quarterly, Diplomatic History*, and the *Washington Quarterly*.

Christopher P. Twomey is associate professor of national security affairs at the U.S. Naval Postgraduate School (NPS) in Monterey, California. He received his Ph.D. from MIT. Since joining the faculty at NPS, he has also served as associate chair for research and as director of the Center for Contemporary Conflict from 2007–2009. Today he works closely with the Office of the Secretary of Defense (Policy) and the State Department on a range of diplomatic engagements across Asia and regularly advises PACOM, STRATCOM, and the Office of Net Assessment. His book *The Military Lens: Doctrinal Differences and Deterrence Failure in Sino-American Relations* (2010) explains how differing military doctrines complicate diplomatic signaling, interpretations of those signals, and assessments of the balance of power. Its empirical work centers on contemporary and historic Sino-American cases. He edited *Perspectives on Sino-American Strategic Nuclear Issues* (2008), and his articles have appeared in journals such as *Asian Survey, Security Studies, Arms Control Today, Contemporary Security Policy, Asia Policy, Current History,* and *Journal of Contemporary China.* He has previously taught or researched at Harvard, Boston College, RAND, the Chinese Academy of Social Sciences, and IGCC and is currently a Research Fellow at the National Bureau of Asian Research. He has lived in China several times, speaks and reads Chinese, and regularly travels to Asia.

Wu Xinbo is professor and deputy director at the Center for American Studies and associate dean at the School of International Relations and Public Affairs, at Fudan University in Shanghai. He teaches China-U.S. relations and U.S. Asia-Pacific policy and writes widely about China's foreign policy, Sino-American relations, and Asia-Pacific issues. Professor Wu received his B.A. in history and Ph.D. in international relations from Fudan University. He has been a visiting scholar George Washington University's Sigur Center for Asian Studies, the Asia-Pacific Research Center at Stanford University, and the Henry Stimson Center, the Brookings Institution Center for Northeast Asian Policy Studies (CNAPS), and was a Jennings Randolph Senior Fellow at the United States Institute of Peace. Professor Wu is the author of *Dollar Diplomacy and Major Powers in China, 1909–1913* (1997), *Turbulent Water: The U.S. Asia-Pacific Security Strategy in the Post–Cold War Era* (2006), *Managing Crisis and Sustaining Peace Between China and the United States* (2008), and *The New Landscape in Sino-U.S. Relations in the Early 21st Century* (2011). He also has published numerous articles and book chapters in China, the U.S., Japan, Germany, South Korea, Singapore, and India. Dr. Wu is on the editorial board of *The Washington Quarterly* published by the Center for Strategic and International Studies (CSIS), and the International Board of the *Studies in Asian Security* book series sponsored by the East-West Center and published by the Stanford University Press.